Wagner,
Thanks for your
leadership and
work possible for
David

Aggression and Violence:
Genetic, Neurobiological, and Biosocial Perspectives

Aggression and Violence:
Genetic, Neurobiological,
and Biosocial Perspectives

Edited by

David M. Stoff
National Institute of Mental Health

and

Robert B. Cairns
University of North Carolina

 LAWRENCE ERLBAUM ASSOCIATES, PUBLISHERS
1996   Mahwah, New Jersey

Lawrence Erlbaum Associates, Inc., Publishers
10 Industrial Avenue
Mahwah, New Jersey 07430

Library of Congress Cataloging-in-Publication Data

Aggression and violence : genetic, neurobiological, and biosocial
perspectives / edited by David M. Stoff and Robert B. Cairns.
     p. cm.
   Includes bibliographical references and index.
   ISBN 0-8058-1755-7 (c : acid-free paper). —ISBN
0-8058-2504-5 (p : acid-free paper)
    1. Violence—Physiological aspects. 2. Aggressive-
ness—Physiological aspects. I. Stoff, David M. II. Cairns,
Robert B., 1933– .
RC569.5.V55A28 1996
616.85'82—dc20
                         95-42601
                           CIP

Books published by Lawrence Erlbaum Associates are printed on
acid-free paper, and their bindings are chosen for strength and
durability.

Printed in the United States of America
10 9 8 7 6 5 4 3 2 1

CONTENTS

v

INTRODUCTION

This volume[1] was conceived at a time when biological research on aggression and violence was drawn into controversy because of sociopolitical questions about its study (Stone, 1992[2]). A group of dedicated scientists recognized the importance of freedom of inquiry, deemed it vital to address the state of the art of biological studies in the field, and generated this volume. The challenge for biological research in aggression and violence will be the courage to pursue responsible research so that opinions and political decisions can be informed by reliable and valid facts.

This volume is intended to familiarize readers with the rapidly growing and increasingly significant body of knowledge on the biological bases of human antisocial, aggressive, and violent behaviors. We concentrated on biological influences that support the basic physiological and biochemical processes of the brain and did not include those biological influences that impact on the health of the individual (e.g., head injury, pregnancy and birth complications, diet, exposure to lead and other toxins). We focused on biological influences to illuminate their role in the complex behavioral phenomenon of violence. This focus does not imply that biological variables are paramount as a determinant of violence. Rather, biological variables operate in conjunction with numerous other variables contributing to violence. A complete understanding of violence requires consideration of *all* influences that bear on it.

A century ago, the Italian physician Cesare Lombroso proposed a constitutional theory claiming that sloping foreheads, jutting chins, and long arms were signs of born criminals. In the 1960s, scientists advanced the now discounted notion that men who carry an XYY chromosome pattern, rather than the normal XY pattern, were predisposed to becoming violent criminals. Recent advances in the neurosciences have given researchers new tools to search for biological clues to aggression and violence. Fresh interest in the field reflects the recognition that violence has become one of the country's worst public health threats.

---

[1] The opinions expressed herein are the views of the authors and do not necessarily reflect the official position of the National Institute of Mental Health or any other part of the U.S. Department of Health and Human Services.

[2] Stone, R. (1992). HHS "violence initiative" caught in a cross-fire. *Science, 258,* 212–213.

Three different approaches to the biological study of human antisocial, aggressive, and violent behaviors are represented here: Genetic (Part I), *Neurobiological* (Part II), and *Biosocial* (Part III). Generally speaking, investigators following these different approaches have experience in different scientific backgrounds, select different methods, generate different analyses, employ different conceptual definitions for some of the same terms, and assume a different philosophic stance in attempting to explain violence. Nevertheless, all are united in their efforts to understand the biological underpinnings of violence. For this reason, it is incumbent on us all to assume a comprehensive approach wherein different levels of analysis and different approaches inform each other.

Part I, the "Genetic Perspective," includes three chapters. The studies discussed in these chapters employ quantitative genetic designs to assess the importance of genetic and nongenetic influences in behavior and molecular genetic strategies to identify some of the gene(s) involved. Some of the questions asked are: (a) Is aggressive, antisocial behavior familial? If so, (b) To what extent is the familial aggregation of aggressive antisocial behavior due to environmental and genetic factors? (c) What is transmitted within families that predisposes an individual to aggressive antisocial behavior? If genetic factors play an important role in the familial transmission of aggressive antisocial behavior, (d) What is their mode of genetic transmission, and (e) What is the location of any major gene(s) as well as their pathophysiological expression?

In chapter 1, Carey reviews the human behavioral genetic literature and concludes that aggressive antisocial behavior has an important heritable component that is probably multifactorially transmitted. According to this view, it is unlikely that there is a "genetic marker" for aggressive antisocial behavior and the most likely role for genetics is to unravel the neurobiology of aggressive antisocial behavior. In chapter 2, Goldman reports data in humans that the tryptophan hydroxylase gene, which codes for the rate-limiting enzyme in the synthesis of serotonin, may be a factor influencing serotonin turnover and impulsive aggressive behaviors that appear to be controlled by serotonin. These promising findings, detected in a population of impulsive offenders, need to be confirmed in additional population samples, by genetic linkage in families more definitively, or by identification of a functional variant of the human tryptophan hydroxylase gene. In chapter 3, Gariépy, Lewis, and Cairns present data that challenge traditional assumptions about the relationships between genes and development, neurobiology, and social behaviors, using a selective breeding program for aggression in mice. These investigators conclude that social behavior constitutes a leading edge for biological adaptation and an integrative, developmental analysis is required for understanding the operation of genetic and neurochemical processes in aggressive behavior.

Part II, the "Neurobiological Perspective," includes nine chapters. The challenge for the neurobiological perspective is to identify specific brain structures and functions that operate through basic physiological and biochemical processes to regulate behavior. Steroid and peptide hormones, as well as peptides and biogenic amines, are critically important in the neural and physiologic mechanisms initiating, executing, and coping with violent behavior. It is here that important endocrine and pharmacologic interventions are targeted. These neurochemical systems mediating violent behavior are specific to discrete neuroanatomic networks.

The first series of chapters in the neurobiology section is devoted to the role of serotonin in aggressive antisocial behavior. This neurotransmitter has received the most attention due to the confluence of animal and behavior literature suggesting that serotonin is critical in the regulation of aggressive antisocial behavior. Coccaro and Kavoussi (chap. 4) review the role of neurotransmitter systems in impulsive–aggressive behavior, primarily serotonin and, to a lesser extent, norepinephrine, dopamine, and endogenous opiates. Using neuropsychopharmacological challenges and the consequent measurement of hormones mediated by the hypothalamic-pituitary-adrenal axis, these investigators propose a comprehensive model of impulsive–aggressive behavior that focuses on the interaction of inhibitory, stimulatory, and permissive biological and environmental factors associated with aggressive behavior. Noting an extensive literature describing central serotonin deficits in alcoholic, impulsive, violent offenders and fire setters, Virkkunen and Linnoila (chap. 5) report studies on biochemical concomitants of impulsivity and aggressiveness (reduced cerebrospinal fluid 5-hydroxyindoleacetic acid, CSF 5-HIAA) and its physiological consequences (abnormalities of glucose metabolism) in alcoholic impulsive offenders. Many of the offenders exhibited both low CSF 5-HIAA concentration and low blood glucose nadirs after an oral glucose administration. However, further study is needed to elucidate the basic physiological mechanisms mediating the interrelationships between serotonin and glucose metabolism dysregulation. In chapter 6, Stoff and Vitiello review the biochemistry and pharmacology of serotonin in the aggression of children and adolescents. These authors conclude that the more peripheral 5-HT indices, which have an uncertain relationship to central 5-HT function, do not reveal consistent 5-HT abnormalities. Besides a few controlled studies on lithium, the clinical pharmacology of serotonergic agents as possible treatment of childhood aggression is still in an embryonic stage.

The next three chapters in the neurobiology section deal with the most commonly measured psychophysiologic response systems (cardiovascular, electrodermal, cortical) in aggressive antisocial behavior. Mezzacappa, Kindlon, and Earls (chap. 7) discuss the utility of heart rate and heart-rate variability as noninvasive indices of autonomic nervous system regulatory function in disruptive behavior disorder. Methodologic issues make heart rate and heart-rate variability well suited to constructing models of individual differences in the relationship of autonomic nervous system regulatory activity to behavior (behavioral inhibition, conduct disorder, delinquency, and sociopathy). Raine's review of studies assessing autonomic nervous system correlates in aggressive antisocial populations (chap. 8) consistently revealed lower skin conductance activity (reduced arousal, poorer classical conditioning, longer half-recovery times) and resting heart-rate activity. It was argued that these psychophysiological findings should be integrated with other social and cognitive research in antisocial individuals. In chapter 9, Convit et al. present preliminary studies that support a relationship between frontotemporal dysfunction (electroencephalographic [EEG], neuropsychological test performance, neurological evaluation, computerized tomography [CT] findings) and violence in psychiatric and criminal populations. A multidimensional framework is proposed to simultaneously assess these variables which tap frontotemporal lobe activity in the context of disinhibited psychopathology (impulsivity). Frontal dysfunction in violent adults is also suggested by brain-imaging studies in the next two chapters.

Using positron emission tomography (PET), chapters 10 and 11 support an inverse relationship between aggressive impulsive difficulties and regional cerebral metabolic rates of glucose (rCMRG) and regional cerebral blood flow (rCBF). Raine and Buchsbaum (chap. 10) found decreased rCMRG in orbital frontal and prefrontal cortex of murderers and Goyer and Semple (chap. 11) found an inverse correlation between ratings of life history of aggression and cCMRG in the frontal cortex of personality disorder patients. Because ethanol stands out as the drug most frequently associated with violent behavior, the final chapter of the neurobiological section is a discussion of ethanol, central neurotransmitter systems, and animal aggression. Barros and Miczek (chap. 12) pay special attention to the possibility that the progressive effects of ethanol may be mediated through the gamma-aminobutyric acid, GABA, system.

Part III, the "Biosocial Perspective," includes three chapters. The biosocial perspective is based on the idea that biological variables need to be integrated with emotional, social, and cultural factors. Biology, context, experience, and behavior are not independent factors; instead, they are inseparably coalesced in development. This view demands a holistic, interdisciplinary approach for the study of violent behaviors. The notion that biological and psychosocial–environmental factors operate interactively in the production of antisocial behavior suggests that (a) When both psychosocial–environmental and biological factors occur together, an individual is most likely to manifest antisocial behavior, and (b) The interaction between psychosocial–environmental and biological factors accounts for more variance in antisocial behavior than either influence alone.

In chapter 13, Susman et al. discuss mechanisms of hormone–behavior action to advance the notion of reciprocal influences of hormones and behavior. With a specific focus on stress-related hormones, this team of investigators emphasizes the role of experience on hormones to establish neuroendocrine–behavior links in laboratory studies that may be transferable to aggression development in naturalistic settings. Magnusson (chap. 14) presents results indicating that low autonomic activity–reactivity (i.e., low adrenaline excretion) was strongly associated with persistent antisocial behavior, but not with adolescence-restricted antisocial behavior. The role of low autonomic activity–reactivity in the development of antisocial behavior is interpreted in terms of an interactional model between biological factors and other factors in the environment. Hood (chap. 15) provides an analysis of how developmental, genetic, and contextual factors operate in the sex and gender differences for female aggressive behavior. Sex-related developmental changes in aggressive behavior over the life span are employed as a basis for assessing hormonal effects on behavior.

In the concluding chapter we highlight salient findings that are discussed in more detail in the text and recommend some research principles to be followed in future biological studies of aggression and violence. This is presented in the context of an integrative approach that addresses the interaction of biological and socioenvironmental influences. Several myths concerning research on the biology of aggression and violence have hindered progress in the understanding of these interacting influences. These misconceptions are laid out in detail, next, because their clarification is essential for a comprehensive understanding of all influences that bear on aggression and violence.

Myth 1.   Violence can be reduced to and explained on the basis of disordered biological processes. The relation between a biological substrate and aggressive behavior can be understood in terms of a one-to-one coordinate model, a unidirectional causal influence of biology on behavior. While science has traditionally sought to discern the physiologic and hormonal influences that affect behavior, investigators are demonstrating the wide array of circumstances in which social structure and social behavior have a direct influence on physiological and hormonal processes. For example, it is likely that ecological risk factors such as poverty and exposure to violence in the home and neighborhood will be shown to have longstanding traumatic impact on brain structure and function as well as subsequent behavioral adaptation. Therefore, biological variables must be understood in the social context. Biological variables influence social behavior and, vice versa, social behavior influences biological variables. Research needs to examine synergisms between biological and behavioral processes as influences on behavior.

Myth 2.   Biological variables can be measured as increases or decreases at a single time point. Biological (as well as behavioral) variables are best measured as trajectories or patterns of development over time. Individuals should be characterized not as "high" or "low" on a specific biological variable at a single point, but rather as "stable" or "variable" on a specific biological variable over the course of development. Although methodologically difficult, biological variables should be measured prospectively within a more developmental perspective, rather than concurrently with measures of aggression.

Myth 3.   Biological factors directly cause aggression with biology "driving" aggression. Biological factors may exert their effects on aggression via intervening processes which, in turn, influence aggression per se; these intervening processes may include proximal social mechanisms, threshold for aggression, impulsivity, cognition, learning, prosocial behaviors, or other biological events. Research needs to identify the links among biological, intervening, and outcome variables.

Myth 4.   Biological variables can be related to the outcome of violence in general. Violence is heterogeneous in nature, there are different types of violent behaviors, and different biological variables may be related to these different types. However, potentially important biological effects may be masked when violence is conceptualized as a unitary outcome variable. Research needs to develop a taxonomy of qualitatively distinct subtypes of aggressive behavior and relate biological variables to the different subtypes.

Myth 5.   A single biological variable can be related to a single behavioral outcome. Traditionally, researchers have attempted to relate a single biological event, such as one neurotransmitter system, to a single behavioral outcome. The validity of such an approach has now been disproved due to the interaction among biological systems and among related behavioral outcomes. Studies that incorporate multiple measures from a variety of biological subdisciplines are capable of making more powerful statements about violence.

Myth 6. *The existence of biological factors in violence necessitates the view that violence is in part biologically determined, meaning that individuals are born to be violent and one can not change violent behavior.* Notions that "biology is destiny" are not supported by behavioral genetic research in violence. Knowledge of biology restores to individuals more control of their own destinies. Appropriate interventions, whether biological or psychosocial, restore choice and freedom. Biological influences do not act in a vacuum—their expression is highly dependent on environmental parameters and the environment works through a biological substrate. Environmental manipulations can, in theory, be fully successful in reducing the incidence of violence by preventing or re-channeling the full expression of genetic predispositional factors. Biological influences for violence must be seen as a predisposition to violence rather than as destiny for violence.

The previous misconceptions are addressed by research studies throughout the text and in our concluding chapter. It is evident that violence is a multidetermined phenomenon and its comprehensive understanding requires an interdisciplinary approach spanning economic, sociopolitical, psychological, sociological, and criminological, as well as biomedical, considerations. Moreover, it is our view that nature (biology) and nurture (experience, context) are fundamentally inseparable. Biology may affect experience or context, but experience or context also influences biology. Because of the reciprocal interplay we must continue to study both.

ACKNOWLEDGMENTS

In closing, we would like to acknowledge the work of our contributors for their thoughtful and scholarly chapters. We also wish to acknowledge the assistance given to us by Lawrence Erlbaum Associates throughout every phase of the preparation of this book. Finally, we would like to thank our families for their steady encouragement and support.

David M. Stoff
Robert B. Cairns

LIST of CONTRIBUTORS

Helena M. T. Barros. Division of Pharmacology and Toxicology, Federal School of Medical Sciences of Porto Alegre, Brazil.

Monte S. Buchsbaum. Department of Psychiatry, Mount Sinai School of Medicine, New York, New York.

Robert B. Cairns. Center for Developmental Science, University of North Carolina, Chapel Hill, North Carolina.

Louis Camus. Sodona, Arizona.

Gregory Carey. Institute for Behavioral Genetics, University of Colorado, Boulder, Colorado.

Emil F. Coccaro. Department of Psychiatry, Medical College of Pennsylvania and Hahnemann University, Philadelphia, Pennsylvania.

Antonio Convit. Nathan Kline Institute for Psychiatric Research, Orangeburg, New York.

Pal Czobor. Nathan Kline Institute for Psychiatric Research, Orangeburg, New York.

Jose de Asis. Department of Psychiatry, New York University Medical Center, New York, New York.

Richard Douyon. Department of Psychiatry, University of Miami, Miami, Florida.

Felton Earls. Developmental Epidemiology Research Unit, The Judge Baker Children's Center, Boston, Massachusetts.

Colleen A. Frobose. Department of Biobehavioral Health, Pennsylvania State University, University Park, Pennsylvania.

Jean-Louis Gariépy. Department of Psychology, University of North Carolina, Chapel Hill, North Carolina.

David Goldman. Laboratory of Neurogenetics, National Institute on Alcohol Abuse and Alcoholism, Rockville, Maryland.

Peter F. Goyer. Chief of Staff, Department of Veterans Affairs Medical Center, Brecksville, Ohio.

Kathryn E. Hood. Department of Human Development and Family Studies, Pennsylvania State University, University Park, Pennsylvania.

Richard J. Kavoussi. Department of Psychiatry, Medical College of Pennsylvania and Hahnemann University, Philadelphia, Pennsylvania.

Daniel Kindlon. Developmental Epidemiology Research Unit, The Judge Baker Children's Center, Boston, Massachusetts.

Mark H. Lewis. Department of Psychiatry, University of Florida, Gainesville, Florida.

Markku Linnoila. Office of the Scientific Director, National Institute on Alcohol Abuse and Alcoholism, Bethesda, Maryland.

David Magnusson. Department of Psychology, Stockholm University, Stockholm, Sweden.

Enrico Mezzacappa. Developmental Epidemiology Research Unit, The Judge Baker Children's Center, Boston, Massachusetts.

Klaus A. Miczek. Department of Psychology, Tufts University, Medford, Massachusetts.

Elise Murowchick. Department of Human Development and Family Studies, Pennsylvania State University, University Park, Pennsylvania.

Adrian Raine. Department of Psychology, University of Southern California, Los Angeles, California.

Jacqueline E. Schwab. Department of Human Development and Family Studies, Pennsylvania State University, Mont Alto, Pennsylvania.

William E. Semple. Department of Veteran Affairs Medical Center, Case Western Reserve University Medical School, Cleveland, Ohio.

Gwenn Smith. Department of Psychiatry, University of Pittsburgh, Pittsburgh, Pennsylvania.

David M. Stoff. Mood, Anxiety, and Personality Disorders Research Branch, National Institute of Mental Health, Rockville, Maryland.

Elizabeth J. Susman. Department of Biobehavioral Health, Pennsylvania State University, University Park, Pennsylvania.

Matti Virkkunen. Department of Psychiatry, Helsinki University, Helsinki, Finland.

Benedetto Vitiello. Child and Adolescent Disorders Research Branch, National Institute of Mental Health, Rockville, Maryland.

Joseph Vitrai. Nathan Kline Institute for Psychiatric Research, Orangeburg, New York.

Jan Volavka. Nathan Kline Institute for Psychiatric Research, Orangeburg, New York.

Brenda K. Worrall. Department of Biobehavioral Health, Pennsylvania State University, University Park, Pennsylvania.

Kathy F. Yates. Nathan Kline Institute for Psychiatric Research, Orangeburg, New York.

GENETIC PERSPECTIVE

1

FAMILY AND GENETIC EPIDEMIOLOGY OF AGGRESSIVE AND ANTISOCIAL BEHAVIOR

Gregory Carey
University of Colorado

There is an important familial component to aggression, antisocial behavior, crime, and violence. Risk factors of aggression such as parental aggression, poverty, single-parent households, and neighborhood delinquency all contribute to what genetic epidemiologists refer to as "between-family variation." That is, these factors make members of one sibship different from members of another sibship but are common to the individuals within a given sibship—all sibs within a family experience the same factors to a more or less equal degree. However, the *source* of the familial effect is subject to debate. An observable behavior (i.e., a *phenotype*) may run in families for strictly environmental reasons, for genetic reasons, or for some combination of the two. This review explores the source of the familial component to aggressive behavior and examines the relative merits of the genetic and family environmental contributions to the observed correlations among relatives.

Separating genetic from environmental effects is relatively easy in animal studies, where inbred strains have been developed and where matings and environments can be controlled. Aggression among rodents has been a favorite topic of behavioral genetics and results have consistently found heritability for various definitions of aggression in the mouse and rat (see Maxson, 1981, for a review). Research interest has shifted from demonstrating the *fact* of heritability through analysis of inbred strains or artificial selection to using genetics as a tool to explore the potential neurobiological mechanisms behind aggression. Current research suggests that the genetics may be multifactorial. Known or potential genetic factors that have been implicated in rodent aggression include loci on the

Y chromosome (Maxson, Didier-Erikson, & Ogawa, 1989), hormonal influences (Colger-Clifford, Simon, & Jubilan, 1992; Compaan, de Ruiter, Koolhaas, van Oort-merssen, & Bohus, 1992; Svare, 1988), the dopamine system (Nikulina & Kapralova, 1992), the GABA system (Weerts, Miller, Hood, & Miczek, 1992), serotonin receptors (Hen et al., 1993), α-calcium-calmodulin-dependent kinase II deficiencies (Chen, Rainnie, Greene, & Tonegawa, 1994), and developmental effects (Cairns, MacCombie, & Hood, 1983; Gariepy, Hood, & Cairns, 1988; Hood & Cairns, 1988).

The infrahuman literature clearly indicates that genetics cannot be discounted as an important source of individual variation in human aggression, but there is insufficient evidence to prove that point. Clearly, human data are required. Along these lines, the quantitative human behavioral geneticist relies on two major designs. The first is the twin design. Here, the phenotypic similarity of genetically identical twins (monozygotic or MZ twins) is compared to that of genetically nonidentical twins (dizygotic or DZ twins who, like ordinary siblings, share 50% of their genes on average). Greater MZ than DZ similarity implies genetic effects.

The second research strategy is the adoption study. Here, aggressive behavior in adoptees is correlated with aggressive behavior in biological relatives with whom the adoptee shares genes but does not share rearing environments. A positive correlation denotes a significant genetic effect. Also, a correlation between the adoptee's behavior and that of the rearing relatives—with whom the adoptee shares environment but not genes—indicates an environmental effect for family similarity. (Factors that compromise interpretation of the twin and adoption designs are discussed later, after the empirical literature has been reviewed.)

Both the twin and the adoption design partition observable or phenotypic variance into three components. The first component is *heritability*, defined as the proportion of phenotypic variation attributable to individual differences in genotype. Typically, the assumption is made that all gene action is additive, so estimates of heritability must be seen in the context of this assumption. The second component is *common environmentability*. This is the proportion of phenotypic variance attributable to all those environmental variables that cause aggression and at the same time are shared by sibs. The final component is *unique environmentability*, the proportion of phenotypic variance attributable to all those environmental variables that cause aggression but are uncorrelated among siblings. Estimates of unique environmentability often include variance due to measurement errors.[1]

---

[1]The partitioning of variance mentioned here is only a simple introduction to a complicated problem. More elaborate detail about the effects of assortative mating, nonadditive genetic variance, and several other violations of the simple model are provided by Eaves, Eysenck, and Martin (1989) and Neale and Cardon (1990). Eaves, Last, Martin, & Jinks (1977) discussed gene–environment covariance and interaction—factors important for rodent aggression. The general conclusion is that violations of the assumptions of the simple model will not give "genetic looking" results when in fact there is no heritability to the trait. The same, however, cannot be said about common environment.

With the rapid development of molecular genetics, two other strategies will play increasingly important roles in the genetic epidemiology of human aggression and antisocial behavior. These two analytical methods are the *linkage* study and the *association* study. The linkage study traces the cosegregation of one or more genes (markers) with a phenotype (a disorder, score on an aggression scale, etc.) within pedigrees. The purpose is to identify regions on chromosomes that may contain a "major gene" or a gene of large effect with respect to the phenotype. In the second strategy, the association study, individuals are genotyped at a locus of interest (a "candidate" gene). One then examines whether aggression differs with respect to the genotypes at that locus.

Both linkage and association studies have advantages and disadvantages. An advantage to both strategies is that they can unambiguously establish a genetic influence uncomplicated by the possible confounding assumptions of the twin and adoption strategy, such as equal twin environments and selective placement. Their chief utility, however, is their potential in identifying a locus that may shed light on neurobiological mechanisms behind aggression.

Both techniques suffer from the disadvantage of having relatively high probabilities of false positive results. The human genome contains about 100,000 active genes, and the number expressed in the central nervous system may be in the tens of thousands. Hence, large numbers of statistical tests will be performed in molecular genetic studies, resulting in a high probability that at least one test will reach significance at the conventional level (see Carey, 1994a; Crowe, 1993). Thus, linkage and association studies must have adjusted p-values and must be replicated before they can be substantively interpreted. To date, I know of no linkage studies of general antisocial behavior, although there are some, reviewed next, of individual Mendelian disorders involving aggression as a symptom. Goldman (chap. 2, this volume) provides an overview of several association studies.

MENDELIAN AND CHROMOSOMAL DISORDERS ASSOCIATED WITH AGGRESSION

Are there known Mendelian disorders or chromosomal anomalies that have aggression or antisocial behavior as important symptoms? An early search through "Mendelian Disorder in Man" on the terms *aggression, antisocial behavior, violence,* and *rage* revealed eight potential disorders that included these terms in their descriptions (Carey, 1994b). Two disorders, alcoholism and Tourette's syndrome, do not segregate as strict Mendelian disorders. The most relevant of the other disorders were Fragile X syndrome and a form of male-limited precocious puberty. In all cases, however, aggression was mentioned as characterizing a few members of a pedigree and could not be considered pathognomonic.

Recently, however, Brunner, Nelen, Breakefield, Ropers, and Van Oost (1993; Brunner et al., 1993) reported a single pedigree with X-linked transmission of a syndrome of mental retardation and behavioral disturbance that included aggression and aberrant sexual behavior. Affected individuals in this pedigree possessed an abnormal chain-terminating codon in the coding region for monoamine oxidase-A. The population genetics of this mutation are unknown. Hence, the abnormal allele may have a frequency on the order of other X-linked Mendelian disorders (e.g., 1 in 1,000 to 1 in 10,000). Similarly, the extent to which the abnormal allele is associated with aggression in the general population is also unknown. Nevertheless, this is an important follow-up lead for future research.

Almost 30 years ago, reports of a high prevalence of XYY syndrome among various types of institutionalized populations sparked considerable (and often acerbic) discussion over the possibility that the chromosomal anomaly was associated with aggressive, antisocial, and criminal behavior. The debate subsided amid a call for careful, prospective investigation. The results of several prospective and population-based studies dispelled the myth of the XYY as a "hyperaggressive, supermasculine sociopath." Instead, development is believed to be largely within the normal range with occasional mild to moderate deficits in cognition and in social and emotive behavior (Bancroft, Axworthy, & Ratcliffe, 1982; Bender, Linden, & Robinson, 1987; Witkin et al., 1976). Although adults XYY may show statistically significant differences in aggression and sexuality from controls, the differences are not so large as to be clinically relevant (Schiavi, Theilgaard, Owen, & White, 1984, 1988; Thielgaard, 1984).

All in all, these results suggest the possible influence of sex hormones, and a gene on the X chromosome on aggression, and possibly some Y chromosomal involvement in aggression. Unless the syndrome described by Brunner, Nelen, Breakefield et al. (1993) can be independently identified in other pedigrees, however, the relationship between single genes or chromosomal disorders must be taken as nonspecific and weak in magnitude. Although these disorders may shed some light on the potential neurobiological mechanisms for aggression, they are unlikely to contribute more than minuscule proportion of the variance in human aggression.

PERSONALITY SCALES

DNA does not code for fighting, rape, or robbery. Instead, genes contain the blueprint for proteins and enzymes that shape and underlie neurobiological systems that in turn influence higher order behavioral phenotypes. It has long been speculated that temperament and personality may be one of the major mediators between the genes and aggression. It is important then to assess how heredity influences personality traits correlated with aggression.

Carey (1994b) presented tables summarizing the results of all twin and adoption studies that used personality scales that were either called aggression scales (e.g., the Aggression scale of the Multidimensional Personality Questionnaire) or were shown to be correlated with aggressive behavior (e.g., the Psychopathic-Deviate scale of the Minnesota Multiphasic Personality Inventory). The overall results of these studies were consistent with those of other personality scales in adults (see Carey & DiLalla, 1994, for a review of this topic). For adults, the pooled correlation for MZ twins was .40 and the pooled correlation for DZ twins was .18. The difference between the MZ and DZ correlation is highly significant ($p < .001$). Heritability is estimated at .44, common environmentability at 0, and unique environmentability at around .56. Data from the Minnesota series of twins raised apart suggested that these results are not due to violations of the assumptions for the twin method. For two scales, the pooled correlation for MZ twins raised apart was .56; for DZ twins raised apart the correlation was .20. Hence, there is an important genetic influence on personality scales that measure aggression and sociopathy in adults. The results for children are more variable and suggest that common environment may play a more important role than it does for adults.

OVERT ANTISOCIAL BEHAVIOR: GENETIC EPIDEMIOLOGY

In the following sections, phenotypes of overt antisocial behavior are considered, including measurement of registered or self-reported criminal acts, symptoms of conduct disorder in children, or symptoms of antisocial personality disorder in adults. To place these studies in perspective, Table 1.1 presents the modern twin studies, the population sampled, and the results. Table 1.2 presents the modern adoption studies, which are discussed in the following section. For clarity, I have separated my review into juvenile versus adult antisocial behavior.

JUVENILE ANTISOCIAL BEHAVIOR

Early twin studies of juvenile antisocial behavior, reviewed in Carey (1994b) and Gottesman and Goldsmith (1994), reported substantial concordance rates that did not differ appreciably for identical and fraternal twins. Hence, common environment may play a more important role than genes in childhood and adolescent aggression. This early literature, however, suffered from many methodological problems, chief among them being small sample sizes and unrepresentative sampling.

Modern samples consistently suggest the importance of both genetic and common environment in juvenile antisocial behavior. Studies of unselected child and adolescent twins using the Delinquent or Aggressive scales of the Child Behavior Checklist report identical twin correlations in the range of .70 with fraternal twin correlations ranging from .31 to .55 (see Gottesman & Goldsmith,

TABLE 1.1

Synopsis of Modern Twin Studies of Antisocial Behavior

Twin Population	Phenotype	References	Evidence for a Genetic Effect?
Norwegian adults	Registered and self-reported criminal acts	Dalgard & Kringlen (1976)	no
USA teenagers	Self-reported delinquent acts	Rowe (1983, 1985, 1986)	yes
Danish adults	Registered criminal acts and/or convictions	Carey (1992); Christiansen (1968, 1970, 1974); Cloninger, Christiansen, Reich, & Gottesman (1978); Cloninger & Gottesman (1987); Gottesman, Carey, & Hansen (1983)	yes
Largely USA/UK adults raised apart	Count of DIS[a] antisocial personality disorder symptoms	Grove et al. (1990)	yes
Children/teenagers	Symptoms of conduct disorder	Eaves et al. (1993)	yes
Adult veterans	Count of DIS[a] antisocial personality disorder symptoms	Lyons et al. (1993)	yes
Adult psychiatric patients	Count of DIS[a] antisocial personality symptoms	Carey (1993)	yes

Note. [a]DIS = Diagnostic Interview Schedule.

TABLE 1.2
Modern Adoption Studies of Antisocial Behavior

Population	Phenotype	References	Evidence for a Genetic Effect?
Offspring of USA female felons	Records and self-reports of arrests and convictions	Crowe (1972, 1974)	yes
Danish adults	Police and court registrations	Hutchings (1972); Hutchings & Mednick (1971, 1975)	yes
USA children	Conduct disorder symptoms	Cadoret (1978; Cadoret et al., 1975)	yes
USA teenagers and young adults	Symptoms of antisocial personality	Cadoret & Cain (1980); Cadoret et al. (1983, 1985, 1986)	yes
Swedish adults	Arrest/court records	Bohman (1978, 1983); Bohman et al. (1982); Bohman, Cloninger, von Knorring, & Sigvardsson (1984); Cloninger et al. (1982); Sigvardsson et al. (1982)	partly
Danish adults[a]	Court convictions	Baker (1986); Baker et al. (1989); Gabrielli & Mednick (1983, 1984); Mednick (1987); Mednick, Brennan, & Kandel (1988); Mednick & Finello (1983); Mednick, Gabrielli, & Hutchings (1987); Moffitt (1987)	yes

Note. [a]Partly overlaps with the other sample of Danish adults given in table.

9

1994, for an overview). Rowe (1983, 1985, 1986) analyzed self-reported delin-quency in a series of junior and senior high school twins and reported correla-tions of .65 for MZ twins and .48 for DZ twins. The heritability estimate was .34 and was statistically significant. Common environmentability was .31, but a statistical test did not reach significance. A recent analysis of conduct disorder symptoms by Eaves et al. (1993) gave greater MZ than DZ concordance for latent classes of the symptoms, but the proportion of variance due to heredity and common environment was not calculated. Analysis of adoption samples by Cadoret, Cain, and Crowe (1983) and by Bohman (1971; Bohman & Sigvardsson, 1985) also implicated importance for the home environment in the development of teenage antisocial behavior.

This line of research tentatively suggests an important developmental influ-ence on aggression and antisocial behavior, but it cannot pinpoint the source of the effect. Nevertheless, the results dictate that future studies in genetic epidemiology must be very concerned with developmental perspectives on antisocial behavior and must try to measure environments in order to isolate the nature of the common environmental influence.

ADULT ANTISOCIAL BEHAVIOR: TWIN STUDIES

In 1976, Dahlgard and Kringlen reported on a series of 139 Norwegian twin pairs where at least one had appeared in the national twin register and could be followed up with either personal interview or family history information. The twins were a decade-long birth cohort who were between the ages of 35 and 45 at the time of follow up. Hence, it would have been uncommon for a twin to be registered for a first offense after this age.

There was a nonsignificant trend for greater MZ than DZ concordance. For a wide definition of criminality (i.e., any legal offense reported on the criminal register), concordance rates were 37% for MZ and 31% for DZ twins. For more serious crimes, concordance rates were 41% and 26% respectively for MZ and DZ twins.

The largest twin study of antisocial behavior was initiated by K. O. Christian-sen (1968). He identified all twins born in Denmark between 1880 and 1910 where both members survived until age 15, giving over 3,000 pairs of twins. The criminal records of the twins were then traced through national and local police and penal registers, and twins were considered "criminal" if convicted of an offense roughly equivalent to a felony according to contemporary U.S. jurisprudence. Among males, MZ concordance was 51% and same-sexes DZ concordance was 30.2%. Although overall concordance was lower in females, MZ similarity still exceed same-sexes DZ similarity—33.3% to 13.3%.

An important adjunct to concordance rates in twin and adoption studies is known as the "correlation of liability." This is a tetrachoric correlation estimated from concordance rates in twins and the baserate in the general population and is based on the assumption that there is a normally distributed variable called liability with an abrupt threshold. Individuals beyond the threshold are affected (i.e., registered for a criminal conviction in this case) whereas individuals below the threshold are unaffected. The tetrachoric correlation measures twin resemblance on the underlying, normally distributed dimension of liability.

In the Danish twins study, the tetrachoric correlation was .74 for MZ twins and .47 for fraternal twins, giving a heritability estimate of .54 and a common environmentability of .20 (Cloninger & Gottesman, 1987). However, there is some evidence in both this sample and others that there may be twin imitation[2] for antisocial behavior (Carey, 1992; Dahlgard & Kringlen, 1976; Rowe, 1983). In this case, estimates of heritability and common environment will be biased. Models that incorporate twin imitation still show a significant genetic effect but lower heritability to around .40 (Carey, 1992).

The aforementioned results for the Danish twins used the phenotype of criminal registration, which includes both crimes against property and crimes against persons. Analysis of crimes against persons (i.e., murder, assault, and sexual offenses) gave tetrachoric correlations of .77 for MZ and .52 for DZ pairs. Although these correlations are consistent with a genetic effect, the difference between them is not significant.

The third modern study of the genetics of antisocial behavior was that of Grove et al. (1990). The phenotype was the number of symptoms of Antisocial Personality Disorder (ASP) as defined by the *DSM–III*. The sample, albeit small, was exceptionally important because it was a series of MZ twins raised apart from an early age. Heritability was estimated at .42 for the number of childhood conduct disorder symptoms and .29 for the number of adult (i.e., over age 18) symptoms of ASP. Moreover, there were important genetic correlations among the number of ASP symptoms and the number of alcohol abuse and drug abuse symptoms. This suggests part of the comorbidity between antisocial behavior and substance abuse in general is genetic in origin.

Two recent abstracts also analyzed twin similarity for symptoms of ASP as specified by the *DSM–III* and *DSM–III–R*. Carey (1993) reported on a mixed-sex twin series in which one member (the proband) has been admitted to a psychiatric facility for any type of disorder. Although there was a gender difference in mean number of ASP symptoms with males having more symptoms than females, there was no detectable gender difference in correlations. There was significant heritability for both ASP symptoms and for diagnostic ratings of ASP.

---

[2]The terms *imitation* (Carey, 1986) and *cooperation* (Eaves, 1976) must be understood in a mathematical context. These terms refer to *all* types of genetic and phenotypic interactions among members of sibships that *increase* similarity. All psychological mechanisms such as reciprocal social learning, coercive interactions, and mutual reinforcement among members of a sibship will be mathematically subsumed under the imitation or cooperation effect.

The second report was that of Lyons et al (1993), who analyzed data from a large series of male Vietnam-era veteran twins. Consistent with the other twin data, they reported significant heritability for ASP symptoms. However, there appeared to be a larger common environmental effect for juvenile and adolescent symptoms than for adult symptoms.

ADULT ANTISOCIAL BEHAVIOR: ADOPTION STUDIES

In contrast to most behavioral genetic phenotypes, until recently, there had been more adoption studies of adult antisocial behavior than twin studies. Crowe (1972, 1974) reported the first modern adoption study. He identified 41 female offenders who had given up children for adoption. Most of the offenders were convicted of felonies. To these probands, he matched a control group of women who also gave children up for adoption but who had no criminal record. Offspring of the criminal women were more likely than the offspring of the control women to have had an arrest (15% vs. 4%) or a criminal conviction (14% vs. 2%). Two small adoption studies by Cadoret (1978; Cadoret and Cain, 1980; Cadoret, Cain, & Crowe, 1983: Cadoret, Cunningham, Loftus, & Edwards, 1975; Cadoret, O'Gorman, Troughton, & Heywood, 1985; Cadoret, Troughton, O'Gorman, & Heywood, 1986) also reported significant heritability for counts of ASP symptoms. Perhaps of more importance than the heritability of ASP per se was the observation that some of the comorbidity between ASP and substance abuse appeared to be genetic in origin (Cadoret et al., 1986).

The most extensive adoption study of antisocial behavior was performed in Denmark. An initial study of adoptees born in the city and county of Copenhagen had evidence consistent with a genetic effect. Of male adoptees with a biological father who was registered for a criminal offense, 22.7% were registered for criminality. The comparable figure among adoptees with unregistered biological fathers was 13.6% (Hutchings, 1972; Hutchings & Mednick, 1977).

The Danish study was later extended to the entire country of Denmark and was reported by Mednick and Finello (1983; Mednick, Gabrielli, & Hutchings, 1983). Using court convictions (as opposed to criminal registration with the police), they found a linear relation between the number of convictions of the biological parents and the number of convictions in the adopted-away offspring. Further and more detailed analyses of this sample have been presented by Baker (1986; Baker, Mack, Moffit, & Mednick, 1989). Of particular importance is the fact that personality disorders and substance abuse in the biological parents predicted court convictions of the adoptees.

An adoption study in Sweden gave more equivocal results (Bohman, Cloninger, Sigvardsson, & von Knorring, 1982; Cloninger, Sigvardsson, Bohman, & von Knorring, 1982; Sigvardsson, Cloninger, Bohman, & von Knorring, 1982). Of 258 male adoptees with either a convicted biological father or biological mother, 13.2% were themselves convicted. The comparable figure for male adoptees with biological parents without convictions was 10.4%, a difference that is not statistically significant. However, alcohol abuse appeared to moderate the relationship. There were significant predictive effects for biological parentage when criminal adoptees were subdivided into those with and without registered alcohol abuse. Violent offenses on the part of the biological father predicted offspring alcohol abuse while paternal property crimes and fraud predicted adoptees who were registered for criminality but not alcohol abuse.

THE QUESTION OF VIOLENCE

It is sometimes assumed that antisocial individuals whose extreme deficits in self-control lead to impulsive and violent acts may be the true "genetic" cases that drive the relationship between heredity and crime. Is there empirical evidence for this?

Three of the aforementioned studies have data relevant to the issue of violence. First, the Swedish adoption data (Bohman et al., 1982) report a significant correlation between violent offenses of the biological father and alcohol abuse in male adoptees. This suggests that there must be some genetic correlation between violence and alcohol abuse. Because one cannot get a genetic correlation between two variables without heritability for each variable, it follows that there must be some heritability for violence.

In stark contrast, the Danish adoption study reported almost no evidence for the heritability of violence, although what constituted a "violent" crime in their sample was undefined by the investigators. Mednick, Brennan, and Kandel (1988; Mednick et al., 1983; Mednick, Gabrielli, & Hutchings, 1984) found no significant relationship between the number of court convictions in biological parents and the presence of a conviction for a violent crime in the adoptee. Mednick et al. (1983) cite other analyses that also failed to reveal a genetic effect for violence.

In the Danish twin sample, Cloninger and Gotttesman (1987) analyzed concordance for "crimes against persons," which includes interpersonal violence and sexual offenses. Because the frequency of this category was so low in females, they restricted analysis to only same-sex, male pairs. The respective identical and fraternal twin correlations were .77 and .52. Although this is suggestive of a genetic effect, the difference between the two correlations is not statistically significant.

Taken together, these three studies do not suggest a strong role for genetics once the phenotype is restricted to violence. That said, there are several qualifications that must be made. All three studies relied on official records and convictions for a violent offense, and all three studies dealt with Scandinavian populations. Although violence may not be rare, adjudication for violent offenses was very rare among these populations. Hence, the studies may have suffered from baserate problems, despite their large sample sizes. As pointed out earlier (Carey, 1994b), the Mednick study might actually not have had sufficient power to detect either a genetic or a family environmental effect for violence given the low baserate. Second, failure to specify exactly what constitutes a *violent* offense makes comparison across studies difficult. Third, extrapolation of violence from Scandinavia to other populations is problematic. And finally, it is possible that small subgroups of violent offenders may exhibit stronger heritability than all offenders lumped together. These results demonstrate how much genetic research needs to be done on violent offenders.

METHODOLOGICAL CONSIDERATIONS
AND PROSPECTS FOR FUTURE RESEARCH

The Interpretation of Existing Results

Research in the genetic epidemiology of antisocial behavior is not experimental. Consequently, the lack of precise, laboratory-like control over such variables as who has twins, how the twins are raised, who gives up children for adoption and who adopts those children, and how the adoptees are raised may compromise a genetic interpretation of the data. Behavioral genetic research has been very sensitive to these issues. Indeed, it is true that:

1. Identical twins tend to be treated more similarly than fraternal twins (Loehlin & Nichols, 1976);
2. Twins as a group have higher rates than singletons of pregnancy and birth complications or PBCs (Kilby, Govind, & O'Brien, 1994; Layde, Erickson, Falek, & McCarthy, 1980; McNeil et al., 1994; Streissguth & Dehaene, 1993);
3. Chorionicity, which is associated with PBCs, differs between MZ and DZ twins leading to the possibility that concordance differences in behavior may reflect intrauterine events (O'Brien & Hay, 1987);
4. Twins as a group may have lower intelligence and higher rates of learning disabilities than singletons (Hay, O'Brien, Johnston, & Prior, 1984);
5. Volunteer twin registries have larger MZ/DZ ratios than expected (Lykken, McGue, & Tellegen, 1987);
6. The biological parents and the adoptive parents of adoptees are not random samples of the population (all adoption studies of antisocial behavior);
7. There is indeed selective placement for adoption.

As in other epidemiological questions such as the causal role of television on violence, the crucial question is whether such confounding influences are large enough to eliminate a putative causal effect. It is here where such criticisms of genetic epidemiology fail. Consider the fact that identical twins are treated more similarly than fraternal twins, for example. If these subtle differences in the rearing environments translated into large differences in MZ and DZ concordances, then two predictions should be shown in the data. First, while some parents treat MZ pairs as a single unit, others accentuate individuality; hence, MZ twins who have been treated more alike should be more similar in behavior than MZ pairs who have been "individualized" or mistaken in zygosity. This, however, has never proven to be the case (Kendler, Neale, Kessler, Heath, & Eaves, 1993; Loehlin & Nichols, 1976). The second prediction is that identical twins raised apart should be much less similar than those raised together. The empirical data, however, suggest very little, if any, difference in similarity for antisocial or aggressivity (Grove et al., 1990; Tellegen et al., 1988). Thus, the conventional thought is that special rearing for MZ pairs is not a major reason for their great similarity (see Shields, 1978, for an insightful discussion of this topic.)

Similar estimates of effect size suggest that PBCs, nonrepresentativeness of families in an adoption design, and selective placement will not dramatically alter observed correlations. For example, consider selective placement. Under this model, the correlation between a biological relative and an adopted-away individual will be the product of two correlations—the correlation between the adoptee and the adoptive family and the correlation between the adoptive and the biological family (i.e., the selective placement correlation). Hence, the patterning of correlations under strong selective placement would be a *large* adoptive family correlation and a *small* biological family correlation. The observed data, however, is in the *opposite* direction (see Baker et al., 1989, for tetrachoric correlations on property crime). Hence, the most likely effect of selective placement is to overestimate the effect of the family environment rather than the effect of the genes.

Perhaps the best argument in favor of a genetic interpretation of these data is the internal consistency of the correlations. Data from volunteer registers of twins (Loehlin & Nichols, 1976; Tellegen et al., 1988) give the same results as those from population-ascertained registers (e.g., Cloninger & Gottesman, 1987). Twins raised apart have correlations consistent with those for twins raised together. Correlation between biological parents and adoptees agree roughly with heritability estimated from twin data. If there were a plethora of biasing factors, it would be very remarkable if their effects would counterbalance each other in studies of adoptees, twins raised together, and twins raised apart to give such a consistent and coherent pattern to the data.

Implications of Genetic Research and the Future

Of what use is finding a "major gene" or "genetic marker" for aggression and antisocial behavior? There are two possible uses—prediction and understanding. The prediction area must grapple with the nature of heritability—it is not small, but neither is it so large as to be called deterministic. A crude estimate based on the Danish twin and adoption data is about 40% of the propensity-liability-predisposition toward antisocial behavior may be attributable to heredity. The major implication of a 40% heritability is that there will probably be no widespread genetic marker for antisocial behavior in the general population (although there may be markers in rare pedigrees). Even if all the genetic influence were due to a single locus (a very implausible situation), there will simply be too many prediction errors to make the locus of any practical significance.

To illustrate, consider a known genotypic risk factor that is detectable at birth—often before birth—such that the high risk genotype stands a hundredfold increase of being convicted for rape compared to the low risk genotype. This genotype, of course, is simply the presence of an XX or an XY genotype for sex determination.[3] The magnitude of the correlation between the chromosomal genotype and rape is not far from the magnitude of the heritability for aggression and antisocial behavior—accounting for between 25% and 50% of the variance, depending on the baserate for rape. Yet it is quite clear that predicting that all men would be rapists will generate more incorrect than correct predictions.

Hence, the usefulness of genetics is likely to be in the understanding of aggression. For neurobiology, studies of the loci behind serotonin receptors and serotonin metabolism as outlined by Goldman (chap. 2, this volume) may elucidate mechanisms correlated with aggression, just as Brown and Goldstein (1986) used familial hypercholesterolemia to unravel mechanisms about synthesis, intracellular transport, and action of the low density lipoprotein receptor. At present, we have no understanding of how the DNA differences inferred from twin and adoption studies translate into behavioral differences in aggression. In the end, the actual genetic mechanisms may be mediated more through the environment than through strict biology. For example, XY genotypes may be socialized into sexual aggressiveness more often than XX genotypes, leading to the observed statistical association with forcible rape. However, given the number of moderately heritable traits correlated with antisocial behavior, ranging from cognitive ability to temperament (Wilson & Herrnstein, 1985), given the emerging data on biochemical correlates of aggression, and given the dramatic advances in molecular genetics, it is clear that genetically informative designs using multivariate techniques will become increasingly important for understanding the complicated pathways for human aggression.

ACKNOWLEDGMENT

Research for this chapter was supported in part by grant DA-05131.

---

[3]I use the term *genotypic risk factor* purely in the statistical or correlational sense of something that is genetic and can *predict* an outcome. The *causal mechanisms* that mediate this prediction are a different matter and may be more social and environmental than biological in nature. The actual sex ratio in this example is a round number taken from Kruttschnitt (1994).

REFERENCES

Baker, L. A. (1986). Estimating genetic correlations among discontinuous phenotypes: An analysis of criminal convictions and psychiatric-hospital diagnoses in Danish adoptees. Special Issue: Multivariate behavioral genetics and development. *Behavior Genetics, 16*, 127–142.

Baker, L. A., Mack, W., Moffitt, T. E., & Mednick, S. A. (1989). Sex differences in property crime in a Danish adoption cohort. *Behavior Genetics, 19*, 355–370.

Bancroft, J., Axworthy, D., & Ratcliffe, S. (1982). The personality and psychosexual development of boys with 47 XXY chromosome constitution. *Journal of Child Psychology and Psychiatry, 23*, 169–180.

Bender, B. G., Linden, M. G., & Robinson, A. (1987). Environment and developmental risk in children with sex chromosome abnormalities. *Journal of the American Academy of Child and Adolescent Psychiatry, 26*, 499–503.

Bohman, M. (1971). A comparative study of adopted children, foster children and children in their biological environment born after undesired pregnancies. *Acta Paediatrica Scandinavica, 60*(Suppl. 221), 5–38.

Bohman, M. (1978). Some genetic aspects of alcoholism and criminality: A population of adoptees. *Archives of General Psychiatry, 35*, 269–276.

Bohman, M. (1983). Alcoholism and crime: Studies of adoptees. *Substance and Alcohol Actions/Misuse, 4*, 137–147.

Bohman, M., Cloninger, C. R., Sigvardsson, S., & von Knorring, A.-L. (1982). Predisposition to petty criminality in Swedish adoptees: I. Genetic and environmental heterogeneity. *Archives of General Psychiatry, 39*, 1233–1241.

Bohman, M., Cloninger, C. R., von Knorring, A.-L., & Sigvardsson, S. (1984). An adoption study of somatoform disorders: III. Cross-fostering analysis and genetic relationship to alcoholism and criminality. *Archives of General Psychiatry, 41*, 872–878.

Bohman, M., & Sigvardsson, S. (1985). A prospective longitudinal study of adoption. In A. R. Nicol (Ed.), *Longitudinal studies in child psychology and psychiatry* (pp. 137–155). Somerset, NJ: Wiley.

Brown, M. S, & Goldstein, J. L. (1986). A receptor mediated pathway for cholesterol homeostasis. *Science, 232*, 34–47.

Brunner, H. G., Nelen, M. R., Breakefield, X. O., Ropers, H. H., & Van Oost, B. A. (1993). Abnormal behavior associated with a point mutation in the structural gene for monoamine oxidase A. *Science 262*, 578–580.

Brunner, H. G., Nelen, M., vanZandvoort, P., Abeling, N. G. G. M., VanGennip, A. H., Wolters, E. C., Kuiper, M. A., Ropers, H. H., & Van Oost, B. A. (1993). X-linked borderline mental retardation with prominent behavioral disturbance: Phenotype, genetic localization, and evidence for disturbed monoamine metabolism. *American Journal of Human Genetics, 52*, 1032–1039.

Cadoret, R. J. (1978). Psychopathology in adopted-away offspring of biologic parents with antisocial behavior. *Archives of General Psychiatry, 35*, 176–184.

Cadoret, R. J., & Cain, C. (1980). Sex differences in predictors of antisocial behavior in adoptees. *Archives of General Psychiatry, 37*, 1171–1175.

Cadoret, R. J., Cain, C., & Crowe, R. R. (1983). Evidence for a gene-environment interaction in the development of adolescent antisocial behavior. *Behavior Genetics, 13*, 301–310.

Cadoret, R. J., Cunningham, L., Loftus, R., & Edwards, J. (1975). Studies of adoptees from psychiatrically disturbed biologic parents: II. Temperament, hyperactive, antisocial, and developmental variables. *Journal of Pediatrics, 87*, 301–306.

Cadoret, R. J., O'Gorman, T. W., Troughton, E., & Heywood, E., (1985). Alcoholism and antisocial personality: Interrelationships, genetic and environmental factors. *Archives of General Psychiatry, 42*, 161–167.

Cadoret, R. J., Troughton, E., O'Gorman, T. W., & Heywood, E. (1986). An adoption study of genetic and environmental factors in drug abuse. *Archives of General Psychiatry, 43*, 1131–1136.

Cairns, R. B., MacCombie, D. J., & Hood, K. E. (1983). A developmental-genetic analysis of aggressive behavior in mice: I. Behavioral outcomes. *Journal of Comparative Psychology, 97*, 69–89.

Carey, G. (1986). Sibling imitation and contrast effects. *Behavior Genetics, 18*, 329–338.

Carey, G. (1992). Twin imitation for antisocial behavior: Implications for genetic and family environment research. *Journal of Abnormal Psychology, 101*, 18–25.

Carey, G. (1993). Multivariate genetic relationships among drug abuse, alcohol abuse and antisocial personality. *Psychiatric Genetics, 3*, 141.

Carey, G. (1994a). The genetic association study in psychiatry: Analytical evaluation and a recommendation. *American Journal of Medical Genetics, 54*, 311–317.

Carey, G. (1994b). Genetics and violence. In A. J. Reiss, Jr. & J. A. Roth (Eds.), *Understanding and preventing violence: Biobehavioral influences on violence, Vol. 2* (pp. 21–58). Commmittee on Law and Justice, National Research Council. Washington, DC: National Academy Press.

Carey, G., & DiLalla, D. L. (1994). Personality and psychopathology: Genetic perspectives. *Journal of Abnormal Psychology, 103*, 32–43.

Chen, C., Rainnie, D. G., Greene, R. W., & Tonegawa, S. (1994). Abnormal fear response and aggressive behavior in mutant mice deficient for α-calcium-calmodulin kinase II. *Science, 266*, 291–294.

Christiansen, K. O. (1968). Threshold of tolerance in various population groups illustrated by results from Danish criminological twin study. In A. V. S. de Reuck & R. Porter (Eds.), *Ciba Foundation symposium on the mentally abnormal offender* (pp. 107–116). London: Churchill.

Christiansen, K. O. (1970). Crime in a Danish twin population. *Acta Geneticae Medicae Gemellologicae: Twin Research, 19*, 323–326.

Christiansen, K. O. (1974). Seriousness of criminality and concordance among Danish twins. In R. Hood (Ed.), *Crime, criminology, and public policy*. London: Heinemann.

Cloninger, C. R., Christiansen, K. O., Reich, T., & Gottesman, I. I. (1978). Implications of sex differences in the prevalences of antisocial personality, alcoholism, and criminality for familial transmission. *Archives of General Psychiatry, 35*, 941–951.

Cloninger, C. R., & Gottesman, I. I. (1987). Genetic and environmental factors in antisocial behavior disorders. In S. A. Mednick, T. E. Moffitt, & S. A. Stack (Eds.), *The causes of crime: New biological approaches* (pp. 92–109). New York: Cambridge University Press.

Cloninger, C. R., Sigvardsson, S., Bohman, M., & von Knorring, A.-L. (1982). Predisposition to petty criminality in Swedish adoptees: II. Cross-fostering analysis of gene-environment interaction. *Archives of General Psychiatry, 39*, 1242–1247.

Cologer-Clifford, A., Simon, N. G., & Jubilan, B. M. (1992). Genotype, uterine position, and testosterone sensitivity in older female mice. *Physiology and Behavior, 51*, 1047–1050.

Compaan, J. C., de Ruiter, A. J., Koolhaas, J. M., van Oortmerssen, G. A., & Bohus, B. (1992). Differential effects of neonatal testosterone treatment on aggression in two selection lines of mice. *Physiology and Behavior, 51*, 7–10.

Crowe, R. R. (1972). The adopted offspring of women criminal offenders: A study of their arrest records. *Archives of General Psychiatry, 27*, 600–603.

Crowe, R. R. (1974). An adoption study of antisocial personality. *Archives of General Psychiatry, 31*, 785–791.

Crowe, R. R. (1993). Candidate genes in psychiatry: An epidemiological perspective. *American Journal of Medical Genetics, 48*, 74–77.

Dalgard, O. S., & Kringlen, E. (1976). A Norwegian twin study of criminality. *British Journal of Criminology, 16*, 213–232.

Eaves, L. J. (1976). A model for sibling effects in man. *Heredity, 36*, 205–214.

Eaves, L. J., Eysenck, H. J., & Martin, N. G. (1989). *Genes, culture, and personality*. New York: Academic Press.

Eaves, L. J., Last, K. A., Martin, N. G., & Jinks, J. L. (1977). A progressive approach to non-additivity and genotype-environment covariance in the analysis of human differences. *British Journal of Mathematical and Statistical Psychology, 30,* 1–42.

Eaves, L. J., Silberg, J. L., Hewitt, J. K., Rutter, M., Meyer, J. M., Neale, M. C., & Pickles, A. (1993). Analyzing twin resemblance in multisymptom data: Genetic applications of a latent class model for symptoms of conduct disorder in juvenile boys. *Behavior Genetics, 23,* 5–19.

Gabrielli, W. F., & Mednick, S. A. (1983). Genetic correlates of criminal behavior: Implications for research, attribution, and prevention. *American Behavioral Scientist, 27,* 59–74.

Gabrielli, W. F., & Mednick, S. A. (1984). Urban environment, genetics, and crime. *Criminology, 22,* 645–652.

Gariépy, J.-L., Hood, K. E., & Cairns, R. B. (1988). A developmental-genetic analysis of aggressive behavior in mice (Mus musculus): III. Behavioral mediation by heightened reactivity or immobility? *Journal of Comparative Psychology, 102,* 392–399.

Gottesman, I. I., Carey, G., & Hanson, D. H. (1983). Pearls and perils in epigenetic psychopathology. In S. G. Guze, E. J. Earls, & J. E. Barrett (Eds.), *Childhood psychopathology and development* (pp. 287–300). New York: Raven.

Gottesman, I. I., & Goldsmith, H. H. (1994). Developmental psychopathology of antisocial behavior: Inserting genes into its ontogenesis and epigenesis. In C. A. Nelson (Ed.), *Threats to optimal development: Integrating biological, psychological and social risk factors.* Hillsdale, NJ: Lawrence Erlbaum Associates.

Grove, W. M., Eckert, E. D., Heston, L. L., Bouchard, T. J., Jr., Segal, N. L., & Lykken, D. T. (1990). Heritability of substance abuse and antisocial behavior: A study of monozygotic twins raised apart. *Biological Psychiatry, 27,* 293–304.

Hay, D. A., O'Brien, P. J., Johnston, C. J., & Prior, M. (1984). The high incidence of reading disability in twin boys and its implication for genetic analysis. *Acta Geneticae Medicae et Gemellogiae (Roma), 33,* 223–236.

Hen, R., Boschert, V., Lemeur, M., Dierich, A., Ait Amara, D., Buhot, M. C., Segu, L., Misslin, R., & Sandou, F. (1993, July). *5HT1B Receptor "knockout": Pharmacological and behavioral consequences.* Paper presented at the 23rd Annual Meeting of the Society for Neuroscience, Washington, DC.

Hood, K. E., & Cairns, R. B. (1988). A developmental-genetic analysis of aggressive behavior in mice. II. Cross-sex inheritance. *Behavior Genetics, 18,* 605–619.

Hutchings, B. (1972). *Environmental and genetic factors in psychopathology and criminality.* Unpublished master's thesis, University of London.

Hutchings, B., & Mednick, S. A. (1971). Criminality in adoptees and their adoptive and biological parents: A pilot study. In S. A. Mednick & K. O. Christiansen (Eds.), *Biosocial bases of criminal behavior* (pp. 127–141). New York: Gardner.

Hutchings, B., & Mednick, S. A. (1975). Registered criminality in the adoptive and biological parents of registered male criminal adoptees. In R. R. Fieve, D. Rosenthal, & H. Brill (Eds.), *Genetic research in psychiatry.* Baltimore, MD: Johns Hopkins University Press.

Kendler, K. S., Neale, M. C., Kessler, R. C., Heath, A. C., & Eaves, L. J. (1993). A test of the equal environments assumption in twin studies of psychiatric illness. *Behavior Genetics, 23,* 21–27.

Kilby, M. D., Govind, A., & O'Brien, P. M. (1994). Outcome of twin pregnancies complicated by a single intrauterine death: A comparison with viable twin pregnancies. *Obstetrics and Gynecology, 84,* 107–109.

Kruttschnitt, C. (1994). Gender and interpersonal violence. In A. J. Reiss, Jr. & J. A. Roth (Eds.), *Understanding and preventing violence. Vol. 3. Social Influences* (pp. 293–376). Washington, DC: National Academy Press.

Layde, P. M., Erickson, J. D., Falek, A., & McCarthy, B. J. (1980). Congenital malformation in twins. *American Journal of Human Genetics, 32,* 69–78.

Loehlin, J. C., & Nichols, R. C. (1976). Heredity, environment, and personality: A study of 850 sets of twins. Austin: University of Texas Press.

Lykken, D. T., McGue, M., & Tellegen, A. (1987). Recruitment bias in twin research: The rule of two-thirds reconsidered. *Behavior Genetics, 17*, 343–362.

Lyons, M. J., Eaves, L. J., Tsuang, M. Y., Eisen, S. E., Goldberg, J., & True, W. T. (1993). Differential heritability of adult and juvenile antisocial traits. *Psychiatric Genetics, 3*, 117.

Maxson, S. C. (1981). The genetics of aggression in vertebrates. In P. F. Brain & D. Benton (Eds.), *The biology of aggression*. Amsterdam: Sijthoff & Noordhoff.

Maxson, S. C., Didier-Erikson, A., & Ogawa, S. (1989). The Y chromosome, social signals, and offense in mice. *Behavioral and Neural Biology, 52*, 251–259.

McNeil, T. F., Cantor-Graae, E., Torrey, E. F., Sjostrom, K., Bowler, A., Taylor, E., Rawlings, R., & Higgins, E. S. (1994). Obstetric complications in histories of monozygotic twins discordant and concordant for schizophrenia. *Acta Psychiatrica Scandinavica, 89*, 196–204.

Mednick, S. A. (1987). Introduction—Biological factors in crime causation: The reactions of social scientists. In S. A. Mednick, T. E. Moffitt, & S. A. Stack (Eds.), *The causes of crime: New biological approaches*. New York: Cambridge University Press.

Mednick, S. A., Brennan, P., & Kandel, E. (1988). Predisposition to violence. Special Issue: Current theoretical perspectives on aggressive and antisocial behavior. *Aggressive Behavior, 14*, 25–33.

Mednick, S. A., & Finello, K. M. (1983). Biological factors and crime: Implications for forensic psychiatry. *International Journal of Law and Psychiatry, 6*, 1–15.

Mednick, S. A., Gabrielli, W. F., & Hutchings, B. (1983). Genetic influences in criminal behavior: Evidence from an adoption cohort. In K. T. Van Dusen & S. A. Mednick (Eds.), *Prospective studies of crime and delinquency* (pp. 39–56). Boston: Kluwer-Nijhoff.

Mednick, S. A., Gabrielli, W. F., & Hutchings, B. (1984). Genetic influences in criminal convictions: Evidence from an adoption cohort. *Science, 224*, 891–894.

Mednick, S. A., Gabrielli, W. F., & Hutchings, B. (1987). Genetic factors in the etiology of criminal behavior. In S. A. Mednick, T. E. Moffitt, & S. A. Stack (Eds.), *The causes of crime: New biological approaches* (pp. 74–91). New York: Cambridge University Press.

Moffitt, T. E. (1987). Parental mental disorder and offspring criminal behavior: An adoption study. *Psychiatry, 50*, 346–360.

Neale, M. C., & Cardon, L. R. (1990). *Methodology for genetic studies of twins and families*. Dordrecht, The Netherlands: Kluwer Academic Publishers.

Nikulina, E. M., & Kapralova, N. S. (1992). Role of dopamine receptors in the regulation of aggression in mice: Relationship to genotype. *Neuroscience and Behavioral Physiology, 22*, 364–369.

O'Brien, P. J., & Hay, D. A. (1987). Birthweight differences, the transfusion syndrome and the cognitive development of monozygotic twins. *Acta Geneticae Medicae et Gemellogiae (Roma), 32*, 181–196.

Rowe, D. C. (1983). Biometrical genetic models of self-reported delinquent behavior: A twin study. *Behavior Genetics, 13*, 473–489.

Rowe, D. C. (1985). Sibling interaction and self-reported delinquent behavior: A study of 265 twin pairs. *Criminology, 23*, 223–240.

Rowe, D. C. (1986). Genetic and environmental components of antisocial behavior: A study of 265 twin pairs. *Criminology, 24*, 513–532.

Schiavi, R. C., Theilgaard, A., Owen, D. R., & White, D. (1984). Sex chromosome anomalies, hormones, and aggressivity. *Archives of General Psychiatry, 41*, 93–99.

Schiavi, R. C., Theilgaard, A., Owen, D. R., & White, D. (1988). Sex chromosome anomalies, hormones, and sexuality. *Archives of General Psychiatry, 45*, 19–24.

Shields, J. (1978). MZA twins: Their use and abuse. In W. E. Nance, G. Allen, & P. Parisi (Eds.), *Progress in clinical and biological research: Vol. 24A* (pp. 79–93). New York: Alan R. Liss.

Sigvardsson, S., Cloninger, C. R., Bohman, M., & von Knorring, A.-L. (1982). Predisposition to petty criminality in Swedish adoptees: III. Sex differences and validation of the male typology. *Archives of General Psychiatry, 39*, 1248–1253.

Streissguth, A. P., & Dehaene, P. (1993). Fetal alcohol syndrome in twins of alcoholic mothers: Concordance of diagnosis and IQ. *American Journal of Medical Genetics, 47,* 857–861.

Svare, B. (1988). Genotype modulates the aggression-promoting quality of progesterone in pregnant mice. *Hormones and Behavior, 22,* 90–99.

Tellegen, A., Lykken, D. T., Bouchard, T. J., Jr., Wilcox, K. J., Segal, N., & Rich, S. (1988). Personality similarity in twins reared apart and together. *Journal of Personality and Social Psychology, 54,* 1031–1039.

Theilgaard A. (1984). A psychological study of the personalities of XYY and XXY men. *Acta Psychiatrica Scandinavica, Supplementum 69,* 1–133.

Weerts, E. M., Miller, L. G., Hood, K. E., & Miczek, K. A. (1992). Increased GABAA-dependent chloride uptake in mice selectively bred for low aggressive behavior. *Psychopharmacology, 108,* 196–204.

Wilson, J. Q., & Herrnstein, R. J. (1985). *Crime and human nature.* New York: Simon and Schuster.

Witkin, H. A., Mednick, S. A., Schulsinger, F., Bakkestrom, E., Christiansen, K. O., Goodenough, D. R., Hirschhorn, K., Lundsteen, C., Owen, D. R., Philip, J., Rubin, D. B., & Stocking, M. (1976). Criminality in XYY and XXY men. *Science, 193,* 547–555.

2

THE SEARCH FOR GENETIC ALLELES CONTRIBUTING TO SELF-DESTRUCTIVE AND AGGRESSIVE BEHAVIORS

David Goldman
National Institute on Alcohol Abuse and Alcoholism

The interactions of genetic and environmental sources of variation produce powerful individual differences in the development of neural mechanisms that are permissive for a variety of aggressive behaviors. Ultimately, profound differences in these behaviors are therefore observable both between species and within species. Numerous genes are essential for the normal development and function of the neural systems mediating aggressive behaviors. Detection of the variants of these genes will not reduce behavior to the nucleotide, but could help explain the origins of behavior and the origins of behavioral variation. The development and eventual function of the neural systems involved in aggression are powerfully modulated in many ways by the animal's experiences, and the animal's experiences are shaped by gene–environment interactions. The domain of this chapter is the detection of gene variants which, in part, mediate the interindividual variation.

The variety of behaviors that may be labeled *aggressive* is large, and *aggression* is therefore not a phenotype for genetic analysis. Narrower or better-defined categories of aggression can be utilized; much of the relevant work on aggression is on neuropsychological phenotypes and psychiatric diagnoses, which are associated with forms of aggression but which represent goals in their own right. A full appreciation of the genetic antecedents of aggression would require a better understanding of what aggression is, as well as the identification of genetic and nongenetic origins of interindividual differences in a wide variety of behaviors. Changing the definition of aggressive behavior will obviously change the genes involved.

Both within and outside the laboratory, pharmacological manipulations of neurochemical systems moderate and augment impulsive and aggressive behaviors. By manipulating serotonin, particular murine-aggressive behaviors can be augmented or reduced. Androgen levels also play a role in determining aggressiveness, for example, rough-and-tumble play (Levine, 1966; see also Gariépy, Lewis, and Cairns, chap. 3, this volume). In humans, aggressive behavior is frequently released only when the individual is intoxicated. These interactions between aggression and drugs resemble gene–environment interactions in behavior. More importantly, for the purpose of discovering the determinants of aggression, results from behavioral pharmacology may also serve to identify the neurochemical pathways where genetic variants alter individual variation in the predisposition to such behaviors.

Functionally variant alleles cause heritable behavioral variation in impulsiveness and aggressivity. In animals, the behavioral variation resulting from the differential action of these alleles is exemplified by behavioral differences between species and between strains of animals (Plomin, 1990). Across species and across strains within species, genetic differences in temperament, including aggressiveness, are apparent. The allelic differences affecting behavior have in various cases been deliberately selected, randomly fixed, or determined by natural selection. In the same fashion, variant alleles are also responsible for heritable differences in temperament and disease liability in humans. In humans and in other mammalian species, the inherited behavioral differences are mediated by differences in neural systems that are homologous in their origins and similar in important functional aspects across species. This knowledge enables investigators to learn some things about the genetics of human behavior by studying animals and to learn some things about the genetics of animal behavior by studying humans.

Recently, linked (or associated) genetic markers and functionally significant alleles for self-destructive and aggressive behaviors have been discovered in the human. This chapter discusses the relationship of genetic variation in serotonin function to impulsive and aggressive behaviors and describes approaches, limitations of these approaches, and recent progress in identifying alleles determining interindividual variation in these behaviors.

Phenotypes

Aggressive behaviors are exhibited in a variety of contexts, for different purposes, and through different underlying mechanisms. Aggressive behaviors that are stereotyped, individual (rather than part of group or collective aggression [May, 1968]) and accompanied by distinct neurochemical or neuropsychological markers are likely to be relatively more homogeneous on an etiologic basis.

Because various psychiatric disorders that are significantly heritable are accompanied by increased or decreased liabilities for aggressive behavior, identification of genetic vulnerability factors contributing to these disorders will contribute to understanding the antecedents of aggressiveness. For example, more than half of violent crimes occur under the influence of alcohol (see Barros and Miczek, chap. 12, this volume) and the violent behavior is frequently triggered by relatively small amounts of alcohol (Mark & Ervin, 1970). Thus, one genetic mechanism mediating liability for aggressive behaviors would be genetic vulnerabilities for alcoholism. In addition, various other neuropsychiatric disorders increase the likelihood of violent behaviors. These phenotype-diagnosis associations include suicide in depression (Tsuang, 1983), schizophrenia (Niskanen & Achte, 1972; Tsuang, 1983), and alcoholism. Self-directed violence in borderline personality disorder, self-mutilation, and other self-destructive behaviors characteristic of Lesch Nyhan syndrome are also observed in other mental retardation syndromes. The substantial heritability of several psychiatric diseases sometimes associated with aggressiveness has been reviewed (e.g., schizophrenia [Gottesman & Shields, 1982], affective illness [Berrettini, Goldin, Nurnberger, & Gershon, 1984; Loehlin, Willerman, & Horn, 1988], alcoholism [Goldman, 1993]), and are not addressed here. Other behaviors that are associated with aggressiveness and for which heritability studies are strongly suggestive of a major genetic component are suicide, delinquency, sociopathy, criminal behavior, and violent behavior (Coccaro, Bergeman, & McClearn, 1993).

Reliable and accurate psychiatric diagnoses are available both in clinical research and in practice at the majority of academic medical centers. Using a structured clinical interview and defined diagnostic criteria, diagnoses are assigned that have validity across groups of investigators and across centers. Therefore, a particular advantage of studying psychiatric disorders associated with aggressiveness is that the phenotypes tend to be portable, replicable, and understandable.

Studying genetic factors for psychiatric disorders introduces two difficulties for understanding trait differences in aggressiveness: (a) the genetic epidemiology of the psychiatric disorders—including their incomplete penetrance, genetic heterogeneity, and phenocopies has made identification of determinant alleles difficult, and (b) the variety of aggressive behaviors and the variation in the propensity to these behaviors is probably incompletely encompassed through the psychiatric disorders. The latter problem could be approached by studying a wide range of psychiatric traits, by evaluating underlying traits and marker traits, and simply by adding dimensional measures of whatever type of aggressiveness that is of interest. Incomplete penetrance diminishes the power of family linkage studies but can be dealt with conservatively by studying only affected individuals. Phenocopies are nonproblematic for rare disorders but will complicate linkage analyses on common traits, such as alcoholism, in which as many as half of all cases may be sporadic. For both traits and diseases, genetic heterogeneity is more the rule than the exception and should be presumed for common behavioral traits and diseases, even if at their surfaces they do not reveal evidence of underlying heterogeneity.

Several approaches should ultimately be successful in resolving genetic determinants in the face of the problem of heterogeneity: the use of underlying traits and marker traits that isolate more homogeneous subgroups; the use of large, high density families or genetically more homogeneous populations; direct scanning of the candidate genes for mutations. The direct gene scanning approach has only recently become practical with the advent of automated sequencing methods and rapid methods for scanning for the genetic variants (Ellison, Dean, & Goldman, 1993). Direct scanning for genetic variants turns the problem of heterogeneity into an advantage because heterogeneity only increases the likelihood that analysis of one particular candidate gene will result in the detection of a functional gene variant from among an unrelated population of individuals with the phenotype of interest.

Heritability

Not all behavioral variation is from genetic sources but all human behaviors arise within a matrix of genetically determined mechanisms. Heritability studies provide a minimum estimate of the extent to which variance in a behavior across a human population is genetically determined. Heritability studies led to current efforts to identify and elucidate the roles in behavior of inherited differences and, to some extent, they may help guide the design of such studies. Alleles determining or influencing traits may be detected when heritability of a trait is low or undetectable (due to etiologic heterogeneity). Also, identification of high heritability for a trait or discovery of an allele determining variation does not preclude the manipulation of the environment to modify the trait, for example, by aiding an individual to shaping his or her emotional or intellectual development along avenues self-perceived as favorable. To the contrary, inborn differences are one starting point for understanding the web of interactions that create complex traits such as individual personality and behavior, as well as individual psychopathological problems.

It has occasionally been argued that nonreplicability of a particular genetic finding indicates that genetic factors are not involved in the behavior in question (Horgan, 1993). However, current views on heritability of psychiatric diseases and behavioral traits rest on a different foundation: twin, adoptive and family studies in humans, and selection and strain comparisons in animals. Therefore, the overall approach of seeking the genetic variants is not invalidated by the "discovery" that the determinant DNA differences are difficult to identify or by failure to replicate any particular finding.

Heritabilities for behavioral (and other) variables are minimum estimates for the genetic variance. This is due to the error variance associated with personality measurement and to various other factors including nonadditive genetic effects and gene–environment interactions. A heritability of 0.4 represents 40% of the variance (not 16%), however, heritability is a ratio and the precise heritability may depend more on the denominator than it does the numerator. The denominator includes all sources of variance including measurement error, genetic factors, and interactions—but also sources of environmental variance that may wax or wane over time, space, and culture. The numerator is the genetic variance. Large sociocultural effects on aggressiveness could be completely missed by a heritability estimate derived within one sample. The prevalence of certain aggressive criminal behaviors, including murder, is dramatically higher in the United States, for example, as compared to populations with the same genetic background, and the prevalence may be lower in cultures that place more value on minimizing aggressive behaviors (Montagu, 1968). The *precise* heritability is therefore largely irrelevant in terms of guiding either public policy, treatment, prevention, or research aimed at finding the alleles influencing liability for aggressive behaviors, except that the heritability estimates for aggressiveness are sufficient to verify that genetic determinants are present and available to be isolated.

Results on twin studies of impulsive aggression were reviewed by Coccaro et al. (1993). Including that study, 6 of 12 studies reported evidence for heritability of aggressiveness and there was considerable variability in heritability depending on both the measure of aggression or impulsiveness and the age of the twins. Three of 5 twin studies conducted on children and reviewed by Coccaro et al. (1993) detected signicant heritability for aggressiveness and the average was 0.80, while two other negative studies in children appear to have used other measures of aggressiveness, which may be less strongly influenced genetically (Coccaro et al., 1993). Among adolescents there were three negative studies. Three of 4 studies in adults found that heritability of aggressiveness was significant. In these positive studies the heritabilities were 0.72 (Rushton, Fulker, Neale, Nias, & Eysenck, 1986), 0.44 (Tellegen et al., 1988), and 0.41 for the "irritable impulsiveness" factor of Coccaro et al. (1993). The weight of the evidence indicates that measures of hostile–aggressive behaviors demonstrate higher heritability than measures focusing on aggressive ideation and that shared environmental influences account for little of the variability in the dimensional measures of aggressiveness (Coccaro et al., 1993). Heritability for aggressiveness is probably comparable to that of various other dimensions of personality, which exhibit heritabilities ranging from 0.4–0.6 (Cattell, 1982; Loehlin, 1989). As discussed in the preceding paragraph, the point of these numbers is that there appears to be a significant genetic contribution to the variance in aggressiveness. The actual percentage of the variance which is genetic is an artifact of technique, phenotype, and sampling frame, so concerns over whether the percentage seems *high, low,* or *just right* are unwarranted.

Important influences that will determine differences in aggressive behavior already appear to be active during childhood. Distinct interindividual differences in aggressiveness and behavioral inhibition become evident early in life and show some continuity across developmental periods both in humans (Kagan, Resnick, & Snidman, 1988) and in other primates in which systematic alteration of early rearing conditions can also modulate aggressive behaviors that appear later in life (Suomi, 1982). In primates, and due to androgen exposure, male–female differences appear in aggression, including gender differences in rough-and-tumble play. Differences in shared environmental influences appear to play a minor role in aggressiveness (Coccaro et al., 1993) and the measurable effect of shared environmental influences is small for other personality variables as well (Plomin, 1990). Therefore, important determinants of interindividual variance in aggressiveness begin to show early in childhood and include both genetic differences and nonshared environmental factors which could include teratogens and birth trauma.

Serotonin and Aggressiveness

Serotonin inhibits a variety of behaviors including ingestive behaviors and aggressiveness (Soubrie, 1986), and this neurotransmitter also lowers body temperature and stimulates slow-wave sleep. Serotoninergic neurotransmission modulates impulsivity and diminution of serotonergic activity releases punishment-suppressed behaviors (Linnoila et al., 1983). The resulting behavioral disinhibition is accompanied by an increase in aggressiveness and disinhibited aggressive acts directed against both self and others (Traskman-Bendz, Asberg, Nordstrom, & Stanley, 1989).

Brain concentrations of serotonin's principal metabolite, 5-hydroxyindoleacetic acid (5-HIAA), reflect rate of serotonin release (Aghajanian, Rosecrans, & Sheard, 1967) and 5-HIAA levels in lumbar cerebrospinal fluid (CSF) correlate with levels in brain (Stanley, Traskman-Bendz, & Dorovini-Zis, 1985). CSF 5-HIAA is lower in violent suicides (Asberg, Traskman, & Thoren, 1976a; Asberg, Thoren, & Traskman, 1976b; Lidberg, Tuck, Asberg, Scalia-Tomba, & Bentilsson, 1985; van Praag & Korf, 1971) and in impulsive–aggressive individuals (Brown, Goodwin, Ballenger, Goyer, & Major, 1979; Brown et al., 1982; Brown et al., 1985; Linnoila et al., 1983; Virkkunen, de Jong, Bartko, Goodwin, & Linnoila, 1989; Virkkunen, de Jong, Bartko, & Linnoila, 1989). In a population of impulsive–violent Finns, many with exceptionally low CSF 5-HIAA concentrations, all met criteria for alcoholism and more than half had a history of suicide attempts (Linnoila et al., 1983). Most of the impulsive subjects studied by Brown et al. (1979, 1982, 1985), although young, were also alcoholic. The more than random comorbidity and co-occurence of alcoholism, suicidal behavior, and impulsive–aggressive behaviors in some individuals may be due to underlying variation in the function of serotonergic pathways.

There are parallels but also potentially important differences connecting serotonin function to aggressiveness and impulsivity in the data derived from animals and humans. The concordance in the data is probably remarkable given the difficulties of equating different models of aggression. In rodents, the data on association of brain serotonin and 5-HIAA levels to aggressiveness are inconsistent (see in Barros and Miczek, chap. 12, this volume). Serotonin turnover is lower, however, when aggressiveness is induced by isolation, diet, or administration of parachlorophenylalanine, an inhibitor of serotonin synthesis, and these aggressive states are partially reversed by orally administered L-tryptophan, by the serotonin reuptake inhibitor fluoxetine, and by 5-HT1A receptor agonists (Berzenyi, Galateo, & Valzelli, 1983; Kantak, Hegstrand, & Eichelman, 1981; Katz, 1980; Valzelli, Bernasconi, & Dalessandro, 1981; Valzelli & Garratini, 1968). However, an extensive literature also exists on the inhibition of rodent aggression by serotonin antagonists (see Barros & Miczek, chap. 12, this volume). In humans, lithium, which is thought to enhance serotoninergic neurotransmission, has been reported to reduce impulsive–aggressive behavior in those subjects (Myers & Melchior, 1977; Sheard, 1971, 1975; Tupin et al., 1973). Finally, in both Rhesus macaque monkeys (Higley, Suomi, & Linnoila, 1991, 1992) and African green monkeys (Raleigh, Brammer, & McGuire, 1983) there appears to be an inverse correlation, as there is in the human, between aggressiveness and CSF 5-HIAA concentrations.

Heritability of serotonin function has been difficult to study because of the relative inaccessability to measurement of serotonin function in brain. The available data are therefore somewhat limited, but, taken together, positive. A study of platelet serotonin uptake in monozygotic and dizygotic twins demonstrated significant heritability (Meltzer & Arora, 1988). Oxenstierna et al. (1986) directly examined the heritability of CSF 5-HIAA in a small number of twin pairs. Calculated heritabilities were therefore crude estimates and heritability for 5-HIAA (0.35) although positive, did not reach statistical significance. However, in a larger study on Rhesus macaque monkeys raised under various conditions, Higley et al. (1993) determined that heritability for CSF 5-HIAA was greater than 50%.

A program to identify the genetic variants that would provide the mechanism by which variation in aggressiveness can be inherited could focus on genes crucial for the function of several neurochemical systems; scenarios can be constructed whereby genetic developmental variation in function of a variety of neurotransmitter systems (most or all of them) could increase or decrease aggressiveness. My laboratory is identifying genetic variants at genes involved in serotonin function. These candidate genes are being studied because of the information available that altered serotonin function is particularly likely to underlie the vulnerability of certain individuals to alcoholism (see, for example, Brown et al., 1979, 1982, 1985; Linnoila et al., 1983). As described later, the phenotype of this particular subgroup of alcoholics frequently includes impulsive and aggressive behaviors, and there is also a genetic overlap in that other problems associated with aggression–impulsivity are often vertically transmitted across generations in the families of these alcoholics (Bohman, 1978; Cloninger, Bohman, & Sigvardsson, 1981; Cloninger, Bohman, Sigvardsson, & von Knorring, 1985).

IDENTIFICATION OF GENETIC LOCI SIMULTANEOUSLY INFLUENCING SEROTONIN, AGGRESSIVENESS, AND OTHER TRAITS

Population Associations to TPH and DRD2

Genes determining differences in serotonin function are likely to include trypto-phan hydroxylase (TPH). TPH catalyzes the rate-limiting step in serotonin biosyn-thesis (Kaufman & Fisher, 1974) and the TPH cDNA and gene have been cloned (Stoll, Kozak, & Goldman, 1989; Stoll & Goldman, 1991) and genetically mapped in mouse (Stoll et al., 1989) and in the human (Nielsen, Dean, & Goldman, 1992). Under ordinary conditions, concentrations of substrate are thought to be nonsaturat-ing—5-hydroxytrophan being rapidly decarboxylated to 5-hydroxytryptamine.

A population association between a DNA marker within intron seven of the TPH gene to CSF 5-HIAA concentration and to suicidal behavior was found in a population of alcoholic Finnish Whites incarcerated for their criminal offenses (Nielsen et al., 1994). These individuals were studied while inpatients on a psychiatric ward where diet could be controlled, and they were abstinent from alcohol so that differences in CSF monoamine were unlikely to be due to ethanol withdrawal. The association to 5-HIAA concentration was only observable within individuals who, by the nature of their crimes, were impulsive. This could indicate that functional TPH variants capable of altering 5-HIAA concentration may be rare (too rare to yield an association) in the general population and in nonimpulsive individuals.

Population associations are frequently sought using genetic markers that do not themselves alter function but which may be in linkage disequilibrium (non-random association in the population) with DNA variants which do alter func-tion. If authentic (i.e., not due to chance or inadvertant racial–ethic stratification of patients and controls), the TPH association would be such an association. To be authentic in terms of localizing a genetic determinant of a behavioral pheno-type, a population group will usually require two levels of linkage disequilibrium: namely linkage disequilibrium of the phenotype to the unknown determinant (or vulnerability) allele and linkage disequilibrium of the determinant allele to the marker polymorphism.

Spurious associations usually arise by chance or due to ethnic stratification of patient and control groups. Ethnic stratification can explain some conflicting reports on the association of the dopamine DRD2 receptor to alcoholism and to other behaviors, because four-fold DRD2 allele frequency differences are found between ethnic groups (Goldman et al., 1993). Furthermore, DRD2 asso-ciation studies conducted in ethnically well-defined populations have generally been negative (Arinami et al., 1993; Goldman et al., 1992, 1993; Schwab et al., 1991), as have linkage studies in families (Bolos et al., 1990; Parsian et al., 1991). Following the initial study by Blum, Nobel, and Sheridan (1990), the DRD2 association was never as strong in subsequent positive reports (Blum et al., 1991; Blum et al., 1993; Parsian et al., 1991), or in negative reports (Arinami et al., 1993; Bolos et al., 1990; Cook, Wang, Crowe, Hauser, & Freimer, 1992; Gelernter et al., 1991; Goldman et al., 1992, 1993; Schwab et al., 1991; Suarez et al., 1994; Turner et al., 1992). Although the statistical signal for the DRD2 association to alcoholism has dwindled, perhaps to nonsignificance (Gelernter, Goldman, & Risch, 1993), several recently reported associations of DRD2 to other traits, including substance abuse (Noble et al., 1993; Smith et al., 1992), P300 latency, and other conditions (Comings et al., 1991) have neither been verified nor refuted. Chance associations may be difficult to invalidate because of the natural tendency to submit and publish confirmations and positive findings. The DRD2 coding sequence was scanned in large samples of alcoholics and schizophrenics without detection of a functional variant that can account for an association to any of the conditions named earlier (Gejman et al., 1994). However, even this analysis (which detected three rare, possibly functional, variants) cannot completely rule out the possibility that there exists an abundant functional variant within the DRD2 promotor region, in an intron, or in a completely different, but genetically linked, gene.

The TPH population association to suicide and CSF 5-HIAA concentration was found in a sample that was relatively extreme behaviorally and neurochemically. The TPH sample was also genetically relatively homogeneous. These factors enhance the plausibility of the association. However, the implication of the discussion just provided on the DRD2 association is that the logical next step for the TPH association would be to identify any functional mutations that may be present at the TPH locus.

Genetic Linkage and Functional Variant Identification at MAO-A

The oxidation of serotonin to 5-HIAA is catalyzed by MAO-B in raphe neurons of the brain. This mitochondrially associated enzyme is also found in the platelet, where however, its activity does not well correlate with MAO-B activity in brain (Young, Laws, Sharbrough, & Weinshilbaum, 1986). MAO-A is not found in the platelet, but is located in the brain where it metabolizes other monoamines including dopamine and norepinephrine. Both MAO-A and MAO-B are X-linked (Kochersperger et al., 1986) and located at Xp11-p21 (Ozelius et al., 1988).

A family with X-linked nondysmorphic borderline mental retardation in several males was described. This trait was found to be genetically linked to a CA-repeat polymorphism located in Xp11-21 (Brunner, Nelen, Breakfield, Ropers, & Van Oost, 1993) and a stop codon mutation was identified within the structural gene for MAO-A (Brunner, Nelen, vanZandvoort, et al., 1993), which was previously localized to this region of the X chromosome. Behavior of affected males within this family was markedly abnormal in that the affected males were shy, withdrawn, often without friends, and showed aggressive outbursts, either un-provoked or after minimal provocation. Other prominent behaviors, present in some but not all of these males, included arson and sexually aggressive behaviors. Reduced urinary excretion for metabolites of dopamine, norepinephrine, and serotonin produced by the action of MAO-A was detected.

The definitive demonstration of a causal link between an MAO-A gene variant and aggressive behavior in this single family makes it likely that the same MAO-A defect or other inactive MAO-A alleles will be demonstrated in additional families in which aggressive and impulsive behaviors are transmitted. However, preliminary data indicate that the MAO-A stop codon mutation is rare in individuals with aggressivity–impulsivity and low CSF 5-HIAA. Discovery of the MAO-A mutation also leaves many other issues unsettled. For example, failure to metabolize serotonin could have led to an increase in concentrations of this neurotransmitter effective at receptors, leading to behavioral inhibition rather than impulsivity. Thus the mechanism by which an MAO-A mutation would increase aggressivity or impulsivity is at this point unknown and may be difficult to elucidate. The mechanism which is involved may include increased dopaminergic or noradrenergic neurotransmission, both of which have been implicated in studies of aggressive behavior (reviewed in Brunner, Nelen, van Zandvoort, et al., 1993).

Situations in which the mutation is found but the etiologic mechanism at least temporarily remains elusive, are not unprecedented. For example, the pathway by which deficiency of hypoxanthine-guanine phosphoribosyltransferase (also encoded by an X-linked gene) causes mental retardation and self-mutilation remains unknown decades after the discovery of the defect, although there is some evidence for a relatively specific deficit in dopamine systems within the basal ganglia of mice in which the gene has been inactivated (Jinnah et al., 1994). Presence of a common X-linked determinant in the population could also have helped to explain the preponderance of males with pathological impulsive aggressiveness. Because of the high frequency of father–son transmission, however, it is unlikely that an X-linked locus could account for all or most of the genetic liability for impulsive–aggressive behaviors.

Other Candidate Serotonin Genes for Variation in Aggressiveness

At the present time, and focusing only on serotoninergic neurotransmission, there are more than a dozen genes in addition to MAO that have been cloned and that should be considered as candidate genes, which may determine individual differences in aggressiveness and related behaviors. Due to the roles of these genes in serotonin synthesis (TPH and signal transduction, or reuptake), many or most of the genes may alter behavior. The functionally variant alleles may generally be infrequent, acting to cause behavioral variation only in small numbers of individuals. The cloned candidate genes include the transporter for L-tryptophan across the blood–brain barrier and neuronal membrane and into the raphe neuron where concentrations of L-tryptophan are limiting for serotonin synthesis. Also to be considered is the serotonin transporter, which inactivates serotonin released into the synapse by reuptake. Expressed in the liver is another candidate gene, tryptophan oxidase, which converts L-tryptophan to kynurenine, reducing tryptophan availability. Eight and possibly more serotonin receptors have been cloned, including three (5-HT1A [Fargin et al., 1988], 5-HT1Da, and 5-HT1Db), which are found presynaptically, as well as 5-HT1C and 5-HT2 (Lubbert et al., 1986; Julius, MacDermott, Axel, & Jessell, 1988), 5-HT3, 5-HT4, and 5-HT7. A number of these receptor genes are of great interest. For example, 5-HT1A agonists reduced aggressive and defensive behavior and increased passivity in wild rats in anxiety producing situations (Blanchard, Rodgers, Hendrie, & Hori, 1988). In animal studies on the 5-HT3 subtype, the antagonist GR38032F reduced anxiety, aggressive behavior, agitation, and restlessness (Butler, Hill, Ireland, Jordan, & Tyers, 1988). Mice in which the 5-HT1B receptor (equivalent to the 5-HT1Db) has been "knocked out" show greatly enhanced intruder confrontation aggression (Sadou et al., 1994) and various 5-HT1B agonists and antagonists (both) reduce aggression in intruder confrontation paradigms (see Barros and Miczek, chap. 12, this volume).

METHODOLOGICAL CONSIDERATIONS AND PROSPECTS FOR FUTURE RESEARCH

Genetic linkage strategies have the advantage of being able to detect phenotypically significant genetic variation wherever that variation exists in the genome, including regions involved in regulation of gene expression. However, families of impulsive aggressive probands with low levels of CSF monoamine metabolites are ascertainable but are also often fragmented. Affected individuals within such families are frequently unavailable for studies, for example, because they are deceased, incarcerated, or uncooperative. Therefore, identification of loci by genetic linkage may falter if, for example, genetic heterogeneity is extensive. One solution to this problem is to screen for genetic association using large samples of individuals with the target phenotype and using a dense map of genetic markers. Although spurious associations can arise due to ethnic stratification (*vide supra*), this problem can be avoided by careful matching for ethnicity and by sampling parents and using the nontransmitted alleles of parents to derive the population allele frequency.

A definitive and, in some ways, more comprehensive strategy for finding alleles contributing to a heterogeneous phenotype is direct analysis of the genes which could contribute to the phenotype. Both direct analysis of candidate genes and genetic linkage analysis permit exclusion mapping; linkage analysis excludes regions of the genome and direct gene analysis generally excludes only coding sequences of genes. Linkage analysis is capable of scanning much larger regions of DNA for determinants, but scanning by genetic linkage may be ineffective, depending on the abundance and effect on phenotype of the functionally divergent allele. The genetic variant scanning techniques include the single-strand conformational polymorphism (SSCP) method (see, e.g., Nielsen et al., 1992), denaturing gradient electrophoresis (see, e.g., Gejman et al., 1994), and direct sequencing including automated sequencing.

In direct gene scanning, genetic heterogeneity and multifactorial inheritance increase the likelihood that a functional variant will be discovered in a particular candidate gene (if unrelated subjects are studied). With direct gene analysis, an *n* of *one* is in some cases sufficient to identify a phenotypically significant gene variant. After the variant is found, functionality of the encoded protein may be shown to have been eliminated or modified in a major way. Also, population association to definitively relate the presence of the phenotype to the variant can subsequently be performed. Low abundance alleles can be efficiently typed across thousands of DNA samples by using mass allele detection (MAD) in which pooled DNA samples are amplified using allele-specific primers and the presence of a specifically amplified allele is detected using a highly sensitive method such as electrochemiluminescence (ECL; Bergen, Wang, Nakhai, & Goldman, in press). Also, families of probands can be collected for linkage analysis even if the variant is rare. The availability of DNA sequences for a substantial number of candidate genes and rapid DNA sequence analysis methods that take advantage of the polymerase chain reaction for DNA amplification make feasible this approach, which was impractical only several years ago.

TABLE 2.1
Polymorphic Candidate Genes for Serotonin Function

Gene	Protein Variant	Frequency	DNA Variant	Reference
5-HT1A	yes (2)	< 0.01	yes	Nakhai, Nielsen, Linnoila, & Goldman (1995)
5-HT1Da			yes	Ozaki et al. (1995)
5-HT1Db			yes	Lappalainen, Dean, et al. (1995)
5-HT1E				Lappalainen, Goldman, Ozaki, & Dean
			yes	(personal communication)
5-HT1F			yes	Lappalainen et al. (personal communication)
5-HT2A	yes (2)	< 0.01, 0.09	yes	Ozaki, Rosenthal, et al. (1995)
5-HT2C	yes (1)	0.13	yes	Lappalainen, Zhang, et al. (1995)
5-HT7	yes (1)	< 0.01	yes	Pesonen et al. (in press)
TPH			yes	Nielsen et al. (1992); Nielsen et al. (1994)
TO				
MAO-A	yes	< 0.01	yes	Brunner et al. (1993)
MAO-B			yes	Brunner et al. (1993)
GTPC1	yes (4)	< 0.01	yes	Ichinose et al. (in press)

Note: 5-HT1A etc. = Various serotonin receptor genes; TPH = tryptophan hydroxylase; TO = Tryptophan 2,3 dioxygenase; GTPC1 = GTP Cyclohydrolase I.

Primarily using the SSCP method and scanning Finnish alcoholic offenders, we have detected naturally occurring amino acid substitutions at 4 of 8 different serotonin receptors (included in Table 2.1) and the other serotonin receptors show synonymous substitutions. All of the variants have been observed in more than one unrelated individual. However, only the 5-HT2A and 5-HT2C protein sequence variants are abundant, as compared to rare sequence variants that have been detected at GTP cyclohydrolase I, MAO-A and other serotonin receptors as listed in the table. Thus, using the direct gene analysis approach, a list can be assembled of all the structural variants that could cause variation in a phenotype. The gene scanning approach obviously becomes more powerful as the number of genes available for this type of analysis increases and intense interest in the genes expressed in brain has made them a prime target for initial cloning and sequencing.

Conclusions

1. Aggression is not a unitary phenotype but a set of sometimes interrelated behaviors. These behaviors overlap in their origins with each other and with personality traits and psychiatric diseases. Studies which identify genetic biologic factors in a variety of personality traits and psychiatric diseases could shed light on the origins of aggression.

2. Aggressive behaviors and relevant personality traits and psychiatric disorders show substantial heritability. These high heritability values help justify analyses to identify the genetic variants that, in part, are the basis of interindividual variation in behavior.

3. A multiplicity of genetic and nongenetic variables contribute to interindividual variability in the propensity to aggressive behaviors.

4. The neurochemistry and neuropharmacology of aggression point to a major role for the serotonin system in aggression.

5. Gene variants influencing aggression, such as the rare MAO-A stop codon variant, can be identified by genetic linkage or by direct gene scanning—two general approaches with different advantages and limitations.

REFERENCES

Adamson, D., Dean, M., Virkkunen, M., Linnoila, M., & Goldman, D. (1995). DRD4 dopamine receptor and CSF monoamine metabolites in Finnish alcoholics and controls. *Neuropsychiatric Genetics, 60*, 199–205.

Aghajanian, G. K., Rosecrans, J. A., & Sheard, M. H. (1967). Serotonin release in the forebrain by stimulation of midbrain raphe. *Science, 15*, 402–403.

Arinami, T., Itokawa, M., Komiyama, T., Mitsushio, H. Mori, H., Mifune, H., Hamaguchi, H., & Toru, M. (1993). Association between severity of alcoholism and the A1 allele of the dopamine D2 receptor gene Taql A RFLP in Japanese. *Biological Psychiatry, 33*(2), 108–114.

Asberg, M., Thoren, P., & Traskman, L. (1976b). Serotonin depression—a biochemical subtype within the affective disorders? *Science, 191,* 478.

Asberg, M., Traskman, L., & Thoren, P. (1976a). 5-HIAA in the cerebrospinal fluid—a biochemical suicide predictor? *Archives of General Psychiatry, 33,* 1193–1197.

Bergen, A., Wang, C-Y., Nakhai, B., & Goldman, D. (in press). Mass allele detection (MAD) of rare 5HT1A structural variants with allele specific amplification and electrochemiluminescence detection. *Human Mutation.*

Berrettini, W. H., Goldin, L. R., Nurnberger, J. I., Jr., & Gershon, E. S. (1984). Genetic factors in affective illness. *Journal of Psychiatric Research, 18,* 329–350.

Berzenyi, P., Galateo, E., & Valzelli, L. (1983). Fluoxetine activity on muricidal aggression induced in rats by p-chlorophenylalanine. *Aggressive Behavior, 9,* 333–338.

Blanchard, C. D., Rodgers, R. J., Hendrie, C. A., & Hori, K. (1988). 'Taming' of wild rats (*Rattus rattus*) by 5HT1a agonists buspirone and gepirone. *Pharmacology and Biochemical Behavior, 31,* 269–278.

Blum, K., Noble, E. P., & Sheridan, P. J. (1990). Allelic association of human dopamine D2 receptor gene in alcoholism. *Journal of the American Medical Association, 263,* 2055–2060.

Blum, K., Noble, E. P., Sheridan, P. J., Finley, O., Montgomery, A., Ritchie, T., Ozkaragoz, T., Fitch, R. J., Sadlack, F., Sheffield, D., Dahlmann, T., Halbardier, S., & Nogami, H. (1991). Association of the A1 allele of the D2 dopamine receptor gene. *Alcohol, 8,* 409–416.

Blum, K., Noble, E. P., Sheridan, P. J., Montgomery, A., Ritchie, T., Ozkaragoz, T., Fitch, R. J., Wood, R. C., Finley, O., & Sadlack, F. (1993). Genetic predisposition in alcoholism: Association of the D2 dopamine receptor Taql B1 RFLP with severe alcoholics. *Alcohol, 10*(1), 59–67.

Bohman, M. (1978). Some genetic aspects of alcoholism and criminality: A population of adoptees. *Archives of General Psychiatry, 35,* 269–276.

Bolos, A. M., Dean, M., Lucas-Derse, S., Ramsburg, M., Brown, G. L., Goldman, D. (1990). Population and pedigree studies reveal a lack of association between the dopamine D2 receptor gene and alcoholism. *Journal of the American Medical Association, 264,* 3156–3160.

Brown, G. L., Ebert, M. H., Goyer, P. F., Jimerson, D. C., Klein, W. J., Bunney, W. E., & Goodwin, F. K. (1982). Aggression, suicide and serotonin: Relationships to CSF amine metabolites. *American Journal of Psychiatry, 139,* 741–746.

Brown, G. L., Goodwin, F. K., Ballenger, J. C., Goyer, P. F., & Major, L. F. (1979). Aggression in humans correlates with cerebrospinal fluid metabolites. *Psychiatric Research, 1,* 131–139.

Brown, G. L., Kline, W. J., Goyer, P. F., Minichiello, M. D., Krusei, M. J. P., & Goodwin, F. K. (1985). Relationship of childhood characteristics to cerebrospinal fluid 5-hydroxyindoleacetic acid in aggressive adults. In C. Chagass (Ed.), *Biological psychiatry* (pp. 177–179). New York: Elsevier.

Brunner, H. G., Nelen, M., Breakefield, X. O., Ropers, H. H., & Van Oost, B. A. (1993). Abnormal behavior associated with a point mutation in the structural gene for monoamine oxidase A. *Science, 262,* 578–580.

Brunner, H. G., Nelen, M. R., van Zandvoort, P., Abeling, N. G. G. M., van Gennip, A. H., Wolters, E. C., Kuiper, M. A., Ropers, H. H., & Van Oost, B. A. (1993). X-linked borderline mental retardation with prominent behavioral disturbance: Phenotype, genetic localization, and evidence for disturbed monoamine metabolism. *American Journal of Human Genetics, 52,* 1032–1039.

Butler, A., Hill, J. M., Ireland, S. J., Jordan, C. C., & Tyers, M. B. (1988) Pharmacological properties of GR38032F, a novel antagonist at 5-HT3 receptors. *British Journal of Pharmacology, 94,* 397–412.

Cattell, R. B. (1982). *The inheritance of personality and ability.* New York: Academic Press.

Cloninger, C. R., Bohman, M., & Sigvardsson, S. (1981). *Archives of General Psychiatry 38,* 861.

Cloninger, C. R., Bohman, M., Sigvardsson, S., & von Knorring, A.-L. (1985). Psychopathology in adopted-out children of alcoholics. *Recent Developments in Alcoholism, 3,* 37.

Coccaro, E. F., Bergeman, C. S., & McClearn, G. E. (1993). Heritability of irritable impulsiveness: A study of twins reared together and apart. *Psychiatric Research, 48,* 229–242.

Comings, D. E., Comings, B. G., Muhleman, D., Dietz, G., Shahbahrami, B., Tast, D., Knell, E., Kocsis, P., Baumgarten, R., Kovacs, B., Levy, D. L., Smith, M., Borison, R. L., Evans, D. D., Klein, D. N., MacMurray, J., Tosk, J. M., Sverd, J., Gysin, R., & Flanagan, S. D. (1991). The dopamine D2 receptor locus as a modifying gene in neuropsychiatric disorders. *Journal of the American Medical Association, 56,* 1793–1800.

Cook, B. L., Wang, Z. W., Crowe, R. R., Hauser, R., & Freimer, M. (1992). Alcoholism and the D2 receptor gene. *Alcoholism, Clinical and Experimental Research, 16,* 806–809.

Ellison, J., Dean, M., & Goldman, D. (1993). Efficacy of fluorescence-based PCR-SSCP for detection of point mutations. *Biotechniques, 15,* 684–691.

Ellison, J., Squires, G., & Goldman, D. (1994). Detection of mutations and polymorphisms using fluorescence-based dideoxy fingerprinting (F-ddF). *Biotechniques, 17*(4), 742–753.

Fargin, A., Raymond, J. R., Lohse, M. J., Kobilka, B. K., Caron, M. G., & Lefkowitz, R. J. (1988). The genomic clone G-21 which resembles a B adrenergic receptor sequence encodes the 5-HT1A receptor. *Nature, 335,* 358–360.

Gejman, P. V., Ram, A., Gelernter, J., Friedman, E., Cao, Q., Pickar, D., Blum, K., Noble, E. P., Kranzler, H. R., O'Malley, S., Hamer, D., Whitsitt, F., Rao, P., DeLisi, L. E., Virkkunen, M., Linnoila, M., Goldman, D., & Gershon, E. S. (1994). No structural mutation in the dopamine D2 receptor gene in alcoholism or schizophrenia. *Journal of the American Medical Association, 271,* 204–208.

Gelernter, J., Goldman, D., & Risch, N. (1993). The A1 allele at the D2 dopamine receptor gene and alcoholism: A reappraisal. *Journal of the American Medical Association, 269,* 1673–1677.

Gelernter, J., O'Malley, S., Risch, N., Kranzler, H. R., Krystal, J., Merikangas, K., Kennedy, J. L., & Kidd, K. K. (1991). No association between an allele at the D2 dopamine receptor gene (DRD2) and alcoholism. *Journal of the American Medical Association, 256,* 1801–1807.

Goldman, D. (1993). Alcoholism: Genetic transmission. In M. Galanter (Ed.), *Recent developments in alcoholism* (Vol. II, pp. 231–248). New York: Plenum.

Goldman, D., Brown, G. L., Albaugh, B., Robin, R., Goodson, S., Trunzo, M., Akhtar, L., Lucas-Derse, S., Long, J., Linnoila, M., & Dean, M. (1993). DRD2 dopamine receptor genotype, linkage disequilibrium and alcoholism in American Indians and other populations. *Alcoholism, Clinical and Experimental Research, 17,* 199–204.

Goldman, D., Dean, M., Brown, G. L., Bolos, A. M., Tokola, R., Virkkunen, M., & Linnoila, M. (1992). D2 dopamine receptor genotype and cerebrospinal fluid homovanillic acid, 5-hydroxyindoleacetic acid and 3-methoxy-4-hydroxyphenylglycol in Finnish and American alcoholics. *Acta Psychologia Scandinavica, 86,* 351–357.

Gottesman, I. I., & Shields, J. (1982). *The epigenetic puzzle.* Cambridge, England: Cambridge University Press.

Higley, J. D., Suomi, S. J., & Linnoila, M. (1991). CSF monoamine metabolite concentrations vary according to age, rearing and sex, and are influenced by the stressor of social separation in rhesus monkeys. *Psychopharmacology, 103,* 551–556.

Higley, J. D., Suomi, S. J., & Linnoila, M. (1992). A longitudinal assessment of CSF monoamine metabolite and plasma cortisol concentrations in young rhesus monkeys. *Biological Psychiatry, 32,* 127–145.

Higley, J. D., Thompson, W. T., Champoux, M., Goldman, D., Hasert, M. F., Kraemer, G. W., Scanlan, J. M., Suomi, S. J., & Linnoila, M. (1993). Paternal and maternal genetic contributions to CSF monoamine metabolites in rhesus monkeys (*Macaca mulatta*). *Archives of General Psychiatry, 50,* 615–623.

Horgan, J. (1993, June). Eugenics revisited. *Scientific American,* 123–131.

Ichinose, H., Ohye, T., Takahashi, E., Seki, N., Hori, T., Segawa, M., Nomura, Y., Endo, K., Tsuji, S., Fujita, K., & Nagatsu, T. (in press). Hereditary progressive dystonia with marked diurnal fluctuation caused by mutations in the GTP cyclohydrolase I gene. *Nature Genetics.*

Julius, D., MacDermott, A. B., Axel, R., & Jessell, T. M. (1988). Molecular cloning of a functional cDNA encoding the serotonin 1c receptor. *Science, 241,* 558–556.

Jinnah, H. A., Wojcik, B. E., Narang, N., Lee, K. Y., Goldstein, M., Wamsley, J. K., Langlais, P. J., & Friedmann, T. (1994). Dopamine deficiency in a genetic mouse model model of Lesch-Nyhan disease. *Journal of Neuroscience, 14,* 1164–1175.

Kagan, J., Reznick, J. S., & Snidman, N. C. (1988). Biological bases of childhood shyness. *Science, 240,* 167–171.

Kantak, K. M., Hegstrand, L. R., & Eichelman, B. (1981). Facilitation of shock-induced fighting following intraventricular 5,7 dihydroxytryptamine and 6-hydroxy DOPA. *Psychopharmacology, 74,* 157–160.

Katz, R. J. (1980). Role of serotonergic mechanisms in animal models of predation. *Progress in Neuro-Psychopharmacology, 4,* 219–231.

Kaufman, S., & Fisher, D. B. (1974). Pterin-requiring aromatic amino acid hydroxylases. In O. Hayaishi (Ed.), *Molecular mechanisms of oxygen activation* (pp. 285–339). New York: Academic Press.

Kochersperger, L. M., Parker, E. L., Siciliano, M., Park, M., Darlington, D. J., & Denney, R. M. (1986). Assignment of genes for human monoamine oxidases A and B to the X chromosome. *Journal of Neuroscience Research, 16,* 601–616.

Lappalainen, J., Dean, M., Charbonneau, L., Virkkunen, M., Linnoila, M., & Goldman, D. (1995). Mapping of the 5-HT1Db autoreceptor gene on chromosome 6 and direct analysis for sequence variants. *Neuropsychiatric Genetics, 60,* 157–161.

Lappalainen, J., Zhang, L., Dean, M., Oz, M., Ozaki, N., Yu, D.-H., Virkkunen, M., Weight, F., Linnoila, M., & Goldman, D. (1995). Identification, expression and pharmacology of a cys23-ser23 substitution in the human 5-HT2C receptor gene. *Genomics, 27,* 274–279.

Lester, H. A., & Davidson, N. (1987). cDNA cloning of a serotonin 5-HT1c receptor by electrophysiological assays of mRNA-injected Xenopus oocytes. *Proceedings of the National Academy of Sciences, USA, 84,* 4332–4336.

Levine, S. (1966). Sex differences in the brain. In J. L. McGaugh, N. M. Weinberger, & R. E. Whalen (Eds.), *Psychobiology* (p. 76). San Francisco, CA: Freeman.

Lidberg, L., Tuck, J. R., Asberg, M., Scalia-Tomba, G. P., & Bertilsson, L. (1985). Homocide, suicide and CSF 5HIAA. *Acta Psychologia Scandanavia, 71,* 230–236.

Linnoila, M., Virkkunen, M., Scheinin, M., Nuutila, A., Rimon, R., & Goodwin, F. K. (1983). Low cerebrospinal fluid 5-hydroxyindoleacetic acid concentration differentiates impulsive from nonimpulsive violent behavior. *Life Science, 33,* 2609–2614.

Loehlin, J. C. (1989). Partitioning environmental and genetic contributions to behavioral development. *Behavioral Genetics, 144,* 1285–1292.

Loehlin, J. C., Willerman, L., & Horn, J. M. (1988). Human behavior genetics. *Annual Review of Psychology, 39,* 101–233.

Lubbert, H., Hoffman, B. J., Snutch, T., Van Dyke, T., Levine, A. J., Hartig, P. R., Markstein, H. A., Hoyer, R. D., & Engel, G. (1986). 5-HT1A receptors mediate stimulation of adenylate cyclase in rat hippocampus. *Naunyn-Schmiedeberg's Archives of Pharmacology, 129,* 333–337.

Mark, V. H., & Ervin, F. R. (1970). *Violence and the brain.* New York: Harper & Row.

May, M. A. (1968). War, peace and social learning. In L. Bransom & G. W. Goethals (Eds.), *War* (p. 151). New York: Basic Books.

Meltzer, H. M., & Arora, R. C. (1988). Genetic control of serotonin uptake in blood platelets: A twin study. *Psychiatric Research, 24,* 263–269.

Montagu, M. F. A. (1968). *Man and aggression.* New York: Oxford University Press.

Myers, R. D., & Melchior, C. L. (1977). Alcohol and alcoholism: Role of serotonin. In W. B. Essman (Ed.), *Serotonin in health and disease, Vol. II* (p. 373). New York: Spectrum.

Nakhai, B., Nielsen, D. A., Linnoila, M., & Goldman, D. (1995). Two naturally-occurring amino acid substitutions in the human 5HT1A receptor: 5HT1A-ZZ Gly→Ser and 5HT1A-28 Ile→Val. *BBRC, 210,* 530–536.

Nielsen, D. A., Dean, M., & Goldman, D. (1992). Genetic mapping of the human tryptophan hydroxylase gene to chromosome 11p15.5 using an intronic conformational polymorphism. *American Journal of Human Genetics, 51,* 1366–1371.

Nielsen, D. A., Goldman, D., Virkkunen, M., Tokola, R., Rawlings, R., & Linnoila, M. (1994). Serotonergic traits associate with a tryptophan hydroxylase polymorphism. *Archives of General Psychiatry*.

Niskanen, P., & Achte, K. A. (1972). *The course and prognoses of schizophrenic psychoses in Helsinki: A comparative study of first admissions in 1950, 1960 and 1965.* Monographs from the psychiatric clinic of the Helsinki University Central Hospital (No. 4).

Noble, E. P., Blum, K., Khalsa, M. E., Ritchie, T., Montgomery, A., Wood, R. C., Fitch, R. J., Ozkaragoz, T., Sheridan, P. J., Anglin, D. A., Paredes, A., Treiman, L. J., & Sparkes, R. S. (1993). Allelic association of the D2 dopamine receptor gene with cocaine dependence. *Drug and Alcohol Dependence, 33,* 271–285.

Oxenstierna, G., Edman, G., Iselius, L., Oreland, L., Ross, S. B., & Sedvall, G. (1986). Concentrations of monoamine metabolites in the cerebrospinal fluid of twins and unrelated individuals—a genetic study. *Journal of Psychiatric Research, 20,* 19–29.

Ozaki, N., Lappalainen, J., Dean, M., Virkkunen, M., Linnoila, M., & Goldman, D. (1995). Mapping of the serotonin 5-HT1Dα autoreceptor gene (HTR1D) on chromosome 1 using a silent polymorphism in the coding region. *Neuropsychiatric Genetics, 60,* 162–164.

Ozaki, N., Rosenthal, N. E., Pesonen, U., Lappalainen, J., Naim, S., Schwartz, E., & Goldman, D. (1995). Identification of two naturally occurring amino acid substitutions of the 5HT2A receptor in patients with seasonal affective disorder and controls. *Biochemical and Biophysical Research Communications*.

Ozelius, L., Hsu, Y.-P., Bruns, G., Powell, J. F., Chen, S., Weyler, W., Utterback, M., Zucker, D., Haines, J., Trofatter, J. A., Conneally, P. M., Gusella, J. F., & Breakefield, X. O. (1988). Human monoamine oxidase gene (MAOA): Chromosome position (Xp21-p11) and DNA polymorphism. *Genomics, 3,* 53–58.

Parsian, A., Todd, R. D., Devor, E. J., O'Malley, K. L., Suarez, B. K., Reich, T., & Cloninger, C. R. (1991). Alcoholism and alleles of the human D2 dopamine receptor locus. *Archives of General Psychiatry, 48,* 655–663.

Pesonen, U., Koulu, M., Ozaki, N., Eggert, M., Virkkunen, M., Linnoila, M., & Goldman, D. (in press). *Multiple polymorphisms of 5-hydroxytryptamine 2A receptor gene in Finnish alcoholic violent offenders*.

Plomin, R. (1990). The role of inheritance in behavior. *Science, 248,* 183–188.

Raleigh, M. J., Brammer, G. L., & McGuire, M. T. (1983). Male dominance, serotonergic systems and the behavioral and physiological effects of drugs in vervet monkeys (*Cercopithecus aethiops sabaeus*). In K. A. Miczek (Ed.), *Ethnopharmacology: Primate models of neuropsychiatric disorders* (pp. 185–198). New York: Alan R. Liss.

Rushton, J. P., Fulker, D. W., Neale, M. C., Nias, N. K. B., & Eysenck, H. J. (1986). Altruism and aggression: The heritability of individual differences. *Journal of Personality and Social Psychology, 50,* 1192–1198.

Sadou, F., Amara, D. A., Dierich, A., Lemeur, M., Ramboz, S., Segu, L., Buhot, M. C., & Hen, R. (1994). Enhanced aggressive behavior in mice lacking 5-HT1B receptor. *Science, 265,* 1875–1878.

Schwab, S., Soyka, M., Niederecker, M., Ackenheil, M., Scherer, J., & Wildenauer, D. B. (1991). Allelic association of human D2-receptor DNA polymorphism ruled out in 45 alcoholics. *American Journal of Human Genetics, 49*(Suppl.), 203.

Sheard, M. H. (1971). Effect of lithium on human aggression. *Nature, 230,* 113.

Sheard, M. H. (1975). Lithium in the treatment of aggression. *Journal of Nervous and Mental Disorders, 100,* 108.

Smith, S. S., O'Hara, B. F., Persico, A. M., Gorelick, D. A., Newlin, D. B., Vlahov, D., Solomon, L., Pickens, R., & Uhl, G. R. (1992). Genetic vulnerability to drug abuse: The D2 dopamine receptor Taq1 restriction fragment length polymorphism appears more frequently in substance abusers. *Archives of General Psychiatry, 49,* 723–727.

Soubrie, P. (1986). Reconciling the role of central serotonin neurons in human and animal behavior. *Behavioral Brain Science, 9,* 319–364.

Stanley, M., Traskman-Bendz, L., & Dorovini-Zis, K. (1985). Correlations between amine concentrations simultaneously obtained from samples of CSF and brain. *Life Science, 37,* 1279–1286.

Stoll, J., & Goldman, D. (1991). Molecular cloning and analysis of the mouse tryptophan hydroxylase gene. *Journal of Neuroscience Research 28,* 457–465.

Stoll, J., Kozak, C., & Goldman, D. (1989). Characterization and chromosomal mapping of a cDNA encoding tryptophan hydroxylase from a mouse mastocytoma cell line. *Genomics, 7,* 88–96.

Suarez, B. K., Parsian, A., Hampe, C. L., Todd, R. D., Reich, T., & Cloninger, C. R. (1994). Linkage disequilibria at the D2 dopamine receptor locus (DRD2) in alcoholics and controls. *Genomics, 19,* 12–20.

Suomi, S. J. (1982). Abnormal behavior in nonhuman primates. In J. Forbes & J. King (Eds.), *Primate behavior* (pp. 171–175). New York: Academic Press.

Tellegen, A., Lykken, D. T., Bouchard, T. J. J., Wilcox, K., Jr., Seagal, N., & Rish, S. (1988). Personality similarity in twins reared apart and together. *Journal of Personality and Social Psychology, 54,* 1031–1039.

Traskman-Bendz, L., Asberg, M., Nordstrom, P., & Stanley, M. (1989). Biochemical aspects of suicidal behavior. *Progress in Neuropsychopharmacology and Biological Psychiatry, 13,* S35–44.

Tsuang, M. T. (1983). Risk of suicide in relatives of schizophrenics, manic depressives and controls. *Journal of Clinical Psychiatry, 44,* 396–400.

Tupin, J. P., Smith, D. B., Classon, T. L., Kim, L. I., Nugent, A., & Groupe, A. (1973). The long-term use of lithium in aggressive prisoners. *Comprehensive Psychiatry, 14,* 311.

Turner, E., Ewing, J., Shilling, P., Smith, T. L., Irwin, M., Schuckit, M. A., & Kelsoe, J. R. (1992). Lack of association between an RFLP near the D2 dopamine receptor gene and severe alcoholism. *Biological Psychiatry, 31,* 285–290.

Valzelli, L., Bernasconi, S., & Dalessandro, M. (1981). Effect of tryptophan administration on spontaneous and p-PCA-induced muricidal aggression in laboratory rats. *Pharmacology Research Communication, 13,* 891–897.

Valzelli, L., & Garratini, S. (1968). Behavioral changes and 5-hydroxytryptamine turnover in animals. *Advances in Pharmacology, 6B,* 249–260.

van Praag, H. M., & Korf, J. (1971). Endogenous depressions with and without disturbances in 5-hydroxytryptamine metabolism: A biochemical classification. *Psychopharmacology, 19,* 148–152.

Virkkunen, M., de Jong, J., Bartko, J., Goodwin, F. K., & Linnoila, M. (1989). Relationship of psychobiological variables to recidivism in violent offenders and impulsive fire setters. *Archives of General Psychiatry, 46,* 600–603.

Young, W. F., Laws, E. R., Sharbrough, F. W., Weinshilbaum, R. M. (1986). Human monoamine oxidase: Lack of brain and platelet correlation. *Archives of General Psychiatry, 43,* 604–609.

3

GENES, NEUROBIOLOGY, AND AGGRESSION: TIME FRAMES AND FUNCTIONS OF SOCIAL BEHAVIORS IN ADAPTATION

Jean-Louis Gariépy
University of North Carolina, Chapel Hill

Mark H. Lewis
University of Florida

Robert B. Cairns
University of North Carolina, Chapel Hill

The proposition that social behaviors may be partitioned into components of nature or nurture has endured over the past century. At least part of the contemporary debate stems from the different levels of analysis that are employed in addressing the matter. At one level, the focus has been on the identification of the mechanisms supporting their integration within the developing organism (Scott, 1977). At another level, the concern has been with the psychometric quantification of how much variance each component contributes to social behavioral characteristics in a specifiable population (Plomin, 1990). The two levels of analyses appear to aspire to a common goal—namely, the understanding of gene–behavior interrelations—but they differ in methods, generate different analyses, and, unhappily, employ different conceptual definitions for some of the same terms. Although the assumption that genetic and environmental factors are separate and additive has proved to be productive in the psychometric tradition and in neurobiological investigations where it introduces an additional level of control, it encounters difficulties when social adaptations are examined in their functional context.

The results of recent programs of selection for aggressive behavior challenge commonly accepted assumptions on the relations between genes, development, neurobiology, and social behaviors. In their place, a new framework has emerged in which the analysis of the multiple factors cannot be divorced from their proximal controls, developmental functions, and experiential contexts. This research has provided, as a byproduct, fresh information on related problems, including the heritability of sex differences, the age- and context-relativity of genetic effects, and the reversibility of social patterns. Rather than complicating the picture, an integrated view of aggressive behaviors in terms of development, social learning, neurobiology, and intergenerational transfer now appears to make the phenomena more accessible to general biobehavioral theory. In this chapter, we summarize some of the findings that have been obtained on these matters and discuss their implications for social development and the consolidation of aggressive behaviors. In closing, we offer some comments on the special properties of behavior—especially social behaviors—in organismic adaptation.

GENETIC BACKGROUND AND AGGRESSIVE BEHAVIOR IN MICE

The first modern research effort to selectively breed mice for aggressive behavior was initiated by Kirsti Lagerspetz in the early 1960s. Lagerspetz began with the establishment of aggressive lines of mice through selective breeding, then analyzed for behavioral and physiological mediators. The detailed analysis of between-line behavioral similarities and differences has proceeded over the past 30 years in the Turku laboratory (e.g., Lagerspetz, 1964; Lagerspetz & Lagerspetz, 1975; Sandnabba, Lagerspetz, & Jensen, 1994).

Another selective breeding program was initiated in the early 1970s in the United States and focused initially on the social interactional and developmental controls of aggression (e.g., Cairns, 1973, 1976; Cairns, Gariépy, & Hood, 1990; Gariépy, Hood, & Cairns, 1988; Hood & Cairns, 1988). Once these controls were fairly well understood, genetic methods were employed to uncover otherwise inexplicable sources of variance in the data. The detailed information obtained on proximal controls was then used in the ontogenetic study of successive generations of animals at the time new lines were being established through selective breeding. The integration of short-term analyses of social interactions, longitudinal designs, and genetic methods permitted us to identify the likely points of developmental entry for ontogenetic and microevolutionary changes.

Despite differences in assessment procedures, data coding, and selection criteria, the two research programs have yielded convergent answers on key questions about the genetic regulation of aggressive behavior. Both research teams find that lines that differ markedly in aggressive behavior can be produced rapidly, within 1 to 5 generations of selective breeding. Moreover, they both find powerful effects of rearing conditions, social interactions, and learning that modify the level of aggressive behavior in the selected lines, regardless of genetic background. The similarities in outcomes have been striking in the light of the separate establishment and evolution of the investigations for more than 2 decades. The confirmation seemed especially important because the findings had independently challenged widely held assumptions on the relations between development, genes, and social behavior.

Detailed accounts of the technical features of the selection programs are provided in Cairns, MacCombie, and Hood (1983) and Gariépy et al. (1988), so a brief account should suffice. In the foundational generation of our selective breeding research, the males that attacked most rapidly and frequently were identified, and they were subsequently mated with females who were non-littermates but whose brothers had also been selected for high levels of attack. From the first selection generation onward, the same procedures were duplicated within the initially selected high-aggressive line. This meant that the males who failed to attack were, in each generation, removed from the reproduction colony for that line, along with the females in their litters. Exactly comparable procedures were followed in establishing the low-aggressive line, except that low-aggressive males were selected and more aggressive ones were eliminated. Thus, attack behavior among the males was the only criterion for selection. In the following discussion, "NC100" and "NC900" refer to the low-aggressive and the high-aggressive lines thus produced.

A nonselectively bred line derived from the original Institute for Cancer Research (ICR) stock was also maintained throughout our research program. These animals were reared in groups of 4 or 5 males and were used as partners in the dyadic tests. Rearing this line of animals under such conditions dramatically reduced their tendency to initiate attacks, which permitted us to obtain relatively independent measures of agonistic tendencies among the selected subjects. This interesting effect of housing conditions on aggressive behavior is discussed later. All housing and testing procedures have been continued virtually unmodified since the work began.

In each generation, two tests were administered on consecutive days when the animals reached the specified age for testing. On the first day, subjects were tested for reactivity to tactile stimulation. Six stimulations were delivered by lightly tapping the subject on its flank with a cotton swab. Reactivity ratings reflected the extent to which the subject responded with any combination of reflexive kicks, vocalizations, and jumps. On the second day, a dyadic test was conducted. For this purpose, the subject was placed alone for 5 minutes in one side of a Plexiglas compartment in order to habituate to the test environment, then a sliding sheet-panel wall was removed, exposing the subject to a same-age, randomly selected group-reared male that had been placed in the other half of the compartment. In the succeeding 10 minutes, all social interactions were recorded following a dyadic syntax by an observer who was blind to the experimental condition or genetic background of the subject. These interactions were recorded in successive 5-second blocks. The coding categories included various forms of mild (e.g., sniff, climb), and more intense (vigorous grooming) investigative behaviors, agonistic behaviors (bite, feint, attack, chase, box posture, escape), behavioral indices of social reactivity (startle, kick, vocalize, escape

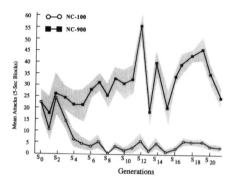

FIG. 3.1. Generational changes in rates of attacks for the high-aggressve (NC900) and low-aggressive lines (NC100). The abcissa shows the successive generations of selection and the ordinate shows attack frequency. Shading indicates standard error.

and/or jump *in response to mild* investigative behaviors), and an index of behavioral inhibition (freezing or rigid immobility on social contact).[1]

The number of 5-second blocks during which the selected subjects were observed to attack in the dyadic tests is depicted in Fig. 3.1 for 22 consecutive generations of selective breeding. In each generation a total of 20 to 35 animals were observed in each line. This figure shows that the line differentiation began as early as the first generation. Differences in attack frequencies reached statistical significance in S_4, and a clear separation of the lines was maintained thereafter. Note that the outcome of the selective breeding program has been largely unidirectional even though the procedures were bidirectional. In the high-aggressive line attack frequencies did not change from the foundational level across the successive generations of selective breeding. Line differentiation occurred principally as a result of the rapid decrease of attacks in the low-aggressive line and the stabilization of frequencies near zero in the subsequent generations of low-aggressive animals.[2] Instead of attacking, these animals exhibited a strong tendency to freeze and become immobile upon social contact. This tendency was virtually absent from the behavioral repertoire of the high-aggressive line, but increased systematically across the successive generations of low-aggressive animals, in spite of the floor effect attained much earlier in attack behavior.

---

[1]These procedures differ on several counts from those employed in other laboratories (e.g., Sandnabba, Lagerspetz, & Jensen, 1994; van Oortmerssen & Bakker, 1981), including the criteria for coding and determining attacks, age of assessment, and foundational strains.

[2]These findings essentially replicate an earlier selective program conducted in this laboratory (Cairns, MacCombie, & Hood, 1983).

The subjects observed in the dyadic tests had had no prior experience of dominance or subordination in fighting interactions with other males. At 45 days-of-age, they were exposed to a conspecific for the first time since weaning. In the absence of prior learning relevant to the dyadic situation, the differences observed between the lines strongly suggested that aggressive behavior in mice is under genetic control. Lagerspetz (1964) and van Oortmerssen and Bakker (1981) made the same observation on the basis of their own selective breeding for high and low aggression.

These findings on the heritability of aggressive behavior differences do not stand by themselves. Reviewing the last 50 years of research in behavior genetics, Fuller and Thompson (1978) showed that most behavioral characteristics, even the most complex, are readily amenable to genetic selection. What is striking about the present findings is that *this complex social behavior in a mammalian species is highly sensitive to selection pressure.* Not only is the effect robust, it was obtained within a remarkably few generations (i.e., 2–7 generations) in all of the published attempts to select for aggressive behavior. This phenomenon indicates that (a) aggressive behavior in mice is heritable, and (b) the genetic effects can be demonstrated much more rapidly than is generally recognized in the human or animal literature.

INTERACTIONS, EXPERIENCE, AND THE PLASTICITY OF AGGRESSION

In the generations following line differentiation in the NC selective breeding program, a series of experiments was conducted to verify if the genetic effects could be attenuated or magnified through either or both maturation or experiential input. These experiments permitted us to determine the relative importance of the multiplicative component (gene × environment interaction) in the otherwise additive model of phenotypic variance advocated in classic behavior genetics. As we are about to see, simple manipulations can significantly enhance or reduce aggressive behavior in our selected lines. Taken together, our findings on these issues have demonstrated considerable plasticity in the aggressive behavior of both selectively bred lines. Instead of favoring the view that behavior can be fixed by genes or experience, our results favor the opposite view that behavior is essentially an adaptive device, an "organizer," whereby efficient and rapid changes in patterns of ecological adaptation and in their supportive systems can be achieved. By way of summary, the empirical evidence includes:

Contextual Adjustment. A most effective and powerful manipulation whereby line differences in aggressive behavior can be altered is through a simple change in rearing conditions. As depicted in Fig. 3.1, a large difference is observed between the lines when, following isolation rearing, the animals are exposed for the first time to an unfamiliar male at puberty. Remarkably, the robust genetic effect is lost when the males are reared with other males instead of social isolation. Under such rearing conditions, high-aggressive animals rarely attack an unfamiliar mouse, the low-aggressive ones rarely freeze, and no line differences are observed (Cairns, Hood, & Midlam, 1985). Lagerspetz and Sandnabba (1982) reported similar effects for their high-aggressive males, as they observed a sharp decline of their aggressiveness following repeated punishment by cagemates. In independent observations of the same phenomenon, Brain and Benton (1983) described the effects of isolation as the removal of the fighting inhibition acquired in the presence of male conspecifics. In all cases, the findings demonstrate clearly that the expression of genetic differences is essentially context-dependent.

Adjustment to the Interactive Context. Additional information on the proximal controls regulating the effects described earlier was obtained by conducting short-term analyses of social interaction sequences. One of the effects of social isolation is to make the subject more readily startled and reactive, such that even mild investigatory actions by the partner trigger high intensity responses, which in turn augment reactivity in the partner mouse. In order to control for reciprocal reactivity, Cairns and Scholz (1973) systematically decreased the amount of stimulation provided by the partner mouse by injecting it with various doses of chlorpromazine. As dose levels were increased and reactive responding diminished proportionately, so did reactivity in the isolated subject, such that the probability that an attack would evolve in their interactions followed the same trend (see also Banks, 1962). In this regard, the low reactivity observed among group-reared animals facilitates their cohabitation by diminishing the likelihood of their attacking other cage mates. The same dynamic explains the social interactions involving the dihydrexidine-treated animals (see next section), although in this case it worked the other way around, in that their high reactivity made them twice as likely to be attacked than the control noninjected animals. One methodological implication of these results is that the analysis of genetic or pharmacological effects can not be divorced from their proximal controls.

Age and Experience-Related Changes. Another question that was addressed was whether maturational changes and prior social experience in a dyadic test may have long-term effects that could either attenuate or magnify the expression of genetic differences. In order to examine this question, four males from the same litter were assigned to be tested either repeatedly or only once at different points during ontogeny. This design involved a total of 23 litters, where each was represented on each assessment point. The result reported in Cairns et al. (1983) showed that the magnitude of the line difference depends on the age of the subjects at testing. For the earliest testing point, which involved prepubertal animals (30 days-of-age), virtually no attacks were observed and the lines did not differ in aggressive performance. Among the animals that were tested only once on each of the successive points, the large difference appeared at puberty, was maintained among young adults, and some convergence between the lines was observed later in adulthood. Although in the single test condition the genetic influence on aggressive behavior was confirmed, the results also showed that this effect is itself under maturational control.

The repeated testing condition revealed an entirely different story. It turned out that four short 10-minute exposures to a conspecific, with long intertest intervals, were sufficient to wipe out completely the line difference among older animals. A clear attenuation of the line difference was already observed at 45 days, even if no attacks had occurred in the previous test. This attenuation continued until the fourth test where high- and low-aggressive animals attacked equally fiercely. Taken together, the cross-sectional and the longitudinal series indicated that genetic and experiential factors do not affect behavior in an additive manner but are intimately fused within the developing organism (Schneirla, 1966).

Timing and Behavioral Reorganization. Further research was conducted with the goal of determining whether the same experiential effects could take place over intervals of hours or days instead of weeks and months. To this end, extended triadic tests (8 to 24 hours) were conducted, which involved placing together in a large enclosure a high- and a low-aggressive male, and a female. As expected, high-aggressive subjects were invariably the first to attack in every test (Gariépy, 1994). However, in 22 out of 54 of these tests, low-aggressive subjects achieved full dominance—generally within 2 hours—over their high-aggressive opponent. In these cases of line reversal, the initial inhibition/avoidance typical of low-aggressive animals was gradually replaced by more frequent approaches, and attacks were initiated at a higher rate when some of the high-aggressive partners, because they were counterattacked, decreased their own rate of aggressive initiation and became more reactive. After the establishment of social dominance, the high degree of behavioral homogeneity normally found within lines for the dyadic test vanished, and attack measures no longer differentiated the lines. We see in the next section that this rapid reorganization of behavioral patterns was supported at least in part by changes in the activity of the endocrine system.

Behavioral Reorganization Across Generations. When our selected mice attack, they do so in a species-typical, stereotyped fashion regardless of selection line. The line differences arise not in forms of aggressive behavior, but in the thresholds for inhibition-elicitation. In this regard, one of the effects of selective breeding has been to alter the developmental rates of social inhibition in the low-aggressive line, such that prepubertal levels were retained progressively longer in the ontogeny of the descendant generations (Cairns et al., 1990). A most important aspect of the findings is that whatever the time frame considered, transgenerational, developmental, or short-term experiential, quantitative variations in the same thresholds seem sufficient to support rapid and efficient reorganizations in behavior and social interactions.

GENETICS, EXPERIENCE, AND THE NEUROBIOLOGY OF AGGRESSION

The detailed behavioral characterization of the NC selected lines provided a solid basis for examining the physiological pathways mediating the expression of aggressive and correlated social behaviors. This investigation focused on line differences in endocrine, immune, and neurochemical functions and their pharmacological manipulation. A special attention was given to identifying the physiological pathways, hormonal and neurobiological, supporting the rapid changes in behavioral organization observed as a result of both punctual and long-term adjustments to changes in social–ecological conditions.

Hormonal Differences in NC100 and NC900 Mice: Effects of Line, Experience, and Gender

Marked differences occur in the expression of aggressive behavior as a result of maturation. This effect is thought to be due, at least in part, to increases in circulating concentrations of testosterone. Thus we have assayed this hormone in high- and low-aggressive mice at either Day 24 or Day 45 of life. Our results indicate a substantial increase in testosterone as a function of age, with no significant differences in testosterone being observed at either age. We have since repeated the line comparison in 45-day-old mice and confirmed that no line difference occurs in testosterone, and that social isolation does not alter testosterone levels in either NC100 or NC900 mice. These findings, although negative, were important in demonstrating that the effects of selective breeding on aggressive behavior are not mediated through the Y chromosome (see Michard & Carlier, 1985, for a review), and suggested instead, the involvement of autosomal pathways.

Our measures of circulating levels of corticosterone also failed to reveal differences between the two selected lines. These levels were essentially the same for NC100 and NC900 mice, and did not appear to be affected by conditions of rearing, isolation, or group housing. Again, this negative finding was important in its own right, showing as it did, that the line differences observed in aggressive behavior following isolation rearing do not reflect a difference in how much stress is experienced under social isolation (see Essman, 1966, and Valzelli, 1969, for a coherent statement of this hypothesis).

Our findings on testosterone levels are consistent with results published by the Lagerspetz group with regard to the effects of early exposure to this steroid in their selected lines (e.g., Lagerspetz & Lagerspetz, 1975). Recent attempts to enhance aggressiveness in their low-line of animals by injections of testosterone propionate replicate earlier findings; namely, negative results for both low-aggressive males and females but positive results for high-aggressive females (Sandnabba, Lagerspetz, & Jensen, 1994). High-aggressive females that normally do not attack in the usual dyadic test, become as aggressive as high-line males when chronically exposed to testosterone. Testosterone apparently interacts with other features of the central nervous system (CNS), and constitutes a necessary but insufficient component of a neurobiological system that supports aggressive behaviors. These results are consistent with earlier findings of Hood and Cairns (1988) who, using postpartum assessments of females, found line differences in aggressive behavior that paralleled those of the male lines.

In the previous section we demonstrated that genetic differences in aggression could be modified by repeated social experience, and that similarly strong effects could be observed over hours as opposed to weeks and months. Recall that after an extended period of interaction, a substantial number of our low-aggressive mice achieved full dominance over their high-aggressive opponent. In an attempt to identify possible mechanisms supporting the rapid line reversals observed in these extended tests, levels of circulating testosterone and corticosterone were measured for all male dyads immediately after the test. Large differences were found between the males that had achieved a dominant or a submissive status. These differences were very consistent. Corticosterone levels for the submissive member of *each* dyad were twice as high as that of the dominant member. In the same pairs of animals, testosterone levels showed an inverse pattern, with the highest levels always observed for the dominant member. The dyadic differences for the two steroids were observed irrespective of line. In fact, when the data were pooled with respect to line instead of social status, no differences were observed, and measured concentrations were virtually the same for the two lines (Gariépy, 1994). The results suggested that otherwise strong and well established differences in genetic background could be easily overridden when other systems are activated in a supportive way during the course of ongoing demands for behavioral reorganization.

Line Differences in Immune Function

The availability of two lines of mice that exhibit robust and stable genetic differences in social behavior allowed us to test the hypothesis that certain heritable traits may correlate with altered immune function and increased vulnerability to disease. We have demonstrated that NC100 males are significantly more vulnerable to 3-methylcholanthrene-induced tumors and exhibit reduced natural killer (NK) cell function (Petitto, Lysle, Gariépy, Cairns, & Lewis, 1991). In this study, all NC100 mice developed tumors compared to only 44% of the high-aggressive mice (NC900). Baseline NK activity was also significantly lower among NC100 mice. Conversely, there was no difference in NK activity between

NC900 mice and nonselected isolated mice (NC600), a finding that was consistent with other unidirectional outcomes of this selective breeding program. These results support the hypothesis that social "traits" may be related to immune function and tumor susceptibility.

The foregoing experiments were done in mice reared in social isolation post-weaning, the conditions that produce robust differences in social behaviors. In a recent study, we sought to extend those findings to other measures of cellular immune responsiveness. Then, because the full expression of these genetic differences in behavior can be influenced by differential social experience, we sought to determine whether social experience affected the line differences observed in immune function. To this end, a cosibial design was used to examine whether social isolation versus group-housing postweaning modified the magnitude of the line differences in immune function. Compared to aggressive (NC900) mice low-aggressive (NC100) mice had significantly lower T-cell proliferative responses to ConA, lower IL-2 and gamma-interferon production as well as significantly lower NK activity (Petitto, Lysle, Gariépy, & Lewis, 1994). These marked line differences appear to be largely genetically mediated, as rearing condition did not influence significantly the line differences in cellular immune function. These data demonstrate that genetic selection for differences in social behavior are associated with individual differences in several parameters of cellular immune function, and that the expression of these differences does not seem to be affected by rearing conditions. The absence of rearing effects on immune function was consistent with the fact that differences in rearing conditions do not alter stress levels in our selected lines. Future studies are planned where stress levels will be experimentally manipulated and the effects on immune functions determined for the two lines.

Line Differences in Dopaminergic Function

On the basis of the known behavioral line differences and the current literature on the neurobiological substrates for the same behaviors, it appeared promising to conduct for the two lines neurochemical analyses of the mesolimbic and striatal sensorimotor structures. Indeed, earlier lesion studies have shown that the nucleus accumbens is an important terminal area and output system of the mesolimbic dopaminergic pathway, and that it plays a key role in the initiation of responses to both social and nonsocial stimuli (Louilot, LeMoal, & Simon, 1986). More specifically, this nucleus has been shown to be involved in the mediation of the adaptive response toward an aggressive intruder, even though the response to such an intruder was freezing or immobility (Taghzouti, Simon, Louilot, Herman, & LeMoal, 1985).

Research also demonstrated a role for the nigrostriatal dopaminergic system in regulating the ability to initiate adaptive responses rapidly (Kelly, Domestik, & Nauta, 1982; Nabeshima, Katoh, Hiramatsu, & Kameyama, 1986). On this issue, there is evidence that dopaminergic activity increases in the preparatory phase of appetitive or instrumental behavior, but not in the following, consummatory phase. According to Scheel-Krüger and Willner (1991) the dopaminergic systems function as motivators to activate and direct behavior toward the goal. In general, both signals predicting reward and approach behavior, and stressors which predict punishment and result in avoidance or escape, activate the mesolimbic and nigrostriatal dopaminergic systems.

In a series of studies begun in the 16th selectively bred generation (S_{16}), monoamine (e.g., dopamine, norepinephrine, serotonin) and metabolite concentrations were determined for the two selected lines. The initial analyses were conducted using brain tissue of animals that had been sacrificed at Day 45 without being tested and who had been in continuous isolation since weaning. Brain samples were obtained using microdissection by punch and were assayed by high performance liquid chromatography (HPLC) with electrochemical detection. The primary line differences that were apparent from these initial studies were discrete and limited to dopamine and metabolite concentrations in the nucleus accumbens and the caudate nucleus (Lewis, Gariépy, Southerland, Mailman, & Cairns, 1988). These two nuclei are, respectively, important terminal areas of the mesolimbic and nigrostriatal dopaminergic pathways. In these two areas, but especially in the nucleus accumbens, dopamine concentrations and its acidic metabolites were lower in the low-aggressive line. These line differences have been replicated in analyses of the same nuclei conducted over five different generations.

An analysis of dopamine receptor densities was also performed for our two lines by determining the concentrations of recognition sites for dopaminergic D_1 and D_2 ligands in both the nucleus accumbens and the caudate nucleus. Quantitative receptor autoradiographic techniques indicated a significantly increased density of these receptors in the low-aggressive line. Specifically, for the two nuclei investigated, D_1 receptor densities were higher among low-aggressive animals. Similar measures obtained for the D_2 receptor revealed higher densities in the rostral caudate nucleus of low-aggressive animals (Lewis et al., 1988). Additional measures taken at the origin of the two dopaminergic systems showed, by contrast, that the density of D_2 receptors in the substantia nigra and the ventral tegmental area was significantly lower in the low-aggressive line. Because these receptors lie on the bodies of the dopaminergic cells where they act as autoreceptors, the finding suggested that low-aggressive animals may have fewer of these cells. Fewer dopaminergic cells at the origin of the mesolimbic and nigrostriatal pathways would explain the reduced dopamine concentrations observed in the terminal areas.

The foregoing results are consistent with the proposal that central dopamine is an important mediator of how neocortical and limbic areas influence complex motor behavior (Louilot, LeMoal, & Simon, 1986). The significance of a line difference in the nucleus accumbens lies especially in the integrative role played by this nucleus as an interface between limbic and striatal sensorimotor structures. As such, this nucleus mediates the integration of emotional responding, motivational states, and the initiation of action.

Genetic Differences in Biogenic Amine Neurochemistry

In a more recent investigation, we assessed monoamine and metabolite concentrations in other key limbic areas, including the amygdala, the thalamus, and the frontal cortex. In this study, untested mice from both lines were sacrificed at Day 45 following continuous isolation, and selected brain regions were microdissected. We have demonstrated multiple times that low-aggressive mice have lower dopamine concentrations in the caudate nucleus and nucleus accumbens than their high-aggressive counterpart. Interestingly, in the amygdala, we found higher dopamine and DOPAC concentrations among NC100 mice than among NC900 mice. In addition, serotonin, and its major metabolite 5-HIAA were also lower in NC100 mice in thalamus as well as 5-HIAA in substantia nigra/ventral tegmental area. Finally, norepinephrine, serotonin, and its metabolite 5-HIAA were lower in NC100 mice in frontal cortex. These results are particularly provocative and suggest an important role for serotonin and possibly norepinephrine in mediating line differences in social behavior. The new evidence on genetic differences in biogenic amine neurochemistry is entirely consistent with the view proposed earlier by Darwin (his "law of correlated growth," 1859), and more recently by Mayr (1988) to the effect that the genome is a cohesive unit, and that even small changes in any part necessarily involve a global reorganization and the establishment of new functional relations between its constituents. These findings will permit interesting studies of how limbic–motor interactions may mediate social behavior.

BEHAVIORAL AND NEUROBEHAVIORAL EFFECTS OF EARLY SOCIAL EXPERIENCE

The effects of social experience on genetic differences was also examined and yielded provocative results. This study has demonstrated that repeated, early social experience (4 tests from Day 24 to Day 45) decreased freezing and increased attacks in NC100 mice, whereas it had opposite effects (increased freezing and decreased attacks) in NC900 mice. Thus, when tested at 45 days-of-age, few if any line differences were observed. This early social experience was found to affect turnover ratios (DOPAC/Dopamine concentrations) in the caudate nucleus and nucleus accumbens of high-aggressive animals. Specifically, repeatedly tested high-aggressive animals had significantly lower turnover ratios than either low-aggressive animals or high-aggressive animals that were tested for the first time at Day 45. The finding that there were high negative correlations between social reactivity and dopamine turnover or basal concentrations of DOPAC in the nucleus accumbens of repeatedly tested high-aggressive mice suggests that their high level of social reactivity following repeated testing can be accounted for by a decreased activity in mesolimbic dopamine neurons. The negative correlations that were found between attacks and dopamine turnover or basal concentrations of DOPAC in the caudate nucleus in low-aggressive animals that were tested either once or repeatedly is interesting inasmuch as the same correlations in high-aggressive animals are positive (Milko, 1992). This is supportive of differences in neurobiological activity between the lines even in the absence of the effects of social experience. Replication and further research is suggested in order to clarify these differences.

Effects of Benzodiazepine Administration on Freezing

A key question for this research is whether the low levels of aggression and the high levels of freezing observed in NC100 mice reflect a specific response to social stimulation, or a nonspecific "emotionality" or "fearfulness." We now have several lines of evidence to support the former hypothesis. First, NC100 and NC900 mice do not differ in their behavior in the elevated plus-maze (Petitto et al., 1991). This test has been shown to be a reliable measure of the level of fearfulness or emotional response to novelty in mice. Additionally, we have not been able to demonstrate line differences in corticosterone, under either basal or social challenge conditions. It should also be pointed out that over many generations, no systematic line differences have appeared in reactivity to tactile stimulus (Gariépy et al., 1988). Finally, treatment with a benzodiazepine appeared to have little effect on line differences observed in the social interaction test. We had hypothesized that the freezing behavior characteristic of the low-aggressive line in response to mild social stimulation was fear mediated, and that this propensity could be diminished by treatment with a benzodiazepine. We tested both NC100 and NC900 mice with either vehicle, 1.0, 3.0, or 10mg/kg of chlordiazepoxide. This treatment failed to have any dramatic effects on freezing, although somewhat reduced levels were observed at the lower doses. The anxiolitic failed also to affect aggressive behavior and social reactivity (Tancer, Gariépy, Mayleben, Petitto, & Lewis, 1992). These data provide largely negative but informative results on the mediation of freezing and confirm the hypothesis that it constitutes a specific response to social stimulation.

Effects of Monoamine Oxidase Inhibition
on Social Behavior

The marked social inhibition observed in NC100 mice have suggested that our ongoing studies may be useful in understanding the neurobiological basis of phobias in humans. The treatment of choice for this clinical disorder is the monoamine oxidase inhibitor, phenelzine. Previously, we showed that chronic phenelzine (10 mg/kg) had little effect on freezing or attack. In a recent study, phenelzine was administered to mice of both lines via osmotic minipump. The results of this study showed that even when administered chronically, phenelzine has little effect on attack and freezing. Moreover, this MAOI did not affect reactivity. The drug, however, did alter the latency of socially inhibited animals to counterattack. This effect on the speed of escalation to aggression following an initial provocation, mirrors the effects of phenelzine in humans, where the effects of the drug are often seen only after social exposure.

D_1 Dopamine Receptor Activation and Reactivity to Social Stimuli

As described earlier, we have established that compared to NC900 animals, NC100 mice have lower dopamine concentrations in nucleus accumbens and caudate nucleus, with increased dopamine receptor densities in these same regions. Thus we wished to determine the effects of administration of a dopamine receptor agonist on social behavior. Mice of both lines were administered either saline, 1, 3, or 10 mg/kg (s.c) of the selective, full efficacy D_1 receptor agonist dihydrexidine and their behavior assessed in the social interaction test. The results of this study were both surprising and striking. Dihydrexidine dose-dependently reduced aggression in NC900 mice and similarly reduced nonagonistic approaches in the low-aggressive line, without affecting its characteristic freezing behavior. In both cases, the effects were related to a marked increase in reactivity to the mild social stimulation provided by the partner mouse, as measured by increases in behaviors such as escape, reflexive kicking, and vocalization. In independent experiments, mice of both lines were pretreated with the selective D_1 antagonist SCH23390 (0.1 mg/kg) or the selective D_2 antagonist remoxipride (1.0 mg/kg), after which they received dihydrexidine (10 mg/kg) and were tested as before. The effects of dihydrexidine on social reactivity were significantly antagonized in both lines by SCH23390 but not attenuated by remoxipride. These experiments confirmed further the role that D_1 dopamine receptors play in the mediation of social reactivity (Lewis, Gariépy, Gendreau, Nichols, & Mailman, 1994).

The mechanism by which social isolation induces marked differences in social behavior in selectively bred lines has been a major question for this research. On this issue, our hypothesis has been that social isolation causes a significant increase in the sensitivity of postsynaptic dopamine receptors. We tested this hypothesis by examining the effects of the same D_1 receptor agonist on the social behavior of both isolated and group-housed mice of each line. The effects of dihydrexidine on social behaviors essentially replicated those previously observed by Lewis et al. (1994). The "supersensitivity" to the D_1 dopamine agonist observed among isolated mice confirmed the role of this receptor in the mediation of the isolation effects. Finally, the fact that NC900 mice were the most sensitive to the pharmacological challenge suggested that social isolation has a differential effect on the two lines (Gariépy, Gendreau, & Lewis, 1995).

D_1 Dopamine Receptor Function: Effect of Experience

Because both social isolation and administration of a D_1 dopamine agonist can induce social reactivity in mice, we hypothesized that isolation rearing must exert its effects, at least in part, by up-regulation of D_1 dopamine receptors. To test this hypothesis, we have conducted radioligand binding experiments using striatal tissue taken from mice of both lines. Half of the animals were socially reared from weaning until sacrifice (Day 45), whereas half were group reared for the same period of time. Relative to the group condition, homogenate binding data revealed a substantial increase in striatal densities of D_1 dopamine receptors among isolated animals. The fact that such an increase was observed in the striatum is entirely consistent with the known functions of this area in the integration of affective, emotional and motivational states, and would explain the strong propensity of isolated animals to react strongly to novel social stimulation. Moreover, the significantly greater increase in D_1 receptor density observed in NC900 mice was consistent with their known tendency to be more reactive to social stimuli following isolation than NC100 mice (Gariépy et al., 1995). Future experiments will include further tests of the effects of social isolation on specific dopamine receptor subtypes and examining the behavioral effects of pharmacologically down-regulating these receptors during the period of social isolation.

D_1 Dopamine Receptor Upregulation and Social Reactivity: Reversal by Social Experience

The previous experiments on the linkages between social reactivity, rearing conditions, and the D_1 dopamine receptor indicated that both genetic differences and differential rearing conditions can alter the sensitivity of this receptor. In order to examine further the influence of experiential input on D_1 receptor function we verified the possibility of altering its sensitivity by having our animals to experience a dramatic change in social experience over their life time. Accordingly, we initially isolated both NC900 and NC100 mice at weaning. At Day 45, half the animals of each line were placed into social groups. At Day 64, ca. 12 mice per line per housing condition were tested in a social interaction test. A second set of animals representing both lines and housing conditions was challenged as before with dihydrexidine prior to the social test. A final set of animals was sacrificed for receptor studies at Day 64. We hypothesized that returning animals to social groups would reduce social reactivity, attenuate the dihydrexidine-induced social reactivity, and reduce D_1 dopamine receptor sensitivity. Our results supported these hypotheses. Mice of both lines that experienced a change in rearing condition exhibited significantly less reactivity, a reduced response to dihydrexidine, and a decreased density of D_1 receptors when compared to animals that remained singly caged. This experiment constituted a striking demonstration of the plasticity of the neurobiological system supporting reactive responses, and confirmed the view that its functional organization is eminently open to experiential input.

TOWARD A DEVELOPMENTAL SYNTHESIS

It is a well-established tradition to treat behavior as a dependent variable, or an outcome to be explained in terms of its biological and environmental controls. The earlier findings, however, raise questions concerning the validity of the underlying mechanistic–deterministic assumptions. In most of our experimental manipulations, changes in behavioral patterns did not occur because, but *in spite of*, the genetic, neurobiological, and environmental controls. Recall, for example, the case of those low-aggressive animals that faced a high-aggressive opponent for the first time, or those animals that were introduced to a group situation after a prolonged period of isolation. The behavioral outcomes in these cases seem more appropriately described as *accommodations* to changes in stimulative conditions than as determined by those same conditions. Moreover, closer examination of the findings suggest that these accommodations served as inducers of change in the biological and environmental systems rather than vice versa. When the investigative work is explicitly focused on the analysis of behavior, as opposed to the "preparation" of a "behavioral assay," behavioral phenomena appear highly dynamic and reveal their essential function of supporting flexible and malleable adaptations. In this section, we evaluate some of the theoretical and methodological implications of the findings.

The Special Functions of Social Behavior

Behavioral actions and cognitions—the stuff of psychology—have a special status for organismic adaptation and functional integration. The accommodations achieved through behavior can be relatively fail-safe, and reversible. These actions permit to rapidly change environmental conditions, on the one hand, and they promote changes in the structure of the organism, on the other. By creating "enduring changes" within and without, behavioral actions further create a supportive context for their own consolidation. Perhaps the special functions of behavior are best illustrated in the context of social adaptations where the organism must serve two masters. One master is within, which may be described as the functional alignment created by virtue of reciprocal influences between the different organismic systems over the course of previous adaptations. The other master is without, and represents the need to preserve the external conditions supporting these adaptations, given the actions of others and their effects on these conditions. Under such constraints, any behavior that would become stereotyped or frozen, whether by genes, neurochemistry, or early experience, would lose its most vital function of promoting flexible and reversible adaptations.

This line of reasoning implies that behavior can be reduced to "biological structure" or "environmental influence" only in a trivial and misleading sense. The dual synchrony involved in all complex social patterns precludes reduction to any single source of regulation, whether internal or external. Instead, we propose that behavioral adaptations occupy the space between the relatively enduring structures of the organism, on the one hand, and the relatively enduring properties of the physical and social environment, on the other. Although uncommon in the behavioral sciences, these proposals are not entirely new. In essence, they were suggested by the evolutionist Rensch (1959) who defined progressive evolution (anagenesis) in terms of an enhanced behavioral command and independence of environmental factors. Similarly, Schneirla (1949) and Tobach (1969) defined behavior as the activity whereby organisms promote their own integrity-promoting tonicity. Together, these proposals suggest that the internal and external conditions that define the state of an adapted system, are instantiated by the very act of adapting, and not the reverse as is commonly assumed. To put it differently, it might be of greater heuristic value to situate behaviors—particularly social behaviors—at the origin of a process whereby internal and external conditions are brought into alignment, in ways that support preservation and development. In brief, there are substantial reasons why behavior should be viewed as the leading edge of biological adaptation.

Correlated Constraints and Systemic Vulnerability to Change

It may be useful to define first what we mean by adaptation, or more specifically, what is the general state of an adapted system. Such a definition may be arrived at by examining the implications of the bidirectional nature of influences between organismic levels as recently stated by Gottlieb (1992). This concept specifies that it is the functional relationship between components—the interactive activity taking place between them—that promotes structural–functional changes within living systems. At the gene-cell level, for example, this bidirectionality implies that the set of genes that are being turned on or off at any point in time depends on the existing conditions within the cell, and reciprocally, that these conditions are themselves linked to genetic activity. A logical consequence of bidirectionality between these two structures is that their organizational states—the patterning of on–off genes on the one hand, and the chemical composition of the cell on the other—are strongly correlated. Similarly, the cellular release of specific enzymes is not independent of the state of organization and activity within the host organ, and reciprocally. Because bidirectional influences are found between all organismic levels, what applies to lower levels applies to systemic organization as a whole, such that over time a strong network of correlations is created among all organismic levels, from genetic to neurobiological activity. When these correlations extend to the organization of extraorganismic structures, the biological system may be said to be in an adapted state.

As an example, we argue elsewhere that "it should not be surprising to find hot-tempered, impulsive children growing up with family members who themselves exhibit and reward these traits, or subcultures of aggressive adolescents in which aggressive behavior is viewed as an asset rather than a liability. More broadly, social systems are usually formed in ways that are correlated with and support bio-behavioral dispositions" (Cairns, McGuire, & Gariépy, 1993, p. 110). The idea that continuity in adaptive patterns arises as a result of the developmental emergence of systemic correlations explicitly precludes a causal interpretation in terms of genetic or neurological influence, early experience, antecedent events, or environmental contingencies. Instead, conservatism in adaptive patterns reflects a state of homeostatic equilibrium which tends to perpetuate itself by virtue of the correlated constraints that systemic activity generates over time.

A related perspective on conservatism is the suggestion by Hegmann and DeFries (1970) that correlations between genetic influences and correlations between features of the environment often tend to be themselves correlated. On this point, they commented that a correlation between genetic and environmental effects can enhance the biological efficiency of the adaptational process because both forces "push" behavior in the same direction. Their observation is particularly interesting because it suggests a linkage between developmental accommodations and evolutionary modifications. Extending this proposal further, Cairns et al. (1990) observed that "in periods of severe challenges, parallel and mutually supportive behavioral modifications may be rapidly mobilized in ontogeny and evolution by separate routes that act jointly to consolidate the same forms of adaptations" (p. 56).

A direct consequence of the existence of correlations between systemic components is that adapted systems tend to exhibit a good deal of inertia in which certain forms of equilibrium are maintained over time. But circumstances also occur when this equilibrium is threatened. Although behavioral activity is necessarily constrained by the trace effects created internally and externally by previous adaptations, what actually precedes any systemic change, is not a change in external or internal conditions, or in their blind interactions, but a change in how the organism–environment relationship is constructed through behavioral activity. It is this activity that sets the stage for systemic changes, including the initiation of new functional relationships between the constituent levels. In order to make sense of the process of adaptation, from the initial phase of behavioral accommodation to the systemic consolidation of the new adaptive directions, it is necessary to examine the dynamic interplay that exists between different systemic levels and their respective time frames for reorganization (Gariépy, 1995).

Time and Relations Between Systemic Levels

It is well documented that the different systems of the organism, the neurobiological, endocrinological, or genetic are not forever fixed in a given state of activity, but are eminently open to changes in stimulative conditions. The analysis of the adaptive process requires attention to the fact that functional changes within these different systems do not occur all at once, but may potentially take place over vastly different time frames. From the standpoint of adaptability, the fact that the various systems of the organism are differentially open for change over different periods of time provides for both conservatism and the possibility of fail-safe, innovative, and reversible changes in adaptive patterns. In this way, when new adaptive challenges arise, those systems open for change over the short-term may minimize the constraints imposed by other systems that change over longer periods of time. If those conditions only represented transient changes from the normative context, the overall systemic support for adjustment to the norm was not lost, and a return to the previous adaptation is equally facilitated. However, if those same conditions endure, by virtue of bidirectionality, activity within other systems eventually become aligned with the changed adaptive directions, such that new correlations are established in which a new systemic equilibrium is created. Over generations, it is the same process that forces reorganization at the genetic level and its eventual alignment with adaptive directions, which in their initial stage of behavioral accommodation, appeared as punctual adjustments.

Examples of the foregoing proposals were given earlier in this chapter. In one case, behavioral accommodations were supported by a change in the activity of the endocrine system, and in the other, they were supported by a change in the sensitivity of the D_1 dopamine receptor. A similar example was provided by Fuller (1967) in his short-term analysis of the relations between time and genetic expression. In a provocative article, he observed that the primary differences among breeds of dogs—namely, a propensity to become inhibited in a novel context following isolation rearing—occurred during the initial stages of assessment. Once past the initial stage, the animals responded similarly to the demands of the assessment context. Accordingly, Fuller viewed the "emergence response" to be the phase where genetic biases in terms of emotional responses and temperamental differences were maximal. Once beyond the introductory stage, other context-bound systems, in this case, the perceptual–cognitive systems, took over in behavioral support. What works for adaptation in the short term may not be the most effective in the long term, in the light of inevitable changes in the nature of the internal and external context.

Such illustrations of short-term processes of changes overtaking the constraints imposed by systems established over the long-term should not be overdrawn, however. Existing evidence on mechanisms of development indicates that bidirectionality and mutual support is more often the rule than the exception. The example provided earlier by Cairns et al. (1993) of hot-tempered aggressive adolescents seeking peer affiliations that further consolidate the behaviors and values characteristic of their family background was an illustrative case. Perhaps a most remarkable aspect of behavioral activity is its capacity to force reorganization between the different levels of systemic activity such that their mutual effects may be either cancelled or brought back into alignment. It is precisely because of this function that behavior can serve as an adaptive device in a system that otherwise tends to conservation and continuity in structure and function.

SUMMARY AND CONCLUSIONS

The studies reported in this chapter demonstrate that selective breeding for high and low levels of aggression in mice creates robust and replicable genetic effects on aggressive behaviors. It was also demonstrated that the same manipulation creates profound and nontrivial line differences in neurochemistry. Perhaps a most striking aspect of the findings was that in spite of the genetic and neurobiological constraints new patterns of behavioral adaptation were observed that were hardly predictable on the basis of these constraints alone. Rapidity and effective changes in forms of social adaptation was the rule whatever the time frame over which such changes were investigated, transgenerational, ontogenetic, or even in the moment-to-moment context of social interactions. The search for mediating factors across these time frames pointed to the primacy of behavioral accommodations in promoting changes in the biological system and its environmental support.

It appears to be an important property of the hierarchical organization of living systems, both within and without the organism, to offer multiple levels whereby rapid and fail-safe adaptive reorganizations may be initiated. To be sure, behavioral actions are always correlated with the organizational states of the internal and external systems. The impression that behavior is a product of these systems is created by the difficulty of experimentally generating conditions in which systemic correlations are temporarily broken. In the absence of control for these correlations, the assumptions of determination remain unchallenged and the special properties of behavior, unrecognized. By focusing explicitly on conditions where established patterns of adaptation are compromised, our research showed that rapid and fail-safe behavioral accommodations occur whereby systemic changes are initiated. By implication, study of these changes should begin with a systematic analysis of the behavioral accommodations observed under challenging conditions, along with appropriately time-framed analyses of the supportive changes taking place in the other systems of the organism and its environment.

REFERENCES

Banks, E. M. (1962). A time and motion study of prefighting behavior in mice. *Journal of Genetic Psychology, 101*, 165–183.

Brain, P. F., & Benton, D. (1983). Conditions of housing, hormones, and aggressive behavior. In B. B. Svare (Ed.), *Hormones and aggressive behavior* (pp. 351–372). New York: Plenum.

Cairns, R. B. (1973). Fighting and punishment from a developmental perspective. In J. K. Coles & D. D. Jensen (Eds.), *Nebraska Symposium on Motivation* (Vol. 20). Lincoln: University of Nebraska Press.

Cairns, R. B. (1976). The ontogeny and phylogeny of social behavior. In M. E. Hahn & E. C. Simmel (Eds.), *Evolution and communicative behavior*, (pp. 115–139). New York: Academic Press.

Cairns, R. B., Gariépy, J.-L., & Hood, K. E. (1990). Development, microevolution, and social behavior. *Psychological Review, 97*, 49–65.

Cairns, R. B., Hood, K. E., & Midlam, J. (1985). On fighting in mice: Is there a sensitive period for isolation effects? *Animal Behaviour, 33*, 166–180.

Cairns, R. B., MacCombie, D. J., & Hood, K. E. (1983). A developmental-genetic analysis of aggressive behavior in mice: I. Behavioral outcomes. *Journal of Comparative Psychology, 97*, 69–89.

Cairns, R. B., McGuire, A. M., & Gariépy, J.-L. (1993). Developmental behavior genetics: Fusion, correlated constraints, and timing. In D. F. Hay & A. Angold (Eds.), *Precursors and causes in development and psychopathology* (pp. 87–122). New York: Wiley.

Cairns, R. B., & Scholz, S. D. (1973). Fighting in mice: Dyadic escalation and what is learned. *Journal of Comparative and Physiological Psychology, 85*, 540–550.

Darwin, C. (1859). *On the origin of species by means of natural selection*. London: Murray.

Essman, W. B. (1966). The development of activity differences in isolated and aggregated mice. *Animal Behaviour, 14*, 406–409.

Fuller, J. L. (1967). Experiential deprivation and later behavior. *Science, 158*, 1645–1652.

Fuller, J. L., & Thompson, W. R. (1978). *Foundations of behavior genetics*. St. Louis, MO: Mosby.

Gariépy, J.-L. (1994). The mediation of aggressive behavior in mice: A discussion of approach-withdrawal processes in social adaptations. In G. Greenberg, K. E. Hood, & E. Tobach (Eds.), *Behavioral development in comparative perspective: The approach-withdrawal theory of T. C. Schneirla* (pp. 231–284). New York: Garland.

Gariépy, J.-L. (1995). The evolution of a developmental science: Early determinism, modern interactionism, and a new systemic approach. In R. Vasta (Ed.), *Annals of Child Development, Vol. 11* (pp. 167–224). Bristol, PA: Jessica Kingsley.

Gariépy, J.-L., Gendreau, P. J., & Lewis, M. H. (1995). Rearing conditions alter social reactivity and D_1 dopamine receptors. *Psychopharmacology Biochemistry and Behavior, 51*, 767–773.

Gariépy, J.-L., Hood, K. E., & Cairns, R. B. (1988). A developmental-genetic analysis of aggressive behavior in mice: III. Behavioral mediation by heightened reactivity or increased immobility? *Journal of Comparative Psychology, 102*, 392–399.

Gottlieb, G. (1992). *Individual development and evolution: The genesis of novel behavior*. New York: Oxford University Press.

Hegmann, J. P., & DeFries, J. C. (1970). Are genetic correlations and environmental correlations correlated? *Nature, 226*, 284–286.

Hood, K. E., & Cairns, R. B. (1988). A developmental-genetic analysis of aggressive behavior in mice: II. Cross-sex inheritance. *Behavior Genetics, 18*, 605–619.

Kelly, A. E., Domestik, V. B., & Nauta, W. H. J. (1982). The amydalostriatal projection in the rat: An anatomical study by anterograde and retrograde tracing methods. *Neuroscience, 7*, 615–630.

Lagerspetz, K. (1964). Studies on the aggressive behavior of mice. *Annals Acadamiae Scientiarum Fennicae, Sarja-ser. B, 131*, 1–131.

Lagerspetz, K., & Lagerspetz, K. Y. H. (1975). The expression of the genes of aggressiveness in mice: The effect of androgen on aggression and sexual behavior in females. *Aggressive Behavior, 1*, 291–296.

Lagerspetz, K., & Sandnabba, K. (1982). The decline of aggressiveness in male mice during group caging as determined by punishment delivered by cage mates. *Aggressive Behavior, 8*, 319–334.

Lewis, M. H., Gariépy, J.-L., Gendreau, P. J., Nichols, D. E., & Mailman, R. B. (1994). Social reactivity and D_1 dopamine receptors: Studies in mice selectively bred for high and low levels of aggression. *Neuropsychopharmacology, 10*, 115–122.

Lewis, M. H., Gariépy, J.-L., Southerland, S. B., Mailman, R. B., & Cairns, R. B. (1988). Alterations in central dopamine induced by selective breeding. *Society for Neuroscience Abstracts, 14*, 969.

Louilot, A., LeMoal, M., Simon, H. (1986). Differential reactivity of dopaminergic neurons in the nucleus accumbens in response to different behavioral situations: An in vivo voltammetric study in free moving rats. *Brain Research, 400*, 395–397.

Mayr, E. (1988). *Toward a new philosophy of biology: Observations of an evolutionist.* Cambridge: Harvard University Press.

Michard, C., & Carlier, M. (1985). Les conduites d'agression intraspécifique chez la souris domestique: Différences individuelles et analyses génétiques [Intraspecific aggressive behaviors in the domestic mouse: Individual differences and genetic analyses]. *Behavioral Biology, 10*, 123–146.

Milko, J. E. (1992). *Effects of social experience on the dopaminergic systems of mice selectively bred for high and low levels of aggressiveness.* Unpublished honors thesis, University of North Carolina at Chapel Hill.

Nabeshima, T., Katoh, A., Hiramatsu, M. & Kameyama, T. (1986). A role played by dopamine and opioid neuronal systems in stress-induced motor suppression (conditioned suppression of motility) in mice. *Brain Research, 398*, 354–360.

Petitto, J. M., Lysle, D. T., Gariépy, J.-L., Cairns, R. B. & Lewis, M. H. (1991). Genetic differences in social behavior: Relation to natural killer cell function and susceptibility to cancer. *Neuropsychopharmacology, 8*, 35–43.

Petitto, J. M., Lysle, D. T., Gariépy, J.-L. & Lewis, M. H. (1994). Association of genetic differences in social behavior and cellular immune responsiveness: Effects of social experience. *Brain, Behavior and Immunity, 8*, 111–122.

Plomin, R. (1990). *Nature and nurture: An introduction to human behavior genetics.* Monterey, CA: Brooks/Cole.

Rensch, B. (1959). *Evolution above the species level.* New York: Columbia University Press.

Sandnabba, N. K., Lagerspetz, K., & Jensen, E. (1994). Effects of testosterone exposure and fighting experience on the aggressive behavior of female and male mice selectively bred for intermale aggression. *Hormones and Behavior, 28*, 219–231.

Scheel-Krüger, L., & Willner, P. (1991). The mesolimbic system: Principles of operation. In P. Willner & J. Scheel Krüger (Eds.), *The mesolimbic dopamine system: From motivation to action.* New York: Wiley.

Schneirla, T. C. (1949). Levels in the psychological capacities of animals. In R. W. Sellars, V. J. McGill, & M. Farber (Eds.), *Philosophy for the future: The quest of modern materialism* (pp. 243–286). New York: Macmillan.

Schneirla, T. C. (1966). Behavioral development and comparative psychology. *Quarterly Review of Biology, 41*, 283–302.

Scott, J. P. (1977). Social genetics. *Behavior Genetics, 7*, 327–346.

Taghzouti, K., Simon, H., Louilot, A., Herman, J. P., & LeMoal, M. (1985). Behavioral study after local injection of 6-hydroxydopamine into the nucleus accumbens in the rat. *Brain Research, 344*, 9–20.

Tancer, M. E., Gariépy, J.-L., Mayleben, M. A., Petitto, J. M., & Lewis, M. H. (1992, April). NC100 mice: A putative animal model for social phobia. *Society of Biological Psychiatry*, Washington, DC.

Tobach, E. (1969). Developmental aspects of chemoreception in the wistar (DAB) rat: Tonic processes. *Annals of New York Academy of Science, 290*, 226–267.

Valzelli, L. (1969). Aggressive behavior induced by isolation. In S. Garattini & E. B. Sigg (Eds.), *Aggressive behavior* (pp. 70–76). Amsterdam: Excepta Medica Foundation.

van Oortmerssen, G. A., & Bakker, Th. C. M. (1981). Artificial selection for short and long attack latencies in wild *Mus musculus domesticus*. *Behavior Genetics, 11*, 115–126.

NEUROBIOLOGICAL PERSPECTIVE

4

Neurotransmitter Correlates of Impulsive Aggression

Emil F. Coccaro
Richard J. Kavoussi
Medical College of Pennsylvania

This chapter focuses on the putative role that central neurotransmitters play in impulsive–aggressive behavior in humans. Although there is a growing literature in this area, other factors (both biological and nonbiological) also contribute to the development and display of this behavior in humans. Many of these factors are discussed in other chapters in this volume. However, one of the appeals of studying neurotransmitter correlates in relation to behavior is that abnormalities in neurotransmitter function often translate directly into psychopharmacological interventions. For example, if individuals with a prominent history of impulsive–aggressive behavior have a deficit in a particular central neurotransmitter system, treatment with agents that enhance the function of that system may well diminish the frequency or severity of the behavior. Conversely, if impulsive–aggressive behavior seems to be enhanced by activation of certain neurotransmitter systems, then inhibition of that system by agents that blockade the relevant receptors or inhibit neurotransmitter synthesis may diminish the behavior in selected individuals.

At this time there is much data to support the role of serotonin in impulsive–aggressive behavior. Serotonin (5-HT) is thought to function as a behavioral inhibitor and, as such, appears to display an inverse relationship with impulsive–aggressive behavior (Coccaro, 1992). That is, the lower the 5-HT activity the more impulsive–aggressive the individual. However, biological systems are rarely influenced by one biological factor. Usually there are inhibitory and excitatory influences, which interact and lead to some form of balance between the factors, which may then be observed behaviorally. If 5-HT functions as an important inhibitory influence in impulsive–aggressive behavior, there should be central neurotransmitters that function as excitatory influences in this regard. Although limited at this time, there is empiric data to support the roles of non-5-HT neurotransmitter systems, including those acted upon by central norepinephrine, dopamine, and the endogenous opiates. Accordingly, we focus on each of these neurotransmitter systems to the extent that there is empiric data to support a role for each in impulsive–aggressive behavior. These data are derived from both psychobiological and treatment studies.

SEROTONIN (5-HT) AND IMPULSIVE AGGRESSION

Biochemical Studies in Human Subjects

The first set of studies that implicated 5-HT in aggressive-related behaviors in humans were postmortem brain studies of individuals who had committed suicide and of individuals who had died in accidents. Three of these 4 mid-1960s studies found reduced 5-HT levels, in the brain stem, raphe, or other structures within the limbic system, in suicide victims compared with accident victims (Coccaro & Astill, 1990). A decade later, Asberg and colleagues (Asberg, Traksman, & Thoren, 1976) reported that depressed patients with a past history of suicidal behavior had lower levels of the cerebrospinal fluid (CSF) 5-HT metabolite, 5-hydroxyindolacetic acid (5-HIAA) than depressed patients who had never attempted suicide. Moreover, all the individuals who had used violent means to attempt suicide, or who ultimately committed suicide on follow-up, had low levels of CSF 5-HIAA. Struck by the fact that low 5-HT activity predisposes lower mammalian animals to aggressive behavior (see Valzelli, 1981), Asberg and colleagues suggested that low levels of CSF 5-HIAA might be a correlate of violent suicidal behavior in humans. Although low levels of CSF 5-HIAA do not always seem to correlate with violent suicide attempts, this measure has been replicated many times as a correlate of suicidal behavior in general (Coccaro & Astill, 1990).

Brown and colleagues (Brown et al., 1982; Brown, Goodwin, Ballenger, Goyer, & Major, 1979; Fig. 4.1) were the first to report a clear relationship between CSF 5-HIAA concentration and aggression in humans. Brown et al. reported a strong inverse correlation between CSF 5-HIAA levels and a history of aggressive events ($r = -0.78$) in 24 young male naval recruits being evaluated for fitness of duty. These individuals were all personality disordered (by *DSM–II*) and were nondepressed and nonsubstance abusing. Aggression ratings were performed by review of medical and military charts by several raters. These ratings had very high interrater reliability, probably because only actual aggressive events were counted for purposes of the rating. A replication study with 12 similarly recruited naval subjects with *DSM–III* borderline personality disorder reported similar

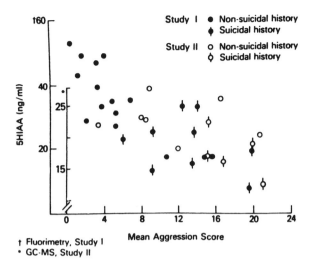

FIG. 4.1. Trivariate relationship between life history of aggression, history of previous suicide attempt, and CSF 5-HIAA concentrations in two studies of personality disordered individuals (Brown et al., 1979; Brown et al., 1982). CSF 5-HIAA and aggression correlation in Study I: $r = -0.78$, $N = 24$, $p < 0.001$; Study II: $r = -0.53$, $N = 12$, $p < 0.08$. CSF 5-HIAA by Fluorimetry in Study I; by GC-MS in Study II. From the *American Journal of Psychiatry, 139*, pp. 741–746, 1982. Copyright 1982, the American Psychiatric Association. Reprinted by permission.

inverse correlations with the Psychopathic Deviance subscale of the MMPI ($r = -0.77$, $p < 0.01$), Buss–Durkee "irritability" ($r = -0.66$, $p < 0.05$; Brown & Goodwin, 1984), and with the history of aggressive events ratings ($r = -0.53$, $p < 0.08$) used in the previous study (Brown et al., 1979). Of greater interest, however, was the observation that in both studies, subjects with a history of suicidal behavior had lower CSF 5-HIAA concentrations and higher ratings of aggressive events than subjects who did not have a history of suicidal behavior. This suggested that, in some populations at least, reduced CSF 5-HIAA concentration predisposes humans to aggression directed both at the self (suicidal behavior) and at others (aggression). Although this finding has been replicated in samples of abstinent alcoholics (Limson et al., 1991) and nonhuman primate monkeys (Higley et al., 1992), we have not been able to identify an inverse relationship between a measure of aggression and basal CSF 5-HIAA concentration in two separate samples in our laboratory (Coccaro, Kavoussi, Trestman, & Siever, 1993).

Although the nature of the population studied by Brown et al. (1979, 1982), suggested that the type of aggression being studied was impulsive in nature, Linnoila and colleagues (1983) were the first to provide evidence that low CSF 5-HIAA concentrations were more specifically associated with impulsive–aggressive behavior in humans. Violent offenders in a Finnish forensic facility were studied as a function of the number of violent crimes committed and as a function of whether the violent acts resulting in incarceration were impulsive or premeditated. CSF 5-HIAA concentrations of repeated violent offenders (67.9 ± 12.2 nM; $n = 17$) were significantly ($p < 0.02$) lower than those of offenders with a history of only one violent crime (87.1 ± 23.7 nM; $n = 19$). Similarly, CSF 5-HIAA concentrations of impulsive violent offenders were significantly lower than those of the premeditated violent offenders ($p < 0.01$). Moreover, violent offenders with a history of a suicide attempt also had lower CSF 5-HIAA concentrations than violent offenders without a history of a suicide attempt. This suggested that impulsive–aggression (whether directed at others or the self), rather than aggression in general, is the specific correlate of low CSF 5-HIAA concentrations. This same group of investigators later reported that impulsive firesetters (i.e., those without a financial motive to commit arson) have CSF 5-HIAA concentrations comparable to those of violent offenders (Virkunnen, Nuutila, Goodwin, & Linnoila, 1987). It is of interest that most of the impulsive firesetters met *DSM–III* criteria for borderline personality disorder (95%) and for having had a history of at least one violent suicide attempt (60%), because both groups have been shown to have generalized problems with aggression and reduced 5-HT function (Coccaro et al., 1989).

Biochemical Studies in Nonhuman Primates

At least two studies in nonhuman primate subjects demonstrate evidence consistent with an inverse relationship between CSF 5-HIAA concentration and aggression. The first study by Higley et al. (1992) reported a significant inverse relationship between ratings of overt aggression and cisternal CSF 5-HIAA concentration in 18 free-ranging juvenile and adolescent rhesus monkeys living on an island preserve. Overt aggressive behavior was evaluated by researchers experienced in rhesus monkey behavior using photography, transcribed descriptions of aggressive behavior, and number of old scars and recent wounds. From these data, but blind to CSF 5-HIAA concentration, the raters ranked the monkeys from the *most* to the *least* aggressive. The correlation between this aggression rating and CSF 5-HIAA was: $r = -0.52$ ($p < 0.002$). In a second study by the same group (Mehlman et al., 1994), aggressive behavior was directly observed over seven 30-minute periods distributed over different times of several days. Aggressive behavior rated included displacements, stationary threats, chases, and physical assaults. A derived variable, "escalated aggression" (i.e., number of chases and assaults divided by all aggressive acts), was also calculated as a way of ranking animals along the dimension using the most severe form of aggressive behavior. Another derived variable, *percent (%) long leaps* (number of long leaps divided by total number of leaps in the tree canopy) was used to assess impulsive risk-taking (long leaps are leaps between trees greater than 3 meters in length at a height of 7 or more meters high and therefore likely to be lethal if unsuccessful). Among the 23 rhesus monkeys studied, there were no correlations between cisternal CSF 5-HIAA concentration and total aggression or total leaping behavior. However, there were significant inverse correlations between CSF 5-HIAA and number of wounds, and the two derived variables of escalated aggression ($r = -0.42$, $p < 0.05$) and percentage of long leaping ($r = -0.44$, $p < 0.05$). These data suggest that lower concentrations of CSF 5-HIAA are associated with manifestations of severe aggression and impulsive risk-taking as observed in the social setting of these monkeys. As such, these data are consistent with the findings of several clinical investigators in aggressive human subjects.

Brain Receptor Studies

Studies of brain receptors, in general, support the hypothesis that self-directed aggression (suicide) is associated with reduced 5-HT activity. Three of 5 studies of ^{3}H-imipramine binding in brains of suicide and accident victims report reduced numbers of ^{3}H-imipramine binding sites in suicide compared to accident victims (Coccaro & Astill, 1990). Although ^{3}H-imipramine binding is a somewhat controversial parameter of 5-HT activity, ^{3}H-imipramine binding in the brain is thought to reflect either the number of 5-HT neurons in the brain tissue assayed or the number of 5-HT uptake sites. In the former case, these findings are consistent with brain 5-HT levels and CSF 5-HIAA concentrations in suicide victims; in the latter case, these findings may reflect a diminished ability of the 5-HT terminal to recapture synaptic 5-HT for re-release. Three of 6 studies reflective of 5-HT_2 receptor binding in the brain report an increase in the number of 5-HT_2 receptor binding sites in the frontal cortex of suicide victims compared to accident controls. This may be consistent with previous findings if this reflects an inadequate level of compensatory receptor upregulation in the face of reduced 5-HT presynaptic output. Alternately, it is possible that increased 5-HT_2 receptor binding reflects a primary abnormality which results in increased activity in 5-HT_2 receptor mediated pathways. This possibility is consistent with the observation in preclinical studies that activation of 5-HT_2 receptors is associated with neuronal excitation, rather than inhibition (as is true for 5-HT_1 receptors). In contrast to this literature, one of the most recent studies suggest that 5-HT_2 receptor binding may be decreased in the brains of young suicide victims (less than age 50; Gross-Isseroff, Salama, Israeli, & Biegon, 1990) and unchanged in the brain of old suicide victims (greater than age 50).

Platelet Receptor Studies

Studies of platelet receptor elements have also tended to support the findings of the brain 5-HT receptor studies. Three studies of platelet ^{3}H-imipramine binding have reported reduced numbers of ^{3}H-imipramine binding sites in: (a) nondepressed suicide attempters compared with healthy volunteers (Marazziti, DeLeo, & Conti, 1989); (b) aggressive, hyperactive psychiatric inpatients with "mental deficiency" compared to healthy volunteers (Marazziti & Conti, 1991); and (c) conduct disordered children compared with age-matched nonaffected children (Stoff, Pollock, Vitiello, Behar, & Bridger, 1987). As with brain receptor studies, platelet 5-HT$_2$ receptor binding is elevated in depressed patients with a history of suicide attempts compared to depressed patients without this history (Biegon et al., 1990). Finally, at least one study reports an inverse correlation between a self-report measure of impulsivity and the velocity of platelet 5-HT uptake in individuals with episodic aggression (Brown et al., 1989).

Neuropsychopharmacologic Challenge Studies in Humans

The bulk of biochemical and brain–platelet receptor studies are consistent with animal data, which suggest that impulsive–aggressive (or suicidal) behavior is inversely related to overall central 5-HT activity. Although 5-HT hypofunction is easy to reconcile with data from presynaptic measures of 5-HT, it is harder to reconcile this hypothesis with data from postsynaptic measures of 5-HT (i.e., 5-HT$_2$ receptor binding; see earlier discussion). Does decreased 5-HT output and increased postsynaptic receptor numbers result in a decrease, increase (or no change) in net downstream 5-HT activity? Does an increased number of post-synaptic 5-HT receptors lead to an increased physiologic response on 5-HT stimulation? Is it possible that the increased number of receptors represent a compensatory response to having receptors that are already impaired in sensitivity?

Unfortunately, the answers to physiological questions like these cannot even be inferred from biochemical or 5-HT receptor studies. This is because these parameters are static in nature and because pathology at one side of the synapse may not correlate with what is present on the other side. Examination of physiological (e.g., hormonal) responses to challenge with neurotransmitter "selective" agents, however, can yield data to give insight regarding the functional status of the synapse or receptors in question. The paradigm used to obtain this type of data is referred to as a neuropsychopharmacologic challenge. In this paradigm, single doses of selective agents, which display a dose-related relationship with a specific hormonal or behavioral response, are given to subjects under controlled conditions. The magnitude of the hormonal–behavioral response is used as an index of either the functional level of the synaptic apparatus or the sensitivity of certain postsynaptic receptors. It is important to understand (particularly in the case of hormonal outcome parameters) that while physiological responses are being utilized, these responses may be the result of a complex series of events occurring distal to the synapse in question.

Accordingly, these data are thought to allow a window into the brain and view the physiological nature of the synapse in question (Coccaro & Kavoussi, 1994).

Neuropsychopharmacological challenges using 5-HT selective agents have been performed in several studies with patients with either prominent histories of impulsive–aggressive or suicidal behavior. These probes include the 5-HT precursor 5-hydroxytryptophan (5-HTP), the 5-HT releaser-uptake inhibitor fenfluramine (FEN: both d- and d,l- forms), and 5-HT direct agonists m-chlorophenylpiperazine (m-CPP) and buspirone.

Cortisol (CORT) responses to 5-HTP challenge were examined in mood-disordered (depressed and manic) patients with a previous history of a suicide attempt compared with similar patients without this history, and healthy volunteers (Meltzer, Perline, Tricou, Lowy, & Robertson, 1984). Although mood-disordered patients as a group had higher CORT[5-HTP] responses than healthy volunteers, mood-disordered patients with a history of suicidal behavior (not simply ideation) had an even higher CORT[5-HTP] response to challenge than those patients without this history. Similarly, prolactin (PRL) responses to d,l-fenfluramine challenge were found to be positively correlated with indices of "aggression" and "impulsivity" in a mixed group of patients with substance abuse (Fishbein, Lozovsky, & Jaffe, 1989). Both studies have been interpreted as evidence that 5-HT receptors are "supersensitive" in individuals with histories of suicidal or aggressive behavior. Accordingly, this "receptor supersensitivity hypothesis" was considered to be consistent with data from brain receptor studies of increased numbers of 5-HT_2 receptor binding and of CSF studies that suggest decreased presynaptic output of 5-HT in such subjects.

Subsequent challenge studies, however, do not support a receptor supersensitivity hypothesis. Another d,l-fenfluramine challenge study, conducted in mood and personality disordered patients, published at about the same time as the Fishbein et al. (1989) study, found that PRL responses to d,l-fenfluramine were reduced in mood and personality disordered patients who had a previous history of a suicide attempt (Coccaro et al., 1989). In addition, both clinical and self-report assessments of aggression (see Brown et al., 1979) and assulativeness and irritability (on the Buss–Durkee Hostility Inventory) were inversely correlated with PRL[d,l-FEN] responses in the personality disordered patients (r's of −0.57, −0.65, − 0.68, respectively). Although these correlations with aggression were not seen in the depressed sample, the authors hypothesized that concomitant hypofunction in central norepinephrine function in the depressives (Siever et al., 1992) might explain this lack of a relationship with externally directed aggression (see p. 78).

Most, though not all, subsequent studies support the hypothesis that overall 5-HT function, or 5-HT postsynaptic receptor sensitivity, is reduced in individuals with histories of suicidal behavior and impulsive aggression. A second d,l-fenfluramine study conducted in Spain reported that patients with a history of a suicide attempt had blunted PRL[d,l-FEN] responses compared to similar pa-tients without this history (Lopez-Ibor, Lana, & Saiz Ruiz, 1990). Another d,l-fen-fluramine study, this time in nonhuman primates, reported that macaques with low PRL[d,l-FEN] responses had greater ratings of overt aggressive behavior than macaques with high PRL[d,l-FEN] responses (Botchin, Kaplan, Manuck, & Mann, 1993). Two of 3 studies with d-fenfluramine are also in agreement with these findings. Reduced PRL[d-FEN] responses have been reported in a small sample of incarcerated individuals with antisocial personality disorder (O'Keane et al., 1992). In addition, preliminary data from ongoing studies in our laboratory, suggest an inverse relationship with aggression and PRL[d-FEN] responses in personality disordered patients as well (Fig. 4.2). Finally, there are at least two negative studies with d-, or d,l-fenfluramine in this area. One study reports no

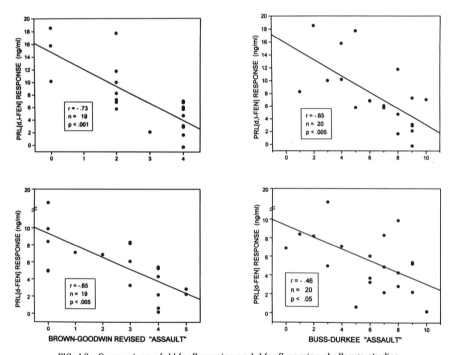

FIG. 4.2. Comparison of d,l-fenfluramine and d-fenfluramine challenge studies in two separate samples of personality disordered patients as a function of the Specific Assault item on the clinician administered Life History of Aggression assessment (BGA; Brown et al., 1979; left) and as a function of the Assault subscale on the self-report Buss–Durkee Hostility Inventory (Buss, 1961; right). The BGA assessment used for the d-fenfluramine study was revised to have six (0–5), rather than five (0–4), levels of severity. Data from the d,l-fenfluramine challenge studies are from the Coccaro et al., 1989 study; those from the d-fenfluramine challenge studies are from the authors' laboratory and are previously unpublished.

difference in PRL[d,l-FEN] responses between (aggressive) behavior-disruptive disordered children and adolescents compared to healthy volunteer subjects (Stoff et al., 1992). The other reports no difference in PRL[d-FEN] responses in depressed patients as a function of a history of suicidal behavior (O'Keane & Dinan, 1991). The absence of findings in either sample may be secondary to differences in the nature of the samples in the first study (i.e., adults vs. nonadults) and in the limited variance in the PRL[d-FEN] responses in the second (i.e., PRL[d-FEN] responses among the depressives were very low).

Studies with direct 5-HT agonist challenge are mixed, but also offer evidence to support a 5-HT "hypofunction" hypothesis. As with the d-fenfluramine challenge, reduced PRL[m-CPP] responses have also been reported in substance abusing patients with antisocial personality disorder (Moss, Yao, & Panzak, 1990). In addition, there was a significant inverse correlation between PRL[m-CPP] responses and the Buss–Durkee subscale on assaultiveness ($r = -0.52$) among all subjects including the healthy volunteers. This finding appears to be confirmed in a study of alcohol and cocaine abusers. Preliminary data from an ongoing study suggests that PRL responses to both d,l-fenfluramine and m-CPP challenge are inversely correlated with Buss–Durkee subscales in alcohol abusers and positively correlated with the same scales in cocaine abusers (Handelsman, Holloway, Shiekh, Sturiano, & Bernstein, 1993). The latter finding may give some insight into why the substance abusing patients of the Fishbein et al. (1989) study found positive, rather than inverse, correlations with assessments of aggression and impulsivity. Finally, an inverse correlation between PRL[BUSP] responses the Buss–Durkee subscale on irritability ($r = -0.72$) has been reported in a small sample of personality disordered patients (Coccaro et al., 1991).

Two negative studies examining PRL[m-CPP] responses have also been reported. The first (Wetzler, Kahn, Asnis, Korn, & van Praag, 1991), reported no difference in PRL[m-CPP] responses among depressed and panic disordered patients as a function of either a history of suicidal behavior or currently rated levels of subjective or overt anger (conducted by use of a general structured diagnostic interview). The second study, conducted by Coccaro et al. (1993), reported a nonsignificant, though inverse, correlation between PRL[m-CPP] responses and the Buss–Durkee assaultiveness subscale in patients with *DSM–III* personality disorder.

Core Phenomenological–Psychobiological Correlates of Reduced 5-HT Function

Based on the work summarized earlier, the behavioral constructs of irritability and assaultiveness appear to be critical to the relationship between 5-HT and impulsive–aggressive behavior. Accordingly, we reanalyzed the data from our first study with d,l-fenfluramine in order to gain greater insight into the specific phenomenological relationships that might exist with 5-HT in this context. In order to compare a group of subjects with low and normal 5-HT system function (i.e., PRL[FEN] values), we subdivided our patients into PRL[FEN] "blunters" and "nonblunters" by median split. The median value for this sample was 6.9 ng/ml and produced a blunter group ($N = 10$) with a mean PRL[FEN] value of 3.9 ± 2.3 ng/ml and a nonblunter group ($N = 10$) of 11.4 ± 4.4 ng/ml; mean PRL[FEN] values of the healthy volunteers of same sex and age ($N = 14$) was 12.5 ± 6.9 ng/ml. Despite the fact that PRL[FEN] values of nonblunters and healthy volunteers were similar, nonblunters scored higher on Buss–Durkee irritability scale than healthy volunteers (7.5 ± 2.5 vs. 3.8 ± 2.5: $p < 0.01$). Also, while blunters and nonblunters had similar scores on irritability (8.7 ± 1.4 vs. 7.5 ± 2.5), the two groups differed in their Buss–Durkee assault and verbal aggression scores with blunters having higher assault scores (7.7 ± 1.4 vs. 5.2 ± 3.0: $p < 0.05$) and nonblunters showing a trend for higher verbal aggression scores (9.6 ± 1.6 vs. 7.7 ± 2.9: $p < 0.10$). This suggests that PRL[FEN] values (i.e., central 5-HT function) may differentially correlate in personality disordered patients as a function of reduced or nonreduced PRL[FEN] values. Indeed, Buss–Durkee irritability scores were found to correlate highly with PRL[FEN] values in both blunter and non-blunter groups, but that PRL[FEN] values correlate differentially with Buss–Durkee assault, indirect aggression, and verbal aggression depending on whether blunter or nonblunter data was analyzed. The same differential relationships were noted when Buss–Durkee irritability was correlated with Buss–Durkee assault, indirect aggression, and verbal aggression in these two groups. Figure 4.3 demonstrates this graphically as a function of the degree of variance (i.e., r^2) that is shared by the Buss–Durkee irritability score or PRL[FEN] value and Buss–Durkee assault, indirect aggression, and verbal aggression, respectively. It appears that both Buss–Durkee irritability and PRL[FEN] values correlate best with Buss–Durkee assault in blunters and with indirect and verbal aggression in nonblunters. This suggests that although Buss–Durkee irritability may have an inverse relationship across the spectrum of PRL[FEN] values, that reduced 5-HT function (i.e., as reflected by reduced PRL[FEN] values) is specifically associated with physically assaultive behaviors whereas nonreduced (i.e., in the range of comparable healthy volunteers), PRL[FEN] values are associated more specifically with less marked (or severe) manifestations of aggressive behavior. This is consistent with the notion that central 5-HT function is associated with behavioral inhibition. Hence, the less central 5-HT activity the less inhibition and the greater the display of aggressive behavior, not only with regards to frequency but possibly severity of the individual behaviors as well. Put another way, individuals with less central 5-HT activity may have less ability to inhibit their response to aversive stimuli and may be more likely to resort to a more

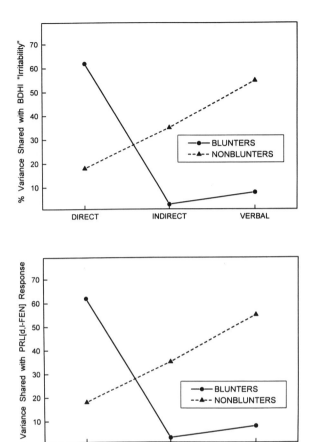

FIG. 4.3. Figure on top displays the relationship between the percent variance shared by Buss–Durkee irritability scores and Buss–Durkee scores for direct, indirect, and verbal assault in PRL[FEN] blunters and nonblunters. The lower figure displays the relationship between the percent variance shared by PRL[FEN] values and Buss–Durkee scores for direct, indirect, and verbal assault in PRL[FEN] blunters and nonblunters. Data have been reanalyzed from the raw data set published by Coccaro et al., 1989.

severe display of aggression. This is in contrast with someone who has greater central 5-HT activity, and who may have sufficient behavioral inhibition to constrain behavioral responses as severe as physical assault to self or others and therefore may stop at indirect (i.e., throwing things, etc.) or verbal (i.e., screaming, etc.) displays of aggression.

OTHER CENTRAL NEUROTRANSMITTER SYSTEMS: NOREPINEPHRINE, DOPAMINE, AND OPIATES

Evidence supporting a role in aggression for other neurotransmitter systems such as norepinephrine (NE), dopamine (DA), and endogenous opiates is much more limited than that for 5-HT. However, there are a number of animal studies that support the hypothesis that these systems have a direct (e.g., as opposed to an inverse) role in aggression.

Indices of increased NE function in brain correlate positively with the number of shock-induced aggressive episodes in rodents (Stolk, Connor, Levine, & Barchas, 1974). Moreover, agents that enhance central NE function (i.e., tricyclic/MAOI antidepressants) increase shock-induced fighting in rodents (Eichelman & Barchas, 1975). The most recent evidence suggests that facilitation of aggression is mediated through stimulation of postsynaptic alpha$_2$ noradrenergic receptors in the hypothalamus (Barrett, Edinger, & Siegel, 1990). Clinical treatment with these agents has also been associated with agitation and irritability, especially in subsets of patients with *DSM–III* borderline personality disorder (Cowdry & Gardner, 1988; Soloff, George, Nathan, Schulz, & Perel, 1986). Conversely, agents that diminish noradrenergic function, such as propranolol, appear to have antiaggressive properties (Yudofsky, Silver, Schneider, 1987). Similar findings in humans may be inferred from the limited biological data published to date. Roy, de Jong, and Linnoila (1989) reported a positive correlation between CSF (and plasma) measures of NE and the "extroversion" factor of Eysenck in a group of pathological gamblers. While extroversion may appear to have little relevance to aggression, the Eysenck's extraversion subscale is largely comprised of two personality dimensions related to *sociability* and *impulsiveness* (Schalling & Asberg, 1985). Impulsiveness, in turn, has been shown to correlate with irritability (which also correlates with assaultiveness) in patients with personality disorder (Coccaro et al., 1989). More specifically, however, growth hormone responses to challenge with the alpha-2 NE agonist, clonidine, has been reported to correlate positively with irritability in a preliminary sample of patients with personality disorder and healthy volunteers (Coccaro et al., 1991; also see Barrett et al., 1990). In contrast, several clinical studies suggest either no relationship or an inverse relationship between indices of NE function and aggression. Neither Brown et al. (1979) nor Linnoila et al. (1983), reported any relationship between CSF MHPG and aggression or impulsive violence, respectively. On the other hand, a later work by Virkunnen et al. (1987) reported a reduction of CSF–MHPG in violent offenders and impulsive arsonists compared with healthy volunteers. Given the intriguing animal and clinical psychopharmacologic data, more research is needed to fully elucidate the role of NE in human aggression.

Like NE, animal data tend to support a positive relationship between central DA function and aggression. Treatment with either the DA precursor l-DOPA or the receptor agonist apomorphine induces aggressive behavior in rodents (Lammers & vanRossum, 1968; Senault, 1970). Pretreatment with DA neurotoxins increases the effect of these agents (Thoa, Eichelman, & Ng, 1972), suggesting that the effect of DA activation on enhancing aggressive behaviors is working through the postsynaptic DA receptor. Similarly, foot-shock induced aggression in rats is enhanced by treatment with a variety of D_2 agonists (Datla, Sen, & Bhattacharya, 1992; Nikulina & Kapralova, 1991) and may be decreased by treatment with D_2 antagonists (Nikulina & Kapralova, 1991). Experimental work where humans are challenged with DA agents is limited although it is widely appreciated that stimulants, such as amphetamines and cocaine (both of which acutely enhance DA function), can induce or increase aggressive behavior in humans. Correlational studies suggest that there is a relationship between DA and aggression in humans. In addition, two reports suggest an inverse relationship between impulsive aggression and CSF HVA concentration. Roy, Adinoff, and Linnoila (1988) reported a trend towards an inverse relationship between "acting out hostility" (similar to Buss–Durkee irritability) and CSF HVA in healthy volunteers. Later, Limson et al. (1991) reported a modest, but statistically significant, inverse correlation between Brown's life history assessment of aggression and CSF HVA. Moreover, there are a number of studies that report reduced CSF HVA concentrations in patients with a history of suicide attempt compared to those without history of this behavior. It is possible, however, that since CSF HVA concentrations are highly correlated with CSF 5-HIAA concentrations that reductions in CSF HVA may simply be reflecting a primary abnormality in CSF 5-HIAA. Another possibility is that reduced CSF HVA concentration is associated with an increase in DA neurotransmission secondary to the development of receptor supersensitivity (see animal study by Thoa et al., 1972). Recent data from Pichot, Hansennes, Gonzalez-Moreno, and Asseau (1992), however, suggests that depressed patients with history of suicidal behavior have blunted, rather than enhanced, growth hormone responses to the DA agonist apomorphine. On the other hand, data from preclinical (Nikulina & Kapralova, 1991) and clinical psychopharmacological studies suggest generally that blockade of D_2 receptors decreases aggression in humans (Coccaro, 1993). Moreover, treatment with the neuroleptic flupenthixol has been reported to decrease the incidence of suicide attempts in highly suicidal-prone personality disordered patients in a placebo-controlled study; the antidepressant mianserin was unsuccessful in this regard in a similar, but separate, study (Montgomery & Montgomery, 1982).

Except for one preliminary study reporting a positive correlation between CSF opioid binding protein and the Buss–Durkee subscale assaultiveness ($r = 0.77, N = 18, p < 0.0002$) in healthy male volunteers (Post, Pickar, Ballenger, Naber, & Rubinow, 1984), evidence for a role of endogenous opiates in aggression has been studied most frequently in the context of self-injurious behavior (SIB). The few studies published in this area suggest that individuals with SIB (most often the mentally retarded) have elevated circulating levels of metenkephalins (Coid, Allolio, & Rees, 1983). Other studies suggest that treatment with opiate antagonists (naloxone, naltrexone) can diminish SIB in selected individuals (see Konecki & Schulz, 1989, for a review). Similar results have been obtained in nonhuman primates with SIB (see Kraemer & Clarke, 1990, for review). One interpretation for these findings is that individuals with SIB may have greater sensitivity to pain sensation and that the SIB is a mechanism to stimulate the release of endogenous opiates. It is possible that increased pain sensitivity could be secondary to a 5-HT deficiency (5-HT and nociception are inversely related). Brown and Goodwin (1984) noted that low CSF 5-HIAA concentration correlated with a number of MMPI measures including somatization and suggested that impulsive–aggressive individuals may also have an abnormal pain threshold. On the other hand, others have reported that individuals with SIB feel numb before an episode of SIB and appear to hurt themselves in order to "feel something" even if the feeling is painful (Gardner & Cowdry, 1985). This picture is also consistent with increased circulating levels of endogenous opiates. Most importantly, there is preliminary evidence of increased number of opiate receptors in the brains of young suicide victims (less than age 40; Gross-Isseroff, Dillon, Israeli, & Biegon, 1990) and of the antisuicidal efficacy of naltrexone (Sonne, Rubey, Brady, Malcolm, & Morris, 1993).

A HYPOTHETICAL MODEL OF IMPULSIVE AGGRESSION IN HUMANS

Based on existing data, a reasonably comprehensive model of impulsive–aggressive behavior would focus on the interaction of inhibitory, stimulatory, and permissive biological and environmental factors associated with aggressive behavior. Given the subanalysis of the PRL[FEN] data at the end of the section on 5-HT, one such model would hypothesize that the threshold to "act" aggressively, given the proper environmental circumstances, is modulated by overall 5-HT system function. The lower the functional status of the 5-HT system, the more likely the individual is to respond to similar degrees of threat, frustration, or aversive circumstances with an aggressive outburst. Also, the lower the functional status of the 5-HT system, the more severe the manifestation of aggression the individual is likely to use. Specifically, verbal aggression is less severe than direct physical aggression against others or the self, and vice versa. This is consistent with the notion that 5-HT functions as a behavioral inhibitor. The role of other neurotransmitter systems (e.g., NE, DA, Opiates?) in modulating aggression lies in their role in perceiving the threat or frustration (e.g., NE?) and in activating the cognitive and motor systems (DA?) necessary to mount the aggressive response. In this model, potential psychosocial interventions could be targeted towards decreasing the level of arousal of the individual and redirecting one's thinking away from a confrontational view of the external world (i.e., and reduce NE–DA activity?).

METHODOLOGICAL CONSIDERATIONS
AND PROSPECTS FOR FUTURE RESEARCH

Research into the neurotransmitter roots of aggressive behavior is still in its infancy. Future research in this area should proceed on a variety of fronts. These include the addition of: (a) experimental paradigms that putatively assess aggressive behavior under controlled laboratory conditions; (b) multiple measures of the activity of a specific neurotransmitter (e.g., 5-HT); (c) measures of the activity of different neurotransmitter systems (e.g., 5-HT and NE) and subsystems (e.g., 5-HT-1a and 5-HT-2a/2c); and (d) genetic markers of specific neurotransmitter function.

Future research will require the availability of experimental paradigms of aggression because there is a clear limit to the amount of information that may be provided by historical and self-reported assessments of aggression. More importantly, experimental testing of the serotonergic, noradrenergic, or dopaminergic hypotheses of aggression cannot be performed using historical and self-reported assessments of aggression. Although there are some experimental paradigms available to study aggression in the laboratory, these have only recently been employed in this area of research. In addition to allowing for experimental study of neurotransmitter function in aggression, these paradigms offer a view of aggressive behavior not captured by standard nonexperimental assessments. Specifically, Atkins, Stoff, Osbourne, and Brown (1993) have reported that hostile aggressive responses during an experimental assessment of aggression in aggressive boys was highly correlated with impulsive commission errors during a continous performance task, while historical–interview assessments of aggression and delinquency were unrelated to both the experimental assessment of aggression and impulsivity. In our own laboratory we have observed that simultaneous analysis of historical, self-report, and experimental assessments of aggression yield to a stronger correlation with PRL[d-FEN] responses than does any aggression variable alone. Hence, the incorporation of experimental assessments of aggression to the standard assessment battery should yield more accurate correlation between biological and behavioral variables in this area.

The notion that several, overlapping assessments of aggression may lead to a more accurate picture of the nature of brain–behavioral relationships with respect to aggression also applies the assessment of central neurotransmitter systems. Simultaneous assessment of multiple indices of 5-HT function, for example, may yield a stronger correlation between 5-HT activity and any one (if not several) assessments of aggressive behavior. Similarly, simultaneous assessment of multiple neurotransmitter systems (e.g., 5-HT-1a, 5-HT-2a/2c, NE, or DA) may also yield a stronger correlations between neurotransmitter variables and assessments of aggression. Finally, assessment of genetic markers of neurotransmitter function in appropriate populations (e.g., aggressive vs. nonaggressive;

see Nielsen et al., 1994) should yield important information about the constitutional role of neurotransmitter function or abnormalities in aggressive behavior. Such data may even enable researchers to disentangle the genetic and environmental influences there might be on neurotransmitter function.

REFERENCES

Asberg, M., Traskman, L., & Thoren, P. (1976). 5-HIAA in the cerebrospinal fluid: A biochemical suicide predictor? *Archives of General Psychiatry, 33,* 1193–1197.

Atkins, M. S., Stoff, D. M., Osbourne, M. L., & Brown, B. (1993). Distinguishing instrumental and hostile aggression: Does it make a difference? *Journal of Abnormal Child Psychology, 21,* 355–365.

Barrett, J. A., Edinger, H., & Siegel, A. (1990). Intrahypothalamic injections of norepinephrine facilitate feline affective aggression via alpha-2 adrenoceptors. *Brain Research, 525,* 285–293.

Biegon, A., Grinspoon, A., Blumenfeld, B., Bleich, A., Apter, A., & Mester, R. (1990). Increased serotonin 5-HT$_2$ receptor binding on blood platelets of suicidal men. *Psychopharmacology, 100,* 165–167.

Botchin, M. B., Kaplan, J. R., Manuck, S. B., & Mann, J. J. (1993). Low versus high prolactin responders to fenfluramine challenge: Marker of behavioral differences in adult male cynmolgus macaques. *Neuropsychopharmacology, 9,* 93–99.

Brown, C. S., Kent, T. A., Bryant, S. G., Gevedon, R. M., Campbell, J. L., Felthous, A. R., Barratt, E. S., & Rose, R. M. (1989). Blood platelet uptake of serotonin in episodic aggression. *Psychiatry Research, 27,* 5–12.

Brown, G. L., Ebert, M. H., Goyer, P. F., Jimerson, D. C., Klein, W. J., Bunney, W. E., & Goodwin, F. K. (1982). Aggression, suicide, and serotonin: Relationships to CSF amine metabolites. *American Journal of Psychiatry, 139,* 741–746.

Brown, G. L., & Goodwin, F. K. (1984). Diagnostic, clinical and personality characteristics of aggressive men with low CSF 5-HIAA. *Clinical Neuropharmacology, 7,* S408–S409.

Brown, G. L., Goodwin, F. K., Ballenger, J. C., Goyer, P. F., & Major, L. F. (1979). Aggression in humans correlates with cerebrospinal fluid amine metabolites. *Psychiatry Research, 1,* 131–139.

Buss, A. H. (1961). *The psychology of aggression.* New York: Wiley.

Coccaro, E. F. (1989). Central serotonin and impulsive aggression. *British Journal of Psychiatry, 155* (Suppl. 8), 52–62.

Coccaro, E. F. (1992). Impulsive aggression and central serotonergic system function in humans: An example of a dimensional brain-behavioral relationship. *International Journal of Clinical Psychopharmacology, 7,* 3–12.

Coccaro, E. F. (1993). Psychopharmacologic studies in patients with personality disorder: Review and perspective. *Journal of Personality Disorders (Spring Suppl.),* 181–192.

Coccaro, E. F., & Astill, J. L. (1990). Central serotonergic function in parasuicide. *Progressive Neuro-Psychopharmacology and Biological Psychiatry, 14,* 663–674.

Coccaro, E. F., & Kavoussi, R. J. (1994). The neuropsychopharmacologic challenge in biological psychiatry. *Clinical Chemistry, 40,* 319–327.

Coccaro, E. F., Kavoussi, R. J., Trestman, R. L., & Siever, L. J. (1993). 5-HT and aggression: Assessment of pre- and post-synaptic indices of 5-HT. *Biological Psychiatry, 33,* 87A.

Coccaro, E. F., Lawrence, T., Trestman, R., Gabriel, S., Klar, H., & Siever, L. J. (1991). Growth hormone responses to intravenous clonidine challenge correlates with behavioral irritability in psychiatric patients and in healthy volunteers. *Psychiatry Research, 39,* 129–139.

Coccaro, E. F., Siever, L. J., Klar, H. M., Maurer, G., Cochrane, K., Cooper, T. B., Mohs, R. C., & Davis, K. L. (1989). Serotonergic studies in affective and personality disorder patients: Correlates with suicidal and impulsive aggressive behavior. *Archives of General Psychiatry, 46*, 587–599.

Coid, J., Allolio, B., & Rees, L. H. (1983). Raised plasma metenkephalin in patients who habitually mutilate themselves. *Lancet, 2*, 545–546.

Cowdry, R. W., & Gardner, D. L. (1988). Pharmacotherapy of borderline personality disorder: Alprazolam, carbamazepine, trifluroperazine, and tranylcypromine. *Archives of General Psychiatry, 45*, 111–119.

Datla, K. P., Sen, A. P., & Bhattacharya, S. K. (1992). Dopaminergic modulation of footshock induced aggression in paired rats. *Indian Journal of Experimental Biology, 30*, 587–591.

Eichelman, B., & Barchas, J. D. (1975). Facilitated shock-induced aggression following antidepressant medication in the rat. *Pharmacology, Biochemistry, and Behavior, 3*, 601–604.

Fishbein, D., Lozovsky, D., & Jaffe, J. H. (1989). Impulsivity, aggression, and neuroendocrine responses to serotonergic stimulation in substance abusers. *Biological Psychiatry, 25*, 1049–1066.

Gardner, D. L., & Cowdry, R. W. (1985). Suicidal and parasuicidal behavior in borderline personality disorder. *Psychiatric Clinics North America, 8*, 389–403.

Gross-Isseroff, R., Dillon, K. A., Israeli, M., & Biegon, A. (1990). Regionally selective increases in mu opioid receptor density in the brains of suicide victims. *Brain Research, 530*, 312–316.

Gross-Isseroff, R., Salama, D., Israeli, M., & Biegon, A. (1990). Autoradiographic analysis of ^{3}-H-ketanserine binding in the human brain post-mortem: Effect of suicide. *Brain Research, 507*, 208–215.

Handelsman, L., Holloway, K., Shiekh, I., Sturiano, C., & Bernstein, D. (1993). Serotonergic challenges in cocaine addicts and alcoholics. *New Research Abstracts (NR 433)*, 146th Meeting of the American Psychiatric Association, San Francisco.

Higley, J. D., Mehlman, P. T., Taub, D. M., Higley, S. B., Suomi, S. J., Linnoila, M., & Vickers, J. H. (1992). Cerebrospinal fluid monoamine and adrenal correlates of aggression in free-ranging rhesus monkeys. *Archives of General Psychiatry, 49*, 436–441.

Konecki, P. E., & Schulz, S. C. (1989). Rationale of clinical trials of opiate antagonists in treating patients with personality disorders and self-injurious behavior. *Psychopharmacology Bulletin, 25*, 556–563.

Kraemer, G. W., & Clarke, A. S. (1990). The behavioral neurobiology of self-injurious behavior in rhesus monkeys. *Progressive Neuro-Psychopharmacology and Biological Psychiatry, 14*, S141–S168.

Lammers, A. J. J. C., & vanRossum, J. M. (1968). Bizarre social behavior in rats induced by a combination of a peripheral decarboxylase inhibitor and DOPA. *European Journal of Pharmacology, 5*, 103–106.

Limson, R., Goldman, D., Roy, A., Lamparski, D., Ravitz, B., Adinoff, B., & Linnoila, M. (1991). Personality and cerebrospinal fluid monoamine metabolites in alcoholics and controls. *Archives of General Psychiatry, 48*, 437–441.

Linnoila, M., Virkkunen, M., Scheinin, M., Nuutila, A., Rimon, R., & Goodwin, F. K. (1983). Low cerebrospinal fluid 5-hydroxyindolacetic acid concentration differentiates impulsive from nonimpulsive violent behavior. *Life Science, 33*, 2609–2614.

Lopez-Ibor, J. J., Lana, F., & Saiz Ruiz, J. (1990). Conductas autoliticas impulsivas y serotonina. *Actas Luso-Esp. Neurol. Psiquiatr., 18*, 316–325.

Marazziti, D., & Conti, L. (1991). Aggression, hyperactivity and platelet imipramine binding. *Acta Psychiatr. Scand., 84*, 209–211.

Marazziti, D., DeLeo, D., & Conti, L. (1989). Further evidence supporting the role of the serotonin system in suicidal behavior: A preliminary study of suicide attempters. *Acta Psychiatr. Scand., 80*, 322–324.

Mehlman, P. T., Higley, J. D., Faucher, I., Lilly, A. A., Taub, D. M., Vickers, J. H., Suomi, S. J., & Linnoila, M. (1994). Low CSF 5-HIAA concentrations and severe aggression and impaired impulse control in non-human primates. *American Journal of Psychiatry, 151*, 1485–1491.

Meltzer, H. Y., Perline, R., Tricou, B. J., Lowy, M. T., & Robertson, A. (1984). Effect of 5-hydroxytryptophan on serum cortisol levels in major affective disorders. II. Relation to suicide, psychosis, and depressive symptoms. *Archives of General Psychiatry, 41*, 379–387.

Montgomery, S. A., & Montgomery, D. (1982). Pharmacological prevention of suicidal behavior. *Journal of Affective Disorders, 4*, 219–298.

Moss, H. B., Yao, J. K., & Panzak, G. L. (1990). Serotonergic responsivity and behavioral dimensions in antisocial personality disorder with substance abuse. *Biological Psychiatry, 28*, 325–338.

Nielsen, D. A., Goldman, D., Virkkunen, M., Tokola, R., Rawlings R., & Linnoila, M. (1994). Suicidality and 5-hydroxyindolacetic acid concentration associated with a tryptophan hydroxylase polymorphism. *Archives of General Psychiatry, 51*, 34–38.

Nikulina, E. M., & Kapralova, N. S. (1991). The role of dopamine receptors in controlling mouse aggressivity: The genotype dependence. *Zhurnal Vysshei Nervnoi Deiatelnosti Imeni, 41*, 734–740.

O'Keane, V., & Dinan, T. G. (1991). Prolactin and cortisol responses to d-fenfluramine in major depression: Evidence for diminished responsivity of central serotonergic function. *American Journal of Psychiatry, 148*, 1009–1015.

O'Keane, V., Moloney, E., O'Neill, H., O'Connor, A., Smith, C., & Dinan, T. G. (1992). Blunted prolactin responses to d-fenfluramine in sociopathy: Evidence for subsensitivity of central serotonergic function. *British Journal of Psychiatry, 160*, 643–646.

Pichot, W., Hansennes, M., Gonzalez-Moreno, A., & Asseau, M. (1992). Suicidal behavior and growth hormone response to the apomorphine test. *Biological Psychiatry, 31*, 1213–1219.

Post, R. M., Pickar, D., Ballenger, J. C., Naber, D., & Rubinow, D. R. (1984). Endogenous opiates in cerebrospinal fluid: Relationship to mood and anxiety. In R. M. Post & J. C. Ballenger (Eds.), *Neurobiology of mood disorders* (pp. 356–368). Baltimore, MD: Williams & Wilkins.

Roy, A., Adinoff, B., & Linnoila, M. (1988). Acting out hostility in normal volunteers: Negative correlation with levels of 5-HIAA in cerebrospinal fluid. *Psychiatry Research, 24*, 187–194.

Roy, A., de Jong, J., & Linnoila, M. (1989). Extraversion in pathological gamblers: Correlates with indexes of noradrenergic function. *Archives of General Psychiatry, 46*, 679–681.

Schalling, D., & Asberg, M. (1985). Biological and psychological correlates of impulsiveness and monotony avoidance. In J. Strelau, F. H. Farley, & A. Gale (Eds.), *The biological bases of personality and behavior* (pp. 181–194). Washington, DC: Hemisphere.

Senault, B. (1970). Comportement d'agressivite intraspecifique induit par l'apomorphine chez le rat. *Psychopharmacologia, 18*, 271–287.

Siever, L. J., Trestman, R. L., Coccaro, E. F., Bernstein, D., Gabriel, S. M., Owen, K., Moran, M., Lawrence, T., Rosenthal, J., & Horvath, T. B. (1992). The growth hormone response to clonidine in acute and remitted depressed male patients. *Neuropsychopharmacology, 6*, 165–177.

Soloff, P. H., George, A., Nathan, R. S., Schulz, P. M., & Perel, J. M. (1986). Paradoxical effects of amitriptyline in borderline patients. *American Journal of Psychiatry, 143*, 1603–1605.

Sonne, S., Rubey, R., Brady, K. T., Malcolm, R., & Morris, T. (1993). Naltrexone for self-injurious thoughts and actions. *New Research Abstracts (NR 138)*, 146th Meeting of the American Psychiatric Association, San Francisco.

Stoff, D. M., Pastiempo, A. P., Yeung, J., Cooper, T. B., Bridger, W. H., & Rabinovich, H. (1992). Neuroendocrine responses to challenge with d,l-fenfluramine and aggression in disruptive behavior disorders of children and adolescents. *Psychiatry Research, 43*, 263–276.

Stoff, D. M., Pollock, L., Vitiello, B., Behar, D., & Bridger, W. H. (1987). Reduction of [3]-H-Imipramine binding sites on platelets of conduct disordered children. *Neuropsychopharmacology, 1*, 55–62.

Stolk, J. M., Connor, R. L., Levine, S., & Barchas, J. D. (1974). Brain norepinephrine metabolism and shock induced fighting behavior in rats: Differential effects of shock and fighting on the neurochemical response to a common footshock stimulus. *Journal of Pharmacology and Experimental Therapeutics, 190*, 193–209.

Thoa, N. B., Eichelman, B., & Ng, K. Y. (1972). Shock-induced aggression: Effects of 6-hydroxy-dopamine and other pharmacological agents. *Brain Research, 43*, 467–475.

Valzelli, L. (1981). *Psychobiology of aggression and violence*. New York: Raven.

Virkkunen, M., Nuutila, A., Goodwin, F. K., & Linnoila, M. (1987). Cerebrospinal fluid metabolite levels in male arsonists. *Archives of General Psychiatry, 44*, 241–247.

Wetzler, S., Kahn, R. S., Asnis, G. M., Korn, M., & van Praag, H. M. (1991). Serotonin receptor sensitivity and aggression. *Psychiatry Research, 37*, 271–279.

Yudofsky, S. C., Silver, J. M., & Schneider, S. E. (1987). Pharmacologic treatment of aggression. *Psychiatric Annals, 17*, 397–406.

5

SEROTONIN AND GLUCOSE METABOLISM IN IMPULSIVELY VIOLENT ALCOHOLIC OFFENDERS

Matti Virkkunen
Helsinki University

Markku Linnoila
National Institute on Alcohol Abuse and Alcoholism

HUMAN BRAIN SEROTONIN TURNOVER, PERIPHERAL GLUCOSE METABOLISM, AND IMPULSIVE VIOLENCE

A low concentration of cerebrospinal fluid (CSF) 5-hydroxyindoleacetic acid (5-HIAA) has been associated with an increased risk of suicide attempts, unprovoked interpersonal violence, and early onset alcoholism in men. These findings have been among the most replicated in modern biological psychiatry (Roy, Virkkunen, & Linnoila, 1991).

In a series of studies, we have observed that compared to Finnish alcoholic, nonimpulsive violent offenders and American healthy volunteers, Finnish alcoholic, impulsive violent offenders and fire setters have relatively low CSF 5-hydroxyindoleacetic acid (5-HIAA) concentrations (Linnoila et al., 1983; Virkkunen, Nuutila, Goodwin, & Linnoila, 1987). They also have low blood glucose nadirs during oral glucose tolerance tests and sleep irregularly while on the forensic psychiatry ward (Roy, Virkkunen, Guthrie, & Linnoila, 1986). Based on these observations we have postulated that in alcoholic, impulsive violent offenders deficient central serotonin turnover is conducive to disturbances of diurnal activity rhythm and glucose metabolism (Linnoila & Virkkunen, 1994; Linnoila, Virkkunen, & Roy, 1986). The neuroanatomical substrate whose dysfunction, secondary to reduced central serotonin turnover, could explain the constellation of our psychobiological findings is the suprachiasmatic nucleus. It receives a serotonergic input from the dorsal and median raphe nuclei (Palkovits et al., 1977) and functions as an endogenous circadian pacemaker (Moore & Eichler, 1972) and also as a regulator of glucose metabolism (Yamamoto, Nagai, & Nagakawa, 1984).

In follow-up and family history studies on offenders, we have found that a low CSF 5-HIAA concentration and propensity to low blood glucose concentrations are predictive of recidivist violent criminality after release from prison (Virkkunen, DeJong, Bartko, Goodwin, & Linnoila, 1989). Suicide attempts and completed suicides are primarily associated with low 5-HIAA and 3-methoxy-4-hydroxyphenylglycol (MHPG) concentrations in the CSF (Virkkunen, DeJong, Bartko, & Linnoila, 1989). Moreover, alcoholic sons of alcoholic fathers, who have been convicted of violent crimes, have the lowest CSF 5-HIAA concentrations (Linnoila, de Jong, & Virkkunen, 1989). This latter finding suggests that there may exist a familial trait associated with early onset alcohol abuse, impulsive and violent criminality, and low CSF 5-HIAA concentration.

BRAIN SEROTONIN (5-HT) AND PERIPHERAL GLUCOSE METABOLISM

There is clear evidence that the central serotonin (5-HT) systems play an important role in the regulation of glucose metabolism (Wozniak & Linnoila, 1991). Especially 5-HT1-like receptors may be involved because nonselective antagonists, metergoline and methysergide, are hyperglycemic at doses which usually antagonize 5-HT1-like receptors. In contrast, ritanserin (a 5-HT2A and 5-HT2C antagonist) is effective only at very high doses.

The exact mechanism by which 5-HT receptor antagonism produces hyperglycemia is unclear. 5-HT and its precursors and tryptamine release insulin in vitro (Gagliardino, Nierle, & Pfeiffer, 1974; Gagliardino, Zieher, Iturriza, Hernandez, & Rodriquez, 1971; Telib, Raptis, Schroder, & Pfeiffer, 1968) and in vivo (Wilson & Furman, 1982; Yamada, Sugimoto, Kimura, Takeuchi, & Horisaka, 1989). This suggests that there may be a physiologically significant relationship, direct or indirect, between insulin and 5-HT, which affects a number of variables regulating glucose homeostasis. Insulin, on the other hand, has a facilitating effect on 5-HT metabolism (Kwok & Juorio, 1987) by increasing the transport of the 5-HT precursor, tryptophan, to the brain.

Furthermore, 5-hydroxytryptophan (5-HTP), the immediate precursor of 5-HT, produces hypoglycemia in monoamine oxidase inhibitor-pretreated mice (Furman & Wilson, 1980). The hypoglycemia associated with 5-HTP administration involves mechanisms that are additional to changes in insulin (Furman & Wilson, 1980; Smith & Pogson, 1977). For example, some 5-HT receptor antagonists increase glucagon secretion (Marco, Hedo, Martinell, Calle, & Villaneuva, 1976) whereas 5-HT or 5-HTP are inhibitory to basal and stimulated glucagon release (Marco, Hedo, & Villaneuva, 1977).

5-HT antagonists, cyproheptadine and methysergide, have been reported to improve glucose tolerance (GTT) in diabetic patients (Ferrari et al., 1979). Pontiroli, Viberti, Tognetti, and Pozza (1975) found similar improvement in GTT in normal subjects following metergoline. This finding was not evident in diabetics. Wozniak and Linnoila (1991) have suggested that serotonin exerts variable effects on insulin release depending on the state of the organism, as the different effects in normal and diabetic subjects suggest.

So, it is clear that central serotonin (5-HT) and peripheral glucose metabolism are interrelated, but the exact physiological mechanisms involved await further elucidation.

BRAIN SEROTONIN (5-HT) AND CEREBRAL GLUCOSE METABOLISM

Studies with serotonergic ligands have revealed brain structures whose neuronal activity is altered by serotonin agonism and antagonism. 5-HT1A partial agonists gepirone, ipsapirone and buspirone reduce glucose utilization in the hippocampus and dentate gyrus and increase glucose utilization in the lateral habenular nucleus, which serves as an important connection between striatal and limbic structures and the raphe nuclei (Grasby, Sharp, Allen, Kelly, & Grahame-Smith, 1992). The 5-HT1A agonist 8-OH-DPAT increases glucose utilization in the hippocampus and the sensorimotor cortex (Kelly, Davis, & Goodwin, 1988).

Metachlorophenylpiperazine (mCPP) binds in vitro to several 5-HT receptor subtypes but has the highest affinity to the 5-HT2C (earlier 5-HT1C) receptor. A high dose of MCPP increases the regional cerebral metabolic rate for glucose (rCMRglc) particularly in cortical areas but low doses reduce central glucose uptake possibly due to presynaptic autoreceptor agonism (Freo, Larson, Tolliver, Rapoport, & Soncrant, 1991; Freo et al., 1990). On the other hand, 1-(2,5-dimethoxy-4-iodophenyl)-2-aminopropane (DOI) a relatively selective serotonergic 5-HT2A agonist reduces rCMRglc in many brain regions that have high densities of 5-HT2A receptors (Freo, Soncrant, Holloway, & Rapoport, 1991). Also clomipramine reduces rCMRglc dose—dependently in the same brain regions (Freo, Pietrini, Dam, Pizzolato, & Battistin, 1993).

In a preliminary positron emission study (PET) to examine cerebral metabolic rates of glucose (CMRg) among patients with personality disorders (6 borderline, 6 antisocial, 5 other personality disorders), Goyer and colleagues (1994) found that life history of aggressive, impulsive behaviors correlated inversely with frontal CMRg ($r = -.56$; $p;0,17$). The borderline group showed the greatest difference when compared to normal controls. This is the first study to relate measures of impulse control to neuronal activity within specific brain areas (Goyer et al., 1994). Other groups have also found selective reductions in prefrontal glucose metabolism in murderers and habitually violent offenders (Raine et al., 1994; Volkow et al., 1995). Also, among rhesus monkeys, changes in frontal glucose metabolism were observed to be associated with increased aggressiveness and low concentrations of CSF-5HIAA when measured under standardized anesthesia (Doudet et al., 1995).

The borderline patients, studied by Goyer et al. and Raine et al., who did not meet diagnostic criteria for ASP, but who had high lifetime aggression scores may be similar to our patients with intermittent explosive disorder. They also commonly fulfill diagnostic criteria for borderline personality disorder and have both low CSF 5-HIAA and low blood glucose nadir during the oral GTT.

A *post mortem* human study found that 5-HIAA concentration in the prefrontal cortex, but not in other brain regions, correlated positively with lumbar CSF 5-HIAA concentration (Stanley, Traskman-Bendz, & Dorovini-Zis, 1985). This apparent anatomic–neurochemical relationship is intriguing, because of the postulated role of the prefrontal cortex in impulse control (Miller, 1992).

It is also of interest that brain glucose uptake and regional cerebral blood flow in patients with obsessive compulsive disorder have been found to be increased in neuronal circuits, which include the orbitofrontal cortex (Baxter et al., 1987, 1988; Rauch, Jenike, Albert, et al., 1994; Swedo et al., 1989). There is evidence that obsessive compulsive disorder is associated with serotonergic dysfunction which, in certain respects, may be opposite to that in patients with impaired impulse control (Insel & Winslow, 1992).

RECENT STUDIES ON FINNISH VIOLENT OFFENDERS

In the most recent studies (Virkkunen, Kallio, et al., 1994; Virkkunen, Rawlings, et al., 1994) we have elucidated in greater depth interactions between brain serotonin turnover (low CSF 5-HIAA) and peripheral glucose metabolism among alcoholic violent offenders and age- and sex-matched healthy volunteers.

We investigated age- and sex-matched Finnish healthy volunteers as inpatients in the same psychiatry department as the alcoholic, violent offenders who underwent forensic psychiatric examinations. Furthermore, we examined relationships between symptoms of putative functional deficits of the suprachiasmatic nucleus and CSF 5-HIAA concentrations. The a priori hypotheses were as follows:

1. Low CSF 5-HIAA concentration is associated with impulsivity of the index crime, a history of suicide attempts, a disturbance of diurnal activity rhythms, and abnormalities of glucose metabolism. (Also other monoamine metabolites, several neuropeptides and hormones were quantified in the CSF but these results are not discussed in this chapter.)

2. We have postulated as a part of our proposed model to explain psychobiological concomitants of impulsivity (Linnoila et al., 1986) that it is particularly during episodes of hypoglycemia experienced during inebriation that the alcoholic impulsive offenders are most likely to exhibit unprovoked, interpersonally violent behavior or set fires impulsively. To test this hypothesis, we chose the Rosenzweig Picture Frustration Test to measure aggressiveness after an oral

glucose load (Rosenzweig, 1981). Our choice of the test was influenced by a report describing a strong negative correlation between the outward directed aggression score on the Rosenzweig test and blood glucose nadir in healthy volunteers after an oral glucose load (Benton, Kumari, & Brain, 1982).

The Rosenzweig test is a structured projective procedure which gauges responses to 24 cartoon pictures depicting conflict situations in everyday life (Rosenzweig, 1981). There is a blank caption box above the person on the right in each picture. The subject is instructed to imagine himself as this person and asked to write the first thought elicited by the picture into the box. Direction of aggression and reaction type bias scores are assigned to each response. Direction of aggression is scored as extrapunitiveness (E: directed to the environment), intropunitiveness (I: directed to oneself), and impunitiveness (M: aggression avoided). Type of reaction is scored as obstacle dominance (O–D: frustration), ego defense (E–D: dominated by the ego of the subject), and need persistence (N–P: solving the problem).

Materials and Methods

Alcoholic, violent offenders and impulsive fire setters were ordered to undergo forensic psychiatric examinations by their trial judges. They spent an average of one month on the low monoamine diet, drug free in the research ward. The offenders wore the physical activity monitors on their left wrist continuously for 10 days and nights. Following the lumbar punctures, they underwent double blind, random order, oral glucose, and aspartame tests on 2 consecutive days.

The activity monitors are small watch size devices that have a movement sensor as well as clock and memory functions that permit continuous recording of activity for a period of 10 days (Wehr, Goodwin, Wirz-Justice, Breitmeir, & Craig, 1982). The data were decoded and stored on an Apple Macintosh computer.

Healthy volunteers were recruited by advertisements in the local newspapers. They were paid for their participation. The advertisement defined that the volunteers had to be free of current or past drinking problems and mental disorders. They were asked to follow a low monoamine and caffeine free diet, not to use any alcohol or medicines for a week prior to admission, and to stay as inpatients on the research ward for 3 days and 3 nights. Only volunteers free of lifetime and family histories of major mental disorders, alcohol dependence, and substance abuse in their first degree relatives were included in the sample.

On the first full day after a night on the ward, they underwent a lumbar puncture between 8:00 a.m. and 9:00 a.m. On the next 2 days they received double blind, random order, oral glucose, or aspartame tests starting at 8:00 a.m. Throughout their stay, the volunteers wore physical activity monitors on their left wrist.

Diagnoses

As in our previous studies, the alcoholic offenders were divided into impulsive and nonimpulsive groups by the forensic research psychiatrist (M.V.) based on the characteristics of the index crime described in the police report.

A crime was called impulsive when the victim was previously unknown to the offender, when no provocation or only verbal altercation preceded the attack, no premeditation could be documented, and no economic motivation such as robbery or burglary was evident. Impulsive fire setting excluded setting fires for insurance fraud. Nonimpulsive crimes were all clearly premeditated.

The alcoholic, impulsive offender group was further subdivided into groups with antisocial personality and intermittent explosive disorders. This was done to examine whether these two clinically distinct disorders are psychobiologically different as well. Ten subjects in the alcoholic, impulsive offender group were fire setters.

All subjects, including the volunteers, were administered an SADS-L (Schedule of Affective Disorders and Schizophrenia-Lifetime Version; Spitzer, Endocott, & Robbins, 1978) and a clinical interview (by M.V.) to derive lifetime *DSM–III–R* (American Psychiatric Association, 1987) diagnoses. To maintain reasonable continuity with diagnostic practices in our previous studies, intermittent explosive disorder was diagnosed according to *DSM–III* (American Psychiatric Association, 1980) criteria which unlike *DSM–III–R* permits the diagnosis when the behavior is exhibited under the influence of alcohol.

Thus, the analyses included four groups: alcoholic, antisocial personality disorder; alcoholic, intermittent explosive disorder; alcoholic, nonimpulsive violent offender; and normal male control group.

Biochemical Variables

All biochemical variables were quantified by investigators who were blind to the clinical characteristics of the subjects.

Monoamine Metabolites. The CSF samples were obtained by a neurologist at 8:00 a.m. after one night's bed rest with only water permitted after 8:00 p.m. The samples were collected into a large polypropylene tube on wet ice. After the first 12 mL had been drawn, the tube was capped, inverted, and the CSF was aliquotted into 1 mL tubes on dry ice. The samples were stored in a –80° C freezer and shipped air freight on dry ice from Helsinki to Bethesda, Maryland, where 5-HIAA concentration was quantified with a liquid chromatographic procedure using electrochemical detection (Scheinin, Chang, Kirk, & Linnoila, 1983).

Glucose and Aspartame Tolerance Tests. After a 12-hour overnight fast, at 8:00 a.m. the subjects consumed 1 g/kg of body weight (4mL/kg) of glucose solution or an identical volume of an aspartame solution of indistinguishable sweetness. Fifteen mL blood samples were drawn from an antecubital vein into an aprotinin-containing test tube (12.5 mIU/mL, Antagosan[R]) prior to and 15, 30, 60, 90, 120, 180, 240, and 300 minutes after the administration of the liquid. For the first 2 hours of the test, the subjects rested in bed. Thereafter, they were allowed to move on the ward, but resting was encouraged. Blood glucose concentration was measured with an enzymatic assay. Glucagon was quantified immediately after the samples were thawed with a double antibody separation radioimmunoassay. Insulin was quantified in antibody coated test tubes (Coat-A-Count[R]). Between-assay variation for insulin was 4.6% at 30.2 uU/mL and for glucagon 5.1% at 44.8 pg/mL. All samples were assayed in duplicate. When the results of the duplicate determinations were discrepant by more than 5%, the samples were reanalyzed.

Results and Discussion

CSF 5-HIAA. Mean CSF 5-HIAA concentration was significantly lower among the alcoholic, impulsive than the alcoholic, nonimpulsive offenders ($p < .01$). The alcoholic, nonimpulsive offenders had significantly higher mean CSF 5-HIAA concentration than the healthy volunteers. Among the alcoholic, impulsive offenders, subjects with antisocial personality and intermittent explosive disorder had similar mean CSF 5-HIAA concentrations. Of the alcoholic, violent offenders, 25 had made a suicide attempt. Their mean CSF 5-HIAA was lower than the nonattempting offenders' CSF 5-HIAA concentration ($58.8 + 25.2$ vs. $68.5 + -24.7$ nmol/L; $p < .05$, one-tailed probability).

In the discriminant analysis on the impulsive–nonimpulsive grouping of the alcoholic offenders, the only variable that contributed significantly to the variance was CSF 5-HIAA. It produced an overall correct jackknife classification rate of .78.

In our previous studies, alcoholics, as opposed to healthy volunteers, showed a lack of seasonal variation in CSF 5-HIAA (Roy et al., 1991). In accordance with this observation, we again did not find any seasonal variation in CSF monoamine metabolite concentrations in the alcoholic offenders despite adequate sampling during all four seasons.

The present results replicate our earlier observation (Linnoila et al., 1983) of a low mean CSF 5-HIAA concentration in alcoholic offenders with a history positive for suicide attempts compared to alcoholic offenders without suicide attempts. Recently, among these offenders a genetic variant of the tryptophan hydroxylase (TPH) gene was found to be associated with low CSF 5-HIAA concentrations and suicidal behavior (Nielsen et al., 1994).

Oral Glucose and Aspartame Tolerance Tests

Alcoholic, impulsive offenders with intermittent explosive disorder had significantly lower mean blood glucose nadir during the glucose tolerance test than healthy volunteers ($p = .0049$). Plasma, insulin, and glucagon concentrations did not, however, differ significantly between the groups at any time point during the oral glucose tolerance test. There were no significant differences in any of the biochemical variables at any time between the groups in the aspartame tolerance test.

In accordance with Virkkunen's previous findings (Virkkunen, 1986; Virkkunen & Närvänen, 1987), mean blood glucose nadir was significantly lower in the alcoholic, impulsive violent offenders with intermittent explosive disorder than in the healthy volunteers. There was, however, no difference between the alcoholic impulsive and nonimpulsive offenders on this variable. Thus, the low blood glucose nadir was not correlated to CSF 5-HIAA concentration across the different groups of offenders. The difference between the intermittent explosive offenders and healthy volunteers could be secondary to alcohol dependence. No differences between any of the groups were found in glucagon and insulin concentrations at any point during the oral glucose tolerance tests.

The conclusive investigation of glucose metabolism in these subjects requires further studies utilizing the technique of euglycemic insulin clamp and carefully correlating the glucose metabolism related variables to alcohol consumption history.

Rosenzweig Results

Alcoholic nonimpulsive offenders had a significantly larger difference in the mean Rosenzweig EO-D scores between the glucose and the aspartame tolerance tests than the healthy volunteers with higher scores during the glucose tolerance test ($p = .0274$). There were no other significant differences in any of the total or change scores on any of the dimensions of the Rosenzweig test.

Even though the differences were neither robust, nor statistically significant, outward directed aggression was higher in alcoholic, nonimpulsive offenders compared to healthy volunteers during the oral glucose tolerance test than during the aspartame tolerance test. This difference in general did not, however, covary with either CSF 5-HIAA or blood glucose concentrations. Furthermore, we could not replicate in either our healthy volunteers or alcoholic offenders an earlier healthy volunteer study reporting a relatively high negative correlation between blood glucose nadir during oral glucose tolerance test and E-OD score on the Rosenzweig Picture Frustration Test. The reasons for the apparent discrepancy between our and Benton et al.'s (1982) findings remain obscure.

Physical Activity Monitoring

Alcoholic, impulsive offenders with antisocial personality disorder had significantly higher mean total 10 day–night activity counts than healthy volunteers (ANOVA = .0181). Alcoholic, impulsive offenders with intermittent explosive disorder had indistinguishable day and night activity counts in a striking difference from the other groups.

The present results demonstrate that alcoholic, impulsive violent offenders with intermittent explosive disorder exhibit a profound diurnal activity rhythm disturbance. In rodents, intact serotonergic input to the suprachiasmatic nucleus facilitates entrainment of the circadian activity rhythm by light (Morin & Blanchard, 1991). If the same principle holds for humans, the disturbed diurnal activity rhythm observed in these offenders may also be secondary to deficient central serotonergic neurotransmission. On the other hand, roughly half of the alcoholic, impulsive offenders with antisocial personality disorder exhibited a clear activity difference between the day and night times despite an equally low mean CSF 5-HIAA concentration. Compared to the healthy volunteers they showed, however, increased mean total 24-hour activity counts throughout the monitoring period. This finding is commensurate with the history of attention deficit disorder and hyperactivity in many of alcoholic offenders with antisocial personality disorder (ASP). Attention deficit disorder with hyperactivity has been reported to be associated with increased diurnal physical activity (Porrino et al., 1983).

METHODOLOGICAL CONSIDERATIONS
AND FUTURE RESEARCH DIRECTIONS

In future studies, the following issues need to be addressed:

1. Direct behavioral observation in concert with functional brain imaging and CSF studies will be necessary to support or refute the hypothesized relationships between reduced frontal serotonin turnover, reduced glucose uptake in frontal brain areas, low CSF 5-HIAA concentration, and impaired impulse control.

2. Interrelationships between serotonin and glucose metabolism dysregulation need further study to elucidate the basic physiological mechanisms.

3. We found in the most recent studies (Virkkunen, Kallio et al., 1994; Virkkunen, Rawlings et al., 1994) no differences between any of the groups (violent offenders vs. normal controls) in glucagon and insulin concentrations in glucose tolerance tests. Early communications by Virkkunen reported higher insulin secretion in alcoholic violent offenders with intermittent explosive but not with antisocial personality disorder compared to healthy volunteers with similar age, gender, and weight (Virkkunen, 1986; Virkkunen & Närvänen, 1987). It, is possible that altered insulin sensitivity contributes to low blood glucose nadirs among violent offenders. To elucidate these apparently discrepant findings further investigation of glucose metabolism in these subjects requires utilizing the technique of euglycemic insulin clamp.

4. How serotonin receptors within the central nervous system regulate insulin and glucagon secretion and peripheral glucose metabolism also requires additional studies.

5. It appears that glucose metabolism in violent offenders with ASP differs from glucose metabolism in violent offenders with intermittent explosive disorder. The lowest glucose values in the Glucose Tolerance Test (GTT) have repeatedly been observed in the latter group (Virkkunen 1986; Virkkunen & Närvänen, 1987; Virkkunen, Rawlings et al., 1994). Offenders with ASP have low 24-hour urinary cortisol secretion (Virkkunen, 1985), and recently we found that they have also low CSF ACTH concentration (Virkkunen, Rawlings et al., 1994). These findings parallel observations by Fishbein, Dax, Lozovsky, & Jaffe (1992) and Bergman and Brismar (1994), but they need to be examined in an independent sample.

6. How brain serotonin, glucose, and testosterone metabolisms are regulated and influence impaired impulse control and increased aggressiveness conducive to interpersonal violence is not clear at this time. Serotonin and testosterone metabolisms may be coregulated (Martinez-Conde, Leret, & Diaz, 1985) as castration causes an increase in limbic forebrain serotonin turnover in experimental animals (Carlsson, Svensson, Erikkson, & Carlsson, 1985). Mechanistically, this finding is, however, poorly understood. According to Archer's (1991) review a repetitive pattern of aggressive behavior that starts early in life and occurs usually under the influence of alcohol is associated with elevated salivary testosterone concentrations.

SUMMARY

In this chapter we have examined literature concerning brain serotonin and brain and peripheral glucose metabolism and their possible interrelationships in laboratory animals and humans. Clearly, our understanding of the basic mechanisms involved is still rudimentary. This state of affairs provides an exciting research opportunity and the emerging findings may be important in areas of investigation seemingly unrelated to impulse control, such as diabetes research.

The emerging interactions between serotonin and testosterone metabolisms may further clarify understanding concerning determinants of human aggressive behavior.

REFERENCES

American Psychiatric Association. (1980). *Diagnostic and statistical manual of mental disorders* (3rd. ed.). Washington, DC: Author.

American Psychiatric Association. (1987). *Diagnostic and statistical manual of mental disorders* (3rd. ed., revised). Washington, DC: Author.

Archer, J. (1991). The influence of testosterone on human aggression. *British Journal of Psychology, 82,* 1–28.

Baxter, L. R., Phelps, M. E., Mazziotta, J. C., Guze, B. H., Schwartz, J. M., & Selin, C. E. (1987). Local cerebral glucose metabolic rates in obsessive-compulsive disorder: A comparison with rates in unipolar depression and in normal controls. *Archives of General Psychiatry, 44,* 211–218.

Baxter, L. R., Schwartz, J. M., Mazziotta, J. C., Phelps, M. E., Pahl, J. J., Guze, B. H., & Fairbanks, L. (1988). Cerebral glucose metabolic rates in nondepressed patients with obsessive-compulsive disorder. *American Journal of Psychiatry, 145,* 1560–1563.

Benton, D., Kumari, N., & Brain, P. F. (1982). Mild hypoglycemia and questionnaire measures of aggression. *Biological Psychology, 14,* 129–135.

Bergman, B., & Brismar, B. (1994). Hormone levels and personality traits in abusive and suicidal male alcoholics. *Alcoholism: Clinical and Experimental Research, 18,* 311–316.

Carlsson, M., Svensson, K., Eriksson, E., & Carlsson, A. (1985). Rat brain serotonin: Biochemical and functional evidence for a sex difference. *Journal of Neural Transmission, 63,* 297–313.

Doudet, D., Hommer, D., Dee Higley, I., Andreason, P. J., Moneman, R., Suomi, S. J., & Linnoila, M. (1995). Cerebral glucose metabolism, CSF 5HIAA levels, and aggressive behavior in rhesus monkeys. *American Journal of Psychiatry, 152,* 1782–1787.

Ferrari, C., Barbieri, C., Caldara, R., Magnoni, V., Testori, G. P., & Romussi, M. (1979). Improved oral glucose tolerance following antiserotonin treatment in patients with chemical diabetes. *European Journal of Clinical Pharmacology, 15,* 395–399.

Fishbein, D. H., Dax, E., Lozovsky, D., & Jaffe, J. H. (1992). Neuroendocrine response to a glucose challenge in substance users with high or low levels of aggression, impulsivity, and antisocial personality. *Neuropsychobiology, 25,* 106–114.

Freo, U., Larson, D. M., Tolliver, T., Rapoport, S. I., & Soncrant, T. T. (1991). Parachloroamphetamine selectively alters regional cerebral metabolic responses to the serotonergic agonist metachlorophenylpiperazine in rats. *Brain Research, 544,* 17–25.

Freo, U., Pietrini, P., Dam, M., Pizzolato, G., & Battistin, L. (1993). The tricyclic antidepressant clomipramine dose-dependently reduces regional cerebral metabolic rates for glucose in awake rats. *Psychopharmacology, 113,* 53–59.

Freo, U., Soncrant, T. T., Holloway, H. W., & Rapoport, S. I. (1991). Dose- and time-dependent effects on 1-(2,5-dimethoxy-4-iodophenyl)-2-aminopropane (DOI), a serotonergic 5-HT2 receptor agonist, on local cerebral glucose metabolism in awake rats. *Brain Research, 541,* 63–69.

Freo, U., Soncrant, T. T., Ricchieri, G. L., Wozniak, K. M., Larson, D. M., & Rapoport, S. I. (1990). Time courses of behavioral and regional cerebral metabolic responses to different doses of meta-chlorophenylpiperazine in awake rats. *Brain Research, 511,* 209–216.

Furman, B. L., & Wilson, G. A. (1980). Further studies on the effects of 5-hydroxytryptophan on plasma glucose and insulin in the mouse. *Diabetologia, 19,* 386–390.

Gagliardino, J. J., Nierle, C., & Pfeiffer, E. F. (1974). The effect of serotonin in vitro insulin secretion and biosynthesis in mice. *Diabetologia, 10,* 411–414.

Gagliardino, J. J., Zieher, L. M., Iturriza, F. C., Hernandez, R. E., & Rodriquez, R. R. (1971). Insulin release and glucose changes induced by serotonin. *Hormone and Metabolic Research, 3,* 145–150.

Goyer, P. F., Andreason, P. J., Semple, W. E., Clayton, A. H., King, A. C., Schultz, S. C., & Cohen, R. M. (1994). Positron emission tomography and personality disorders. *Neuropsychopharmacology, 10,* 21–28.

Grasby, P. M., Sharp, T., Allen, T., Kelly, P. A. T., Grahame-Smith, D. G. (1992). Effects of the 5-HT$_{1A}$ partial agonists gepirone, ipsapinone and buspirone on local cerebral glucose utilization in the conscious rat. *Psychopharmacology, 106,* 97–101.

Insel, T. R., & Winslow, J. T. (1992). Neurobiology of obsessive-compulsive disorder. *Psychiatric Clinics of North America, 15,* 813–824.

Kelly, P. A. T., Davis, C. J., & Goodwin, G. M. (1988). Differential patterns of local cerebral glucose utilization in response to 5-hydroxytryptamine 1 agonists. *Neuroscience, 25,* 907–915.

Kwok, R. P. S., & Juorio, A. V. (1987). Facilitating effect of insulin on 5-hydroxytryptamine metabolism. *Neuroendocrinology, 45,* 267–273.

Linnoila, M., de Jong, J., & Virkkunen, M. (1989). Family history of alcoholism in violent offenders and impulsive fire setters. *Archives of General Psychiatry, 46,* 613–616.

Linnoila, M., & Virkkunen, M. (1994). Testing a proposed model on central serotonergic function and impulsivity. In S. A. Montgomery & T. H. Corn (Eds.), *Psychopharmacology of Depression* (pp. 170–184). Oxford, England: Oxford University Press.

Linnoila, M., Virkkunen, M., & Roy, A. (1986). Biochemical aspects of aggression in man. In W. E. Bunney, Jr., E. Costa, & S. C. Potkin (Eds.), *Clinical Neuropharmacology* (Suppl. 1), 377–379.

Linnoila, M., Virkkunen, M., Scheinin, M., Nuutila, A., Rimón, R., & Goodwin, F. K. (1983). Low cerebrospinal fluid 5-hydroxyindoleacetic acid concentration differentiates impulsive from nonimpulsive violent behavior. *Life Sciences, 33,* 2609–2614.

Marco, J., Hedo, J. A., Martinell, J., Calle, C., & Villaneuva, M. L. (1976). Potentiation of glucagon secretion by serotonin antagonists in man. *Journal of Clinical Endocrinology and Metabolism, 42,* 215–221.

Marco, J., Hedo, J. A., & Villaneuva, M. L. (1977). Inhibition of glucagon release by serotonin in mouse pancreatic islets. *Diabetologia, 13,* 585–588.

Martinez-Conde, E., Leret, M. L., & Diaz, S. (1985). The influence of testosterone in the brain of the male rat on levels of serotonin (5-HT) and hydroxyindole-acetic acid (5-HIAA). *Comparative Biochemistry and Physiology, 80C,* 411–414.

Miller, L. A. (1992). Impulsivity, risk-taking, and the ability to synthesize fragmented information after frontal lobectomy. *Neuropsychologia, 30,* 69–79.

Moore, R. Y., & Eichler, V. B. (1972). Loss of a circadian adrenal corticosterone rhythm following suprachiasmatic lesions in the rat. *Brain Research, 42,* 201–206.

Morin, L. P., & Blanchard, J. (1991). Depletion of brain serotonin by 5,7-DHT modifies hamster circadian rhythm response to light. *Brain Research, 566,* 173–185.

Nielsen, D. A., Goldman, D., Virkkunen, M., Tokola, R., Rawlings, R., & Linnoila, M. (1994). Suicidality and 5-hydroxyindoleacetic acid concentration associated with tryptophan hydroxylase polymorphism. *Archives of General Psychiatry, 51,* 34–38.

Palkovits, M., Saavedra, J. M., Jakowits, D. M., Kizer, J. S., Zaborsky, L., & Brownstein, M. J. (1977). Serotonergic innervation of the forebrain: Effects of lesions on serotonin and tryptophan hydroxylase levels. *Brain Research, 130,* 121–134.

Pontiroli, A. E., Viberti, G. C., Tognetti, A., & Pozza, G. (1975). Effect of metergoline, a powerful and long-acting antiserotoninergic agent, on insulin secretion in normal subjects and in patients with chemical diabetes. *Diabetologia, 11,* 165–167.

Porrino, L. J., Rapoport, J. L., Behar, D., Sceery, W., Ismond, D. R., & Bunney, W. E. (1983). A naturalistic assessment of the motor activity of hyperactive boys. I. Comparison with normal controls. *Archives of General Psychiatry, 40,* 681–687.

Raine, A., Buchsbaum, M. S., Stanley, J., Lottenberg, S., Abel, L., & Stoddard, J. (1994). Selective reductions in prefrontal glucose metabolism in murderers. *Biological Psychiatry, 36,* 365–373.

Rauch, S. L., Jenike, M. A., Alpert, N. M., Baer, L., Breiter, H. C. R., Savage, C. R., & Fischman, A. J. (1994). Regional cerebral blood flow measured during symptom prevocation in obsessive-compulsive disorder using oxygen 15-labeled carbon dioxide and positron emission tomography. *Archives of General Psychiatry, 51,* 62–70.

Rosenzweig, S. (1981). The current status of the Rosenzweig Picture-Frustration study as a measure of aggression in personality. In P. F. Brain & D. Benton (Eds.), *Multidisciplinary approaches to aggression research* (pp. 113–115). The Netherlands: Elsevier: North Holland.

Roy, A., Virkkunen, M., Guthrie, S., & Linnoila, M. (1986). Indices of serotonin and glucose metabolism in violent offenders, arsonists and alcoholics. In J. J. Mann & M. Stanley (Eds.), *Psychobiology of suicidal behavior* (pp. 202–220). New York: The New York Academy of Sciences.

Roy, A., Virkkunen, M., & Linnoila, M. (1991). Serotonin in suicide, violence, and alcoholism. In E. F. Coccaro & D. L. Murphy (Eds.), *Serotonin in major psychiatric disorders* (pp. 187–208). Washington, DC: American Psychiatric Press, Inc.

Scheinin, M., Chang, W-H., Kirk, K. L., & Linnoila, M. (1983). Simultaneous determination of 3-methoxy-4-hydroxyphenylglycol, 5-hydroxyindoleacetic acid, and homovanillic acid in cerebrospinal fluid with high-performance liquid chromatography using electrochemical detection. *Analytical Biochemistry, 131,* 246–253.

Smith, S. A., & Pogson, C. I. (1977). Tryptophan and the control of plasma glucose concentrations in the rat. *Biochemical Journal, 168,* 495–506.

Spitzer, R. L., Endocott, J., & Robbins, E. (1978). Research diagnostic criteria: Rationale and reliability. *Archives of General Psychiatry, 35,* 773–782.

Stanley, M., Traskman-Bendz, L., & Dorovini-Zis, K. (1985). Correlations between aminergic metabolities simultaneously obtained from human CSF and brain. *Life Sciences, 37,* 1279–1286.

Swedo, S. E., Schapiro, M. B., Grady, C. L., Cheslow, D. L., Leonard, H. L., Kumar, A., Friedland, R., Rapoport, S. I., & Rapoport, J. L. (1989). Cerebral glucose metabolism in childhood-onset obsessive-compulsive disorder. *Archives of General Psychiatry, 46,* 518–523.

Telib, M., Raptis, R., Schroder, K. E., & Pfeiffer, E. F. (1968). Serotonin and insulin release in vitro. *Diabetologia, 4,* 253–256.

Virkkunen, M. (1985). Urinary free cortisol secretion in habitually violent offenders. *Acta Psychiatria Scandinavia, 72,* 40–44.

Virkkunen, M. (1986). Insulin secretion during the glucose tolerance test among habitually violent and impulsive offenders. *Aggressive Behavior, 12,* 303–310.

Virkkunen, M., de Jong, J., Bartko, J., Goodwin, F. K., & Linnoila, M. (1989). Relationship of psychobiological variables to recidivism in violent offenders and impulsive fire setters: A follow up study. *Archives of General Psychiatry, 46,* 600–603.

Virkkunen, M., de Jong, J., Bartko, J., & Linnoila, M. (1989). Psychobiological concomitants of history of suicide attempts among violent offenders and impulsive fire setters. *Archives of General Psychiatry, 46,* 604–606.

Virkkunen, M., Kallio, E., Rawlings, R., Tokola, R., Poland, R. E., Guidotti, A., Nemeroff, C., Bissette, G., Kalogeras, K., Karonen, S. -L., & Linnoila, M. (1994). Personality profiles and state aggressiveness in Finnish alcoholic, violent offenders, fire setters, and healthy volunteers. *Archives of General Psychiatry, 51,* 28–33.

Virkkunen, M., & Närvänen, S. (1987). Plasma insulin, tryptophan and serotonin levels during the glucose tolerance test among habitually violent and impulsive offenders. *Neuropsychobiology, 17,* 19–23.

Virkkunen, M., Nuutila, A., Goodwin, F. K., & Linnoila, M. (1987). Cerebrospinal fluid monoamine metabolites in male arsonists. *Archives of General Psychiatry, 44,* 241–247.

Virkkunen, M., Rawlings, R., Tokola, R., Poland, R. E., Guidotti, A., Nemeroff, C., Bissette, G., Kalogeras, K., Karonen, S. L., & Linnoila, M. (1994). CSF biochemistries, glucose metabolism, and diurnal activity rhythms, in alcoholic, violent offenders, impulsive fire setters, and healthy volunteers. *Archives of General Psychiatry, 51,* 20–27.

Volkow, N. D., Tancredi, L. R., Grant, G., Gillespie, H., Valentie, A., Mullani, N., Wang, G.-J., & Hollister, L. (1995). Brain glucose metabolism in violent psychiatric patients: A preliminary study. *Psychiatry Research: Neuroimaging, 61,* 243–253.

Wehr, T. A., Goodwin, F. K., Wirz-Justice, A., Breitmeir, J., & Craig, C. (1982). 48 hour sleep-wake cycles in manic-depressive illness: Naturalistic observations and sleep deprivation experiments. *Archives of General Psychiatry, 39,* 559–565.

Wilson, G. A., & Furman, B. L. (1982). Effects of inhibitors of 5-hydroxytryptamine uptake on plasma glucose and their interaction with 5-hydroxytryptophan in producing hypoglycemia in mice. *European Journal of Pharmacology, 78,* 263–270.

Wozniak, K. M., & Linnoila, M. (1991). Hyperglycemic properties of serotonin receptor antagonists. *Life Sciences, 49,* 101–109.

Yamada, J., Sugimoto, Y., Kimura, I., Takeuchi, N., & Horisaka, K. (1989). Serotonin-induced hypoglycemia and increased serum insulin levels in mice. *Life Sciences, 45,* 1931–1936.

Yamamoto, H., Nagai, K., & Nagakawa, H. (1984). Additional evidence that the suprachiasmatic nucleus is the center for regulation of insulin secretion and glucose homeostasis. *Brain Research, 304,* 237–241.

6

ROLE OF SEROTONIN IN AGGRESSION OF CHILDREN AND ADOLESCENTS: BIOCHEMICAL AND PHARMACOLOGICAL STUDIES

David M. Stoff
Benedetto Vitiello
National Institute of Mental Health

Neurobiological research in human aggression stems mainly from systematic manipulations of central neurotransmitters in different animal models of aggression. Animal behavioral studies have indicated that increasing or decreasing serotonin (5-HT) activity pharmacologically produces decreases or increases in aggression, respectively (Soubrie, 1986). It is notable that human data coincide with those suggested by animal research because there is considerable clinical evidence that links impulsive-aggressive behaviors in adults to reduced brain 5-HT function (Coccaro & Kavoussi, chap. 4, this volume). Similar relationships between aggression and brain 5-HT function may exist in children and adolescents in view of continuities from childhood to adulthood in both aggressive behavior and in central 5-HT function. One of the clearest findings concerning adolescent and adult aggressive and antisocial behavior is that such behavior is predictable statistically from early antisocial, aggressive, and hyperactive behavior (Cairns, Cairns, Neckerman, Ferguson, & Gariépy, 1989; Farrington, 1990; Huesmann, Eron, Lefkowitz, & Walder, 1984; Moffitt, 1990; Olweus, 1979; Pulkkinen & Pitkanen, 1993). The more aggressive child is likely to become both the more aggressive adult and the more antisocial and criminal adult. Although the development of the serotonergic system is difficult to characterize, there is relatively good intraindividual stability over the life cycle for concentrations of the principal 5-HT metabolite, 5-hydroxyindoleacetic acid (5-HIAA), in cerebrospinal fluid (CSF) (Leckman et al., 1980; Shaywitz, Cohen, Leckman, Young, & Bowers, 1980; Traskman-Bendz, Asberg, Bertilsson, & Thoren, 1984).

This chapter first presents the rationale behind the use of different 5-HT indices in the context of some background studies in adults. We then review studies in children and adolescents with aggressive behavior in which the functional status of brain serotonergic systems is assessed using central (CSF 5-HIAA concentration, neuroendocrine responses to 5-HT agonists) and peripheral (plasma tryptophan, imipramine binding and 5-HT uptake in platelets, platelet 5-HT content, platelet $5-HT_2$ receptors) 5-HT indices (see Table 6.1). Because these biochemical findings may have implications for the pharmacological treatment of aggression and for drug development we conclude this chapter with a review of reports of serotonergic agents in the treatment of childhood aggression (see Table 6.2).

CENTRAL INDICES

CSF 5-HIAA

A widely applied approach to studying serotonergic function in humans is the measurement of CSF concentrations of 5-HIAA obtained from lumbar punctures. CSF 5-HIAA concentrations are closely correlated with frontal cortex 5-HIAA concentrations (Knott et al., 1989; Stanley, Traskman-Bendz, & Dorovini-Zis, 1985) but specific regional brain contributions cannot be identified using this method. Also, it is difficult to assess the physiologic state of the 5-HT system on the basis of neurotransmitter–metabolite concentrations in CSF because central serotonergic systems are dynamic, and possibly have multiple self-regulatory sites.

Over the past decade multiple reports have described decreased CSF 5-HIAA in various populations of adults characterized as having violent and impulsive–destructive behaviors, or both (Coccaro and Kavoussi, chap. 4, this volume). Case studies in childhood aggression suggested diminished CSF 5-HIAA concentrations in an impulsive child with conduct disorder (CD) manifesting carbohydrate craving (Kruesi, Linnoila, Rapoport, Brown, & Petersen, 1985), and in children who torture animals (Kruesi, 1989). Indirect evidence was also provided by the report of a negative correlation between CSF 5-HIAA levels measured in early adulthood and self-rated childhood problems related to excessive aggression (Brown, Kline, Goyer, Minichiello, Kruesi, & Goodwin, 1986). More direct evidence for similar CSF 5-HIAA-aggression relationships in children, as in adults, is supported by two studies conducted by Kruesi and colleagues. In the first report Kruesi et al. (1990) found significantly lower CSF 5-HIAA in a group of children and adolescents with at least one disruptive behavior disorder, compared to a matched group of youths with obsessive–compulsive disorder. These authors found several statistically significant negative correlations between various assessments of aggression and CSF 5-HIAA concentration in the raw data set but only two remained significant after correcting for the effect of age on CSF 5-HIAA concentration ("aggression

TABLE 6.1
Studies of Central and Peripheral 5-HT Indices in Aggression of Children and Adolescents

Study	Patient Group	5-HT Index	Result
Greenberg & Coleman (1976)	30 institutionalized mentally retarded patients (age range, 4 to 39 yrs) with aggressive and often destructive behavior	Whole blood 5-HI levels	Lower in mentally retarded patients compared to age- and sex-matched healthy controls
Stoff, Pollack, Vitiello, Behar, & Bridger (1987)	17 (14M, 3F) prepubertal (mean age, 10.8 yrs) DSM-III CD, most also had ADHD; 10 (4M, 6F) adolescents (mean age, 15.5 yrs) with mixed DSM-III diagnoses (3 CD, 3 CD and mood disorder, 2 dysthymia, 1 depression, 1 schizoaffective)	Platelet IB	Reduction in prepubertal CD plus ADHD compared to age/sex matched normal children; Reduction in adolescents with mixed DSM-III diagnoses compared to pediatric contrast group; Inverse correlations in adolescents with the aggressive $(r = -0.72)$, delinquent $(r = -0.70)$ and externalizing $(r = -0.72)$ factors of the parent-rated CBCL
Pliszka, Rogeness, Renner, Sherman, Broussard (1988)	27M juvenile offenders (mean age, 15.3 yrs) with CD, K-SADS-III-R	Whole blood 5-HT levels	Higher in juvenile offenders compared to younger comparison group of adolescents with depressive or anxiety disorders; Positively correlated $(r = 0.53)$ with CD rating, K-SADS-III-R
Brown et al. (1989)	15M outpatients (mean age, 21.8 yrs) with episodic aggression	Platelet 5-HT uptake	Reduced V_{max} compared to sex and age matched healthy controls; Inverse correlation $(r = -0.62)$ with BIS-10 impulsivity scale
Modai et al. (1989)	34 inpatient adolescents of various diagnoses (borderline personality disorder, affective and schizoaffective, schizophrenia, other), most with suicide attempts and aggressive behavior	Platelet 5-HT uptake	V_{max} inversely correlated with recent aggressive behavior (based on history and observation) in schizophrenia $(r = -0.87)$ and CD symptom scale, K-SADS in "other diagnoses" $(r = -0.62)$
Birmaher et al. (1990)	23 boys (mean age, 12.6 yrs) with history of recurrent aggressive behavior and impulsivity but no suicidal behavior; all boys met DSM-III criteria for CD (16 boys also had ADHD)	Platelet IB	B_{max} inversely correlated with clinician-rated CBCL scales: Total Behavior $(r = -0.47)$, Externalizing $(r = -0.48)$, Hostility $(r = -0.53)$, Aggression $(r = -0.50)$ (omitting one outlier)
Kruesi et al. (1990)	29 children and adolescents (mean age, 11.3 yrs) with one or more DBD, DSM-III	CSF 5-HIAA	Low CSF 5-HIAA compared to age- sex- and race-matched contrast group with obsessive-compulsive disorders; Inverse correlations for age-corrected CSF 5-HIAA with child's report of aggression toward people, DICA $(r = -0.40)$ and with expressed emotionality of child about mother $(r = -0.39)$

(Continued)

TABLE 6.1
(Continued)

Study	Patient Group	5-HT Index	Result
Stoff et al. (1991)	42 prepubertal (mean age, 9.5 yrs) boys with one or more DBD, *DSM-III-R*	Platelet IB (38); Platelet 5-HT Uptake (27); Plasma AAGP (17)	No differences between prepubertal DBD patients and normal controls
Marrazziti & Conti (1991)	16 institutionalized patients (8M, 8F; mean age, 26 yrs) with mental deficiency and history of other- and inner-directed aggression	Platelet IB	Reduced B_{max} in mentally deficient patients compared to age- and sex-matched healthy controls
Kruesi et al. (1992)	29 children and adolescents (mean age, 13.8 yrs) with one or more DBD, *DSM-III-R*	CSF 5-HIAA	At 2-yr follow-up, age-corrected CSF 5-HIAA inversely correlated with severity of physical aggression, Modified Overt Aggression Scale ($r = -0.53$)
Stoff, Pasatiempo, Yeung, Bridger, et al. (1992)	15 prepubertal boys (mean age 10.2) with one or more DBD, *DSM-III-R* and rated $2SD_s$ above norm on aggressive factor of CBCL; 8M adolescents (mean age, 14.7 yrs) with one or more DBD, *DSM-III-R*	PRL (FEN 1.0 mg/kg) and CORT (FEN 1.0 mg/kg)	No correlations with Child Hostility Inventory or Inventory for Antisocial Behavior in prepubertals; No correlations with Brown–Goodwin Assessment for History of Lifetime Aggression or Buss–Durkee Hostility Inventory or aggression subscale of Multidimensional Personality Inventory in adolescents; No difference between adolescent DBD patients and normal controls
Marrazziti et al. (1993)	25 mentally handicapped subjects (mean age, 27.5 yrs) institutionalized since childhood because of aggression	Platelet IB	B_{max} reduced in mentally handicapped subjects, compared to healthy controls; B_{max} reduced in suicide attempters; B_{max} does not differ between violent and nonviolent suicide methods
Halperin et al. (1994)	25 prepubertal boys with aggressive ADHD	PRL (FEN 1.0 mg/kg); Platelet 5-HT levels	Larger PRL (FEN) in aggressive ADHD compared to nonaggressive ADHD; No differences in platelet 5-HT levels, plasma MHPG or plasma HVA

Note. Abbreviations (by column): Patient Group: M = Male; F = Female; CD = Conduct Disorder; ADHD = Attention Deficit Hyperactivity Disorder; DBD = Disruptive Behavior Disorder; CBCL = Child Behavior Checklist. 5-HT Index: 5-HT = 5-hyrdroxytryptamine = serotonin; 5-HI = 5-hydroxyindole; IB = imipramine binding; CSF 5-HIAA = cerebrospinal fluid 5-hydroxyindoleacetic acid; AAGP = alpha₁ acid glycoprotein; PRL (FEN) = prolactin response to fenfluramine challenge; CORT (FEN) = cortisol response to fenfluramine challenge. Result: V_{max} = maximal rate of uptake; BIS-10 = Barratt Impulsivity Scale; B_{max} = maximal binding capacity; MHPG = 3-methoxy-4-hydroxyphenylglycol; HVA = homovanillic acid.

TABLE 6.2
Reports of Serotonergic Agents in the Treatment of Aggression in Children and Adolescents

Authors	Drug	N	Sample	Design	Dose (mg per day)	Results
Selective Serotonergics						
Realmuto, August, & Garfinkel (1989)	buspirone	4	9–10 year old with autism	open	15	2 improved
Quiason, Ward, & Kitchen (1991)	buspirone	1	8 year old	open	45	improved
Gedye (1991)	trazodone	1	17 year old with mental retardation	open	250	improved
Zubieta & Alessi (1992)	trazodone	22	5–12 year old	open	185 ± 117	13 improved
Ghaziuddin & Alessi (1992)	trazodone	3	7–9 year old	open	75	improved
Markowitz (1992)	fluoxetine	1	17 year old with mental retardation	open	40	improved
Tiihonen, Hakola, Paanila, & Turtiainen (1993)	eltoprazine	1	17 year old with mental retardation	open	30–60	unchanged
Stanislav, Fabre, Crismon, & Childs (1994)	buspirone	1	17 year old	chart review	15	improved
Nonselective Serotonergics						
Campbell et al. (1984)	lithium	61	5–13 year old	double-blind	500–2000; mean serum: 0.9 mEq/L	better than placebo, as effective as haloperidol
Kuperman & Stewart (1987)	propranolol	16	4–24 year old	open	80–280	16 improved
Klein (1991)	lithium	35	6–15 year old	double-blind	serum: 0.6–1.2 mEq/L	not better than placebo
Carlson, Rapport, Pataki, & Kelly (1992)	lithium	11	6–12 year old	double-blind in 7 pts.	600–1500; serum: 0.7–1.1 mEq/L	mixed
Campbell et al. (1995)	lithium	50	5–12 year old	double-blind	600–2100; mean serum: 1.1 mEq/L	better than placebo

105

against people," "negative expressed emotion about mother"). Statistical adjustment for the large number of correlations examined and the use of a normal control group of healthy children and adolescents would have been beneficial. In a 2-year prospective follow-up study, Kruesi et al. (1992) found that initial CSF 5-HIAA concentrations predicted the severity of physical aggression during follow-up, which ranged from 14 to 65 months.

Fenfluramine Challenge Test

In recent years neuroendocrine challenge tests have been widely used to assess the responsivity of serotonergic neuronal circuits in the CNS and postsynaptic 5-HT receptors (Coccaro and Kavoussi, chap. 4, this volume). These tests are a more practical clinical method than CSF analyses to evaluate the role of central monoamine neurotransmitters in youth. This method depends on the ability of agents with major effects on 5-HT function to elicit specific neuroendocrine responses. Such responses are taken to reflect the functional status of central 5-HT systems. Prolactin responses to a variety of central 5-HT agents are thought to reflect pre- or postsynaptic aspects of 5-HT activity in the limbic hypothalamic pituitary axis (Preziosi, 1983). Because there are no 5-HT receptors on pituitary lactotroph cells (Lamberts & MacLeod, 1978), this effect is indirect and thought to occur proximal to this site. It must be noted that neuroendocrine responses to 5-HT agonists cannot assess the relative sensitivity of specific postsynaptic 5-HT receptors located in hypothalamic nuclei, and such responses reflect the activity of only a circumscribed portion of the CNS serotonergic system. Drug challenge with selective 5-HT receptor probes is a promising strategy in the armamentarium of the clinical investigator, especially in view of demonstrated stability for the prolactin response to fenfluramine challenge (Stoff, Pasatiempo, Yeung, Bridger, & Rabinovitch, 1992). However, the method suffers from several drawbacks, which may restrict its usefulness only to specific situations, that is, assessment of the mechanism of action of psychotropic drugs in humans. More specific agents, with better pharmacokinetic and side effect profiles, continue to be needed.

Inverse correlations have been demonstrated between the prolactin response to indirect- and direct-acting 5-HT agonists and aggressive–impulsive behaviors in adult patients with personality disorders (Coccaro et al., 1989; Moss, Yao, & Panzak, 1990), but a positive correlation has been found in substance abusers (Fishbein, Lozovsky, & Jaffe, 1989). Consistent with results of inverse correlations, O'Keane, Moloney, O'Neill, O'Connor, Smith, and Dinan (1992) reported that the prolactin response to d-fenfluramine was blunted in violent offenders with antisocial personality disorder. There have been two neuroendocrine challenge studies of the 5-HT system in children or adolescents with aggressive behavior. The first study (Stoff, Pasatiempo, Yeung, Cooper, Bridger, & Rabinovich, 1992) reported no relationship between the prolactin or cortisol responses to d,l-fenfluramine and measures of aggression or impulsivity in pre- and postpubertal patients with disruptive behavior disorders. Further, adolescent patients with aggressive forms of disruptive behavior disorder demonstrated basal prolactin–cortisol levels and d,l-fenfluramine-induced prolactin–cortisol release similar to those of matched normal healthy controls. The second study found enhancement in the prolactin response to d,l-fenfluramine in aggressive children with attention deficit hyperactivity disorder (ADHD), compared to nonaggressive children with ADHD (Halperin et al., 1994). Unfortunately, the absence of a normal control group in this study makes it difficult to know which group had the deviant response.

PLATELET MODEL

Platelets and 5-HT neurones show many common similarities including active transport systems for tryptophan and 5-HT, storage granules for 5-HT, embryological ancestry, the presence of ^{3}H-imipramine and 5-HT_2 binding sites as well as MAO and neuron-specific enolase. Many investigators believe that the 5-HT uptake site in platelets and in CNS serotonergic neurons may be virtually identical and, moreover, that the activity of the platelet 5-HT transporter may closely parallel that of the CNS 5-HT neurons (Da Prada, Cesura, Launay, & Richards, 1988; Pletscher, 1988). Thus, the measurement of platelet 5-HT uptake or platelet 5-HT transporter sites may provide a "window to the brain," potentially a useful, easily available laboratory "marker" to aid in the diagnosis and prediction of aggression and in the monitoring of response to pharmacotherapy. It remains open to question whether in vivo physiological changes in the platelet accurately reflect changes in brain; however, such a possibility is a major motivation for studying platelets. It has been shown that changes in serotonergic parameters of blood platelets do not accompany changes in brain 5-HT neurones in laboratory animals (Moret & Briley, 1991; Twist, Mitchell, Brazel, Stahl, & Campbell, 1990). Furthermore, even if the serotonergic systems in platelets reflect central serotonergic systems, the diversity of brain serotonergic systems should be taken into account. For example, only in the hypothalamus is the B_{max} of ^{3}H-imipramine binding controlled by photoperiod (Rovescalli, Brunello, Riva, Galimberti, & Racagni, 1989). In addition, platelets apparently possess only one of the many molecularly identified 5-HT receptors so that a presumed CNS abnormality in the 5-HT_{2C} receptor can not be studied in platelets.

CORRELATIONS BETWEEN CENTRAL
AND PERIPHERAL 5-HT MEASURES

Little is known regarding the relationship of central 5-HT measures to peripheral 5-HT measures. The theoretical importance lies in studying peripheral 5-HT-related proteins because they may be abnormal due to the systematic manifestation of a genetic abnormality involving such a protein or due to the systemic effect of a humoral factor or hormone. The practical importance lies in determining what information about brain 5-HT systems can be inferred from platelet indices by studying the relationship of such indices to brain or central 5-HT indices. For routine clinical purposes, lumbar punctures cannot be performed as readily as blood sampling, and therefore, alternative approaches to a lumbar puncture would facilitate the conduct of biologic studies of the serotonergic system.

CSF 5-HIAA concentration correlated with B_{max} for platelet ^{3}H-imipramine binding (IB) in Parkinson's disease (Sano et al., 1991) but no correlation was observed in neurosurgical patients (Stoff, Goldman, Bridger, Jain, & Pylypiw, 1990) or in major affective disorder (Wagner, Aberg-Wistedt, Asberg, Bertilsson, Martinsson, & Montero, 1987). In a study of the relationship of several peripheral and CNS basal serotonergic measures in humans, Sarrias, Cabre, Martinez, and Artigas (1990) reported a correlation only between the ratio of platelet to plasma 5-HT levels and CSF 5-HIAA levels and suggested that this correlation may be explained by the action of monoamine oxidase (MAO), which is partly under genetic control. However, human brain MAO and platelet MAO activity do not correlate with each other (Young, Laws, Sharbrough, & Weinshilboum, 1986). Fenfluramine-stimulated prolactin release, but not CSF 5-HIAA level, correlates positively with platelet 5-HT$_2$ receptor number in depressed/suicidal inpatients (Mann, McBride, Anderson, & Mieczkowski, 1992). Similarly, the maximal prolactin response induced by fenfluramine also correlates positively with the magnitude of 5-HT amplified platelet aggregation, mediated by the 5-HT$_2$ receptor complex, in young adult autistic subjects (McBride et al., 1989). The significance of these correlations is strengthened by the findings that the binding characteristics and the inhibition of binding of 5-HT$_2$ receptors in the brain and in platelets appear to be similar (Elliott & Kent, 1989).

PLATELET–BLOOD 5-HT INDICES

Plasma Tryptophan

Availability of tryptophan, the amino acid precursor of 5-HT, in brain may contribute to the regulation of central presynaptic activity in aggression. Because tryptophan hydroxylase (TH) is the rate-limiting enzyme involved in 5-HT synthesis and TH is not normally saturated by its substrate, changes in brain tryptophan levels by the administration of tryptophan can increase the synthesis of brain 5-HT up to twofold. The behavioral effects of decreased 5-HT function can be studied in clinical populations using an amino acid drink to reduce levels of plasma tryptophan, the precursor of 5-HT. Thus, the use of amino acid mixtures alters tryptophan availability and therefore 5-HT synthesis. Evidence from several studies of aggression with acute tryptophan depletion in primates and humans suggests that a selected provocation may be required to demonstrate a relationship between 5-HT function and impulsive–aggressive behavior (Chamberlain, Ervin, Pihl, & Young, 1987; Salomon, Mazure, Delgado, Mendia, & Charney, 1994; Smith, Pihl, Young, & Ervin, 1986). It also must be noted that in addition to affecting 5-HT, acute dietary manipulation of tryptophan levels may affect neuropeptides, second messenger systems, receptor synthesis or some other nonspecific aspect of brain function as well as the balance between 5-HT and some other neurotransmitter systems.

In determining what controls the concentration of tryptophan in brain, studies in recent years have focused on the importance of free (unbound) versus total plasma tryptophan and the ratio of tryptophan to large neutral amino acids competing with tryptophan for transport. Data showing a relationship between tryptophan availability to the brain and aggression in adults are scarce. Decreased plasma tryptophan ratio has been associated with aggressive and depressive tendencies in alcoholics (Branchey, Branchey, Shaw, & Lieber, 1984; Buydens-Branchey, Branchey, Noumair, & Lieber, 1989) but increased plasma tryptophan ratio has been found in habitually violent impulsive offenders with intermittent explosive and antisocial personality disorders (Virkkunen & Narvanen, 1987). In the only study of tryptophan availability in aggressive youth (prepubertal boys codiagnosed with CD and ADHD), there were no abnormalities in plasma tryptophan ratio or plasma free or total tryptophan. No correlations were obtained for these plasma tryptophan indices with aggression rating scales or with cognitive measures of impulsivity (see Table 6.3).

Imipramine Binding and Serotonin Uptake in Platelets

Another strategy to assess serotonergic function is tritiated IB which has been examined in platelets and brain (Langer, Galzin, Poirer, Loo, Sechter, & Zarifian, 1987) as a measure of presynaptic serotonergic receptor sites associated with the 5-HT transporter (Marcusson, Baeckstroem, & Ross, 1986). At first, it was reported that platelet IB capacity was reduced in depressed patients (e.g., Raisman, Sechter, Briley, Zarifian, & Langer, 1981) but subsequent studies have shown a similar decrease in a broad spectrum of mental disorders that have been linked to a 5-HT disturbance common to them all (Marrazziti, Placidi, Cassano, & Akiskal, 1989). In studies of young adults reduced platelet IB capacity has been found in severely mentally handicapped subjects who had been institutionalized since childhood due to aggression (Marrazziti & Conti, 1991; Marrazziti et al., 1993). A similar reduction has also been reported in children with conduct disorder (most with attention deficit hyperactivity disorder comorbidity) in two out of three studies (Birmaher et al., 1990; Stoff et al., 1987, 1991). In our first study we found a reduction in platelet IB capacity in prepubertal conduct-disordered patients and an inverse relation between platelet IB capacity and aggression ratings in inpatient adolescents (Stoff et al., 1987). However, we were unable to replicate these findings in another sample of less symptomatic

TABLE 6.3
Peripheral 5-HT Indices in Disruptive Behavior Disorder

5-HT Index	Disruptive Behavior Disorder	Controls
Plasma Free Tryp[a,e] (nMol/ml)	12.60 ± 0.54 (24)	11.90 ± 0.40 (38)
Plasma Total Tryp[b,e] (nMol/ml)	49.50 ± 2.45 (24)	43.0 ± 1.82 (40)
Plasma Tryp Ratio[b,e]	0.106 ± 0.005 (18)	0.105 ± 0.004 (18)
Plasma Free 5-HT[c,e] (ng/ml)	0.62 ± 0.007 (23)	0.70 ± 0.138 (16)
Whole Blood 5-HT[c,e] (ng/ml)	52.30 ± 9.23 (27)	67.89 ± 12.25 (21)
Platelet 5-HT$_2$: B$_{max}$[d,e] (fmol/mg prot)	20.37 ± 2.15 (27)	25.45 ± 3.28 (21)

Note. Values are mean ± SEM (N). No differences between patients and controls by independent *t* tests.

[a]Determined in an ultrafiltrate of plasma by the fluorimetric method (Denckla & Dewey, 1967).

[b]Total plasma tryptophan and all amino acids measured using HPLC by precolumn fluorescence derivitization with o-phthaldialdehyde (Lindroth & Mopper, 1967). Tryptophan ratios determined by dividing the values obtained for tryptophan by the sum of the values obtained for large neutral amino acids phenylalanine, valine, tyrosine, isoleucine, and leucine.

[c]Analyzed according to a modification of Wester, Gottfries, and Winblad (1987) by HPLC with amperometric detection.

[d]Maximum number of binding sites (B$_{max}$) and apparent dissociation constant (K$_d$), determined for ^{125}Iodo-spiroperidol in the presence and absence of 10uM mianserin (Perry, Cook, Leventhal, Wainwright, & Freedman, 1991).

[e]No correlations with aggression rating scales or cognitive measures of impulsivity: *DSM–III–R* Conduct Disorder Symptom Checklist, Aggression factor of Parent rated-Child Behavior Checklist (Achenbach & Edelbrock, 1983), IOWA Inattention/Overactivity and Aggression scales (Loney, 1987), Inventory for Antisocial Behavior (Kazdin & Esveldt-Dawson, 1986), Vigilance Task and Delayed Responding Test (Gordon, 1986), Matching Familiar Figures Test (Kagan, 1964).

boys with one or more disruptive behavior disorders even though platelet IB capacity correlated inversely with cognitive measures of impulsivity (Stoff et al., 1991). Consistent with our first study, an inverse correlation has been reported between platelet IB capacity and factors of the child behavior checklist related to aggression in prepubertal children with predominantly conduct disorder and coexisting attention deficit hyperactivity disorder but without suicidal behavior (Birmaher et al., 1990). Because IB sites may label the 5-HT transporter it would be worthwhile to directly measure platelet 5-HT uptake sites in aggressive youth. Platelet 5-HT uptake is reduced in young adult outpatients with episodic aggression and inversely correlated with ratings of nonaggressive impulsivity (Brown et al., 1989). Similar studies in youth report either inverse correlations or no group differences (see Table 6.1). Maximal platelet 5-HT uptake velocity correlated inversely with conduct disorder symptoms and recent aggressive behavior in schizophrenic adolescents (Modai et al., 1989). We failed to obtain differences on maximal platelet 5-HT uptake velocity comparing prepubertal conduct-disordered boys with attention deficit hyperactivity comorbidity to normal controls (Stoff et al., 1991). We also did not find differences in the plasma concentration of alpha$_1$-acid glycoprotein, a putative endogenous inhibitor of the 5-HT transporter, in boys with conduct disorder and attention deficit hyperactivity disorder (Stoff et al., 1991). An alternative way to assess 5-HT uptake in platelets is to measure ^{3}H-paroxetine binding, a much more selective ligand for the platelet 5-HT transporter than ^{3}H-imipramine. There are no reported studies of paroxetine binding in the aggression of children.

Whole Blood–Platelet 5-HT Content

Measurement of the amount of 5-HT in whole blood which has not been separated into a platelet fraction is the best estimate of platelet 5-HT content in a given volume of blood because of the high concentration of 5-HT in platelets. The potential utility of relating blood 5-HT levels to a behavioral trait such as aggression is underscored by the finding that whole blood 5-HT levels are remarkably stable over time in normoserotonemic, adult control subjects with normal levels of blood 5-HT (Yuwiler, Plotkin, Geller, & Ritvo, 1970). However, whole blood or platelet 5-HT levels are affected by multiple physiological and pathological factors, which must be considered in the interpretation of findings. Moreover, the precise relationship of whole blood 5-HT to central serotonergic functioning is unclear. Most evidence suggests that platelets do not synthesize 5-HT (Stahl, 1985); rather, tryptophan is taken up and converted to 5-HT by the enterochromaffin cells of the gut. Newly synthesized platelets have storage granules and transport mechanisms, but they do not contain 5-HT until they reach the gut circulation, where they obtain 5-HT by exchanging with the enterochromaffin cells. 5-HT concentrations in platelets are probably not a good direct indicator of central 5-HT activity, but because the neuron and the platelet share similar receptor, release, and transport mechanisms (Pletscher, 1988), platelet 5-HT concentrations may be a useful biological marker in the study of psychiatric disorders.

Greenberg and Coleman (1976) found an inverse relationship between whole blood 5-HT and hyperactivity and aggression in mentally retarded patients, whereas Pliszka et al. (1988) reported a positive correlation between whole blood 5-HT and conduct disorder ratings in adolescent males at a juvenile detention center and a community mental health clinic. Consistent with the report by Pliszka et al. (1988) of a trend for higher blood 5-HT in violent juvenile offenders, depressed inpatients with comorbid borderline personality disorder exhibit a positive correlation between whole blood 5-HT content and aggressivity traits (as measured by the Brown–Goodwin assessment for history of lifetime aggression as well as the BPRS hostility subscale; Mann et al., 1992). Similarly, Raleigh, McGuire, Brammer, and Yuwiler (1984) have also reported elevated whole blood 5-HT in dominant male adult vervet monkeys. In prepubertal boys co-diagnosed with CD and ADHD, we investigated free plasma 5-HT, in addition to whole blood 5-HT levels, because free plasma 5-HT represents the physiologically active fraction which is able to interact with receptors (Anderson, Feibel, & Cohen, 1987), in contrast to whole blood 5-HT that reflects 5-HT stored in platelets. Free plasma 5-HT levels and whole blood 5-HT levels were not different between CD + ADHD patients and controls and did not correlate with aggression rating scales or cognitive measures of impulsivity (see Table 6.3).

Platelet 5-HT$_2$ Receptors

Many investigators reported the presence of functional 5-HT$_2$ receptors in human platelets with pharmacologic and functional characteristics that are similar to those in human frontal cortex (Elliott & Kent, 1989; Geaney, Schachter, Elliott, & Grahame-Smith, 1984; Peters & Grahame-Smith, 1980). The binding characteristics of the 5-HT$_2$ receptor in cortical synaptosomes and platelet membranes are correlated in humans and they are similarly regulated (Andres, Rao, Ostrowitzki, & Entzian, 1993). Phosphoinositide hydrolysis serves as the signal transducing system for the platelet (DeChaffoy de Courcelles, Leysen, DeClerck, Vanbelle, & Janssen, 1985; DeChaffoy de Courcelles, Roevans, Wynants, & Vanbelle, 1987) as well as the brain (Conn & Sanders-Bush, 1985, 1986). The platelet 5-HT$_2$ receptor is an attractive model for the study of 5-HT$_2$ receptor function in neuropsychiatric disorders and problem behavior because it is readily accessible, and because techniques have beeen devised to evaluate both receptor binding indices and receptor-mediated physiological responses. These responses include serotonin-induced platelet shape change and serotonin-induced and amplified platelet aggregation (DeClerck, David, & Janssen, 1982; DeClerck, Xhonneux, Leysen, & Janssen, 1984).

A negative correlation was found between the magnitude of 5-HT-amplified platelet aggregation responses and the total score on the Brown–Goodwin assessment for history of lifetime aggression in adult patients with major depression (McBride et al., 1994). In contrast, 5-HT$_2$ receptor number and the ratio of the 5-HT-amplified platelet aggregation response to platelet 5-HT$_2$ receptor number, an index of the mean responsivity of an individual receptor complex, was not significantly correlated with the aggression score. In order to examine the role of 5-HT$_2$ receptors in child aggression, we measured 5-HT$_2$ receptors using ^{125}I-iodo-spiroperidol as the binding ligand in platelets obtained from drug-free prepubertal male patients with CD + ADHD ($n = 21$) and normal control subjects ($n = 27$). We observed that the mean B_{max} of ^{125}I-iodo-spiroperidol binding in platelets of CD + ADHD patients was not significantly different when compared with normal control subjects (see Table 6.3). There was also no significant difference in K_d values between patients and normal controls. To examine whether 5-HT$_2$ receptors are related to the magnitude of aggression or of cognitive impulsivity, we determined the relationships of B_{max} and K_d with scores on various aggression rating scales and on laboratory indices of cognitive impulsivity. We found no significant correlations between B_{max} and K_d with these aggression and impulsivity measures (Table 6.3). Our results do not indicate abnormal 5-HT$_2$ receptors in platelets of patients with CD + ADHD.

SEROTONERGIC AGENTS IN THE TREATMENT OF CHILDHOOD AGGRESSION

On the whole, clinical reports on the use of serotonergic drugs in childhood aggression are still too few and uncontrolled to help clarify the role of these agents as antiaggressive drugs. Several compounds that have activity on the serotonergic system have been used in an attempt to control aggression in pediatric age. None of them can be considered specifically active upon aggression, because their antiaggressive activity is accompanied by other effects on mood, seizure threshold, or cardiovascular parameters. Furthermore, there is no clinical evidence in children that the serotonergic system is specifically involved in aggression. In fact, among the drugs known to have antiaggressive properties in children, methylphenidate, d-amphetamine, and neuroleptics are active on the dopaminergic and noradrenergic systems (Amery, Minichiello, & Brown, 1984; Klorman et al., 1988). Controlled studies on the effects of serotonergic agents on aggression in pediatric age are few. Most of the available data come from single case reports and open label trials in limited numbers of patients. In many of these reports, gross organic brain pathology is the underlying cause of aggression, a fact that limits the inference of the results to other types of aggression that are unaccompanied by brain damage. Table 6.2 summarizes the clinical reports currently available. At the moment, there are no adequately controlled data to support the efficacy of any selective serotonergic drugs in childhood aggression. Lithium, which can be considered a nonselective serotonergic drug, has been shown to be more effective than placebo in decreasing impulsive aggression in hospitalized children.

Among the selective serotonergic drugs, buspirone, a partial agonist at the 5-HT$_{1A}$ receptor (Peroutka, 1985), was associated with a gradual decrease in aggression when given 15 mg three times a day to an 8-year-old boy (Quiason, Ward, & Kitchen, 1991). It is of interest that this child's coexistent hyperactivity did not improve while on buspirone. Similarly, in a sample that also included adults with organic-induced aggression, a 17-year-old boy with organic personality disorder, psychotic features, and recurrent aggressive behavior improved on buspirone 5 mg three times a day (Stanislav et al., 1994). Moreover, buspirone 5 mg three times a day was also given to four autistic children and two of them showed improvement in their behavioral symptoms (Realmuto et al., 1989).

Trazodone, which acts on the 5-HT system in a complex way, has been shown to ameliorate aggression in a few reports. Trazodone is an antagonist at $5\text{-}HT_2$ and $5\text{-}HT_1$ receptors and also weakly blocks 5-HT re-uptake, while its main metabolite, m-chlorophenylpiperazine (m-CPP), is a $5\text{-}HT_1$ agonist (Fuller, Snoddy, & Cohen, 1984; Maj, Palider, & Rawlow, 1979). Dose amount and duration of treatment may influence the balance of the agonist–antagonist effects. Trazodone (mean dose 185 ± 117 mg per day) decreased aggression in 13 out of 22 children with mean IQ 83 ± 13 (Zubieta & Alessi, 1992). In this sample, one of the nonresponders improved when lithium was added to trazodone. The administration of trazodone 75 mg per day was also associated with decreased aggression in three children of normal IQ (Ghaziuddin & Alessi, 1992). Likewise, in an on-off–on-off design, trazodone (250 mg per day) was shown to decrease the aggressive and self-injurious behavior of a 17-year-old boy with severe mental retardation (Gedye, 1991). With the current limited clinical data, it is difficult to speculate on antiaggressive mechanism of action of this drug, which certainly deserves more attention.

Fenfluramine, a drug that acutely enhances 5-HT transmission by increasing its release and blocking its re-uptake, but which chronically depletes serotonin (Garattini, Jori, Buczko, & Sunanin, 1975), has been studied in autistic children (Ritvo, Freeman, Geller, & Yuwiler, 1983). At this time, there is no evidence for its antiaggressive activity.

On the other hand, serotonergic agents have also been associated with emergence or worsening of aggression. Clomipramine (100–200 mg per day) given to two obsessive–compulsive children (aged 11 and 14 years, respectively) was associated with a sudden appearance of aggression and self-injurious behavior (Alarcon, Johnson, & Lucas, 1991). One of them was also receiving buspirone 5 mg twice a day. After discontinuing clomipramine and buspirone, there was improvement on the combination of carbamazepine 200 mg per day and fluoxetine 10 mg per day. A similar reaction was observed in an 11-year-old boy with Tourette and obsessive–compulsive disorder who received clomipramine 25–50 mg per day for 2 weeks (Cruz, 1992). Likewise, fluoxetine, another 5-HT re-uptake inhibitor, was associated with emergence of self-injurious thoughts and behaviors in six patients aged 10–17 years who were given doses of 20 mg per day for obsessive–compulsive disorder (King et al., 1991). The exact biochemical mechanism underlying these episodes is not yet clear. They cannot be merely explained as an acute effect of blocking the presynaptic 5-HT re-uptake because they have often emerged after several weeks of treatment. One could speculate that the blockade of 5-HT re-uptake may abnormally turn down the serotonergic system in some patients by acting on the presynaptic receptors. Attesting to the complexity of the interaction between aggression and 5-HT re-uptake inhibitors, fluoxetine was also associated with decreased self-inflicted aggression in a group of mentally retarded patients, including a 17-year-old girl (Markowitz, 1992). Self-injurious behavior in mental retardation can have stereotypic or compulsive features and its response to fluoxetine might be related to the anticompulsive properties of this drug.

Also employed in the management of aggression in children and adolescents are psychotropic agents which are active on several other neurotransmitters besides 5-HT. However, given the amount of evidence that 5-HT is involved in impulsive aggression, it is not implausible to hypothesize that their interaction with 5-HT plays a paramount role in their antiaggressive activity. Among these agents, lithium carbonate has been the most extensively studied. The mechanism of action of lithium is unknown, but there are data showing that lithium enhances serotonergic transmission (Blier & De Montigny, 1985). Lithium has been shown to decrease aggression in children, at serum levels ranging from 0.3–1.5 mEq/L (mean 0.9 mEq/L; Campbell et al., 1984). This study is remarkable because it is one of the few controlled studies in this field. Sixty-one aggressive children aged 5–13 years (mean 9 years) and with IQ 64–108 (mean 82) were randomly assigned to receive lithium 500–2000 mg per day, haloperidol 1–6 mg per day, or placebo for 4 weeks. Both lithium and haloperidol were more effective than placebo. In addition, lithium had fewer side effects than haloperidol, particularly from a cognitive point of view (Platt, Campbell, Green, & Grega, 1984). In this study, the efficacy of lithium in this sample was unrelated to the presence of affective symptoms in the patients or their families, thus suggesting that lithium has antiaggressive properties that are independent of its antimanic effects. The same investigators have, in part, replicated these findings with a double-blind placebo-controlled study in 50 children aged 5–12 years who were hospitalized for aggressive conduct disorder (Campbell et al., 1995). In this study, patients on lithium (500–2100 mg per day, mean serum level 1.1 mEq/L) fared better than the placebo group on some but not all the outcome measures. In another study, lithium (600–1500 mg per day; serum level: 0.7–1.1 mEq/L) was given to 11 inpatient children aged 6–12 years, of which 7 were studied in double-blind fashion (Carlson et al., 1992). The results were mixed with suggestions of an antiaggressive activity of lithium, even though only three children improved enough to be discharged. The antiaggressive effect of lithium may be less clear in children with less severe aggression lacking the element of explosiveness (Klein, 1991). Open studies suggest that lithium is effective also in mentally retarded children and adolescents suffering from explosive aggression (Dale, 1980; Dostal, 1972).

Another drug used in the management of explosive aggression is propranolol, which is primarily known as an adrenergic beta-blocker, but also acts on 5-HT as a 5-HT$_{1A}$ receptor antagonist and a 5-HT$_{1B}$ agonist (Nishio, Nakakura, & Segawa, 1989; Pierson, Lyon, Titeler, Kowalski, & Glennon, 1989). In an open study, propranolol 80–280 mg (mean 164 ± 55 mg) was administered to 16 aggressive patients aged 4–24 years (mean 13 years) and with IQ of 15–118 (mean 70). A decrease in aggression was observed in 16 of them (Kuperman & Stewart, 1987). These antiaggressive effects were not limited to the subjects with mental retardation nor were they related to its cardiovascular effects. Finally, carbamazepine, for which there are preliminary indications of efficacy in children with explosive aggression (Kafantatris et al., 1992), may, in part, act through enhancement of serotonergic transmission (Yan et al., 1992).

Future studies should look at the effects on aggression of more specific serotonergic agents, such as the 5-HT$_{1A}$ receptor agonists ipsapirone, gepirone, and tandospirone (White, Kucharik, & Moyer, 1991). Recently, eltoprazine has been proposed as prototype for a new category of specific antiaggressive agents, called the "serenics" (Rasmussen, Olivier, Raghoebar, & Mos, 1990). Eltoprazine acts as a serotonergic agonist at the 5-HT$_{1B}$ receptor and has been tried in mentally retarded adults with mixed results (Kohen, 1993; Verhoeven et al., 1992). In another study (Tiihonen et al., 1993), 6 out of 9 patients with schizophrenia or mental retardation became less aggressive when given eltoprazine up to 30–60 mg per day. They were all adults, except for a 17-year-old adolescent girl with mental retardation whose behavior did not improve on eltoprazine. As more specific serotonergic agents become available, one could expect that more light may be shed on the biochemical mechanisms of aggression, or at least of some types of affective and explosive aggression. This could provide the clinicians with the effective and specific antiaggressive drugs that they are now lacking.

SUMMARY AND FUTURE DIRECTIONS

Taken together, the relatively few studies of central 5-HT indices in child and youth aggression (only four; two by the same research group), do not reveal the consistent pattern of reduced 5-HT function that has been found in numerous reports of adult aggression (see references in Coccaro and Kavoussi, chap. 4, this volume). There is a hint of a relation between lower CSF 5-HIAA levels and aggression of youth with disruptive disorders but these data must be replicated under more controlled conditions by other investigators. In addition to practical and ethical difficulties in employing more invasive procedures to assess central 5-HT function in younger populations, there are other reasons that complicate conducting central 5-HT studies of aggression in children and youth. These include: (a) problems in repetitive measurement of central 5-HT indices for prospective longitudinal studies, (b) age- or developmentally-related changes in central 5-HT function and aggression, or both, and (c) problems in assessing central 5-HT indices in interaction with the ongoing social context (which has a powerful effect on poorly modulated, developing behaviors). Studies that employ the more peripheral 5-HT indices are still in a stage of infancy and results do not reveal consistent 5-HT abnormalities. In addition to problems mentioned earlier, which also apply to peripheral 5-HT indices, these studies are further limited by the unacceptably low correlations between central 5-HT indices and peripheral 5-HT indices, arguing against the use of indirect peripheral indices.

Biological studies of the serotonergic system have just begun to contribute useful information about the nature of the dysfunction of the 5-HT system in aggression and impulsivity. CSF, pharmacologic challenge, plasma and platelet studies have begun to be supplanted by PET studies using ligands to identify uptake sites, presynaptic and postsynaptic receptors, and measures of 5-HT turnover. All these methods may provide evidence for specific disturbances in 5-HT physiology, which could direct the strategy for pharmacologic intervention. It is important to recognize that neurotransmitter systems do not function in isolation. Studies that examine both noradrenergic and serotonergic systems allow us to begin to approach the complexity of interactive neurochemical systems in the brain. Neurotransmission mediated by dopamine, norepinephrine, acetylcholine, glutamate, and neuropeptides is influenced by 5-HT and vice versa. More information is needed on the potential efficacy of simultaneous pharmacological interventions to more than one neurotransmitter system agent. Especially in developing organisms, it will also be important to examine 5-HT's role in regulating the maturation of the brain during early development. 5-HT may act as a neurodevelopmental signal and its actions may occur in concert with other early developmental systems such as cholinergic and catecholaminergic. We have come a long way in measuring neurotransmitter functioning in individuals with behavior problems, and comparing it to that in normals. The notion underlying most of this work that biological processes determine behavior must be reconciled with a growing body of evidence that experiential events may have a significant impact on biological processes, which ultimately influence aggressive behavior (see Susman et al., chap. 13, this volume). We need to go now beyond the linear model of investigating biological abnormalities in patient groups and look at the bidirectionality of biological and behavioral influences to address the reciprocal interplay between biology and behavior.

The clinical pharmacology of serotonergic agents as possible treatment of childhood aggression is still in an embryonic stage. Most of the reports currently available are anecdotal, except for a few controlled studies on lithium, whose activity however is difficult to ascribe merely to a serotonergic mechanism given its multiple biochemical effects. Future controlled studies using specific serotonergic agents are needed. New drug development must consider the range of altered patterns of serotonergic activity that may exist in aggression, their interaction with other transmitter system abnormalities, and their association with possible dimensions of symptomatology that cut across diagnostic categories.

ACKNOWLEDGMENT

The opinions expressed herein are the views of the authors and do not necessarily reflect the official position of the National Institute of Mental Health or any other part of the U.S. Department of Health and Human Services.

REFERENCES

Achenbach, T. M., & Edelbrock, C. (1983). *Manual for the child behavior checklist and revised behavior profile.* Burlington, VT: Thomas Achenbach.

Alarcon, R. D., Johnson, B. R., & Lucas, J. P. (1991). Paranoid and aggressive behavior in two obsessive-compulsive adolescents treated with clomipramine. *Journal of the American Academy of Child and Adolescent Psychiatry, 30,* 999–1002.

Amery, B., Minichiello, M. D., & Brown, G. L. (1984). Aggression in hyperactive boys: Response to d-amphetamine. *Journal of the American Academy of Child and Adolescent Psychiatry, 23,* 291–294.

Anderson, G. M., Feibel, F. C., & Cohen, D. J. (1987). Determination of serotonin in whole blood, platelet-rich plasma, platelet-poor plasma and plasma ultrafiltrate. *Life Sciences, 40,* 1063–1070.

Andres, A. H., Rao, M. L., Ostrowitzki, S., & Entzian, W. (1993). Human brain cortex and platelet serotonin-2-receptor binding properties and their regulation by endogenous serotonin. *Life Sciences, 52,* 313–321.

Birmaher, B., Stanley, M., Greenhill, L., Twomey, J., Gavrilescu, A., & Rabinovich, H. (1990). Platelet imipramine binding in children and adolescents with impulsive behavior. *Journal of the American Academy of Child and Adolescent Psychiatry, 29,* 914–918.

Blier, P., & De Montigny, C. (1985). Short-term lithium administration enhances serotonergic neurotransmission: Elecrophysiological evidence in the rat. *European Journal of Psychopharmacology, 113,* 69–77.

Branchey, L., Branchey, M. H., Shaw, S., & Lieber, C. S. (1984). Depression, suicide, and aggression in alcoholics and their relationship to plasma amino acids. *Psychiatry Research, 12,* 219–226.

Brown, C. S., Kent, T. A., Bryant, S. G., Vevedon, R. M., Campbell, J. L., Felthous, A. R., Barratt, E. S., & Rose, R. M. (1989). Blood platelet uptake of serotonin in episodic aggression. *Psychiatry Research, 27,* 5–12.

Brown, G. L, Kline, W. J., Goyer, P. F., Minichiello, M. D., Kruesi, M. J. P., & Goodwin, F. K. (1986). Relationship of childhood characteristics to cerebrospinal fuid 5-hydroxyindoleacetic acid in aggressive adults. In C. Shagass, R. Josiassen, W. H. Bridger, K. J. Weiss, D. M. Stoff, G. M. Simpson (Eds.), *Proceedings of IVth World Congress of Biological Psychiatry* (Vol 7, pp. 177–179). New York: Elsevier.

Buydens-Branchey, L., Branchey, M. H., Noumair, D., & Lieber, C. S. (1989). Age of alcoholism onset. II. Relationship of susceptibility to serotonin precursor availability. *Archives of General Psychiatry, 46,* 231–236.

Cairns, R. B., Cairns B. D., Neckerman, H. J., Ferguson, L. L., & Gariépy, J-L. (1989). Growth and Aggression: I. Childhood to Early Adolescence. *Developmental Psychology, 25,* 320–330.

Campbell, M., Adams, P. B., Small, A. M., Kafantaris, V., Silva, R. R., Shell, J., Perry, R., & Overall, J. E. (1995). Lithium in hospitalized aggressive children with conduct disorder: A double-blind and placebo controlled study. *Journal of the American Academy of Child and Adolescent Psychiatry, 34,* 445–451.

Campbell, M., Small, A. M., Green, W. H., Jennings, S. J., Perry, R., Bennett, W. G., & Anderson, L. (1984). Behavioral efficacy of haloperidol and lithium carbonate: A comparison in hospitalized aggressive children with conduct disorder. *Archives of General Psychiatry, 41,* 650–656.

Carlson, G. A., Rapport, M. D., Pataki, C. S., & Kelly, K. L. (1992). Lithium in hospitalized children at 4 and 8 weeks: Mood, behavior and cognitive effects. *Journal of Child Psychology and Psychiatry, 33,* 411–425.

Chamberlain, B. G., Ervin, F. R., Pihl, R. O., & Young, S. N. (1987). The effect of raising or lowering tryptophan levels on aggression in vervet monkeys. *Pharmacology, Biochemistry and Behavior, 28,* 503–510.

Coccaro, E. F., Siever, L. J., Klar, H., Maurer, G., Cochrane, K., Cooper, T. B., Mohs, R. C., & Davis, K. L. (1989). Serotonergic disorders: Correlates with suicidal and impulsive aggressive behavior. *Archives of General Psychiatry, 46,* 587–599.

Conn, P. J., & Sanders-Bush E. (1985). Serotonin-stimulated phosphoinositide turnover: Mediated by the S_2 binding site in rat cerebral cortex but not in the subcortical regions. *Journal of Pharmacology and Experimental Therapeutics, 234,* 195–203.

Conn, P. J., & Sanders-Bush E. (1986). Biochemical characterization of serotonin stimulated phosphoinositide turnover. *Life Sciences, 38,* 633–669.

Cruz, R. (1992). Clomipramine side effects. *Journal of the American Academy of Child and Adolescent Psychiatry, 31,* 1168–1169.

Dale, P. G. (1980). Lithium therapy in aggressive mentally subnormal patients. *British Journal of Psychiatry, 137,* 469–474.

Da Prada, M., Cesura, A. M., Launay, J. M., & Richards, J. G. (1988). Platelets as a model for neurones? *Experientia, 44,* 115–126.

DeChaffoy de Courcelles, D., Leysen, J. E., DeClerck, F., Vanbelle, H., & Janssen, P. A. J. (1985). Evidence that phospholipid turnover is the signal transducing system coupled to serotonin-S_2 receptor sites. *Journal of Biological Chemistry, 260,* 7603–7608.

DeChaffoy de Courcelles, D., Roevans, P., Wynants, J., & Vanbelle, H. (1987). Serotonin-induced alterations in inositol phospholipid metabolism in human platelets. *Biochimica et Biophysica Acta, 927,* 291–302.

DeClerck, F., David, J. L., & Janssen, P. A. J. (1982). Inhibition of 5-hydroxytryptamine-induced and-amplified human platelet aggregation by ketanserin (R41468), a selective 5-HT$_2$ receptor antagonist. *Agents and Actions, 12,* 388–397.

DeClerck, F., Xhonneux, B., Leysen, J. E., & Janssen, P. A. J. (1984). Evidence for functional 5-HT$_2$ receptor sites on human blood platelets. *Biochemical Pharmacology, 33,* 2807–2811.

Denckla, W. D., & Dewey, H. K. (1967). The determination of tryptophan in plasma, liver and urine. *Journal of Laboratory and Clinical Medicine, 69,* 160–169.

Dostal, T. (1972). Antiaggressive effects of lithium salts in mentally retarded adolescents. In A. L. Annell (Ed.), *Depressive states in childhood and adolescents* (pp. 491–498). Stockholm, Almquist & Wiksell.

Elliott, J. M., & Kent, A. (1989). Comparison of [^{125}I] Iodolysergic Acid Diethylamide binding in human frontal cortex and platelet tissue. *Journal of Neurochemistry, 53,* 191–196.

Farrington, D. P. (1990). Childhood aggression and adult violence: Early precursors and later-life outcomes. In D. J. Pepler & K. H. Rubin (Eds.), *The development of childhood aggression.* Hillsdale, NJ: Lawrence Erlbaum Associates.

Fishbein, D., Lozovsky, D., & Jaffee, J. H. (1989). Impulsivity, aggression and neuroendocrine responses to serotonergic stimulation in substance abusers. *Biological Psychiatry, 25,* 5–12.

Fuller, R. W., Snoddy, H. D., & Cohen, M. L. (1984). Interaction of trazodone with serotonin neurons and receptors. *Neuropharmacology, 23,* 539–544.

Garattini, S., Jori, A., Buczko, W., & Sunanin, R. (1975). The mechanism of action of fenfluramine. *Postgraduate Medical Journal, 51*(Suppl. 1), 27–35.

Geaney, D. P., Schachter, M., Elliott, J. M., & Grahame-Smith, D. G. (1984). Characterization of [^{3}H]-lysergic acid diethylamide binding to a 5-hydroxytryptamine receptor on human platelet membranes. *European Journal of Pharmacology, 97,* 87–93.

Gedye, A. (1991). Trazodone reduced aggressive and self-injurious movements in a mentally handicapped male patient with autism. *Journal of Clinical Psychopharmacology, 11,* 275–276.

Ghaziuddin N., & Alessi, N. E. (1992). An open clinical trial of trazodone in aggressive children. *Journal of Child and Adolescent Psychopharmacology, 2,* 291–297.

Gordon, M. (1986). Microprocessor-based assessment of Attention Deficit Disorders (ADD). *Psychopharmacology Bulletin, 22,* 288–290.

Greenberg, A. S., & Coleman, M. (1976). Depressed 5-hydroxyindole levels associated with hyperactive and aggressive behavior. *Archives of General Psychiatry, 46,* 237–241.

Halperin, J. M., Sharma V., Siever L. J., Schwartz S. T., Matier K., Wornell G., & Newcorn J. H. (1994). Serotonergic function in aggressive and nonaggressive boys with attention deficit hyperactivity disorder. *American Journal of Psychiatry, 151,* 243–248.

Huesmann, L. R., Eron, L. D., Lefkowitz, M. M., & Walder, L. O. (1984). Stability of aggression over time and generations. *Developmental Psychology, 20,* 1120–1134.

Kafantatris, V., Campbell, M., Padron-Gayol, M. V., Small, A. M., Locascio, J. J., & Rosenberg, C. R. (1992). Carbamazepine in hospitalized aggressive conduct disorder children: An open pilot study. *Psychopharmacology Bulletin, 28,* 193–199.

Kagan, J. (1964). Reflection-impulsivity: The generality and dynamics of conceptual tempo. *Journal of Abnormal Psychology, 71,* 17–24.

Kazdin, A. E., & Esveldt-Dawson, E. (1986). The Interview for Antisocial Behavior: Psychometric characteristics and concurrent validity with child psychiatric inpatients. *Journal of Psychopathology, 8,* 289–303.

King, R. A., Riddle, M. A., Chappell, P. B., Hardin, M. T., Anderson, G. M., Lombroso, P., & Scahill, L. (1991). Emergence of self-destructive phenomena in children and adolescents during fluoxetine treatment. *Journal of the American Academy of Child and Adolescent Psychiatry, 30,* 179–186.

Klein, R. (1991). Preliminary results: Lithium effects in conduct disorders. *Proceedings Summary, 144th Annual Meeting of the American Psychiatric Association* (pp. 119–120). New Orleans, LA.

Klorman, R., Brumaghim, J. T., Salzman, L. F., Strauss, J., Borgstedt, A. D., McBride, M. C., & Loeb, S. (1988). Effects of methylphenidate on attention deficit hyperactivity disorders with and without aggressive/noncompliant features. *Journal of Abnormal Psychology, 97,* 413–422.

Knott, P., Haroutunian, V., Bierer, L., Perl, D., Handler, M., de Leon, M., Yang, R-K, & David, K. (1989). Correlations post-mortem between ventricular CSF and cortical tissue concentrations of MHPG, 5-HIAA and HVA in Alzheimer's disease. *Biological Psychiatry, 25*(Suppl. 7A), 112A.

Kohen, D. (1993). Eltoprazine for aggression in mental handicap. *Lancet, 341,* 628–629.

Kruesi, M. J. P. (1989). Cruelty to animals and CSF 5-HIAA. *Psychiatry Research, 28,* 115–116.

Kruesi, M. J. P., Hibbs, E. D., Kahn, T. P. Keysor, C. S., Hamburger, S. D., Bartko, J., & Rapoport, J. L. (1992). A 2 year prospective follow-up study of children and adolescents with disruptive behavior disorders: Prediction by cerebrospinal fluid 5-hydroxyindoleacetic acid, homovanillic acid, and automonic measures. *Archives of General Psychiatry, 49,* 429–435.

Kruesi, M. J. P., Linnoila, M., Rapoport, J. L., Brown, G. L., & Petersen, R. (1985). Carbohydrate craving, conduct disorder and low CSF 5-HIAA. *Psychiatry Research, 16,* 83–86.

Kruesi, M. J. P., Rapoport, J. L., Hamburger, S. D., Hibbs, E. D., Potter, W. Z., Lenane, M., & Brown, G. L. (1990). CSF monoamine metabolites, aggression and impulsivity in disruptive behavior disorder of children and adolescents. *Archives of General Psychiatry, 47,* 419–426.

Kuperman, S., & Stewart, M. A. (1987). Use of propranolol to decrease aggressive outbursts in younger patients. *Psychosomatics, 28,* 315–319.

Lamberts, S. W. J, & MacLeod, R. M. (1978). The interaction of the serotonergic and dopaminergic systems on prolactin secretion in the rat. *Endocrinology, 103,* 287–295.

Langer, S. Z., Galzin, A. M., Poirier, M. F., Loo, H., Sechter, D., & Zarifian, E. (1987). Association of the (^{3}H)-imipramine and (^{3}H)-paroxetine binding with the 5HT transporter in brain and platelets: Relevance to studies in depression. *Journal of Receptor Research, 7,* 499–521.

Leckman J. G., Cohen D. J., Shaywitz B. A., Capurol B. K., Heninger G. R., & Bowers M. B., Jr. (1980). CSF monoamine metabolites in child and adult psychiatric patients: A developmental perspective. *Archives of General Psychiatry, 37,* 677–681.

Lindroth, P., & Mopper, K. (1979). High performance liquid chromatographic determination of picomole amounts of amino acids by precolumn fluorescence derivatization with o-phthaldialdehyde. *Analytical Chemistry, 51,* 1667–1674.

Loney, J. (1987). Hyperactivity and aggression in the diagnosis of attention deficit disorder. In B. B. Lahey & A. E. Kazdin (Eds.), *Advances in Child Psychology* (Vol. 10, pp. 99–135). New York: Plenum.

Maj, J., Palider, W., & Rawlow, A. (1979). Trazodone, a central serotonin antagonist and agonist. *Journal of Neural Transmission, 44*, 237–248.

Mann J. J., McBride, P. A., Anderson, G. M., & Mieczkowski, T. A. (1992). Platelet and whole blood serotonin content in depressed inpatients: Correlations with acute and life-time psychopathology. *Biological Psychiatry, 32*, 243–257.

Marcusson, J. O., Baeckstroem, I., & Ross, S. B. (1986). Single-site model of the neuronal 5-hydroxytryptamine uptake and imipramine binding site. *Molecular Pharmacology, 30*, 121–128.

Markowitz, P. (1992). Effect of fluoxetine on self-injurious behavior in the developmentally disabled: A preliminary study. *Journal of Clinical Psychopharmacology, 12*, 27–31.

Marrazziti, D., & Conti, L. (1991). Aggression, hyperactivity and platelet imipramine binding. *Acta Psychiatrica Scandinavica, 84*, 209–211.

Marrazziti, D., Placidi, G. F., Cassano, G. B., & Akiskal, S. H. (1989). Lack of specificity of reduced platelet imipramine binding in different psychiatric conditions. *Psychiatry Research, 30*, 21–29.

Marrazziti, D., Rotondo, A., Presta, S., Pancioli-Guadagnucci, M. L., Palego, L., & Conti, L. (1993). Role of serotonin in human aggressive behavior. *Aggressive Behavior, 19*, 347–353.

McBride, F. A., Anderson, G. M., Hertzig, M. E., Sweeney, J. A., Kream, J., Cohen, D. J., & Mann, J. J. (1989). Serotonergic responsivity in male young adults with autistic disorder. *Archives of General Psychiatry, 46*, 213–221.

McBride P. A., Brown R. P., DeMeo M., Keilp J., Mieczkowski T. A., & Mann J. J. (1994). The relationship of platelet 5-HT$_2$ receptor indices to major depressive disorder, personality traits, and suicidal behavior. *Biological Psychiatry, 35*, 295–308.

Modai, I., Apter, A., Meltzer, M., Tyano, S., Walevski, A., & Jerushalmy, Z. (1989). Serotonin uptake by platelets of suicidal and agressive adolescent psychiatric inpatients. *Neuropsychobiology, 21*, 9–13.

Moffitt, T. E. (1990). Juvenile delinquency and attention deficit disorder: Developmental trajectories from age 3 to 15. *Child Development, 61*, 893–910.

Moret, C., & Briley M. S. (1991). Platelet ^{3}H-paroxetine binding to the serotonin transporter is insensitive to changes in central serotonergic innervation in the rat. *Psychiatry Research, 38*, 97–104.

Moss, H. B., Yao, J. K., & Panzak, G. L. (1990). Serotonergic responsivity and behavioral dimensions in antisocial personality disorder. *Biological Psychiatry, 28*, 325–338.

Nishio, H., Nagakura, Y., & Segawa, T. (1989). Interaction of carteolol and other beta-adrenoreceptor blocking agents with serotonin receptor subtypes. *Archives Internationales de Pharmacodynamie et de Therapie, 302*, 96–106.

O'Keane, V., Moloney, E., O'Neill, H., O'Connor, A., Smith, C., & Dinan, T. G. (1992). Blunted prolactin responses to d-fenfluramine in sociopathy: Evidence for subsensitivity of central serotonergic function. *British Journal of Psychiatry, 160*, 643–646.

Olweus, D. (1979). The stability of aggressive reaction patterns in human males: A review. *Psychological Bulletin, 85*, 852–875.

Pandey, G. N., Pandy, S. C., Janicak, P. G., Marks, R. C., & Davis, J. M. (1990). Platelet serotonin-2 receptor binding sites in depression and suicide. *Biological Psychiatry, 28*, 215–222.

Peroutka, S. (1985). Selective interaction of novel anxiolytics with 5-hydroxytryptamine-1A receptors. *Biological Psychiatry, 20*, 971–979.

Perry, B. D., Cook, E. H., Jr., Leventhal, B. L., Wainwright, M. S., & Freedman, D. X. (1991). Platelet 5-HT2 serotonin receptor binding sites in autistic children and their first-degree relatives. *Biological Psychiatry, 30*, 121–130.

Peters, J. R., & Grahame-Smith, D. G. (1980). Human platelet 5HT$_2$ receptors: Characterization and functional associations. *European Journal of Pharmacology, 68*, 243–256.

Pierson, M., Lyon, R., Titeler, M., Kowalski, P., & Glennon, R. (1989) Design and synthesis of propranolol analogues as serotonergic agents. *Journal of Medicinal Chemistry, 32*, 859–868.

Platt, J. E., Campbell, M., Green, W. H., & Grega, D. M. (1984). Cognitive effects of lithium carbonate and haloperidol in treatment resistant aggressive children. *Archives of General Psychiatry, 41*, 657–662.

Pletscher, A. (1988). Platelets as models: Uses and limitations. *Experientia, 44,* 152–155.

Pliszka, S. R., Rogeness, G. A., Renner, P., Sherman, J., & Broussard, T. (1988). Plasma neurochemistry in juvenile offenders: *Journal of the American Academy of Child and Adolescent Psychiatry, 27,* 588–594.

Preziosi, P. (1983). Serotonin control of prolactin release. *Trends in Pharmacological Science, 4,* 171–174.

Pulkkinen, L., & Pitkanen, T. (1993). Continuities in aggressive behavior from childhood to adulthood. *Aggressive Behavior, 19,* 249–263.

Quiason, N., Ward, D., & Kitchen, T. (1991). Buspirone for aggression *Journal of Clinical Psychiatry, 30,* 1026.

Raisman, R., Sechter, D., Briley, M. S., Zarifian, E., & Langer, S. Z. (1981). High-affinity ^{3}H-imipramine binding in platelets from untreated and treated patients compared to healthy volunteers. *Psychopharmocology, 75,* 368–371.

Raleigh, M. J., McGuire, M. T., Brammer, G. L., & Yuwiler, A. (1984). Social and environmental influences on blood serotonin concentrations in monkeys. *Archives of General Psychiatry, 41,* 405–410.

Rasmussen, D. L., Olivier, R., Raghoebar, M., & Mos, J. (1990). Possible clinical applications of serenics and some implications of their preclinical profile for their clinical use in psychiatric disorders. *Drug Metabolism and Drug Interactions, 6,* 159–186.

Realmuto, G. M., August, G. J., & Garfinkel, B. D. (1989). Clinical effect of buspirone in autistic children. *Journal of Clinical Psychopharmacology, 9,* 122–125.

Ritvo, E. R., Freeman, B. J., Geller, E., & Yuwiler, A. (1983). Effects of fenfluramine on fourteen outpatients with the syndrome of autism. *Journal of the American Academy of Child Psychiatry, 22,* 549–558.

Rovescalli, A. C., Brunello, N., Riva, M., Galimberti, R., & Racagni, G. (1989). Effect of different photoperiod exposure on [^{3}H]imipramine binding and serotonin uptake in the rat brain. *Journal of Neurochemistry, 52,* 507–514.

Salomon, R. M., Mazure, C. M., Delgado, P. L., Mendia, P., & Charney, D. S. (1994). Serotonin function in aggression: The effect of acute plasma tryptophan depletion in aggressive patients. *Biological Psychiatry, 35,* 570–572.

Sano, M., Stanley, M., Lawton, A., Cote, L., Williams, J., Stern, Y., Marder, K., & Mayeux, R. (1991). Tritiated imipramine binding: A peripheral marker for serotonin in Parkinson's Disease. *Archives of Neurology, 48,* 1052–1054.

Sarrias, M. J., Cabre, P., Martinez, E., & Artigas, F. (1990). Relationship between serotoninergic measures in blood and cerebrospinal fluid simultaneously obtained in humans. *Journal of Neurochemistry, 54,* 783–786.

Shaywitz, B. A., Cohen, D. J., Leckman, J. F., Young, J. G., & Bowers, M. B., Jr. (1980). Ontogeny of dopamine and serotonin metabolites in the cerebrospinal fluid: Epilepsy and neurological disorders of childhood. *Developmental Medicine and Child Neurology, 22,* 749–754.

Smith, S. E., Pihl, R. O., Young, S. N., & Ervin, F. R. (1986). Elevation and reduction of plasma tryptophan and their effect on aggression and perceptual sensitivity in normal males. *Aggressive Behavior, 12,* 393–407.

Soubrie, P. (1986). Reconciling the role of central serotonin neurons in human and animal behavior. *Behavioral and Brain Sciences, 9,* 319–364.

Stahl, S. M. (1985). Platelets as pharmacologic models for the receptors and biochemistry of monoaminergic neurons. In G. L. Longnecker (Ed.), *The Platelets: Physiology and Pharmacology* (pp. 307–319). New York: Academic.

Stanislav, S. W., Fabre, T., Crismon, M. L., & Childs, A. (1994). Buspirone's efficacy in organic-induced aggression. *Journal of Clinical Psychopharmacology, 14,* 126–130.

Stanley, M., Traskman-Bendz, L., & Dorovini-Zis, K. (1985). Correlations between aminergic metabolites simultaneously obtained from human CSF and Brain. *Life Sciences, 37,* 1279–1286.

Stoff, D. M., Pollack, L., Vitiello, B., Behar, D., & Bridger, W. H. (1987). Reduction of [³H]-imipramine binding sites on platelets of conduct-disordered children. *Neuropsychopharmacology, 1*, 55–62.

Stoff, D. M., Goldman, W., Bridger, W. H., Jain, A. K., & Pylypiw, A. (1990). No correlation between platelet imipramine binding and CSF 5-HIAA in neurosurgical patients. *Psychiatry Research, 33*, 323–326.

Stoff, D. M., Ieni, J., Friedman, E., Bridger, W. H., Pollock, L., & Vitiello, B. (1991). Platelet ³H-imipramine binding, serotonin uptake, and plasma alpha₁ acid glycoprotein in disruptive behavior disorders. *Biological Psychiatry, 29*, 494–498.

Stoff, D. M., Pasatiempo, A. P., Yeung, J., Bridger, W. H., & Rabinovich, H. (1992). Test-retest reliability of the prolactin and cortisol response to D., L-fenfluramine challenge in disruptive behavior disorders. *Psychiatry Research, 42*, 65–72.

Stoff, D. M., Pasatiempo, A. P., Yeung, J., Cooper, T. B., Bridger, W. H., & Rabinovich, H. (1992). Neuroendocrine responses to challenge with dl-fenfluramine and aggression in disruptive behavior disorders of children and adolescence. *Psychiatry Research, 43*, 263–276.

Tiihonen, J., Hakola, P., Paanila, J., & Turtiainen, M. (1993). Eltoprazine for aggression in schizophrenia and mental retardation. *Lancet, 341*, 307.

Traskman-Bendz, L., Asberg, M., Bertilsson, L., & Thoren, P. (1984). CSF monoamine metabolites of depressed patients during illness and after recovery. *Acta Psychiatrica Scandinavica, 69*, 333–342.

Twist, E. C., Mitchell, S., Brazell, C., Stahl, S. M., & Campbell, I. C. (1990). 5-HT₂ receptor changes in rat cortex and platelets following chronic ritanserin and clorgyline administration. *Biochemical Pharmacology, 39*, 161–166.

Verhoeven, W. M., Tuinier, S., Sijben, N. A., van der Berg, Y. H., de Witte van der Schoot, E. P., Pepplinkhuizen, L., & van Nieuwenhuizen, O. (1992). Eltoprazine in mentally retarded self-injurious patients. *Lancet, 340*, 1037–1038.

Virkkunen, M., & Narvanen, S. (1987). Plasma insulin, tryptophan and serotonin levels during the glucose tolerance test among habitually violent and impulsive offenders. *Neuropsychobiology, 17*, 19–23.

Wagner, A., Aberg-Wistedt, A., Asberg, M., Bertilsson, L., Martensson, B., & Montero, D. (1987). Effects of antidepressant treatment on platelet tritiated imipramine binding in major affective disorder. *Archives of General Psychiatry, 44*, 870–877.

Wester, P., Gottfries, J., & Winblad, B. (1987). Simultaneous liquid chromatographic determination of seventeen of the major monoamine neurotransmitters, precursors and metabolites. II. Assessment of human brain and cerebrospinal fluid concentrations. *Journal of Chromatography, 415*, 275–288.

White, S. M., Kucharik, R. F., & Moyer, J. A. (1991). Effects of serotonergic agents on isolation-induced aggression. *Pharmacology, Biochemistry, and Behavior, 39*, 729–736.

Yan, Q. S., Mishra, P. K., Burger, R. L., Bettendorf, A. F., Jobe, P. C., & Dailey, J. W. (1992). Evidence that carbamazepine and antiepilepsirine may produce a component of their anticonvulsant effects by activating serotonergic neurons in genetically epilepsy-prone rats. *Journal of Pharmacology and Experimental Therapeutics, 261*, 652–659.

Young, W. F., Laws, E. R., Jr., Sharbrough, F. W., & Weinshilboum, R. M. (1986). Human monoamine oxidase: Lack of brain and platelet correlation. *Archives of General Psychiatry, 43*, 604–609.

Yuwiler, A., Plotkin, S., Geller, E., & Ritvo, E. R. (1970). A rapid accurate procedure for the determination of serotonin in whole human blood. *Biochemical Medicine, 3*, 521–531.

Zubieta, J. K., & Alessi, N. E. (1992). Acute and chronic administration of trazodone in the treatment of disruptive disorders in children. *Journal of Clinical Psychopharmacology, 12*, 346–351.

7

METHODOLOGIC ISSUES IN THE USE OF HEART RATE AND HEART-RATE VARIABILITY IN THE STUDY OF DISRUPTIVE BEHAVIOR DISORDERS

Enrico Mezzacappa
Daniel Kindlon
Felton Earls
The Judge Baker Children's Center, Boston, MA

Individual differences in autonomic regulatory functions and their relationships to cognition, emotions, and behavior have long interested researchers in psychophysiology. Heart rate (HR) and HR variability have received considerable attention for their utility as noninvasive indices of autonomic nervous system (ANS) regulatory activity (Boomsma & Plomin, 1986; Fox & Porges, 1985; Hare, 1982; Izard et al., 1991; Kagan, Reznick, & Snidman, 1988; Matthews, Woodall, & Stoney, 1990; Raine, Venables, & Williams, 1990a, 1990b; van der Molen, Somsen, Jennings, Nieuwboer, & Orlebeke, 1987; Wadsworth, 1976).

As is well known, autonomic regulation of HR is mediated via the parasympathetic and sympathetic nervous systems. The highly localized parasympathetic influences affecting only HR and mediated via the cardiac vagus nerves, have been much easier to study than the more diffuse sympathetic influences that affect HR, cardiac contractility, and peripheral vascular resistance. Therefore, most empirical work and theoretical modeling in psychophysiology with few exceptions, has focused on the relationship of vagal modulation of HR to various psychologic indices.

In this chapter, identification of some of the principle sources of the HR variability, the physiology of the mediating effects of autonomic regulatory influences, the analysis of beat-to-beat HR variability using spectral estimation techniques, and developmental aspects of HR regulation are presented. With this background, selected issues on the relationship of HR regulatory patterns to behavioral inhibition, conduct disorder, delinquency, and sociopathy are then examined. Finally, the potential utility of the HR indices for constructing models of individual differences in the relationship of ANS regulatory activity to behavior, and the use of spectral techniques towards these ends are discussed.

Physiologic Aspects of Autonomic Heart Rate Regulation

Variability in HR can be determined over a wide range of time intervals, from milliseconds to decades (Appel, Berger, Saul, Smith, & Cohen, 1989; Saul, Albrecht, Berger, & Cohen, 1988). For the study of autonomic influences on HR, interest is focused on the changes evident in the beat-to-beat variability of HR (Appel et al., 1989; Saul, 1990).

Autonomic responses to perturbations in cardiovascular dynamics mediated through the parasympathetic and sympathetic nervous systems are active and in balance at all times. The resulting effects include the beat-to-beat modulation of HR, which continuously and imperceptibly responds to the constantly changing demands and inputs brought to bear on the sinus node or pacemaker by the parasympathetic and sympathetic nervous systems. Without these autonomic regulatory influences, the heart would beat monotonically somewhere in the range of 80 to 110 beats per minute (bpm), the intrinsic rate of the pacemaker itself.

Under normal circumstances the perturbations and modulatory responses affecting HR, occur at rates of up to 30 times per minute (.5 Hz; Appel et al., 1989; Saul, 1990); but can reach rates of 60 times per minute (1 Hz). Event rates in infants related to respiratory activity extend higher still, up to 80 times per minute (1.3 Hz), due to their rapid breathing (Fox & Porges, 1985; Izard et al., 1991). Changes in the direction and the magnitude of HR will depend on the source(s) of the perturbations to cardiovascular dynamics, and the balance of the parasympathetic and sympathetic regulatory influences mediating the HR response to those perturbations.

SYMPATHETIC CONTROL OF HEART RATE

Increased efferent sympathetic activity results in cardioacceleration, while decreased activity results in cardiodeceleration. The effects of sympathetic modulation of HR in response to perturbations in circulatory dynamics are delayed in onset, and sustained (Berger, Saul, & Cohen, 1989). The rate at which this system normally responds to perturbations in cardiovascular dynamics through instantaneous changes in HR, is up to .20 Hz (12 times per min), though the impact on the HR variability beyond .15 Hz is small (Akselrod et al., 1981, 1985; Berger et al., 1989; Pomeranz et al., 1985; Saul, Berger, Chen, & Cohen, 1989; Saul et al., 1991). This range is commonly referred to as low frequency HR variability, or low power (see Figs. 7.3 and 7.4 on p. 131).

Sympathetic effects on HR variability are enhanced in the upright position and by exercise. They are more easily identified under these circumstances, or in subjects who have received pharmacologic parasympathetic blockade.

PARASYMPATHETIC CONTROL OF HEART RATE

Increased efferent parasympathetic activity results in cardiodeceleration, whereas decreased activity results in cardioacceleration. Parasympathetic or vagal modulatory influences on HR are nearly immediate in onset and short lived (Berger et al., 1989). The normal frequency response range of this system to perturbations in cardiovascular dynamics is broader than that of the sympathetic system, ranging from 0 Hz to > 1 Hz (> 60 times per min), though the effects on HR variability beyond .5 Hz (except in infants) are small. The preponderance of autonomically mediated changes of instantaneous HR beyond .15 Hz (9 times per min) occur via the cardiac vagus nerves (Akselrod et al., 1981, 1985; Berger et al., 1989; Pomeranz et al., 1985; Saul et al., 1989, 1991). This range is commonly referred to as high frequency HR variability, or high power (see Figs. 7.3 and 7.4).

Parasympathetic influences on HR are enhanced in the supine position and by increasing the depth and frequency of respiration. They are more easily identified under these circumstances, or in subjects who have received pharmacologic sympathetic blockade.

SINUS ARRHYTHMIA, RESPIRATORY TYPE

Respiratory sinus arrythmia (RSA; Figs. 7.3 and 7.4) represents the changes in heart rate resulting from the alternation of inspiration and expiration. This cyclical activity is accompanied by alternating increases and decreases of output through the cardiac sympathetic and vagus nerves. Other influences affecting RSA include mechanical forces impinging on the heart from the changes in intrathoracic pressure which accompany respiration (Saul et al., 1989, 1991; Saul & Cohen, 1994). Because abolition of cardiac parasympathetic input has been shown to dramatically reduce HR variability from RSA at the normal respiratory frequencies (.15 to .3 Hz, or 9 to 20 times per min) (Akselrod et al., 1981, 1985; Fouad, Tarazi, Ferrario, Fighaly, & Alicandri, 1984; Pomeranz et al., 1985; Saul et al., 1989, 1991), the mechanical forces and sympathetic effects are considered to play a minor role in the genesis of RSA over these frequencies. It is for this reason that estimates of RSA are commonly thought to represent, and are referred to as indices of vagal tone. Sympathetic effects become more prominent at lower frequencies (< .15 Hz), and mechanical influences on the HR variability figure more prominently at higher frequencies (> .5 Hz).

CARDIOVASCULAR BARORECEPTOR REFLEXES

These reflexes respond to acute variations in blood pressure (Figs. 7.3 and 7.4). Transient elevations in blood pressure lead to decreased sympathetic and increased parasympathetic outflow to the heart, resulting in decreased HR. Sudden lowering of blood pressure, such as occurs during supine to standing postural changes, results in increased sympathetic and decreased parasympathetic outflow to the heart, and increased HR (Saul et al., 1991). The frequency range over which the HR variability is affected by these reflexes is similar to that for RSA for the parasympathetically mediated HR responses, and less than .20 Hz for the sympathetically mediated contributions to the HR response.

RESPONSE CHARACTERISTICS OF THE SINUS NODE OR PACEMAKER TO AUTONOMIC REGULATORY INPUT

Until recently, studies of HR variability did not take into account the end organ or pacemaker's (sinus node) responses to incoming autonomic regulatory signals. Spectral estimation techniques (discussed shortly) have revealed important information about how the sinus node responds to autonomic regulatory input (Berger et al., 1989; Saul et al., 1989, 1991). These investigators found the response characteristics of the sinus node, in both canines and healthy young adults, to differ for parasympathetic and sympathetic influences. Their findings led the authors to characterize the sinus node as a low-pass filter. That is, one that preferentially allows the passage of lower frequencies, with different upper limits or cutoff frequencies for the parasympathetic (higher cutoff) and sympathetic (lower cutoff) inputs. Furthermore, it was observed that the magnitude of the sinus node response was dependent on the mean levels of neural input or tone. For both parasympathetic and sympathetic input, the greatest effects on the HR variability were observed at lower mean levels of input tone.

Therefore, the actual measured HR response to various perturbations is reflective of the sinus node response characteristics, as much as it is an index of autonomic regulatory influences impinging on the sinus node. This finding raises questions about the advisability of utilizing HR indices obtained noninvasively to estimate autonomic input tone, as is commonly done in the case of parasympathetic (vagal) control of HR (Mezzacappa, Kindlon, Saul, & Earls, 1994).

Spectral Analysis of Heart Rate Variability

Before proceeding to a description of spectral estimation techniques, the reader is directed to Fig. 7.1. The four diagrams each represent hypothetical time-series information. They are quite distinct from each other when the information is presented in this way. However, if each diagram is summarized by descriptive statistics they are no longer distinguishable, since they share the same means and standard deviations. Distinctions such as this have led some investigators to adopt frequency domain analyses such as those described shortly, to examine time-series information.

The time related changes in HR associated with the repetition of the cardiac cycle constitute the HR variability signal. The components of this signal are derived from both periodic and aperiodic influences on HR, which together contribute to the total HR variability. The HR variability mediated by the regulatory influences of the parasympathetic and sympathetic nervous systems are to a large extent periodic (Appel et al., 1989; Rompelman, 1986; Saul, 1990).

Spectral analysis of this sequential cardiac activity represents the adaptation of signal analysis to the study of beat-to-beat changes in HR over time (Rompelman, 1985). Spectral estimation techniques applied to time-series data involve mathematical operations known as Fourier transformations (Brigham, 1974). This transformation of time-series information can be likened to the effects of a prism on white light, separating the whole light signal into its component frequencies or colors. Each frequency dependent component or color contributes to the power or variance in the signal (Fig. 7.2).

The spectral analysis of a time-series signal results in a power spectrum that portrays the variance in signal power accounted for by each component of the signal as a function of its respective frequency of change. The area under the entire spectrum is the total variance or power in the signal (Cook & Miller, 1992). The units of power are beats per minute $(bpm)^2/Hz$ (Figs. 7.3 and 7.4). Thus, the power spectrum portrays in the frequency domain an estimate of both the total variance in the signal, as well as the distribution of that variance over the frequency range of the signal. These frequency-dependent characteristics, not previously identified by techniques that limited the study of HR to the time domain, in the case of the HR variability have been associated with particular sources of the HR variability and corresponding regulatory responses mediated by the parasympathetic and sympathetic nervous systems, as noted earlier (van Dellen, Aasman, Mulder, & Mulder, 1985).

In instances where sources of the HR variability can be quantified and portrayed in a concomitant time-series, such as for changes in lung volume or blood pressure over time, transfer functions portraying the frequency-dependent distribution of the magnitude of the HR responses to the corresponding measured changes in lung volume and blood pressure can be calculated. Transfer functions also provide estimates of the timing (phase) of the HR responses to the changes in the sources of the HR variability (Berger et al., 1989; Saul et al., 1989, 1991).

Time-series analyses, whether they are conducted in the time domain or the frequency domain are based on the assumption of "stationarity" of the data. This assumption requires that the mean, variance, and autocovariance of the

Power is analogous in signal analysis to variance and is represented by the area under the power spectrum. The units of power are beats per minute $(bpm)^2/Hz$. Low power is defined as the variance between .02 and .15 Hertz (Hz) and high power is defined as the variance between .15 and .5 Hz. These two frequency bands together account for the preponderance of the HR variability mediated by the autonomic nervous system. Below .02 Hz, HR variability is affected primarily by processes related to thermoregulation and metabolic demands. Above .5 Hz, mechanical forces related to changes in intrathoracic pressure figure prominently in the HR variability.

Low power represents a mixture of parasympathetic and sympathetically mediated HR variability due primarily to blood pressure regulation (sympathetic). Sympathetic influences predominate in this band when subjects are upright, thereby calling into play the baroreceptor reflexes, particularly if breathing is controlled so that it exceeds 12 breaths per minute (.2 Hz). High power is the HR variability due to higher frequency respiratory activity, mediated through the parasympathetic nervous system. This variable is relatively free of other influences when subjects are supine and breathing at 12 breaths per minute or more.

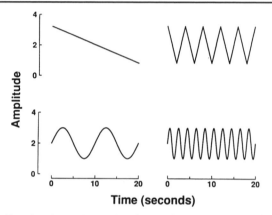

FIG. 7.1. Four imaginary time series sharing the same means and standard deviations. See the text for an explanation.

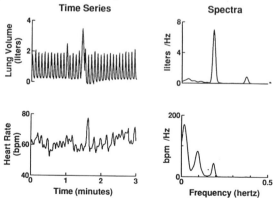

FIG. 7.2. Simultaneous heart rate and respiratory time series and corresponding power spectra. Note the principle peak in the respiratory power spectrum, representing the prevalent breathing frequency, and the corresponding peak in the heart rate power spectrum, representing the HR variability driven by the respiratory changes.

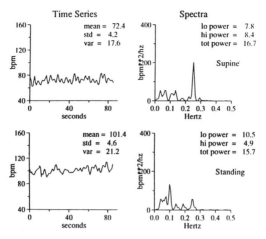

FIG. 7.3. Time-series and corresponding power spectra in a subject breathing rhythmically 15 times per minute (.25 Hz) in the supine and standing positions. Note the spectral peak at .25 Hz, reflecting the HR variability due to respiratory activity, and the peak in the vicinity of .1 Hz, reflecting the HR variability due to the baroreceptor reflexes. Note the shift in the HR variability distribution as the latter reflexes influence both the mean HR and its regulatory pattern following the supine to standing challenge. In this subject there is little difference in the total HR variability between the two positions; only the distribution of the HR variability changes. (Lo power = HR variability below .15 Hz; Hi power = HR variability above .15 Hz; Tot power = Total HR variability.)

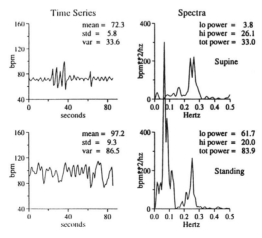

FIG. 7.4. In this subject there are marked differences in the total HR variability due primarily to a large increase in low frequency HR variability in the vicinity of .1 Hz, related to the baroreceptor reflex.

131

time-series are unchanging over time. Physiologic time-series data usually violate the requirements of stationarity. Nonstationarities in the time series, such as linear trends, introduce effects on spectral estimates that must be considered in their interpretation (Gottman, 1990; Porges & Bohrer, 1990).

Strategies to reduce the impact of nonstationarities on spectral estimates can be both statistical and physiological. It is best to first establish physiologic stationarity, to the extent that this is possible, by specifying and maintaining the conditions associated with data collection. For instance, estimates of parasympathetically mediated respiratory effects on HR are improved by having subjects breathe rhythmically while in the supine position at predetermined frequencies greater than those associated with sympathetically mediated HR variability (i.e., > .2 Hz). This will impose and maintain the regularity and periodicity of the respiratory activity on that component of the HR variability. The supine position also minimizes the effects of low frequency influences on HR variability associated with blood pressure regulation. In a similar fashion, rhythmic breathing patterns at frequencies at or above .2 Hz (12 times per min.) will minimize the possibility that unpredictable variations in respiratory induced HR variability will be introduced into the low frequency HR variability when subjects are standing upright, and blood pressure effects on the HR variability are being studied.

Following the collection of data, several strategies may be employed to improve the stationary qualities of the time-series data:

1. Epochs of data that are adequately stationary can be selected from the time series for spectral analysis, and then subsequently combined, provided the segments are taken from data obtained under the same physiologic conditions. Recently, a test for nonstationarity of time-series data has been developed and tested by Weber, Molenaar, and van der Molen (1992). This method essentially "searches" the time series information for the longest stationary segments identifiable, extracting only those segments, prior to submission for power spectral analysis.

2. The time-series data can be mathematically modeled into components, separating nonstationary components such as aperiodic linear trends from more stationary ones (Gottman, 1990). An example of this strategy is found in the method of Porges (Porges & Bohrer, 1990), which essentially generates a new, filtered time series, presumed devoid of undesired elements contributing to the HR variability.

The process of assessing HR responses to challenges presents a particularly thorny problem, given the requirement of stationarity. In such instances, it is advisable to carefully maintain the pre- and postconditions around the challenge influencing the physiology, and to adopt the strategy of using stationary epochs of data immediately preceding and following the challenge.

Developmental Changes in Heart Rate
and HR Variability

Efforts to study developmental changes in HR and HR variability include a diversity of samples, measurement, and analytic strategies, rendering the comparison and generalization of findings difficult. Longitudinal designs emphasize such aspects as temporal stability of mean heart rate and total HR variability. Other designs have utilized cross-sectional assessment of subjects spanning different age ranges. Some studies have limited analytic strategies to descriptive statistics; others have also examined the distribution of heart rate variability and its developmental changes using spectral techniques.

Several points seem to emerge from the integration of the findings in these methodologically diverse studies of the developmental changes in HR and HR variability. There is evidence suggesting that the autonomic regulation of HR is changing both quantitatively and qualitatively over the entire life span (Finley, Nugent, & Hellebrand, 1987; Shannon, Carley, & Benson, 1987). Maturation of parasympathetic and sympathetic influences does not necessarily proceed at the same rate, and there can be marked differences in the rate at which these regulatory influences mature among individuals of similar ages (Finley et al., 1987; Shannon et al., 1987). Large differences in mean HR and HR variability are expectable within groups of subjects of similar age, especially in younger subjects (Attuel et al., 1986; Davignon et al., 1980; Finley et al., 1987; Shannon et al., 1987).

Heart Rate Patterns and Models of Autonomic
Regulatory Functions

A range of cognitive, emotional, and behavioral correlates has been reported in relation to differences across samples in mean HR and HR variability. These findings have engendered theories of differences in central autonomic regulation of HR among groups originally distinguished by their behavioral characteristics. For instance, Kagan and colleagues (Kagan, Reznick, Clarke, Snidman, & Garcia-Coll, 1984; Kagan et al., 1987, 1988; Reznick et al., 1986) studying children from 21 months to 7.5 years-of-age, explored the relationship of a number of physiologic indices believed to be under sympathetic control, including heart period and heart period variability, and compared them to a measure of behavioral inhibition to unfamiliar situations. When comparing extreme groups taken from a behavioral continuum, they found that children with high, stable heart rates under both baseline conditions and during cognitive tasks were more likely to show behavioral manifestations of inhibition to unfamiliar situations, than were those children with lower and more variable heart rates. In addition, spectral estimation techniques were used in these studies to assess changes in the distribution of the HR variability during baseline conditions and under the stress of cognitive tasks. Subjects who were classified as inhibited demonstrated not only greater increases in mean HR, but greater shifts in the distribution of the HR variability towards the low frequency contributions, where sympathetic influences predominate. The authors interpreted these findings as reflective of heightened sympathetic reactivity in inhibited subjects when compared to their uninhibited counterparts.

Different patterns of HR regulation have been associated with conduct disorder and juvenile delinquent behavior. Lower mean pulse rate taken during a medical examination at age 11 was found to predict delinquent behavior, particularly that involving interpersonal aggression, in British boys by age 21 (Wadsworth, 1976). Boys with the lowest heart rates, went on to commit the most violent crimes.

Raine et al. (1990a, 1990b) found resting HR in a cross section of inner-city English schoolboys at age 15 predictive of criminal status by age 24. In a more detailed examination of boys who were already antisocial at age 15, Raine and colleagues (Raine, Venables, & Williams, 1994) found that those boys who desisted in their antisocial behaviors by age 24 showed significantly higher mean levels of resting HR than those boys who continued to be antisocial at age 24.

Raine and Jones (1987) obtained significant negative correlations between pulse rate and concurrent teacher ratings of conduct disorder and aggression in a sample of 7- to 15-year-old White, British boys.

Although these studies provide empirical evidence for a relationship between individual differences in HR and behavior, information about the nature of this relationship is lacking. The repeated observation of lower mean HR in samples of conduct disordered and delinquent subjects (Raine, 1988) has led to at least two theories of autonomic regulatory function to explain this HR–behavior relationship. Autonomic underarousal (Raine et al., 1990a, 1990b), generally understood as reduced sympathetic influence, and passive vagal coping, understood as increased parasympathetic influence (vagal tone; Raine & Jones, 1987; Raine & Venables, 1984), have both been advanced as plausible explanations. How one would determine which of these models is operative is not clear, if the information available is limited to mean HR and the total HR variability. One must bear in mind that both the parasympathetic and sympathetic branches of the ANS are continuously and actively responsive under normal circumstances. A response on the part of either, regardless of the direction, will lead to manifest changes in measurable physiologic functions. The HR response to changes in autonomic input will reflect the balance of the quantitative and directional changes of these two systems. The frequency-dependent distribution of the HR variability derived from spectral analytic techniques is sensitive to such quantitative and directional changes, and may prove useful in understanding the HR–disruptive behavior relationship.

A complementary conceptual approach to understanding the HR–behavior relationship has been the temperament model. This approach implies that stable individual differences in the regulatory balance between the two branches of the ANS, either underlie or are related to observed differences in HR and in behavior. Heart rate regulatory patterns have been related to temperamental traits defined along dimensions of approach–withdrawal (McGuire & Turkewitz, 1979), behavioral inhibition–disinhibition (Kagan et al., 1988), or emotionality (Buss & Plomin, 1984). Such work proposes that a relative dominance of para-sympathetic regulatory activity is related to a lack of inhibition or a diminished tendency for withdrawal in novel situations. Or conversely, withdrawal tenden-cies are seen as reflecting greater reactivity associated with sympathetic regu-latory functions.

A temperament model alone cannot fully account for the observed HR–behav-ior relationships. Environmental influences on this relationship are found in twin studies of temperament (Boomsma & Plomin, 1986), cross fostering studies of criminality (Mednick, Gabrielli, & Hutchings, 1983), the relationship of HR to divorce or early separation (Wadsworth, 1976), and social class (Raine & Venables, 1984; Raine & Mednick, 1989). Social class is most problematic in this regard, given its own relationship to antisocial behaviors.

There is research indicating that HR–behavior relationships represent stable individual difference phenomena, but these studies are largely confined to mid and upper income groups (Boomsma & Plomin, 1986; Kagan et al., 1988; Matthews et al., 1990; C. A. Stifter, personal communication, September 28, 1992). Further-more, they do not directly address the HR–disruptive behavior relationship. The demographic homogeneity of these studies is problematic because of data indi-cating that the HR–aggression relationship does not appear to hold in low-socio-economic status (SES) groups (Raine & Mednick, 1989; Raine & Venables, 1984). As noted, the relationship between HR and antisocial behaviors is complicated by the apparent effect of social class on the latter, and by the fact that temporal stability has not yet been demonstrated for HR indices in lower SES populations. In order for a variable to qualify as a measure of temperament, it must yield similar results over time (Goldsmith et al., 1987). Without knowing whether the HR indices themselves are stable in such samples, it is difficult to determine whether there are conditions present to a greater degree in low-SES environments that may affect HR directly (e.g., chronic stress), or whether a stable autonomic regulatory pattern exists within such groups, but the environmental pressures towards antisocial behaviors are so strong that they obscure the expression of the autonomic trait.

A related problem in interpreting HR–behavior relationships is the general absence of a developmental perspective. As Venables (1987) noted in a review of research on autonomic factors in criminal behavior: "It may be that there are entirely different relations between autonomic and behavioral variables at one stage of a child's life and between the same variables at a later stage" (p. 111). For example, the HR–aggression relationship found in juvenile samples does not appear to hold in adult samples of criminals or psychopaths (Raine, 1988). A relevant example is found in the work of Hare (1982). Heart rate obtained under baseline conditions (supine), and the HR response following exposure to an aversive auditory stimulus did not discriminate among healthy, incarcerated males classified according to severity of psychopathy. Sample characteristics that included only incarcerated subjects has been implicated by the author as a probable source for the lack of observed differences. However, it is also not clear whether subgroups within this sample would demonstrate differences in the baseline distribution of the total HR variability, or different shifts in that distribution following the aversive stimulus, even though mean HR and total HR variability were not distinctive.

Furthermore, there are no reported data describing a lower HR–disruptive behavior relationship below the age of 11. It is possible that this relationship may not be stable over the life course, making it important to delineate its developmental course as a step toward understanding the link between physiology and behavior. Or again, it may be that the analytic strategies adopted thusfar may not be sensitive to potential differences, such as changes in the distribution of the HR variability at baseline and following experimental challenges.

Sensitivity to developmental change also involves the investigation of factors that covary with age, given that HR diminishes with increasing age through childhood and on into adolescence (Davignon et al., 1980). Two such factors are body size and pubertal status.

A final point complicating research in this domain is the choice of operational definitions of aggression, conduct disorder, delinquency, criminality, and antisocial behavior (Earls, 1994; Gottfredson & Hirshi, 1990; Wolf, 1987). There are findings that suggest that a subtype of conduct disorder involving early-onset, stable patterns of physical assaultiveness may be the one most related to a presumptive autonomic trait. Studies have shown such children to be qualitatively different from, and at greater risk for persistent criminality and violence than children with later onset of delinquent behavior, or those with unstable patterns of aggressiveness (Moffitt, 1990; Robins, 1966). This may be consistent with Wadsworth's (1976) finding that the lowest heart rate was found in persons who later committed the most violent crimes.

In an attempt to address some of these methodologic considerations, namely those regarding the stability of HR indices (including spectral estimates of the distribution of the HR variability) in samples of children with disruptive behavior disorders, the stability of HR–behavior relationships in such samples, the effects of SES, family adversity, physical maturation, and the matter of defining more homogenous subgroups of children; two studies have recently been completed in our laboratory. The first study was designed to examine the short-term temporal stability, and the validity of a battery of measures of impulsivity in samples of children with and without disruptive behavior disorders (Kindlon, Mezzacappa, & Earls, 1995). The second study examined the developmental stability of the HR–aggression relationship in subjects from a low-SES sample (Kindlon et al., 1995).

In the first study, temporal stability was found for mean HR and high frequency HR variability in both the supine and standing positions, and for the proportion of low frequency HR variability to total HR variability in the standing position, in children ($N = 66$ boys, 5 girls) aged 6–16 years. Subjects all attended therapeutic school programs for children unable to be managed in regular public schools at the time of assessment. Levels of behavioral disturbance from teacher ratings on the Revised Behavior Problem Checklist (Quay & Peterson, 1987) were at least 1 standard deviation above the mean for normal samples on the scales related to conduct disorder, attentional problems, and motor excess.

In the second study, boys ($N = 202$) characterized by stable developmental patterns of frequent fighting showed lower mean resting HR at age 11 than those who were nonaggressive. At age 12, boys with developmental patterns of both persistent and intermediate frequencies of fighting differed from nonaggressive subjects, the absence of aggression being associated with a higher mean HR.

Groups were established on the basis of teacher questionnaire reports. The sample was divided into three categories of physical aggression using three items from the disruptive behavior scale of the Social Behavior Questionnaire: fights with other children; kicks, bites, and hits other children; bullies or intimidates other children. The psychometric properties of the disruptive behavior scale itself, and the derived 3-item scale are reported in Tremblay et al. (1991).

Stable, high fighters (SHF) scored above the 70th percentile on the 3-item aggression scale at a minimum of 4 of 5 time points over 6 years. Intermediate fighters (IF) scored above the 70th percentile at 1, but no more than 3 time points. Stable, low fighters (SLF) never had a score above the 70th percentile. Of note are the observations that greater family adversity, a body mass index, and pubertal status were not found to influence the HR–aggression relationship in this particular sample at this stage in development.

Heart Rate Relationships to Cognitive and Motivational Factors

To this point, the discussion has focused on HR–behavior relationships, with emphasis on disruptive, aggressive and antisocial behaviors. Relationships of HR, with the cognitive and motivational domains have also been explored.

Indices such as the change in the cardiac cycle time or heart period duration, have been used to infer the onset of unobservable cognitive processes, as well as to reflect the effort related to the effects of cognitive demands. The timing, depth, and duration of the cardiac deceleration associated with stimulus perception and evaluation, and the onset and magnitude of the anticipatory cardiac acceleration during preparation and activation of motor responses are relevant examples (Jennings, 1986; van der Molen, Bashore, Halliday, & Callaway, 1991; van der Molen et al., 1987).

The relationship of HR to the motivational domain has been reviewed by Fowles (1980, 1982, 1988) and studied by Fowles (1988). Elaborating on the theory of Jeffrey Gray, Fowles has drawn an association between HR and an appetitive motivational system, the behavioral activation system (BAS), driving approach and active avoidance behaviors, while relating electrodermal activity to an aversive motivational system, the behavioral inhibition system (BIS), driving extinction, and passive avoidance behaviors. However, the focus on mean HR and cardioacceleration solely, as reflective of arousal and motivational salience, may have limited the scope and understanding of the interactions involved in the HR–motivational relationship. It is not clear whether examining both cardio-acceleration and deceleration, related to differing levels of activation of the two autonomic branches, and the corresponding differences in the distribution of the HR variability, would shed light on both appetitive and aversive influences on HR and the HR variability.

Methodologic Considerations and Prospects for Future Research

Autonomic regulation of beat-to-beat HR variability is changing throughout the life span. Under normal circumstances, the HR response is strongly influenced by the parasympathetic and sympathetic nervous systems. Developmental changes in parasympathetic and sympathetic influences do not necessarily proceed in parallel, and in younger subjects especially, different maturational rates in persons of similar age are likely across these two systems. Furthermore, each of the two autonomic branches is characterized by unique influences on HR depending on the nature of the perturbations to cardiovascular dynamics and the response characteristics of the sinus node to their respective inputs.

Therefore, the interpretation of the observations from an output measure such as HR is far from straightforward. The cardiac sympathetic and vagal influences represent final common pathways mediating regulatory influences on HR to a multiplicity of perturbations affecting cardiovascular dynamics. Interpretation must take into account the sources of the perturbations, the balance of the mediating parasympathetic and sympathetic regulatory influences impinging on the sinus node, the response characteristics of the latter to those inputs, and developmental changes affecting the regulatory inputs and the sinus node responses.

It is not correct to assume a priori that an increased or higher mean HR is the result of increased sympathetic regulatory input, or that a decreased or lower mean HR derives only from heightened parasympathetic input. The former can result from reduced parasympathetic input, and the latter from diminished sympathetic influences. Similarly, the degree of HR variability is not to be construed as the sole result of parasympathetic (vagal) regulatory influences. Sympathetic and nonautonomic influences all contribute to the HR variability over more or less characteristic frequency ranges.

The usage of terms such as mean autonomic tone and autonomic arousal may be misleading. In the case of the vagus for instance, RSA, the index commonly used to represent mean vagal tone, actually represents an estimate of the *variability in heart rate* due to respiratory activity that is mediated through *alternating increases and decreases* in parasympathetic (and sympathetic, up to .2 Hz) input to the sinus node. The common understanding of autonomic arousal refers to observable phenomena such as an increased HR, which are presumed to result from heightened sympathetic drive. This restrictive interpretation of the notion of arousal does not include parasympathetic activation, which on its own would result in cardiodeceleration.

The application of spectral techniques to the study of beat-to-beat HR variability has enhanced the knowledge of the complex regulatory patterns governing HR. This particular noninvasive method is a valuable tool for the detection of both qualitative and quantitative differences in the HR variability, which in turn may then be related to differences in autonomic regulatory patterns. Differential effects on components of the HR variability are discernable with this technique, even when the total variability does not change. Spectral techniques are preferable to other noninvasive techniques when it is important to understand in greater detail the relationships between the source(s) of the HR variability, the mediating autonomic regulatory mechanisms, and the distribution of the HR variability. When quantifiable sources of HR variability are studied in conjunction with HR, the calculation of transfer functions may ultimately prove useful in drawing further inferences about central autonomic processing of peripheral signals associated with the HR variability.

In addition to the limitations inherent in using only mean HR and total HR variability to explain differences in autonomic regulatory functions, researchers have also tended to focus on vagal HR effects, because it is comparatively easier to identify and manipulate the parasympathetically mediated influences on HR variability originating from respiratory activity. However, this practice has limited what can be learned about the HR response over the entire physiologic range relevant to autonomic control. By referring to the high- and low-frequency HR variability obtained from spectral techniques, differences or changes in the distribution of the HR variability over these frequency bands as a function of sample characteristics, experimental challenges, developmental maturation, and so on, may provide a more complete understanding of how the autonomic regulatory influences mediate the influences of the sources of the HR variability under different conditions.

The replication of normative, developmental studies on HR regulation, including those involving transfer function analyses, in samples of diverse socioeconomic and ethnic backgrounds, and in different clinical samples, is needed. It will be important to identify homogenous clinical subgroups, and particularly in younger samples, groups with acceptable temporal stability of the HR indices. Furthermore, standardization of the circumstances under which HR data are obtained, including the position of subjects, their cognitive, motoric, and respiratory activity, and the duration of data collection, is necessary for comparability. General guidelines for the collection of heart rate data have been reported by Jennings and colleagues (Jennings et al., 1981). Baseline physiologic conditions should include states of quiet spontaneous and controlled breathing in the supine and erect postures. When possible, time-series data on respiration and blood pressure should also be collected. Using the knowledge of the physiology of HR regulation, challenges can be selected that include the manipulation of any respiratory, positional, motoric, cognitive, emotional or motivational factors considered pertinent to the detection or enhancement of theorized differences in the autonomic regulation of HR among comparison groups.

The integrated study of the HR variability–cognitive–motivational relationships, utilizing careful analysis of cardiac cycle time effects and spectral estimation techniques under different cognitive and motivational demands, is essentially lacking in the realm of the disruptive behavior disorders. Sergeant (in press), and Sergeant and van der Meere (in press), have written of the importance in this area of psychopathology, of investigating and understanding potential differences in information processing and higher level influences on information processing likely to be affected by motivational salience. The utility of HR indices to enhance the understanding of information processing mechanisms and the influence on these of higher level controls, has been described by Jennings and van der Molen and colleagues (Jennings, 1986; van der Molen et al., 1987, 1991).

Although spectral estimations of the HR variability at baseline and following challenges can enhance the understanding of autonomic regulatory mechanisms for the purposes of generating and testing psychophysiologic models, investigators must remain mindful of the limitations and constraints imposed by the requirements of stationarity of physiologic time-series data. It will be important therefore, to make use of experimental and analytic techniques to maintain physiologic stationarity during data collection, and to enhance stationarity of the time-series data prior to the application of spectral estimation techniques.

REFERENCES

Akselrod, S., Gordon, D., Madwed, J. B., Snidman, N. C., Shannon, D. C., & Cohen, R. J. (1985). Hemodynamic regulation: Investigation by spectral analysis. *American Journal of Physiology, 249* (Heart Circulatory Physiology, 18), H867–H875.

Akselrod, S., Gordon, D., Ubel, F. A., Shannon, D. C., Barger, A. C., & Cohen, R. J. (1981). Power spectrum analysis of heart rate fluctuation: A quantitative probe of beat-to-beat cardiovascular control. *Science, 213,* 220–222.

Appel, M. L., Berger, R. D., Saul, J. P., Smith, J. M., & Cohen, R. J. (1989). Beat to beat variability in cardiovascular variables: Noise or music? *Journal of the American College of Cardiology, 14*(5), 1139–1148.

Attuel, P., Leporho, M. A., Ruta, J., Lucet, V., Steinberg, A., Azancot, A., & Coumel, P. (1986). The evolution of the sinus heart rate and variability as a function of age from birth to 16 years. In E. F. Doyle (Ed.), *Pediatric Cardiology: Proceedings of the Second World Congress, 1985.* New York: Springer-Verlag.

Berger, R. D., Saul, J. P., & Cohen, R. J. (1989). Transfer function analysis of autonomic regulation I. Canine atrial response. *American Journal of Physiology, 256* (Heart Circulatory Physiology, 25), H142–H152.

Boomsma, D. I., & Plomin R. (1986) Heart rate and behavior of twins. *Merrill-Palmer Quarterly, 32,* 141–151.

Brigham, E. O. (1974). *The Fast Fourier Transform.* Englewood Cliffs, NJ: Prentice-Hall.

Buss, A. H., & Plomin, R. (1984). *Temperament: Early developing personality traits.* Hillsdale, NJ: Lawrence Earlbaum Associates.

Cook, E. W., & Miller, G. A. (1992). Digital filtering: Background and tutorial for psychophysiologists. *Psychophysiology, 29*(3), 350–367.

Davignon, A., Rautaharju, P., Boisselle, E., Soumis, F., Megalas, M., & Choquette, A. (1980). Normal ECG standards for infants and children. *Pediatric Cardiology, 1,* 123–131.

Dellen, van, H. J., Aasman, J., Mulder, L. J. M., & Mulder, G. (1985). Time domain versus frequency domain measures of heart-rate variability. In J. F. Orlebeke, G. Mulder, & L. J. P. van Doornen (Eds.), *Psychophysiology of Cardiovascular Control. Models, Methods and Data* (pp. 353–374). New York: Plenum.

Earls, F. (1994). Oppositional-defiant and conduct disorders. In M. Rutter, L. Hersov, & E. Taylor (Eds.), *Child and Adolescent Psychiatry* (3rd ed., pp. 308–329). Oxford, England: Blackwell Scientific Publications.

Finley, J. P., Nugent, S. T., & Hellebrand, W. (1987). Heart-rate variability in children. Spectral analysis of developmental changes between 5 and 24 years. *Canadian Journal of Physiology and Pharmacology, 65,* 2048–2052.

Fouad, F. M., Tarazi, R. C., Ferrario, C. M., Fighaly, S., & Alicandri, C. (1984). Assessment of parasympathetic control of heart rate by a noninvasive method. *American Journal of Physiology, 246* (Heart Circulatory Physiology, 15), H838–H842.

Fowles, D. C. (1980). The three arousal model: Implications of Gray's two-factor learning theory for heart rate electrodermal activity, and psychopathy. *Psychophysiology, 17,* 87–104.

Fowles, D. C. (1982). Heart rate as an index of anxiety: Failure of a hypothesis. In J. T. Cacioppo & R. E. Petty (Eds.), *Perspectives in Cardiovascular Physiology* (pp. 93–126). New York: Guilford Press.

Fowles, D. C. (1988). Psychophysiology and psychopathology: A motivational approach. *Psychophysiology, 25,* 373–391.

Fox, N. A., & Porges, S. W. (1985). The Relation between neonatal heart period patterns and developmental outcome. *Child Development, 56,* 28–37.

Goldsmith, H. H., Buss, A. H., Plomin, R., Rothbart, M. K., Thomas, A., Chess, S., Hinde, R. A., & McCall, R. B. (1987). Roundtable: What is temperament? Four approaches. *Child Development, 58,* 505–529.

Gottfredson, M. R., & Hirschi, T. (1990). *A general theory of crime.* Stanford, CA: Stanford University Press.

Gottman, J. (1990). Time-series analysis applied to physiological data. In J. T. Cacioppo & L. G. Tassinary (Eds.), *Principles of Psychophysiology. Physical, Social and Inferential Elements* (pp. 754–774). New York: Cambridge University Press.

Hare, R. D. (1982). Psychopathy and physiological activity during anticipation of an aversive stimulus in a distraction paradigm. *Psychophysiology, 19*(3), 266–271.

Izard, C. E., Porges, S. W., Simons, R. F., Haynes, O. M., Hyde, C., Parisi, M., & Cohen, B. (1991). Infant cardiac activity: Developmental changes and relations with attachment. *Developmental Psychology, 27*(3), 432–439.

Jennings, J. R. (1986). Bodily changes during attending. In M. G. H. Coles, E. Donchin, & S. Porges (Eds.), *Psychophysiology: Systems, Processes and Applications* (pp. 268–289). Amsterdam: Elsevier.

Jennings, J. R., Berg, W. K., Hutcheson, J. S., Obrist, P., Porges, S. W., & Turpin, G. (1981). Publication guidelines for heart rate studies in Man. *Psychophysiology, 18*(3), 226–231.

Kagan, J., Reznick, J. S., Clarke, C., Snidman, N. C., & Garcia-Coll, C. (1984). Behavioral inhibition to the unfamiliar. *Child Development, 55*, 2212–2225.

Kagan, J., Reznick, J. S., & Snidman, N. C. (1987). The physiology and psychology of behavioral inhibition in children. *Child Development, 58*, 1459–1473.

Kagan, J., Reznick, J. S., & Snidman, N. C. (1988). Biological bases of childhood shyness. *Science, 240*, 167–171.

Kindlon, D., Mezzacappa, E., & Earls, F. (1995). Psychometric properties of impulsivity measures: Temporal stability, validity and factor structure. *Journal of Child Psychology and Psychiatry and Allied Disciplines, 36*(4), 645–661.

Kindlon, D., Tremblay, R. E., Mezzacappa, E., Earls, F., Laurent, D., & Benoist, S. (1995). Longitudinal patterns of heart rate and fighting behavior in 9 to 12 year old boys. *Journal of the American Academy of Child and Adolescent Psychiatry, 34*(3), 371–377.

Matthews, K. A., Woodall, K. L., & Stoney, C. M. (1990). Changes in and stability of cardiovascular responses to behavioral stress: Results from a four-year longitudinal study of children. *Child Development, 61*, 1134–1144.

McGuire, I., & Turkewitz, G. (1979) Approach-withdrawal theory and the study of infant development. In M. Bortner (Ed.), *Cognitive Growth and Development* (pp. 57–84). New York: Brunner/Mazel.

Mednick, S. A., Gabrielli, W. F., Jr., & Hutchings, B. (1983). Genetic influences on criminal behavior: Evidence from an adoption cohort. In K. T. van Dusen & S. A. Mednick (Eds.) *Prospective Studies of Crime and Delinquency* (pp. 39–56). Boston: Kluver Nijhoff.

Mezzacappa, E., Kindlon, D., Saul, J. P. & Earls, F. (1994). The utility of spectral analytic techniques in the study of the autonomic regulation of beat-to-beat heart rate variability. *International Journal of Methods in Psychiatric Research, 4*, 29–44.

Moffitt, T. E. (1990) Juvenile delinquency and attention deficit disorder: Boys developmental trajectories from age 3 to age 15. *Child Development, 61*, 893–910.

Molen van der, M. W., Bashore, T. R., Halliday, R., & Callaway, E. (1991). Chronopsychophysiology: Mental chronometry augmented by psychophysiologic time markers. In J. R. Jennings & M. G. H. Coles (Eds.), *Handbook of Cognitive Psychophysiology: Cognitive and Autonomic Nervous System Approaches* (pp. 9–178). Chichester, England: Wiley.

Molen van der, M. W., Somsen, R. J. M., Jennings, J. R., Nieuwboer, R. T., & Orlebeke, J. F. (1987). A psychophysiologic investigation of cognitive-energetic relations in human information processing: A heart rate/additive factors approach. *Acta Psychologica, 66*, 251–289.

Pomeranz, B., Macaulay, R. J. B., Caudill, M. A., Kutz, I., Adam, D., Gordon, D., Kilborn, K. M., Barger, A. C., Shannon, D. C., Cohen, R. J., & Benson, H., (1985). Assessment of autonomic function in humans by heart rate spectral analysis. *American Journal of Physiology, 248* (Heart Circulatory Physiology, 17), H151–H153.

Porges, S. W., & Bohrer, R. E. (1990). The analysis of periodic processes in psychophysiological research. In J. T. Cacioppo & L. G. Tassinary (Eds.), *Principles of Psychophysiology: Physical, Social and Inferential Elements* (pp. 708–753). New York: Cambridge University Press.

Quay, H. C., & Peterson, D. R. (1987) *Manual for the revised behavior problem checklist.* Coral Gables, FL: University of Miami.

Raine, A. (1988). Antisocial behavior and social psychophysiology. In H. L. Wagner (Ed.), *Social Psychophysiology and Emotion: Theory and Clinical Applications* (pp. 231–250). New York: Wiley.

Raine, A., & Jones, F. (1987). Attention, autonomic arousal, and personality in behaviorally disordered children. *Journal of Abnormal Child Psychology, 15*, 583–599.

Raine, A., & Mednick, S. A. (1989) Biosocial longitudinal research into anti-social behavior. *Revue Epidemiologique et Sante Publique, 37*, 515–524.

Raine, A., & Venables, P. H. (1984). Tonic heart rate level, social class, and antisocial behavior in adolescents. *Biological Psychology, 18*, 123–132.

Raine, A., Venables, P. H., & Williams, M. (1990a). Autonomic orienting responses in 15-Year-Old male subjects and criminal behavior at age 24. *American Journal of Psychiatry, 147,* 933–937.

Raine, A., Venables, P. H., & Williams, M. (1990b). Relationships between central and autonomic measures of arousal at age 15 years and criminality at age 24 years. *Archives of General Psychiatry, 47,* 1003–1007.

Raine, A., Venables, P. H., & Williams, M. (1994, February). Autonomic nervous system factors that protect against crime. Paper presented at the *Annual Meeting of the American Association for the Advancement of Science,* San Francisco, CA. 18–23.

Reznick, J. S., Kagan, J., Snidman, N. C., Gersten, M., Baak, K., & Rosenberg, A. (1986). Inhibited and uninhibited children: A follow-up study. *Child Development, 57,* 660–680.

Robins, L. N. (1966). *Deviant children grow up.* Baltimore, MD: Williams & Wilkins.

Rompelman, O. (1985). Spectral analysis of heart rate variability. In J. F. Orlebeke, G. Mulder, & L. J. P. van Doornen (Eds.), *Psychophysiology of Cardiovascular Control. Models, Methods and Data* (pp. 315–331). New York: Plenum.

Rompelman, O. (1986). Tutorial review on processing the cardiac event series: A signal analysis approach. *Automedica, 7,* 191–212.

Saul, J. P. (1990). Beat-to-beat variations of heart rate reflect modulation of cardiac autonomic outflow. *News in Physiologic Science, 5,* 32–37.

Saul, J. P., Albrecht, P., Berger, R. D., & Cohen, R. J. (1988). Analysis of long term heart rate variability: Methods, 1/f scaling and implications. *Proceedings of the Computers in Cardiology Conference* (1987, September), Leuven, Belgium. Washington, DC: IEEE Computer Society Press.

Saul, J. P., Berger, R. D., Albrecht, P., Stein, S. P., Chen, M. H., & Cohen, R. J. (1991). Transfer function analysis of the circulation: Unique insights into cardiovascular regulation. *American Journal of Physiology, 261* (Heart Circulatory Physiology, 30), H1231–H1245.

Saul, J. P., Berger, R. D., Chen, M. H., & Cohen, R. J. (1989). Transfer function analysis of autonomic regulation II. Respiratory sinus arrhythmia. *American Journal of Physiology, 256* (Heart Circulatory Physiology, 25), H153–H161.

Saul, J. P., & Cohen, R. J. (1994). Respiratory sinus arrhythmia. In P. Schwartz & M. Levy (Eds.), *Vagal Control of the Heart* (pp. 511–536). Mount Kisco, NY: Futura.

Sergeant, J. A. (in press). Lower and upper information processing mechanisms in hyperactivity. *Canadian Journal of Psychology.*

Sergeant, J. A., & Meere, van der, J. J. (in press). Towards an empirical child psychopathology. In D. Routh (Ed.), *Disruptive Behavior in Children. Essays in honor of H.C. Quay.* NY: Plenum.

Shannon, D. C., Carley, D. W., & Benson, H. (1987). Aging of modulation of heart rate. *American Journal of Physiology, 253,* H874–H877.

Tremblay, R. E., Loeber, R., Gagnon, C., Charlesbois, P., Larivee, S., & Leblanc, M. (1991). Disruptive boys with stable and unstable high fighting behavior patterns during junior elementary school. *Journal of Abnormal Child Psychology, 19,* 285–300.

Venables, P. H. (1987). Autonomic nervous system factors in criminal behavior. In S. A. Mednick, T. E. Moffitt, & S. A. Stack (Eds.), *The Causes of Crime: New Biological Approaches* (pp. 110–136) Cambridge, England: Cambridge University Press.

Wadsworth, M. E. J. (1976). Delinquency, pulse rates, and early emotional deprivation. *British Journal of Criminology, 16,* 245–256.

Weber, E. J. M., Molenaar, P. C. M., & Molen, van der, M. W. (1992). A nonstationarity test for the spectral analysis of physiologic time series with an application to respiratory sinus arrhythmia. *Psychophysiology, 29,* 55–65.

Wolf, P. (1987) Definitions of antisocial behavior in biosocial research. In S. A. Mednick, T. E. Moffitt, & S. A. Stack (Eds.), *The Causes of Crime: New Biological Approaches* (pp. 65–73). Cambridge, England: Cambridge University Press.

8

AUTONOMIC NERVOUS SYSTEM ACTIVITY AND VIOLENCE

Adrian Raine
University of Southern California

Since the 1940s an extensive body of research has been built up on the psycho-physiological basis of antisocial, delinquent, criminal, psychopathic, and violent behavior. For example, there have been at least 150 studies on electrodermal and cardiovascular activity in such populations. This body of research has received little attention in the broader field of criminology, and is rarely if ever referred to in textbooks of crime. This chapter proposes to bring this body of knowledge to wider attention. For readers who have some familiarity with this area, a second aim is to provide an update on recent findings in this literature, highlight some of the more salient issues, and to provide some directives for future research.

I focus here on autonomic nervous system (ANS) correlates of violent and antisocial behavior, in particular skin conductance (SC) and heart rate (HR). EEG and violence is reviewed elsewhere in this volume (see Convit et al., chap. 9), and a recent review of event-related potentials (ERPs) and antisocial–psychopathic behavior may be found in Raine (1989). Only a very brief overview of ANS measures and what they reflect is provided here; detailed introductions to ANS measures and recording techniques may be found in Stern, Ray, and Davis (1980) and Cacioppo, Tassinary, and Fridlund (1991). These are not the only psychophysiological measures that have been applied to violent and antisocial behavior, however. More extensive knowledge is available on ANS correlates of violent and antisocial behavior and, consequently, such measures form the focus of this chapter.

A brief, general introduction to psychophysiological measures is followed by an introduction to the measurement of skin conductance (SC) activity. Findings from studies on skin conductance activity in offenders conducted since the last main review (Hare, 1978) will be subdivided into five main areas: arousal, orienting, classical conditioning, responsiveness to aversive stimuli, and SC half-recovery time. Findings on heart rate are then reviewed after a brief introduction to this measure, focusing on the finding of lowered resting heart rate in violent and antisocial populations and its theoretical interpretation. The issue of specificity of autonomic findings to violent offending per se is then addressed, together with theoretical implications stemming from SC and HR data. Finally, conceptual and methodological directions for future research in this area are outlined. The key point in this review is that low resting heart rate in noninstitutionalized offenders is: (a) a highly replicated finding that may be relatively specific to violent offending, (b) can be easily and cheaply integrated into research focusing on social variables, and (c) may interact with social variables in the prediction of violence.

INTRODUCTION TO PSYCHOPHYSIOLOGY

Psychophysiological measures have a number of important strengths with respect to violence research. First, psychophysiology is uniquely placed to provide important insights into violent behavior because it rests at the interface between psychology and physiology. As such, there is a greater potential for psychophysiological findings to be integrated with broader concepts such as learning, emotion, arousal, and cognition than for some other biological measures. Second, a relative advantage over other physiological measures such as hormones, neurotransmitters, and brain glucose metabolism is the excellent temporal resolution of psychophysiological measures. That is, measures such as skin conductance and heart rate are sensitive to changes in the environment (e.g., experimental manipulations or presentation of stimuli) occurring over periods of 1 or 2 seconds. In contrast, the measure of brain glucose metabolism in murderers reported elsewhere in this volume (Raine and Buchsbaum, chap. 10, this volume) reflect brain processes occurring over a pooled period of about half an hour. A third and important advantage is that they are relatively noninvasive compared to neurotransmitter assays which require a spinal tap or the withdrawal of blood, and PET and CT, which involve exposure to radiation. Fourth, relative to brain-imaging technology, psychophysiological recordings are relatively cheap, and recent technical advances in both software and hardware promise to make the technology of psychophysiology available on a much wider scale.

Set against these advantages are several potential limitations. One such limitation is that psychophysiological measures are relatively indirect measures of specific brain functioning (i.e., poor spatial resolution). We know relatively little about the neuroanatomical mediators of skin conductance and heart rate, though as seen shortly, recent brain-imaging data has produced new findings on the neuroanatomy and neurophysiology of measures such as skin conductance orienting. A second potential limitation is that psychophysiological measures are more sensitive to changes in the environment, a factor necessitating careful standardization and control of the laboratory environment. Relatedly, we know almost nothing about how the early rearing environment can modify autonomic nervous system activity. For example, are differences in arousal levels in antisocials a reflection of a genetic predisposition, or conversely, are such levels produced by a very stressful early environment? Many of these limitations to psychophysiological measures are also limitations of more advanced functional brain-imaging measures, and, on balance, the benefits to be obtained from psychophysiological measures outweigh their disadvantages.

SKIN CONDUCTANCE (SC)

Introduction to SC Activity

Skin conductance (SC) is usually measured from electrodes placed on two sites of the hand (fingers or palms), and involves the passage of an imperceptible current across the electrodes. Changes in SC activity reflect very small changes in the electrical activity of the skin, with increased sweating leading to an increase in skin conductance activity. Individual differences in the size of a subject's response to an orienting stimulus has been taken to reflect differences in the extent to which a subject allocates attentional resources to the processing of that stimulus. Although peripheral by virtue of the fact that SC is an autonomic nervous system measure, SC is nevertheless a simple but powerful measure of central nervous system (CNS) processing. Extensive experimental research indicates that SCRs represent a very sensitive measure of attention allocation (e.g., Dawson, Schell, & Filion, 1991).

Because the ANS plays an important role in emotional behavior, and because SC is a direct measure of sympathetic ANS activity, SC has also been taken to reflect states such as anxiety and fearfulness. It is important to recognize that no unique, one-to-one relationships exist between psychophysiological measures and specific emotions. Nevertheless, because the sympathetic nervous system is sensitive to stress and emotional arousal, in general terms SC activity can be used to index stress reactivity to aversive or arousing events. In this context, SC is an excellent and direct measure of autonomic arousal.

Findings on SC Activity

Most previous discussions of SC and antisocial behavior have focused specifically on that subgroup of criminals who are psychopathic (Blackburn, 1983; Fowles, 1980, 1993; Hare, 1970, 1978; Siddle, 1977; Siddle & Trasler, 1981; Zahn,

1986), though Venables (1987) provides one exception to this. Because psychopaths tend to be more violent and recidivistic than nonpsychopaths (Hare, 1980), this population is of special relevance in the present context, though it must also be remembered that not all psychopaths are violent. The most comprehensive review of SC activity has been conducted by Hare (1978), and consequently it is worth reiterating the conclusions drawn for research conducted up to this date. Psychopaths are characterized by (a) reduced tonic arousal as measured by SCL (though not nonspecific fluctuations), (b) reduced SCRs to aversive but not neutral tones, (c) reduced SCRs in conditioning and quasi-conditioning paradigms, and (d) longer SC half-recovery times to aversive stimuli. Finding (a) is relatively weak in terms of effect size, however, as it only emerges when data are pooled together across several studies.

SC Arousal. Arousal in 10 studies has been assessed by measurement during an initial "rest" period of either skin conductance levels (SCLs) or nonspecific fluctuations (NSFs). Key findings are outlined in Table 8.1. Four of the 10 studies find significant effects, with 3 of these 4 finding differences for NSFs. Only 1 of the 4 found effects for SCL, although one of these studies found trends for lower SCLs (Raine, Venables, & Williams, 1990a). NSFs may produce stronger support for SC underarousal in antisocials relative to SCLs because the latter are more influenced by factors such as local peripheral conditions of the skin, and the thickness and hydration of the stratum corneum (Venables & Christie, 1973), factors that are unrelated to autonomic arousal. An interesting study by Buikhuisen, Bontekoe,

TABLE 8.1
Key Findings for SC Arousal Measured by SCL
(Skin Conductance Level) and NSF (Nonspecific Fluctuations)

Authors	Subjects	Findings
Significant Findings		
Hinton et al. (1979)	Public offenders	Low NSF
Buikhuisen et al. (1985)	Crimes of evasion	Low NSF, low SCL
Venables (1989)	Conduct disorder (age 18)	Low SCL (age 11) (males and females)
Raine et al. (1990a)	Crime (age 24)	Low NSF (age 15)
Nonsignificant Findings		
Tharp et al. (1980)	Psychopathic gamblers	n.s.d. SCL
Hemming (1981)	Criminals from good homes	n.s.d. NSF
Hare (1982)	Psychopaths	n.s.d. NSF, SCL
Buikhuisen et al. (1985)	General crime	n.s.d. NSF, SCL
Raine & Venables (1988)	Psychopaths	n.s.d. SCL
Schmidt, Solanto, & Bridger (1985)	Conduct disorder	n.s.d. SCL, NSF

Note. n.s.d. = no significant differences.

Plas-Korenhoff, and Buuren (1985) found effects specific to type of crime, that is, underarousal characterizes crimes of evasion (e.g., customs offenses) but not other forms of crime. It could be speculated that being autonomic underaroused is particularly conducive to escaping detection of covert crime. Regarding more violent offenders, the two studies of psychopaths both observed nonsignificant results, although one study of murderers (Hinton, O'Neill, Dishman, & Webster, 1979) observed fewer NSFs in this group (see Table 8.1).

SC Orienting. Key findings from nine studies that have assessed SC orienting in antisocial groups are given in Table 8.2. All studies assess orienting to neutral tone stimuli, with the exception of Damasio, Tranel, and Damasio (1990) who measured responses to socially meaningful stimuli. Five out of 9 studies find evidence for an orienting deficit as indicated by reduced frequency of SCRs to orienting stimuli. Frequency measures of SC orienting appear to produce stronger findings in these studies, perhaps because frequency measures tend to be more reliable than amplitude measures; this in turn may be because amplitude is more affected by non-ANS factors such as the number and size of sweat glands (Venables & Christie, 1973). The most striking finding from Table 8.2, however, is that reduced SC orienting appears to be specific to psychopathic, criminal, and antisocial individuals with schizoid or schizotypal features. But 3 of these 4 findings are from the same laboratory and, consequently, stronger conclusions await confirmatory findings from other researchers. However, Crider (1993) has also argued for a link between antisocial personality and schizotypal personality with respect to reduced frequency of nonspecific skin conductance responses based on additional data from the field of personality research.

TABLE 8.2
Key Findings for SC Orienting to Neutral Stimuli

Authors	Subjects	Finding
Significant Findings		
Blackburn (1979)	Secondary schizoid psychopaths	Reduced frequency
Raine & Venables (1984a)	Conduct disorder with schizoid personality	Reduced frequency
Raine (1987)	Schizotypal criminals	Reduced frequency
Raine et al. (1990a)	Criminals	Reduced frequency
Nonsignificant Findings		
Aniskiewitz (1973)	Psychopaths	n.s.d. (% responding)
Hinton et al. (1979)	Public offenders	n.s.d. (amplitude)
Schmidt et al. (1985)	Conduct disorder	n.s.d. (amplitude)
Raine & Venables (1988)	Psychopaths	n.s.d. (amplitude & frequency)

Note. n.s.d. = no significant differences.

Reduced skin conductance orienting has also been found to be a well-replicated finding in schizophrenic patients (Bernstein et al., 1982; Ohman, 1981). With respect to schizotypal personality, findings are more varied although there is some evidence that the more "negative" aspects of schizotypal personality such as anhedonia are related to reduced SC orienting (Gruzelier & Raine, 1994). The fact that reduced orienting is a feature of both schizophrenia, and perhaps also schizophrenia-spectrum disorders is consistent with the notion that reduced orienting is most frequently found in antisocial groups with schizotypal features. Whether reduced orienting is also observed more specifically in violent offenders with schizotypal personality features is a hypothesis that remains to be tested, because the studies in Table 8.2 have not divided subjects into those with and without violence.

The study by Damasio et al. (1990) is of particular interest in that it measured SC responsivity to "socially significant stimuli" (pictures depicting mutilation, social disasters, or nudity) in five patients who had bilateral lesions to orbital frontal and lower medial frontal cortex with "sociopathic behavior" (defined by severe deficits in social conduct, judgment, and planning following brain damage). Psychopaths with frontal lesions showed reduced SCR amplitudes to the socially meaningful stimuli compared to six control patients with nonfrontal lesions, but showed normal responses to neutral tone stimuli. Although preliminary, these results suggest that frontal dysfunction may underlie both psychopathic behavior and deficits in SC orienting to meaningful social stimuli. Such findings are broadly consistent with recent findings implicating frontal cortex in the mediation of SC orienting responses reported next (Hazlett, Dawson, Buchsbaum, & Neuchterlein, 1993; Raine, Reynolds, & Sheard, 1991). In a broad sense they are also consistent with reports of frontal EEG abnormalities in violent patients (Convit, Czobor, & Volavka, 1991; Convit et al., this volume), and with recent findings from functional brain imaging studies of prefrontal deficits in violent offenders (Goyer et al., 1994; Goyer and Semple, chap. 11, this volume; Raine, 1993; Raine et al., 1994; Raine and Buchsbaum, chap. 10, this volume). This theme is pursued in a later section.

SC Classical Conditioning. The notion that offenders have a deficit in classical conditioning has been a key feature in several theories of crime (Eysenck, 1977; Lykken, 1957; Trasler, 1987). Theoretically, lack of a conditioned fear response would be expected to predispose to lack of conscience development and lack of socialized behavior. The last systematic review of conditionability was reported by Hare (1978). Of the 14 studies reported by Hare covering classical conditioning and quasi-conditioning, 12 indicated that psychopaths, criminals, delinquents, and antisocials showed poorer SC conditioning than control groups. Consequently, this review indicates general support for the notion of poorer conditionability in antisocial groups.

In order to assess whether this general conclusion remains true, findings from conditioning studies conducted since 1978 have been assessed. Six studies since 1978 have reported findings on SC classical conditioning; their key findings are noted in Table 8.3. SC conditioning in these studies is assessed either by SCRs occurring to the conditional stimulus (what has been termed the conditioned "A" response) or by the SCR occurring in between the CS and the unconditional stimulus (the conditioned "B" response). In two of the studies (Hare, 1982; Tharp, Maltzman, Syndulco, & Ziskind, 1980) the paradigm consists of a "count-down" procedure in which the subject awaits the onset of an aversive stimulus whose onset is signaled several seconds beforehand—a paradigm referred to by Hare (1978) as "quasi-conditioning."

All six of these studies showed some evidence indicating significantly poorer SC conditionability in antisocials. Not all of these studies provide unequivocal evidence for poor conditioning however. Hemming (1981) found group differences for conditioned discrimination in extinction, but not for conditioning discrimination during acquisition. Similarly, Raine and Venables (1981) found poor conditioning specifically in antisocial children from higher social class, but not in those from lower social classes. Findings are unusual in that they all observe significant group differences even though there are wide variations in the paradigms used (vicarious conditioning, quasi-conditioning, classical CS–UCS paradigm) and subject populations (uninstitutionalized antisocial children, adult criminals, institutionalized criminal psychopaths, psychopathic gamblers). The fact that all studies showed significant effects in the predicted direction indicates that poor conditioning is related to the general development of antisocial behavior.

Perhaps one of the greatest future challenges in violence research concerns the integration between social and psychophysiological risk factors. Such social-psychophysiological interactions are suggested by at least three SC conditioning studies. Hemming (1981) found poorer SC conditioning specifically in criminals from relatively good social backgrounds. Similarly, Raine and Venables (1981) found poorer SC conditioning in antisocial children from the higher social classes, but not from the lower social classes. The first study to report conditioning deficits

TABLE 8.3
Key Findings From Studies on Classical Conditioning in Antisocials,
Criminals, and Psychopaths as Measured by Skin Conductance

Authors	Subjects	Finding
Significant Findings		
Ziskind, Syndulko, & Malzman (1978)	Psychopathic gamblers	Poor differential conditioning but verbal awareness
Aniskiewitz (1973)	Primary psychopaths	Poor vicarious conditioning
Tharp et al. (1980)	Psychopathic gamblers	Less anticipatory responding
Raine & Venables (1981)	Conduct disorder	Poor conditioning in high social class antisocials
Hemming (1981)	Criminals from good homes	Less conditioned discrimination in extinction
Hare (1982)	Psychopaths	Less anticipatory responding

also excluded psychopaths if they came from a "markedly sociopathic or deviant" family background (Lykken, 1957, p. 111a), and consequently studied a population of psychopaths from relatively good home backgrounds. Such findings suggest that biological predispositional variables may have greater explanatory power in antisocials from relatively benign family backgrounds where the "social push" towards antisocial behavior is relatively lower; if individuals from good homes become antisocial, then it may be more for biological reasons than social reasons (Raine, 1988; Raine & Mednick, 1989).

SCRs to Aversive Stimuli.   Eight analyses providing data on SCR amplitudes to aversive stimuli are shown in Table 8.4. All studies assessed responsivity using auditory stimuli ranging from 90 dB to 120 dB in intensity. Only 2 of the 8 analyses showed evidence for lower responsivity in antisocials. Three studies testing adult psychopaths all failed to find significant group differences. Two of the studies that failed to find effects used stimuli that were unlikely to have been strongly aversive (90 and 95 dB intensity). Nevertheless, Hare (1982) used 120 dB stimuli and failed to find significant effects for adult psychopaths, indicating that stimulus intensity cannot easily account for the failure to find effects. These data are not supportive of the generally accepted view that offenders are less responsive to punishment. Conversely, the classical conditioning data together with data reported in the next section are more supportive of the view that offenders show deficient processing of stimuli associated with aversive consequences.

SC Half-Recovery Time.   SC half-recovery time is the time it takes the SC response to recover or dissipate to half of its original size. As indicated earlier, pre-1978 studies have shown that criminals and psychopaths have longer SC

TABLE 8.4
Key Findings for SCRs to Aversive Stimuli

Authors	Subjects	Findings
	Significant Findings	
Buikhuisen et al. (1985)	Crimes of evasion	Low SCR (120 dB)
Schmidt et al. (1985)	Conduct disorder	Low SCR (90 dB)
	Nonsignificant Findings	
Tharp et al. (1980)	Psychopathic gamblers	n.s.d. (95 dB)
Hare (1982)	Psychopaths	n.s.d. (120 dB)
Raine & Venables (1981)	Conduct disorder	n.s.d. (105 dB)
Buikhuisen et al. (1985)	General crime	n.s.d. (120 dB)
Raine & Venables (1988)	Psychopaths	n.s.d. (90 dB)
Raine (1990)[a]	Psychopaths	n.s.d. (105 dB)

[a]SC measured at age 15 years and related to psychopathic personality also measured at age 15 in those who became criminal by age 24 years. n.s.d. = no significant differences.

recovery times (Hare, 1978; Loeb & Mednick, 1977; Mednick, 1977; Siddle, Mednick, Nichol, & Foggitt, 1976). Findings of the eight studies on SC half-recovery time published since Mednick's review in 1977 are reported in Table 8.5. Seven of the 8 observe statistically significant group differences in the predicted direction. Only one study that assessed adult institutionalized psychopaths (Raine & Venables, 1988) failed to observe this effect. This may be because stimulus intensity was relatively low (90 dB) compared to other studies that tended to use intensities of 100 dB or above, although some studies do obtain significant effects with lower stimulus intensities. Findings are not specific to aversive stimuli, because three studies found effects using intensities (65, 75, and 83 dB) not generally considered to elicit responses which, in psychophysiological terms, are viewed as "defensive." This finding is associated with all types of antisocial and violent behavior (aggressive behavior in children, young antisocial adults, public recidivistic offenders, criminal characterized by low socialization scores) and in institutionalized as well as noninstitutionalized samples.

Several researchers have questioned how half-recovery time can be interpreted (Siddle & Trasler, 1981; Trasler, 1987). Mednick (1975, 1977) has argued that slow SC half-recovery time reflects the rate at which fear dissipates; according to this theory slow fear dissipation would predispose to antisocial behavior because

TABLE 8.5
SC Half-Recovery Time (T2): Key Findings

Authors	Subjects	Findings
Significant Findings		
Hinton et al. (1979)	Public offenders[a]	Long T2 (83 dB)
Levander, Shalling, Lidberg, Bartfai, & Lidberg (1980)	Undersocialized[b] criminals	Long T2 (93 dB)
Hemming (1981)	Criminals from good homes	Long T2 (100 dB)
Buikhuisen et al. (1985)	General crime	Long T2 (120 dB)
	Crimes of evasion	Long T2 (120 dB)
Buikhuisen, Eurelings-Bontekoe, & Host (1989)	Early crime	Long T2 (98 dB)
	Violence against police	Long T2 (98 dB)
Venables (1989)[c]	Fighting at age 9	Long T2 (75 dB) (at age 3)
Raine (1990)[d]	Psychopathic personality	Long T2 (65 dB)
Nonsignificant Findings		
Raine & Venables (1988)	Psychopaths	n.s.d. (75 and 90 dB)

[a]Public offenders were recidivists committing offenses against strangers.

[b]Undersocialization measured by the Socialization scale of the California Personality Inventory.

[c]SC measured at age 3 and related to fighting at age 9 in a normal sample.

[d]SC measured at age 15 and related to psychopathic personality also measured at age 15 in a group who had developed a criminal record by age 24 years.

it results in reduced reinforcement for passive-avoidance learning. Others have suggested that SC half-recovery time measures a dimension of "openness–closed-ness to the environment," whereas long recovery measures closedness or "shut-ting out" of environmental stimuli, and screening out the aversive qualities of punishments (Hare, 1978; Siddle & Trasler, 1981; Venables, 1974, 1987). Despite problems in clearly interpreting the psychological significance of long SC recovery time, the strength of the foregoing empirical data indicate the potential signifi-cance of this measure for violent and antisocial behavior.

HEART RATE AND CRIME

Introduction to Heart Rate (HR)

Resting HR level is probably the easiest psychophysiological measure to record. It can be recorded from cheap portable equipment (under $50), as opposed to a polygraph, without significant loss in quality of data. Furthermore, it is one of the few psychophysiological measures that can be easily recorded without any equipment at all, because an excellent measure of resting HR can be obtained from the pulse. Heart rate reflects both sympathetic and parasympathetic nerv-ous system activity, unlike SC activity which reflects only sympathetic processes. As with SC activity, HR has been commonly used to assess the extent of auto-nomic arousal.

Most studies on antisocial populations in the past 15 years have focused on resting HR rather than phasic HR responses to neutral or aversive stimuli. Consequently, findings for phasic heart rate are not reviewed in detail. Very briefly, Raine, Venables, and Williams (1990b) in a prospective study found that reduced heart rate orienting at age 15 predicted outcome for crime at age 24, findings that confirm similar effects for skin conductance orienting deficits. Hare and Craigen (1974) and Hare, Frazelle, and Cox (1978) showed larger anticipatory HR acceleratory responses to a loud (120 dB) tone in psychopaths, with under-socialized psychopaths also showing reduced SC responses to the aversive tone. Hare (1982) also demonstrated that psychopaths showed greater anticipatory HR acceleration and reduced SC responses to an aversive 120 dB tone. Hare (1978) has interpreted these findings as indicating that psychopaths have a very proficient active coping mechanism that allows them to "tune out" aversive events. Siddle and Trasler (1981) have criticized Hare's position on several methodological and theoretical counts, and Tharp et al. (1980) have failed to replicate the phasic heart rate findings. Because there appears to have been no active research in this area in the past 10 years, these findings, although con-sistent with the general tenor of this review on autonomic factors, should be treated with due caution.

Findings for Resting Heart Rate

There is a major contrast in research findings for resting HR for institutionalized offender populations on the one hand, and uninstitutionalized populations on the other. Reviews by Hare (1970, 1975, 1978) reveal no successes and at least 15 failures to obtain lower resting heart rate in institutionalized, criminal psychopaths. In stark contrast, studies on younger and noninstitutionalized populations reveal very clear effects, showing that antisocial, aggressive, and criminal individuals are characterized by lower resting HR.

Thirteen studies that have assessed resting HR in these younger or noninstitutionalized populations are shown in Table 8.6. These 13 studies report on 17 analyses. Two of these 17 analyses represent re-analyses or extensions of earlier studies. One by Raine et al. (1990a) represents a 9-year follow-up of those tested at age 15 (Raine & Venables, 1984a). The other by Farrington (1987) re-analyzes HR data collected by West and Farrington (1977) and presents new analyses for violent offending. One of the studies (Rogeness, Cepeda, Macedo, Fischer, & Harris, 1990) presents HR data for three independent samples of antisocial behavior, and another (Little, 1978) reports findings for three separate age groups. Altogether, these 13 studies report on 15 independent samples of antisocial subjects.

All 13 studies find significantly lower resting HRL in antisocial groups. No failures to replicate this finding have been found to date. Out of the 15 samples analyzed in these 13 studies, 14 find significant effects; the only failure comes from the study by Little (1978) who observed significant effects in 9- and 11-year-olds, but not in 7-year-olds.

Several features of these studies should be noted. Heart rate is measured in these studies in childhood or adolescence (between the ages of 7 and 15), with the exception being West and Farrington (1977) who measured HR at age 18. Almost all of these samples are uninstitutionalized, with the one exception being Rogeness et al. (1990) who assessed children in a private psychiatric hospital. Eleven of the 13 studies assessed children drawn from the normal population and therefore are not restricted to "unsuccessful," caught criminals which characterized the subject samples of previous studies.

These 13 studies were heterogenous in many aspects. Resting HR level is measured in a wide variety of ways (polygraphs, pulsimeters, stopwatches). A wide number of definitions of antisocial behavior were used, ranging from legal criminality and delinquency to teacher rating of antisocial behavior in school, self-report socialization measures, diagnostic criteria for conduct disorder, and genetically inferred law-breaking. Subjects were assessed in a wide variety of settings (medical interview, study office, school, university psychophysiological laboratory, hospital), and lower HR was found both in males and females and across both sides of the Atlantic. Such heterogeneity attests to the robustness of the observed effects. Importantly, there has been good cross-laboratory replication of this finding.

TABLE 8.6

Studies on Resting Heart Rate Level (HRL) in Nonpsychopathic,
Noninstitutionalized Antisocial Populations

Authors	Subjects	Key Finding	Effect Size
Davies & Maliphant (1971)	13.6-year-old schoolboys	Lower resting HRL in antisocials	1.44
Wadsworth (1976)	11-year-old schoolboys	Lower resting HRL (11 years) related to delinquency measured from ages 8–21 years. Lowest HRL found in nonsexual violent offenders.	0.39
West & Farrington (1977)	18–19-year-old noninstitutionalized males	Convicted offenders more represented in low resting HRL category.	–
Farrington (1987)	" " "	Lowest HRLs in those convicted of violent offenses at age 25. Lower HRLs in children of criminal parents	0.40
Little (1978)	7-, 9-, 11-year-old schoolchildren	Lower resting HRL linked to antisocial behavior in 9 and 11 year olds	–
Raine & Venables (1984b)	15-year-old schoolboys	Lower resting HRL in antisocials	0.58
Bullock (1988)	15-year-old schoolgirls	Lower resting HRL in girls rated as antisocial	1.60
Venables (1987)	11-year-old offspring of criminal or control parents (male and female)	Lower resting HRL in children with criminal parents.	–
Raine & Jones (1987)	11-year-old boys with behavior problems	Lower resting HRL in those characterized by conduct disorder and socialized aggression	0.63
Rogeness et al. (1990)	12-year-old boys with conduct disorder (unsocialized)	Lower resting HRL in conduct disordered boys relative to depression and anxiety controls	0.50
Rogeness et al. (1990)	12-year-old boys with conduct disorder (socialized)	Lower resting HRL in socialized conduct disorder relative to controls	0.50
Rogeness et al. (1990)	13-year-old girls with conduct disorder (both types combined)	Lower resting HRL in conduct disordered girls relative to controls	0.35
Maliphant, Hume, & Furnham (1990)	12–13-year-old schoolgirls	Lower resting HRL in disruptive, badly behaved girls.	1.28
Raine et al. (1990a)	15-year-old schoolboys	Lower resting HRL (age 15) in those who are criminal at 24 years	0.63
Maliphant, Watson, & Daniels (1990)	7–9-year-old schoolboys	Lower resting HRL in disruptive, badly-behaved boys.	1.91
Bice (1992)	8–10-year-old schoolboys	Lower resting HRL in prosocial aggressives.	0.68

Note. All reported findings are statistically significant.

Effect sizes, d, in these studies, were not small. In the 12 analyses where effect sizes can be calculated, the average d (Cohen, 1988) across all studies was 0.85. The average effect sizes in the three female samples ($d = 1.08$) were somewhat higher than for the average of the nine male samples ($d = 0.79$). This effect may be partially due to the fact that three of the male studies were prospective in nature, and due to the time lag between measurement of heart rate in adolescence and breakdown for crime in adulthood. The average effect size for these three prospective studies is lower ($d = 0.47$). Average effect size for the six male studies which concurrently collected heart rate is calculated as 0.94, a more similar rate to females ($d = 1.08$). One of the lowest effect sizes (0.4 in Farrington, 1987) was for a sample in which heart rate was recorded at the end of a 2-hour interview whereas much larger effect sizes have been observed in studies where resting HR is measured prior to other experiments and procedures.

These effect sizes are not trivial. For example, an effect size of .85 found for heart rate and antisocial behavior is larger than the effect size of 0.80 for the difference in height between 13- and 18-year-old girls (Cohen, 1988). As another comparison, low serotonin in violent and antisocial populations is a strong finding in the area of neurochemistry and violence, yet the averaged effect size calculated in a recent review of this literature is 0.47, or just over half the effect size for low heart rate. In the guidelines drawn up by Cohen (1988), an effect size of 0.85 as observed for low heart rate would be classified as *large*.

Interpretation of Lower Resting HR in Antisocials

Lower resting HR levels in antisocials can be interpreted in a number ways. First, low HR in violent and antisocial individuals may reflect lack of fear. Psychologically, low HR has been thought to reflect "fearlessness." For example, field studies show that bomb disposal experts have lower heart rates than soldier controls; furthermore, those decorated for their bravery and particular fearlessness have even lower heart rates than other bomb disposal experts (Cox, Hallam, O'Connor, & Rachman, 1983; O'Connor, Hallam, & Rachman, 1985). Low heart rates, particularly in infants and young children, have also been associated with a relative lack of anxiety and a fearless temperament (Kagan, 1989; Scerbo, Raine, Venables, & Mednick, 1992). Such an analysis would be more widely consistent with theories of antisocial behavior based on a reduced fear concept (e.g., Mednick, 1977). Reduced fear would predispose to antisocial and violent behavior because such behavior (e.g., fights and assaults) requires a degree of fearlessness to execute, while lack of fear, especially in childhood, would help explain poor socialization inasmuch as low fear of punishment would reduce the effectiveness of conditioning. It should be remembered that although the previous studies recorded HR in a "resting" state, this measurement period frequently preceded a series of other experiments or procedures (e.g., medical examination, exposure to aversive tone stimuli). As such, low HR may be viewed as reflecting lack of anticipatory fear to mild or moderate stressors.

A second possibility is that low heart rate simply reflects underarousal, although underarousal in turn could equally be viewed as a predisposition toward fearlessness. A third interpretation put forward by Raine and Venables (1984b) is that low heart rate reflects a vagal passive coping response to a mildly stressful testing situation, which serves to disengage the individual from the environment and produce a passive state of emotional withdrawal which could serve to dampen the effects of socializing punishments. Fourth, Venables (1988) has suggested that low heart rate reflects predominance of parasympathetically tuned ANS, or vagotonia, and has linked such a finding with findings on EEG (Convit et al., 1991) and hypoglycemia (Virkkunen, 1986) in violent offenders.

A fifth and more speculative suggestion is that low resting HR in antisocials may reflect enlargement of the lateral ventricles of the brain. Low heart rate has been associated with enlargement of the third ventricle of the brain (Cannon et al., 1992); such ventricular enlargement may reflect reductions in hypothalamic area, a periventricular structure known to be involved in mediating heart rate (Larsen, Schneiderman, & Pasin, 1986). Enlargement of the third ventricle has also been linked to reduced SC orienting (Cannon et al., 1988; Raine & Lencz, 1993), which in turn has been found in antisocial populations. Birth complications have been linked to enlargement of the third ventricle (Cannon, Mednick, & Parnas, 1989), and also appear to predispose to violence (Brennan, Mednick, & Mednick, 1993). Ventricular enlargement and damage to periventricular structures, possibly linked to birth complications, may therefore represent the neuroanatomical underpinnings of reduced orienting and lowered heart rate in antisocials. This hypothesis needs to be further tested by assessing ventricular size in antisocial populations using MRI, as previous studies using CT scans with poorer spatial resolution than MRI provide conflicting evidence on ventriculomegaly in forensic populations (Convit et al., this volume; Hucker et al., 1986; see Raine and Buchsbaum, chap. 10, this volume for a more detailed analysis).

Although there are a number of theoretical interpretations that can be made of the strong empirical finding of low heart rate in young uninstitutionalized, violent and antisocial individuals, the notion that it reflects fearlessness may be currently the most parsimonious explanation to date. Parenthetically, it should be noted that lower resting HR in antisocials does not appear to be an artifact of other factors such as age, cigarette smoking, exercise and engagement in sporting activities, alcohol intake, or body size (Raine, 1993).

SPECIFICITY OF AUTONOMIC UNDERAROUSAL AND POOR ORIENTING TO VIOLENT OFFENDERS?

It is clear from the foregoing reviews that there has been little systematic research on whether autonomic deficits found in antisocial populations are specific to violence per se. This is particularly true for SC data where there is no indication of specificity for violence. By the same token, there is no good evidence indicating *lack* of specificity for violence; it is more the case that good tests have not been conducted to answer this important question.

The fact that some studies find heart rate particularly low in violent offenders than nonviolent offenders (e.g., Farrington, 1987; Wadsworth, 1976) constitutes somewhat better evidence for the specificity of this effect for violence, though again, findings to date should be regarded as suggestive only. This would make this measure a particularly important psychophysiological variable to utilize in future studies of violence. One of the problems is that sample sizes in psychophysiological studies to date have generally precluded the division of offenders into violent and nonviolent offenders.

To provide some initial data on this issue, however, data from a recent prospective psychophysiological study of crime are re-analyzed here to assess for possible trends. The original study (Raine et al., 1990a) found that HR and SC measures of arousal measured at age 18 in 101 normal 15-year-old schoolboys were predictive of criminality status as measured by official records at age 24. Seventeen subjects eventually broke down for crime. Five of these 17 had convictions for violence (assault or wounding) and these were compared to the other 12 nonviolent offenders and 84 controls on resting heart rate. Results of this analysis for resting HR (measured at the start and end of a rest period prior to an orienting paradigm) are shown in Fig. 8.1. Note the effect sizes between each of the two offender groups relative to normal controls.

The violent group had the lowest heart rates of all, with the nonviolent offender group being intermediate between violent offenders and controls. The averaged effect size of 1.0 for the violent group is slightly higher than that of 0.85 obtained for previous studies on HR reviewed earlier. Despite the lack of

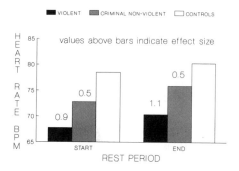

FIG. 8.1. Resting heart rate in violent criminals, nonviolent criminals, and controls. Values above bars represent effect size differences for the experimental groups when compared to controls.

statistical power due to small N size, HR level for the violent offender group was significantly lower than the normal control at the end of the rest period ($p <$ .05, two-tailed), with a trend ($p < .08$) for the start of the rest period. Conversely, nonviolent offender versus control comparisons were nonsignificant. Similar analyses for nonspecific SC responses and SCL did not produce statistically significant differences between violent offenders and controls, but in all cases the violent offenders had the lowest values of all, with the nonviolent offenders in between violent and control groups.

The foregoing analysis is clearly limited and, as such, strong conclusions cannot be drawn. Taken together with the findings of the review, however, they suggest that low HRL may be a particularly strong characteristic of the violent offender.

THEORETICAL INTERPRETATION OF AUTONOMIC ACTIVITY AND VIOLENT, CRIMINAL BEHAVIOR

In summary, offenders and other antisocials are characterized by reduced arousal, poorer orienting, and poorer classical conditioning in the electrodermal domain. In addition, they are characterized by long SC half-recovery time which might in cognitive terms reflect either a shutting out of aversive events or slow fear dissipation, or possibly both. Most strikingly of all however, antisocial noninstitutionalized populations and children have been very consistently shown to have lower heart rate in a resting state which precedes exposure to other experimental manipulations.

Theoretically, two related ideas can encapsulate these findings. The first idea is that a lack of fear may predispose an individual to criminal and violent behavior, and is most clearly linked to arousal and conditioning data. As outlined before, low arousal has been linked with fearlessness, perhaps because under-arousal also predisposes the individual to seek out stimulation to compensate for pathologically low levels of arousal. Because such stimulation-seeking would more frequently place the individual in conditions of threat, this individual would eventually habituate responses to such stimuli, and consequently show reduced reactivity to situations involving threat. Underarousal and lack of anticipatory fear to aversive events may also account for poorer conditionability because the unconditional stimulus may be perceived in less threatening terms.

The second and related idea is that offenders have a cognitive deficit linked to the processing of aversive events and punishments, and is most clearly linked with orienting and SC recovery time data. Orienting deficits could contribute to conditioning deficits because lack of attentional processing to initially neutral stimuli which warn of impending punishment would be expected to result in poorer conditioning (as might low arousal). If slow half-recovery time does indeed reflect a cognitive strategy typified by a tuning out of aversive events, this would also be consistent with poor conditioning. Lack of orienting and responsivity to other salient events in the environment might also help account for underarousal, inasmuch as arousal reflects tonic levels of activity or, more loosely, "physiological idling speed," which may in part be a function of moment-to-moment responsivity to events in the environment. Although this theoretical analysis must be viewed heuristically, it illustrates the possibility that different psychophysiological deficits may reflect a similar process, or at least different aspects of the same general process.

Finally, a very different theoretical interpretation of one specific deficit (reduced SC orienting) in offenders should be raised. This is the notion that frontal dysfunction may underlie both reduced SC orienting and violent/criminal behavior. This view is generated by recent brain-imaging data on the neuroanatomy and neurophysiology of SC orienting. Raine et al. (1991) found that number of skin conductance orienting responses correlated between .44 and .60 with area of prefrontal cortex as measured by MRI in a normal sample. The direction of the effects (reduced orienting associated with reduced prefrontal area) is consistent with the notion that prefrontal cortex plays an important role in mediating orienting. Similarly, Hazlett et al. (1993) found significant associations between glucose metabolism in frontal cortex (measured by positron emission tomography [PET]) and SC orienting in the same direction of reduced frontal activity, reduced SC orienting. Neuropsychological test data have been suggestive of frontal dysfunction in adult and juvenile violent offenders (Moffitt, 1990; Moffitt & Henry, 1991; Raine and Buchsbaum, chap. 11, this volume). Other chapters in this volume also report evidence for prefrontal dysfunction in violent offenders as measured by PET (Goyer, chap. 11, this volume; Raine & Buchsbaum, chap. 8, this volume; Raine et al., 1994). As reviewed earlier, reduced orienting may be specifically related to offenders with schizotypal features, or psychopaths with frontal damage. Because schizophrenics and schizotypals have also been reported to show structural and function prefrontal dysfunction (Buchsbaum et al., 1990; Raine et al., 1992; Raine, Sheard, Reynolds, & Lencz, 1992), the prediction generated from this analysis is that it would be specifically a subgroup of offenders—those who are *both* violent and possess schizotypal features, who would be most likely to show both SC orienting deficits and frontal dysfunction as measured by brain imaging or neuropsychological testing.

METHODOLOGICAL CONSIDERATIONS AND PROSPECTS FOR FUTURE RESEARCH

This chapter has so far focused on empirical issues at the expense of conceptual issues. Seven methodological and conceptual issues that form directives for future research into the psychophysiological basis of violence and crime can, however, be identified.

A first, crucially important, issue lies with attempting to integrate psychophysiological findings with other social and cognitive research. In particular, it is quite possible that the interaction between social and biological factors is more important in explaining violence than either factor alone; for example, poorer electrodermal conditioning appears to characterize antisocials from good but not poor home environments. The lack of communication between social scientists and biologically orientated researchers has resulted in relatively few tests of this proposition for violent and aggressive behavior. Biologically oriented researchers have ignored social influences on violence just as much as socially oriented researchers have ignored biological influences. Findings for resting HR probably represent both the strongest and best replicated psychophysiological data in the field to date. Given the ease and low cost of measuring resting HR, it is perhaps this measure that can be most easily incorporated by nonbiologically orientated researchers of crime into more socially orientated research studies.

Second, while the field is beginning to accrue knowledge on psychophysiological risk factors for violence, we know virtually nothing about psychophysiological *protective* factors for violence. Specifically, some children who are at risk for later violence by virtue of having a negative family and peer environment or by showing antisocial behavior in adolescence, do not become violent adults. Is this because they possess psychophysiological characteristics that contributes to desistence to later violence? Answers to such questions are crucially important to fully understanding violence and what may retard its development, yet, from the standpoint of psychophysiology, there appears to be no published research to date on this issue. New findings show that antisocial 15-year-old boys who *desist* from adult crime and violence by age 29 have significantly *higher* skin conductance and heart rate arousal, higher skin conductance orienting, better skin conductance conditioning, and shorter skin conductance half-recovery times relative to antisocial adolescents who do become criminal in later life (Raine, Venables, & Williams, 1995; Raine, Venables, & Williams, in press). These initial findings suggest that heightened autonomic activity may serve as a protective factors against later crime and violence.

Third, dividing offenders into violent and nonviolent groups only goes partway to establishing specificity of effects for violence. For example, the larger effect size for resting heart rate in the re-analysis of the Raine et al. (1990a) data reported earlier may simply reflect that the violent offenders are more severely antisocial and recidivistic, rather than being violent. To this author's knowledge, there have been no psychophysiological studies that have controlled for this effect. Future studies need to identify factors specific to violence versus recidivism per se.

Fourth, the literature has paid very little attention to one potentially very important moderator variable—the presence or absence of alcohol abuse. It is quite possible that the etiological underpinnings of violence and crime differ substantially depending on whether or not the violent individual abuses alcohol (Barros and Miczek, chap. 12, this volume; Reiss & Roth, 1993). For example, violent offenders who abuse alcohol may drink in order to reduce tension and anxiety due to *high* levels of arousal and reactivity, whereas violent offenders who do not drink may be the subgroup most clearly characterized by low arousal. Alcohol and drug use therefore need to be assessed more consistently in future research.

Fifth, while research on institutionalized adult violent offenders is clearly important, prospective longitudinal studies are capable of making more powerful statements on the etiology and development of violence. As findings for heart rate showed, much stronger findings may be obtained in younger, noninstitutionalized samples than in samples of prisoners. Although they can never demonstrate causality, such studies can help rule out artifactual relationships such as the possibility that early violent behavior in some way causes underarousal. Furthermore, the use of self-report measures of violence would be helpful in tapping those individuals in the general population who commit nontrivial violence yet are never featured in research studies of caught, "unsuccessful" offenders. Use of such measures are essential for a more unbiased theoretical perspective of violent offending. Unfortunately, few such studies have been conducted. Until violence is viewed within a more developmental, community perspective, it will be difficult to conduct substantial tests of theories of violence and to generate new biological perspectives that have widespread generality.

Sixth, psychophysiological risk factors for violence and crime need to be integrated more closely with other biological risk factors such as neurochemistry (Coccaro and Kavoussi, chap. 4, this volume; Kreusi, Rapoport, Hamberger, & Hibbs, 1990; Linnoila, Virkkunen, & Scheinin, 1983; Stoff and Vitiello, chap. 6, this volume; Virkkunen and Linnoila, chap. 5, this volume; Virkkunen, Nuutila, Goodwin, & Linnoila, 1987), birth complications (Brennan et al., 1993), and brain dysfunction (Goyer et al., 1994). Without such integration, it will be much more difficult to put together pieces in the biological jigsaw of violence perpetration.

Finally, studies that adopt these suggestions will not, in and of themselves, result in advances in our understanding of violence. Well-conceptualized theories that generate testable predictions lie at the heart of our ability to make genuine advances in our understanding and conceptualization of this complex phenomenon.

SUMMARY

This chapter reviews all studies measuring skin conductance and heart rate activity conducted on violent and antisocial populations since the last main review in this area by Hare (1978). With respect to skin conductance, offenders and other antisocials are characterized by reduced arousal, poorer classical conditioning, and long half-recovery times. Poorer orienting is also found, but this seems to be specific to violent and antisocial individuals with schizotypal features. With respect to heart rate, 14 studies of noninstitutionalized violent and antisocial children and adults have been very consistently shown to have lower heart rate in a resting state with no failures to replicate this finding to date. Reduced HR level, representing an averaged effect size of 0.85, appears to be strongest in violent populations. It is hypothesized that low heart rate may predispose to the development of fearlessness, which predisposes to violent and antisocial behavior. This fearlessness may, in turn, underlie the skin conductance arousal and conditioning deficits found in antisocials. It is argued that low resting heart rate in noninstitutionalized offenders is a highly replicated finding that may be relatively specific to violent offending, which can be easily and cheaply integrated into research focussing on social variables, and may interact in important ways with social variables in the prediction of violence.

ACKNOWLEDGMENTS

This chapter was written while the author was supported by NIMH grant RO1 MH46435-02 and an NIMH Research Scientist Development Award (1 KO2 MH01114-01).

REFERENCES

Aniskiewitz, A. (1973). Autonomic components of vicarious conditioning and psychopathy. *Journal of Clinical Psychology, 35*, 60–67.

Bernstein, A. S., Frith, C. D., Gruzelier, J. H., Patterson, T., Straube, E., Venables, P. H., & Zahn, T. P. (1982). An analysis of skin conductance orienting response in samples of American, British and German schizophrenics. *Biological Psychology, 14*, 155–211.

Bice, T. (1992). *Cognitive and psychophysiological differences in proactive and reactive aggressive boys.* Unpublished doctoral dissertation, Department of Psychology, University of Southern California, Los Angeles.

Blackburn, R. (1979). Cortical and autonomic responses arousal in primary and secondary psychopaths. *Psychophysiology, 16*, 143–150.

Blackburn, R. (1983). Psychopathy, delinquency and crime. In A. Gale & J. A. Edwards (Eds.), *Physiological correlates of human behavior* (Vol. 3, pp. 187–205). London: Academic Press.

Brennan, P., Mednick, B. R., & Mednick, S. A. (1993). Parental psychopathology, congenital factors, and violence. In S. Hodgins (Ed.), *Crime and mental disorder.* Beverly Hills, CA: Sage.

Buchsbaum, M. S., Neuchterlein, K. H., Haier, R. J., Wu, J., Sicotte, N., Hazlett, E., Asarnow, R., Potkin, S., & Guich, S. (1990). Glucose metabolic rate in normals and schizophrenics during the continuous performance test assessed by positron emission tomography. *British Journal of Psychiatry, 156*, 216–227.

Buikhuisen, W., Bontekoe, E. H. M., Plas-Korenhoff, C. D., & Buuren, S. (1985). Characteristics of criminals: The privileged offender. *International Journal of Law and Psychiatry, 7*, 301–313.

Buikhuisen, W., Eurelings-Bontekoe, E. H. M., & Host, K. B. (1989). Crime and recovery time: Mednick revisited. *International Journal of Law and Psychiatry, 12*, 29–40.

Bullock, J. (1988). *Tonic heart rate, social class, and antisociality in adolescent girls.* Unpublished manuscript, University of York, England.

Cacioppo, J. T., Tassinary, L. G., & Fridlund, A. (1991). *Principles of psychophysiology: Physical, social and inferential elements.* Cambridge, England: Cambridge University Press.

Cannon, T. D., Fuhrmann, M., Mednick, S. A., Machon, R. A., Parnas, J., & Schulsinger, F. (1988). Third ventricle enlargement and reduced electrodermal responsiveness. *Psychophysiology, 25,* 153–156.

Cannon, T. D., Mednick, S. A., & Parnas, J. (1989). Genetic and perinatal determinants of structural brain deficits in schizophrenia. *Archives of General Psychiatry, 46,* 883–889.

Cannon, T. D., Raine, A., Herman, T. M., Mednick, S. A., Schulsinger, F., & Moore, M. (1992). Third ventricle enlargement and lower heart rate levels in a high risk sample. *Psychophysiology, 29,* 294–301.

Cohen, J. (1988). *Statistical power analysis for the behavioral sciences* (2nd. ed.). Hillsdale, NJ: Lawrence Erlbaum Associates.

Convit, A., Czobor, P., & Volavka, J. (1991). Lateralized abnormality in the EEG of persistently violent psychiatric inpatients. *Biological Psychiatry, 30,* 363–370.

Cox, D., Hallam, R., O'Connor, K., & Rachman, S. (1983). An experimental study of fearlessness and courage. *British Journal of Psychology, 74,* 107–117.

Crider, A. (1993). Electrodermal response lability–stability: Individual difference correlates. In J. C. Roy, W. Boucsein, D. C. Fowles, & J. Gruzelier (Eds.), *Electrodermal activity: From physiology to psychology.* New York: Plenum.

Damasio, A. R., Tranel, D., & Damasio, H. (1990). Individuals with sociopathic behavior caused by frontal damage fail to respond autonomically to social stimuli. *Behavioral Brain Research, 41,* 81–94.

Davies, J. G. V., & Maliphant, R. (1971). Autonomic responses of male adolescents exhibiting refractory behavior in school. *Journal of Child Psychology and Psychiatry, 12,* 115–127.

Dawson, M., Schell, A. M., & Filion, D. (1991). The electrodermal system. In J. T. Cacioppo, L. G. Tassinary, & A. Fridlund (Eds.), *Principles of psychophysiology: Physical, social and inferential elements* (pp. 295–324). Cambridge, England: Cambridge University Press.

Eysenck, H. J. (1977). *Crime and personality* (3rd. ed.). St. Albans, U.K.: Paladin.

Farrington, D. P. (1987). Implications of biological findings for criminological research. In S. A. Mednick, T. E. Moffitt, & S. A. Stack (Eds.), *The causes of crime: New biological approaches* (pp. 42–64). New York: Cambridge University Press.

Fowles, D. C. (1980). The three arousal model: Implications of Gray's two-factor learning theory for heart rate, electrodermal activity, and psychopathy. *Psychophysiology, 17,* 87–104.

Fowles, D. C. (1993). Electrodermal activity and antisocial behavior. In J. C. Roy, W. Boucsein, D. C. Fowles, & J. Gruzelier (Eds.), *Electrodermal activity: From physiology to psychology.* New York: Plenum.

Goyer, P. F., Andreason, P. J., Semple, W. E., Clayton, A. H., King, A. C., Compton-Toth, B. A., Schulz, S. C., & Cohen, R. M. (1994). Positron-emission tomography and personality disorders. *Neuropsychopharmacology, 10,* 21–28.

Gruzelier, J. G., & Raine, A. (1994). Bilateral electrodermal activity and cerebral mechanisms in syndromes of schizophrenia and the schizotypal personality. *International Journal of Psychophysiology, 16,* 1–16.

Hare, R. D. (1970). *Psychopathy: Theory and practice.* New York: Wiley.

Hare, R. D. (1975). Psychophysiological studies of psychopathy. In D. C. Fowles (Ed.), *Clinical applications of psychophysiology* (pp. 77–105). New York: Cambridge University Press.

Hare, R. D. (1978). Electrodermal and cardiovascular correlates of psychopathy. In R. D. Hare & D. Schalling (Eds.), *Psychopathic behavior: Approaches to research* (pp. 107–144). New York: Wiley.

Hare, R. D. (1980). Psychopathy and violence. In J. R. Hays, K. Roberts, & K. Solway (Eds.), *Violence and the violent individual* (pp. 53–74). New York: Spectrum.

Hare, R. D. (1982). Psychopathy and physiological activity during anticipation of an aversive stimulus in a distraction paradigm. *Psychophysiology, 19,* 266–271.

Hare, R. D., & Craigen, D. (1974). Psychopathy and physiological activity in a mixed motive game situation. *Psychophysiology, 11,* 197–206.

Hare, R. D., Frazelle, J., & Cox, D. (1978). Psychopathy and physiological responses to threat of an aversive stimulus. *Psychophysiology, 15,* 165–172.

Hazlett, E., Dawson, M., Buchsbaum, M. S., & Neuchterlein, K. H. (1993). Reduced regional brain glucose metabolism assessed by PET in electrodermal nonresponder schizophrenics: A pilot study. *Journal of Abnormal Psychology, 102,* 39–46.

Hemming, J. H. (1981). Electrodermal indices in a selected prison sample and students. *Personality and Individual Differences, 2,* 37–46.

Hinton, J., O'Neill, M., Dishman, J., & Webster, S. (1979). Electrodermal indices of public offending and recidivism. *Biological Psychology, 9,* 297–309.

Hucker, S., Langevin, R., Wortzman, G., Bain, J., Chambers, J., & Wright, S. (1986). Neuropsychological impairment in pedophiles. *Canadian Journal of Behavioral Sciences, 18,* 440–448.

Kagan, J. (1989). Temperamental contributions to social behavior. *American Psychologist, 44,* 668–674.

Kreusi, M. J., Rapoport, J. L., Hamburger, S., D. & Hibbs, E. D. (1990). Cerebrospinal fluid monoamine metabolites, aggression, and impulsivity in disruptive behavior disorders of children and adolescents. *Archives of General Psychiatry, 47,* 419–426.

Larsen, P. B., Schneiderman, N., & Pasin, R. D. (1986). Physiological bases of cardiovascular psychophysiology. In M. G. H. Coles, E. Donchin, & S. W. Porges (Eds.), *Psychophysiology: Systems, processes, and applications* (pp. 122–165). New York: Guilford.

Levander, S. E., Schalling, D., Lidberg, L., Bartfai, A., & Lidberg, Y. (1980). Skin conductance recovery time and personality in a group of criminals. *Psychophysiology, 17,* 105–111.

Linnoila, M., Virkkunen, M., & Scheinin, M. (1983). Low cerebrospinal fluid 5-hydroxyindoleacetic acid concentration differentiates impulsive from nonimpulsive violent behavior. *Life Sciences, 33,* 2609–2614.

Little, B. (1978, December). *Physiological correlates of antisocial behavior in children and young adults.* Paper presented at the British Psychophysiology Society, London.

Loeb, J., & Mednick, S. A. (1977). A prospective study of predictors of criminality: 3. Electrodermal response patterns. In S. A. Mednick & K. O. Christiansen (Eds.), *Biosocial bases to criminal behavior* (pp. 245–254). New York: Gardner.

Lykken, D. T. (1957). A study of anxiety in the sociopathic personality. *Journal of Abnormal and Social Psychology, 55,* 6–10.

Maliphant, R., Hume, F., & Furnham, A. (1990). Autonomic nervous system (ANS) activity, personality characteristics and disruptive behavior in girls. *Journal of Child Psychology and Psychiatry, 31,* 619–628.

Maliphant, R., Watson, S. A., & Daniels, D. (1990). Disruptive behavior in school, personality characteristics, and heart rate (HR) levels in 7–9 year old boys. *Educational Psychology, 10,* 199–205.

Mednick, S. A. (1975). Autonomic nervous system recovery and psychopathology. *Scandinavian Journal of Behavior Therapy, 4,* 55–68.

Mednick, S. A. (1977). A bio-social theory of the learning of law-abiding behavior. In S. A. Mednick & K. O. Christiansen (Eds.), *Biosocial bases of criminal behavior* (pp. 1–8). New York: Gardner.

Moffitt, T. E. (1990). The neuropsychology of juvenile delinquency: A critical review. In M. Tonry & N. Morris (Eds.), *Crime and justice: A review of the literature* (pp. 99–169). Chicago: University of Chicago Press.

Moffitt, T. E., & Henry, B. (1991). Neuropsychological studies of juvenile delinquency and juvenile violence. In J. S. Millner (Ed.), *Neuropsychology of aggression* (pp. 131–146). Boston: Kluwer.

O'Connor, K., Hallam, R., & Rachman, S. (1985). Fearless and courage: A replication experiment. *British Journal of Psychology, 76,* 187–197.

Ohman, A. (1981). Electrodermal activity and vulnerability to schizophrenia: A review. *Biological Psychology, 12,* 87–145.

Raine, A. (1987). Effect of early environment on electrodermal and cognitive correlates of schizotypy and psychopathy in criminals. *International Journal of Psychophysiology, 4,* 277–287.

Raine, A. (1988). Antisocial behavior and social psychophysiology. In H. Wagner (Ed.), *Social psychophysiology and emotion: Theory and clinical application* (pp. 231–253). London: Wiley.

Raine, A. (1989). Evoked potentials and psychopathy. *International Journal of Psychophysiology, 8,* 29–36.

Raine, A. (1990). *Electrodermal correlates of psychopathic personality in 15-year olds who become adult criminals.* Unpublished manuscript, Department of Psychology, University of Southern California, Los Angeles.

Raine, A. (1993). *The psychopathology of crime: Criminal behavior as a clinical disorder.* San Diego, CA: Academic Press.

Raine, A., Buchsbaum, M. S., Stanley, J., Lottenberg, S., Abel, L., & Stoddard, J. (1994). Selective reductions in pre-frontal glucose metabolism assessed with positron emission tomography in accused murderers pleading not guilty by reason of insanity. *Biological Psychiatry, 36,* 365–373.

Raine, A., & Jones, F. (1987). Attention, autonomic arousal, and personality in behaviorally disordered children. *Journal of Abnormal Child Psychology, 15,* 583–599.

Raine, A., & Lencz, T. (1993). The neuroanatomy of electrodermal activity. In J. C. Roy (Ed.), *Electrodermal activity: From Physiology to psychology* (pp. 115–135). New York: Plenum.

Raine, A., Lencz, T., Harrison, G., Reynolds, G. P., Sheard, S., & Cooper, J. E. (1992). An evaluation of structural and functional prefrontal deficits in schizophrenia using MRI and neuropsychological measures. *Psychiatry Research, 45,* 123–137.

Raine, A., & Mednick, S. A. (1989). Biosocial longitudinal research into antisocial behavior. *Review d'Epidemiologie et de Sante Publique, 37,* 515–524.

Raine, A., Reynolds, G. P., & Sheard, C. (1991). Neuroanatomical mediators of electrodermal activity in normal human subjects: A magnetic resonance imaging study. *Psychophysiology, 28,* 548–558.

Raine, A., Sheard, S., Reynolds, G. P., & Lencz, T. (1992). Pre-frontal structural and functional deficits associated with individual differences in schizotypal personality. *Schizophrenia Research, 7,* 237–247.

Raine, A., & Venables, P. H. (1981). Classical conditioning and socialization—A biosocial interaction? *Personality and Individual Differences, 2,* 273–283.

Raine, A., & Venables, P. H. (1984a). Electrodermal non-responding, schizoid tendencies, and antisocial behavior in adolescents. *Psychophysiology, 21,* 424–433.

Raine, A., & Venables, P. H. (1984b). Tonic heart rate level, social class, and antisocial behavior. *Biological Psychology, 18,* 123–132.

Raine, A., & Venables, P. H. (1988). Skin conductance responsivity in psychopaths to orienting, defensive, and consonant-vowel stimuli. *Journal of Psychophysiology, 2,* 221–225.

Raine, A., Venables, P. H., & Williams, M. (1990a). Relationships between CNS and ANS measures of arousal at age 15 and criminality at age 24. *Archives of General Psychiatry, 47,* 1003–1007.

Raine, A., Venables, P. H., & Williams, M. (1990b). Orienting and criminality: A prospective study. *American Journal of Psychiatry, 147,* 933–937.

Raine, A., Venables, P. H., & Williams, M. (1995). High autonomic arousal and orienting at age 15 years as protective factors against crime development at age 29 years. *American Journal of Psychiatry, 152,* 1595–1600.

Raine, A., Venables, P. H., & Williams, M. (in press). Better autonomic conditioning and faster electrodermal half-recovery time at age 15 years as protective factors against crime at age 29 years. *Developmental Psychology.*

Reiss, A., & Roth, J. A. (1993). *Understanding and preventing violence.* Washington, DC: National Academy Press.

Rogeness, G. A., Cepeda, C., Macedo, C. A., Fischer, C., & Harris, W. R. (1990). Differences in heart rate and blood pressure in children with conduct disorder, major depression, and separation anxiety. *Psychiatry Research, 33,* 199–206.

Scerbo, A., Raine, A., Venables, P. H., & Mednick, S. A. (1992). *Heart rate and skin conductance in behaviorally inhibited Mauritian children.* Manuscript submitted for publication.

Schmidt, K., Solanto, M. V., & Bridger, W. H. (1985). Electrodermal activity of undersocialized aggressive children: A pilot study. *Journal of Child Psychology and Psychiatry and Allied Disciplines, 26,* 653–660.

Siddle, D. A. T. (1977). Electrodermal activity and psychopathy. In S. A. Mednick & K. O. Christiansen (Eds.), *Biosocial bases of criminal behavior* (pp. 199–212). New York: Gardner.

Siddle, D. A. T., Mednick, S. A., Nichol, A. R., & Foggitt, R. H. (1976). Skin conductance recovery in antisocial adolescents. *British Journal of Social and Clinical Psychology, 15,* 425–428.

Siddle, D. A. T., & Trasler, G. (1981). The psychophysiology of psychopathic behavior. In M. J. Christie & P. G. Mellett (Eds.), *Foundations of psychosomatics* (pp. 283–303). Chichester, U.K.: Wiley.

Stern, R. M., Ray, W. J., & Davis, C. M. (1980). *Psychophysiological recording.* New York: Oxford University Press.

Tharp, V. K., Maltzman, I., Syndulko, K., & Ziskind, E. (1980). Autonomic activity during anticipation of an aversive tone in noninstitutionalized sociopaths. *Psychophysiology, 17,* 123–128.

Trasler, G. (1987). Biogenetic factors. In H. C. Quay (Ed.), *Handbook of juvenile delinquency* (pp. 184–216). New York: Wiley.

Venables, P. H. (1974). The recovery limb of the skin conductance response. In S. A. Mednick, F. Schulsinger, J. Higgins, & B. Bell (Eds.), *Genetics, environment and psychopathology* (pp. 117–133). Oxford, England: North-Holland.

Venables, P. H. (1987). Autonomic and central nervous system factors in criminal behavior. In S. A. Mednick, T. Moffitt, & S. Stack (Eds.), *The causes of crime: New biological approaches* (pp. 110–136). New York: Cambridge University Press.

Venables, P. H. (1988). Psychophysiology and crime: Theory and data. In T. E. Moffitt & S. A. Mednick (Eds.), *Biological contributions to crime causation.* Dordrecht: Martinus Nijhoff.

Venables, P. H. (1989). The Emanuel Miller Memorial Lecture 1987: Childhood markers for adult disorders. *Journal of Child Psychology and Psychiatry and Allied Disciplines, 30,* 347–364.

Venables, P. H., & Christie, M. J. (1973). Mechanisms, instrumentation, recording techniques, and quantification of responses. In W. F. Prokasy & D. C. Raskin (Eds.), *Electrodermal activity in psychological research.* New York: Wiley.

Virkkunen, M. (1986). Reactive hypoglycemia tendency among habitually violent offenders. *Nutrition Reviews, 44,* 94–103.

Virkkunen, M., Nuutila, A., Goodwin, F. K., & Linnoila, M. (1987). Cerebrospinal fluid monoamine metabolite levels in male arsonists. *Archives of General Psychiatry, 4,* 241–247.

Wadsworth, M. E. J. (1976). Delinquency, pulse rate and early emotional deprivation. *British Journal of Criminology, 16,* 245–256.

West, D. J., & Farrington, D. P. (1977). *The delinquent way of life.* London, England: Heinemann.

Zahn, T. P. (1986). Psychophysiological approaches to psychopathology. In M. G. H. Coles, E. Donchin, & S. W. Porges (Eds.), *Psychophysiology: Systems, processes, and applications* (pp. 508–609). New York: Guilford.

Ziskind, E., Syndulko, K., & Malzman, J. (1978). Aversive conditioning in the sociopath. *Pavlovian Journal of Biological Science, 13,* 199–205.

9

FRONTOTEMPORAL ABNORMALITIES AND VIOLENT BEHAVIOR

Antonio Convit
Nathan Kline Institute for Psychiatric Research
New York University

Richard Douyon
University of Miami

Kathy F. Yates
Nathan Kline Institute for Psychiatric Research
New York University

Gwenn Smith
University of Pittsburgh

Pal Czobor
Nathan Kline Institute for Psychiatric Research
New York University

Jose de Asis
New York University

Joseph Vitrai
Nathan Kline Institute for Psychiatric Research
New York University

Louis Camus
Sodona, Arizona

Jan Volavka
Nathan Kline Institute for Psychiatric Research
New York University

Attempts to elucidate some of the etiological contributions to violence have met with limited success. First, the intricacies of violence research such as the separate contributions from biology and environment and their resulting interactions make this a very complex issue. Second, the study of violence has been plagued with lack of uniform definitions for violent behaviors and by unidimensional approach to its study. Furthermore, the field of violence has been studied by scientists from diverse disciplines that include criminology, sociology, and different biological perspectives (physiology, psychobiology, and neurobiology). These diverse disciplines use different language, tools, ways to conceptualize the problem, and have studied developmentally different violent populations. To compound these problems investigators from these different disciplines frequently do not read each others work, and consequently the amount of cross-fertilization has been, until quite recently, somewhat limited.

Research in violence has, to date, lacked clear hypotheses and has been mostly descriptive and correlational. Our knowledge of the risk factors for violent behavior remains simplistic and unidimensional. Etiological theories of violence have undergone numerous transformations over the years. Theories stressing biological factors have been supplanted by theories stressing psychosocial factors and then back again to those stressing biological factors. What has been lacking is a clear conceptual framework, which will then generate specific hypotheses that can then be tested.

This chapter presents a simple conceptual framework based on the construct that frontotemporal abnormality is related to violent behavior. Some of the supporting evidence we present is derived from different populations and uses varying assessment techniques. Moreover, we attempt to link this abnormality with more general constructs such as poor impulse control. The chapter is separated into three sections. First, we review the literatures on aspects of brain function, drawing specifically from the literature that links frontotemporal dysfunction and violence among psychiatric and criminal populations. We briefly make some linkages to the literature on poor impulse control (impulsivity) and its neurochemical substrate. Impulsivity, its possible serotonin substrate, and its relationship to violence is the focus of other work presented in this volume and detailed here. Second, we present two pilot studies, which together with some of our prior work, support the contention that there may be a relationship between frontotemporal dysfunction and violence among schizophrenic inpatients. Third, we describe limitations of our work as well as that of others, propose a theoretical framework for future research that expands on the concept of frontotemporal brain dysfunction, and propose specific tools for the implementation of such a framework.

GENERAL CONSIDERATIONS ON THE LINK BETWEEN VIOLENT BEHAVIOR AND BRAIN DYSFUNCTION

Research utilizing neurological and neuropsychological assessments has uncovered multiple brain impairments associated with violence in criminal and noncriminal populations. Because most of these studies are cross-sectional, the origin of the impairments and their role in the perpetuation of the violent behavior remains unclear. In a study of patients who sustained head injury, with at least 2 days of posttraumatic amnesia, Brooks et al. (1986) found that at 5-year follow-up, 54 of the patients made threats and 20% actually exhibited violent behavior, when none had been present prior to the head injury. However, it is possible that individuals who are violent sustain head injuries as a result of being involved in fights or other risk-taking behaviors. Alternatively, it is possible that brain dysfunction predates the violent behavior, which in turn leads to further head injuries, and so on.

The issue of whether brain damage predates violent behavior or is the consequence of it can only be addressed in longitudinal studies. There is a small body of literature suggesting that brain dysfunction, assessed by neuropsychological measures (Moffitt, 1990b; Moffitt & Silva, 1988) or by slowing of the EEG (Petersen, Matousek, Mednick, Volavka, & Pollock, 1982; Raine, Venables, & Williams, 1990), may predate criminal behavior rather than result from it.

A relationship has consistently been demonstrated between neuropsychological test scores and delinquency (see Moffitt, 1990b; Moffitt & Henry, 1991, for a review). Despite the varied definitions of delinquency and diversity of utilized neuropsychological measures, studies have consistently shown delinquency-related deficits in self-control functions (such as planning, inhibiting inappropriate responses, attention, and concentration) and in verbal skills (including abstract reasoning and language comprehension).

The possible links between violent behavior and brain dysfunction take on added importance given the fact that in the United States both the prevalence of brain dysfunction and the incidence of violent criminal behavior may be on the rise. With the widespread use of cocaine and alcohol, an increasing number of children are exposed to cocaine and alcohol in utero. In inner cities, up to 12% of women giving birth have cocaine metabolites in their urine (McCalla, 1991). The babies exposed to cocaine *in utero* have lower weights and lower Apgar scores at 5 minutes and are likely to have neurological sequelae (McCalla, 1991). Akin to electrical kindling (Goddard, McIntyre, & Leech, 1969), one could hypothesize that the brains of these children may be functionally changed and may respond differently to cocaine exposure later in life. Another group of children, those with fetal alcohol syndrome, have brain impairments that can be expressed in the form of mental retardation, learning disabilities, and an increasing vulnerability to stress (Yellin, 1984). Anecdotally, it has been suggested that these children have high rates of assaultive and violent behavior.

Even when a child had a "safe" intrauterine environment, he or she may not have a safe childhood environment. A child does not need to be struck on the head to sustain brain injury. Dykes (1986) has reported that infants who are shaken vigorously by the extremities or shoulders may sustain intracranial and intraocular bleeding with no sign of external head trauma. Insults during pregnancy as well as those suffered early in life are on the rise, therefore, increasing the number of children with potential brain dysfunction, adding to the number of people at risk for violence.

THEORETICAL RATIONALE FOR LINKING THE FRONTAL AND TEMPORAL BRAIN REGIONS TO VIOLENCE

Although unanimity of opinion is lacking as to the morphophysiological substrates of aggression, the hypothalamus, the medial temporal lobe (amygdaloid complex), and orbital frontal cortex have been found to be involved in the regulation and expression of aggression (Bear, 1991). Weiger and Bear (1988) have illustrated a distinctive relationship of aggression to these three specific brain structures. They further suggest that the degree and nature of the interaction between organic and functional influences on aggression is strongly dependent on the anatomical location of the organic lesion. For purposes of this chapter, we focus on the temporal and frontal lobes.

Episodic rage and aggression due to frontal lobe dysfunction has been mentioned in the neurologic literature (mostly with patients of normal intelligence). Gedye (1989) has been the first to pursue such links in a psychiatric population. The author has suggested that episodic rage and aggression in some mentally handicapped individuals may be involuntary (needing recognition as neural dysfunction—not as a "behavior problem" under voluntary control) and is reflective of frontal lobe dysfunction.

The amygdaloid complex, a limbic structure within the temporal lobe with extensive connections to and from the orbitofrontal cortex (Fuster, 1989) plays a fundamental role in the regulation of aggression, and also in new learning and memory. In monkeys, the fundamental effect of an amygdalectomy is a modification of the previously acquired pattern of linking stimuli with aggressive responses, which suggests that the amygdala may be particularly relevant for recall of the affective significance of stimuli (Rosvold, Mirsky, & Pribram, 1954). Behavioral improvement after amygdalectomy has been demonstrated in aggressive patients (Hitchcock & Cairns, 1973).

The frontal lobes can also be implicated in the regulation and expression of aggression because of their critical role in planning and regulation of behavior. Reports of cases involving lesions to the frontal lobes and most consistently to its orbitomedial area have described impulsive and socially inappropriate behavior executed without any apparent regard for its consequences (Damasio, Grabowski, Frank, Galaburda, & Damasio, 1994; Harlow, 1868). Damage to the orbital undersurface of the frontal lobe results in a severe impairment of foresight and consideration of remote consequences of action. Conversely, it is also associated with superficial, reflexive emotional responses to external stimuli. Lesions of the orbitofrontal region lead to episodes of transient irritability, brief outbursts of anger, or impulsive action in response to trivial provocations (Blumer & Benson, 1975). Individuals with these lesions are usually indifferent to what they have done (Weiger & Bear, 1988). Perhaps both amygdaloid complex and orbitofrontal integrity (and perhaps even an appropriate level feedback balance between the activity of these regions) is required for proper control of violent impulses and for prosocial behaviors.

LINKS OF FRONTOTEMPORAL LOBE REGIONS TO IMPULSIVITY

Certain childhood characteristics such as an "uninhibited and fearless temperament" may be risk factors for later violence (National Research Council Report, 1993). Adult violent offenders tend to have certain personality features as children: they are hyperactive, impulsive, take risks, and show poor ability to defer gratification (National Research Council Report, 1993). The characteristic of an individual acting with no forethought and without regard to consequences links the criminologists' explanations of criminal propensity by inadequate "self control" (Gottfredson & Hirschi, 1990) or impaired "impulse control" (Wilson & Herrnstein, 1986) and to results suggested by a role of serotonin in impulsive violence (Virkkunen & Linnoila, 1993). The mechanism(s) for impulsive behavior remain unclear. However, most brain researchers would agree that the frontal lobes are crucial in complex tasks where planning is required and that their main function is inhibitory or regulatory. When a person suffers head trauma (irrespective of severity), the temporal and frontal regions (especially the supraorbital) are the areas most likely injured because of their position relative to skull bones (Alexander, 1982; Reitan & Wolfson, 1986). Stevens and Hermann (1981) speculated that there may be damage to the basal forebrain which could be implicated in rage attacks or aggression in temporal lobe epileptic patients. Both the animal and human literature has consistently found impulsive individuals to have reductions in central nervous system serotonin metabolism (Brown & Linnoila, 1990; Higley et al., 1992; Moss, 1987; Virkkunen & Linnoila, 1990). Given the fact that these same reductions are found in individuals with frontotemporal brain damage (Van Woerkom, Teelken, & Minderhoud, 1977) and that orbitomedial frontal lobe damage can lead to impulsive behavior (Blumer & Benson, 1975; Harlow, 1868; Weiger & Bear, 1988), perhaps serotonergic dysfunction is the final common mechanism to the impulsive behavior. This potential dysfunction could be the result of one or a combination of the following factors: varying levels of structural damage, genetic, and experiential influences.

There are individuals who are impulsive but who have no history of head trauma. Perhaps this predisposition to an impulsive behavioral style in these individuals results from either or both genetic and experiential influences. These individuals with an impulsive-response style (originating perhaps in childhood) have a diminished capacity to control their impulses, and tend to fly off the handle when the situation does not require it or when it is not adaptive to do so. Adult violent offenders tend to exhibit evidence of an impulsive-response style as children: they are hyperactive, take risks, and show poor ability to defer gratification (National Research Council Report, 1993). Evidence exists from longitudinal work that children with behavioral problems and certain personality disorders are at increased risk for delinquency and adult offending (Farrington, 1982; McCord, 1979; Moffitt, 1990b; Moffitt & Henry, 1991; Robins & Ratcliff, 1979). Some investigators have hypothesized that such life experiences as victimization during childhood may have an impact on adult behavioral styles. For example, "These early experiences may lead to the development of impulsive behavioral styles that, in turn, are related to deficiencies in problem-solving skills or inadequate school performance that, in turn, predispose those affected towards delinquency or adult criminality" (Widom, 1989, p. 185).

Impulsivity is frequently linked in the literature with alcohol abuse and violent behavior (Kroll, Stock, & James, 1985; Linnoila, de Jong, & Virkkunen, 1989; Muntaner, Walter, & Nagoshi, 1990; Sher & Levenson, 1982; Virkkunen, de Jong, Goodwin, & Linnoila, 1989). Although there are a number of uncertainties about the relationship between impulsivity and violence and alcoholism, there is convergent evidence pointing to a common central serotonin mechanism.

DESCRIPTION OF VIOLENT BEHAVIOR AND EVIDENCE OF FRONTOTEMPORAL DYSFUNCTION IN PSYCHIATRIC AND CRIMINAL POPULATIONS

Psychiatric Populations

Given the great deal of media attention received by the violent crimes committed by the mentally disordered, most lay people believe that there is a clear relationship between mental illness and violent behavior. However, there has been considerable debate as to whether such an association actually exists or whether it results from methodological problems intrinsic in most of the studies to date. Most studies looking at this relationship have concentrated on violence among mentally ill populations or psychiatric disorders among criminal populations (Monahan, 1992). The biases imparted by the selection of these populations for the study of this putative relationship has made the interpretation and generalization of their results very problematic.

To validly test the possible relationship between mental illness and violence, violence among persons with mental disorders in community samples should be assessed. To date there are only a handful of such studies. Swanson and collaborators (Swanson, Holzer, Ganju, & Tsutumo Jono, 1990), using data from the Epidemiologic Catchment Area program (Regier et al., 1984), found an increased prevalence of self-reported violent behavior among those respondents with a mental disorder. Moreover, they reported that persons with multiple disorders were more likely to report violence than those with only one disorder. The presence of an association between mental illness and violent behavior was replicated in two other studies (Hodgins, 1992; Link, Cullen, & Andrews, 1992). These two studies, although using somewhat different definitions of violent behavior and sampling methods, clearly indicated that the presence of major mental disorders elevated the risk for violent behavior.

Prevalence of Psychiatric Violence. Violent behavior by psychiatric patients in the community was an important reason for psychiatric inpatient admission (Craig, 1982; Lagos, Perlmutter, & Saexinger, 1977; McNiel, Binder, & Greenfield, 1988; Rossi, Jacobs, & Monteleone, 1985; Tardiff & Sweillam, 1980). Once inside the hospital, the reported rates of violent behavior depend, in part, on the definition of violent behaviors and on their method of detection (Convit, Isay, Otis, & Volavka, 1990). The rates of violent behavior while in the hospital among psychiatric inpatients differ widely across reports. A middle-of-the-road estimate for the New York State mental health system suggests that 7% of all inpatients will commit at least one aggressive act against another person over a 3-month period (Tardiff & Sweillam, 1980).

There appears to be a continuity of violent behavior: The best predictor of future violence is past violent behavior. Different investigators describe that a high percentage of the inpatient violence is accounted by a small group of patients (Convit et al., 1990; Depp, 1983; Fottrell, 1980; Ionno, 1983). The most common characteristics among violent psychiatric inpatients were that they are male, young, and predominantly schizophrenic (Convit et al., 1990; Fottrell, 1980; Karson & Bigelow, 1987). There was some evidence that the diagnoses of organic brain syndrome and personality disorders may also be overrepresented among violent inpatients (Convit et al., 1990; Evenson, Sletten, Altman, & Brown, 1974). Other correlates of psychiatric inpatient violence included histories of violent crime, deviant family rearing environment, and violent suicide attempts as well as subtle neurological abnormality (Convit, Jaeger, Lin, Meisner, & Volavka, 1988). After this initial report, in a companion study, our group further described the presence of diffuse neurological and neuropsychological abnormalities among the violent inpatients and found that these abnormalities were related to their level of violence (Krakowski, Convit, Jaeger, Lin, & Volavka, 1989).

Relationship Between Psychiatric Violence and Brain Dysfunction. There is little work characterizing the brain functioning of violent psychiatric patients. In this section we review studies linking brain function (neurological, neuropsychological, and EEG) and violence in subjects who had psychiatric diagnoses ranging from psychoses to substance abuse.

There have been a few reports linking diffuse brain dysfunction with violence among psychiatric patients as assessed by the Luria–Nebraska Neuropsychological Battery (Adams, Meloy, & Moritz, 1990), a structured Quantified Neurological Examination (Convit et al., 1988; Convit, Volavka, Czobor, de Asis, & Evangelista, 1994), and a history of head injury with loss of consciousness (Felthous, 1980). In addition to the studies that have shown an association between violence and diffuse brain dysfunction, there are a few studies reporting frontal and temporal abnormalities related to the violent behavior. Among a group of 45 neuropsychiatric inpatients, frontal lesions (confirmed by means of computerized axial tomography) as opposed to general cerebral damage were related to their in-hospital violent incidents (Heinrichs, 1989). Using the Luria–Nebraska Neuropsychological Battery, Adams and coinvestigators found that in a group of adult schizophrenics in a psychiatric unit within a jail, a history of violent acts in the community was associated with more neuropsychological impairment (Adams et al., 1990). Our group described that in a group of right-handed adult male violent psychiatric inpatients, the level of the violence was related to the relative power of delta activity over the frontal lobes (Convit, Czobor, & Volavka, 1991). These results were independent of concurrent antipsychotic medication. In a similar study of drug abusers, who had been drug free for 48 hours prior to the EEG examination, Fishbein and colleagues (1989) found that the level of aggressiveness, assessed using the Buss–Durkee hostility inventory (Buss & Durkee, 1957), was associated with slowing of the EEG over frontocentral areas. Volkow and Tancredi (1987), employing positron emission tomography (PET), found dysfunction of the frontal lobes in 2 of 4 forensic patients.

Although there is some evidence that violence is more prevalent among certain broad diagnostic categories (including schizophrenia and organic brain syndrome), this apparent relationship may be related to the higher level of neurological abnormality in these populations (Heinrichs & Buchanan, 1988). Some investigators have suggested that these broad diagnostic categories are not predictive, in their own right, of violent behavior (Heinrichs, 1989). There is some literature on the interplay of neurological variables and affective behavior (Heinrichs, 1987; Stuss & Benson, 1984). Heinrichs (1989) identified two neurological variables that he felt could contribute to an understanding of violence in chronic neuropsychiatric populations: frontal cerebral lesions and a history of seizures. He also found that chronic hospitalization could predict some aspects of patient violence. The nature of the neurological associations to violence was unclear and requires closer examination.

The violent psychiatric populations we have studied report a high rate of violent criminal offenses (Convit et al., 1988). Perhaps the violent inpatients we have studied simply represent a subgroup of violent offenders and consequently share some characteristics with them. Some populations have both psychiatric disorders and criminal offenses, such as drug abusers and forensic patients. Studies involving these populations are reviewed next.

Criminal Populations

In contrast to the few studies exploring brain function in violent psychiatric populations, there have been numerous neurobiological studies in criminal populations. In psychiatric populations, there appears to be a continuity of violence across different settings (Convit et al., 1988). We provide a selected review of the biological literature on offenders here. For a more comprehensive and critical review of the literature on the psychobiology of aggression refer to Volavka (1994).

Using cross-sectional designs, a number of authors have described a link between violence and brain dysfunction (Bryant, Scott, Golden, & Tori, 1984; Gudjonsson & Roberts, 1981; Langevin, Ben-Aron, Wortzman, Dickey, & Handy, 1987; Lewis, Shanook, Pincus, & Glaser, 1979; Lewis et al., 1985; Lewis et al., 1988; Lewis, Lovely, Yeager, & Femina, 1989; Pontius & Yudowitz, 1980; Spellacy, 1977, 1978; Volkow & Tancredi, 1987). Yeudall (1977) reported abnormal patterns on the Halstead–Reitan Neuropsychological Battery (HRNB) in 90% of violent offenders. The HRNB has also differentiated psychopathic and nonpsychopathic criminals (Fedora & Fedora, 1983; Hare & Jutai, 1983; Hare & McPherson, 1984; Yeudall, Fromm-Auch, & Davies, 1982). Langevin et al. (1987) found that HRNB scores differentiated murderers, other violent offenders, and nonviolent controls. Finally, Lewis and colleagues found impairments on EEG, neurological examination, and the HRNB in an uncontrolled study of juveniles on death row (Lewis et al., 1988). Persistently-violent offenders showed left ear advantage (poorer right ear functioning) on dichotic listening paradigms indicating left hemisphere dysfunction (Nachshon, 1988). Other researchers have also found impairments lateralized to the dominant hemisphere is a sample of violent offenders (Yeudall & Fromm-Auch, 1979). Langevin and coauthors examined the brain structure and function of 91 sexual aggressives and found some striking brain abnormalities. Forty-one percent of 22 identified sexual sadists (admitters) had right temporal horn dilatation as compared to 11% of the nonsadistic sexual aggressives ($N = 21$) and 13% of the offender controls ($N = 36$). This was a subtle but statistically significant phenomenon (Langevin et al., 1988). Taken together, these diverse reports suggest that neuropsychological, neurological, and neuroradiological findings are related to criminal violence and that perhaps the dominant hemisphere is preferentially affected. However, the nature, extent, and type of interaction with other biological, personality, and historical risk factors remains to be determined.

Apart from the neurological, structural neuroimaging, and neuropsychological studies described, there is also evidence demonstrating that EEG slowing in childhood may predispose to later criminal behavior, including violent crime (Raine et al., 1990). In the largest study of its type, Williams (1969), using 333 offenders who committed violent crimes, found that EEG slowing (delta and theta activity) over frontotemporal areas was associated with a history of repetitive violent crime. Using reliable computerized EEG analyses, the following studies have reported an association between EEG and violence: generalized slowing of the EEG in aggressive boys (Surwillo, 1980); and frontocentral slowing associated with a history of aggressive behavior in adult male drug abusers (Fishbein et al., 1989). Please note the parallel of these findings to those reported by our group in violent psychiatric patients cited earlier. We found that anterior slowing related to degree of violent behavior in violent psychiatric inpatients and that the findings lateralized to the dominant hemisphere (Convit et al., 1991).

There appears to be a higher prevalence of epilepsy among adult prisoners than in the general populations. Whitman and coworkers found that among a group of adult prisoners in Illinois the prevalence of epilepsy was fourfold that of comparable nonprisoner groups (Whitman, Coleman, Patmon, Desai, & Cohen, 1984). However, the importance to violence of this higher prevalence remains unclear; two groups have reported that epileptic prisoners did not commit more serious or more violent crimes than their nonepileptic counterparts (Gunn & Bonn, 1971; Whitman et al., 1984). In summary, the EEG–violence literature indicates: Frontotemporal EEG slowing is a relatively reliable finding in violent criminals; the slowing is more expressed in repeated offenders; and the development of slowing perhaps precedes the onset of the criminal careers. A detailed review of this literature has been published elsewhere (Volavka, 1990).

PILOT STUDIES

Our group has carried out a series of studies in a special state hospital inpatient unit, which was specially designed to evaluate and treat violent psychiatric inpatients who can not be managed on their home wards. In a first set of studies of this population we described that diffuse subtle neurological dysfunction, assessed with the Quantified Neurological Scale (QNS) developed by Dr. Convit (Convit et al., 1988), differentiates violent from matched nonviolent psychiatric inpatients (Convit, Jaeger, Lin, Meisner, & Volavka, 1988), and is related to the degree of violence (Krakowski, Convit, Jaeger, Lin, & Volavka, 1989), and to poor treatment response (Krakowski, Convit, Jaeger, & Volavka, 1989). We speculated that repeatedly violent schizophrenics may represent a distinct group characterized by early onset of illness, neurological abnormality, and poor response to treatment (Krakowski, Convit, Jaeger, Lin, & Volavka, 1989).

After this first set of studies we wanted to test if more localized brain dysfunction was related to the degree of violence. To this end we assessed, in a subgroup of patients evaluated in the special violence unit, the relationship between quantified computerized EEG characteristics and the level of their violent behavior. We found that a higher level of violence was accompanied by slowing of the EEG (larger power in the delta band) and that there was a relationship between lateralization of the EEG and the amount of violence. We found that the amount of violence was significantly related to the EEG hemispheric asymmetry for the frontotemporal derivations: With an increased level of violence, there was a greater level of power of delta band activity in the left hemisphere when compared with the right hemisphere (Convit et al., 1991). Most of the subjects in this uncontrolled EEG study were schizophrenic. We could, therefore, not rule out that this relationship was limited to schizophrenia. To assess whether these findings were not due to the diagnosis of schizophrenia, we carried out two pilot studies utilizing a nonviolent schizophrenic control group. In the first study we contrasted the computed tomography (CT) scans of a group of violent schizophrenics with gender and age-matched nonviolent schizophrenics; in the second study we contrasted a new group of violent schizophrenic inpatients with a group of age-matched nonviolent schizophrenic inpatients by using computerized EEG and a quantified neurological assessment. These pilot studies are discussed next.

Brain Computed Tomography (CT) Differences Between Violent and Nonviolent Schizophrenic Inpatients

Subjects. A group of 9 consenting violent schizophrenic males (age 32.1 ± 5.4; 5 African American, 2 Hispanic, and 2 Caucasian) selected from consecutive admissions to the Intensive Psychiatric Service described earlier, were taken to the New York University Medical Center for a CT scan of the brain. Control schizophrenic males, matched on age and race (age 31.2 ± 4.1; 5 African American, 2 Hispanic, and 2 Caucasian) were selected from patients who had participated in different studies at New York University and had received a brain CT scan using the same protocol.

CT Evaluations. Scans were obtained with a GE 9800 CT scanner. All subjects were placed in the scanner using a head holder. Patients were positioned using a laser coordinate system and according to external landmarks were "secured" in place by foam wedges. Two protocols were used:

1. In the first protocol we obtained 10-mm thick contiguous slices from the base of the brain to the vertex in a conventional plane parallel to the cantho-meatal (CM) line. Using this CM protocol we rated the overall extent of ventricular enlargement and sulcal prominence (cortical atrophy) in the different regions (frontal, temporal, parietal, occipital, and cerebellar) using a 4-point scale which included anchor reference cases for each of the points (de Leon et al., 1980). We also obtained linear measurements by using a transparent metric ruler placed directly on the hard copy of the scan. The linear measurements, which were assessed from the one or two slices that best depicted the basal ganglia, foramen of Monroe, and third ventricle, were bifrontal span of the lateral ventricle, width of the lateral ventricles at the level of the head of the caudate nucleus, the width of the third ventricle, and the separate width of each of the

frontal horns. The methodology for these linear measurements has been described elsewhere (de Leon et al., 1980). Each linear measurement was corrected for brain size, and an overall ventricular–brain ratio (VBR) was calculated. This procedure produces a linear VBR that is highly correlated with ventricular volume VBRs and which is highly reliable across observers (de Leon et al., 1993). The scans were also rated for the presence of white matter lesions.

2. The second protocol included six contiguous 5-mm thick slices through the temporal lobes at an infraorbital-meatal angulation of 20–25 degrees negative to the cantho-meatal (CM) plane. This negative angle of scanning runs parallel to the long axis of the temporal lobe and allows evaluation of the peri-hippocampal CSF and improves the ability to visualize the temporal horn and Sylvian Fissure. Using the images from this second protocol subjective ratings of the hippocampus, using the 4-point scale, where 0 = *normal*, 1 = *questionable*, 2 = *mild–moderate*, 3 = *severe* (de Leon et al., 1993), were also carried out. The Sylvian Fissure was rated using the same 4-point scale by examining the images from both protocols.

In order to rate the CT scans blind to group membership, an opaque tape was placed over all the identifying information on the films. All the subjective ratings were done by consensus by two investigators (AC and GS).

Results. There were no differences between the violent and nonviolent schizophrenics for any of the ventricular linear measurements; namely there was no evidence of increased ventricular size for the violent group. The regional ratings of cortical atrophy were in each case larger for the violent than for the nonviolent group. However, none of them came close to reaching statistical significance; the means and standard deviations were as follows: *frontal* 0.89 ± 0.78 vs. 0.56 ± 0.72; *temporal* 0.11 ± 0.33 vs. 0.0 ± 0.0; *parietal* 0.44 ± 0.53 vs. 0.11 ± 0.33; *occipital* 0.33 ± 0.50 vs. 0.0 ± 0.0; *cerebellar* 0.67 ± 0.71 vs. 0.33 ± 0.50 for the violent and nonviolent groups respectively. The ratings of hippocampal atrophy or of white matter lesions also did not differentiate the two groups. The subjective rating for the Sylvian Fissure was significantly larger for the violent subjects (0.89 ± 0.93 vs. 0.22 ± 0.44; $t = 1.91$, $df = 16$, $p < 0.05$ one-tailed). The subjective enlargement of the Sylvian Fissure was present bilaterally.

Comment. We did not find any difference in ventricular size or level of cortical atrophy between the violent and nonviolent schizophrenic groups. The enlargement of the Sylvian Fissure (SF) in the violent schizophrenic group probably reflects brain loss in the areas adjoining the fissure. This brain volume loss could give rise to some level of dysfunction in the frontotemporal region, which adjoins the Sylvian Fissure. The enlargement of the SF in the violent group is consistent with our prior finding of frontotemporal slowing in the EEG being related to the level of violence. In this small number of subjects who had received a CT scan we found no preferential enlargement of the left SF to parallel the EEG hemispheric asymmetry in frontotemporal derivations that we had found in the EEG study mentioned earlier.

We found that although both groups were quite chronic, the violent schizophrenics tended to have a longer duration of psychiatric illness (15.4 ± 7.54 vs. 9.3 ± 4.72; $F = 4.25$, $p = 0.06$). We had only matched the violent and nonviolent schizophrenic groups on age, gender, and race. There is considerable literature in schizophrenia linking chronicity of illness with ventricular enlargement. However, despite the trend for the violent schizophrenic group to have a larger number of years ill, we found a practically identical ventricular size between the violent and nonviolent groups. To our knowledge, no relationship between chronicity of illness and SF enlargement has been described in schizophrenia. Therefore, it appears that the enlargement of the SF in the violent group is related to the chronicity of the illness. Perhaps SF enlargement is another characteristic of this group of repeatedly violent schizophrenic patients, who we know to have neurological impairment, early age of illness onset, and poor response to treatment. We have speculated that perhaps these repeatedly violent schizophrenics with neurological dysfunction and who fail to respond to conventional psychopharmacologic treatment constitute a distinct subgroup of schizophrenics. Given that the number of subjects we studied was small, our findings need to be interpreted with caution. Future imaging studies of violent schizophrenics should control for age, gender, *duration of illness*, and utilize larger samples.

Neurological and EEG Differences between Violent and Matched Nonviolent Schizophrenics

The main purpose for this pilot was to replicate, using a controlled design, the EEG findings demonstrating a relationship between frontotemporal EEG slowing and violence.

Subjects. Thirteen repeatedly violent schizophrenic males (age 32.8 ± 6.6; years ill 15.2 ± 8.1) who did not overlap with the subjects reported on previously (Convit et al., 1991) and who were being treated on the special violence unit received a computerized EEG and a quantified neurological assessment. These violent schizophrenics were contrasted with a group of 13 nonviolent schizophrenic males (age 31.4 ± 5.2; years ill 15.1 ± 6.1) who had received the same evaluations and who had participated in a drug efficacy study (Volavka et al., 1992).

Neurological Evaluation. Neurological abnormality was assessed using the Quantified Neurological Scale (QNS; Convit et al., 1988). The level of abnormality on the QNS has been found to differentiate violent from nonviolent psychiatric inpatients (Convit et al., 1988; Krakowski, Convit, Jaeger, & Volavka, 1989; Krakowski, Convit, Jaeger, Lin, & Volavka, 1989) and to be related to their response to treatment (Krakowski, Convit, and Volavka, 1988). Since these original studies, we have expanded the QNS to 96 items. Thirty-six items, which assess cranial nerves, reflexes, cerebellar function, pyramidal tract function, and muscle strength, are used to screen for gross neurological dysfunction. The remaining items measure more subtle forms of neurodysfunction. The QNS generates some subscores: an overall neurological abnormality score (which we call NEURO), frontal, soft-signs and cerebellar function. All items on the scale were rated as 0 for *normal* and 1 for *abnormal*. The sum of item scores in each subscale reflected the abnormality score for that subscale. The QNS is a highly reliable instrument. To assess reliability of the expanded QNS, two trained physicians independently rated 30 patients. For the individual items, the interrater reliabilities kappa [K] ranged from 0.69 to 1. Eighty-seven items (96%) had a K of 0.75 or greater. We attribute the high level of reliability to the very detailed administration and coding instructions that we have developed. The scale has been published elsewhere (Convit et al., 1994); instructions for administration and coding can be obtained from the first author.

To assess the validity of the QNS we contrasted, in a separate group of 28 psychiatric inpatients, the NEURO scores with the Halstead–Reitan Impairment Index (HRII) of the Halstead–Reitan neuropsychological battery (Reitan, 1979) and the frontal score with the number of errors on the Wisconsin Card Sort (WCS) (Berg, 1948), a widely accepted measure of frontal lobe function. The total QNS abnormality was significantly related to the HRII ($r = 0.43$, $N = 28$, $p = 0.02$). The frontal abnormality subscore, which uses the newly added items, was significantly related to the number of errors on the WCS ($r = 0.47$, $N = 28$, $p = 0.01$).

Electroencephalogram (EEG). A Cadwell Spectrum 32 system was utilized to measure the quantified computerized EEG (John, Prichep, Fridman, & Easton, 1988). Recordings were obtained using an electrode cap, available in three different head sizes, to minimize discomfort for the subject and to optimize the electrode placement. These are the same EEG procedures we have previously utilized successfully with a similar population of violent mentally ill subjects (Convit et al., 1991). A 10- to 15-minute sample of resting EEG was recorded from 19 electrodes of the International 10–20 System, referenced to linked earlobes, in an eyes closed situation. Prior to data collection all electrode contact impedances were below 3 k Ohm. The sampling rate was 205/sec, the time constant 0.3 sec, and the upper cut off frequency 30 Hz. During recording, the ongoing EEG was visually monitored. Electrooculogram was used (with electrode locations at the right and left ocular canthi) to recognize and eliminate eye-movement artifacts. Whenever a decrease in vigilance was detected on the ongoing EEG, the technician instructed the subject to open his eyes; a short pause was allowed, when needed, to minimize drowsiness.

After the 10–15 minute sample of resting EEG was recorded, off-line, epochs with artifacts (eye blinks, eye movements, muscle activity, and movement potentials) were identified visually and rejected. From each recording, 2.5 sec samples of artifact-free EEG (total duration: 60–120 sec) were collected. The EEG slows when the subject becomes drowsy. To ensure that only baseline resting EEG segments were included, without the contamination of segments when the individual was becoming drowsy, specific criteria for recognizing drowsiness were employed. Principal criteria for recognizing drowsiness were: (a) spread and shift of alpha to anterior regions followed by a disintegration and fragmentation of occipital alpha, and (b) a general dissolution of resting activity into theta waves with superimposed beta activity (Bente, 1979; Streitberg, Rohmel, Herrmann, & Kubicki, 1987).

For the analyses, bipolar derivations were created from the monopolar ear-referenced recordings. Statistical analysis of the selected EEG epochs were based on procedures described elsewhere (John, Prichep, & Easton, 1987; John et al., 1988). Briefly, first, power spectral analysis was performed to yield log-transformed values of relative power in the delta (1.5–3.5 Hz), theta (3.5–7.5 Hz), alpha (7.5–12.5 Hz), and beta (12.5–19.5 Hz) frequency bands for each bipolar channel. Measures of relative power were then used as they demonstrate small variability and provide excellent test–retest reliability (John et al., 1980). Second, the relative power values were transformed into standard scores. Standard scores express the deviations of the above relative power features from the predicted age-normative values expressed in standard deviation units. Description of the age regression equations and the rationale behind their use are provided elsewhere (John et al., 1980; John et al., 1987).

Statistical Method. In a prior EEG study we found a link between frontotemporal slowing and lateralization to the dominant hemisphere and the level of violence (Convit et al., 1991). The current study was designed to replicate those findings in a group of violent schizophrenics using a control nonviolent group. Given that we had only 13 matched pairs, a relatively small number of subjects, we selected the derivations and frequency bands that had shown the relationship to violence in the previous study in order to minimize the number of analyses run. We selected 12 EEG variables: 8 reflected the relative delta and alpha power from the right and left frontotemporal derivations (F7–T3 and F8–T4) and 4 reflected the asymmetry measures for those derivations and frequency bands. From the QNS we chose three variables: the total abnormality score (NEURO), the soft-sign score, and the frontal abnormality score (FRONTAL).

The violent (V) and nonviolent (NV) schizophrenics were contrasted by repeated measures analysis of variance. Group (V and NV) was used as a between-subject factor. The within-subject factors were: laterality, derivation, and frequency band. If any of the neurological subscales were significantly different between V and NV those ratings were used as covariates. In these analysis of variance models, the interactions between grouping and within-subject factors tested an EEG difference between the two groups. Namely, we tested if there was a difference between the groups on lateralization by head location (LATERALIZATION*DERIVATION*GROUP) or a difference between the groups on lateralization by frequency band (LATERALIZATION*BAND*GROUP).

Results. The only neurological subscale that differentiated the two groups significantly was the frontal (FRONTAL) subscale. The violent schizophrenic group had significantly more number of frontal abnormalities than the schizophrenic control group (9.48 ± 6.1 vs. 4.2 ± 3.0; $F[1,23]$ = 8.76, $p < 0.01$). The repeated measures ANOVAs indicated the absence of a third-order interaction between group laterality and derivation and the presence a third-order interaction between group, laterality, and band ($F = 4.28$; $df = 1,23$; $p < .04$).

Comment. This pilot study confirmed, using a case-control design, that there is an excess of delta activity in the left hemisphere (for both the frontotemporal and temporotemporal derivations) as compared to the right hemisphere for the violent group. This effect was not present for the nonviolent group. Furthermore, we also found that the violent schizophrenics had a significantly higher level of frontal abnormality on the QNS. The EEG effect seen was beyond and above the effect seen for the frontal abnormality on the QNS. These findings lend support to our contention that there may be a relationship between frontotemporal dysfunction and violence among schizophrenic inpatients and that perhaps this relationship is more pronounced for the dominant hemisphere.

Although we have not shown that dysfunction of the frontotemporal region causes violent behavior, we have presented some preliminary data demonstrating an association between the two. Given the theoretical and empirical support associating these anterior brain regions with poor impulse control and violent behavior, we propose a conceptual framework for the future study of those brain–behavior relationships.

CONCLUSIONS AND SUGGESTIONS FOR FUTURE RESEARCH

In its recent report on *Understanding and Prevention of Violence*, the National Research Council (NRC, 1993), stressed that "Violence is a complex and multifaceted form of behavior. It is likely that there are no simple explanations of violence" (p. 381). At the same time, members of the MacArthur Foundation effort on risk assessment, write: "no such (big "T") Theory of violence exists. . . . given that violence has multiple causes, it may be that a single coherent theory linking each of these causal influences is not feasible" (Steadman et al.,

1994). However, a broad conceptual framework, albeit short of a single unifying theory, is essential. This broad conceptual framework would represent the structure that will generate and integrate specific correlational and potential etiological hypotheses.

Biological, behavioral, and social literature suggest that a lowered impulse control could be the nucleus of such a framework. The appeal of this approach is its compatibility with contributions drawn from different disciplines. For example, reduced impulse control could result from brain influences (i.e., brain "damage" and abnormalities in the serotonin system), behavioral influences (i.e., substance use and abuse, certain personality characteristics, and certain psychiatric diagnoses such as borderline and antisocial personality disorders), and life experiences (i.e., peer system, witnessing violence, and child abuse and neglect). This multidimensional approach integrating biological views with behavioral and environmental (psychosocial) influences will give rise to more relevant etiological theories which can be tested. It is important to develop an understanding of which risk factors (and the interactions among those risk factors) contribute to violence. This understanding will guide the development of realistic intervention and prevention strategies. Research should examine violent behavior in the context of a multidimensional framework that builds on univariate linkages established in past research.

The best way to test a causal theory of criminal violence is a longitudinal prospective design. By using a longitudinal prospective design, one could tease apart perinatal, developmental, family, and environmental contributions to criminal violence. However, as general population longitudinal studies of delinquent and criminal activity have demonstrated (Moffitt, 1990a), the number of truly violent individuals in these samples is very low, which makes it difficult to identify risk factors. We have a crisis of violence in our society. Given the great time and monetary costs of longitudinal research, it behooves us first to identify risk factors (and their interactions) associated with criminal violence, which could then be used to target assessments in longitudinal studies of *high-risk* populations. To examine clearly identified violent individuals, we suggest using a cross-sectional design. For example, by studying adult repeat offenders, investigators would be concentrating their efforts on those individuals with serious criminal violence after a "life pattern" of violence has been established. The most productive and least expensive way to study large numbers of violent individuals is in a prison setting.

New technologies allow more direct and sophisticated views of the brain. Moreover, we believe these brain evaluations should be carried out using various modalities of assessment. We recommend an anatomic view such as MRI, a functional view such as Functional Magnetic Resonance Imaging (FMRI), Positron Emission Tomography (PET), Single Photon Emission Tomography (SPECT), or (Electroencephalogram) EEG, and a behavioral view such as Neuropsychological assessment. However, studying clearly identified violent individuals has limitations. Apart from the problems of generalizability to violence in general, there are practical limitations inherent in the security considerations of the prison system. It is almost impossible to transport violent prisoners to centers that offer many of the new technologies. One is therefore restricted to the technologies that can be used on the actual prison site; these are the EEG and neuropsychological testing.

Methodological shortcomings of early research into the relationship between neuropsychological test scores and delinquent or violent behavior have made it difficult for current research to corroborate results. Many of these methodological problems have been remedied in recent research, but should be noted to minimize the occurrence of future design flaws. These methodological problems have included: (a) problems with the definitions of violence; (b) absence or poorly matched control groups; time elapsed between the neuropsychological assessment and the beginning of the violent behavior allowing potential confounds such as substance abuse, head injury, truancy, and incarceration to intervene in lowering the test scores; and (c) the creation of a univariate view where in addition little effort has been spent in controlling for the potential confounds of race, gender, or social class. Clearly these limitations have to be addressed in future work.

Moffitt, Lynam, and Silva (1994) suggest that neuropsychological research can make inferences about the developmental origins of crime by offering a fine grained analysis of mental functions beyond the IQ, and by supporting inferences that observable behavior is linked to the physical health of the brain. Neuropsychological batteries can assess a variety of functions such as memory, motor skill, language processing, judgment, and mental self-control. Many different investigation methods have provided evidence that neuropsychological test scores are linked to brain function and to behavior. For example, neuropsychological performance tests of self-control were originally designed to document presence of injury or disease in the frontal areas of the brain of neurological patients. These tests have discriminated patients with frontal brain damage from patients with focal disease elsewhere in the brain (Lezak, 1983). Subsequent research has further demonstrated the validity of these tests by showing that nonclinical subjects who perform poorly on tests of self-control are also described as impulsive by teachers, parents, and others (White, Moffitt, & Silva, 1989); show poor blood flow to the frontal lobes of the brain (Lou, Henriksen, & Bruhn, 1984); and exhibit abnormalities in electroencephalographic recordings from electrode sites over the temporal and parietal regions (Raine, 1988).

With respect to the brain functioning aspect of a multidimensional approach, we feel that future work should be guided by a model concentrating on frontal and temporal lobe assessments. Some specific or specialized functions are related principally to a particular region of cerebral cortex whereas other higher-level brain functions are diffusely distributed throughout the cerebral cortex.

Clearly it would not be accurate to describe any one cognitive function as localizing to an exact part of the brain. Thus, the following descriptions of functional localization for the cognitive tests should only be regarded as an illustration of how such cognitive tests would fit into a frontal-temporal lobe model. We briefly review some of the cognitive manifestations of the two brain components of this frontotemporal model (individually and collectively). A few examples (not intended as an exhaustive list) of some specific neuropsychological measures for assessing these abilities are provided.

Frontal Lobe

Luria (1966a, 1966b) suggested that the anterior frontal lobes were responsible for executive functions that he felt were involved in every complex behavioral process. More specifically, frontal lobe damage was associated with deficits in judgment, insight, mental flexibility, reasoning, abstraction, planning, and sequencing. The aspects of attention that depended on response inhibition and on the ability to sustain behavioral output were also associated with frontal lobe disturbance. Furthermore, lesions in the orbital part of the frontal lobes may lead to memory disturbances.

Judgment and insight are difficult to test objectively and no formal tests are currently available. However, insight can be judged by a patient's awareness and understanding of his or her illness. Denial or minimization of disease is an example of poor insight. Socially inappropriate behavior may also be indicative of impaired judgment and insight. Mental flexibility can be assessed by tasks such as The Trail Making Test, forms A and B (Reitan, 1979). Reasoning and abstraction are best measured by tasks such as the Comprehension and Similarities subtests of the Wechsler Adult Intelligence Scale–Revised (Wechsler, 1981), proverb interpretation (such as found in the Mental State Examination or the Gorham Proverbs Test [Gorham, 1956]), and The Wisconsin Card Sorting Test (Grant & Berg, 1980). The Raven Progressive Matrices (Raven, 1956) and the Hooper Test (Hooper, 1958) specifically assess nonverbal reasoning abilities. Although there are very few formal tests of planning and sequencing abilities, Alternating Sequences Test (Luria, 1966a, 1966b) and drawing of a clock (Mesulam, 1985) have been used. The Porteus Maze Test (Porteus, 1959, 1965) has also been used to assess one's ability to plan a strategy for negotiating visual mazes. Digit Span and Visual Memory Span (from the Wechsler Memory Scale–Revised, WMS-R; Wechsler, 1984) are measures of attention and concentration and Finger Tapping assesses sustained behavioral output (Reitan, 1979).

Temporal Lobe

The temporal lobes contain auditory cortex, visual association cortex, and medially situated limbic and paralimbic structures. The left temporal lobe also contains Wernicke's area and has traditionally been assessed by tests of naming and language comprehension. Corresponding parts of the right temporal lobe can be tested with nonverbal complex auditory tasks such as identification of environmental sounds and discrimination of memory for tones, timbre, and pitch. Integrity of temporal limbic and paralimbic regions can be tested with the help of memory tests. For the left temporal lobe, verbal measures such as the Logical Memory II and Verbal Paired Associates II (subtests from the WMS-R [Wechsler, 1984]) and the Rey Auditory Verbal Learning Test (Rey, 1964) have been used. Visual Reproduction II, another subtest from the WMS-R is a nonverbal memory test frequently used to assess right temporal lobe functioning. Bilateral lesions that damage the visual association areas of the temporal lobe or their connectivity with other parts of the brain can result in very complex deficits that include visual amnesia, prosopagnosia, object agnosia, and visual anomia. Unilateral lesions in the auditory association cortex are best detected clinically with the Dichotic Listening Test (Kimura, 1961).

A number of higher level brain functions are associated with adjoining regions on different lobes. The posterior inferior frontal lobe, temporal lobe, and adjacent lower parts of the parietal lobe are involved in expressive and receptive aspects of language and verbal functioning (Penfield & Roberts, 1959). The Boston Diagnostic Aphasia Examination (Goodglass & Kaplan, 1983) is a standardized test for examining the variety of linguistic components of language, both spoken and written. Other abilities that are a product of the interrelatedness between the frontal and temporal lobes can be assessed by such measures as Visual Memory Span (a subtest of the WMS-R [Wechsler, 1984]) and the Digit Symbol Substitution Test (a subtest of the WAIS-R [Wechsler, 1981]).

In conclusion, we advocate the study of violence within a broad multidimensional framework that will allow the differences and interactions between biology and environment to be assessed. We advocate the assessment of brain dysfunction as one of the biological risk factors to be considered. Moreover, we propose that such brain functioning assessment should utilize a multifaceted approach, utilizing several partly overlapping and complementary techniques. Finally, given our reading of the literature and our own pilot studies reported on here, we advocate the brain assessment to be focused predominantly on the frontal and temporal regions.

REFERENCES

Adams, J. J., Meloy, J. R., & Moritz, M. S. (1990). Neuropsychological deficits and violent behavior in incarcerated schizophrenics. *Journal of Nervous and Mental Disease, 178,* 253–256.

Alexander, M. (1982). Traumatic brain injury. In D. F. Benson & D. Blumer (Eds.), *Psychiatric aspects of neurologic disease Vol. 2* (pp. 219–249). New York: Grune & Stratton.

Bear, D. M. (1991). Neurological perspectives on aggressive behavior. *Journal of Neuropsychiatry, 3*(2), 53–58.

Bente, D. (1979). Vigilance and evaluation of psychotropic drug effects on EEG. *Pharmakopsychiatry, 12,* 137–147.

Berg, E. A. (1948). A simple objective test for measuring flexibility of thinking. *Journal of General Psychology, 39*, 15–22.

Blumer, D., & Benson, D. F. (1975). Personality changes with frontal and temporal lobe lesions. In D. F. Benson & D. Blumer (Eds.), *Psychiatric Aspects of Neurologic Disease*. New York: Grune & Stratton.

Brooks, N., Campsie, L., Symington, C., Beattie, A., & McKinlay, W. (1986). The five year outcome of severe blunt head injury. *Journal of Neurology, Neurosurgery, and Psychiatry, 49*, 764–770.

Brown, G. L., & Linnoila, M. (1990). CSF serotonin metabolite studies in depression, impulsivity, and violence. *Journal of Clinical Psychiatry, 51*, 31–41.

Bryant, E. T., Scott, M. L., Golden, C. J., & Tori, C. D. (1984). Neuropsychological deficits, learning disability, and violent behavior. *Journal of Consulting and Clinical Psychology, 52*(2), 323–324.

Buss, A., & Durkee, A. (1957). An inventory for assessing different kinds of hostility. *Journal of Consulting Psychology, 21*(4), 343–349.

Convit, A., Czobor, P., & Volavka, J. (1991). Lateralized abnormality in the EEG of persistently violent psychiatric inpatients. *Biological Psychiatry, 30*, 363–370.

Convit, A., Isay, D., Otis, D., & Volavka, J. (1990). Characteristics of repeatedly assaultive psychiatric inpatients. *Hospital and Community Psychiatry, 41*, 1112–1115.

Convit, A., Jaeger, J., Lin, S. P., Meisner, M., Brizer, D., & Volavka, J. (1988). Prediction of violence in psychiatric inpatients. In T. Moffitt & S. Mednick (Eds.), *Biological contributions to crime causation* (pp. 223–245). Amsterdam: Martinus Nijhoff.

Convit, A., Jaeger, J., Lin, S. P., Meisner, M., & Volavka, J. (1988). Prediction of assaultiveness in psychiatric inpatients: A pilot study. *Hospital and Community Psychiatry, 39*, 429–434.

Convit, A., Volavka, J., Czobor, P., de Asis, J., & Evangelista, C. (1994). Effect of subtle neurodysfunction on haloperidol treatment response in schizophrenia. *American Journal of Psychiatry, 151*, 49–56.

Craig, T. J. (1982). An epidemiologic study of problems associated with violence among psychiatric inpatients. *American Journal of Psychiatry, 139*, 1262–1266.

Damasio, H., Grabowski, T., Frank, R., Galaburda, A. N., & Damasio, A. R. (1994). The return of Phineas Gage: Clues about the brain from the skull of a famous patient. *Science, 264*, 1102–1105.

de Leon, M., Ferris, S., George, A., Reisberg, B., Kricheff, I., & Gershon, S. (1980). Computed tomography evaluations of brain-behavior relationships in senile dementia of the Alzheimer's type. *Neurobiology of Aging, 1*, 60–69.

de Leon, M., Golomb, J., George, A. E., Convit, A., Tarshish, C. Y., McRae, T., De Santi, S., Smith, G., Ferris, S., Noz, M., & Rusineck, H. (1993). The radiologic prediction of Alzheimer's disease: The atrophic hippocampal formation. *American Journal of Neuroradiology, 14*, 897–906.

Depp, F. C. (1983). Assaults in a public mental hospital. In J. R. Lion & W. H. Reid (Eds.), *Assaults within psychiatric facilities* (pp. 21–45). New York: Grune & Stratton.

Dykes, L. (1986). The whiplash shaken infant syndrome: What has been learned? *Child Abuse and Neglect, 10*, 211–221.

Evenson, R. C., Sletten, I. W., Altman, H., & Brown, M. L. (1974). Disturbing Behavior: A study of incident reports. *Psychiatric Quarterly, 48*, 66–275.

Farrington, D. P. (1982). Delinquency from 10–25. In S. A. Mednick (Ed.), *Antecedents of aggression and antisocial behavior*. Boston, MA: Kluwer.

Fedora, O., & Fedora, S. (1983). Some neuropsychological and psychophysiological aspects of psychopathic and non-psychopathic criminals. In P. Flor-Henry & J. H. Gruzelier (Eds.), *Laterality and psychopathology*. Amsterdam: Elsevier.

Felthous, A. R. (1980). Childhood antecedents of aggressive behaviors in male psychiatric patients. *Bulletin of the American Academy of Psychiatry and the Law, 8*, 104–110.

Fishbein, D., Herning, R., Pickworth, W., Haertzen, C. A., Hickey, J. F., & Jaffe, J. H. (1989). EEG and brainstem auditory evoked potentials in adult male drug abusers with self-reported histories of aggressive behavior. *Biological Psychiatry, 26*, 595–611.

Fottrell, E. (1980). A study of violent behavior among patients in psychiatric hospitals. *British Journal of Psychiatry, 136*, 216–121.

Fuster, J. M. (1989). *The prefrontal cortex: Anatomy, physiology, and neuropsychology of the frontal lobe*. New York: Raven.

Gedye, A. (1989). Episodic rage and aggression attributed to frontal lobe seizures. *Journal of Mental Deficiency Research, 33*, 369–379.

Goddard, G., McIntyre, D., & Leech, C. (1969). A permanent change in brain function resulting from daily electrical stimulation. *Experimental Neurology, 25*, 295–330.

Goodglass, H., & Kaplan, E. (1983). *The assessment of aphasia and related disorders* (2nd ed.). Philadelphia: Lea & Febiger.

Gorham, D. R. (1956). A proverbs test for clinical and experimental use. *Psychology Reports, 1*, 1.

Gottfredson, M. R., & Hirschi, T. (1990). *A general theory of crime*. Stanford, CA: Stanford University Press.

Grant, D. A., & Berg, E. A. (1980). *The Wisconsin card sort test random layout: Directions for administration and scoring*. Madison, WI: Wells Printing Co.

Gudjonsson, G. H., & Roberts, J. C. (1981). Trail making scores as a prediction of aggressive behavior in personality-disordered patients. *Perceptual and Motor Skills, 52*, 413–414.

Gunn, J., & Bonn, J. (1971). Criminality and violence in epileptic prisoners. *British Journal of Psychiatry, 118*, 337–343.

Hare, R. D., & Jutai, J. (1983). Criminal history of the male psychopath: Some preliminary data. In K. Van Dusen & S. Mednick (Eds.), *Prospective studies of crime and delinquency*. Boston: Kluwer-Nijhoff.

Hare, R. D., & McPherson, L. M. (1984). Violent and aggressive behavior by criminal psychopaths. *International Journal of Law & Psychiatry, 7*, 35–50.

Harlow, J. M. (1868). *Pub. Mass. Medical Society, 2*, 327.

Heinrichs, R. W. (1987). Does depression in patients with known or suspected cerebral disease contribute to impairment in the Luria-Nebraska Neuropsychological Battery? *International Journal of Neuroscience, 32*, 895–899.

Heinrichs, R. W. (1989). Frontal cerebral lesions and violent incidents in chronic neuropsychiatric patients. *Biological Psychiatry, 25*, 174–178.

Heinrichs, D. W., & Buchanan, R. W. (1988). Significance and meaning of neurological signs in schizophrenia. *American Journal of Psychiatry, 145*, 11–18.

Higley, J. D., Mehlman, P. T., Taub, D. M., Higley, S. B., Suomi, S. J., Linnoila, M., & Vickers, J. H. (1992). Cerebrospinal fluid monoamine and adrenal correlates of aggression in free-ranging rhesus monkeys. *Archives of General Psychiatry, 49*, 436–441.

Hitchcock, E., & Cairns, V. (1973). Amygdalotomy. *Postgraduate Medical Journal, 49*, 894–904.

Hodgins, S. (1992). Mental disorder, intellectual deficiency, and crime. Evidence from a birth cohort. *Archives of General Psychiatry, 49*, 476–483.

Hooper, H. W. (1958). *The Hooper visual organization test manual*. Los Angeles: Western Psychological Services.

Ionno, J. A. (1983). A prospective study of assaultive behavior in female psychiatric inpatients. In J. R. Lion & W. H. Reid (Eds.), *Assaults within psychiatric facilities* (pp. 21–45). New York: Grune & Stratton.

John, E. R., Ahn, H., Prichep, L. S., Trepetin, M., Brown, D., & Kaye, H. (1980). Developmental equations for the electroencephalogram. *Science, 210*, 1255–1258.

John, E. R., Prichep, L. S., & Easton, P. (1987). Normative data banks and neurometrics: Basic concepts, methods and results of norm constructions. In A. S. Gevins & A. Remond (Eds.), *Methods of analyzing bioelectric and magnetic signals. EEG handbook. Revised series V. II* (pp. 449–495). New York: Elsevier.

John, E. R., Prichep, L. S., Fridman, J., & Easton, P. (1988). Neurometrics: Computer-assisted differential diagnosis of brain dysfunctions. *Science, 239*, 162–169.

Karson, C., & Bigelow, L. B. (1987). Violent behavior in schizophrenic inpatients. *Journal of Nervous and Mental Disease, 175,* 161–164.

Kimura, D. (1961). Cerebral dominance and the perception of verbal stimuli. *Canadian Journal of Psychology, 15,* 166.

Krakowski, M., Convit, A., Jaeger, J., Lin, S. P., & Volavka, J. (1989). Neurological impairment in violent schizophrenics. *American Journal of Psychiatry, 146,* 849–853.

Krakowski, M., Convit, A., Jaeger, J., & Volavka, J. (1989). Inpatient violence: Trait and state. *Journal of Psychiatric Research, 23,* 57–64.

Krakowski, M., Convit, A., & Volavka, J. (1988). Patterns of inpatient assaultiveness: Effect of neurological impairment and deviant family environment on response to treatment. *Neuropsychiatry, Neuropsychology, and Behavioral Neurology, 1,* 21–29.

Kroll, P., Stock, D., & James, M. (1985). The behavior of adult alcoholic men abused as children. *Journal of Nervous and Mental Disease, 173,* 689–693.

Lagos, J. M., Perlmutter, K., & Saexinger, H. (1977). Fear of the mentally ill: Empirical support for the common man's response. *American Journal of Psychiatry, 134,* 1134–1136.

Langevin, R., Ben-Aron, M., Wortzman, G., Dickey, R., & Handy, L. (1987). Brain damage, diagnosis, and substance abuse among violent offenders. *Behavioral Sciences and the Law, 5,* 77–94.

Langevin, R., Bain, G., Wortzman, G., Hucker, S., Dickey, R., & Wright, P. (1988). Sexual Sadism: Brain, blood, and behavior. *Annals of the New York Academy of Sciences* (Vol. 528), pp. 163–171.

Lewis, D. O., Lovely, R., Yeager, C., & Femina, D. (1989). Toward a theory of the genesis of violence: A follow-up study of delinquents. *Journal of the American Academy of Child Psychiatry, 28,* 431–436.

Lewis, D. O., Moy, E., Jackson, L. D., Aaronson, R., Restifo, N., Serra, S., & Simos, A. (1985). Biopsychosocial characteristics of children who later murder: A prospective study. *American Journal of Psychiatry, 142,* 1161–1167.

Lewis, D. O., Pincus, J. H., Bard, B., Richardson, E., Prichep, L. S., Feldman, M., & Yeager, C. (1988). Neuropsychiatric, psychoeducational, and family characteristics of 14 juveniles condemned to death in the United States. *American Journal of Psychiatry, 145,* 584–589.

Lewis, D. O., Shanook, S. S., Pincus, J. H., & Glaser, G. H. (1979). Violent juvenile delinquents: Psychiatric, neurological, psychological, and abuse factors. *Journal of the American Academy of Child Psychiatry, 18,* 307–319.

Lezak, M. (1983). *Neuropsychological assessment.* New York: Oxford University Press.

Link, B. G., Cullen, F. T., Andrews, H. (1992). The violent and illegal behavior of mental patients reconsidered. *American Sociological Review, 57,* 275–292.

Linnoila, M., de Jong, J., & Virkkunen, M. (1989). Family history of alcoholism in violent offenders and fire setters. *Archives of General Psychiatry, 46,* 613–616.

Lou, H., Henriksen, L., & Bruhn, P. (1984). Focal cerebral hypoperfusion in children with dysphasia and/or attention deficit disorder. *Archives of Neurology, 41,* 825–829.

Luria, A. R. (1966a). *Higher cortical functions in man.* New York: Basic Books.

Luria, A. R. (1966b). *Human brain and psychological processes.* New York: Harper & Row.

McCalla, S. (1991). The biological and social consequences of perinatal cocaine use in an inner-city population: Results of an anonymous cross-sectional study. *Obstetrics and Gynecology, 264,* 625–630.

McCord, J. A. (1979). Some child rearing antecedents of criminal behavior in adult men. *Journal of Personality and Social Psychology, 9,* 1477–1486.

McNiel, D. E., Binder, R. L., & Greenfield, T. K. (1988). Predictors of violence in civilly committed acute psychiatric patients. *American Journal of Psychiatry, 145,* 965–970.

Mesulam, M. M. (1985). *Principles of behavioral neurology.* Philadelphia: F. A. Davis.

Moffitt, T. E. (1990a). Juvenile delinquency and attention-deficit disorder: Developmental trajectories from age 3 to 15. *Child Development, 61,* 893–910.

Moffitt, T. E. (1990b). The neuropsychology of juvenile delinquency: A critical review. In N. Morris & M. Tonry (Eds.), *Crime and justice: An annual review of research.* Chicago: University of Chicago Press.

Moffitt, T. E., & Henry, B. (1991). Neuropsychological studies of juvenile delinquency and juvenile violence. In J. S. Milner (Ed.), *The neuropsychology of aggression.* Boston: Kluwer.

Moffitt, T. E., Lynam, D. R., & Silva, P. A. (1994). Neuropsychological tests predicting persistent male delinquency. *Criminology, 32*(2), 277–300.

Moffitt, T. E., & Silva, P. A. (1988). Neuropsychological deficit and self-reported delinquency in a nonselected birth cohort. *Journal of the American Academy of Child and Adolescent Psychiatry, 27,* 233–240.

Monahan, J. (1992). Mental disorder and violent behavior. Perceptions and evidence. *American Psychologist, 47,* 511–521.

Moss, H. (1987). Serotonergic activity and disinhibitory psychopathy in alcoholism. *Medical Hypotheses, 23,* 353–361.

Muntaner, C., Walter, D., Nagoshi, C. (1990). Self-reports vs. laboratory measures of aggression as predictors of substance abuse. *Drug and Alcohol Dependence, 25,* 1–11.

Nachshon, I. (1988). Hemisphere function in violent offenders. In T. Moffitt & S. Mednick (Eds.), *Biological contributions to crime causation* (pp. 55–67). Amsterdam: Martinus Nijhoff.

National Research Council Report (1993). *Understanding and preventing violence.* Reiss, A. & Roth, J. (Eds.). Washington, DC: National Academy Press.

Penfield, W., & Roberts, L. (1959). *Speech and brain mechanisms.* Princeton, NJ: Princeton University Press.

Petersen, K. G. I., Matousek, M., Mednick, S. A., Volavka, J., & Pollock, V. (1982). EEG antecedents of thievery. *Acta Psychiatrica Scandinavica, 65,* 331–338.

Pontius, A. A., & Yudowitz, B. S. (1980). Frontal lobe dysfunction in some criminal actions shown in the narratives test. *Journal of Nervous and Mental Diseases, 168,* 111–117.

Porteus, S. D. (1959). *The maze test and clinical applications.* Palo Alto, CA: Pacific.

Porteus, S. D. (1965). *The maze test. Fifty years' application.* New York: Psychological Corporation.

Raine, A. (1988). Evoked potentials and antisocial behavior. In T. E. Moffitt, S. A. Mednick, & S. A. Stack (Eds.), *Biological contributions to crime causation.* Dordecht: Nijhoff.

Raine, A., Venables, P. H., & Williams, W. (1990). Relationships between central and autonomic measures of arousal at age 15 years and criminality at age 24 years. *Archives of General Psychiatry, 47,* 1003–1007.

Raven, J. C. (1956). *Guide to using the coloured progressive matrices.* New York: Psychological Corporation.

Regier, D. A., Myers, J. K., Kramer, M., Robins, L. N., Blazer, D. G., Hough, R. L., Eaton, W. W., & Locke, B. Z. (1984). Epidemiologic catchment area program. Historical context, major objectives, and study population characteristics. *Archives of Genral Psychiatry, 41,* 934–941.

Reitan, R. M. (1979). *Manual for administration of neuropsychological test batteries for adults and children.* Tucson, AZ: Neuropsychology Laboratory.

Reitan, R. M., & Wolfson, D. (1986). *The Halstead-Reitan neuropsychological battery: Theory and clinical interpretation.* Tucson, AZ: Neuropsychology Press.

Rey, A. (1964). *L'examen clinique en psychologie.* Paris: Presses Universitaires de France.

Robins, L. N., & Ratcliff, K. S. (1979). Risk factors in the continuation of childhood antisocial behavior into adulthood. *International Journal of Mental Health, 7,* 96–116.

Rossi, A. M., Jacobs, M., Monteleone, M. (1985). Violent or fear-inducing behavior associated with hospital admission. *Hospital and Community Psychiatry, 36,* 643–647.

Rosvold, H. E., Mirsky, A. F., & Pribram, K. H. (1954). Influence of amygdalectomy on social behavior in monkeys. *Journal of Comparative and Physiological Psychology, 47,* 173–178.

Sher, K., & Levenson, R. (1982). Risk for alcoholism and individual differences in the stress-response-dampening effect of alcohol. *Journal of Abnormal Psychology, 91,* 350–367.

Spellacy, F. (1977). Neuropsychological differences between violent and nonviolent adolescents. *Journal of Clinical Psychology, 33*, 966–969.

Spellacy, F. (1978). Neuropsychological discrimination between violent and nonviolent men. *Journal of Clinical Psychology, 34*(1), 49–52.

Steadman, H., Monahan, J., Applebaum, P., Grisso, T., Mulvey, E., Roth, L., Clark Robbins, P., & Klassen, D. (1994). Designing a new generation of risk assessment research. In J. Monahan & H. Steadman (Eds.), *Violence and mental disorder: Developments in risk assessment*. Chicago: University of Chicago Press.

Stevens, J. R., & Hermann, B. P. (1981). Temporal lobe epilepsy, psychopathology, and violence: The state of the evidence. *Neurology, 31*, 1127–1132.

Streitberg, B., Rohmel, J., Herrmann, W. M., & Kubicki, S. (1987). COMSTAT rule for vigilance classification based on spontaneous EEG activity. *Neuropsychobiology, 17*, 105–117.

Stuss, D. T., & Benson, D. F. (1984). Neuropsychological studies of the frontal lobes. *Psychological Bulletin, 95*, 3–28.

Surwillo, W. (1980). The electroencephalogram and childhood aggression. *Aggressive Behavior, 6*, 9–18.

Swanson, J., Holzer, C., Ganju, V., & Tsutumo Jono, R. (1990). Violence and psychiatric disorder in the community: Evidence from the epidemiologic catchment area survey. *Hospital and Community Psychiatry, 41*, 761–770.

Tardiff, K., & Sweillam, A. (1980). Assault, suicide, and mental illness. *Archives of General Psychiatry, 37*, 164–169.

Van Woerkom, T. C., Teelken, A. W., Mindehoud, J. M. (1977). Differences in neurotransmitter metabolism in fronto-temporal lobe contusion and diffuse cerebral contusion. *Lancet, 1*, 812–813.

Virkkunen, M., de Jong, J., Goodwin, F. K., & Linnoila, M. (1989). Relationship of psychobiological variables to recidivism in violent offenders and impulsive fire setters. *Archives of General Psychiatry, 46*, 600–603.

Virkkunen, M., & Linnoila, M. (1990). Serotonin in early onset, male alcoholics with violent behavior. *Annals of Internal Medicine, 22*, 327–331.

Virkkunen, M., & Linnoila, M. (1993). Serotonin in personality disorders with habitual violence and impulsivity. In S. Hodgins (Ed.), *Mental disorder and crime*. Newbury Park: Sage.

Volavka, J. (1990). Aggression, EEG, and evoked potentials: A critical review. *Neuropsychiatry, Neurophysiology, and Behavioral Neurology, 3*, 249–259.

Volavka, J. (1994). *Psychobiology of violence*. Washington DC: American Psychiatric Association Press.

Volavka, J., Cooper, T. B., Czobor, P., Bitter, I., Meisner, M., Laska, E., Gastanaga, P., Krakowski, M., Chou, J., Crowner, M., & Douyon, R. (1992). Haloperidol blood levels and clinical effects. *Archives of General Psychiatry, 49*, 354–361.

Volkow, N. D., & Tancredi, L. R. (1987). Neural substrates of violent behavior. *British Journal of Psychiatry, 151*, 668–673.

Wechsler, D. (1981). *WAIS-R manual*. New York: Psychological Corporation.

Wechsler, D. (1984). *Wechsler Memory Scale-Revised Manual*. New York: Psychological Corporation.

Weiger, W. A., & Bear, D. M. (1988). An approach to the neurology of aggression. *Journal of Psychiatric Research, 22*(2), 85–98.

White, J., Moffitt, T., & Silva, P. A. (1989). A prospective replication of the protective effects of IQ in subjects at high risk for juvenile delinquency. *Journal of Clinical and Consulting Psychology, 57*, 719–724.

Whitman, S., Coleman, T. E., Patmon, C., Desai, P. T., & Cohen, R. (1984). Epilepsy in prison: Elevated prevalence and no relationship to violence. *Neurology, 34*, 775–782.

Widom, C. S. (1989). The intergenerational transmission of violence. In N. Weiner & M. E. Wolfgang (Eds.), *Pathways in criminal violence*. Newbury Park, CA: Sage.

Williams, D. (1969). Neural factors related to habitual aggression—consideration of differences between those habitual aggressives and others who have committed crimes of violence. *Brain, 92,* 503–520.

Wilson, J. Q., & Herrnstein, R. (1986). *Crime and human nature* (2nd ed.). New York: Simon & Schuster.

Yellin, A. (1984). The study of brain function in fetal alcohol syndrome: Some fruitful directions for research. *Neuroscience and Biobehavioral Reviews, 8,* 1–4.

Yeudall, L. T. (1977). Neuropsychological assessment of forensic disorders. *Canadian Mental Health, 25,* 7.

Yeudall, L. T., Fromm-Auch, D., & Davies, P. (1982). Neuropsychological impairment in persistent delinquency. *Journal of Nervous and Mental Disease, 70,* 257–265.

Yeudall, L. T., & Fromm-Auch, D. (1979). Neuropsychological impairments in various psychopathological populations. In J. Gruzelier & P. Flor-Henry (Eds.), *Hemisphere asymmetries of function in psychopathology* (pp. 401–428). North Holland: Elsevier.

10

VIOLENCE, BRAIN IMAGING, AND NEUROPSYCHOLOGY

Adrian Raine
University of Southern California

Monte S. Buchsbaum
Mount Sinai School of Medicine

Perhaps the most exciting development in clinical neuroscience in recent years has been the development and increased use of several brain-imaging techniques. These new techniques allow for much better visualization of both structural and functional properties of the brain than earlier methods. The disadvantage with more traditional neuropsychological measures is that they are inevitably only indirect indices of brain dysfunction. New brain-imaging techniques hold great promise for an exponential increase in our understanding of the type of brain abnormalities and dysfunctions that may underlie different disorders because they constitute more direct indices of CNS structure and function.

Within the field of crime and violence, these new techniques are just beginning to be applied, and to date there have been only 14 studies that have applied new methods to further our understanding of violence. It is expected that such techniques will have more widespread application to antisocial populations as they become cheaper and more available. More than any other methodology, there is the potential for a revolution in our understanding of the neurophysiological and neuroanatomical underpinnings of crime and violence.

This chapter outlines the limited knowledge that has been gained to date from brain-imaging studies. In addition, a brief overview of neuropsychological findings on violent offenders is provided. See Raine (1993) for more in-depth reviews. We argue here that frontal and temporal lobe dysfunction appears to be related to violence. More specifically, a dimension of frontal-to-temporal dysfunction may exist, with violence aligned most closely with frontal dysfunction, and sexual offending aligned with temporal lobe dysfunction—with both sexual and violent offending being characterized by both frontal and temporal dysfunction.

There are two basic types of information that brain-imaging techniques yield: information on brain structure, and information on brain function. It should be noted that a brain can be structurally impaired without any obvious functional abnormality, and, by the same token, there can be brain dysfunction even though the brain appears structurally normal. As such, structural and functional brain-imaging techniques provide different information about the brain. The two main structural brain-imaging techniques consist of computerized tomography (CT) and magnetic resonance imaging (MRI); the two main functional brain-imaging techniques consist of positron emission tomography (PET) and regional cerebral blood flow (RCBF).

NEUROPSYCHOLOGICAL STUDIES

This chapter briefly reviews the neuropsychological literature on violence. Much more detailed reviews of neuropsychological impairments in various antisocial groups may be found in Moffitt (1988, 1990), Kandel and Freed (1989), Moffitt and Henry (1991), and Raine (1993); good overviews of specifically aggressive behavior may be found in Milner (1991). This section discusses two neuropsychological theories of violence: frontal dysfunction theory and the related left frontotemporal dysfunction theory, and reduced lateralization theory.

Neuropsychological studies do not always make distinctions between prefrontal and more posterior frontal brain areas, partly because neuropsychological tests are limited in the extent of their specificity, with some being relatively sensitive to dysfunction localized to one brain site (e.g., Wisconsin Card Sorting and dorsolateral prefrontal cortex), whereas others are sensitive to damage in almost any cerebral region (e.g., Digit Symbol). As such, finer distinctions cannot always be drawn. This is particularly true with respect to the even finer distinctions between medial, dorsolateral, and orbitofrontal regions of the prefrontal cortex, which have not to date been accurately "mapped" by neuropsychological tests. In this context, more modern brain-imaging techniques clearly have superior spatial resolution.

Frontal Dysfunction

Neurological studies examining damage to the frontal cortex have shown a pattern of changes including argumentativeness, lack of concern for consequences of behavior, loss of social graces, impulsivity, distractibility, shallowness, lability, violence, and reduced ability to utilize symbols—a pattern of deficits known as the Frontal Lobe Syndrome (MacKinnon & Yudofsky, 1986; Mesulam, 1986; Silver & Yudofsky, 1987). More direct evidence for frontal dysfunction in crime comes from neuropsychological studies that have implicated anterior and frontal dysfunction in violent criminals (Flor-Henry, 1973). Yeudall and Fromm-Auch (1979), for example, compared 86 violent criminals to 79 normal controls using the Halstead–Reitan Neuropsychological Test Battery (HRNTB) and found significantly more anterior neuropsychological dysfunction in the violent group. Yeudall, Fromm-Auch, and Davies (1982), however, failed to find differences between violent and nonviolent delinquents on the HRNTB and 12 other neuropsychological tests, indicating that frontal dysfunction may be specific to adult offenders.

In a study using the Luria–Nebraska Neuropsychological Battery (LNNB), Bryant, Scott, Golden, and Tori (1984) found violent crimes in 73% of subjects classified as brain damaged compared to 28% of those classified as normal. In addition, significant impairment was found in the violent relative to nonviolent groups on LNNB tasks, which have been described by Luria (1980) as associated with adult-onset frontal lobe disorders. In contrast to these findings, Brickman, McManus, Grapentine, and Alessi (1984) compared violent and nonviolent subjects on the LNNB, and found impaired functioning for the violent group to lie in tasks more indicative of temporal rather than frontal lobe dysfunction. Psychopaths have also been studied to examine deficits in frontal lobe functioning with some researchers finding response perseveration deficits (e.g., Gorenstein, 1982; Newman, Patterson, & Kosson, 1987) whereas others have failed to observe effects (e.g., Hare, 1984; Hoffman, Hall, & Bartsch, 1987).

It seems clear that although frontal deficits are implicated at some level in antisocial behavior, there are some inconsistencies that require elaboration. First, violent offenders may be more likely to have frontal deficits than nonviolent criminal offenders. Second, psychopaths per se may not be characterized by significant damage to frontal cortex; alternatively, they may be characterized by damage to orbitofrontal cortex, which results in personality changes rather than the type of cognitive deficits tapped by traditional frontal neuropsychological tasks. Third, perhaps frontal dysfunction is maximally found in violent or psychopathic offenders who also have schizotypal features (Raine, 1993; Raine & Venables, 1992), and who have dysfunction to both orbitofrontal and dorsolateral regions of prefrontal cortex. Fourth, violent offenders with an early history of childhood aggression may be more likely to have frontal dysfunction whereas environmental and learning factors may contribute more significantly to late-onset violence. Although speculative at this point, these notions can be empirically tested in future studies.

Left Frontotemporal–Limbic Damage

In the context of the previous discussion, it is also possible that frontal deficits are localized largely to the left hemisphere (Flor-Henry, 1973), and that neuropsychological tasks that are not sensitive to laterality effects will not detect this more localized deficit. This laterality notion has also been applied to the fron-totemporal–limbic dysfunction theory of violence.

Yeudall (1978) and Yeudall, Fedora, Fedora, and Wardell (1981) have argued that crime and violence is in part determined by damage to the left frontal-anterior temporal cortex, and left hippocampal–amygdala areas. Empirical evidence for this view is based on numerous neuropsychological studies of habitually violent and aggressive subjects. In an extensive neuropsychological investigation of aggressive criminals, Yeudall and Flor-Henry (1975) found that 76% of such subjects had dysfunction localized to the frontal and temporal regions of the brain. Of these, 79% showed frontotemporal abnormalities lateralized to the left hemisphere. Similar localization to the dominant temporal lobe in violent–aggressive adolescents has been reported by Yeudall (1978).

Yeudall (1978, Yeudall et al., 1981) has used this neuropsychological evidence of anterior temporal dysfunction to implicate the limbic regions of the temporal lobe, in particular the amygdala and hippocampus. Lesion studies in both animals and humans are cited to support the role of the amygdala in generating violence, as are studies linking temporal lobe epilepsy to violence (Yeudall, 1978). The episodic dyscontrol syndrome (Monroe, 1970) is also invoked to link temporal-limbic systems with frontal inhibitory control mechanisms. Specific brain areas argued to be dysfunctional by Yeudall et al. (1981) included dorsolateral prefrontal cortex, orbitofrontal cortex, temporal cortex, basal ganglia, hypothalamus, amygdala, and hippocampus.

Although at one level the evidence in favor of this theory appears substantial, there are limitations to this approach (see Raine, 1993, for a detailed discussion). In spite of these criticisms, the left frontotemporal–limbic theory of violence is potentially important and further empirical testing of this theory is warranted. The notion that violent, and particularly sexual, offenders are characterized by temporal lobe dysfunction is reviewed in the section on brain imaging.

Reduced Lateralization for Neuropsychological Functions

The traditional left hemisphere dysfunction theory of violence essentially argues for a type of structural damage to the left hemisphere that can be detected by neuropsychological tests validated against patients with brain lesions. A more subtle, recent, and potentially more plausible theory of violence concerns the notion that violent individuals are less lateralized for speech processes. Evidence for this viewpoint stems largely from two sources: studies on handedness, and studies of dichotic listening in psychopaths, although the following section on brain imaging comments briefly on some initial support for this view based on dysfunction of the corpus callosum in violent offenders.

Regarding handedness, the prediction generated by a reduced lateralization theory of crime is that delinquents and criminals should be more likely to be left-handed, since left-handers are more likely to have bilateral language representation relative to right-handers, who are more likely to be left-hemisphere dominant for language. Several studies have observed this finding. Gabrielli and Mednick (1980) in a prospective study of 265 Danish children found that a left-side preference measured at age 11 was predictive of delinquency measured at age 17. However, left-handedness in delinquents could not be accounted for by low verbal IQ, suggesting that gross left-hemisphere dysfunction does not account for the effect. Ellis (1990) reported that there have been at least seven studies finding significantly higher left-handedness in criminal and delinquent groups. Nevertheless, some studies have failed to find this link (see Ellis, 1990, for a detailed review).

More direct evidence for reduced lateralization is provided by studies of lateralization of linguistic functions in both adult and juvenile psychopaths. Hare and McPherson (1984) administered a verbal dichotic listening task to adult prisoners divided into three groups (high, medium, and low psychopathy) on the basis of scores on the Psychopathy Checklist and *DSM–III–R* criteria for antisocial personality disorder. A significant Group × Ear interaction was observed whereby the high-psychopathy group was less lateralized than the low-psychopathy group (see Fig. 10.1). Hare and McPherson interpreted their results as indicating reduced lateralization for language in psychopaths.

A similar and more recent study confirms that these findings are not spurious. Raine, O'Brien, Smiley, Scerbo, and Chan (1990) administered a verbal dichotic listening task to juvenile offenders aged 13–18 years. Four self-report and behavioral measures were used to define psychopathy using cluster analytic techniques. Results of this study are shown in Fig. 10.1. Whereas nonpsychopaths showed the expected normal right-ear (left hemisphere) advantage for verbal material, psychopaths evidenced a reduction in this lateralization. This was confirmed by a significant Group × Ear interaction; while right-ear performance was significantly greater than the left ear for nonpsychopaths, no significant ear differences were observed for psychopaths. Between-group analyses also indicated that psychopaths had higher left-ear and lower right-ear scores than nonpsychopaths. Although subjects in the two studies (Hare & McPherson, 1984; Raine et al., 1990) differed in age, ethnic background, type of dichotic listening task, and method of psychopathy assessment, Fig. 10.1 shows that the pattern of results in the two studies are strikingly similar, indicating robustness of the effect.

This reduced ear asymmetry again indicates that psychopaths are less lateralized for linguistic processes. This effect does not seem to be modality specific; the same reduction in hemisphere asymmetries has also been observed in the visual modality in psychopaths (Hare & Jutai, 1988). Other neuropsychological and psychophysiological studies provide additional support for the notion of

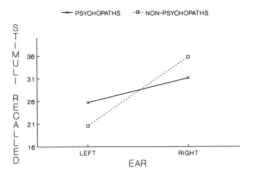

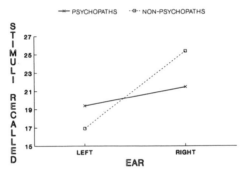

FIG. 10.1. Verbal dichotic listening in (top) adult psychopaths (Hare & McPherson, 1984) and (bottom) juvenile psychopaths (Raine et al., 1990) illustrating a reduction in the right-ear advantage for psychopaths and consequently reduced lateralization for linguistic functions.

abnormal linguistic processing in psychopaths (see e.g., Gillstrom & Hare, 1988; Jutai, Hare, & Connolly, 1987; Raine & Venables, 1988).

An important unresolved issue concerns the way reduced lateralization for verbal material translates itself into criminal and violent behavior. A number of alternatives seem feasible. If reduced lateralization for language results in poorer verbal comprehension and communication, this could contribute to misinterpretation of events and motives in an interpersonal encounter that could precipitate violence. Similarly, a child with poor linguistic skills may be less able to talk him- or herself out of trouble with parents or peers. Poor verbal abilities and communication skills per se could contribute to peer rejection in childhood, which in combination with other later social and situational factors could predispose one to alienation and violence. Alternatively, linguistic abnormalities could result in verbal deficits leading to school failure, which in turn could predispose to later alienation and violence. Future lateralization research should be conducted within the context of other cognitive and social research to better tease out these possible explanations and confirm the importance of linguistic processes and speech lateralization in predisposing to crime.

BRAIN IMAGING RESEARCH

CT Studies of Violence

Key Findings. To date, there are nine studies (seven Canadian) that report CT data on violent and sexual offenders. Key findings are outlined in Table 10.1. Most of these studies do not look at CT data in isolation, but in combination with other data such as EEG or neuropsychological testing.

Initial inspection of Table 10.1 indicates two points. First, half of the studies have not found any differences between experimental and control groups. This may indicate that offender groups do not suffer from structural brain abnormalities. Alternatively, CT is limited in terms of spatial resolution, particularly because slice thickness of 10 mm results in significant partial volume effect. Although it has been an important technique for visualizing the whole brain, assessing size of the lateral ventricles, and revealing presence of gross anatomical abnormalities, CT scanning is not as sensitive as MRI in assessing more subtle reductions in size of specific brain structures. Consequently, lack of significance may reflect a Type 2 error.

The second observation that can be made from Table 10.1 is that if there is any difference between groups, it lies with respect to greater temporal lobe abnormalities in the sex offender group, especially with respect to pedophiles and violent sexual assaulters (Hucker et al., 1986; Hucker et al., 1988; Langevin, Wortzman, Dickey, Wright, & Handy, 1988; Wright, Nobrega, Langevin, & Wortzman, 1990). On the other hand, temporal lobe abnormality is clearly not universally found. Specifically, this abnormality does not seem to characterize aggressive, assaultive, and murderous individuals or exhibitionists (Herzberg & Fenwick, 1988; Langevin, Ben-Aron, Wortzman, Dickey, & Handy, 1987; Langevin, Lang, Wortzman, Frenzel, & Wright, 1989).

Frontal abnormalities are generally not reported in CT studies, suggesting that frontal dysfunction does not characterize sex offender groups. CT does not lend itself to accurate assessment of discrete frontal abnormalities, however. Indeed, it appears that frontal abnormalities were only assessed in one study in Table 10.1, and in this case, significant differences were found for pedophiles (Wright et al., 1990). Furthermore, anterior horn enlargement would be expected to indicate loss of frontal tissue, and in the study where this is measured, significant effects were again obtained (Hucker et al., 1986). The question of whether frontal dysfunction characterized violent offenders therefore remains an open one.

TABLE 10.1

Structural Brain Imaging: Overview of Key Findings From
CT (Computerized Tomography) and MRI (Magnetic
Resonance Imaging) Studies of Offender Groups

Authors	Subjects	Technique	Key Finding
Hucker et al. (1986)	39 pedophiles 14 property offenders	CT	Left and bilateral temporal horn dilation; dilation of anterior horn of lateral ventricles in pedophiles
Langevin et al. (1987)	18 murderers 21 assaulters 16 property offenders	CT	n.s.d.
Herzberg & Fenwick (1988)	14 aggressive TLE 7 non-aggressive TLE	CT	n.s.d.
Hucker et al. (1988)	22 sadistic sex assaulters 21 nonsadistic sex assaulters 36 property offenders	CT	Right temporal horn abnormalities in sadists
Langevin et al. (1988)	91 incest offenders 36 property offenders	CT	n.s.d. for main group comparisons, but violence within incest group associated with temporal lobe abnormalities
Langevin, Wortzman, Wright, & Handy (1989)	84 pedophiles 32 property offenders	CT	n.s.d.
Langevin, Lang, et al. (1989)	15 exhibitionists 36 property offenders	CT	n.s.d.
Wright et al. (1990)	18 pedophiles 12 incest offenders 34 rapists 12 controls	CT	smaller left frontal and temporal areas in sex offenders
Tonkonogy (1991)	14 violent OBS 9 nonviolent OBS	MRI and CT	anterior–inferior temporal lobe lesions in 5 violent OBS patients

Note. TLE = temporal lobe epilepsy, OBS = organic brain syndrome.

Although based on a sample of schizophrenics as opposed to criminals, a recent CT study by Convit et al. (chap. 9, this volume) is of relevance. This study found that nine violent schizophrenics had bilateral enlargement of the Sylvian Fissure relative to nonviolent schizophrenic controls, a finding they interpreted as indicating dysfunction of the frontotemporal region in violent schizophrenics. Conversely, no effects were obtained for ventricular size, cortical atrophy, hippocampal atrophy, and white matter lesions.

Assessment of Findings. Several other general observations may be made from CT studies. One striking aspect of many of these studies is that there are dissociations between CT and neuropsychological measures of brain abnormality (e.g., Langevin et al., 1987; Langevin et al., 1988; Langevin, Wortzman, Wright, & Handy, 1989; Wright et al., 1990). Although this may seem contradictory, it must be remembered that the former is a structural measure and the latter is a functional measure. Such findings may therefore reflect dissociations between structure and function, and underlie the need for the assessment of both types of brain abnormality wherever possible.

One general methodological issue that restricts generalizability of findings to date is that many of the studies in Table 10.1 are from the same laboratory with a common control group; studies from other laboratories are therefore needed to provide a good test of the robustness of these findings. Finally, an interesting possibility in some studies is that the lack of significant group differences may conceivably be due to relatively high rates of structural brain abnormality in the control group, where this is made up of property offenders (Langevin et al., 1987; Langevin et al., 1988; Langevin et al., 1989). It may be a mistake to assume that nonviolent offenders do not have genetically mediated brain abnormalities, particularly since there appears to be a stronger genetic basis to property offending than violent offending (e.g., Mednick, Gabrielli, & Hutchings, 1984).

Magnetic Resonance Imaging (MRI)

Key Findings. Only one study to date has included MRI in assessments of offenders. Tonkonogy (1991) used both MRI and CT on 87 patients with disorders such as schizophrenia and bipolar disorder referred for neuropsychiatric examination due to alcohol abuse, cerebrovascular accidents, or head injury. CT, MRI, EEG, and neurological examinations were used to diagnose organic mental disorder in 23 of the 87 patients. Fourteen of these patients had what was termed "frequent episodes of violent behavior" (p. 190). The main finding to emerge is that the 14 psychiatric patients with both organic mental disorder and violent behavior were significantly more likely to have lesions in the anterior–inferior area of the temporal lobe than the 9 organic mental disorder patients without violence, with 5 of the patients having identifiable lesions to this area. In 4 of these 5 cases lesions were lateralized to the right hemisphere. Three were male; and 2 were female. The authors speculated that violence may result from unilateral tissue loss in the amygdala–hippocampal region of the temporal lobe.

Assessment of Findings. This study is valuable because it is the first to use MRI on a forensic sample. On the other hand, results must be regarded as preliminary for several reasons. First, MRI was only used on a subset of subjects, and of the five violent cases with lesions, it appears from the case studies presented that only one is assessed with MRI. This study is therefore much more representative of a CT study than an MRI study, and as such findings should not be weighted more heavily than other CT studies, as the study does not benefit substantially from MRI methodology. Second, it is clear that all cases are a selected sample of those who have already been shown to have substantial brain pathology as indicated by CT or MRI. However, this selection does not explain why such pathology should be localized to a specific brain area in the subgroup of violent patients. Nevertheless, findings are clearly limited to this selected sample. Third, because all patients had a severe mental illness, deficits might be related to illness rather than violence per se. Fourth, there are no methodological details of how CT and MRI were conducted. Fifth, there are no details of what constitute brain pathology, how lesions were localized, and whether the person who rated the scans was blind to group membership. Sixth, there are no details on how violence was assessed or defined. These are significant methodological limitations.

Positron Emission Tomography and Regional Cerebral Blood Flow Studies

Key Findings. There appear to have been only five studies reporting data on PET and regional cerebral blood flow in violent offenders. Because these studies are preliminary, findings must be interpreted with caution, particularly because sample sizes tend to be small and frequently few procedural details are reported. The fifth study by Raine and colleagues (Raine et al., 1994) is reported in detail later; only the first four are discussed in this section.

Key findings from functional brain-imaging studies are reported in Table 10.2. Excluding the study by Raine et al. (1994), which finds selective prefrontal dysfunction in murderers, 2 of the 4 other studies find nonlocalized differences in glucose metabolism in offenders. The other two studies find more localized differences (Volkow & Tancredi, 1987; Hendricks et al., 1988). In both cases

TABLE 10.2
Key Findings From Positron Emission Tomography (PET)
and Regional Cerebral Blood Flow (RCBF) Studies

Authors	Subjects	Techniques	Key Findings
Graber et al. (1982)	3 pedophiles 3 rapists	RCBF	reduced RCBF in pedophiles but not rapists.
Volkow & Tancredi (1987)	4 violent patients 4 normal controls	PET	left temporal dysfunction and hypofrontality
Garnett et al. (1988)	1 sexual sadist 2 normal controls	PET	bilateral cortical activation in sadist, right hemisphere activation in controls.
Hendricks et al. (1988)	16 child molesters 16 normal controls	RCBF	reduced RCBF in child molesters greatest over frontal areas.
Raine et al. (1994)	22 murderers (NGRI) 22 normals	PET	selective prefrontal dysfunction in murderers.

Note. NGRI = pleading not guilty by reason of insanity.

frontal dysfunction is implicated, and in one case (Volkow & Tancredi, 1987) left temporal dysfunction is also observed. If any conclusions can be drawn from these initial studies, it would tentatively be that frontal and temporal dysfunction may be linked to violent and assaultive behavior.

Assessment of Findings. A number of limitations in these studies indicate that any conclusions should be interpreted cautiously. First, only Garnett, Nahmias, Wortzman, Langevin, and Dickey (1988) appear to have employed an activation condition (sexually arousing tape). This is an important strength because the investigators attempt to activate or "challenge" those brain areas that they believe may be involved in sexual activity. An additional advantage of such a challenge task is that one has some degree of control over what the subject is doing. In contrast, artifactual group differences may occur in "resting baseline" nonchallenge conditions because one group is differentially engaged in some type of mental activity.

Second, the two studies that measured both structure and function (CT and PET; Volkow & Tancredi, 1987; Hendricks et al., 1988) found a dissociation between these measures. This confirms the same dissociation noted earlier in CT studies, and suggests that caution must be exerted in generalizing from one type of study to another. Clearly, functional deficits can exist without structural deficits, and vice versa.

Third, studies measuring glucose metabolism are inevitably based on small sample sizes, precluding the use of statistical tests of significance. For example, 3 of the 4 studies had sample sizes of 4 or less. As such, firm conclusions cannot be drawn from these studies. In particular, factors such as head injury, ethnicity, and psychopathology within the experimental group remain uncontrolled. Nevertheless, the study by Volkow and Tancredi (1987) supports CT data in indicating a moderate degree of converging evidence suggesting that frontal and temporal brain regions may be implicated in some forms of criminal behavior.

A fourth issue concerns subject sampling and control groups. For example, subjects in the study by Hendricks et al. (1988) were incarcerated in a psychiatric facility. Because other institutionalized groups were not used as controls, differences in RCBF in the child molesters may be a function of generalized underarousal due to institutionalization. Such a criticism does not, however, easily account for their second finding of a Group × Site interaction whereby the offender group had lower blood flow values particularly in the frontal lobe. However, the fact that this study contained female controls when all experimental subjects were male may be a nontrivial factor in accounting for higher CBF in controls, inasmuch as females have been found to have higher CBF than males (Gur & Gur, 1990).

Fifth, a criticism of PET studies that also applies to CT studies is that the extent to which deficits are *relative* are often not assessed. Whereas CT scans may reveal abnormalities in temporal areas, a question remains as to whether these abnormalities are greater relative to another brain area. Similarly for PET data, it is important to establish that a certain brain site shows reduced glucose metabolism relative to another brain site if one wants to establish specificity of findings. Two studies that have demonstrated such a relative deficit indicate relatively lower frontal activity, and as such these data constitute more powerful evidence of specific brain dysfunction (see Volkow & Tancredi, 1987; Hendricks et al., 1988). Although the advantage of PET relative to CT lies in better localization of dysfunction, localization is very general in some studies (e.g., frontal lobe, temporal lobe), and in some studies findings are not localized at all (e.g., Garnett et al., 1988; Graber, Hartmann, Coffman, Huey, & Golden, 1982).

Despite these criticisms, these four studies are important in providing unique information on brain function in offender samples. Although there are clear limitations, such limitations are frequent in groundbreaking studies, which at the least provide a basis for methodologically better studies. Furthermore, although not dealing with a criminal sample, Goyer et al. (1994, and chap. 11, this volume) have recently reported significant correlations ($r = -0.54$ to -0.56) between lower prefrontal glucose metabolism and increased ratings of aggressive behavior in 17 personality-disordered psychiatric patients, findings that support the general link between prefrontal dysfunction and violence. The fifth study reported in detail next, when taken together with results of these earlier studies, suggests that frontal dysfunction may be a predisposition for violent behavior and sexual assault.

Reduced Prefrontal Glucose Metabolism in Murderers. One theme that arises from the imaging data described earlier is the notion that violent offenders may be characterized by frontal dysfunction. At the time of writing, the most recent brain-imaging study of a criminal population has tested this hypothesis by assessing glucose metabolism using PET in murderers pleading not guilty by reason of insanity (Raine et al., 1994). Although it has a number of important limitations in its own right, the study also addresses some of the limitations already described for earlier imaging studies, and also provides some assessment of temporal lobe functioning that has been implicated in earlier imaging studies. This section describes the methodology and initial findings from this study and attempts to place the observed findings within a wider etiological context. Further details of this study may be found in Raine et al. (1994).

The experimental group consisted of 22 homicide cases tried in the state of California (20 male, 2 female) with a mean age of 35.4 years ($SD = 10.4$). Subjects were referred to the University of California, Irvine (UCI) imaging center to obtain evidence relating to an insanity defense (not guilty by reason of insanity–NGRI) or to capability for understanding the judicial process (incompetence to stand trial).

A control group was formed by matching each murderer with a normal subject of same gender and age who had been tested using identical PET imaging procedures in the same laboratory. Three of the 22 murderers (all male) had been diagnosed as schizophrenic according to court-appointed psychiatrists. In order to control for this raised prevalence of schizophrenia in the group of murderers, these three schizophrenic murderers were individually matched on age and gender with three schizophrenics from a larger sample tested under identical procedures at the Brain Imaging Center at UCI.

The FDG tracer was injected into the subject in the test room and taken up by the brain as a tracer of brain metabolic rate for a 32-minute period during which the subject completed the continuous performance task. A degraded stimulus version of the CPT was employed as the frontal challenge task because it is traditionally viewed as a frontal task in the neuropsychology literature and has been shown to produce increases in relative glucose metabolic rates in the frontal lobes in normals, in addition to increases in right temporal and parietal lobes.

Significant group differences found in analyses from both box and cortical peel techniques support the hypothesis that murderers are characterized by prefrontal dysfunction. The box analyses indicated strongest effects for anterior medial cortex and for the higher, supraventricular superior frontal cortex, with significantly reduced glucose metabolism in these areas in murderers. At lower levels, medial frontal glucose levels did not differentiate the two groups. At the lowest, infraventricular levels however, prefrontal deficits were again indicated by significant reductions in orbitofrontal glucose metabolism in murderers, although this effect was weaker and more specific to the left hemisphere. The peel analyses corroborated the general finding of widespread prefrontal dysfunction in murderers, particularly when values were expressed relative to posterior (occipital) cortex. Values for nonprefrontal motor areas, on the other hand, did not differ across groups, indicating specificity of findings to the prefrontal area. An illustration of the localization of the effects to frontal areas for one murderer and one control is shown in Fig. 10.2.

The fact that the prefrontal deficit in murderers is relatively specific and does not reflect generalized brain dysfunction is indicated in four ways. First, glucose levels for a particular area were expressed as a ratio of all other brain areas in that slice, and therefore reflect *relative* glucose metabolic deficits. Second, one prefrontal area (medial frontal at the level of the lateral ventricles) did not distinguish the two groups, indicating some specificity within prefrontal cortex for the observed deficit. Third, posterior frontal glucose metabolism levels were the same in both groups, indicating that within the frontal lobe, the deficit was localized to the more anterior (prefrontal) region. Fourth, no deficits were observed in temporal and parietal regions, again localizing the deficit to anterior prefrontal regions. As such, the relatively specific nature of the deficit indicates that it cannot be easily explained by general factors such as motivational deficits and underarousal, which have been previously implicated in crime and violence.

Although prefrontal deficits have also been observed in schizophrenia (Buchsbaum et al., 1990), murderers are differentiated from schizophrenics in terms of the extent of this deficit. For example, schizophrenics have been found not only

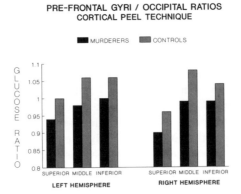

FIG. 10.2. Left and right hemisphere superior, middle, and inferior prefrontal
gyri relative glucose metabolic rates in murderers and controls (cortical peel
technique).

to show reduced frontal glucose metabolism during the continuous performance
task, they also show deficits relative to controls at right temporal and right parietal
sites, areas that are also activated by the continuous performance task
(Buchsbaum et al., 1990). In contrast, murderers show deficits specific to prefrontal cortex that do not extend to temporal and parietal regions. Group differences
in prefrontal activity were not found to be a function of group differences in age,
sex, schizophrenia, handedness, ethnicity, motivation, or history of head injury.

Taken together, these results indicate selective prefrontal dysfunction in
murderers. Although findings need to be generalized to unselected populations
of violent offenders, these data provide some striking support for a prefrontal
theory of violence. Finally, a preliminary analysis of data from this study has
recently indicated evidence for significantly reduced glucose metabolism in the
corpus callosum in murderers. Such a finding would provide some related
support for the neuropsychological test data reported earlier in this chapter,
indicating that there may be deficits in brain lateralization in violent offenders.

Overview of Brain-Imaging Studies—
Frontal Dysfunction in Violent Offenders
and Temporal Dysfunction in Sexual Offenders?

The number of brain-imaging studies conducted to date on offender groups is
too small for the conduction of a formal meta-analysis. However, an informal
analysis of Tables 10.1 and 10.2 yield some patterns that suggest preliminary

hypotheses on different brain areas that may predispose to different type of crime.

Of the 14 CT, PET, and MRI studies conducted to date, 8 suggest some specificity of findings. In all cases, selective deficits are found in the anterior region of the brain (either frontal or temporal areas). Although temporal findings are more frequently observed than frontal findings, it must be remembered that the more numerous CT studies frequently do not assess frontal deficits. Furthermore, all three functional brain-imaging studies that report specificity of findings indicate frontal dysfunction, indicating that future functional studies may find more evidence for frontal than temporal dysfunction.

Four of the studies provide evidence for selective frontal dysfunction. One of these studies involved murderers (Raine et al., 1994), one violent subjects (Volkow & Tancredi, 1987), one sex offenders in which the largest subgroup consisted of rapists (Wright et al. 1990), and one child molesters charged with sexual assault (Hendricks et al., 1988). As such, frontal dysfunction tends to be found either in violent offenders, child assaulters, or sex offenders containing a large proportion of rapists who may be more likely to be violent than incest offenders or pedophiles.

Seven studies found evidence for deficits partly localized to the temporal lobe. The 6 samples being tested in these studies were as follows: pedophiles, sadistic sexual assaulters, incest offenders, sex offenders (34 rapists, 18 pedophiles, 12 incest offenders), sadistic sexual offenders, violent offenders, and violent psychiatric patients with organic brain syndrome. As such, these seven studies contain a larger proportion of sex offenders, including more passive sexual offenders such as pedophiles and incest offenders.

The hypothesis being suggested here is that there is a tendency for frontal dysfunction to be associated with violent offending and rape, while temporal dysfunction may be more associated with less violent sexual offending including incest and pedophilia. The data are only suggestive of this hypothesis, however, because the studies finding temporal dysfunction also contain samples of violent sexual offenders. It may be that a continuum exists, with frontal dysfunction and violence at one end of the continuum and temporal dysfunction and sexual offending at the other. The middle of this continuum may involve some degree of both temporal and frontal dysfunction, and a mix of both sexual and violent behavior. Interestingly, one of the two studies that found evidence for both temporal and frontal dysfunction used a sample made up almost evenly of rapists (53%) and incest offenders–pedophiles (47%) (Wright et al., 1990). The other study found that frontal dysfunction characterized violent individuals who had no remorse for their actions (Volkow & Tancredi, 1987), suggesting the possibility that psychopathy may also feature at this end of the continuum.

One difficulty making this analysis speculative is the fact that, as outlined earlier, many of the CT studies on sex offenders come from the same group of researchers (Garnett et al., 1988; Hucker et al., 1986; Hucker et al., 1988; Langevin et al., 1987; Langevin et al., 1988; Langevin, Lang, et al., 1989; Langevin, Wortzman, Wright, & Handy, 1989). Though these researchers cannot be faulted for being productive, a more complete analysis would ideally included studies from many different laboratories. Although speculative at the present time, this hypothesis may at least provide some basis for hypothesis testing in future imaging studies, since studies to date have been empirically driven rather than theory driven. The following section attempts to provide some conceptual underpinnings for future brain-imaging studies of offender populations.

THEORETICAL INTERPRETATIONS
OF FRONTAL DYSFUNCTION

Discussion here focuses on the finding of relative frontal dysfunction because temporal lobe deficits in relation to abnormal sexual functioning have been covered elsewhere. Briefly, both animal and human patient research indicates that changes in sexual functioning are linked with damage to temporal-limbic areas of the brain. A temporal lobe–sexual activity link has also been found in normal humans. For example, early research by Mosovich and Tallafero (1954) indicated that six normal subjects who masturbated to orgasm showed EEG changes in temporal lobe regions (see Garnett et al., 1988; Hucker et al., 1988; Langevin et al., 1989 for further details on temporal dysfunction).

Turning to frontal dysfunction, findings of functional brain-imaging studies have implications for theoretical accounts of violence. A number of brain deficits have been postulated as potential predispositional factors to violence, including left hemisphere dysfunction, lateralization abnormalities, and temporal dysfunction. Little evidence was observed for temporal dysfunction in studies involving PET and CBF, and 3 of the 4 studies found some evidence for frontal dysfunction. Findings for some nonmedial structures (orbitofrontal, superior, middle, and inferior surface; see Raine et al., 1994) indicated that prefrontal deficits were greatest over the left hemisphere, but these must be regarded as only suggestive, as laterality effects were not obtained in other analyses. Although Volkow and Tancredi (1987) have found evidence for deficits to be lateralized to the left hemisphere, evidence for lateralization is not strong.

Regarding the interpretation of frontal dysfunction in violent offenders, such dysfunction may be best viewed as a *predisposition* to violence rather than prefrontal dysfunction, in and of itself, causing violence. One predispositional model for the link between prefrontal dysfunction and violence would be to suggest that: (a) there are a number of pathways by which prefrontal dysfunction can contribute to violence; (b) the greater the prefrontal dysfunction, the greater the likelihood that several of these pathways will be activated; (c) the more pathways that are activated, the greater the risk for serious violence. These putative pathways can be viewed at several levels. At a neurophysiological level, reduced prefrontal functioning could result in a loss of inhibition normally exerted by the frontal cortex on phylogenetically older subcortical structures which are thought to play a role in facilitating aggression (Gorenstein & Newman, 1980; Weiger & Bear, 1988). At a neurobehavioral level, damage to prefrontal cortex in clinical patients has been found to result in behavioral changes that include risk taking, rule breaking, emotional and aggressive outbursts, and argumentative behavior, which in turn could predispose to more violent acts (Damasio, 1980; Mesulam, 1986). At a personality level, frontal damage has been found to result in impulsivity, loss of self-control, immaturity, lack of tact, inability to modify and inhibit behavior appropriately, and poor social judgment, which could predispose to serious violence (Luria, 1980). At a social level, the loss of intellectual flexibility, concept formation skills, problem-solving skills and reduced ability to use information provided by verbal cues resulting from prefrontal dysfunction (Kolb & Wishaw, 1990) could impair social skills essential for formulating nonaggressive solutions to fractious interpersonal encounters. At a cognitive level, poor concentration, divergent thinking, and reasoning ability could result in school failure, employment failure, and economic deprivation, thereby predisposing to a criminal way-of-life, which in turn could predispose to violence. This model should be viewed from a heuristic standpoint, illustrating that although prefrontal function may be related to violence, it may be essentially a predisposition only, requiring other environmental, psychological, and social factors to enhance or diminish this biological predisposition.

From an etiological standpoint, although the findings of this study implicate a biological factor as predisposing to violence, it is important to emphasize that the cause of this dysfunction could be environmental as well as biological or genetic. Birth complications have been implicated in later violent offending (Mungas, 1983), and represent only one of a number of early environmental agents that could contribute to prefrontal dysfunction. Alternatively, the deficit could be neurodevelopmental in nature. Homicide rates in both Whites and non-Whites show a step increase between the ages of 15 and 19 before peaking in the 20s (O'Carroll & Mercy, 1990), an age at which prefrontal cortex is reaching full maturity (Huttenlocher, 1979) and when there are important environmental demands (e.g., leaving school, starting work, getting married) placed on the individual that require prefrontal executive functions. Breakdown of prefrontal functions at this age, in conjunction with environmental stressors, could in part explain the increase in homicide rates in the late teens and into the 20s.

APPLICATIONS AND IMPLICATIONS
OF BRAIN IMAGING RESEARCH

Results of brain-imaging studies of violent individuals are potentially of key importance in the contexts of law, psychiatry, and society. Although individual murderers are often suspected of some brain dysfunction, the foregoing study is the first indicating that, as a group, murderers show a clear dysfunction of a *specific* cortical brain region. If offenders as a group, such as murderers, show evidence of a relatively focal brain abnormality relative to control groups, this would have potential implications for judgments in contexts of the insanity defense and competence to stand trial. Tancredi and Volkow (1988) have argued that new imaging techniques offer the promise of giving psychiatric evaluations of dangerousness and violence much greater objectivity.

Applications of brain imaging need to proceed cautiously however. First and foremost, there needs to be much more extensive evaluation of brain imaging in offender groups to both establish that certain groups do have clear and significant brain pathology, and also to establish reliable normative data to provide a context for the evaluation of such pathology. Even if clear deficits can be demonstrated in certain offender groups, the fact that an individual offender has this characteristic does not demonstrate, in and of itself, that such individuals are legally insane. Brain imaging is necessarily a post hoc test, and questions will always remain as to whether identifiable brain dysfunction existed at the time the offense took place. More importantly, the causal relationship of brain dysfunction to commission of the offense must, in many cases, be very much open to question.

The key question asked in an insanity defense is whether the person, at the time of committing the act, was unable to appreciate the wrongfulness of the act due to a severe mental disease or defect and, as such, was not responsible for his or her actions. Brain-imaging findings can only provide data that may or may not be consistent with such a state of mind or with a proposed severe mental illness, and cannot by themselves provide a clear answer to what is effectively a legal question. Bearing these limitations in mind, however, brain-imaging studies have the potential to make nontrivial contributions to such decision making.

METHODOLOGICAL CONSIDERATIONS AND PROSPECTS FOR FUTURE RESEARCH

The foregoing review suggests a number of important methodological and conceptual issues that need to be attended to in future studies. These may be identified as follows:

1. Simply having more brain-imaging studies would provide valuable empirical data to help establish or disconfirm claimed relationships. A major limitation in the field to date is that there are so few studies, with such small N sizes, that it is difficult to draw any firm conclusions about violence.

2. Any such future studies would be even more valuable if they aimed to test hypotheses based on theoretical models of violence in both humans and animals

(e.g., Eichelman, 1992). Although new empirical findings are of great value, they are more valuable if set within a hypothetico-deductive framework. Such a framework has been generally lacking in previous studies.

3. Functional brain-imaging studies need to use neuropsychological uptake tasks that challenge those brain areas thought to be dysfunctional in violence. Such studies have very rarely been conducted, yet they provide stronger tests and help develop a more theoretical approach to understanding violence.

4. The literature is notable for dissociations between structure and function. Future studies combining structural with functional brain imaging would clearly be very important toward resolving issues arising from such dissociations. In this context, the emergence of fast MRI, which combines the structural MRI techniques with the functional technique of blood flow assessment, provides an ideal vehicle for such research. Although this technology is only recently available, it should be in relatively widespread use in the next few years.

5. Both spatial and temporal resolution in studies to date have been limited. Future studies using new-generation imaging equipment should be capable of delineating more precisely which specific brain regions (including subcortical areas) may be dysfunctional in violent offenders.

6. The challenges facing neuropsychological research on violence lie in two areas. First, it is conceivable that a new generation of neuropsychological tests validated against brain-imaging measures of brain functioning will provide stronger evidence for localized neuropsychological impairment in violent offenders. Second, neuropsychologists can play a key role in working with neuroradiologists in developing the type of neuropsychological challenge tasks that can best test theories of violence using brain-imaging techniques.

7. Finally, many of the conceptual issues surrounding violence outlined by Raine (chap. 8, this volume) with respect to autonomic nervous system factors also applies to brain-imaging research. These include integration of findings with other social and cognitive risk factors for violence, assessment of brain mechanisms which protect against violence development, controlling for recidivism per se, examining alcohol abuse as a moderator variable, and setting research within a theoretical context.

SUMMARY

Brain-imaging research provides a unique opportunity to make direct assessments of structural and functional brain abnormalities, and thereby provide a new body of knowledge on factors predisposing to the perpetration of violence. This chapter reviews 14 brain-imaging studies using CT, PET, RCBF, and MRI conducted to date on offender groups, in addition to briefly overviewing findings from neuropsychological research. Neuropsychological test research provides some limited support for frontal and left temporal dysfunction, and reduced lateralization for linguistic functions in violent offenders. CT and MRI studies suggest that violent and sexual offenders are characterized by frontal and temporal structural deficits. PET and RCBF studies also indicate frontal dysfunction in violent offenders, and additionally some evidence for temporal lobe dysfunction. One recent study of 22 murderers finds evidence for selective prefrontal dysfunction during performance of a frontal challenge task in addition to deficits in the corpus callosum, which may be related to lateralization abnormalities in violent offenders. It is argued that frontal dysfunction may represent a predisposition to violence by virtue of the neurobehavioral, cognitive, personality, and social implications of such frontal dysfunction. It is also speculated that frontal-temporal dysfunction may represent a predispositional continuum for violent and sexual offending, with violent offending most clearly related to frontal dysfunction, and sexual offending more related to temporal dysfunction. Applications and implications of this research, together with directive for future research, are drawn here.

ACKNOWLEDGMENTS

This chapter was written while the first author was supported by NIMH grant RO1 MH46435-02 and an NIMH Research Scientist Development Award (1 KO2 MH01114-01).

REFERENCES

Brickman, A. S., McManus, M., Grapentine, W. L., & Alessi, N. E. (1984). Neuropsychological assessment of seriously delinquent adolescents. *Journal of the American Academy of Child Psychiatry, 23,* 453–457.

Bryant, E. T., Scott, M. L., Golden, C. J., & Tori, C. D. (1984). Neuropsychological deficits, learning disability, and violent behavior. *Journal of Consulting and Clinical Psychology, 52,* 323–324.

Buchsbaum, M. S., Nuechterlein, K. H., Haier, R. J., Wu, J., Sicotte, N., Hazlett, E., Asarnow, R., Potkin, S., & Guich, S. (1990). Glucose metabolic rate in normals and schizophrenics during the continuous performance test assessed by positron emission tomography. *British Journal of Psychiatry, 156,* 216–227.

Damasio, A. R. (1980). The frontal lobes. In K. M. Heilman & E. Valenstein (Eds.), *Clinical neuropsychology* (pp. 339–375). New York: Oxford University Press.

Eichelman, B. (1992). Aggressive behavior: From laboratory to clinic. *Archives of General Psychiatry, 49,* 488–492.

Ellis, L. (1990). Left- and mixed-handedness and criminality: Explanations for a probable relationship. In S. Coran (Ed.), *Left handedness: Behavioral implications and anomalies.* North Holland: Elsevier.

Flor-Henry, P. (1973). Psychiatric syndromes considered as manifestations of lateralized temporal-limbic dysfunction. In L. Laitiner & K. Livingston (Eds.), *Surgical approaches in psychiatry.* Lancaster, England: Medical and Technical Publishing Co.

Gabrielli, W. F., & Mednick, S. A. (1980). Sinstrality and delinquency. *Journal of Abnormal Psychology, 89*, 654–661.

Garnett, E. S., Nahmias, C., Wortzman, G., Langevin, R., & Dickey, R. (1988). Positron emission tomography and sexual arousal in a sadist and two controls. *Annals of Sex Research, 1*, 387–399.

Gillstrom, B. J., & Hare, R. D. (1988). Language-related hand gestures in psychopaths. *Journal of Personality Disorders, 2*, 21–27.

Gorenstein, E. E. (1982). Frontal lobe functions in psychopaths. *Journal of Abnormal Psychology, 91*, 368–379.

Gorenstein, E. E., & Newman, J. P. (1980). Disinhibitory psychopathology: A new perspective and a model for research. *Psychological Review, 87*, 315–355.

Goyer, P. F., Andreason, P. J., Semple, W. E., Clayton, A. H., King, A. C., Compton-Toth, B. A., Schulz, S. C., & Cohen, R. M. (1994). Positron-emission tomography and personality disorders. *Neuropsychopharmacology, 10*, 21–28.

Graber, B., Hartmann, K., Coffman, J. A., Huey, C. J., & Golden, C. J. (1982). Brain damage among mentally disordered offenders. *Journal of Forensic Science, 27*, 125–134.

Gur, R. E., & Gur, R. C. (1990). Gender differences in regional cerebral blood flow. *Schizophrenia Bulletin, 16*, 247–254.

Hare, R. D. (1984). Performance of psychopaths on cognitive tasks related to frontal lobe dysfunction. *Journal of Abnormal Psychology, 93*, 133–140.

Hare, R. D., & Jutai, J. (1988). Psychopathy and cerebral asymmetry in semantic processing. *Personality and Individual Differences, 9*, 329–337.

Hare, R. D., & McPherson, L. M. (1984). Psychopathy and perceptual asymmetry during verbal dichotic listening. *Journal of Abnormal Psychology, 93*, 141–149.

Hendricks, S. E., Fitzpatrick, D. F., Hartmann, K., Quaife, M. A., Stratbucker, R. A., & Graber, B. (1988). Brain structure and function in sexual molesters of children and adolescents. *Journal of Clinical Psychiatry, 49*, 108–112.

Herzberg, J. L., & Fenwick, P. B. C. (1988). The aetiology of aggression in temporal lobe epilepsy. *British Journal of Psychiatry, 153*, 50–55.

Hoffman, J. J., Hall, R. W., & Bartsch, T. W. (1987). On the relative importance of "psychopathic" personality and alcoholism on neuropsychological measures of frontal lobe dysfunction. *Journal of Abnormal Psychology, 96*, 158–160.

Hucker, S., Langevin, R., Wortzman, G., Bain, J., Handy, L., Chambers, J., & Wright, S. (1986). Neuropsychological impairment in pedophiles. *Canadian Journal of Behavioral Science, 18*, 440–448

Hucker, S., Langevin, R., Wortzman, G., Dickey, R., Bain, J., Handy, L., Chambers, J., & Wright, S. (1988). Cerebral damage and dysfunction in sexually aggressive men. *Annals of Sex Research, 1*, 33–47.

Huttenlocher, P. R. (1979). Synaptic density in human frontal cortex—developmental changes and effects of aging. *Brain Research, 163*, 195–205.

Jutai, J., Hare, R. D., & Connolly, J. F. (1987). Psychopathy and event-related brain potentials (ERPs) associated with attention to speech stimuli. *Personality and Individual Differences, 8*, 175–184.

Kandel, E., & Freed, D. (1989). Frontal lobe dysfunction and antisocial behavior: A review. *Journal of Clinical Psychology, 45*, 404–413.

Kolb, B., & Wishaw, I. Q. (1990). *Fundamentals of human neuropsychology* (3rd ed.). New York: Freeman.

Langevin, R., Ben-Aron, M., Wortzman, G., Dickey, R., & Handy, L. (1987). Brain damage, diagnosis, and substance abuse among violent offenders. *Behavioral Sciences and the Law, 5*, 77–94.

Langevin, R., Lang, R. A., Wortzman, G., Frenzel, R. R., & Wright, P. (1989). An examination of brain damage and dysfunction in genital exhibitionists. *Annals of Sex Research, 2*, 77–87.

Langevin, R., Wortzman, G., Dickey, R., Wright, P., & Handy, L. (1988). Neuropsychological impairment in incest offenders. *Annals of Sex Research, 1*, 401–415.

Langevin, R., Wortzman, G., Wright, P., & Handy, L. (1989). Studies of brain damage and dysfunction in sex offenders. *Annals of Sex Research, 2*, 163–179

Luria, A. R. (1980). *Higher cortical functions in man.* New York: Basic Books.

MacKinnon, R. A., & Yudofsky, S. C. (1986). *Psychiatric evaluation in clinical practice.* Philadelphia: Lippincott.

Mednick, S. A., Gabrielli, W. H., & Hutchings, B. (1984). Genetic influences in criminal convictions: Evidence from an adoption cohort. *Science, 224*, 891–894.

Mesulam, M. M. (1986). Frontal cortex and behaviors. *Annals of Neurology, 19*, 319–323.

Milner, J. (1991). *Neuropsychology of aggression.* Boston: Kluwer.

Moffitt, T. E. (1988). Neuropsychology and self-reported early delinquency in an unselected birth cohort. In T. E. Moffitt & S. A. Mednick (Eds.), *Biological contributions to crime causation* (pp. 93–120). New York: Martinus Nijhoff.

Moffitt, T. E. (1990). The neuropsychology of juvenile delinquency: A critical review. In M. Tonry & N. Morris (Eds.), *Crime and justice: A review of the literature* (pp. 99–169). Chicago: University of Chicago Press.

Moffitt, T. E., & Henry, B. (1991). Neuropsychological studies of juvenile delinquency and juvenile violence. In J. S. Milner (Ed.), *Neuropsychology of aggression* (pp. 131–146). Boston: Kluwer.

Monroe, R. R. (1970). *Episodic behavioral disorders—A psychodynamic and neurophysiologic analysis.* Cambridge, MA: Harvard University Press.

Mosovich, A., & Tallafero, A. (1954). Studies on EEG and sex function orgasm. *Disease of the Nervous System, 15*, 218–220.

Mungas, D. (1983). An empirical analysis of specific syndromes of violent behavior. *Journal of Nervous and Mental Disease, 171*, 354–361.

Newman, J. P., Patterson, C. M., & Kosson, D. S. (1987). Response perseveration in psychopaths. *Journal of Abnormal Psychology, 96*, 145–148.

O'Carroll, P. W., & Mercy, J. A. (1990). Patterns and recent trends in black homicides. In N. A. Weiner, M. A. Zahn, & R. J. Sagi (Eds.), *Violence: Pattern, causes, public policy* (pp. 55–58). San Diego: Harcourt, Brace Jovanovich.

Raine, A. (1993). *The psychopathology of crime: Criminal behavior as a clinical disorder.* San Diego: Academic Press.

Raine, A., Buchsbaum, M. S., Stanley, J., Lottenberg, S., Abel, L., & Stoddard, J. (1994). Selective reductions in pre-frontal glucose metabolism assessed with positron emission tomography in accused murderers pleading not guilty by reason of insanity. *Biological Psychiatry, 36*, 365–373.

Raine, A., O'Brien, M., Smiley, N., Scerbo, A. S., & Chan, C. J. (1990). Reduced lateralization in verbal dichotic listening in adolescent psychopaths. *Journal of Abnormal Psychology, 99*, 272–277.

Raine, A., & Venables, P. H. (1988). Skin conductance responsivity in psychopaths to orienting, defensive, and consonant-vowel stimuli. *Journal of Psychophysiology, 2*, 221–225.

Raine, A., & Venables, P. H. (1992). Antisocial behavior: Evolution, genetics, neuropsychology, and psychophysiology. In A. Gale & M. Eysenck (Eds.), *Handbook of individual differences: Biological perspectives.* London: Wiley.

Silver, J. M., & Yudofsky, S. C. (1987). Aggressive behavior in patients with neuropsychiatric disorders. *Psychiatric Annals, 17*, 367–370.

Tancredi, L., & Volkow, N. D. (1988). Neural substrates of violent behavior: Implications for law and public policy. *International Journal of Law and Psychiatry, 11*, 13–49.

Tonkonogy, J. M. (1991). Violence and temporal lobe lesion: Head CT and MRI data. *Journal of Neuropsychiatry, 3*, 189–196.

Volkow, N. D., & Tancredi, L. (1987). Neural substrates of violent behavior: A preliminary study with positron emission tomography. *British Journal of Psychiatry, 151*, 668–673.

Weiger, W. A., & Bear, D. M. (1988). An approach to the neurology of aggression. *Journal of Psychiatry Research, 22,* 85–98.

Wright, P., Nobrega, J., Langevin, R., & Wortzman, G. (1990). Brain density and symmetry in pedophilic and sexually aggressive offenders. *Annals of Sex Research, 3,* 319–328.

Yeudall, L. T. (1978). *The neuropsychology of aggression.* Clarence Hinks Memorial Lecture. University of Western Ontario.

Yeudall, L. T., Fedora, O., Fedora, S., & Wardell, D. (1981). *Australian Journal of Forensic Science, 13*(4) and *14*(1).

Yeudall, L. T., & Flor-Henry, P. (1975). *Lateralized neuropsychological impairments in depression and criminal psychopathy* Paper presented at the conference of the Psychiatric Association of Alberta, Calgary, Alberta.

Yeudall, L. T., & Fromm-Auch, D. (1979). Neuropsychological impairments in various psychopathological populations. In J. Gruzelier & P. Flor-Henry (Eds.), *Hemisphere asymmetries of function and psychopathology* (pp. 5–13). New York: Elsevier/North Holland.

Yeudall, L. T., Fromm-Auch, D., & Davies, P. (1982). Neuropsychological impairment of persistent delinquency. *Journal of Nervous and Mental Disease, 170,* 257–265.

11

PET STUDIES OF AGGRESSION IN PERSONALITY DISORDER AND OTHER NONPSYCHOTIC PATIENTS

Peter F. Goyer
William E. Semple
Department of Veterans Affairs Medical Center
and
Case Western Reserve University Medical School

In 1979, Brown, Goodwin, Ballenger, Goyer, and Major studied cerebrospinal fluid (CSF) samples from a group of patients with personality disorder and found a statistically significant inverse relationship between their life history of aggression scores and the serotonin metabolite, 5-hydroxyindole acetic acid (5-HIAA). A similar study by Brown et al. (1982) focused on the specific diagnostic group of borderline personality disorder (BPD) and replicated the findings of the earlier study with respect to CSF 5-HIAA and life history of aggression scores. Linnoila et al. (1983) used frequency scoring in a group of 36 character disorders who had killed or attempted to kill and found that offenders with more than one violent crime had lower average CSF 5-HIAA than offenders with only one. There was also a significantly lower average CSF 5-HIAA in personality disorders grouped as impulsive (i.e., explosive or antisocial) compared to personality disorders grouped as nonimpulsive (i.e., passive–aggressive). In another study of criminal offenders, Virkkunen, Nuutila, Goodwin, and Linnoila (1987) reported that arsonists had significantly lower CSF 5-HIAA than a group of violent offenders and that both were significantly lower than a group of normal controls. Roy and Linnoila (1988) examined CSF 5-HIAA in a group of 17 normal controls and found a significant negative correlation with the urge to act out hostility subscale of the Hostility and Direction of Hostility Questionnaire.

Although these noninclusive examples focused on a biological finding which correlated to aggressive behavior that was directed primarily away from oneself, there is also an extensive literature on CSF 5-HIAA in aggressive or destructive behavior directed toward oneself (e.g., suicide, self-mutilation, substance abuse). Confounding the issue of aggressive behavior and CSF 5-HIAA, is the likelihood of comorbidity in those diagnostic groups that may be more likely to have higher aggression scores such as personality disorder, substance abuse, and or posttraumatic stress disorder (PTSD). Nonetheless, a consistent theme that is present in the findings reported to date, is that biological links for aggressive behavior exist and statistically correlate with frequency scoring of either specific aggressive behaviors or life history of multiple aggressive behaviors.

One of the authors (PFG) was involved in the earlier work by Brown et al. (1979, 1982) and has subsequently worked on modifying the Life History of Aggression Scale and its extension from a military population to a civilian population. Ratings from these modifications and extensions are among the topics discussed in this chapter.

Irrespective of which scale is used to measure a life history of aggression, there is not necessarily a one-to-one relationship between CSF metabolites and their parent neurotransmitter. Consequently, the in situ role of cortical serotonin or other neurotransmitters in human aggressive behavior remains problematic. One approach to this problem is positron emission tomography (PET). On the assumption that increases or decreases in regional presynaptic and postsynaptic activity are directly related to regional energy usage, regional cerebral metabolic rate of glucose (rCMRG) and whole brain metabolic rate of glucose (CMRG) have been measured with PET in numerous psychiatric disorders. Furthermore, in functional psychiatric disorders, CMRG is assumed to be directly coupled with cerebral blood flow (CBF). Consequently, whole brain CBF and regional CBF (rCBF) have also been measured in psychiatric illness. Depending on the diagnostic category examined, statistically significant increases or decreases in rCMRG and rCBF have been localized to specific areas of the frontal cortex.

Consistent with animal and human postmortem studies documenting serotonin subtype 2 receptors ($5-HT_{2A}$) in frontal cortex, Wong et al. (1984) documented in vivo $5-HT_{2A}$ receptor uptake in human frontal cortex using PET and ^{11}C-N-methylspiperone (^{11}C-NMSP). (In accordance with the Serotonin Receptor Nomenclature Committee [Watson and Girdlestone, 1993], $5-HT_{2A}$ will be the notation used for receptors previously denoted as $5-HT_2$.) Benkelfat et al. (1989) found that increased rCMRG in the orbital frontal cortex of obsessive-compulsive disorder (OCD) patients returned to levels found in normal controls, after the OCD patients received successful clinical treatment with the serotonergic agent clomipramine. Thus, if there is a relationship between in situ cortical serotonin activity and a life history of aggressive behavior, the serotonin (or other) neurotransmitter activity could, if the increases or decreases were of sufficient magnitude, be reflected in changes of rCMRG or rCBF. Our findings on these correlations are reported here.

PET AND LIFE HISTORY OF AGGRESSION

Aggression Rating Procedures

Patients were administered a Modified Aggression Scale (MAS) during personal interviews. The MAS is modified from the Life History of Aggression Rating Scale previously published by Brown et al. (1979). Items 1 through 3 were modified as previously described (Goyer et al., 1994) and Items 4 through 9 were unchanged. Per item scoring was maintained in a range of 0 to 4. See Table 11.1 for a listing of the MAS items.

Because both the Life History of Aggression Scale (Brown et al., 1979) and the MAS (Goyer et al., 1994) were designed for military populations, additional revisions were necessary for application to civilians. The concept of a 9-item scale with scores from 0 to 4 on each item was maintained in order to provide some relationship between results from previously reported scales and results from a Civilian Aggression Scale (CAS). Items 8 and 9, which were identical on both the Brown et al. (1979) scale and the MAS, dealt specifically with military disciplinary problems and were incorporated in the civilian version as a type of "law enforcement agency." Item 2 on the MAS, which had included physically aggressive behavior toward other humans (Table 11.1) with no distinction between family and nonfamily members, was divided into Items 1 and 2. In the CAS, Item 1 became "physical aggression toward family members" and Item 2 became "physical aggression toward nonfamily members" (Table 11.2). Item 3 on the MAS, which had included physically aggressive behavior toward both self or animals (Table 11.1), was divided into Items 3 and 4. In the CAS, Item 3 became "physical aggression toward self" and Item 4 became "physical aggression toward nonhuman animals." The remaining items on the MAS were maintained but reordered (Table 11.2). Though not counted in the overall scoring, an Item 10 was used to record illicit drug usage.

Intergroup comparison of aggression scores on the MAS and CAS have not been previously reported. Consequently, we compared previously unpublished gender and personality disorder differences on the MAS in a group of military

TABLE 11.1
Modified Aggression Scale (MAS)

---

1. Aggressive behavior directed toward inanimate objects.
2. Aggressive behavior directed toward other humans.
3. Aggressive behavior directed toward self or animals.
4. School discipline.
5. Relationship with civilian supervisors.
6. Antisocial behavior not involving the police.
7. Antisocial behavior involving the police.
8. Military disciplinary problems not involving the military judicial system.
9. Military disciplinary problems involving the military judicial system.

Note. From Goyer et al. (1994).

TABLE 11.2
Civilian Aggression Scale (CAS)

---

1. Physical aggression toward family members.
2. Physical aggression toward nonfamily members.
3. Physical aggression toward self.
4. Physical aggression toward nonhuman animals.
5. Physical aggression toward inanimate objects.
6. Suspensions or expulsions from school.
7. Authority conflicts with job supervisors resulting in termination, voluntary, or involuntary.
8. Antisocial behavior apprehended by law enforcement agencies.
9. Antisocial behavior not apprehended by law enforcement agencies.

---

personality disorders whom we had previously studied with PET (Goyer et al., 1991; Goyer et al., 1994). We also compared differences on the CAS in a group of civilian subjects with respect to gender, PTSD, and OCD, and these results are also included.

PET Scans and Image-Analysis Procedures

PET scanning and image-analysis procedures for those studies, which were performed by the authors and their collaborators, were conducted in the PET center at the National Institute of Mental Health (NIMH) in Bethesda or at University Hospitals (UH) in Cleveland.

The PET scan and image-analysis procedures for the military subjects from the Bethesda National Naval Medical Center (NNMC) and for the civilian normal control group from the National Institute of Mental Health (NIMH) were identical to those previously reported in other NIMH studies which used 18-fluoro-deoxy-glucose (^{18}FDG) to measure rCMRG during cortical activation by an auditory continuous performance task (CPT). The protocol has been described by several authors including Goyer et al. (1992; Goyer et al., 1994). A schematic of the regions of interest (ROI) used in those studies is illustrated for the left cortical hemisphere (Fig. 11.1). The statistical analysis of the PET scan ROI data, using analysis of covariance (ANCOVA) with age and sex covaried and Spearman rank ordering correlation, has also been described elsewhere (Goyer et al., 1994).

The PET scans performed at UH used oxygen-15-water (H_2O^{15}) to measure rCBF during an auditory CPT in a group of PTSD patients from the Cleveland VA Medical Center (CVAMC) and in a group of normal controls. Although the auditory CPT was identical to that used in the NIMH studies, the PET scanning and image-analysis procedures were different and have been described elsewhere (Goyer, Berridge, et al., 1993; Goyer, Semple, et al., 1993; Semple et al., 1993). A schematic of these ROI is illustrated for the left cortical hemisphere in Fig. 11.2.

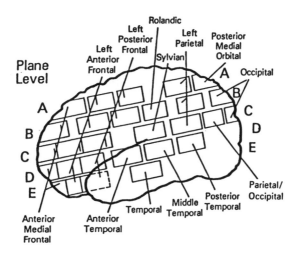

FIG. 11.1. Left hemisphere schematic of rectangular regions of interest in five transaxial planes.

Subjects

Twenty-four inpatients from the NNMC signed informed consent to voluntarily participate in the NIMH–NNMC study on personality disorders. PET scan correlations with MAS scores have previously been reported for 16 of the 24 patients (Goyer et al., 1991; Goyer et al., 1994) and are summarized here. An extended analysis of the MAS scores with the eight additional subjects and their intragroup comparisons has not been previously reported and is included in this chapter.

The NIMH–NNMC study used the MAS and positron emission tomography to examine the relationship between cerebral metabolism and a life history of aggression. There were 16 males and 8 females with an average age and standard deviation (*SD*) of 23.3 ± 4.6 years. All 24 patients were administered the MAS and 17 patients received PET scans. To be included each patient had to receive, by consensus of the treatment team, an Axis II diagnosis of personality disorder according to DSM-IIIR. A diagnosis of "personality disorder, not otherwise specified" with the features of a specific diagnosis was grouped under the specific diagnosis. A comorbid diagnosis on Axis I was not an exclusion criteria and 19 patients also had an Axis I diagnosis.

The normal control group for between-group comparisons of PET scans consisted of 43 subjects who signed informed consent to voluntarily participate in the study. There were 21 males and 22 females with an average age of 30.2 ± *SD* = 9.2 years. All of them had responded to advertisements sponsored by the NIMH and all received remuneration. They were screened for present or past psychiatric and other medical illness by interview and physical exam (PFG and colleagues). Routine laboratory screening tests were also performed.

Aggression ratings were compared with the PET scans as a dimensional study of a symptom complex across all Axis II diagnostic groups within the NNMC military population. PET scan differences between the military patient group and the civilian normal controls were compared as a categorical study for the Axis II diagnostic groups of antisocial personality disorder and borderline personality disorder (BPD).

Because the CAS was not yet implemented when the NIMH civilian normal control group received PET scans, life history of aggression ratings could not be compared between the NNMC military patients and the NIMH civilian control subjects.

In an ongoing continuation of our aggression work, we have recently studied a group of 10 male combat veterans with PTSD who were being treated at the CVAMC and a normal control group of 35 subjects who responded to advertisements at Case Western Reserve University Medical School (CWRU) and University Hospitals (UH) in Cleveland. All subjects signed informed consent to participate in the study and all received remuneration. Routine laboratory screening tests were performed for subjects in both groups. Subjects in both groups were administered the CAS by the first author (PFG). The average age of the PTSD patients was 43.3 years $\pm SD = 2.2$ years. All had a history of substance abuse but were currently drug and alcohol abstinent; all had received treatment for their substance abuse and during their treatment had been monitored with weekly blood and urine drug screens. They were also tested on the day of the PET scan and all patients were negative for toxicology on that day. PET scans were performed on all 10 of the PTSD patients. In the normal control group, there were 21 males and 14 females with an average age of $27.3 \pm SD = 7.5$ years and they were screened for present or past psychiatric and other medical illness by interview and by physical exam (PFG and colleagues). Fourteen of the 21 control males received CBF scans. The average age of these 14 was $30.4 \pm SD = 10.3$ years.

Exclusion criteria for all subjects in both the NIMH–NNMC and UH–CVAMC studies, included no neurological illnesses or head trauma; no current alcohol or substance abuse; and medication free for at least 2 weeks prior to the PET scan. An additional exclusion criteria for the NIMH and UH normal control groups was no present or past psychiatric illness.

As part of their ongoing evaluation, eight male patients at UH with OCD were administered the CAS (PFG), but they did not receive PET scans.

MAS and CAS Results

Average MAS scores $\pm SD$ were 8.9 ± 3.8 ($N = 8$) for the female non-antisocial personality disorder group, 15.1 ± 6.6 ($N = 7$) for the male non-antisocial personality disorder group, and 18.1 ± 6.2 ($N = 9$) for the male antisocial personality disorder group. These mean scores are listed in Table 11.3. Differences in scores between the male and female non-antisocial personality disorders were statisti-

TABLE 11.3
Mean Scores on the Modified Aggression Scale (MAS) for
Different Diagnostic Groups of Male and Female Military Personnel

Population[a]	DSM–IIIR Diagnosis	MAS Scores Mean ± SD
Military Females	non-antisocial personality disorders	8.9 ± 3.8 $(N = 8)$[b]
Military Males	non-antisocial personality disorders	15.1 ± 6.6 $(N = 7)$[b]
Military Males	antisocial personality disorders	18.1 ± 6.2 $(N = 9)$

[a]12 of 16 males and 5 of 8 females previously reported (from Goyer et al., 1994).
[b]Female non-antisocial personality disorder compared to male non-antisocial personality disorder, $p < .01$, two-tailed t test.

cally significant, $p < .01$, two-tailed t test. Although the male antisocial personality disorders scored higher on the MAS than the male non-antisocial personality disorders, the difference in this small sample was not statistically significant, $p = .37$, two-tailed t test.

Previously unpublished results for average CAS scores ± SD in the four groups more recently examined from UH–CVAMC were as follows: UH male controls = 4.0 ± 5.3, $N = 21$; UH female controls = 2.7 ± 3.5, $N = 14$; CVAMC male PTSD patients = 18.8 ± 5.7, $N = 10$; UH male OCD patients = 8.4 ± 6.0; $N = 8$. The average age of each of the four groups ± SD, respectively, was 29.0 ± 9.0 years, 24.6 ± 3.1 years, 43.3 ± 2.2 years, and 38.0 ± 7.8 years.

Based on previous findings with the life history of aggression scales, we expected males to score higher than females and patients to score higher than controls, so all t tests on the CAS are one-tailed. Although normal males have higher CAS scores than normal females, the difference was not statistically significant, $p < .22$. When CAS scores for each of the two male patient groups were compared to the group of control males, there was a statistically significant increase in a life history of aggression in both patient groups, $p < .001$ for PTSD patients and $p < .03$ for OCD patients. There was also a statistically significant difference in CAS scores between the two patient groups, $p < .001$.

The 16 military males and 8 females with personality disorders have a statistically significant increase in aggression scores compared to the 21 males and 14 females in the civilian control group, $p < .001$, two-tailed t test. Although the MAS and CAS are similar, the reader is reminded that they are not identical, so in this instance comparison of diagnostic groups across these scales may be problematic. The differences in structure between the two scales is, however, such that scores tend to be higher on the CAS than on the MAS so that statistically significant differences in the opposite direction, as in this example, are probably more robust than indicated. Summaries of average scores for different population groups on their group specific aggression rating scales are listed in Tables 11.3 and 11.4.

TABLE 11.4

Mean Scores on the Civilian Aggression Scale (CAS) for Male and
Female Normal Controls, Posttraumatic Stress Disorder (PTSD)
Males, and Obsessive–Compulsive Disorder (OCD) Males

Population	DSM-IIIR Diagnosis	CAS Scores Mean ± SD
Males	normal controls	4.0 ± 5.3 (N = 21)
Females	normal controls	2.7 ± 3.5 (N = 14)
Males	PTSD	18.8 ± 5.7 (N = 10)[a,c]
Males	OCD	8.4 ± 6.0 (N = 8)[b,c]

[a]Male PTSD patients compared to male normal controls, $p < .001$, one-tailed t test.
[b]Male OCD patients compared to male normal controls, $p < .03$, one-tailed t test.
[c]Male PTSD patients compared to male OCD patients, $p < .001$, one-tailed t test.

PET Scan Results

Some of the following PET results were originally published in abstract (Goyer et al., 1991) and subsequently more fully analyzed in a later article (Goyer et al., 1994). Other PET correlation results are included here for the first time.

Previously published data (Goyer et al., 1994) comparing normalized rCMRG in the NIMH control group to the NNMC–BPD group, indicated a significant decrease for the NNMC–BPD group in the frontal cortex approximately 81 mm (B plane) above the canthomeatal line (CML), $F(1,45) = 8.65$, $p < .01$, age and sex covaried and a significant increase in the frontal cortex approximately 53 mm (D plane) above the CML, $F(1,45) = 7.68$, $p < .01$, age and sex covaried. These and other ROI in the NIMH–NNMC study are illustrated schematically in Fig. 11.1. An exploratory ANCOVA for comparing mean normalized rCMRG in ROI outside the frontal lobes in each of five planes revealed two ROI in the B plane which were significantly decreased in the BPD group: left parietal, $.93 \pm SEM = .03$, compared to $1.03 \pm SEM = .01$, $p < .02$ and posterior cingulate, $.93 \pm SEM = .05$ compared to $1.03 \pm SEM = .02$, $p < .05$, posterior cingulate ROI not illustrated in the schematic of Fig. 11.1. There were no significant differences in normalized mean rCMRG in any ROI of the antisocial group compared to the NIMH control group.

Within the entire group of 17 personality disorder patients who received a PET scan and who were rated on the MAS (Goyer et al., 1991; Goyer et al., 1994), there was a significant inverse correlation between normalized rCMRG in the orbital frontal cortex in a region of interest (ROI) which was approximately 40 mm (E plane) above the CML and absolute scores on the MAS, $r = -.54$, $p < .03$. Within the E plane orbital frontal cortex, there was a significant inverse correlation between mean normalized rCMRG and MAS scores in the anterior medial frontal, $r = -.63$, $p < .01$ and in the left anterior frontal, $r = -.56$, $p < .02$.

An exploratory analysis of remaining E plane ROI revealed a significant inverse correlation in only one other region, the right temporal, $r = -.49$, $p < .05$.

The E plane was chosen for correlation analysis because the E plane was the only one of the five planes to demonstrate an inverse correlation between group rank on the MAS and normalized mean rCMRG, $r = -.56$, $p < .03$. PET findings discussed to this point have previously been reported by Goyer et al. (1991; Goyer et al., 1994).

In our ongoing and previously unpublished UH–CVAMC aggression studies, we first analyzed rCBF in those ROI that showed trends or had been statistically significant for correlations with rCMRG in our earlier NIMH–NNMC study (cf. earlier). Probability values are one-tailed due to the previously established direction of hypotheses and all correlation coefficients are Spearman (nonparametric). The distance of the parallel planes above the CML is identical in the earlier NIMH work and this ongoing UH–CVAMC work. The ROI in these studies are anatomically similar to the earlier studies (Fig. 11.2). However, the terminology differs somewhat due to the previously noted differences in image analysis procedures. Within the group of 10 PTSD patients, CAS scores showed a tendency to vary inversely with whole brain CBF, $r = -.36$, $p = .15$. In region E-1, right anterior orbital frontal cortex, and in region E-16, left anterior orbital frontal cortex, there was a trend for an inverse correlation between normalized rCBF and CAS scores, $r = -.30$, $p < .2$; and $r = -.50$, $p = .07$, respectively. These findings in PTSD patients tend to support our previous rCMRG finding in personality disorder patients of an inverse relationship between orbital frontal cortex activity and life history of aggression scores.

As noted earlier, borderline personality disorder patients (with life history aggression scores greater than normal military controls) showed decreased frontal cortex activity in the B plane and increased frontal cortex activity in the D plane (Goyer et al., 1991; Goyer et al., 1994). These findings suggested that rCBF in the B and D plane frontal cortex be examined in the PTSD patient group (who also had life history of aggression scores greater than a normal control group). There was a significant inverse relationship between left anterior frontal rCBF (region B-16) and aggression score, $r = -.70$, $p = .01$. The relationship for right anterior frontal cortex (region B-1) was not significant, $r = -.23$, $p > .2$. A similar test for a positive relationship between frontal cortex blood flow in the D plane found a trend relationship at the left frontal cortex (region D-15), $r = .45$, $p < .1$.

LEFT

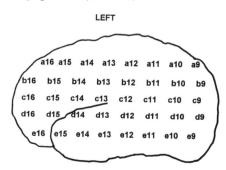

FIG. 11.2. Left hemisphere schematic of cortical peel regions of interest in five transaxial planes.

In the normal PET control group of 14 males, there was a nonsignificant tendency for an inverse correlation between whole brain CBF and CAS scores, $r = -.22$, $p = .22$. In the normal control group, there were no significant correlations between CAS scores and blood flow in the E plane or in orbital frontal regions of the E plane. Aggression scores in normals were negatively correlated with B plane frontal cortex blood flow, $r = -.60$, $p = .01$, at B-2 region; $r = -.35$, $p = .11$, at B-1 region.

One of the procedural differences between scanning with ^{18}FDG for rCMRG and with H_2O^{15} for rCBF is the time required for the scan itself and the time required for five half-lifes of radionuclide decay between successive scans. In the usual 90 minutes required postinjection for a single ^{18}FDG scan, approximately six H_2O^{15} scans can be performed. Consequently, the NIMH–NNMC study consisted of only one ^{18}FDG scan for each subject. In the UH–CVAMC study the normal control group received a minimum of four scans: a resting state, an initial auditory CPT (CPT-1), a repeat auditory CPT (CPT-2), and a forced recall of words beginning with F (FAS). In order to provide comparability to the ^{18}FDG studies which used the auditory CPT, data presented to this point were for the mean of the CBF results during the two auditory CPT studies. Also the data for rCBF analysis, to this point, used one-tailed testing based on regions previously shown to be of interest for ^{18}FDG.

An exploratory analysis of rCBF, not based on regions of interest from previously published ^{18}FDG results, was also performed in the group of normal controls. This analysis examined all four scans using two-tailed, nonparametric, Spearman correlations and revealed robust exploratory findings of inverse correlations between normalized rCBF and CAS scores in the left temporal-parietal cortex of the C plane in the insular region. In ROI = C-12: during rest, $r = -.47$, $p = .08$; during CPT-1, $r = -.34$, $p = .23$; during CPT-2, $r = -.59$, $p = .02$; during FAS, $r = -.64$, $p = .01$. In ROI = C-13: during rest, $r = -.51$, $p = .05$; during CPT-1, $r = -.22$, $p = .4$ during CPT-2, $r = -.47$, $p = .08$; during FAS, $r = -.33$, $p = .25$. A region of interest placed to measure more medial aspects of the insula also indicated a significant inverse relationship between blood flow and aggression scores: during rest, $r = -.68$, $p = .006$; during CPT-1, $r = -.62$, $p = .01$; during CPT-2, $r = -.56$, $p = .03$; and during FAS, $r = -.64$, $p = .01$.

Discussion

The statistically significant differences in mean aggression values between diagnostic groups and between patient groups and normal controls are consistent with previously reported differences in such measures using frequency scoring of physically aggressive behavior. The MAS differentiates between greater life history of aggression scores in male than in female personality disorder groups. The difference in CAS scores, though higher in a group of normal males than in normal females, did not reach statistical significance. This is most likely related to the smaller mean differences in normals (4.0 compared to 2.7) than in personality disorders (15.1 compared to 8.9). It is possible that larger normal control groups with smaller standard deviations would show statistically significant differences in CAS scores between normal males and normal females. These results do, however, seem to indicate that any comparison of life history of aggression scores between different diagnostic groups should correct for gender differences.

All patient subgroups had greater physically aggressive behavior than a control group of normal males and females. This occurred both within the same scoring instrument (CAS) and across scoring instruments (MAS and CAS). In those comparisons that used similar but not identical rating scales, a possible criticism is that normal persons in the military would have higher aggression ratings than normal persons in civilian life. Although extensive studies with the MAS and CAS in large population groups have not yet been performed, a small normal control group of military males had a mean life history of aggression rating of $2.2 \pm SD = 1.5$ (Brown et al., 1979) compared to a mean rating of $4.0 \pm SD = 5.3$ for a civilian male control group on the CAS. One of the authors (PFG) was a rater for the 1979 study (that used a forerunner of the MAS), the MAS scoring at NNMC, and the CAS scoring at UH–CVAMC. Although there may be a time drift even with the same rater and although there is a possibility that normal military males have less behavioral aggression, the more likely explanation is that these two rating scales will have statistically different normative means when applied to larger groups of normal controls and that, in normals, CAS scores will be higher than MAS scores. If this is true, the CAS may be preferred over the MAS and its forerunners even in a military population, because a wider band of scoring will provide more opportunity to examine variations in aggressive behavior within both normal control and patient groups.

With regard to the PET scans, the combined pattern of decreased glucose metabolic rate in the B plane frontal lobes and increased glucose metabolic rate in the D plane frontal lobes is of interest. To the authors' knowledge, this pattern has not been reported in any other diagnostic group. This finding should, however, be approached with caution. First, the study involves only a small group of six BPD patients and hence requires replication. Second, these six patients were mild borderline personality disorders with only one of the six having an unresolved Axis I diagnosis at the time of the scan and a relatively low average group score ($3.7 \pm SD = 1.6$) on the Diagnostic Interview for Borderlines (DIB; Gunderson, Kolb, & Austin, 1981). More severe BPD patients with concomitant Axis I diagnoses and higher DIB or other quantified personality disorder rating scores may have different rCMRG patterns.

Although this specific pattern of B and D plane metabolic findings has not yet been found in other diagnostic groups, statistically significant differences in rCMRG with other ROI patterns have been reported in the B and D planes for other diagnostic groups. For example, Nordahl et al. (1990) reported statistically significant decreases in normalized rCMRG in the left posterior parietal ROI in panic disorder. In bulimia nervosa patients compared to normal controls, Andreason et al. (1992) reported several findings of which one was decreased rCMRG in the right anterior frontal region of the B plane (and of the C plane). Goyer et al. (1992) reported statistically significant decreases in the left posterior parietal and other continquous ROI in patients with summer seasonal affective disorder (SSAD). Patients with SSAD also had decreased rCMRG in the left posterior temporal region of the D plane (Goyer et al., 1992). Several PET studies of rCMRG in D plane frontal lobes of patients with schizophrenia or affective disorders have found significant decreases compared to normal controls (e.g., Baxter et al., 1985; Baxter et al., 1989; Buchsbaum et al., 1984; Cohen et al., 1987; Cohen et al., 1989; Martinot et al., 1990). The findings that this group of patients with BPD exhibited significant rCMRG increases in D plane frontal lobes suggests a difference between this group of BPD patients and patients with psychotic illness.

An additional finding in the NIMH–NNMC study was that personality disorder patients with higher aggression scores on the MAS had lower rCMRG in the orbital frontal region of the E plane. Unpublished results, from our ongoing aggression studies using PET, have extended these findings to rCBF correlations with CAS ratings in a group of 10 combat veterans with PTSD. Although combat veterans with PTSD have high comorbidity for substance abuse and personality disorder, none of the patients in this group of 10 had a clinical diagnosis of personality disorder according to DSM-IIIR. Combat veterans with PTSD do, however, exhibit a wide range of scoring on life history of aggression so that they, like groups of patients with personality disorders, provide opportunities for correlations of aggressive behavior with biological markers such as rCMRG or rCBF. Although repetitive blood and urine screening was used to rule out any current alcohol or illicit drug use, all patients in the PTSD group were comorbid for a history of substance abuse. Whether or not this history will affect CAS correlation with rCBF requires additional work, such as with patients who have PTSD but no substance abuse histories and with patients who have substance abuse histories but no PTSD.

Patients with OCD have been reported to exhibit increased glucose metabolic rates in the orbital frontal and prefrontal cortex (Baxter et al., 1987; Baxter et al., 1988; Baxter et al., 1989; Benkelfat et al., 1989; Nordahl et al., 1989; Swedo et al., 1989). Findings in orbital frontal cortex from the NIMH–NNMC and UH–CVAMC studies imply that higher rCMRG and higher rCBF, respectively, are correlated with lower life history of aggression scores. These findings suggest the possibility that there may be a relationship between some symptoms of OCD and life history of outward directed aggression. Indeed, Semple et al. (1993) did find that those patients with PTSD in the UH–CVAMC study had statistically significant increases in normalized rCBF in orbital frontal cortex compared to normal controls even though none of the PTSD patients had a clinical diagnosis of OCD. In contrast, however, Andreason et al. (1993) used a linear regression analysis to correlate normalized rCMRG with clinical scales in a group of bulimia nervosa patients and found that those patients who had higher rCMRG in their orbital frontal ROI, had lower scores for obsessive–compulsive symptoms on the Maudsley scale.

These findings of higher rCMRG and of higher rCBF are in cortical regions known to contain 5-HT$_{2A}$ receptors and Benkelfat et al. (1989) have shown that the clinical response of OCD patients to the serotonergic agent, clomipramine, correlated with decreases in previously elevated orbital frontal metabolic rate. Serotonergic agents are also used to treat the recurrent intrusive thoughts and other symptoms associated with PTSD. To the authors knowledge, however, no pre- and post-PET scans have been reported in PTSD patients being treated with serotonergic agents.

Serotonergic agents, such as fluoxetine, have also been used to treat impulsive behavior in character disorders (Coccaro, Astill, Herbert, & Schut, 1990; Markowitz, Calabrese, Schulz, & Meltzer, 1991). Impulsive behaviors, such as those described by Coccaro and Markowitz, are rated as items in both the MAS and the CAS and would thus contribute to higher life history of aggression scores on either rating scale. As has been noted, lower rCMRG and lower rCBF in orbital frontal cortex correlates with increased MAS or CAS scores. If either or both rCMRG and rCBF in orbital frontal cortex are related to serotonin neuronal activity in these ROI for patients with impulsive behavior difficulties, then this would be consistent with treatment response to serotonergic agents in such patients. Metabolic or blood flow scans before and after treatment with serotonergic agents in patients with impulsive behavior difficulties would be useful to further examine this possible relationship.

An inverse relationship between upper prefrontal cortex activity and life history of aggression is suggested by findings in personality disorder patients (Goyer et al., 1994). Negative correlations between CAS aggression scores and upper prefrontal cortex blood flow in both PTSD patients and normal controls in the UH–CVAMC studies provide preliminary support to the hypothesized relationship between frontal cortex function and life history of aggressive behavior. Although the effect did not reach statistical significance, whole brain blood flow was associated with correlation coefficients that supported increased aggression scores in the three groups examined to date: personality disorder patients, PTSD patients, and normal controls.

Because correlations may be due to other causal factors associated with both aggression and brain function, caution should be used in the interpretation of correlational data. Further work is needed to replicate and clarify interpretation of these exploratory findings.

Even more tentative is the finding in UH normals of an inverse relationship between left temporal-insular cortex blood flow and life history of aggression. As with the other PET findings, these findings may not be due to differences in aggressive behavior per se but due to other individual differences in cognition or affect that are associated with individual differences in aggressive history.

The overall value of these PET findings may thus be to help develop and formulate hypotheses about brain function and aggressive behavior that can be tested in more definitive paradigms.

PET AND LIFE HISTORY OF HOMICIDAL AGGRESSION

PET and homicidal aggression are discussed more fully in chapter 10. For completeness, two studies are briefly noted here.

To the authors knowledge, one of the first uses of PET to examine homicidal aggression concerned four psychiatric inpatients who had been arrested at least three times for violent behavior (Volkow & Tancredi, 1987). In those four patients, the authors found a lower frontal-occipital ratio and a lower left temporal-right temporal ratio of rCBF.

In a larger and statistically analyzed group, Raine et al. (1992) reported a study that tested "the hypothesis that homicide cases pleading not guilty by reason of insanity or incompetency to stand trial are characterized by pre-frontal dysfunction" (p. S58). To test this hypothesis, the group measured rCMRG using positron emission tomography in subjects who were given a continuous performance task. Subjects consisted of "a group of 22 murderers and 22 age- and sex-matched controls" (p. S58). The murderers were found to have significantly lower rCMRG in prefrontal and orbital frontal cortex. This difference was not related to other variables such as "handedness, schizophrenia, ethnic minority . . . , head injury, or motivation deficits in the murder group" (p. S58).

The more fully analyzed data were subsequently reported by Raine et al. in 1994 and, as mentioned earlier, these and other data on homicidal aggression are presented in chapter 10.

SUMMARY

Although the literature is still sparse with respect to PET studies of aggression, our chapter and chapter 10 (this volume) cover PET and aggression and do seem to support an inverse relationship between aggressive impulse difficulties and rCMRG–rCBF in specific regions of the frontal cortex. Although rCMRG and rCBF are not receptor specific, the known presence of serotonin receptors in frontal cortex is consistent with other biological research in suggesting at least a partial role for serotonergic neurotransmission in the regulation of aggressive behavior.

Findings of an inverse correlation between life history of aggression scores and rCBF in the orbital frontal cortex of the male PTSD patients and in male controls is consistent with previously published results for rCMRG and life history of aggression scores in personality disorders. Additionally in the normal control group, an exploratory ROI analysis revealed a statistically significant inverse correlation between aggression scores and rCBF in three contiguous ROI in the left insular region of the C plane. These rCBF correlations with a life history of aggression have not been previously published. These studies of rCMRG and rCBF in patients and in normal controls suggest that orbital frontal, upper prefrontal, and left insular temporal-parietal regions may be involved in the regulation of aggressive behavior.

PROSPECTS FOR FUTURE RESEARCH

By scanning subjects before and after the administration of pharmacologic probes for specific receptors, future PET studies with sufficient sensitivity to measure the resulting changes in rCMRG or rCBF could further elucidate not only the role of serotonin in aggressive behavior but also the role of other neurotransmitters. Additionally, receptor tracers could be used not only to measure differences in receptor density but also to evaluate receptor occupancy by pharmacologic agents used in the treatment of patients with aggressive impulse difficulties. Furthermore, PET studies before and after pharmacologic treatment of patients with aggressive impulsive difficulty would allow correlation of regional brain function with treatment response.

REFERENCES

Andreason, P. J., Altemus, M., Zametkin, A. J., King, A. C., Lucinio, J., & Cohen, R. M. (1992). Regional cerebral glucose metabolism in bulimia nervosa. *American Journal of Psychiatry, 149*, 1506–1513.

Baxter, L. R., Phelps, M. E., Mazziotta, J. C., Guze, B. H., Schwartz, J. M., & Selin, C. E. (1987). Local cerebral glucose metabolic rates in obsessive-compulsive disorder. A comparison with rates in unipolar depression and in normal controls. *Archives of General Psychiatry, 44*, 211–218.

Baxter, L. R., Phelps, M. E., Mazziotta, J. C., Schwartz, J. M., Gerner, R. H., Selin, C. E., & Sumida, R. M. (1985). Cerebral metabolic rates for glucose in mood disorders. *Archives of General Psychiatry, 42*, 441–447.

Baxter, L. R., Schwartz, J. M., Mazziotta, J. C., Phelps, M. E., Pahl, J. J., Guze, B. H., & Fairbanks, L. (1988). Cerebral glucose metabolic rates in nondepressed patients with obsessive-compulsive disorder. *American Journal of Psychiatry, 145*, 1560–1563.

Baxter, L. R., Schwartz, J. M., Phelps, M. E., Mazziotta, J. C., Guze, B. H., Selin, C. E., Gerner, R. H., & Sumida, R. M. (1989). Reduction of prefrontal cortex glucose metabolism common to three types of depression. *Archives of General Psychiatry, 46*, 243–250.

Benkelfat, C., Murphy, D. L., Zohar, J., Hill, J. L., Grover, G., & Insel, T. R. (1989). Clomipramine in obsessive-compulsive disorder. Further evidence for a serotonergic mechanism of action. *Archives of General Psychiatry, 46*, 23–28.

Brown, G. L., Edert, M. H., Goyer, P. F., Jimerson, D. C., Klein, W. J., Bunney, W. E., & Goodwin, F. K. (1982). Aggression, suicide, and serotonin: Relationships to CSF amine metabolites. *American Journal of Psychiatry, 139*, 741–746.

Brown, G. L., Goodwin, F. K., Ballenger, J. C., Goyer, P. F., & Major, L. F. (1979). Aggression in humans correlates with cerebrospinal fluid amine metabolites. *Psychiatry Research, 1*, 131–139.

Buchsbaum, M. S., Cappelletti, J., Ball, R., Hazlett, E., King, A. C., Johnson, J., Wu, J., & DeLisi, L. E. (1984). Positron emission tomographic image measurement in schizophrenia and affective disorders. *Annals of Neurology, 15*, S157–S165.

Coccaro, E. F., Astill, J., Herbert, J. L., & Schut, A. G. (1990). Fluoxetine treatment of impulsive aggression in DSM-III-R personality disorder patients. *Journal of Clinical Psychopharmacology, 10*, 373–375.

Cohen, R. M., Semple, W. E., Gross, M., Nordahl, T. E., DeLisi, L. E., Holcomb, H. H., King, A. C., Morihisa, J. M., & Pickar, D. (1987). Dysfunction in a prefrontal substrate of sustained attention in schizophrenia. *Life Sciences, 40*, 2031–2039.

Cohen, R. M., Semple, W. E., Gross, M., Nordahl, T. E., King, A. C., Pickar, D., & Post, R. M. (1989). Evidence for common alterations in cerebral glucose metabolism in major affective disorders and schizophrenia. *Neuropsychopharmacology, 2*, 241–254.

Goyer, P. F., Andreason, P. J., Semple, W. E., Clayton, A. H., King, A. C., Compton-Toth, B. A., Schulz, S. C., & Cohen, R. M. (1994). Positron-emission tomography and personality disorders. *Neuropsychopharmacology, 10*, 21–28.

Goyer, P. F., Andreason, P. J., Semple, W. E., Clayton, A. H., King, A. C., Schulz, S. C., & Cohen, R. M. (1991). PET and personality disorders. *Biological Psychiatry (Biological Psychiatry Supplement, 29*(9A), Abstract No. 94A).

Goyer, P. F., Berridge, M., Semple, W. E., Morris, E., Wong, D. F., Schulz, S. C., Miraldi, F., & Meltzer, H. Y. (1993). Dopamine-2 and serotonin-2 receptor indices in clozapine treated schizophrenic patients. *Schizophrenia Research, 9*, 199.

Goyer, P. F., Schulz, P. M., Semple, W. E., Gross, M., Nordahl, T. E., King, A. C., Wehr, T. A., & Cohen, R. M. (1992). Cerebral glucose metabolism in patients with summer seasonal affective disorder. *Neuropsychopharmacology, 7*, 233–240.

Goyer, P. F., Semple, W. E., Morris, E., Muswick, G., Compton, B., Garnett, M. L., Nelson, D., Miraldi, F., Schulz, S. C., & Meltzer, H. Y. (1993). Effects of MK-212 on regional cerebral blood flow in humans. *Schizophrenia Research, 9*, 199.

Gunderson, J. G., Kolb, J. E., & Austin, V. (1981). The diagnostic interview for borderline patients. *American Journal of Psychiatry, 138*, 896–903.

Linnoila, M., Virkkunen, M., Scheinin, M., Nuutila, A., Rimon, R., & Goodwin, F. K. (1983). Low cerebrospinal fluid 5-hydroxyindoleacetic acid concentration differentiates impulsive form nonimpulsive violent behavior. *Life Science, 33*, 2609–2614.

Markowitz, P., Calabrese, J. R., Schulz, S. C., & Meltzer, H. Y. (1991). Fluoxetine in the treatment of borderline and schizotypal personality disorders. *American Journal of Psychiatry, 148*, 1064–1067.

Martinot, J. L., Hardy, P., Feline, A., Huret, J. D., Mazoyer, B., Attar-Levy, D., Pappata, S., & Syrota, A. (1990). Left prefrontal glucose hypometabolism in the depressed state: A confirmation. *American Journal of Psychiatry, 147*, 1313–1317.

Nordahl, T. E., Benkelfat, C., Semple, W. E., Gross, M., King, A. C., & Cohen, R. M. (1989). Cerebral glucose metabolic rates in obsessive compulsive disorder. *Neurospychopharmacology, 2*, 23–28.

Nordahl, T. E., Semple, W. E., Gross, M., Mellman, T. A., Stein, M. B., Goyer, P. F., King, A. C., Uhde, T. W., & Cohen, R. M. (1990). Cerebral glucose metabolic differences in patients with panic disorder. *Neuropsychopharmacology, 3*, 261–272.

Raine, A., Buchsbaum, M. S., Stanley, J., Lottenberg, S., Abel, L., & Stoddard, J. (1992). Selective reductions in pre-frontal glucose metabolism in murderers assessed with positron emission tomography. *Psychophysiology* (From *Psychophysiology Supplements, 29*(4A), S58.

Raine, A., Buchsbaum, M. S., Stanley, J., Lottenberg, S., Abel, L., & Stoddard, J. (1994). Selective reductions in prefrontal glucose metabolism in murderers. *Biological Psychiatry, 36*, 365–373.

Roy, A., & Linnoila, M. (1988). Suicidal behavior, impulsiveness and serotonin. *Acta Psychiatry Scandinavia, 78*, 529–535.

Semple, W. E., Goyer, P. F., McCormick, R., Morris, E. D., Compton, B. A., Muswick, G. J., Nelson, D. A., Donovan, B., Leisure, G., Berridge, M. S., Miraldi, F., & Schulz, S. C. (1993). Preliminary report: Brain blood flow using PET in patients with posttraumatic stress disorder and substance-abuse histories. *Biological Psychiatry, 34*, 115–118.

Swedo, S. E., Schapiro, M. B., Grady, C. L., Cheslow, D. L., Leonard, H. L., Kumar, A., Friedland, R., Rapoport, S. I., & Rapoport, J. L. (1989). Cerebral glucose metabolism in childhood-onset obsessive-compulsive disorder. *Archives of General Psychiatry, 46*, 518–523.

Virkkunen, M., Nuutila, A., Goodwin, F. K., & Linnoila, M. (1987). Cerebrospinal fluid monoamine metabolite levels in male arsonists. *Archives of General Psychiatry, 44*, 241–247.

Volkow, N. D., & Tancredi, L. (1987). Neural substrates of violent behavior; a preliminary study with positron emission tomography. *British Journal of Psychiatry, 151*, 668–673.

Watson, S., & Girdlestone, D. (1993). Receptor nomenclature supplement. *Trends in Pharmacological Science (Suppl.), 14*, 21–72.

Wong, D. F., Wagner, H. N., Dannals, R. F., Links, J. M., Frost, J. J., Ravert, H. T., Wilson, A. A., Rosenbaum, A. E., Gjedde, A., Douglass, K. H., Petronis, J. D., Folstein, M. F., Toung, J. K. T., Burns, D., & Kuhar, M. J. (1984). Effects of age on dopamine and serotonin receptors measured by positron tomography in the living human brain. *Science, 226*, 1391–1396.

12

NEUROBIOLOGICAL AND BEHAVIORAL CHARACTERISTICS OF ALCOHOL-HEIGHTENED AGGRESSION

Helena M. T. Barros
Federal School of Medical Sciences of Porto Alegre

Klaus A. Miczek
Tufts University

Some individuals show increased levels of aggressive behaviors after the use of psychoactive drugs of abuse. The *DSM–IV* describes several possible associations between aggressive behavior and drug use in humans. Characteristically, acute ethanol intoxication produces marked behavioral changes including higher rate and intensity of aggressive behavior; individual drinkers may become atypically belligerent and assaultive. However, the differential diagnosis process must consider the use of other sedative, hypnotic, anxiolytics drugs. Less likely to be associated with aggression, amphetamine and cocaine intoxication may engender maladaptive behavioral changes, such as fighting, whereas belligerence and assaultiveness might happen during either inhalant or PCP intoxications. Irritability, frustration, and anger have also been reported during withdrawal from nicotine or opioids (American Psychiatric Association, 1994). Ethanol clearly stands out as the drug most frequently associated with violent and aggressive behavior in humans (Collins, 1990; Miczek, DeBold, et al., 1994).

IMPLICATIONS OF HUMAN STUDIES ON ETHANOL-ASSOCIATED AGGRESSIVE BEHAVIOR

Epidemiological data show that more than half of the persons known to have committed violent behaviors have consumed ethanol (Miczek, Weerts, & DeBold, 1993a; Roizen, 1993). In agreement with the notion that drinking is almost equally likely among perpetrators and victims of violence (Pernanen, 1991), a recent epidemiological study calculated the risk of violent deaths among nondrinkers, ex-drinkers, and drinkers. The respective risks of death due to suicide, homicide, and motor vehicle accidents were estimated to be six-, seven-, and twofold higher for drinkers than for nondrinkers (Klatsky & Armstrong, 1993). It is remarkable that, up to now, no benchmark data exist on the incidence or prevalence of aggressive acts, after social drinking, among the general population.

Although the incidence of ethanol ingestion associated with violent acts may suggest a *causal* relationship, the epidemiological data are *correlative* and do not elucidate the causal mechanism of the relationship between ethanol drinking and violent acts. Moreover, ethanol is also frequently used by individuals who do not engage in aggressive behavior and the frequency of persons showing less aggressive behavior after drinking ethanol-containing beverages is rarely discussed (Miczek et al., 1993a). Another problem with the epidemiological approach is the multiple and complex relationship found between ethanol and aggressive and violent behavior, rendering it difficult to isolate specific variables to be studied (Roizen, 1993). Many different factors such as the individual's previous experiences, the cultural expectations, and customs seem to contribute to the enhancement of aggressive behavior by ethanol (Lang, Goeckner, Adesso, & Marlatt, 1975). The latter may be exemplified by the description of higher expectation to become aggressive after drinking among college students, males and females, and medium to heavy drinkers (Brennan, Walfish, & Aubuchon, 1986).

Some other factors may be related to the drug itself, such as its direct or indirect effects on different physiological systems, either in the central nervous system (CNS) or in peripheral organs (Pihl, Peterson, & Lau, 1993)—the dose administered and the metabolites that are formed, and the rate of ethanol metabolism. Individual biological factors may be very important; environmental, genetic, and gender differences can be responsible for differences either in ethanol pharmacodynamics or pharmacokinetics. For example, it was demonstrated that the rate of aggressive behavior among females is very low, in comparison to that of males, although the prevalence rates for ethanol use are similar for both genders (White, Brick, & Hansell, 1993).

The biological basis for such complex factors as cultural conventions and social expectations remains elusive. How these social and environmental determinants of ethanol effects interact with the individual's genetic and maturational determinants comprises questions of utmost importance. Several laboratory techniques have been developed for the study of human aggressive behavior, mostly relying on competitive situations in healthy volunteers. With these experimental situations it will be possible to describe in more detail the pharmacological and social factors involved in human ethanol-induced aggressive behavior (e.g., Bond, 1992; Cherek, Steinberg, & Kelly, 1986).

ETHANOL AND AGGRESSIVE BEHAVIOR
IN LABORATORY ANIMALS

Due to the many difficulties in studying the effects of ethanol on human behavior, nonhuman subjects continue to be used particularly to delineate the pharmacological, biochemical, and behavioral aspects of individuals ethanol-enhanced aggression.

The psychopharmacology of aggressive behavior is studied in various animal species, each type with different determinants and functions. These preclinical models of aggressive behavior were developed following the contribution of ethological, experimental psychology, and neurophysiologic concepts and methods. Schemes have been proposed to categorize types of animal aggression in terms of experimental manipulations (e.g., isolated housing, exposure to painful stimuli, brain areas stimulation or lesioning); the type of behavioral phenomena (e.g., affective defense, killing); the potential function of the behavior (e.g., territorial defense, maternal aggression; see Table 12.1). In summary, the experimental models of animal aggression in laboratory research differentiates those that are based on ethological situations, aversive environmental manipulations, and neurological function manipulations. Muricide, or killing behavior, exemplifies the difficulties due to these categorical schemes: Variants of this behavior have been referred to as a form of "predatory aggression" (ethological), "irritable aggression" (aversive environmental manipulations), or it may be produced by brain stimulation or lesioning.

In *ethologically oriented approaches* the effects of ethanol are studied on aggressive behaviors with clear biological functions. The most frequently used include aggressive behaviors during territorial defense ("territorial aggression"); maintenance of dominance in a social group ("dominance" or "rival aggression"); or defense of the newborn by the maternal female ("maternal aggression"). Another approach focuses on a range of *aversive environmental manipulations* such as aggressive behaviors that follow social isolation, REM sleep deprivation, pain- or shock-elicited defense reactions, or the aggressive behavior resulting from the omission of a scheduled reinforcement ("frustration-induced aggression"). The *neurobiological approach* attempts to map neural pathways relevant to aggression by selective brain lesions or electrical stimulation, supposedly mimicking neuropsychiatric diseases (for reviews, see Brain, Miras, & Berry, 1993; Miczek, Haney, Tidey, Vivian, & Weerts, 1994; Miczek et al., 1993a; Mirsky & Siegel, 1994). Whereas the experimental protocols with brain lesions or brain stimulation are disease oriented, the ethological preparations of territorial, dominance or maternal aggression focus on adaptive functions. These preparations differ from each other with regard to motivation, behavioral displays and consequences, reflecting differences in their neurochemical substrata. The behavioral and neurochemical differences between excessive or pathological ag-

TABLE 12.1

Major Experimental Models of Aggression in Laboratory Animals

Experimental Manipulations	Species	Behavioral Topography	Biological Function
A. Aversive environmental manipulations			
Isolation-induced aggression	Mostly in mice	Complete agonistic behavior pattern: isolates attack, threaten, pursue opponent	Territorial defense or compulsive, abnormal, pathological behavior
Pain-elicited or shock-induced aggression	Mostly in rats, also in monkeys	Defensive reactions, including upright postures, bites toward face of opponent, audible vocalizations; bites toward inanimate targets	Some similarity to reaction toward predator or toward large opponent
Aggression due to omission of reward, during schedule-controlled operant behavior	Mostly in pigeons, also in monkeys	Attack - bites or pecks, threat displays towards suitable object or conspecific	Competition for resources such as food, sex, protected niches (?)
B. Brain manipulations			
Brain lesion-induced aggression	Mostly in rats, also in cats	Defensive reactions, biting	Neurological disease
Brain stimulation-induced aggression	Mostly in cats, also in rats	(1) Defensive reactions accompanied by autonomic arousal	Defense against attacker
	Rats	(2) Predatory attack and killing	Predation
		(3) Offensive attacks (no threats)	Pathological, compulsive behavior
C. Ethological situations			
Aggression by resident toward intruder	Most species and in both sexes	Full repertoire of agonistic behavior (attack and threat vs. defense, submission, and flight)	Territorial or group defense (?); rivalry among males and among females
Maternal aggression	Mostly in female lactating rodents	Species-specific repertoire of attack and threat behavior toward intruder	Defense of young, competition for resources and territory
Dominance-related aggression	Mostly in monkeys, mice, and rats	Species-specific repertoire of signals between group members of different social rank; low level and intensity of agonism	Social cohesion and dispersion
D. Killing			
Muricide	Mostly in rats and cats	Stalking, seizing, killing, sometimes consuming prey	Food source; "killer instinct"

Note. Adapted from Miczek et al. (1994).

gressive behavior and adaptive forms of aggression may suggest fundamentally different ethanol effects.

Rats and mice engage in dominance and territorial aggressive behavior, respectively. After they have established "residence" in an environment marked with pheromones, animals will engage in fighting when confronted with an intruder of the same species (Miczek & O'Donnell, 1978). Ethanol can produce a biphasic effect on dominance or territorial aggression. In rats, 0.1 g/kg of ethanol can enhance sideways threats and attack bites, while a 3 g/kg dose sedates the animals and decreases these displays. In mice, territorial aggression is increased in doses ranging from 0.6 to 1 g/kg ethanol, with sedation at 3 g/kg ethanol. This biphasic effect is also observed in dominant monkeys with increased aggressive displays after low doses of ethanol and decreases in these behaviors with doses higher than 1 g/kg (DeBold & Miczek, 1985; Weerts, Tornatzky, & Miczek, 1993; Winslow & Miczek, 1985). The proaggressive effect of ethanol in male mice is influenced by testosterone, as it is not seen after castration and is restored when the castrated mice are treated with this hormone (DeBold & Miczek, 1985). The androgen-dependency of ethanol effects on aggressive behavior in male dominant squirrel monkeys is demonstrated by its annual cyclicity and castration–testosterone effects (Winslow, Ellingboe, & Miczek, 1988; Winslow & Miczek, 1988).

However, not all animals present the same effect in aggressive behaviors when repeatedly given the same low doses of ethanol. Large inter- and intraindividual ethanol effects may be the reason why many previous studies did not detect a reliable increase in aggression after ethanol administration. For example, ethanol in a dose range from 0.5 to 2 g/kg, did not statistically modify maternal aggression of female rats. Nevertheless, the median number of attacks 3 to 4 minutes after the start of the confrontation was around 100% higher for animals treated with 0.5 or 1 g/kg ethanol, when compared to controls (Olivier & Mos, 1986).

The analysis of behavioral alterations in individuals after a low to moderate dose of ethanol allows the identification of subgroups of rats that repeatedly show alcohol-heightened aggression (AHA) or alcohol-suppressed aggression (ASA), using the resident–intruder paradigm (Miczek, Weerts, & DeBold, 1993b; Miczek, Weerts, Tornatzky, DeBold, & Vatne, 1992). In a large population of outbred CFW mice, housed in male–female pairs or isolated, a reliable and repeatable increase in the frequency of attacks toward a standard group-housed intruder is seen after treatment with a low dose of ethanol (1 g/kg) in 20% to 30% of the resident mice (alcohol-heightened aggression, AHA). This percentage contrasts with 6% of mice that show a large increase in attack frequency when given water in control tests, repeatedly, in comparison to their baseline behaviors. In another 15%–20% of mice, ethanol suppressed aggressive behaviors toward the intruder (ASA) on two different occasions, in comparison to the individual baseline behavior of the same animal when treated with control solution. The remaining mice do not show a reliable effect of the drug on aggressive behavior (alcohol nonreliable effects on aggression, ANA). AHA animals show increases in attack bites and sideways threats as high as 200% from their own baselines; by contrast, the ASA animals may even completely cease attacking the intruder at the same ethanol dose (Miczek, Barros, & Weerts, 1995).

Similar to rats, when confronting an intruder, the resident mice follow a sequence of pursuing, threatening, and attacking the intruder, who, in turn, displays defensive and submissive postures or escapes. The aggressive behaviors typically occur in short bursts of fighting, alternating with longer intervals of relative quiescence. Neither ethanol nor benzodiazepine agonists alter the behavioral pattern of aggressive displays of resident male mice and rats or of maternal aggression. In the AHA animals, ethanol prolongs the aggressive bursts and increases the number of aggressive elements per burst. Neither the latency to initiate a burst nor the gaps between the bursts are significantly altered by this agent (Miczek et al., 1992).

An important question regarding the individual differences in the effect of ethanol on aggression is whether it can be predicted. For example, Piazza, Demeniere, le Moal, and Simon (1989, 1990; Piazza et al., 1991) reported that higher locomotor activity exhibited by individual rats in response to d-amphetamine and more rapid acquisition of d-amphetamine self-administration could be predicted on the basis of previously tested higher locomotor response to a novel environment. Using a comparable protocol, the individual differences to the effects of alcohol could not be predicted by their behaviors in a novel environment. When introduced into an open field with a brightly lit center, before the ethanol tests, AHA, ASA, and ANA mice show closely similar exploratory behavior; the frequencies of locomotion in the periphery or in the center of the open field, rearing, and grooming were similar among the three groups. In addition, the initial body weights and weight gain, reproductive behavior, and baseline aggressive behavior of resident mice against an intruder are very similar among mice later classified as AHA, ASA, or ANA (Miczek & Barros, unpublished data), similar to previous observations in rats (Miczek et al., 1992).

Blood ethanol levels above those legally defined as intoxicating are found in individuals involved in violence (Mayfield, 1976; Shupe, 1954). Although pharmacokinetic differences might explain these behavioral dissimilarities, the time course of blood ethanol concentrations is not substantially different between the AHA, ANA, and ASA mice (Miczek, Barros, & Weerts, 1995). All resident mice treated with a 1 g/kg dose showed a peak blood alcohol concentration of 80–130 mg%, 5 to 10 minutes after the drug administration. The proaggressive effects of ethanol start during the elimination phase of the drug (15–20 minutes after drug administration), with blood ethanol levels between 100 and 40 mg%. It remains to be determined if lower peak blood ethanol concentrations can also increase aggressive behavior in this same paradigm.

In sum, under specific experimental conditions, it is possible to detect heightened aggressive behaviors after acute administration of low-moderate doses of alcohol in rats, mice, and primate species. This effect is large, robust, and repeatable, but is limited to a subgroup of subjects of the total population in each species. The defining behavioral and physiological characteristics of these individuals remains to be identified, as well as the neurochemical changes related to ethanol's proaggressive effects.

ETHANOL, AGGRESSION, AND THE CENTRAL NEUROTRANSMITTER SYSTEMS

The approaches used to study the relationship between aggression and ethanol focus on the neurochemical analysis in pertinent brain areas of animals that display the behavior or manipulate each neurotransmitter system with selective agents and analyze its behavioral consequences. To date, most studies deal with the association between aggression and neurochemical changes or the neurochemical changes produced by ethanol; very few describe the possible neurochemical changes related to aggression, under ethanol treatment. The serotonin (5-HT), dopamine (DA) and γ-aminobutyric acid (GABA) systems are shown to be highly relevant for aggressive behavior and ethanol effects, as summarized next.

Serotonin

Human Studies. For the past 3 decades the role of the indoleamine serotonin in the control of aggressive impulses and alcohol abuse has been explored (Everett, 1961; Linnoila et al., 1983; Valzelli & Garattini, 1968; Virkkunen, De Jong, Bartko, Goodwin, & Linnoila, 1989). This link is based on many observations of suicidally depressed, schizophrenic, alcoholic, and explosive antisocial personality disorder patient populations and certain impulsive violent offenders with decreased 5-HIAA concentrations in cerebrospinal fluid (CSF), which reflects low levels of 5-HT metabolism (Asberg, Schalling, Traskman-Bendz, & Wagner, 1987). The assay data from human patient populations indicate that 5-HIAA in CSF is inversely correlated with scores based on the life history of aggression, hostility, anxiety, violent suicidal, or homicidal acts of patients with diverse psychiatric diagnosis or individuals convicted to prison for criminal violence (Brown, Ballenger, Minichiello, & Goodwin, 1979; Brown, Goodwin, Ballenger, Goyer, & Major, 1979; Kruesi, 1989; Lidberg, Tuck, Asberg, Scalia-Tomba, & Bertilsson, 1985; Linnoila, De Jong, & Virkkunen, 1989; Linnoila et al., 1983; Rydin, Schalling, & Asberg, 1982; Van Praag, 1982; Virkkunen et al., 1989; Virkkunen, De Jong, Bartko, & Linnoila, 1989).

In humans presenting violent behavior correlated with low 5-HIAA in CSF, alcohol abuse was an important family characteristic (Linnoila et al., 1989). Moreover, alcoholics who started ethanol abuse early in life show an association between low plasma tryptophan levels just a few days after ceasing to drink, plus displays of depressive and aggressive behaviors. After cessation of drinking, plasma tryptophan levels progressively increase, reaching nonalcoholic levels more than one month after the last drink (Buydens-Branchey, Branchey, & Noumair, 1989a; Buydens-Branchey, Branchey, Noumair, & Lieber, 1989b).

Evidence on alcohol, serotonin, and aggression in humans stems primarily from human subjects who are either long-term alcoholics incarcerated for violent crimes or who are alcohol-treated experimental subjects in tests assessing competitive behavior or hostile tendencies (e.g., Pihl, Peterson, & Lau, 1993; Virkkunen & Linnoila, 1993). It has been hypothesized that the low levels of 5-HIAA in CSF of individuals, who have a family history of male alcohol abuse, render them more vulnerable to engage in violent behavior at late stages of alcohol intoxication (e.g., Linnoila et al., 1989), suggesting the existence of a familiar trait associating low 5-HT activity with ethanol abuse and aggression. However, neither the history of alcoholism nor the commission of violent acts were selectively correlated with low levels of CSF 5-HIAA. Rather, violent acts of an impulsive nature in alcoholics, as assessed from police records or psychiatric personality profiles, were statistically significantly correlated with CSF 5-HIAA in an inverse fashion, as opposed to the findings from nonimpulsive alcoholic offenders (Virkkunen et al., 1994).

Preclinical Studies

Aggression and 5-HT. Assay data on 5-HT or its major metabolite 5-HIAA in CSF or in postmortem brain tissue of mice, hamsters and rats that have just displayed aggressive behavior show either no change (Hadfield & Milio, 1988; Payne, Andrews, & Wilson, 1985), increases (Lasley & Thurmond, 1985) or decreases (Garattini, Giacalone, & Valzelli, 1967; Modigh, 1973). The turnover of 5-HT, as estimated by the 5-HIAA–5-HT ratio, was *increased* in selected brain regions, particularly in the amygdala of rodents who had just exhibited their first episode of attack behavior toward an intruder (Broderick, Barr, Sharpless, & Bridger, 1985; Garris, Chamberlain, & Da Vanzo, 1984; Haney, Noda, Kream, & Miczek, 1990). Determinations of 5-HT metabolite levels in the CSF or blood of very aggressive nonhuman primates, such as squirrel monkeys, vervet monkeys, and rhesus monkeys resulted in inconsistent correlations (Kraemer, Lake, Ebert, & McKinney, 1985; Raleigh, Brammer, & McGuire, 1983; Yodyingyuad, de la Riva, Abbott, Herbert, & Keverne, 1985). More recently, juvenile rhesus monkeys were found to show increased rates of aggressive behavior and wounding that were positively correlated with the developmental age and inversely correlated with CSF 5-HIAA concentration (Higley, Suomi, & Linnoila, 1991, 1992).

More persuasive and consistent than metabolite levels of 5-HT in CSF are the results of direct manipulations of brain 5-HT concentrations and pre- and postsynaptic receptor activation and blockade. Dietary tryptophan supplements, 5-hydroxytryptophan administrations, treatment with postsynaptic receptor agonists or reuptake blockers, suppress many different kinds of aggressive behavior, in various animal species (for extensive review, see Miczek & Donat, 1989; Miczek, Haney, Tidey, Vivian, & Weerts, 1994). However, sedative effects are sometimes observed concomitantly. In apparent contradiction to attributing increased aggressive behavior to reduced serotonergic neurotransmission, are the observations that serotonin receptor antagonists selectively decrease aggressive behaviors in shock-induced, maternal, isolation and territorial confrontations (Lindgren & Kantak, 1987; Malick & Barnett, 1976; Miczek, Haney et al., 1994; Miczek, Weerts, Haney, & Tidey, 1994; Mos, Olivier, Tulp, & Van der Poel, 1992; Sheard, 1981; Wagner, Fisher, Pole, Borve, & Johnson, 1993; Weinstock & Weiss, 1980; Winslow & Miczek, 1983).

Only two of the 5-HT receptor subfamilies are differentially involved in aggression, because 5-HT$_1$ agonists and 5-HT$_2$ antagonists selectively decrease offensive behaviors. The recent developments of compounds that selectively target one of the subtypes of the three 5-HT receptor families have begun to identify highly effective reductions in aggressive behavior due to 5-HT$_{1A}$ or 5-HT$_{1B}$ receptor activation or 5-HT$_2$ receptor blockade (Hen et al., 1994; Mos, Olivier, Poth, Van Oorschot, & Van Aken, 1993; Mos, Olivier, & Tulp, 1992; Olivier, Mos, & Rasmussen, 1990). Ketanserin, a 5-HT$_2$ receptor antagonist, effectively decreases aggressive behavior by male mice confronting an intruder, however, less selectively than the 5-HT$_{1B}$ specific agents (Miczek, Weerts, et al., 1994). Selective 5-HT receptor manipulations, particularly in the 5-HT$_1$ family, are of particular significance in modulating a range of different aggressive behaviors. Reduced aggressive behavior by resident male and female rats and mice toward intruding rivals has been observed after administration of partial 5-HT$_{1A}$ agonists (buspirone, gepirone, ipsapirone, and flesinoxan), and of a full 5-HT$_{1A}$ receptor agonist, 8-OH-DPAT (Haney & Miczek, 1989; Olivier, Mos, & Rasmussen, 1990). Behaviorally selective reduction in dominance, territorial and maternal aggressive behavior was achieved with eltoprazine, a mixed 5-HT$_{1A/B}$ agonist, and TFMPP (m-trifluoromethylphenyl-piperazine), a 5-HT$_{1B}$ agonist, in several animal species (Kruk, 1991; Miczek, Mos, & Olivier, 1989; Mos et al., 1993; Olivier et al., 1987; Sijbesma et al., 1991). Recently it was reported that mice in whom the 5-HT$_{1B}$ receptors were "knocked-out" attacked opponents in less time and at twice the rate of normal controls without any other detectable defects (Saudou et al., 1994).

Ethanol and 5-HT. Earlier evidence from ethanol effects on cortical or hypothalamic tissue slice preparations shows an increase of 5-HT release after initial acute administration and a depletion with continued ethanol administration (Badawy & Evans, 1976; Carmichael & Israel, 1975; Hyatt & Tyce, 1985). Increased firing rate of dorsal raphe neurons observed after low concentrations of ethanol were added in vitro is consonant with the increased extracellular concentrations of 5-HT that may be interpreted as increased release from serotonergic neurons (Chu & Keenan, 1987).

In vivo microdialysis detects increases in either extracellular 5-HT or 5-HIAA in n. accumbens and striatum after acute administration of ethanol in doses from 1–2.0 g/kg (Heidbreder & De Witte, 1993; Imperato & Angelucci, 1989; Yoshimoto, McBride, Lumeng, & Li, 1992). Perfusion of the n. accumbens with 100 mM ethanol via the microdialysis probe increases extracellular 5-HT, which was attenuated by a 5-HT$_3$ antagonist (Wozniak, Pert, Mele, & Linnoila, 1991; Yoshimoto et al., 1992).

It is now apparent that ethanol alters the activity of 5-HT releasing neurons and some of these neurons appear to be part of the circuitry that is targeted by ethanol when increasing aggressive behavior.

Dopamine

Human Studies. Clinical evidence implicates a role for dopamine brain systems in aggression, inasmuch as neuroleptics are drugs frequently used in emergency rooms and found effective for the treatment of acute aggressive episodes of psychiatric patients. Nevertheless, many of the compounds used also sedate the patients (Munizza et al., 1993). As there is discussion in regard to the dopamine system role in different behavioral manifestations of psychotic patients, differences in dopamine receptors are not confirmed to occur in patients with alcohol abuse. In the early 1990s an allelic association between dopamine D2 receptors and alcoholism was reported (Blum et al., 1991), however, association between the DRD2 allele and alcoholism in Cheyenne Indians, other U.S. populations, and Finns was not confirmed (Goldman et al. 1992, 1993).

Preclinical Studies

Aggression and DA. Pharmacological evidence implicates brain dopamine in the neurobiological mechanisms of aggressive behavior, particularly as these behaviors can be increased by dopamine receptor agonists and decreased by neuroleptic drugs that block DA receptors. High doses of amphetamine and apomorphine induce elements of aggressive and defensive behavior in otherwise placid laboratory mice, rats, and cats (Baggio & Ferrari, 1980; Geyer & Segal, 1974; Hasselager, Rolinski, & Randrup, 1972; Puech, Simon, Chermat, & Boisseir, 1974; Thor & Ghiselli, 1975). In confrontations between a resident and an intruder or between dominance rivals, amphetamine and directly acting dopamine agonists mostly disrupt aggressive and social behavior in monkeys and rodents (e.g., Hodge & Butcher, 1975; Miczek & O'Donnell, 1978; Miczek & Yoshimura, 1982). However, when animals are habituated to aggression-provoking opponents or when they are in opiate withdrawal, dopamine releasing agents and dopamine agonists can increase aggressive behavior in mice and rats (Gianutsos & Lal, 1978; Kantak & Miczek, 1988; Tidey & Miczek, 1992b; Winslow & Miczek, 1983).

Increased activity in n. accumbens and prefrontal cortex DA terminal regions were seen in mice and rats that were either aggressive or submissive in social confrontations, nonetheless whole brain measurements of DA or of its metabolites in postmortem tissue resulted in small and often inconclusive changes (e.g., Hadfield, 1983; Haney et al., 1990; Miczek, Weerts, et al., 1994; Puglisi-Allegra & Cabib, 1990). Via in vivo microdialysis, marked increases in extracellular DA and DOPAC in the prefrontal cortex and n. accumbens were found to be synchronized with defensive and submissive behavior in intruders (Tidey, Cohen, Kream, & Miczek, 1993; Tidey & Miczek, 1994). Similarly, the initiation of attack and threat by resident rats also is concomitant with changes in dopaminergic activity, in the n. accumbens (van Erp, Samson, & Miczek, 1994).

Many clinical and preclinical studies demonstrate that typical and atypical neuroleptics effectively reduce diverse forms of aggressive behavior; nevertheless, it is not a selective effect because it is concomitant with secondary effects (Ellenbroek & Cools, 1990; Miczek, 1987; Miczek, Weerts, et al., 1994). These secondary effects could be tentatively explained by the diverse action of neuroleptics on other neurotransmitters, such as the cholinergic or histaminergic systems. Nevertheless, recent studies show that the administration of the more specific D1 and D2 receptor agonists also decreases aggressive components of behavior of pair-housed resident mice against an intruder or of morphine withdrawn mice, in doses equal to or lower than the ones that reduce schedule-controlled conditioned behavior and impair motor behavior (Tidey & Miczek, 1992a; Tidey & Miczek, 1992c). Furthermore, toxic lesioning of dopaminergic pathways in neonatal rats can increase aggressive behavior and self-injury, tentatively related to D1 receptor activity, and modulated by the D2 receptors (Breese, Criswell, & Mueller, 1990). It is expected that with the availability of more specific D1 and D2 receptor antagonists it will be possible to analyze the importance of dopamine receptor specificity and the physiology of the functional balance between D1 and D2 receptor in association with aggressive behavior.

The effect of either D1 and D2 receptor agonists and antagonists is to nonspecifically decrease aggressive behaviors, which argues in favor of a possible modulatory role for mesolimbic and nigrostriatal dopamine systems in the initiation and patterning of aggressive behavior and against an executive role for forebrain dopamine in aggression. These observations point to the importance of the functional state of the dopaminergic synaptic sites as a modulator for aggressive and defensive behavior.

Ethanol and DA. Some behavioral effects of ethanol have been tentatively explained by its action on central dopaminergic pathways. Electrophysiological studies consistently show increased firing rates of cells in the substantia nigra and ventral tegmental area after ethanol injections (Brodie, Shefner, & Dunwiddie, 1990; Gessa, Muntoni, Collu, Vargiu, & Mereu, 1985; Mereu, Fadda, & Gessa, 1984). Increased motor activity and altered endocrine function due to ethanol point to the brain dopamine system as a target of ethanol action, which can be pharmacologically blocked with DA receptor antagonists (Liljequist, Berggren,

& Engel, 1981), but direct measurements of DA in tissue homogenates reveal equivocal results (e.g., review by Dar & Wooles, 1984; Deitrich, Dunwiddie, Harris, & Erwin, 1989; Lynch, Samuel, & Littleton, 1985). However, important determinants for the effects of acute ethanol administration on brain dopamine are the dose and phase of drug action, because low ethanol doses increase nigro-striatal presynaptic activity of dopaminergic neurons, whereas higher doses reduce release and utilization (e.g., Hunt, 1981).

In vivo studies using microdialysis show that specific brain regions, such as the nucleus accumbens and the striatum, are sites of action for ethanol's effect on dopaminergic systems. Acute, low ethanol doses administered either systemically or directly into the n. accumbens increase extracellular concentrations of DA, presumably reflecting increased release (Imperato & DiChiara, 1986; Heidbreder & De Witte, 1993; Wozniak, Pert, Mele, & Linnoila, 1991; Yoshimoto et al., 1992). In striatum, increases in DA turnover are measured, without any detectable changes in dopamine levels, after administration of both low and high doses of ethanol (DiChiara & Imperato, 1986; Fadda, Argiolas, Melis, Serra, & Gessa, 1980; Signs, Yamamoto, & Schecter, 1987). Similar findings are seen in ethanol self-administering rats, which show elevation of DA levels in n. accumbens (Blanchard, Steindorf, Wang, & Glick, 1993) and increased DA release in n. accumbens and firing rate of DA neurons in VTA (Weiss, Lorang, Bloom, & Koob, 1993). Moreover, the behaviorally activating effects of ethanol are synchronized with the increased release of DA in n. accumbens, and both effects can be reversed pharmacologically (Imperato & DiChiara, 1986).

Important differences in the postsynaptic functions in dopaminergic systems have been observed between rat lines selected for ethanol preference (P rats) and their nonpreferring (NP rats) counterparts. For example, 20%–25% lower levels of D2 receptors in the caudate, n. accumbens and VTA were seen in P vs. NP rats (McBride, Chernet, Dyr, Lumeng, & Li, 1993).

The conclusion that the dopaminergic system is an important target in ethanol actions also relies on observations during withdrawal from chronic ethanol administration, that are usually in opposite direction from those after acute ethanol administration. Withdrawal causes a decrease in mesolimbic DA neuronal activity, which is reversed by dopaminergic agonist or acute ethanol administration (Diana, Pistis, Carboni, Gessa, & Rossetti, 1993; Rossetti, Melis, Carboni, & Gessa, 1991).

GABA

Human Studies. Few pharmacological data on the possible role of the GABA system in human aggressive behavior can be found. GABA systems might be implicated in aggressive reactions in epilepsy, because convulsive manifestations are, at least in part, related to a "deficiency" in the GABA system activity (Lloyd et al., 1986). Violent acts directed towards other people during, or immediately after a seizure are extremely rare. However, interictal violence and aggression is more controversial, especially considering (a) the multiple types of epilepsy, (b) the different psychosocial factors related to epilepsy, and (c) the need to destigmatize these patients. Sampling epileptic patients for the presence of aggression shows a relatively elevated incidence rate of violence or hostility (see Mirsky & Siegel, 1994; Perrine & Congett, 1994).

Human alcoholic males have lower systemic GABA levels (Coffman & Petty, 1985). Additionally, alcoholics may have a characteristic benzodiazepine (BZ) recognition site in the cerebellum and frontal cortex. Central BZ receptors were found to be decreased by 30% in hippocampus and by 20% in the frontal cortex of alcoholics submitted to autopsy (Freund & Ballinger, 1988, 1989). The affinity of cerebellar binding of ^{3}H-RO-15-4513 was higher in alcoholics than in control humans and increased muscimol binding was found in frontal cortex of alcoholics (Korpi et al., 1992).

Preclinical Studies

Aggression and GABA. GABA may differentially affect different kinds of aggressive behavior of animals, such as mouse killing behavior, isolation, and shock-induced defense or aggression against intruders (see Paredes & Agmo, 1992). In isolated mice, the tendency to exhibit aggressive behaviors is inversely correlated to GABA concentrations in brain olfactory and striatal areas (Earley & Leonard, 1977). Decreased acid glutamic decarboxilase (GAD) activity in rostral brain areas was demonstrated in isolated mice (Blindermann et al., 1979). The DBA/2 strain of mice, which are aggressive after isolated housing present much lower levels of GABA in olfactory bulb and striatum than other strains (Simler, Puglisi-Allegra, & Mandel, 1982). It is interesting to note the dissociation between the isolation effect on GABA and on aggressive behavior, in C57B1/6 mice, leading to the possibility that other factors than a decrease in central nervous system GABA concentrations are necessary to modulate this behavior.

Indirectly acting GABA agents, which increase cerebral GABA concentrations, and direct GABA$_A$ agonists inhibit responses to shock-induced defense and isolation-enhanced aggressive behavior, while GABA antagonists induce aggressive responses (Allikmets & Rago, 1983; DaVanzo & Sydow, 1979; Poshivalov, 1981; Puglisi-Allegra, Simler, Kempf, & Mandel, 1981). After the administration of indirect GABAergic agents the decrease of aggressive displays of isolated DBA/2 mice occurs at a similar time as the increase of GABA concentrations in different brain areas (DaVanzo & Sydow, 1979; Simler, Puglisi-Allegra, & Mandel, 1983). Nevertheless, the drug-induced increases in GABA levels are maintained for a longer time than the antiaggressive effect.

Whereas the systemic administration or the intraolfactory bulb administration of GABAmimetics decrease aggressive behavior (Molina, Ciesielsky, Gobaille, & Mandel, 1986; Puglisi-Allegra & Mandel, 1980), intracerebroventricular injections of THIP, a GABA$_A$ agonist, increases the offensive behavior towards a

conspecific, in a neutral cage (Depaulis & Vergnes, 1985). Intracerebroventricular bicuculline injections have the opposite effect, decreasing the aggressive
behavior (Depaulis & Vergnes, 1985) and the administration of picrotoxin, a
GABA antagonist, into the midbrain periaqueductal gray area does not affect
the offensive behaviors towards an intruder (Depaulis & Vergnes, 1986). Additionally, in different experimental preparations GABA levels and binding were
increased in limbic regions of aggressive mice, hamsters, and muricidal rats
(DaVanzo, Daugherty, Ruckart, & Kang, 1966; Haug, Simler, Ciesielsky, Mandel,
& Moutier, 1984; Potegal, Perumal, Barkai, Cannova, & Blau, 1982).

Another demonstration of the possible inverse correlation between GABAergic system functions and aggressive behaviors comes from observations that
mice selectively bred for high or low levels of aggressive behavior show differences in BZ receptor binding, GABA-dependent Cl^- flux (low aggression–high Cl^-
uptake) and behavioral effects of BZ treatments (Weerts, Miller, Hood, & Miczek,
1992). Whether these mice bred for different levels of aggression also show
individual effects of ethanol on aggressive behavior as seen with nonselectively
bred animals remains to be determined. In addition, many selected lines for the
different ethanol effects have been obtained, such as ethanol drinking preference (preferring–nonpreferring); sleeping time (short–long); intensity of hy-
pothermia (cold–hot); motor activation (fast–slow), ataxia (AT–ANT). It would
be extremely interesting to learn how animals selectively bred for different
ethanol effects respond in conflict situations when given ethanol. These mouse
lines have been characterized biochemically and pharmacologically especially
regarding the GABA system (Allan & Harris, 1986; Dietrich, 1993).

Ethanol and GABA. The link between ethanol effects and GABAergic action
derive from evidence from neurochemical, electrophysiological, and behavioral
studies, which altogether suggest that activation of the $GABA_A$- benzodiazepine-
Cl^- ionophore receptor complex in specific brain regions plays a major role for its
acute and chronic effects. Ethanol possesses a pharmacological profile similar to
benzodiazepines, with anxiolytic, anticonvulsant, anesthetic, hypnotic-sedative,
and myorelaxant effects. Additionally, many ethanol effects, in low to moderate
doses, are mediated by activating GABA, as revealed by behavioral (Liljequist &
Engel, 1984), neurochemical, and electrophysiological studies (Leidenheimer &
Harris, 1992; Mehta & Ticku, 1988). Similarly to barbiturates, low concentrations
of ethanol enhance the GABA-stimulated $^{36}Cl^-$ uptake into isolated cortical membrane vesicles and in cultured spinal neurons. This effect is antagonized by
picrotoxin, a Cl^- channel antagonist and by bicuculline, a $GABA_A$ receptor blocker
(Mehta & Ticku, 1988; Suzdak, Schwartz, Skolnick, & Paul, 1986). Prolonged
administration of ethanol produces structural modification of the $GABA_A$ receptor
in animals and humans (Mhatre & Ticku, 1994; Ticku, Mahtre, & Mehta, 1992).

GABA brain levels are reported to be either unchanged or to be increased
after ethanol acute treatment to experimental animals, depending on the brain

region considered. For example, low doses of ethanol (0.1 or 1 g/kg) do not change GABA extracellular levels in nucleus accumbens in vivo (Heidbreder & De Witte, 1993). Acute ethanol treatment suppressed GABA catabolism, which allows GABA to accumulate. However, chronic treatment suppressed GABA synthesis (Kulonen, 1983). A confounding factor in ethanol effects in vivo is its metabolism to biologically active compounds. Acetaldehyde, ethanol's main metabolite, reduced the content of GABA and its synthesis enzyme (glutamic acid decarboxylase), more than ethanol, in mice cortical cell cultures (Kuriyama, Ohkuma, Taguchi, & Hashimoto, 1987).

Postsynaptic effects of ethanol and its metabolites are also described. Ethanol and acetaldehyde dose-dependently decrease ^{3}H-flumazenil binding to cultured cells, but ^{3}H-muscimol binding was not modified. Alternatively salsolinol, a tetraisoquinoline that can be produced as a condensation product of acetaldehyde and dopamine, increases ^{3}H-flumazenil binding to cerebral fractions of nontreated mice in a higher proportion than the increase seen in mice withdrawn from prolonged treatment with ethanol (Kuriyama et al., 1987), which renders the whole matter difficult to evaluate in vivo. Acute treatment with ethanol also increased low-affinity GABA receptor binding to whole brain microsomal preparations, while the prolonged treatment with ethanol decreased it (Ticku & Burch, 1980). Prolonged treatment of mice with ethanol decreased ^{3}H-flunitrazepam binding in cortex, cerebellum, and hippocampus, with an increase in the affinity to the ligand. No difference in flumazenil in vivo binding was found (Barnhill, Ciraulo, Greenblatt, Faggart, & Harmatz, 1991). In sum, additional studies considering the acute and chronic effects of low and high doses of ethanol on low-affinity and high-affinity GABAergic receptors are still needed to solve this matter.

Although many studies demonstrate that ethanol potentiates GABA$_A$ receptor functions, not all electrophysiological observations support this conclusion. One explanation for the lack of effects of ethanol in GABA functions in some brain areas could be that the effects of alcohol are limited to specific subtypes of GABA$_A$ receptors, that have a unique regional distribution in brain (Criswell et al., 1993; Givens & Breese 1990). It is possible that, in contrast to barbiturates and benzodiazepines, ethanol potentiated responses are only obtained in the GABA receptors containing a γ2L subunit, in combination with the α and β subunits (Leidenheimer & Harris, 1992). Other distinctive sites of action for ethanol are also proposed, such as the α6 subunit, a binding site of RO-15-4513, a partial inverse agonist at the BZ receptor and a drug that reverses ethanol-depressing effects (Suzdak et al., 1986). Additional sites are revealed after chronic ethanol treatment, which results in decreased α1 subunit mRNA levels and increased α6, β2 and β3 subunit mRNA levels (Mhatre & Ticku, 1994; Morrow, Herbert, & Montpied, 1992; Ticku et al., 1992). The β2 subunit seems to be important for the GABA/ethanol interaction (Criswell et al., 1993).

By now, different studies show that ethanol might act postsynaptically at the GABA-benzodiazepine receptor complex, but elucidation of the contradictory results regarding presynaptic effects on different brain regions and timing after alcohol administration is necessary.

Aggression, Ethanol, and GABA. There are some data suggesting that the proaggressive effect of ethanol might be mediated by the GABA-benzodiazepine receptor complex. Ethanol and BZ share biphasic effects on aggressive behavior, with low doses increasing and high doses decreasing these behaviors (Miczek, 1974; Miczek & Krsiak, 1979; Mos & Olivier, 1988). Additionally, when both ethanol and benzodiazepines are given in ineffective doses to modify aggressive behaviors of resident mice an increase in frequency of attacks towards an intruder is seen (Miczek & O'Donnell, 1980). Moreover, the BZ antagonists flumazenil and ZK93426 reverse the proaggressive effects of low doses of ethanol in both rats and monkeys, without modifying the suppressive component or the sedative effects of high doses (Weerts, Tornatzky, & Miczek, 1993). The benzodiazepine partial inverse agonist, RO 15-4513, binds to the $\alpha6$ subunit of the receptor complex and reduces the behavioral and biochemical effects of ethanol (Bonetti et al., 1989; Glowa, Crawley, Suzdak, & Paul, 1989; Prunell, Escorihuela, Fernandez-Turuel, Nunez, & Tobena, 1994; Suzdak, Schwartz et al., 1986). Because this drug can induce seizures and tremors in primates its use in humans is questioned (Miczek & Weerts, 1987) and other drugs of this group need to be tested for their "antialcohol" effects.

METHODOLOGICAL CONSIDERATIONS AND PROSPECTS FOR FUTURE RESEARCH

Many unsolved questions regarding the proaggressive effect of alcohol deserve further investigation. Different questions should be pursued, in addition to the need in defining proper treatment measures to control the acute crisis involved in aggression and violence related to drinking.

The sources for individual differences in ethanol effects on aggression have to be sought in the interaction between genetic and developmental variables. It would be important to determine if there is a common behavioral or biochemical trait (marker) that would predict which individuals might show ethanol heightening aggression or suppressed aggression. Defining which critical predisposing and early experiential factors interact in order for social and environmental variables to engender excessive aggressive behavior during exposure to specific ethanol doses is also necessary. Such questions conceptualize ethanol effects on neurotransmitter systems that are initially determined by genetic instructions and that are continuously regulated by the demands upon the organism, ranging from interpersonal contacts, stresses, lifestyles, and nutritional, toxic, or drug experiences.

The main neurobiological concerns should center initially in the elucidation of the complex neurotransmitter changes during aggressive bouts associated with the use of ethanol.

Preliminary observation showing a decrease of ethanol-enhanced aggressive behaviors with dietary tryptophan supplementation to animals (Wagner et al., 1993) emphasizes the need of a complete experimental pharmacological analysis of the ethanol–serotonin interactions, with special relevance to aggression, using selective uptake blockers, receptor-selective agonists, and antagonists. Additionally, more knowledge concerning the functional state of the serotonin system after acute and chronic ethanol administration is still needed, to explain the apparent paradox of ethanol stimulating serotonin release *and* enhancing aggressive behavior. Ideally, a comparison within individual subjects presenting different behavioral responses to ethanol should depict diverse serotonin pre- and postsynaptic functional states.

Although ethanol's effects on dopaminergic presynaptic sites have been related to ethanol self-administration and to its effects on motor activity, few data exist to determine whether or not it is possible to modulate ethanol-enhanced aggressive behavior with selective dopaminergic drugs. Stereotyped aggressive postures were shown to be increased in rats chronically treated with ethanol, after the injection of a nonselective dopaminergic agonist (Pucilowski, Trzaskowska, & Kostowski, 1987). And, considering the consistent evidence that neuroleptic drugs suppress many different types of aggressive behavior, it may be predicted that alcohol-stimulated aggressive behavior would be effectively decreased by these drugs. Again, the selectivity of these effects is questionable and the effects of more recently developed substances, with selective action at each dopamine receptor subtypes need to be explored. The advent of selective agonists to the dopamine receptor subtypes and the demonstration that ethanol increases aggressive behavior in only a subgroup of animals will allow conclusions regarding the participation of this neurotransmitter system on the individual effects of low doses of ethanol.

In addition to the pharmacological exploration of the possible association between the GABA system and the effects of ethanol on aggression it would be interesting to elucidate if there are individual differences in GABAergic brain presynaptic or postsynaptic functions underlying the behavioral effects of ethanol. It was verified that alcohol-heightened aggression mice or alcohol-suppressed aggression mice, do not show differences in in vitro ^{3}H-flunitrazepam binding or in vivo flumazenil binding in diverse brain areas. None of these ligands bind to specific α subunit types of the GABA-benzodiazepine receptor complex but ethanol behavioral effects are possibly linked to αv $\alpha 6$ subunit action. Mapping brain densities of the GABA-BZ receptor subunits for individuals who show different behavioral effects of ethanol could be a major progress to the field.

In conclusion, the association between ethanol ingestion and aggression is frequently considered to be related to its pharmacological effects, basically assuming that ethanol stimulates mechanisms related to aggression or disinhibits mechanisms that prevent it. Obviously, this is too simple. The studies from the biological areas, until now, delineate ethanol's proaggressive effects as possibly more related to its presynaptic effects on dopamine and serotonin systems or to its interaction with the GABA-benzodiazepine-Cl⁻ionophore receptor complex. Moving from the past decades of research, when one neurotransmitter was associated with one disease or behavior, nowadays it is recognized that more than one neurotransmitter system participate in the expression of a designated behavior or that different neurotransmitters, neuromodulators or hormones contribute to the fine control of one neurotransmitter's actions. Further exploration of multiple systems interactions in the expression of ethanol-heightened aggression in different species will be easier from now on, due to the development of diverse laboratory and clinical in vivo methods able to detect minute changes of several neurotransmitters and their metabolites at the same time.

REFERENCES

Allan, A. M., & Harris, R. A. (1986). Gamma-aminobutyric acid and alcohol actions: Neurochemical studies of long sleep and short sleep mice. *Life Science, 39*, 2005–2015.

Allikmets, L. H., & Rago, L. K. (1983). The action of benzodiazepine antagonist Ro 15-1788 on the effects of GABA-ergic drugs. *Naunyn-Schmiedeberg's Archives of Pharmacology, 324*, 235–237.

American Psychiatric Association (1994). *Diagnostic and statistical manual of mental disorders* (4th ed.). Washington, DC: Author.

Asberg, M., Schalling, D., Traskman-Bendz, L., & Wagner, A. (1987). Psychobiology of suicide, impulsivity, and related phenomena. In H. Y. Meltzer (Ed.), *Psychopharmacology: The third generation of progress* (pp. 655–668). New York: Plenum.

Badawy, A. A. B., & Evans, M. (1976). The role of free serum tryptophan in the biphasic effect of acute ethanol administration on the concentration of rat brain tryptophan, 5-hydroxytryptamine and 5-hydroxy-3-ylacetic acid. *Biochemistry Journal, 160*, 315–324.

Baggio, G., & Ferrari, F. (1980). Role of brain dopaminergic mechanisms in rodent aggressive behavior: Influence of (+,–) N-n-propyl-norapomorphine on three experimental models. *Psychopharmacology, 70*, 63–68.

Barnhill, J. G., Ciraulo, D. A., Greenblatt, D. J., Faggart, M. A., & Harmatz, J. S. (1991). Benzodiazepine response and receptor binding after chronic ethanol ingestion in a mouse model. *Journal of Pharmacology and Experimental Therapeutics, 258*, 812–819.

Blanchard, B. A., Steindorf, S., Wang, S., & Glick, S. D. (1993). Sex differences in ethanol-induced dopamine release in nucleus accumbens and in ethanol consumption in rats. *Alcoholism: Clinical and Experimental Research, 17*, 968–973.

Blindermann, J. M., DeFeudis, F. V., Maitre, M., Misslin, R., Wolff, P., & Mandel, P. (1979). A difference in glutamate-decarboxilase activity between isolated and grouped mice. *Journal of Neurochemistry, 32*, 1357–1359.

Blum, K., Noble, E. P., Sheridan, P. J., Finley, O., Montgomery, A., Ritchie, T., Ozkaragoz, T., Fitch, R. J., Sadlack, F., Sheffield, D., Dahlmann, T., Halbardier, S., & Nogami, H. (1991). Association of the A1 allele of the D2 dopamine receptor gene with severe alcoholism. *Alcohol, 8*, 409–416.

Bond, A. J. (1992). Pharmacological manipulations of aggressiveness and impulsiveness in healthy volunteers. *Progress in Neuro-psychopharmacology and Biological Psychiatry, 16*, 1–7.

Bonetti, E. P., Burkard, W. P., Gabl, M., Hunkeler, W., Lorez, H.-P., Martin, J. R., Moehler, H., & Osterrieder, W., Pieri, L., Polc, P., Richards, J. G., Schaffner, R., Scherschlicht, R., Schoch, P., & Haeffely, W. E. (1989). Ro 15-4513: Partial inverse agonism at the BZR and interaction with ethanol. *Pharmacology Biochemistry Behavior, 31*, 733–749.

Brain, P. F., Miras, R. L., & Berry, M. S. (1993). Diversity of animal models of aggression: Their impact on the putative alcohol/aggression link. *Journal of Studies of Alcohol*, (Suppl. 11), 140–145.

Breese, G. R., Criswell, H. E., & Mueller, R. A. (1990). Evidence that lack of brain dopamine during development can increase the susceptibility for aggression and self-injurious behavior by influencing d1-dopamine receptor function. *Progress in Neuro-psychopharmacology and Biological Psychiatry, 14*, S65–S80.

Brennan, A. F., Walfish, S., & Aubuchon, P. (1986). Alcohol use and abuse in college students. I. A review of individual and personality correlates. *International Journal of the Addictions, 21*, 449–474.

Broderick, P. A., Barr, G. A., Sharpless, N. S., & Bridger, W. H. (1985). Biogenic amine alterations in limbic brain regions of muricidal rats. *Research Communications in Chemical Pathology and Pharmacology, 48*, 3–15.

Brodie, M. S., Shefner, S. A., & Dunwiddie, T. V. (1990). Ethanol increases the firing rate of dopamine neurons of the rat ventral tegmental area in vitro. *Brain Research, 508*, 65–69.

Brown, G. L., Ballanger, J. C., Minichiello, M. D., & Goodwin, F. K. (1979). Human aggression and its relationship to cerebrospinal fluid 5-hydroxyindoleacetic acid, 3-methoxy-4-hydroxyphenylglycol, and homovanillic acid. In M. Sandler (Ed.), *Psychopharmacology of aggression* (pp. 131–147). New York: Raven.

Brown, G. L., Goodwin, F. K., Ballenger, J. C., Goyer, P. F., & Major, L. F. (1979). Aggression in humans correlates with cerebrospinal fluid amine metabolites. *Psychiatry Research, 1*, 131–139.

Buydens-Branchey, L., Branchey, M. H., & Noumair, D. (1989a). Age of alcoholism onset. I. Relationship to psychopathology. *Archives of General Psychiatry, 46*, 225–230.

Buydens-Branchey, L., Branchey, M. H., Noumair, D., & Lieber, C. S. (1989b). Age of alcoholism onset. II. Relationship to susceptibility to serotonin precursor availability. *Archives of General Psychiatry, 46*, 231–236.

Carmichael, F. J., & Israel, Y. (1975). Effects of ethanol on neurotransmitter release by rat brain cortical slices. *The Journal of Pharmacology and Experimental Therapeutics, 193*, 824–834.

Cherek, D. R., Steinberg, J. L., & Kelly, T. H. (1986). Effects of diazepam on human laboratory aggression: Correlations with alcohol effects and hostility measures. *NIDA research Monograph Series, 76*, 95–101.

Chu, N. S., & Keenan, L. (1987). Responses of midbrain dorsal raphe neurons to ethanol studied in brainstem slices. *Alcohol, 4*, 373–374.

Coffman, J. A., & Petty, F. (1985). Plasma GABA levels in chronic alcoholics. *American Journal of Psychiatry, 142*, 1204–1205.

Collins, J. J. (1990). Summary thoughts about drugs and violence. *NIDA Research Monograph Series, 103*, 265–275.

Criswell, H. E., Simson, P. E., Duncan, G. E., McCown, T. J., Herbert, J. S., Morrow, A. L., & Breese, G. R. (1993). Molecular basis for regionally specific action of ethanol on γ-aminobutyric acid-A receptors: Generalization to other ligand-gated ion channels. *The Journal of Pharmacology and Experimental Therapeutics, 267*, 522–537.

Dar, M. S., & Wooles, W. R. (1984). The effect of acute ethanol on dopamine metabolism and other neurotransmitters in the hypothalamus and corpus striatum of mice. *Journal of Neural Transmission, 60*, 283–294.

DaVanzo, J. P., Daugherty, M., Ruckart, R., & Kang, L. (1966). Pharmacological and biochemical studies in isolation-induced fighting mice. *Psychopharmacology, 9*, 210–219.

DaVanzo, J. P., & Sydow, M. (1979). Inhibition of isolation-induced aggressive behavior with GABA transaminase inhibitors. *Psychopharmacology, 62*, 23–27.

DeBold, J. F., & Miczek, K. A. (1985). Testosterone modulates the effects of ethanol on male mouse aggression. *Psychopharmacology, 86*, 286–290.

Deitrich, R. A., Dunwiddie, T. V., Harris, R. A., & Erwin, V. G. (1989). Mechanism of action of ethanol: Initial central nervous system actions. *Pharmacological Reviews, 41*, 489–537.

Depaulis, A., & Vergnes, M. (1985). Elicitation of conspecific attack or defense in the male rat by intraventricular injection of a GABA agonist or antagonist. *Physiology and Behavior, 35*, 447–453.

Depaulis, A., & Vergnes, M. (1986). Elicitation of intraspecific defensive behaviors in the rat by microinjection of picrotoxin, a gamma-aminobutyric acid antagonist, into the midbrain periaqueductal gray matter. *Brain Research, 367*, 87–95.

Diana, M., Pistis, M., Carboni, S., Gessa, G. L., & Rossetti, Z. L. (1993). Profound decrement of mesolimbic dopaminergic neuronal activity during ethanol withdrawal syndrome in rats— Electrophysiological and biochemical evidence. *Proceedings of the National Academy of Sciences, USA, 90*, 7966–7969.

DiChiara, G., & Imperato, A. (1986). Preferential stimulation of dopamine release in the nucleus accumbens by opiates, alcohol and barbiturates: Studies with transcerebral dialysis in freely moving rats. *Annals of the New York Academy of Sciences, 473*, 367–381.

Dietrich, R. A. (1993). Selective breeding for initial sensitivity to ethanol. *Behavioral Genetics, 23*, 153–162.

Earley, C. J., & Leonard, B. E. (1977). The effect of testosterone and cyproterone acetate on the concentration of γ-aminobutyric acid in brain areas of aggressive and non-aggressive mice. *Pharmacology Biochemistry and Behavior, 6*, 409–413.

Ellenbroek, B. A., & Cools, A. R. (1990). Animal models with construct validity for schizophrenia. *Behavioral Pharmacology, 1*, 469–490.

Everett, G. M. (1961). Some electrophysiological and biochemical correlates of motor activity and aggressive behavior. In E. Rothlin (Ed.), *Neuro-psychopharmacology* (pp. 479–484). Amsterdam: Elsevier.

Fadda, F., Argiolas, A., Melis, M. R., Serra, G., & Gessa, G. L. (1980). Differential effect of acute and chronic ethanol on dopamine metabolism in frontal cortex, caudate nucleus and substantia nigra. *Life Sciences, 27*, 979–986.

Freund, G., & Ballinger, W. E., Jr. (1988). Decrease of benzodiazepine receptors in frontal cortex of alcoholics, *Alcohol, 5*, 275–282.

Freund, G., & Ballinger, W. E., Jr. (1989). Loss of muscarinic and benzodiazepine neuroreceptors from hippocampus of alcohol abusers. *Alcohol, 6*, 23–31.

Garattini, S., Giacalone, E., & Valzelli, L. (1967). Isolation, aggressiveness and brain 5-hydroxytryptamine turnover. *Journal of Pharmacy and Pharmacology, 19*, 338–339.

Garris, D. R., Chamberlain, J. K., & DaVanzo, J. P. (1984). Histofluorescent identification of indoleamine-concentrating brain loci associated with intraspecies, reflexive biting and locomotor behavior in olfactory-bulbectomized mice. *Brain Research, 294*, 385–389.

Gessa, G. L., Muntoni, F., Collu, M., Vargiu, L., & Mereu, G. (1985). Low doses of ethanol activate dopaminergic neurons in the ventral tegmental area. *Brain Research, 348*, 201–203.

Geyer, M. A., & Segal, D. S. (1974). Shock-induced aggression: Opposite effects of intraventricularly infused dopamine and norepinephrine. *Behavioral Biology, 10*, 99–104.

Gianutsos, G., & Lal, H. (1978). Narcotic analgesics and aggression. In L. Valzelli, T. Ban, F. A. Freyhan, & P. Pichot (Eds.), *Modern problems of pharmopsychiatry: Psychopharmacology of aggression* (Vol. 13, pp. 114–138). New York: Karger.

Givens, B. S., & Breese, G. R. (1990). Site-specific enhancement of gamma-aminobutyric acid-mediated inhibition of neural activity by ethanol in the rat medial septal area. *The Journal of Pharmacology and Experimental Therapeutics, 254*, 528–538.

Glowa, J. R., Crawley, J. N., Suzdak, P. D., & Paul, S. M. (1989). Ethanol and the GABA receptor complex: Studies with the partial inverse benzodiazepine receptor agonist Ro 15-4513. *Pharmacology Biochemistry and Behavior, 31,* 767–772.

Goldman, D., Brown, G. L., Bolos, A. M., Tokola, R., Virkkunen, M., & Linnoila, M. (1992). D2 dopamine receptor and cerebral fluid homovanilic acid, 5-hydroxyindoleacetic acid and 3-methoxy-4-hydroxyphenylglycol in alcoholics in Finland and the United States. *Acta Psychiatrica Scandinavica, 86,* 351–357.

Goldman, D., Brown, G. L., Albaugh, B., Robin, R., Goodson, S., Trunzo, M., Akhtar, L., Lucas-Derse, S., Long, J., Linnoila, M., & Dean, M. (1993). DRD2 dopamine receptor genotype, linkage disequilibrium, and alcoholism in American Indians and other populations. *Alcoholism: Clinical and Experimental Research, 17,* 199–204.

Hadfield, M. G. (1983). Dopamine: Mesocortical versus nigrostriatal uptake in isolated fighting mice and controls. *Behavioural Brain Research, 7,* 269–281.

Hadfield, M. G., & Milio, C. (1988). Isolation-induced fighting in mice and regional brain monoamine utilization. *Behavioural Brain Research, 31,* 93–96.

Haney, M., & Miczek, K. A. (1989). d-Amphetamine, MDMA, and PCP effects on aggressive and conditioned behavior: 5-HT and dopamine antagonists. *Society for Neuroscience Abstracts, 15,* 635.

Haney, M., Noda, K., Kream, R., & Miczek, K. A. (1990). Regional 5-HT and dopamine activity: Sensitivity to amphetamine and aggressive behavior in mice. *Aggressive Behavior, 16,* 259–270.

Hasselager, E., Rolinski, Z., & Randrup, A. (1972). Specific antagonism by dopamine inhibitors of items of amphetamine induced aggressive behaviour. *Psychopharmacology, 24,* 485–495.

Haug, M., Simler, S., Ciesielsky, L., Mandel, P., & Moutier, R. (1984). Influence of castration and brain GABA levels in three strains of mice on aggression towards lactating intruders. *Physiology and Behavior, 32,* 767–770.

Heidbreder, C., & De Witte, P. (1993). Ethanol differentially affects extracellular monoamines and GABA in the nucleus accumbens. *Pharmacology Biochemistry and Behavior, 46,* 477–481.

Hen, R., Saudou, F., Ait Amara, D., Dierich, A., Lemeur, M., Segu, L., Misslin, R., & Buhot, M. C. (1994). Mice lacking 5-hydroxytryptamine 1B receptors display aggressive behavior. *Neuroscience Abstracts, 20,* 1266.

Higley, J. D., Suomi, S. J., & Linnoila, M. (1991). CSF monoamine metabolite concentrations vary according to age, rearing, and sex, and are influenced by the stressor of social separation in rhesus monkeys. *Psychopharmacology, 103,* 551–556.

Higley, J. D., Suomi, S. J., & Linnoila, M. (1992). A longitudinal assessment of CSF monoamine metabolite and plasma cortisol concentrations in young rhesus monkeys. *Biological Psychiatry, 32,* 127–145.

Hodge, G. K., & Butcher, L. L. (1975). Catecholamine correlates of isolation-induced aggression in mice. *European Journal of Pharmacology, 31,* 81–93.

Hunt, W. A. (1981). Neurotransmitter function in the basal ganglia after acute and chronic ethanol treatment. *Federation Proceedings, 40,* 2077–2081.

Hyatt, M. C., & Tyce, G. M. (1985). The effects of ethanol on the efflux and release of norepinephrine and 5-hydroxytryptamine from slices of rat hypothalamus. *Brain Research, 337,* 255–262.

Imperato, A., & Angelucci, L. (1989). 5-HT3 receptors control dopamine release in the nucleus accumbens of freely moving rats. *Neuroscience Letters, 101,* 214–217.

Imperato, A., & DiChiara, G. (1986). Preferential stimulation of dopamine release in the nucleus accumbens of freely moving rats by ethanol. *The Journal of Pharmacology and Experimental Therapeutics, 239,* 219–238.

Kantak, K. M., & Miczek, K. A. (1988). Social, motor, and autonomic signs of morphine withdrawal: Differential sensitivities to catecholaminergic drugs in mice. *Psychopharmacology, 96,* 468–476.

Klatsky, A. L., & Armstrong, M. A. (1993). Ethanol use, other traits, and risk of unnatural death: A prospective study. *Alcoholism: Clinical and Experimental Research, 17*, 1156–1162.

Korpi, E. R., Uusi-Oukari, M., Wegelius, K., Casanova, M., Zito, M., & Kleinman, J. E. (1992). Cerebelar and frontal cortical benzodiazepine receptors in human alcoholics and chronically alcohol drinking rats. *Biological Psychiatry, 31*, 774–786.

Kraemer, G. W., Lake, C. R., Ebert, M. H., & McKinney, W. T. (1985). Effects of alcohol on cerebrospinal fluid norepinephrine in rhesus monkeys. *Psychopharmacology, 85*, 444–448.

Kruesi, M. J. P. (1989). Cruelty to animals and CSF 5HIAA. *Psychiatry Research, 28*, 115–116.

Kruk, M. R. (1991). Ethology and pharmacology of hypothalamic aggression in the rat. *Neuroscience and Biobehavioral Reviews, 15*, 527–538.

Kulonen, P. (1983). GABA and ethanol. *Medical Biology, 61*, 147–167.

Kuriyama, K., Ohkuma, S., Taguchi, J., & Hashimoto, T. (1987). Alcohol, acetaldehyde and salsolinol-induced alterations in functions of cerebral GABA/benzodiazepine receptor complex. *Physiology & Behavior, 40*, 393–399.

Lang, A. R., Goeckner, D. J., Adesso, V. J., & Marlatt, G. A. (1975). Effects of alcohol on aggression in male social drinkers. *Journal of Abnormal Psychology, 84*, 508–518.

Lasley, S. M., & Thurmond, J. B. (1985). Interaction of dietary tryptophan and social isolation on territorial aggression, motor activity, and neurochemistry in mice. *Psychopharmacology, 87*, 313–321.

Leidenheimer, N. J., & Harris, R. A. (1992). Acute effects of ethanol on GABA$_A$ receptor function: Molecular and physiological determinants. In G. Biggio, A. Concas, & E. Costa (Eds.), *GABAergic synaptic transmission* (pp. 269–287). New York: Raven.

Lidberg, L., Tuck, J. R., Asberg, M., Scalia-Tomba, G. P., & Bertilsson, L. (1985). Homocide, suicide and CSF 5-HIAA. *Acta Psychiatrica Scandinavica, 71*, 230–236.

Liljequist, S., Berggren, U., & Engel, J. A. (1981). The effect of catecholamine receptor antagonists on ethanol-induced locomotor stimulation. *Journal of Neural Transmission, 50*, 57–67.

Liljequist, S., & Engel, J. A. (1984). The effects of GABA and benzodiazepine receptor antagonists on the anti-conflict actions of diazepam or ethanol. *Pharmacology, Biochemistry and Behavior, 21*, 521–525.

Lindgren, T., & Kantak, K. M. (1987). Effects of serotonin receptor agonists and antagonists on offensive aggression in mice. *Aggressive Behavior, 13*, 87–96.

Linnoila, M., De Jong, J., & Virkkunen, M. (1989). Family history of alcoholism in violent offenders and impulsive fire setters. *Archives of General Psychiatry, 46*, 613–616.

Linnoila, M., Virkkunen, M., Scheinin, M., Nuutila, A., Rimon, R., & Goodwin, F. K. (1983). Low cerebrospinal fluid 5-hydroxyindoleacetic acid concentration differentiates impulsive from nonimpulsive violent behavior. *Life Sciences, 33*, 2609–2614.

Lloyd, K. G., Bossi, L., Morselli, P. L., Munari, C., Rougier, M., & Loiseau, H. (1986). Alterations of GABA-mediated synaptic transmission in human epilepsy. *Advances in Neurology, 44*, 1033–1041.

Lynch, M. A., Samuel, D., & Littleton, J. M. (1985). Altered characteristics of [3H]dopamine release from superfused slices of corpus striatum obtained from rats receiving ethanol in vivo. *Neuropharmacology, 24*, 479–485.

Malick, J. B., & Barnett, A. (1976). The role of serotonergic pathways in isolation-induced aggression in mice. *Pharmacology Biochemistry and Behavior, 5*, 55–61.

Mayfield, D. (1976). Alcoholism, alcohol intoxication and assaultive behavior. *Diseases of the Nervous System, 37*, 288–291.

McBride, W. J., Chernet, E., Dyr, W., Lumeng, L., & Li, T.-K. (1993). Densities of dopamine D(2) receptors are reduced in CNS regions of alcohol-preferring p-rats. *Alcohol, 10*, 387–390.

Mehta, A. K., & Ticku, M. K. (1988). Ethanol potentiation of GABAergic transmission in cultured spinal cord neurons involves gamma-aminobutyric acid$_A$-gated chloride channels. *The Journal of Pharmacology and Experimental Therapeutics, 246*, 558–564.

Mereu, G., Fadda, F., & Gessa, G. L. (1984). Ethanol stimulates the firing of nigral dopaminergic neurons in unanesthetized rats. *Brain Research, 292,* 63–69.

Mhatre, M., & Ticku, M. K. (1994). Chronic ethanol treatment upregulates the GABA receptor β subunit expression. *Molecular Brain Research, 23,* 246–252.

Miczek, K. A. (1974). Intraspecies aggression in rats: Effects of d-amphetamine and chlordiazepoxide. *Psychopharmacology, 39,* 275–301.

Miczek, K. A. (1987). The psychopharmacology of aggression. In L. L. Iversen, S. D. Iversen, & S. H. Snyder (Eds.), *Handbook of psychopharmacology, Vol. 19: New directions in behavioral pharmacology* (pp. 183–328). New York: Plenum.

Miczek, K. A., Barros, H. M. T., & Weerts, E. M. (1995). *Alcohol and heightened aggression in individual mice.* Manuscript submitted for publication to Alcoholism: Clinical and Experimental Research.

Miczek, K. A., DeBold, J. F., Haney, M., Tidey, J. W., Vivian, J., & Weerts, E. M. (1994). Alcohol, drugs of abuse, aggression and violence. In A. J. Reis & J. Roth (Eds.), *Understanding and preventing violence: Social influences on violence* (Vol. 3, pp. 337–570). Washington, DC: National Academy Press.

Miczek, K. A., & Donat, P. (1989). Brain 5-HT system and inhibition of aggressive behaviour. In P. Bevan, A. R. Coold, & T. Archer (Eds.), *Behavioral pharmacology of 5-HT* (pp. 117–144). Hove, UK: Lawrence Erlbaum Associates.

Miczek, K. A., Haney, M., Tidey, J., Vivian, J., & Weerts, E. M. (1994). Neurochemistry and pharmacotherapeutic management of violence and aggression. In A. J. Reis & J. Roth (Eds.), *Understanding and preventing violence: Social influences on violence* (Vol. 2, pp. 244–514). Washington, DC: National Academy Press.

Miczek, K. A., & Krsiak, M. (1979). Drug effects on agonistic behavior. In T. Thompson & P. B. Dews (Eds.), *Advances in behavioral pharmacology* (Vol. 2, pp. 87–162). New York: Academic Press.

Miczek, K. A., Mos, J., & Olivier, B. (1989). Brain 5-HT and inhibition of aggressive behavior in animals: 5-HIAA and receptor subtypes. *Psychopharmacology Bulletin, 25,* 399–403.

Miczek, K. A., & O'Donnell, J. M. (1978). Intruder-evoked aggression in isolated and nonisolated mice: Effects of psychomotor stimulants and l-dopa. *Psychopharmacology, 57,* 47–55.

Miczek, K. A., & O'Donnell, J. M. (1980). Alcohol and chlordiazepoxide increase suppressed aggression in mice. *Psychopharmacology, 69,* 39–44.

Miczek, K. A., & Weerts, E. M. (1987). Seizures in drug-treated animals. *Science, 235,* 1127.

Miczek, K. A., Weerts, E. M., & DeBold, J. F. (1993a). Alcohol, aggression, and violence: Biobehavioral determinants. In S. E. Martin (Ed.), *Alcohol and interpersonal violence: Fostering multidisciplinary perspectives* (NIAAA Research Monograph No. 24, pp. 83–119). National Institutes of Health, Rockville, MD.

Miczek, K. A., Weerts, E. M., & DeBold, J. F. (1993b). Alcohol, benzodiazepine-GABAA receptor complex and aggression: Ethological analysis of individual differences in rodents and primates. *Journal of Studies on Alcohol,* (Suppl. 11), 170–179.

Miczek, K. A., Weerts, E. M., Haney, M., & Tidey, J. (1994). Neurobiological mechanisms controlling aggression: Preclinical developments for pharmacotherapeutic interventions. *Neuroscience and Biobehavioral Reviews, 18,* 97–110.

Miczek, K. A., Weerts, E. M., Tornatzky, W., DeBold, J. F., & Vatne, T. M. (1992). Alcohol and "bursts" of aggressive behavior: Ethological analysis of individual differences in rats. *Psychopharmacology, 107,* 551–563.

Miczek, K. A., & Yoshimura, H. (1982). Disruption of primate social behavior by d-amphetamine and cocaine: Differential antagonism by antipsychotics. *Psychopharmacology, 76,* 163–171.

Mirsky, A. F., & Siegel, A. (1994). The neurobiology of violence and aggression. In J. Reis, K. A. Miczek, & J. Roth (Eds.), *Understanding and preventing violence: Biobehavioral influences on violence* (Vol. 2, pp. 59–172). Washington, DC: National Academy Press.

Modigh, K. (1973). Effects of isolation and fighting in mice on the rate of synthesis of noradrenaline, dopamine and 5-hydroxytryptamine in the brain. *Psychopharmacologia, 33,* 1–17.

Molina, V., Ciesielsky, L., Gobaille, S., & Mandel, P. (1986). Effects of the potentiation of the GABAergic neurotransmission in the olfactory bulbs on mouse-killing behavior. *Pharmacology Biochemistry and Behavior, 24,* 657–664.

Morrow, A. L., Herbert, J. S., & Montpied, P. (1992). Differential effects of chronic ethanol administration on GABA$_A$ receptor α1 and α6 subunit mRNA levels in rat cerebellum. *Molecular and Cellular Neurosciences, 3,* 251–258.

Mos, J., & Olivier, B. (1988). Differential effects of selected psychoactive drugs on dominant and subordinate male rats housed in a colony. *Neuroscience Research Communications, 2,* 29–36.

Mos, J., Olivier, B., Poth, M., Van Oorschot, R., & Van Aken, H. (1993). The effects of dorsal raphe administration of eltoprazine, TFMPP and 8-OH-DPAT on resident intruder aggression in the rat. *European Journal of Pharmacology, 238,* 411–415.

Mos, J., Olivier, B., & Tulp, M. (1992). Ethopharmacological studies differentiate the effects of various serotonergic compounds on aggression in rats. *Drug Development Research, 26,* 343–360.

Mos, J., Olivier, B., & Tulp, M., & Van der Poel, A. M. (1992). Animal models of anxiety and aggression in the study of serotonergic agents. *Serotonin Receptor Subtypes: Pharmacological Significance and Clinical Implications, 1,* 67–79.

Munizza, C., Futlan, P. M., d'Elia, A., D'Onofrio, M. R., Leggero, P., Punzo, F., Vidini, N., & Villari, V. (1993). Emergency psychiatry: A review of the literature. *Acta Psychiatrica Scandinavica, 88* (Suppl. 374), 1–51.

Olivier, B., & Mos, J. (1986). A female aggression paradigm for use in psychopharmacology: Maternal agonistic behaviour in rats. In P. F. Brain & J. M. Ramirez (Eds.), *Cross-disciplinary studies on aggression* (pp. 73–111). Publicaciones de la Universidad de Sevilla.

Olivier, B., Mos, J., & Rasmussen, D. L. (1990). Behavioural pharmacology of the serenic, eltoprazine. *Reviews on Drug Metabolism and Drug Interactions, 8,* 31–83.

Olivier, B., Mos, J., Van der Heyden, J., Schipper, J., Tulp, M., Berkelmans, B., & Bevan, P. (1987). Serotonergic modulation of agonistic behaviour. In B. Olivier, J. Mos, & P. F. Brain (Eds.), *Ethopharmacology of agonistic behaviour in animals and humans* (pp. 162–186). Dordrecht: Martinus Nijhoff.

Paredes, R. G., & Agmo, A. (1992). Gaba and behavior: The role of receptor subtypes. *Neuroscience and Biobehavioral Reviews, 16,* 145–170.

Payne, A. P., Andrews, M. J., & Wilson, C. A. (1985). The effects of isolation, grouping and aggressive interactions on indole- and catecholamine levels and apparent turnover in the hypothalamus and midbrain of the male golden hamster. *Physiology & Behavior, 34,* 911–916.

Pernanen, K. (1991). *Ethanol in human violence.* New York: Guilford.

Perrine, K., & Congett, S. (1994). Neurobehavioral problems in epilepsy. *Neurologic Clinics, 12,* 129–152.

Piazza, P. V., Demeniere, J. M., le Moal, M., & Simon, H. (1989). Factors that predict individual vulnerability to amphetamine self-administration. *Science, 245,* 1511–1513.

Piazza, P. V., Demeniere, J. M., le Moal, M., & Simon, H. (1990). Stress- and pharmacologically-induced behavioral sensitization increases vulnerability to acquisition of amphetamine self-administration. *Brain Research, 514,* 22–26.

Piazza, P. V., Rouge-Pont, F., Demeniere, J. M., Kharoubi, M., le Moal, M., & Simon, H. (1991). Dopaminergic activity is reduced in the profrontal cortex and increased in the nucleus accumbens of rats predisposed to develop amphetamine self-administration. *Brain Research, 567,* 169–174.

Pihl, R. O., Peterson, J. B., & Lau, M. A. (1993). A biosocial model of the alcohol-aggression relationship. *Journal of Studies on Alcohol, 11,* 128–139.

Poshivalov, V. P. (1981). Pharmaco-ethological analysis of social behavior of isolated mice. *Pharmacology Biochemistry and Behavior, 14,* 53–59.

Potegal, M., Perumal, A. S., Barkai, A. I., Cannova, G. E., & Blau, A. D. (1982). GABA binding in the brains of aggressive and non-aggressive female hamsters. *Brain Research, 247,* 315–324.

Prunell, M., Escorihuela, R. M., Fernandez-Teruel, A., Nunez, J. F., & Tobena, A. (1994). Differential interactions between ethanol and Ro 15-4513 on two anxiety tests in rats. *Pharmacology Biochemistry and Behavior, 47,* 147–151.

Pucilowski, O., Trzaskowska, E., & Kostowski, W. (1987). Differential effects of chronic ethanol on apomorphine-induced locomotion, climbing and aggression in rats. *Drug and Alcohol Dependence, 20,* 163–170.

Puech, A. J., Simon, P., Chermat, R., & Boisseir, J. R. (1974). Profil neuropsychopharmacologique de l'apomorphine. [Neuropsychopharmacological profile of apomorphine]. *Journal of Pharmacology, 5,* 241–254.

Puglisi-Allegra, S., & Cabib, S. (1990). Effects of defeat experiences on dopamine metabolism in different brain areas of the mouse. *Aggressive Behavior, 16,* 271–284.

Puglisi-Allegra, S., & Mandel, P. (1980). Effects of sodium n-dipropyl-acetate, muscimol hydrobromide and (R,S) nipecotic acid amide on isolation-induced aggressive behavior in mice. *Psychopharmacology, 70,* 287–290.

Puglisi-Allegra, S., Simler, S., Kempf, E., & Mandel, P. (1981). Involvement of the GABAergic system on shock-induced aggressive behavior in two strains of mice. *Pharmacology Biochemistry and Behavior, 14*(Suppl. 1), 13–18.

Raleigh, M. J., Brammer, G. L., & McGuire, M. T. (1983). Male dominance, serotonergic systems, and the behavioral and physiological effects of drugs in vervet monkeys (Cercopithecus aethiops sabaeus). In K. A. Miczek (Ed.), *Ethopharmacology: Primate models of neuropsychiatric disorders* (pp. 185–198). New York: Alan R. Liss.

Roizen, J. (1993). Issues in epidemiology of alcohol and violence. In S. E. Martin (Ed.), *Alcohol and interpersonal violence: Fostering multidisciplinary perspectives* (NIAAA Research Monograph No. 24, pp. 3–36), National Institutes of Health, Rockville, MD.

Rossetti, Z. L., Melis, F., Carboni, S., & Gessa, G. L. (1991). Marked decrease of extraneuronal dopamine after alcohol withdrawal in rats—Reversal by MK-801. *European Journal of Pharmacology, 200,* 371–372.

Rydin, E., Schalling, D., & Asberg, M. (1982). Rorschach ratings in depressed and suicidal patients with low levels of 5-hydroxyindolacetic acid in cerebrospinal fluid. *Psychiatry Research, 7,* 229–243.

Saudou, F., Ait Amara, D., Dierich, A., Lemeur, M., Ramboz, S., Segu, L., Buhot, M. C., & Hen, R. (1994). Enhanced aggressive behavior in mice lacking 5-HT$_{1B}$ receptor. *Science, 265,* 1875–1878.

Sheard, M. H. (1981). Shock-induced fighting (SIF): Psychopharmacological studies. *Aggressive Behavior, 7,* 41–49.

Shupe, L. M. (1954). A study of the urine alcohol concentration found in 882 persons arrested during or immediately after the comission of felony. *Journal of Criminal Law, Criminology and Police Science, 44,* 661–664.

Signs, S. A., Yamamoto, B. K., & Schecter, M. D. (1987). In vivo electrochemical determination of extracellular dopamine in the caudate of freely moving rats after a low dose of ethanol. *Neuropharmacology, 26,* 1653–1656.

Sijbesma, H., Schipper, J., DeKloet, E. R., Mos, J., Van Aken, H., & Olivier, B. (1991). Postsynaptic 5-HT1 receptors and offensive aggression in rats: A combined behavioural and autoradiographic study with eltoprazine. *Pharmacology Biochemistry and Behavior, 38,* 447–458.

Simler, S., Puglisi-Allegra, S., & Mandel, P. (1982). Gamma-aminobutyric acid in brain areas of isolated aggressive or non-aggressive inbred strains of mice. *Pharmacology Biochemistry and Behavior, 16,* 57–61.

Simler, S., Puglisi-Allegra, S., & Mandel, P. (1983). Effects of n-di-propylacetate on aggressive behavior and brain GABA level in isolated mice. *Pharmacology, Biochemistry and Behavior, 18,* 717–720.

Suzdak, P. D., Glowa, J. R., Crawley, J., Schwartz, R. D., Skolnick, P., & Paul, S. M. (1986). A selective imidazobenzodiazepine antagonist of ethanol in the rat. *Science, 234*, 1243–1247.

Suzdak, P. D., Schwartz, R. D., Skolnick, P., & Paul, S. M. (1986). Ethanol stimulates gamma-aminobutyric acid receptor-mediated chloride transport in rat brain synaptoneurosomes. *Proceedings of the National Academy of Sciences, USA, 83*, 4071–4075.

Thor, D. H., & Ghiselli, W. B. (1975). Suppression of mouse killing and apomorphine-induced social aggression in rats by local anesthesia of the mystacial vibrissae. *Journal of Comparative and Physiological Psychology, 88*, 40–46.

Ticku, M. K., & Burch, T. (1980). Alterations in γ-aminobutyric acid receptor sensitivity following acute and chronic ethanol treatments. *Journal of Neurochemistry, 34*, 417–423.

Ticku, M. K., Mahtre, M., & Mehta, A. K. (1992). Modulation on GABAergic transmission by ethanol. In G. Biggio, A. Concas, & E. Costa (Eds.), *GABAergic synaptic transmission* (pp. 255–268). New York: Raven.

Tidey, J., Cohen, C. A., Kream, R., & Miczek, K. A. (1993). Dopamine release in the nucleus accumbens during social stress: An in vivo microdialysis study. *Neuroscience Abstracts, 19*(2), 1450.

Tidey, J., & Miczek, K. A. (1992a). Effects of SKF38393 and quinpirole on patterns of aggressive, motor and schedule-controlled behaviors in mice. *Behavioural Pharmacology, 3*, 553–565.

Tidey, J., & Miczek, K. A. (1992b). Heightened aggressive behavior during morphine withdrawal: Effects of d-amphetamine. *Psychopharmacology, 107*, 297–302.

Tidey, J., & Miczek, K. A. (1992c). Morphine withdrawal aggression: Modification with D1 and D2 receptor agonists. *Psychopharmacology, 108*, 177–184.

Tidey, J., & Miczek, K. A. (1994). Threat of attack increases in vivo dopamine release in prefrontal cortex and nucleus accumbens. *Neuroscience Abstracts, 20*, 1445.

Valzelli, L., & Garattini, S. (1968). Behavioral changes and 5-hydroxytryptamine turnover in animals. *Advances in Pharmacology, 6B*, 249–260.

van Erp, A. M. M., Samson, H. H., & Miczek, K. A. (1994). Alcohol self-administration, dopamine and aggression in rats. *Neuroscience Abstracts, 20*, 1614.

Van Praag, H. M. (1982). Depression, suicide and the metabolism of serotonin in the brain. *Journal of Affective Disorders, 4*, 275–290.

Virkkunen, M., de Jong, J., Bartko, J., Goodwin, F. K., & Linnoila, M. (1989). Relationship of psychobiological variables to recidivism in violent offenders and impulsive fire setters. *Archives of General Psychiatry, 46*, 600–603.

Virkkunen, M., de Jong, J., Bartko, J., & Linnoila, M. (1989). Psychobiological concomitants of history of suicide attempts among violent offenders and impulsive fire setters. *Archives of General Psychiatry, 46*, 604–606.

Virkkunen, M., Kallio, E., Rawlings, R., Tokola, R., Poland, R. E., Guidotti, A., Nemeroff, C., Bissette, G., Kalogeras, K., Karonen, S.-L., & Linnoila, M. (1994). Personality profiles and state aggressiveness in Finnish alcoholic, violent offenders, fire setters, and healthy volunteers. *Archives of General Psychiatry, 51*, 28–33.

Virkkunen, M., & Linnoila, M. (1993). Brain serotonin, Type II alcoholism and impulsive violence. *Journal of Studies on Alcohol*, (Suppl. 11), 163–169.

Wagner, G. C., Fisher, H., Pole, N., Borve, T., & Johnson, S. K. (1993). Effects of monoaminergic agonists on alcohol-induced increases in mouse aggression. *Journal of Studies on Alcohol*, (Suppl. 11), 185–191.

Weerts, E. M., Miller, L. G., Hood, K. E., & Miczek, K. A. (1992). Increased GABAA-dependent chloride uptake in mice selectively bred for low aggressive behavior. *Psychopharmacology, 108*, 196–204.

Weerts, E. M., Tornatzky, W., & Miczek, K. A. (1993). Prevention of the proaggressive effects of alcohol by benzodiazepine receptor antagonists in rats and in squirrel monkeys. *Psychopharmacology, 111*, 144–152.

Weinstock, M., & Weiss, C. (1980). Antagonism by propranolol of isolation-induced aggression in mice: Correlation with 5-hydroxytryptamine receptor blockade. *Neuropharmacology, 19,* 653–656.

Weiss, F., Lorang, M. T., Bloom, F. E., & Koob, G. F. (1993). Oral alcohol self-administration stimulates dopamine release in the rat nucleus accumbens—Genetic and motivational determinants. *The Journal of Pharmacology and Experimental Therapeutics, 267,* 250–258.

White, H. R., Brick, J., & Hansell, S. (1993). A longitudinal investigation of alcohol use and aggression in adolescence. *Journal of Studies on Alcohol, 11,* 62–77.

Winslow, J. T., Ellingboe, J., & Miczek, K. A. (1988). Effects of alcohol on aggressive behavior in squirrel monkeys: Influence of testosterone and social context. *Psychopharmacology, 95,* 356–363.

Winslow, J. T., & Miczek, K. A. (1983). Habituation of aggression in mice: Pharmacological evidence of catecholaminergic and serotonergic mediation. *Psychopharmacology, 81,* 286–291.

Winslow, J. T., & Miczek, K. A. (1985). Social status as determinant of alcohol effects on aggressive behavior in squirrel monkeys (Saimiri sciureus). *Psychopharmacology, 85,* 167–172.

Winslow, J. T., & Miczek, K. A. (1988). Androgen dependency of alcohol effects on aggressive behavior: A seasonal rhythm in high-ranking squirrel monkeys. *Psychopharmacology, 95,* 92–98.

Wozniak, K. M., Pert, A., Mele, A., & Linnoila, M. (1991). Focal application of alcohols elevates extracellular dopamine in rat brain—A microdialysis study. *Brain Research, 540,* 31–40.

Yodyingyuad, U., de la Riva, C., Abbott, D. H., Herbert, J., & Keverne, E. B. (1985). Relationship between dominance hierarchy, cerebrospinal fluid levels of amine transmitter metabolites (5-hydroxyindole acetic acid and homovanillic acid) and plasma cortisol in monkeys. *Neuroscience, 16,* 851–858.

Yoshimoto, K., McBride, W. J., Lumeng, L., & Li, T.-K. (1992). Alcohol stimulates the release of dopamine and serotonin in the nucleus accumbens. *Alcohol, 9,* 17–22.

BIOSOCIAL PERSPECTIVE

13

EXPERIENCE AND NEUROENDOCRINE PARAMETERS OF DEVELOPMENT: AGGRESSIVE BEHAVIOR AND COMPETENCIES

Elizabeth J. Susman
Brenda K. Worrall
Elise Murowchick
Colleen A. Frobose
Jacqueline E. Schwab
Pennsylvania State University

The behavioral basis for biological development seemingly is a contradiction in logic and in prevailing perspectives on human development. Changes in biological processes most surely are not generally conceived of as products of aggressive encounters. Yet, in various species, cumulative evidence indicates that experiences, including aggressive behavior, lead to changes in physiological processes, specifically, endocrine changes (Booth, Shelley, Mazur, Tharp, & Kittok, 1989; Sapolsky, 1991). The perspective offered herein is that experiences may have a significant impact on neuroendocrine processes. Endocrine changes induced by experience may set in motion neurochemical and morphological changes that affect development in general and aggressive behavior in particular. This experience leading to a biological-change model contrasts with previous models that viewed biology as a determinant of behavior. Given this perspective on biological processes and development, new approaches to conceptualizing and conducting research on the biosocial aspects of aggression seem essential. The problem is to identify those behavioral experiences and contexts that eventuate in neuroendocrine changes that, in turn, may lead to increases or decreases in aggressive behavior. This chapter addresses the notion of reciprocal influences of hormones and behavior by first discussing mechanisms of hormone–behavior action. Findings from past research on hormones and aggression in adult males and adolescents are presented, followed by theory and findings on the role of experience on hormones with a specific focus on stress-related hormones. The chapter concludes with methodological considerations and prospects for future research.

MECHANISMS OF HORMONE–BEHAVIOR INTERACTIONS

Organizational and Activational Influences

The earlier explanations for hormone actions consisted of organizational and activational influences (Phoenix, Goy, Gerall, & Young, 1959). Organizational influences refer to major structural changes that occur during pre- and perinatal development. Activational influences stem from contemporaneous effects of hormones on behavior and refer to regulatory effects of previously established neural circuits. Activational influences originally were thought to involve subtle modifications in synaptic neurochemistry that did not involve changes in neuronal morphology (Arnold & Gorski, 1984). New evidence suggests that adult neural regions can respond to hormonal manipulations with dramatic structural changes (Gould, Woolley, & McEwen, 1991). Much of this new work on structural changes has been on the hippocampal formation, specifically, the sexually dimorphic circuitry of the avian song system (DeVoogd, 1991), the mammalian spinal cord (e.g., DeVoogd, Nixdorf, & Nottebohm, 1985), and the hypothalamus (Block & Gorski, 1988). Hormone-induced changes in reproductive behavior correlate with hormone-induced morphologic changes, both developmentally and in adulthood (Gould et al., 1991). During puberty, gonadal hormone related structural changes in the brain are related to changes in social behavior (Primus & Kellog, 1990). Therefore, it is likely that hormone-induced structural changes are at least partially responsible for behavioral changes throughout development.

In humans, there are hints that prenatal exposure to atypical hormone concentrations, such as diethylstilbestrol (DES), results in changes in brain lateralization. In DES-exposed females, brain lateralization was greater in exposed than in nonexposed sisters (Hines & Shipley, 1984). In future studies large numbers of participants will need to be assessed to document the subtle effects of hormones on behavior given the major influence of the environment on human development (Hines, 1982). Brain-imaging techniques may make it possible to observe structural changes in brain development with changes in hormone exposure.

Direct Effects, Indirect Effects, and Mediators of Hormone Action

Until the last few decades, biological and behavioral aspects of development tended to be considered separately with few theoretical models oriented to integrating biological and behavioral processes. Models for considering hormones and behavior appear in Fig. 13.1. In those instances when both biological and behavioral processes described or explained a developmental process, the integration tended to be deterministic: Biology determines behavior. In the case of aggression, the androgen testosterone (T), for instance, tended to be viewed as a causal agent in aggressive behavior. Recent discoveries in the field of animal behavior and physiology have provided a rationale for the conviction that unidirectional cause–effect thinking between physiology and behavior is far too limiting. This realization has a parallel in the age-old controversy of nature–nurture. The dualism of nature and nurture may be one of convenience rather than reality. Nature and nurture, like physiology and behavior, or hormones and behavior, are most easily studied as components of a larger system by scientists who have tools to assess one aspect of the dualism better than the other.

Contrary to these past approaches, the progression of biological and behavioral research as separate entities now is evolving into a biology–behavior synthesis as reflected in recent theoretical perspectives (Gunnar, 1987; Susman, 1993) and the content of this volume. In the case of aggression, the perspective proposed here is that aggressive tendencies constitute multicausal phenomena. To understand physiological processes and aggression, these processes should not be viewed as separate causal entities. Physiological processes can be viewed as causes, consequences, or mediators of the psychological constructs of development. Magnusson and Cairns (1992) propose that this multidirectional perspective replaces a "paste on" approach to biological variables that has been prominent in the past.

Neuroendocrine processes as consequences or mediators of development have not been represented historically in behavioral endocrinology. The traditional experimental approach to understanding the effects of hormones on behavior is to remove the source of the hormone (ablation), to administer exogenous hormones (replacement), and to measure the effects of the exogenous hormone on behavior. This unidirectional model appears in Fig. 13.1a. The

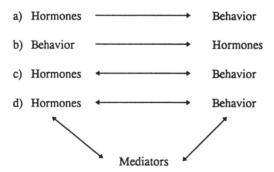

FIG. 13.1. Models used to conceptualize hormones and behavior: hormone to behavior (a), behavior to hormone (b), reciprocal hormones–behavior relations (c), and mediators of hormone and behavior relations (d).

following animal-model example illustrates the effect of hormones on behavior while highlighting the importance of the timing of hormone exposure and behavior. Primus and Kellog (1990) found that in the male rat the gonadal hormones had to be present during puberty for certain behaviors to emerge. If the rat is provided with gonadal hormones at puberty it will express anxiety related behavior in a staged social interaction. If gonadal hormones are not present, anxiety will not occur. Obvious ethical considerations preclude experimental approaches that ablate hormone secretion during puberty in healthy human participants. Perhaps clues from endocrine disordered adolescents (e.g., Turner's syndrome) or puberty inhibitors in female athletes could be used as models for assessing effects of steroid depletion on behavior in humans.

A model of behavioral effects on hormones only recently has begun to emerge (see Fig. 13.1b). One example of this model appears in the work of Booth and colleagues (Booth et al., 1989). An experiment showed that the experience of winning a tennis match elevated T levels in the winners but not in the losers. The effects of these experience-related hormone changes may directly or indirectly affect behavior. Experience may directly affect endocrine processes as a result of changes in arousal and accompanying biochemical processes that involve neurotransmitters, receptors, or other central nervous system (CNS) substances. Experience may indirectly affect behavior through morphological changes in the CNS (e.g., the morphology of dendrites or synapses). In most cases, the mechanisms whereby experience directly or indirectly affects biological processes are unknown.

The contextual or environmental influences on hormones are abundant in the animal literature. For instance, the intrauterine environment, which contains multiple hormones, affects the sexually dimorphic asymmetries in Mongolian gerbils (Clark, Robertson, & Galef, 1993). (In rodents the uterus is a u-shaped horn with the fetuses lined up in a row. Position in this horn has been attributed to many different behavioral effects. A position next to two male siblings has been shown to be more masculinizing than a position next to one male sibling or two female siblings.) Order of eye opening and paw preference are sexually dimorphic in this species. Males open the left eye before the right and females the right before the left. A similar dichotomy occurs in the adult gerbil in which paw is held in the air while maintaining a species-typical tripedal stance (females right paw and males the left). Both the "order of the eye opening and the laterality of paw use while in a tripedal stance varied significantly as a function of the intrauterine position which subjects had occupied as a fetus" (Clark et al., 1993, p. 185). The interpretation here is that the context modifies degree of exposure to androgenic or estrogenic hormones and, in turn, behavior.

Reciprocal influences among hormones and behavior represent a third model for considering hormones and behavior (see Fig. 13.1c). That is, changes in one domain are influenced by changes in the other. Success in aggressive experiences, for instance, may contribute to increases in T (see Sapolsky, 1991) and is reflective of the reciprocal influences between hormones and behavior. Sapolsky (1982) showed that a high-ranking olive baboon, after certain experiences, has a different hormone response than a submissive animal. High ranking males responded to the stress of being captured with transient higher levels of T, whereas in the lower ranked males, the reverse was true. In this instance, social dominance, a behavioral dimension, affected hormone responses to experience such that T tended to increase in socially dominant animals.

The hypothesized effects of anabolic steroids on aggressive behavior is an additional example of the reciprocal influences among hormones and behavior in humans (see Yesalis, Kennedy, Kopstein, & Bahrke, 1993, for a review of anabolic steroid effects). The consumption of anabolic steroids may have direct neurochemical effects that increase aggressive moods and behavior. Anabolic steroids may also have an indirect effect on aggression mediated by presumed steroid-induced morphological changes (growth) in body size and mass. With increases in body size secondary to steroid consumption (hormone effects on morphology), and spurned on by the expectations of fellow athletes, peers, and a conducive environment, the heretofore consummate athlete may become aggressive in nonathletic contexts and participate in violent or antisocial behavior.

Even in those instances when behaviors (or hormones) seem to directly affect hormones (or behavior), multiple factors undoubtedly mediate the reciprocal effects of hormones and behavior (see Fig. 13.1d.) These mediators may include cognition (e.g., perception of events), emotionality, and social contextual processes. Social contextual mediators of hormones may be especially important when aggressive behavior is considered. A close knit community with stable families and effective policing may reduce aggressive behavior in antisocial prone adolescents. An arena that is well studied in relation to the effects of context on behavior occurs in avian species. Schwabl and Kriner (1991) reported that aggressive defense in European Robin (*Erithacus rubecula*) males is facilitated by androgens during the breeding season, but territorial defense during the non-breeding season does not require androgenic activity. Thus, seasonality becomes the contextual mediator of hormones and behavior. Another example of mediation appears in subhuman primates (Zumpe, Bonsall, Kutner, & Michael, 1991). Cynomolgus monkeys (*Macaca fascicularis*) were given medroxyprogesterone acetate (MPA, known as Depro-Provera). Treatment with MPA influenced aggression in males in opposite directions depending on the sex of the recipient. Aggression increased toward males but decreased toward females after treatment. The decrease in male–female aggression was also accompanied by a decline in male sexual activity (Zumpe et al., 1991). Mediational effects of social context on deviance and T have been demonstrated in adult humans as well. In a study examining the effects of T, social integration, and prior involvement in juvenile delinquency, T was significantly related to adult deviance (Booth & Osgood, 1993). This relationship was largely mediated by the influence of T on social integration and prior involvement in juvenile delinquency. The restraining influence of social interaction was less necessary for men with lower levels of T than men with higher levels. The models of hormones and behavior reviewed here included: hormones leading to changes in behavior, behavior leading to changes in hormones, the reciprocal influences of hormones and behavior, and mediators of hormones and behavior. The latter two models share common elements. A shortcoming of these models is that they fail to capture the dynamic changes that occur in hormones, behavior, and environmental circumstances.

Differences in theoretical approaches in animal and human studies further preclude generalizations about hormone–behavior effects. Studies of aggression in humans focus on individual difference correlations whereas much of the research with animals focuses on developmental and situational relationships (e.g., normative age changes and the effects of stress on dominance behavior). These differences in perspective may serve to obscure important relationships in that it is assumed in the human literature that T differences are stable over time and contexts. Specifically, an individual difference perspective assumes that T levels reflect inherent genetic and psychological differences between individuals above and beyond age, context, and time of day variations.

HORMONES AND AGGRESSION

Testosterone and Aggression

Animal model studies, based on a diverse array of species, demonstrate that androgens, primarily T, are related to aggressive tendencies. The consistency of these animal-model findings has enticed scientists to hypothesize that T also facilitates aggressiveness in human males, given that males have higher levels of T and display greater amounts of aggression than females. The findings from human-model studies have been far from conclusive with some reviews of the field concluding that T is related to aggression whereas others do not (see Archer, 1991; Buchanan, Eccles, & Becker, 1992, for reviews). The inconsistency of conclusions regarding T and aggression relations should be anticipated given the disparate ages of the samples included and methods employed in previous studies. Samples have included healthy adolescents (Olweus, Mattsson, Schalling, & Löw, 1988; Inoff-Germain et al., 1988; Nottelmann, Susman, Dorn, et al., 1987; Nottelmann, Susman, Inoff-Germain, et. al., 1987; Susman et al., 1987), college student athletes (Booth et al., 1989), military men (Dabbs & Morris, 1990), and violent and nonviolent criminals (see Archer, 1991). As mentioned earlier, differences in the findings may be due to failure to take into account the context in which individuals act. Additional problems contributing to inconsistencies in findings include different methodological strategies for data collection (questionnaires, interviews, and systematic observation) and failure to assess longitudinal stability in testosterone–behavior links. Research by Constantino and colleagues (1993) suggests that although "aggression is known to be a highly stable trait over the course of the lifespan, there are no longitudinal data on whether the status of being in the top 10% of the testosterone distribution in childhood is predictive of being in the top 10% of the distribution in adulthood" (p. 1218). The cross-sectional descriptive and correlational nature of existing studies cannot be used to ferret out either stability of T or cause–effect inferences between T and aggression. An additional major methodological issue is that there is no reason to expect a one-to-one relation between T and aggression. T is aromatized to other hormones (e.g., estrogen) and may not be the active brain substance implicated in aggressive behavior. Finally, it is known that T is affected by other endocrine systems including the stress system. In the sections that follow, we propose that hormones secreted by the hypothalamic-pituitary-adrenal (HPA) axis, the endocrine system involved in modulating adaptation to stress, exert a major impact on gonadal hormones secretion.

Testosterone and Experience

Although the exact mechanisms involved in mediating testosterone–aggression interactions are unknown, it is now known that experiences and contexts of development affect T levels. In the 1980s and 1990s, the effects of experience on T were examined in both subhuman primates (Sapolsky, 1982, 1986) and human primates (Booth et al., 1989; Mazur, Booth, & Dabbs, 1992). In the subhuman primate studies of Sapolsky (1982, 1986, 1991), the experiences of dominance and social stress were used to examine experiential influences on T and cortisol secretion. The relationship between social status and T and the cortisol-stress response was examined in male olive baboons in natural environments (Sapolsky, 1982). Aggressiveness was associated with higher T. Social status, indexed by copulatory behavior, was also associated with higher T while subordination was associated with lower levels. Similar social status mechanisms might also operate in humans to suppress T secretion in stressful life circumstances.

Dominance and T have been examined in human relationships as well. Mazur (1985) proposed, within a biosocial theory of status, a feedback loop between an individual's T level and assertiveness in attempting to achieve or maintain interpersonal status or dominance rank. As T levels rise, individuals become activated and willing to engage in activities that increase their rank or status. The experience of winning, in turn, further increases T secretion. A corresponding loss of status is accompanied by decreases in T.

The biosocial theory of status provided the theoretical basis for the hypothesis that social status, in the form of competitive winning and losing, affects T levels. Booth and colleagues (Booth et al., 1989) examined T levels in tennis players before a game (anticipatory response) and after winning and losing a match. T levels were higher on the days before and declined the day after a match. Winning or losing the match had an effect on T levels as well. T of winners rose across the match while T of losers decreased. The decline in T levels in winners after the game was greater than that of losers. The findings were moderated by the moods of the players with T levels rising higher in men with highly positive moods than in men with less positive moods. Collectively, the findings indicate that dominance experiences affect T secretion but the changes in T appear to be mediated by emotions.

Developmental Considerations, Hormones, and Experience

A developmental perspective refers to the myriad of changes in biological, psychological, and contextual processes throughout the life span. Given the recent findings that CNS morphological changes, secondary to sex steroid changes, can occur during adulthood in some species (Gould et al., 1991), a developmental perspective seems necessary for explaining mechanisms of hormone action in humans. As reviewed previously, the mechanisms implicated in hormone effects on behavior involve both organizational and activational influences. Adolescence is the period of development when activational influences of hormones are likely to appear, because of the rapid rise in adrenal and gonadal steroids, including T. The increase in T at puberty is hypothesized to be a contributor to the increase in aggressive behavior during adolescence.

This hormone-to-behavior model of aggressive behavior exemplifies the past overemphasis on main effect models of development (Susman, 1993). Main effect models refer to those individual biological or psychological characteristics that directly influence development. Increases in T at puberty probably do not have a direct causal, one-to-one effect on behavior at puberty. Rather, T is one of multiple biological processes that interact with psychological (e.g., emotionality) and contextual (e.g., family conflict) processes to influence aggressive behavior. Direct effects models have been replaced or supplemented by models that consider the indirect, transactional, or interactional effects of multiple influences on development (see Fig. 13.1d). Transactional models include the notion that biological and psychological processes interact with contextual (environmental) contingencies to influence development (Lerner & Kauffman, 1985). Contextual considerations: family, school, and peers, are especially important during adolescence because of the changing amounts of time adolescents spend in these settings. Characteristics of contexts may mediate hormone–behavior relations. An adolescent with aggressive tendencies and higher T, for instance, interacting with temperamentally tolerant and prosocial family members may become a nonaggressive young adult. A hormone–context–behavior model emphasizes complex interactions and transactions between the developing organism and the environment (Kalverboer, 1988). Magnusson and Cairns (1992) state that the essence of the new developmental models is that individuals develop and function as an integrated organism. Maturational, experiential, and cultural contributions are consolidated in ontogeny. For adolescents, in particular, single aspects of the biological transition of puberty, such as increases in T, do not develop and function in isolation to contribute to aggressive behavior.

The Reproductive Transition of Puberty

Given the dramatic changes that occur in endocrine physiology at puberty, it is not surprising that increases in T are hypothesized to be related to increases in aggression. T increases rapidly at puberty beginning at approximately ages 9 for girls and 10 for boys. Puberty is characterized by increases in other hormones as well: gonadotropins (luteinizing hormone [LH] and follicle stimulating hormone [FSH]), estradiol (E_2), and adrenal androgens (dehydroepiandrostenedione [DHEA], dehydroepiandrostenedione sulphate [DHEAS], and androstenedione [Δ4-A]). Figure 13.2 shows the developmental trajectory of T in five age cohorts of boys: 10-, 11-, 12-, 13-, and 14-year-olds; and six age cohorts in girls: 9-, 10-, 11-, 12-, 13-, and 14-year-olds. Time of Measurement indicates that the adolescents were seen three times, at 6-month intervals, across a 1-year period. The age cohorts differ because girls begin puberty 18- to 24-months earlier than boys and it was necessary to enroll a wider age range of girls to cover all five stages of pubertal development (Tanner criterion; Marshall & Tanner, 1969, 1970; Nottelmann, Susman, Dorn, et al., 1987). In males, in all except the 10-year-olds, there is a sharp rise in T across a 1-year period. In the 14-year-olds levels begin to plateau. In females, T shows little change in the 9-year-olds across 1 year. There is a rise in T in the 10- and 11-year-olds. Changes in T becomes more variable in the 12-, 13-, and 14-year-olds because of menstrual cycle variations. For both boys and girls, the standard errors reflect the wide individual differences in T in the same chronological age cohort during early adolescence.

Individual differences in T levels at the same chronological age pose important theoretical and methodological considerations. Genetic factors and timing of puberty contribute to these individual differences. The methodological approach, used to control for individual differences in timing, is to include age as a covariate in analyses when relations among hormones and behavior are examined (Nottelmann, Susman, Inoff-Germain, et al., 1987; Susman, Dorn, & Chrousos, 1991; Susman et al., 1987; Susman et al., 1985). Controlling for chronological age leaves that component of variance attributable to genetic and experiential processes, although age and experiential processes are confounded. Proposed here is the hypothesis that experiences of success and failure, as reflected in competencies and adjustment, contribute to individual differences in hormone levels at puberty.

Puberty-Related Hormone Changes and Aggression

In biological terms, activational influences of hormones are observed with the rise in gonadal and adrenal hormones at puberty. Although the hypothesis that T is linked to the rise in aggression at puberty has been around for sometime,

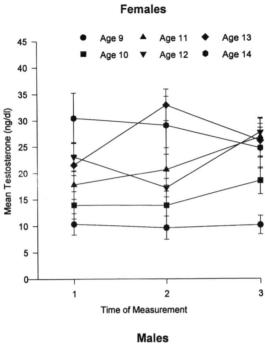

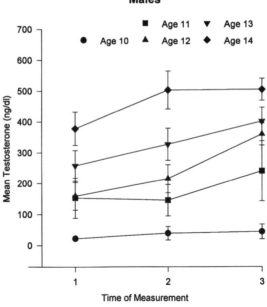

FIG. 13.2. Longitudinal changes in testosterone in pubertal-age cohorts in boys and girls.

only in the last two decades has T actually been measured and related to aggressive behavior and psychological processes in adolescents.

The first study that measured T and levels of aggressive behavior was carried out with Scandinavian boys (Olweus, Mattsson, Schalling, & Löw, 1980). The sample consisted of 15- to 17-year-old boys who were primarily in Stage 5 of pubertal development (Tanner criterion; Marshall & Tanner, 1969) with less than 25% of the boys in Stages 3 and 4. The adolescents completed personality inventories including self-reports of provoked and unprovoked aggression during sixth grade. T was lower at the first than the second time the adolescents were seen and was also related to physical and verbal aggression. Together the findings were interpreted as suggesting that depression of T is likely to follow acute states of anxiety but the suppression is of a short duration. The associations between T level and aggression were accounted for by questionnaire items that involved a response to provocation, including threat or unfair treatment.

In the longitudinal component of the study, the causal role of T on provoked and unprovoked aggression was examined (Olweus, Mattsson, Schalling, & Löw, 1988). Based on path analysis, the findings showed that, at Grade 9, T exerts a direct causal influence on provoked aggressive behavior. The findings also indicated that T lowered the boys' frustration tolerance at Grade 9. The authors conclude that a higher level of T leads to an increased readiness to respond with vigor and assertion to provocation and threat. For unprovoked aggressive behavior (starting fights and saying nasty things) at Grade 9, the findings were somewhat different. T had no direct effects on unprovoked aggressive behavior. There was an indirect effect of T with low frustration tolerance as the mediating variable. The authors conclude that higher levels of aggression in puberty made the boys more impatient and irritable, in turn, increasing readiness to engage in unprovoked aggressive behavior. Overall, the findings indicate that T had causal effects on provoked and unprovoked aggressive behavior when selected causal variables were controlled.

A second study of hormones and behavior, the Adolescent Study Program (Brooks-Gunn & Warren, 1989; Warren & Brooks-Gunn, 1989), was designed to examine puberty-related psychological and biological processes in girls. The sample included 103 White, 10- to 14-year-old, middle- to upper-middle-class girls. The study focused on emotionality, primarily depression and aggressive tendencies, life events, and hormones of gonadal and adrenal origin. One aspect of the study examined whether internal or external pubertal changes, social, or biological factors are more likely to be associated with negative affect (Brooks-Gunn & Warren, 1989). Measures included: self-reports of emotional states, depressed-withdrawal and aggressive affect; life events; stage of pubertal development (Tanner criterion; Marshall & Tanner, 1969); and hormonal assessment, LH, FSH, E_2, T, DHEAS and cortisol.

Given that a nonlinear relation existed, between depressive affect and E_2 the hypothesis was that hormone effects should be most evident during the most rapid hormone increases. Girls were divided into four estrogen groups based on its physiological effect on adolescent pubertal development: little effect on pubertal development, early visible effects, mid- or late puberty effects, and cyclicity in women. Depressive affect increased between the early and midpuberty period and decreased thereafter. The relation between aggressive affect and age, E_2, T, and DHEAS (linear and nonlinear trends) also were examined. Aggressive affect was linearly and negatively associated with DHEAS, but there were no relations with T.

In a third study, an NIMH–NICHD intramural collaboration, psychological processes were examined in relation to physical and endocrine changes at puberty (Dorn, Susman, Nottelmann, Inoff-Germain, & Chrousos, 1990; Inoff-Germain et al., 1988; Nottelmann, Inoff-Germain, Susman, & Chrousos, 1990; Nottelmann, Susman, Inoff-Germain, et al., 1987; Susman et al., 1985, 1987, 1991; see earlier description of the design and sample). The psychological dimensions included concepts hypothesized to be related to hormone changes at adolescence: aggression, competencies, moods, cognition, behavior problems, and parent–adolescent interactions. The biological measures included a physical examination to assess stage of pubertal development (Tanner criterion; Dorn et al., 1990) and hormone concentrations of LH, FSH, T, E_2, DHEA, DHEAS, Δ4-A, testosterone-estradiol binding globulin (TeBG), cortisol, and cortisol binding globulin (CBG).

One aspect of the study focused on relations between adrenal and gonadal axis hormones, emotional dispositions, and aggressive attributes (Susman et al., 1987). The hypothesis was that higher levels of androgens (primarily T, and to a lesser extent the adrenal androgens) are related to higher levels of aggressive behavior. Negative emotions were hypothesized to be involved in the pathway between aggressive attributes and hormones. The general pattern of findings was, for boys only, for hormones and emotional dispositions, higher levels of emotional tone (sad and anxious affect) were related to lower T/E_2 ratio, which is indicative of lower T, TeBG, and higher levels of Δ4-A. For hormones and aggressive attributes, higher scores on delinquent behavior problems were related to lower levels of E_2 and higher levels of Δ4-A. Higher scores on rebellious attitude were related to higher levels of LH, lower levels of FSH, and higher levels of DHEA. When emotional dispositions and aggressive attributes were considered together with hormones, the following pattern of findings emerged: Higher scores on delinquent behavior problems were related to lower T/E_2 ratio, lower levels of TeBG, and lower levels of DHEAS.

From the same sample of adolescents, Nottelmann and colleagues (Nottelmann et al., 1987) reported that adjustment problems were associated with a hormone profile similar to that described earlier for aggressive attributes; higher Δ4-A and lower T levels or a lower T/E_2 ratio. When age and pubertal stage were controlled, the associations between hormone levels and adjustment problems remained relatively the same. The hormone and chronological age profile associated with adjustment problems was characteristic of later maturation; relatively lower sex steroid levels, or lower pubertal stage, and higher Δ4-A levels, sometimes in conjunction with lower chronological age. These findings were interpreted in relation to two different pubertal processes. During the pubertal period, there may be heightened sensitivity of the gonadal axis, which is undergoing reorganization, to stress-related changes in the adrenal axis, resulting in suppression of the gonadal axis. A second interpretation was that higher adrenal and lower gonadal hormone levels, a profile of hormones characteristic of response to stress (see Johnson, Kamilaris, Chrousos, & Gold, 1992, for review of physiology of stress), may be a reflection of a predisposition, in some individuals, to heightened biological reactivity to environmental challenges, which undoubtedly are plentiful during adolescence.

Systematic observations of aggressive behavior of young adolescents interacting with their parents was the focus of another aspect of the same study (Inoff-Germain et al., 1988). Relations among adolescents' hormone levels and their use of anger and power while interacting with their parents were examined. The data consisted of observer ratings of adolescents' expressions of anger and attempts to control or defy their parents during problem-solving tasks. For boys, *expression of modulated anger* was associated with higher levels of DHEA and a lower level of DHEAS. *Shows no sign of anger when aggressed against* was related to a lower T/E_2 ratio and a lower level of TeBG. For girls, there were more significant findings than for boys. *Expresses modulated anger, acts defiantly to mother and father*, and *shows anger toward mother* were related to higher levels of E_2. *Tries to dominate mother, tries to dominate father*, and *shows anger toward father* were related to higher levels of Δ4-A. *Is explosive* was related to higher levels of FSH. In brief, levels of hormones that increase at puberty were associated with adolescent behavioral expressions of anger and power while interacting with their parents. The interpretation, especially with regard to E_2, was that young adolescent girls may be very sensitive to changes in estrogen level, as is hypothesized during the menopausal period. The consistent relationships with Δ4-A, a major source of androgens in girls, indicate that androgens of adrenal origin, as opposed to gonadal origin, may play a role in aggressive behavior in females.

The conclusion drawn from the NIMH–NICHD study was that there are few associations between T and aggression. The relative lack of findings between T and aggressive behavior in the Adolescent Study Program and the NIMH–NICHD study, compared to the consistent findings in the Olweus study (Olweus et al., 1980, 1988) may reflect the developmental maturational status of the adolescents in the different studies. Adolescents were in all 5 stages of pubertal development in the Adolescent Study Program and the NIMH–NICHD study, whereas in the Olweus and colleagues study boys were in the mid and later stages of pubertal development. In the older adolescents, T may have reached a level consistent with the activational influences of hormones. In addition, relations between T and aggression in the Adolescent Study Program and the NIMH–NICHD study may be obscured because the exact conditions and circumstances of assessment, and the interpersonal experiences of challenge, success, and failure in the immediate preceding interval (minutes, hours, or days) are not taken into account.

The consistent relations between aggressive behavior and other negative attributes and hormones of adrenal origin: DHEA, DHEAS, and Δ4-A, raise important theoretical questions regarding the mechanisms of hormone action. Adrenal androgens are secreted under stressful circumstances (Nottelmann et al., 1990). Higher levels of adrenal androgens, in combination with lower E_2, T/E_2, and TeBG, and aggressive tendencies and later maturation, suggest that stressful experiences of adolescents may play a role in the development of the gonadal axis. The hypothesis proposed here is that problems of adjustment, specifically, aggressive behavior may suppress the gonadal axis. Hormones secreted during stress, corticotropin releasing hormone (CRH), adrenocorticotropin hormone (ACTH) and cortisol can suppress the gonadal axis, thereby leading to alterations in timing of puberty and other reproductive processes. Social success during adolescence may have the opposite effect and lead to higher levels of gonadal axis hormones.

The Stress System, Reproduction, and Behavior

Stress provides an instance of how emotional and physical experiences can affect the reproductive endocrine system. The physiological cascade that accompanies stressors emanates from both somatic events (e.g., surgery; Chrousos, Loriaux, & Gold, 1988), emotions (Mason, 1968), and novel and challenging situations (Levine & Weiner, 1989). The mechanism whereby stress affects reproduction involves activation of the HPA axis, by physical or emotional stress, which suppresses the HPG axis (Chrousos & Gold, 1992; Johnson et al., 1992; Susman, Nottelmann, Dorn, Gold, & Chrousos, 1989). The proposed mechanism for suppression of the HPG axis has focused on CRH released by the hypothalamus during stress which acts to inhibit gonadotropin secretion (e.g., Sapolsky, 1991). This effect can occur from a direct affect on the brain or through the mediation of opioids (B-endorphin; Johnson et al., 1992). Glucocorticoids released from the adrenal cortex during stress affect the HPG axis by suppressing gonadotropin releasing hormone (GnRH) from the hypothalamus and gonadotropin release from the pituitary. Glucocorticoids can have an inhibitory effect directly at the gonadal level as well (Johnson et al., 1992).

In animal models, the paradigm for examining the HPA–HPG interactions has included exposure to physical stressors or peripheral administration of CRH. An increase in CRH, ACTH, and cortisol has been shown to induce a fall in T (Olster & Ferin, 1987; Rivier & Vale, 1985), suppress testicular steroidogenesis during puberty (Collu, Gibb, & Ducharme, 1984), and suppress the secretion of gonadal steroids, gonadotropins, growth hormone, and prolactin (Krulich, Hefco, Illner, & Read, 1974; Rivier & Vale, 1985). Given the diverse array of stress effects on reproductive processes in animal models, it should be anticipated that emotions and aversive experiences will lead to individual differences in gonadal and adrenal hormones in humans as well. However, the science of biology–behavior interactions must go beyond an individual difference perspective. The challenge for the future consists of understanding the processes by which behavior and hormones operate in consort, fine tuning each system to meet the challenges of living and reproduction.

Examples of the effects of stress on females include a delay in puberty, failure of ovulation or embryo implantation, amenorrhea, lack of behavioral receptivity, spontaneous abortion, and increased infant mortality (Bullen et al., 1985; Loucks, Mortola, Girton, & Yen, 1989; Warren, 1980). Males may exhibit a suppression in spermatogenesis, T, and libido (Johnson et al., 1992). In these instances, the stressors were high in magnitude, such as intense physical exercise.

Empirical research and theories of reproduction and stress in humans range from sociobiological theory (Belsky, Steinberg, & Draper, 1991) to the molecular biology of stress and reproduction, specifically the reproductive event of pregnancy (Frim, Robinson, Smas, Adler, & Majzoub, 1988). Sociobiology evokes evolutionary notions to link family stress, individual stress, and the timing of puberty with ultimate causes of behavior. Specifically, family stress is viewed as a precipitant to the early timing of puberty. The Belsky et al. (1991) perspective does not propose specific distal or concurrent biological mechanisms whereby stress and timing of puberty are related. Although provocative, the sociobiological theory of stress is antithetical to the known physiological interaction between stress, gonadal and adrenal hormones, and reproduction. Hinde (1991) aptly illustrated this point by noting that the "curvilinear effects of stress make it possible for any general prediction about stress to be confirmed" (p. 674). Under conditions of high levels of stress (e.g., undernutrition and exercise) reproductive functioning in females tends to diminish rather than increase. Maccoby (1991) suggests that in times of high stress, without other social support, women are able to rear fewer children and that it does not make sense "that evolution would have shaped maternal psychological and physiological characteristics toward having more children in the absence of such support when each new child increases the difficulty of raising those already born" (p. 679). Attempts to integrate the physiology of stress with reproduction and evolution will require the interdisciplinary serious efforts of both biologists and social scientists.

The interaction of the HPA and HPG axes hormones is observed in dominance or social status hierarchies in baboons. Dominant baboons showed an increase in T while subordinates showed declines under conditions of changing social status (Sapolsky, 1982). High social status males showed the lowest baseline cortisol level but showed faster and greater cortisol elevations following stress. In humans, the relation between dominance and T remains speculative whereas the relation between social status and aggression is widely accepted.

The mechanism proposed to explain dominance-related changes in T and cortisol are threefold: (a) Inhibition of LH release is caused by the stress-induced release of opiates. Suppression of LH release by opiates is secondary to the suppression of GnRH from the hypothalamus, in turn, leading to reductions in gonadotropins and related reductions of T. (b) Glucocorticoids decrease LH bioactivity. (c) At the testes level, glucocorticoids profoundly inhibit testicular responsiveness to LH. Through these mechanisms, stress appears to play a major role in the suppression of T secretion (Sapolsky, 1991; Sapolsky & Krey, 1988). It is not known whether similar mechanisms operate in children and adolescents experiencing normative life stressors because primarily subhuman primates and adult males have been included in previous studies of stress and reproduction.

Aggressive Experiences and Gonadal and Adrenal Hormones in Adolescents

The work of Booth et al. (1989) and Mazur (1985), cited earlier, and Sapolsky's (Sapolsky, 1991; Sapolsky & Krey, 1988) findings on social stress, dominance, and aggression and accompanying changes in T and cortisol support the hypothesis that social experiences affect the functioning of the HPA and HPG axes. In humans, aggressive and acting out behavior, as well as other behavior problems, may indicate attempts to gain social status through dominance and leadership. If successful in these pursuits, T should increase whereas if the attempts are unsuccessful T should decrease, because of social stress attendant to failure or rejection. The relation between T, aggression, social stress, and dominance have not been separated in humans. High-aggressive boys fare quite well in the social status hierarchy, especially if one looks at actual status of the social network as opposed to peer ratings of likability (Cairns, Cairns, Neckerman, Gest, & Gariepy, 1988). No more than half of aggressive children are rejected (Coie, Dodge, Terry, & Wright, 1991). Those adolescents who are high on aggression and are rejected (low on the social status hierarchy) tend to exhibit more reactive or bullying forms of aggression when older (Coie et al., 1991). Given the difficulty of separating aggression, social status, and developmental issues, a more general hypothesis should first be tested. Aggressive adolescents should have lower levels of T because of their overall stress-related aggressive behavior problem. If the effects of stress on T are mediated by the gonadotropins, LH and FSH, one would expect to see lower levels of LH and FSH in adolescents with aggressive behavior problems. These same individuals would be expected to have higher levels of cortisol.

Success experienced by adolescents should result in a different hormone profile. Successes as well as feelings of efficacy result in self and other perceived competencies. During adolescence, placement in the dominance hierarchy of peer groups becomes increasingly important. The experience of winning in academic, athletic, and interpersonal relations grants adolescents peer popularity. Peer popularity bestows social status and opportunities for engagement with the same and opposite gender peers. If competencies endow social status, then adolescents higher on competencies are expected to be higher on T and lower on cortisol. As was true for aggressive behavior, if the effects of stress on T are mediated by the gonadotropins, one would expect to see higher levels of LH and FSH in competent adolescents.

The hypothesis that experiences with aggressive behavior or competencies will be reflected in hormone levels of gonadal and adrenal origin was tested in a sample of young adolescents (Susman, 1995). The theoretical background for the study included the notion that longitudinal assessment of aggressive or competent behavior in relation to hormones is a better test of the effects of behavior on hormones than a concurrent test of these relations. Aggressive or assertive behavior may have an immediate effect on gonadal or adrenal hormone levels but these fluctuations reflect temporary changes that may not represent usual (baseline) endocrine status.

The sample used to test the hypothesis that experiences of aggressive behavior and competencies affect hormone levels was the NIMH–NICHD collaborative study sample described earlier. Briefly, 56 boys, ages 10–14 years, and 52 girls, ages 9–14 years, were seen three times over the course of 1 year. Adolescents completed measures of emotional, social, and cognitive functioning. Aggressive behavior and competencies are the focus herein. Adolescents were divided into groups based on their scores for acting out behavior on the Child Behavior Checklist (CBCL) subscales (Achenbach & Edelbrock, 1979) and competencies, based on the Perceived Competence Scale for Children (Harter, 1982). For boys, the CBCL subscales used were hostile–withdrawn, delinquent, and aggressive; for girls, the CBCL subscales were delinquent, aggressive, and cruel. The scores for the two broad-band dimensions, internalizing and externalizing, also were included in the analyses. The subscales for the competencies were: cognitive, social, physical, and general competence. Separately by gender, the adolescents were divided into groups above and below the median for the three CBCL subscales and broad-band factors and competencies at three times of measurement across 1 year. The adolescents then were categorized into three additional groups based on the median splits: (a) above the median at all three times of measurement on the CBCL subscales and competency subscales (consistently high-aggressive tendencies or consistently competent), (b) not consistently above or below the median, and (c) below the median at all three times of measurement (consistently low-aggressive tendencies or consistently not competent). Hormone assessments (dependent variables) included plasma levels of LH, FSH, T, E_2, DHEA, DHEAS, Δ 4-A and cortisol. Age was used as a covariate in an analysis of covariance for three groups (consistently above the median, not consistently above or below the median, and consistently below the median on aggressive behaviors or competencies). Age was used as a covariate because of the increase in gonadotropins, gonadal steroids, and adrenal androgens at puberty. The analyses were done separately by sex because of differences in levels of puberty-related hormones and the different within-gender patterns of relations between hormones and behavior described earlier.

The findings provide some support for the hypothesis that experiences with aggressive tendencies or competencies are related to levels of gonadal and adrenal hormones. Males with consistently high social, $F(2,48) = 5.79$, $p = .006$ and cognitive $F(2,49) = 3.20$, $p = .05$ competencies had significantly higher E_2 levels. Females consistently high on internalizing problems had lower LH, $F(2,44) = 2.58$, $p = .08$. Females consistently high on social competencies had lower cortisol levels $F(2,42) = 4.24$, $p = .02$. These findings support a biological–behavioral interaction modified by competencies in males, and internalizing behavior problems and competencies for females. Stressors inherent in behavior problems may suppress the gonadal axis whereas competencies, an indicator of success, may activate the gonadal axis.

Other findings showed that consistent patterns of behavior were related to hormone levels but the findings for the gonadotropins were the reverse of those hypothesized. Males with consistently high externalizing problems, hostile–withdrawn $F(2,47) = 2.92$, $p = .06$, and delinquent $F(2,46) = 3.73$, $p = .031$ behavior, were higher on FSH than males who were unstable or consistently low on these problems. Higher levels of FSH in males with aggressive tendencies contradict the hypothesis that stressors suppress the gonadal axes. Alternatively, these may be males who are high on aggression and are also high on social status. Failure to support the hypothesis relating experience and gonadotropin levels reflect the reality that neuroendocrine behavior processes are more complex than merely a one-to-one coordinate relation between a hormone and a behavior.

A caveat is that the results were based on a large number of analyses and a small sample, with some findings perhaps reflecting chance probabilities. Nonetheless, these findings provide support for further research testing the effects of experience on the development of the gonadal and adrenal axis. Further research on stressors, neuroendocrine processes, and aggressive behavior at puberty may help to explain the wide variation in timing of pubertal maturation and its effects on psychological processes. Even subtle variations in experience-related timing of puberty may alter psychological processes and predispose some adolescents to behavior problems including aggression.

METHODOLOGICAL CONSIDERATIONS AND PROSPECTS FOR FUTURE RESEARCH

Research that integrates neurobiological and behavioral dimensions of human development seldom is based on a specific theory. Rather these integrations tend to be at an empirical level with findings from one level (biological) related to findings from another level (behavior) using correlational or other linear-model statistical procedures. Theories and research on the biological and behavioral aspects of aggression appear in this volume, but such volumes are rare. Theories are needed to integrate antecedents and consequences of aggressive and antisocial behavior and neurobiological processes at all stages of the life span. Specifically, environmental factors, known to affect neuroendocrine development in subhuman species, should be included in the development of theories and hypotheses of aggressive behavior in humans.

Methodologies that exist for establishing neuroendocrine-behavior links in laboratory studies generally fail to be transferable to the naturalistic settings in which individuals develop. This problem is especially acute with regard to aggression. The need is to develop both more and less invasive methodologies for establishing links between neuroendocrine processes and aggressive behavior. Invasive methods are needed to assess the effect of changes in hormones on functional and morphological brain changes and accompanying changes in behavior. Gould and colleagues (Gould et al., 1991) show how changes in gonadal hormones result in dendritic growth and neural sprouting. They propose functional changes secondary to hormone induced morphological changes. Methodologies for establishing morphological changes in brain structures as a result of normative endocrine changes (i.e., at puberty and menopause) are needed. Neuroimaging and other neural scanning procedures may help to solve this methodological deficit.

Less invasive methods for examining links among neuroendocrine processes, contexts, and aggressive behavior are needed as well. Noninvasive methods exist for validly and reliably observing aggressive behavior in naturalistic settings: peer, family, and school contexts. Examining aggressive experiences in relation to neuroendocrine processes in situ has the potential for greatly enhancing understanding of neurobiological–behavior links. Still needed are improved methods for collecting and preserving biological substances in situ. With the improvement of assays for measuring many biological substances in saliva (Malamud & Tabak, 1993), it is becoming increasingly possible to assess interactions among environmental and neuroendocrine processes in field settings.

In summary, although biology and behavior now are theoretically and empirically linked, these interactions need precise and coherent analyses. These analyses must rely on integration from studies of the development of animals, including human ones. Finally, coherent analyses should integrate multiple levels of analysis—cellular, whole organisms, family, and community levels.

ACKNOWLEDGMENT

Preparation of this manuscript was supported in part by grants HD26004 and HD26636 from the National Institute of Child Health and Human Development.

REFERENCES

Achenbach, T. M., & Edelbrock, C. (1979). The child behavior profile: II. Boys aged 12–16 and girls aged 6–11 and 12–16. *Journal of Consulting & Clinical Psychology, 47*, 223–233.

Archer, J. (1991). The influence of testosterone on human aggression. *British Journal of Psychology, 82*, 1–28.

Arnold, A., & Gorski, R. (1984). Gonadal steroid induction of structural sex differences in the central nervous system. *Annual Review of Neuroscience, 7*, 413–442.

Belsky, J., Steinberg, L., & Draper, P. (1991). Childhood experience, interpersonal development, and reproductive strategy: An evolutionary theory of socialization. *Child Development, 62*, 647–670.

Block, G., & Gorski, R. (1988). Estrogen/progesterone treatment in adulthood affects the size of several components of the medial preoptic area in the male rat. *Journal of Comparative Neurology, 190*, 613–622.

Booth, A., & Osgood, D. W. (1993). The influence of testosterone on deviance in adulthood: Assessing and explaining the relationship. *Criminology, 31*, 93–117.

Booth, A., Shelley, G., Mazur, A., Tharp, G., & Kittok, R. (1989). Testosterone, winning and losing in human competition. *Hormones and Behavior, 23*, 556–571.

Brooks-Gunn, J., & Warren, M. P. (1989). Biological and social contributions to negative affect in young adolescent girls. *Child Development, 60*, 40–55.

Buchanan, C., Eccles, J. S., & Becker, J. B. (1992). Are adolescents the victims of raging hormones: Evidence for activational effects of hormones on moods and behavior at adolescence. *Psychological Bulletin, 111*, 62–107.

Bullen, B. A., Skrinar, G. S., Beitens, I. Z., Von Mering, G., Turnbull, B. A., & MacArthur J. W. (1985). Induction of menstrual disorders by strenuous exercise in untrained women. *New England Journal of Medicine, 312*, 1349–1353.

Cairns, R. B., Cairns, B. D., Neckerman, H. J., Gest, S. D., & Gariepy, J.-L. (1988). Social networks and aggressive behvior: Peer support or peer rejection? *Developmental Psychology, 24*, 815–823.

Chrousos, G. P., & Gold, P. W. (1992). The concepts of stress and stress system disorders. *Journal of the American Medical Association, 267*, 1244–1252.

Chrousos, G. P., Loriaux, D. L., & Gold, P. W. (1988). *Mechanisms of physical and emotional stress.* New York: Plenum.

Clark, M. M., Robertson, R. K., & Galef, B. G., Jr. (1993). Intrauterine position effects on sexually dimorphic asymmetries of mongolian gerbils: Testosterone, eye opening, and paw preference. *Developmental Psychobiology, 26*, 185–194.

Coie, J. D., Dodge, K. A., Terry, R., & Wright, V. (1991). The role of aggression in peer relations: An analysis of aggression episodes in boys' play groups. *Child Development, 62*, 812–826.

Collu, R., Gibb, W., & Ducharme, J. R. (1984). Effects of stress on the gonadal function. *Journal of Endocrinological Investigation, 7*, 529–537.

Constantino, J. N., Grosz, D., Saenger, P., Chandler, D. W., Nandi, R., & Earls, F. (1993). Testosterone and aggression in children. *Journal of the American Academy of Child and Adolescent Psychiatry, 32*, 1217–1222.

Dabbs, J. M., Jr., & Morris, R. (1990). Testosterone and antisocial behavior in a sample of 4,462 men. *Psychological Science, 1*, 209–211.

DeVoogd, T. J. (1991). Endocrine modulation of the development and adult function of the avian song system. *Psychoneuroendocrinology, 16*, 41–66.

DeVoogd, T. J., Nixdorf, B., & Nottebohm, F. (1985). Synaptogenesis and changes in synaptic morphology related to acquisition of a new behavior. *Brain Research, 329*, 304–338.

Dorn, L. D., Susman, E. J., Nottelmann, E. D., Inoff-Germain, G. E., & Chrousos, G. P. (1990). Perceptions of puberty: Adolescents and parent ratings of pubertal development. *Developmental Psychology, 26*, 322–329.

Frim, D. M., Robinson, B. G., Smas, C. M., Adler, G. K., & Majzoub, J. A. (1988). Characterization and gestational regulation of corticotropin-releasing hormone messenger RNA in human placenta. *Journal of Clinical Investigation, 82,* 287–292.

Gould, E., Woolley, C. S., & McEwen, B. S. (1991). The hippocampal formation: Morphological changes induced by thyroid, gonadal, and adrenal hormones. *Psychoneuroendocrinology, 16,* 67–84.

Gunnar, M. (1987). Psychobiological studies of stress and coping: An introduction. *Child Development, 58,* 1403–1407.

Harter, S. (1982). Perceived competence scale for children. *Child Development, 58,* 87–97.

Hinde, R. A. (1991). When is an evolutionary approach useful? *Child Development, 62,* 671–675.

Hines, M. (1982). Prenatal gonadal hormones and sex differences in human behavior. *Psychological Bulletin, 92,* 56–80.

Hines, M., & Shipley, C. (1984). Prenatal exposure to diethylstilbestrol (DES) and the development of sexually dimorphic cognitive abilites and cerebral lateralization. *Developmental Psychology, 20,* 81–94.

Inoff-Germain, G. E., Arnold, G. S., Nottelmann, E. D., Susman, E. J., Cutler, G. B., & Chrousos, G. P. (1988). Relations between hormone levels and observational measures of aggressive behavior of early adolescents in family interactions. *Developmental Psychology, 24,* 129–139.

Johnson, E. O., Kamilaris, T. C., Chrousos, G. P., & Gold, P. W. (1992). Mechanisms of stress: A dynamic overview of hormonal and behavioral homeostasis. *Neuroscience and Biobehavioral Reviews, 16,* 115–130.

Kalverboer, A. F. (1988). Follow-up of biological high-risk groups. In M. Rutter (Ed.), *Studies of psychosocial risk: The power of longitudinal data* (pp. 114–137). Cambridge, England: Cambridge University Press.

Krulich, L., Hefco, E., Illner, P., & Read, C. B. (1974). The effects of acute stress on the secretion of LH, FSH, prolactin, and GH in the normal male rat, with comments on their statistical evaluation. *Neuroendocrinology, 16,* 293–311.

Lerner, R. M., & Kauffman, M. B. (1985). The concept of development in contextualism. *Developmental Review, 5,* 309–333.

Levine, S., & Weiner, S. G. (1989). Coping with uncertainty: A paradox. In D. S. Palermo (Ed.), *Coping with uncertainty: Behavioral and developmental perspectives* (pp. 1–16). Hillsdale, NJ: Lawrence Erlbaum Associates.

Loucks, A. B., Mortola, J. F., Girton, L., & Yen, S. S. (1989). Alterations in hypothalamic-pituitary-ovarian and the hypothalamic-pituitary adrenal axis in athletic women. *Journal of Clinical Endocrinology and Metabolism, 68,* 402–411.

Maccoby, E. E. (1991). Different reproductive strategies in males and females. *Child Development, 62,* 676–681.

Magnusson, D., & Cairns, R. B. (1992). *Developmental science: Toward a unitary framework for the investigation of psychological phenomena.* Unpublished manuscript, University of Stockholm.

Malamud, D., & Tabak, L. (Eds.). (1993). *Saliva as a diagnostic fluid* (Vol. 694). New York: Annals of the New York Academy of Sciences.

Marshall, W. A., & Tanner, J. (1969). Variations in the pattern of pubertal change in girls. *Archives of the Disabled Child, 44,* 291–303.

Marshall, W. A., & Tanner, J. (1970). Variations in the pattern of pubertal change in boys. *Archives of the Disabled Child, 45,* 13–23.

Mason, J. W. (1968). A review of the psychoendocrine research on the pituitary-adrenal cortical system. *Psychosomatic Medicine, 30,* 576–608.

Mazur, A. (1985). A biosocial model of status in face-to-face primate groups. *Social Forces, 64,* 377–402.

Mazur, A., Booth, A., & Dabbs, J. M., Jr. (1992). Testosterone and chess competition. *Social Psychological Quarterly, 55,* 70–77.

Nottelmann, E. D., Inoff-Germain, G. E., Susman, E. J., & Chrousos, G. P. (1990). Hormones and behavior at puberty. In J. Bancroft & J. M. Reinisch (Eds.), *Adolescence and puberty* (pp. 88–123). New York: Oxford University Press.

Nottelmann, E. D., Susman, E. J., Inoff-Germain, G. E., Cutler, G. B., Loriaux, D. L., & Chrousos, G. P. (1987). Developmental processes in early adolescence: Relationships between adolescent adjustment problems and chronologic age, pubertal stage and puberty-related serum hormone levels. *Journal of Pediatrics, 110*, 473–480.

Olster, D. H., & Ferin, M. (1987). Corticotropin-releasing hormone inhibits gonadotropin secretion in the ovariectomized rhesus monkey. *Journal of Clinical Endocrinology and Metabolism, 65*, 262–267.

Olweus, D., Mattsson, A., Schalling, D., & Löw, H. (1980). Testosterone, aggression, physical, and personality dimensions in normal adolescent males. *Psychosomatic Medicine, 42*, 253–269.

Olweus, D., Mattsson, A., Schalling, D., & Löw, H. (1988). Circulating testosterone levels and aggression in adolescent males: A causal analysis. *Psychosomatic Medicine, 50*, 261–272.

Phoenix, C. H., Goy, R. W., Gerall, A. A., & Young, W. C. (1959). Organizing action of prenatally administered testosterone propionate on the tissues mediating mating behavior in the female guinea pig. *Endocrinology, 65*, 369–382.

Primus, R. J., & Kellog, C. K. (1990). Gonadal hormones during puberty organize environment-related social interaction in the male rat. *Hormones and Behavior, 24*, 311–323.

Rivier, C., & Vale, W. (1985). Effect of long-term administration of corticotropin-releasing factor on pituitary- and pituitary-gonadal axis in the male rat. *Journal of Clinical Investigation, 75*, 689–694.

Sapolsky, R. M. (1982). The endocrine stress-response and social status in the wild baboon. *Hormones and Behavior, 16*, 279–292.

Sapolsky, R. M. (1986). Stress-induced elevation of testosterone concentrations in high-ranking baboons: Role of catecholamines. *Endocrinology, 118*, 1630–1636.

Sapolsky, R. M. (1991). Testicular function, social rank and personality among wild baboons. *Psychoneuroendocrinology, 16*, 281–293.

Sapolsky, R. M., & Krey, L. (1988). Stress-induced suppression of luteinizing hormone concentrations in wild baboons: Role of opiates. *Journal of Clinical Endocrinology and Metabolism, 66*, 722–726.

Schwabl, H., & Kriner, E. (1991). Territorial aggression and song of male European robins (Erithacus rubecula) in autumn and spring: Effects of antiandrogen treatment. *Hormones and Behavior, 25*, 180–194.

Susman, E. J. (1995, September). Gonadal and adrenal hormones: Developmental transitions and aggression. Paper presented at the New York Academy of Sciences Conference on Understanding Aggressive Behavior in Children. New York.

Susman, E. J. (1993). Psychological, contextual, and psychobiological interactions: A developmental perspective on conduct disorder. *Development and Psychopathology, 5*, 181–189.

Susman, E. J., Dorn, L. D., & Chrousos, G. P. (1991). Negative affect and hormone levels in young adolescents: Concurrent and predictive perspectives. *Journal of Youth and Adolescence, 20*, 167–189.

Susman, E. J., Inoff-Germain, G. E., Nottelmann, E. D., Loriaux, D. L., Cutler, G. B., Jr., & Chrousos, G. P. (1987). Hormones, emotional dispositions, and aggressive attributes in young adolescents. *Child Development, 58*, 1114–1134.

Susman, E. J., Nottelmann, E. D., Dorn, L. D., Gold, P. W., & Chrousos, G. P. (1989). The physiology of stress and behavioral development. In D. S. Palermo (Ed.), *Coping with uncertainty: Behavioral and developmental perspectives* (pp. 17–37). Hillsdale, NJ: Lawrence Erlbaum Associates.

Susman, E. J., Nottelmann, E. D., Inoff, G. E., Dorn, L. D., Cutler, G. B., Jr., Loriaux, D. L., & Chrousos, G. P. (1985). The relation of relative hormonal levels and social-emotional behavior in young adolescents. *Journal of Youth and Adolescence, 14*, 245–252.

Warren, M. P. (1980). The effects of exercise on pubertal progression and reproductive function in girls. *Journal of Clinical Endocrinology and Metabolism, 51,* 1150–1157.

Warren, M. P., & Brooks-Gunn, J. (1989). Mood and behavior at adolescence: Evidence for hormonal factors. *Journal of Clinical Endocrinology and Metabolism, 69,* 77–83.

Yesalis, C., Kennedy, N., Kopstein, A., & Bahrke, M. (1993). Anabolic-androgenic steroid use in the United States. *Journal of the American Medical Association, 270,* 1217–1221.

Zumpe, D., Bonsall, R. W., Kutner, M. H., & Michael, R. P. (1991). Medroxyprogesterone acetate, aggression, and sexual behavior in male cynomolgus monkeys (Macaca fascicularis). *Hormones and Behavior, 25,* 394–409.

14

THE PATTERNING OF ANTISOCIAL BEHAVIOR AND AUTONOMIC REACTIVITY

David Magnusson
Stockholm University

A MODEL

A central theme in a holistic, interactionistic model of man is that an individual functions as a total, integrated whole. The way an individual develops and functions can be described as a dynamic, complex process. The characteristic feature of the process is the continuous, reciprocal interaction among psychological, biological, and social factors (Magnusson, 1988; Magnusson & Törestad, 1993).

A main feature of all individuals' functioning is their interaction with the environment. In the process of interaction the organism has to maintain its integrity and the equilibrium of its internal regulations under varying conditions, even under extreme ones. An individual constantly encounters new situations and the organism has to adjust to the changing conditions, currently and in a developmental perspective, in a process of biological and behavioral adaptation.

Rather early during this century, operating factors and mechanisms in the adaptation process were sought in the functioning of the endocrine system, particularly the sympathetic adrenal and pituitary adrenal system. In classical studies, Cannon (1914) demonstrated the role of the sympathetic adrenal medullary system in emergency situations, by showing how catecholamines—adrenaline and noradrenaline—are released through sympathetic innervation in response to stimuli and situations which the individual experiences as demanding, harmful, and threatening. These biochemicals were supposed to serve in the rapid adaptation of the organism to new situational conditions by preparing the body for fight or flight. The adaptive role of the adrenal cortex, which produces corticosteroids (e.g., cortisol) through release of ACTH from the pituitary, was early advocated by Selye. From the beginning, these theories were mainly concerned with the organism's biological adaptation to physical factors in the environment having biological consequences in terms of cold, hunger, pain, tissue damage, and do on.

During recent decades, research in this area has expanded its focus on the demands of adaptation emanating from the psychosocial environment. In a modern society the frequent demands and challenges of a psychosocial character that an individual encounters, for example, in education, in working life, in traffic and transportation—in almost every aspect of life, may be stronger than the demands coming from the physical environment. These challenges may require emotional and behavioral adjustment, which involves the individual's perceptual–cognitive system (with attached emotions), and behavior, his or her sympathetic autonomic system, and the environment in a continuously ongoing interaction process. A simplified model for this process is presented in Fig. 14.1.

If a person meets a situation that is experienced as harmful, threatening, or demanding, for example, an examination or a work task, the cognitive act of interpretation of the situation stimulates, via the hypothalamus, the excretion of adrenaline from the adrenal medulla, which in turn influences other physi-

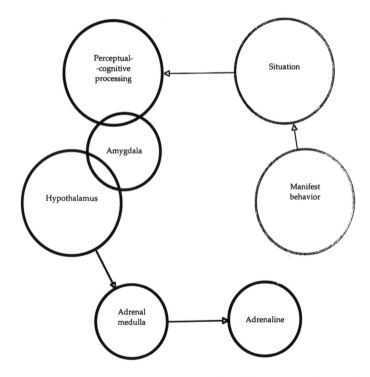

FIG. 14.1. A simplified model for the interplay of environmental, mental, biological, and behavioral factors for an individual in a specific situation.

ological processes. This cognitive–physiological interplay is accompanied by emotional states of fear and anxiety or by generally experienced arousal, which in the next stage of the process of individual functioning affects not only the individual's behavior but also his or her interpretation of the sequence of changes in the situational conditions and, thereby, the physiological reactions in terms of autonomic activity–reactivity.

A central role in this interaction process is played by the individual's perceptual–cognitive system (with attached emotions). In the example presented in Fig. 14.1, it is the way one interprets what happens in the environment that determines if and to what extent the individual reacts with a physiological response, and with concomitant relevant behavior.

As demonstrated in the model, the perceptual–cognitive system, the biological system, and manifest behavior of an individual are involved in a continuous loop of interaction. The way this process functions is dependent, among other things, on the character of the environment, particularly the environment as it is perceived and interpreted by the individual. Once established early in life the total system is rather stable in structure and functioning. However, across time it may change as a result of maturation and experience and of the interaction process itself.

AN EMPIRICAL STUDY

The methodological implications of the theoretical framework briefly summarized before will be illustrated with reference to an empirical study performed in our research group (cf. Magnusson, Klinteberg, & Stattin, 1994).

Large scale longitudinal studies have demonstrated that although a large number of boys commit crime(s) during late puberty and early adolescence, most of them conform before adult age; only a limited number continues criminal activity (Stattin & Magnusson, 1991). This observation raises the question to what extent it is motivated to regard and treat those who commit crime(s) during late puberty and adolescence as one homogeneous group.

The model presented earlier and empirical studies by our research group indicate that factors of particular interest for a discussion of this issue are found in the functioning of the perceptual–cognitive system, in manifest behavior, and in physiological activity/reactivity of the organism. In the study presented here, measures for the first two of these aspects of individual functioning—lack of ability to concentrate and motor restlessness—were combined to form a measure of the clinical syndrome hyperactivity. Physiological activity/reactivity was measured by the excretion of adrenaline from the adrenal medulla of the kidneys.

From clinical and neuropsychological points of view early hyperactivity is recognized as a main precursor of delinquency (Barcai & Rabkin, 1974; Cantwell, 1978; Douglas, 1984; Robins, 1966; Satterfield, 1978, 1987; Schuckit, Petrich & Chiles, 1978; Weiss, 1983). Although there are exceptions (Weiss, Hechtman, Perlman,

Hopkins, & Wenar, 1979), much empirical data, both cross-sectional and longitudinal, support the connection between hyperactivity and antisocial behavior.
Hyperactivity has been found to be strongly related to conduct problems in
children and adolescents (Borland & Heckman, 1976), and a number of follow-up
studies have found children with hyperactive behavior to be at excessive risk of
developing antisocial behavior (Farrington, Loeber, & Van Kammen, 1990; Gittelman, Manuzza, Schenker, & Bonagura, 1985; Hechtman, Weiss, Perlman, & Amsel,
1984; Mendelson, Johnson, & Stewart, 1971; Menkes, Rowe, & Menkes, 1967;
Nylander, 1979; Satterfield, Hoppe, & Schell, 1982; Weiss, Hinde, Werry, Douglas, &
Nemeth, 1971; Weiss & Trockenberg Hechtman, 1986; cf. af Klinteberg, Magnusson,
& Schalling, 1989). Of particular interest here is the finding reported by Farrington et al. (1990). Using data from 411 males in the Cambridge Study of
Delinquency Development, they observed that a hyperactivity–impulsivity–attention deficit measure, obtained at age 8 and 10 years, was especially predictive of
future chronic offending. In a study from the present longitudinal program af
Klinteberg, Andersson, Magnusson, and Stattin (1993) found that hyperactivity in
combination with aggressiveness, studied at age 13 for a large representative
group of males, was a strong indicator of criminal activity at adult age.

Genetic, physiological, and biochemical factors have been proposed to be
causal agents of criminal behavior in the same sense as family and environmental factors (Cadoret, Troughton, Bagford, & Woodworth, 1990; Mednick &
Finello, 1983). In this context, it is of interest that persistent offenders as a group
have been found to have more central nervous system (CNS) dysfunctions than
control groups of nonoffenders. It has also been suggested that unrecognized
cognitive dysfunctions interfere with the development of the socialization process (Buikhuisen, 1982; see also Douglas, 1984), inhibit social adaptation, and
promote delinquency in juveniles (Buikhuisen, 1987).

One area of research in which the role of the sympathetic autonomic system
has been investigated is social and antisocial behavior. Physiological reactivity
has most often been studied in terms of adrenaline excretion in urine or blood.
In an early study, Johansson, Frankenhaeuser, and Magnusson (1973) presented
data showing a positive correlation between amount of adrenaline excretion and
good social and personal adjustment. Similar results were reported by Bergman
and Magnusson (1979) and Lambert, Johansson, Frankenhaeuser, and Klackenberg-Larsson (1969).

In line with these results, a negative relationship between antisocial behavior
and delinquency, on the one hand, and adrenaline excretion, on the other, have
been reported from a number of studies during the 1970s and 1980s (Johansson
et al., 1973; Lidberg, Levander, Schalling, & Lidberg, 1978; Magnusson, 1985a;
Magnusson, Stattin, & Dunér, 1983; Olweus, 1986; Woodman, Hinton & O'Neill,
1977; cf. af Klinteberg & Magnusson, 1989; Susman, 1989).

With reference to these results, the problem under investigation was elucidated by analyses of data for *hyperactivity*, measured as the combination of lack

of ability to concentrate and motor restlessness, and for *autonomic physiological activity–reactivity* in terms of adrenaline excretion at an early age for three categories of males: (a) Those males who have not been recorded for any crime make up *the normative group*; (b) Those who have been recorded only before age 18 and have conformed thereafter compile *the juvenile offenders*; and (c) Those who have been recorded for crime both during the teenage period and in adulthood we refer to as *the persistent offenders.*

(The study is restricted to males. The role of biological factors in the total functioning of the organism is much more complicated in females than in males. A study of females with the same purpose would require consideration of factors that could not be handled here.)

Data

Data come from a longitudinal research program of Individual Development and Adjustment (IDA; Magnusson, 1988; Magnusson, Dunér, & Zetterblom, 1975). The cohort from which the data are fetched consists of all third-grade boys and girls ($N = 1,389$) in the school system in a Swedish community at the time for the first data collections (Magnusson et al., 1975). This implies that the subjects were of an average age of about 10 years at that time. They have been followed since that age up to the age of 30. It should be noted that the total group is homogeneous with respect to chronological age and that comparisons with relevant data from other cohorts show that it is representative of its Swedish age group with respect to the incidence and prevalence of crime (Stattin, Magnusson, & Reichel, 1989).

The number of subjects for which data could be used for the elucidation of the problem under investigation was restricted by the access to data for adrenaline excretion. The total number of individuals in the study was 70.

Hyperactivity. All boys were rated by their teachers at age 10 and again at age 13 with respect to various aspects of person characteristics, including Motor Restlessness and Concentration Difficulties. The ratings were performed on 7-point scales by teachers who had known their pupils for 3 years (Magnusson et al., 1975, pp. 76–79). Different teachers performed the ratings at each age level, which means that the ratings were made by independent raters at the two age levels. In the analyses presented here, the sum of ratings of Motor Restlessness and Concentration Difficulties was used as an indicator of *Hyperactivity*. Ratings for these two variables pooled across the two age levels of 10 and 13 were combined to yield an indicator of *Persistent hyperactivity*.

Autonomic Activity–Reactivity. As a measure of autonomic activity–reactivity, data for the excretion of adrenaline in urine were collected during two different situations at school. This was done for a representative subsample of boys when they were about age 13. Urine samples were collected under standardized conditions, including the same time of the day, on two occasions: first, after a normal, nonstressful situation, viewing a film on ore-mining followed by small talk about what had been seen; second, after what was planned as a stress-inducing situation. The stress element was introduced by the presentation of an achievement-demanding mental arithmetic test of the Kraepelin type, in which the task is to add one number figures, two at a time. In the instruction the subjects were urged to do their best. In order to maintain motivation during the 45-minute test session, a signal was given and the subjects were instructed to make a mark in their protocol each third minute.

Essential for the purpose of the study is that the task serves as stress inducing for all subjects, independent of belongingness to the three experimental groups of subjects. With reference to this demand, the Kraepelin type of test was chosen as stress inducing for the following interrelated reasons: It should make the test stimulating for all subjects; it should avoid experience of failure; and it should make performance independent of knowledge in school subjects and of level of intelligence, as far as possible (for a detailed description of the procedure, see Johansson et al., 1973). So far, the empirical results presented later indicate that the procedure functioned adequately.

Criminal Activity. Data on criminal activity were based on registered instances of law breaking, and were collected from national and local sources. These data cover all offenses leading to public prosecution and conviction for all the males in the cohort, without any dropout. They cover the age period through age 30 (Stattin et al., 1989).

Results

In Fig. 14.2 data for hyperactivity, measured as the sum of ratings of Motor Restlessness and Concentration Difficulties at ages 10 and 13, are shown for the three groups of males differing with respect to frequency of recorded crime.

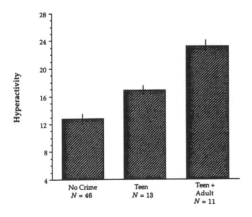

FIG. 14.2. Raw scores for hyperactivity (motor restlessness and lack of concentration) for three groups of males.

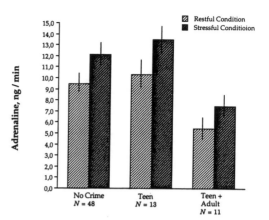

FIG. 14.3. Adrenaline excretion in two situations for three groups of males.

The persistent offenders, that is, those who recurred in criminal registers both in adolescence and in adulthood are, already, at an early age, characterized by high hyperactivity. As an average they have a score of about 5.5 on each of the four 7-point scales from which data are pooled. They differ highly significantly with respect to early persistent hyperactivity from the normative group ($p < .001$) as well as from the juvenile delinquents ($p < .001$).

In Fig. 14.3 the mean adrenaline excretion in the two situations is reported for the three categories of males grouped on the basis of their recorded criminal activity. For all three experimental groups the average level of adrenaline excretion increased from the restful to the stressful situation. This is in line with expectations and is an indication that the experimental conditions functioned adequately.

Of particular interest for a discussion of juvenile delinquency is the result showing that those who commit crimes only before age 18 and then conform do not show the expected *lower* autonomic activity–reactivity than those who have not been recorded at all. They actually showed a somewhat higher adrenaline excretion than those not registered.

On the other hand, the mean adrenaline excretion for persistent offenders differs significantly from the mean adrenaline excretion in the normative group in being lower. This is true for both the normal situation ($p < .004$) and the stressful situation ($p < .007$). The persistent offenders have already, at age 13, only about half the adrenaline excretion as the males in the other two groups. This result is cross-validated by appearance in two independent situations.

A methodological consequence of the theoretical framework for the longitudinal research program is that a variable approach, in which variables and their interrelations form the main interest, has to be complemented with an approach in which individuals are grouped and studied in terms of their characteristic *patterns* of variables which are relevant for the problem under consideration (Magnusson, 1985b; Magnusson, Stattin, & Dunér, 1983).

The earlier results indicate that (a) males with a persistent criminal career are characterized by high persistent hyperactivity *and* low adrenaline excretion, and (b) that males without criminal records are characterized by low hyperactivity and high adrenaline excretion. For juvenile offenders no clear pattern emerges.

The combination of (a) categories with respect to appearance in criminal records, (b) high (20 <) or low (< 20) persistent hyperactivity, and (c) high (M <) or low (< M) adrenaline excretion in the stressful situation yields 12 groupings of the 70 males for whom complete data are available. In order to test which of the 12 patterns occurred more or less often than could be expected from a random model, a Configural Frequency Analysis (CFA; Krauth & Lienert, 1982) was applied. The result of the analysis is presented in Table 14.1.

The result of the pattern analysis is much in line with what was expected from the variable oriented analyses. Eleven males belonged to the category "persistent offenders," that is, they had been registered for crime both before and after the age of 18. Of the 11 persistent offenders, 9 had the combination of high hyperactivity and low adrenaline excretion instead of the expected 1.3, according to a random model. Thus, this pattern forms a significant *type*. Only two persistent offenders had other combinations. Forty-six males had no criminal record. Not one of them had the critical pattern of high hyperactivity and low adrenaline excretion that was characteristic of the persistent offenders:

For the combination of belonging to the normative group, being high in hyperactivity and low in adrenaline excretion, 5.5 individuals were expected. However, the observed frequency was zero. This implies that this combination, characteristic of the persistent offenders, formed a significant *antitype* among

TABLE 14.1
Observed and Expected Frequencies of Patterns of
(a) Belongingness to One of the Three Categories of Males,
(b) Being High or Low in Hyperactivity, and (c) Being High
or Low in Adrenaline Excretion in a Stressful Situation

Crim. Category	Hyperact.	Adrenaline	Observed Freq.	Expected Freq.	p
No crime	low	low	25	20.2	ns
" "	low	high	18	16.0	ns
" "	high	low	0	5.5	< .02
" "	high	high	3	4.4	ns
Crime before 18	low	low	2	5.7	ns
" " "	low	high	8	4.5	ns
" " "	high	low	2	1.6	ns
" " "	high	high	1	1.2	ns
Persistent crime	low	low	1	4.8	ns
" "	low	high	1	3.8	ns
" "	high	low	9	1.3	< .0000
" "	high	high	0	1.0	ns

Note. Hyperact.: low < 20; high > 20
Adrenaline: low = below average; high = above average.

the normatives, that is, it occurs significantly less often than could be expected from a random model.

For juvenile offenders 1.6 were expected to have the pattern of high hyperactivity and low adrenaline excretion that was characteristic of persistent offenders. The observed frequency (two individuals) came as close as possible to this figure.

The result of the analysis presented in Table 14.1 was cross-validated by a pattern analysis based on adrenaline data from the nonstressful situation. The main results were confirmed. The only change that took place for the group of persistent criminals was that one male who was characterized by high hyperactivity and low adrenaline excretion in the first analysis, now was characterized by high hyperactivity and high adrenaline excretion.

CONCLUSIONS AND INTERPRETATIONS

Most research on the development of criminal activity has regarded and treated juvenile delinquents as one homogeneous group. An illustration is the growing number of studies interpreting the results of empirical studies on the role of autonomic physiological activity–reactivity in the process underlying criminal activity as supporting the hypothesis about a systematic relation between low autonomic activity–reactivity in terms of low adrenaline excretion, on the one hand, and antisocial behavior in general, on the other. The analyses presented here suggest a distinction between two categories of juvenile delinquents: Category 1—persistent offenders, with a persistent trait-like disposition of high hyperactivity and low autonomic activity–reactivity; Category 2—juvenile offenders, without this disposition but probably susceptible to conditions in the environment.

This possible distinction has important implications both for further theoretical and empirical research into the processes underlying antisocial behavior and for discussions about appropriate preventive actions. The fact that the distinction has not been made before may explain the incoherent results in previous studies on the relationship between delinquency and autonomic arousal (see McCord, 1990).

The results presented here indicate a strong significant relationship between persistent criminal activity and early adrenaline excretion, whereas there is no systematic relationship between autonomic activity–reactivity in these terms and criminal activity restricted to adolescence. The results demonstrate the importance of including biological factors when striving to understand and explain antisocial behavior. From a perceptual–cognitive point of view low autonomic activity–reactivity might, in line with earlier suggestions, be interpreted as indicating a loss of resources for handling stressful situational demands (Frankenhaeuser, 1979), which may result in difficulties in responding adequately. Low adrenaline output might also be regarded as a biochemical factor mediating between coping deficiency and criminal activity.

There are at least four possible interpretations of the finding of a lower level of adrenaline excretion among hyperactive boys than among nonhyperactive boys. These interpretations also apply to our finding of a lower level of adrenaline excretion among persistent criminal males than among males without reported criminal activity, and males with criminal activity only during adolescence.

The first possible interpretation is biological. Those with a disposition for hyperactive behavior and persistent criminal activity may have been born with a "malfunction" (not necessarily genetic, cf. Offord, Sullivan, Allen, & Abrams, 1979; Raine & Mednick, 1989) in the way the individual system of psychological and physiological factors function. The malfunction may be located at one or several points in the total system.

The second possible interpretation is environmental. In this interpretation the low level of reactivity in terms of adrenaline excretion is learned, that is, a result of early experiences in an inconsistent social environment. As interpreted here, adrenaline excretion occurs as a result of the individual's interpretation of something as threatening or demanding in the environment. If reward and punishment are distributed randomly during the infant socialization process, when biological systems are being established, the psychological and physiological system, which regulates adrenaline production, will not learn when and how to react adequately. As a result the system might become passified. Thus, a consistent set of conduct rules, maintained by distinct, appropriate reactions from the environment is a prerequisite for the physiological system to learn when and how to react to external threats and demands. This explanation is supported by data from a large follow-up study of a sample of Swedish criminals and a control group. Data from the social environments showed that the most important characteristic that differentiated the family background of criminals from that of controls was the lack of consistency in family rules for upbringing (Olofsson, 1973).

The third possible interpretation, and in my mind the most probable one, is interactionistic. The causal explanation to the lower adrenaline excretion in males with a disposition for hyperactivity and for delinquency would then be in the interaction of environmental factors and biological and mental factors in the individual. A child born with an innate biological vulnerability may need an environment characterized by very clear consistency in order to be able to identify the regularities in the patterning of social roles, rules, expectations, etc. A child born with a strong biological system may be able to identify even vague regularities in the social environment and develop adequately even under severe social conditions.

A fourth interpretation is possible, namely that the contemporaneous appearance of hyperactivity and persistent crimes across age levels, on the one hand, and low adrenaline excretion, on the other, does not necessarily imply that they are related to each other. Too often and too easily, wrong conclusions are drawn from contemporaneous events, reflected, for example, in significant correlations.

All four interpretations of the role of low autonomic activity–reactivity in the development of antisocial behavior are made in the frame of reference of the interactional model of individual functioning. The model indicates a multidetermined, stochastic process in which biological factors are involved in a constant, reciprocal interaction with other factors in the individual and the environment.

METHODOLOGICAL IMPLICATIONS: PATTERN ANALYSIS IN A PERSON APPROACH

A prerequisite for success in empirical research in any field is the application of methodologies and research strategies that fit the character of the structures and processes under consideration.

The empirical results and the way the analyses were performed emphasize the importance of an interactionistic theoretical perspective on individual development and its methodological and research strategical implications (Magnusson, 1995). From an interactionistic perspective, individual functioning is regarded as a continuously ongoing process in which psychological and biological factors in the individual and factors in the environment are involved in continuous interaction. An important implication of this view is that in order to understand the individual development process we have to include all these factors in the overriding theoretical framework as has been done in the research program from which the data presented here were fetched. This statement leads to important theoretical, methological, and research strategical issues (Magnusson, 1988).

Developmental research has, for a long time, been dominated by what might be called a variable approach. In a variable approach the focus of interest is in the relations among variables, for example, among independent or dependent variables and between dependent and independent variables. The questions to be answered are formulated in terms of relations among variables, the results are given in terms of relations among variables, and the results are discussed and generalized in such terms. Most often a variable approach is combined with the application of linear and nonlinear regression models for the treatment of data.

Variable-oriented research has contributed much to developmental research and will continue to do so. Sophisticated analyses along these lines, based on careful description and analysis of the phenomena, form an indispensable part of empirical developmental research. Methods, like LISREL, which test theoretical models for causal relations among variables, have been in use for some time, and recent developments of methods for the study of nonlinear relations (e.g., logistic correlations) and of time-series have contributed to make more refined analyses possible (for a review of such methods, see Magnusson, Bergman, Rudinger, & Törestad, 1992).

However, from the perspective of the characteristic features of individual functioning as a complex, dynamic process the variable approach has specific limitations, when the goal is to understand and explain the total process

(Bergman, 1988a; Magnusson, 1995; Magnusson, Andersson, & Törestad, 1993). Thus the variable approach has to be complemented with a person-oriented approach (Magnusson, 1985b; Magnusson, Stattin, & Dunér, 1983). In a person approach the individual is the unit of observation. The specific problem under consideration is formulated in person terms and operationalized and studied empirically in terms of patterns of values for variables that are relevant with reference to the problem under consideration. In other scientific disciplines, which are concerned with dynamic complex processes such as ecology, meteorology, biology, or chemistry, pattern analysis has become an important research methodology.

The analyses presented here demonstrate the fruitfulness of combining a variable approach, in which the interest is directed to the interrelationships among variables, most often studied by the application of linear and nonlinear regression models, with a person approach, in which individuals are studied in terms of their characteristic patterns of the variables under consideration. In the longitudinal research program from which data were used for analysis here, considerable time has been spent on the development and application of appropriate methods for the study of developmental issues in terms of individual patterns (Bergman, 1988b; Bergman & Magnusson, 1983, 1984; Magnusson & Bergman, 1984, 1988, 1990).

A combination of a variable approach and a person approach is a meaningful path for further progress in empirical research on individual development, in general, and in research on social development, in particular.

The characteristic feature of an individual's way of functioning as a psychological and biological organism forms the theoretical basis for the study of individual development in terms of pattern. A basic, well-documented principle in the development of biological systems is their ability for self-organization (Nicolis & Prigogine, 1977). From the beginning of the development of the fetus, self-organization is the guiding principle. Within subsystems the operating components organize themselves in a way that maximizes the functioning of each subsystem with respect to the purpose in the total system. At a higher level subsystems organize themselves in order to fulfill their role in the functioning of the totality. We find this principle in the development and functioning of the biological systems of the brain, the coronary system, and the immune system. It can also be applied to the development and functioning of the cognitive systems and of manifest behavior.

An important aspect of the self-organizing processes is that individuals differ to some extent in the way operational factors are organized and function within subsystems, such as the perceptual–cognitive emotional system, the immune system, the coronary system, and the behavioral system. Individual also differ in subsystem organization and function. These organizations can be described in terms of *patterns* of operating factors within subsystems and in terms of patterns of functioning subsystems (cf. Weiner, 1989, who emphasized that the oscillations produced by natural pacemakers of the heart, the stomach, and the brain are patterned).

This view leads to the conclusion that the main individual differences is to be found in the patterning of operating factors within subsystems, such as those just described, and in the patterning of subsystems in the totality—for example, in the way the perceptual–cognitive–emotive, the behavioral, and the physiological systems function together in the total functioning of the individual.

With reference to this view, person-oriented pattern analyses are based on the fact that the number of biologically and psychologically possible organizations of factors within subsystems and of subsystems within individuals, is limited. This constitutes the theoretical basis for grouping individuals and studying differences among individuals in terms of their characteristic patterns of values for relevant factors. This is, of course, opposed to the view held by extreme advocates of an ideographic notion, that individuals are totally unique.

An empirical illustration to this view on individual differences is presented in Fig. 14.4. In a study of cardiovascular responses (cystolic blood pressure, diastolic blood pressure, and heart rate) in a situation involving psychological challenge during speech preparation, Gramer and Huber (1994) found that subjects could be classified into three groups on the basis of their distinct patterns of reactions.

A basic requirement for successful pattern analyses is that the choice of variables used for classification of individuals is based on careful description and analysis of the phenomena involved in the issue under consideration (Cairns, 1986; Magnusson, 1992). As demonstrated in the empirical study presented in Figs. 14.2, 14.3, and Table 14.1, our empirical research on individual functioning proceeds in two steps (Magnusson, 1993). First, the possible operating factors are identified by variable-oriented analysis. Second, the factors form the basis for a grouping of individuals including their specific patterns of operating factors to identify the basic way in which they operate together. Using this approach, including pattern analyses, a number of studies on antisocial behavior have been performed within our longitudinal research program (e.g., Magnusson & Bergman, 1988, 1990; af Klinteberg et al., 1993). The results have been the object

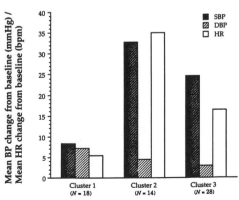

FIG. 14.4. Magnitude of SBP, DBP, and HR reactivity in cardiovascular response clusters during speech preparation. Reprinted with permission.

of cross-validation (Pulkkinen & Tremblay, 1992). A person–pattern approach is not a new term for a typological approach, referring each individual, once and for all, to a certain category. The essential claim in personality research is that analyses of any aspect of individual functioning, in a current and in a developmental perspective, shall be made with reference to the functioning of the subsystems and their role in the functioning of the individual, and that interpretation of results of the analyses shall be made within the same frame of reference.

A number of methods for pattern analysis have been presented and applied; multivariate P-technique factor analysis (Cattell, Cattell, & Rhymer, 1947; Nesselroade & Ford, 1987), Q-sort technique (Asendorpf & van Aken, 1991; Block, 1971), latent profile analysis (LPA; Gibson, 1959; Magnusson et al., 1975); configural frequency analysis (CFA; Krauth & Lienert, 1982; Lienert & zur Oeveste, 1985; von Eye, 1990), and cluster analytical techniques (Bergman, 1993).

So far these methods have been used mainly for description. Pattern description is the first step toward an understanding and explanation of the lawfulness of individual functioning. Its main merit, distinguishing it from a variable approach, is that it considers the holistic character of the functioning of subsystems and of the totality. However, it does not investigate the dynamics of the processes in individual functioning, neither in a current, nor in a developmental perspective.

For further success in handling the important issues in this scientific domain, the development of appropriate methods, which match the character of the processes we are interested in, and the refining of the theoretical basis for such methods are among the most important future tasks (Bergman, Eklund, & Magnusson, 1991). One of these challenges is to develop methods for the analyses of motion and change in the systems, that is, for *dynamic pattern analysis*. At present we are much better at describing states than describing and explaining the change from one state to another or from one age to another (Dannefer & Perlmutter, 1990).

Both the tasks of pattern description and of pattern dynamics are full of conceptual, theoretical, and methodological problems (cf. Bergman, 1993). We are just beginning to develop adequate and effective methods for pattern analyses; most of the work remains to be done. The problems connected with this development need to be solved in order for the analyses to contribute successfully to our understanding and explanations of the lawfulness of the process of individual functioning in general and thus also for understanding and explaining the processes underlying life courses involving antisocial behavior.

ACKNOWLEDGMENTS

This research was supported by grants from the Swedish Council for Planning and Coordination of Research, The Swedish Council for Social Research, and The Bank of Sweden Tercentenary Foundation.

REFERENCES

Asendorpf, J. B., & van Aken, M. A. G. (1991). Correlates of the temporal consistency of personality patterns in childhood. *Journal of Personality, 59*(4), 689–703.

Barcai, A., & Rabkin, L. (1974). A precursor of delinquency: The hyperkinetic disorder of childhood. *Psychiatric Quarterly, 48*, 387–399.

Bergman, L. R., (1988a). Modelling reality. In M. Rutter (Ed.), *Studies of psychosocial risks. The power of longitudinal data* (pp. 354–366). Cambridge, England: Cambridge University Press.

Bergman, L. R. (1988b). You can't classify all of the people all of the time. *Multivariate Behavioral Research, 23*, 425–441.

Bergman, L. R. (1993). Some methodological issues in longitudinal research: Looking forward. In D. Magnusson & P. Casaer (Eds.), *Longitudinal research on individual development: Present status and future perspectives* (pp. 217–241). Cambridge, England: Cambridge University Press.

Bergman, L. R., Eklund, G., & Magnusson, D. (1991). Studying individual development: Problems and methods. In D. Magnusson, L. R. Bergman, G. Rudinger, & B. Törestad (Eds.), *Problems and methods in longitudinal research: Stability and change* (pp. 1–28). Cambridge, England: Cambridge University Press.

Bergman, L. R., & Magnusson, D. (1979). Overachievement and catecholamine excretion in an achievement-demanding situation. *Psychosomatic Medicine, 41*, 181–188.

Bergman, L. R., & Magnusson, D. (1983). *The development of patterns of maladjustment* (Rep. No. 50). Department of Psychology University of Stockholm.

Bergman, L. R., & Magnusson, D. (1984). *Patterns of adjustment problems at age 13* (Rep. No. 620). Department of Psychology, University of Stockholm.

Block, J. (1971). *Lives through time.* Berkeley, CA: Bancroft.

Borland, B. L., & Heckman, H. K. (1976). Hyperactive boys and their brothers: A 25-year follow-up study. *Archives of General Psychiatry, 33*, 669–675.

Buikhuisen, W. (1982). Aggressive behavior and cognitive disorders. *International Journal of Law and Psychiatry, 5*, 205–217.

Buikhuisen, W. (1987). Cerebral dysfunctions and juvenile crime. In S. A. Mednick, T. E. Moffit, & S. A. Stack (Eds.), *The causes of crime. New biological approaches* (pp. 168–184). Cambridge, England: Cambridge University Press.

Cadoret, R. J., Troughton, E., Bagford, J., & Woodworth, G. (1990). Genetic and environmental factors in adopted antisocial personality. *European Archives of Psychiatry and Neurology Sciences, 239*, 231–240.

Cairns, R. B. (1986). Phenomena lost: Issues in the study of development. In J. Valsiner (Ed.), *The individual subject and scientific psychology* (pp. 79–111). New York: Plenum.

Cannon, W. B. (1914). The emergency function of the adrenal medulla in pain and the major emotions. *American Journal of Physiology, 33*, 356–372.

Cantwell, D. P. (1978). Hyperactivity and antisocial behavior. *Journal of American Academy of Child Psychiatry, 17*, 252–262.

Cattell, R. B., Cattell, A. K. S., & Rhymer, R. M. (1947). P-technique demonstrated in determining psycho-physiological source traits in a normal individual. *Psychometrika, 12*, 267–288.

Dannefer, D., & Perlmutter, M. (1990). Development as a multidimensional process: Individual and social constituents. *Human Development, 33*, 108–137.

Douglas, V. (1984). Attentional and cognitive problems. In M. Rutter (Ed.), *Developmental neuropsychiatry* (pp. 280–329). New York: Churchill Livingstone.

Farrington, D. P., Loeber, R., & Van Kammen, W. B. (1990). Long-term criminal outcomes of hyperactivity-impulsivity-attention deficit and conduct problems in childhood. In L. N. Robins & M. Rutter (Eds.), *Straight and devious pathways from childhood to adulthood* (pp. 62–81). Cambridge, England: Cambridge University Press.

Frankenhaeuser, M. (1979). Psychoneuroendocrine approaches to the study of emotion as related to stress and coping. In H. E. Howe & R. A. Dienstbier (Eds.), *Nebraska Symposium on Motivation 1978* (pp. 123–161). Lincoln: University of Nebraska Press.

Gibson, W. A. (1959). Three multivariate models: Factor analysis, latent structure analysis and latent profile analysis. *Psychometrica, 24,* 229–252.

Gittelman, R., Manuzza, S., Schenker, R., & Bonagura, N. (1985). Psychiatric status. *Archives of General Psychiatry, 42,* 937–947.

Gramer, M., & Huber, H. P. (1994). Individual variability in task-specific cardiovascular response patterns during psychological challenge. *German Journal of Psychology, 18,* 766–779.

Hechtman, L., Weiss, G., Perlman, T., & Amsel, R. (1984). Hyperactive as young adults initial predictors of adult outcome. *Journal of the American Academy of Child Psychiatry, 23,* 250–260.

Johansson, G., Frankenhaeuser, M., & Magnusson, D. (1973). Catecholamine output in school children as related to performance and adjustment. *Scandinavian Journal of Psychology, 14,* 20–28.

Klinteberg, B. af, Andersson, T., Magnusson, D., & Stattin, H. (1993). Hyperactive behavior in childhood as related to subsequent alcohol problems and violent offending. *Journal of Personality and Individual Differences, 15*(4), 381–388.

Klinteberg, B. af, & Magnusson, D. (1989). Aggressiveness and hyperactive behaviour as related to adrenaline excretion. *European Journal of Personality, 3,* 81–93.

Klinteberg, B. af, Magnusson, D., & Schalling, D. (1989). Hyperactive behavior in childhood and adult impulsivity: A longitudinal study of male subjects. *Personality and Individual Differences, 1,* 43–50.

Krauth, J., & Lienert, G. A. (1982). Fundamentals and modifications of configural frequency analysis (CFA). *Interdisciplinaria, 3,* 1–14.

Lambert, W. W., Johansson, G., Frankenhaeuser, M., & Klackenberg-Larsson, I. (1969). Catecholamine excretion in young children and their parents as related to behavior. *Scandinavian Journal of Psychology, 10,* 306–318.

Lidberg, L., Levander, S. E., Schalling, D., & Lidberg, Y. (1978). Urinary catecholamines, stress, and psychopathy: A study of arrested men awaiting trial. *Psychosomatic Medicine, 40,* 116–125.

Lienert, G. A., & zur Oeveste, H. (1985). CFA as a statistical tool for developmental research. *Educational & Psychological Measurement, 45,* 301–307.

Magnusson, D. (1985a). Early conduct and biological factors in the developmental background of adult delinquency. *The British Psychological Society, Newsletter, 13,* 4–17.

Magnusson, D. (1985b). Implications of an interactional paradigm for research on human development. *International Journal of Behavior Development, 8,* 115–137.

Magnusson, D. (1988). Individual development from an interactional perspective. In D. Magnusson (Ed.), *Paths through life* (Vol. 1). Hillsdale, NJ: Lawrence Erlbaum Associates.

Magnusson, D. (1992). Back to the phenomena: Theory, methods and statistics in psychological research. *European Journal of Personality, 6,* 1–14.

Magnusson, D. (1993). Human ontogeny: A longitudinal perspective. In D. Magnusson & P. Casaer (Eds.), *Longitudinal research on individual development* (pp. 1–25). Cambridge, England: Cambridge University Press.

Magnusson, D. (1995). Individual development: A holistic, integrated model. In P. Moen, G. H. Elder Jr., & K. Fischer (Eds.), *Examining lives in context: Perspectives on the ecology of human development* (pp. 19–60). Washington, DC: American Psychological Association.

Magnusson, D., Andersson, T., & Törestad, B. (1993). Methodological implications of a peephole perspective on personality. In D. Funder, C. Tomlinson-Keasey, R. Parke, & K. Widaman (Eds.), *Studying lives through time: Approaches to personality and development* (pp. 207–220). Washington, DC: American Psychological Association.

Magnusson, D., & Bergman, L. R. (1984). On the study of the development of adjustment problems. In L. Pulkkinen & P. Lyytinen (Eds.), *Human action and personality essays in honour of Martti Takala* (pp. 163–171). Jyväskylä, Finland: University of Jyväskylä.

Magnusson, D., & Bergman, L. R. (1988). Individual and variable-based approaches to longitudinal research on early risk factors. In M. Rutter (Ed.), *Studies of psychosocial risk: The power of longitudinal data* (pp. 45–61). Cambridge, England: Cambridge University Press.

Magnusson, D., & Bergman, L. R. (1990). A pattern approach to the study of pathways from childhood to adulthood. In L. N. Robins & M. Rutter (Eds.), *Straight and devious pathways from childhood to adulthood* (pp. 101–115). Cambridge, England: Cambridge University Press.

Magnusson, D., Bergman, L. R., Rudinger, G., & Törestad, B. (1992). *Problems and methods in longitudinal research.* Cambridge, England: Cambridge University Press.

Magnusson, D., Dunér, A., & Zetterblom, G. (1975). *Adjustment: A longitudinal study.* Stockholm: Almqvist & Wiksell.

Magnusson, D., Klinteberg, B. af, & Stattin, H. (1994). Juvenile and persistent offenders: Behavioral and physiological characteristics. In R. D. Ketterlinus & M. Lamb (Eds.), *Adolescent problem behaviors* (pp. 81–91). Hillsdale, NJ: Lawrence Erlbaum Associates.

Magnusson, D., Stattin, H., & Dunér, A. (1983). Aggression and criminality in a longitudinal perspective. In K. T. van Dusen & S. A. Mednick (Eds.), *Prospective studies of crime and delinquency* (pp. 277–301). Boston: Kluwer-Nijhoff.

Magnusson, D., & Törestad, B. (1993). A holistic view of personality: A model revisited. *Annual Review of Psychology, 44,* 427–452.

McCord, J. A. (1990). Problem behaviors. In S. S. Feldman & G. R. Elliott (Eds.), *At the threshold: The developing adolescent* (pp. 414–430). Cambridge, MA: Harvard University Press.

Mednick, S. A., & Finello, K. M. (1983). Biological factors and crime: Implications for forensic psychiatry. *International Journal of Law and Psychiatry, 6,* 1–15.

Mendelson, W., Johnson, N., & Stewart, M. A. (1971). Hyperactive children as teenagers: A follow-up study. *The Journal of Nervous and Mental Disease, 153,* 272–279.

Menkes, M., Rowe, J., & Menkes, J. (1967). A twenty-five-year follow-up study on the hyperkinetic child with minimal brain dysfunction. *Pediatrics, 39,* 393–399.

Nesselroade, J. R., & Ford, D. H. (1987). Methodological considerations in modeling living systems. In M. E. Ford, & D. H. Ford (Eds.), *Humans as self-constructing living systems. Putting the framework to work* (pp. 47–79). Hillsdale, NJ: Lawrence Erlbaum Associates.

Nicolis, G., & Prigogine, I. (1977). *Self-organization in non-equilibrium systems.* New York: Wiley.

Nylander, I. (1979). A 20-year prospective follow-up study of 2,164 cases at the child guidance clinics in Stockholm. *Acta Paediatrica Scandinavica,* (Suppl. 276), 1–45.

Offord, D. R., Sullivan, K., Allen, N., & Abrams, N. (1979). Delinquency and hyperactivity. *Journal of Nervous and Mental Disease, 167,* 734–741.

Olofsson, B. (1973). *Unga lagöverträdare III. Hem, uppfostran, skola och kamratmiljöi belysning av intervju- och uppföljningsdata* [Young delinquents III. Home, upbringing, education and peer relations as reflected in interview- and follow-up data], 1973:25. Stockholm: Statens Offentliga Utredningar.

Olweus, D. (1986). Aggression and hormones. Behavior relationship with testosterone and adrenaline. In D. Olweus, J. Block, & M. Radke-Yarrow (Eds.), *The development of antisocial and prosocial behavior: Research, theories and issue* (pp. 51–72). New York: Academic Press.

Pulkkinen, L., & Tremblay, R. E. (1992). Patterns of boys' social adjustment in two cultures and at different ages: A longitudinal perspective. *International Journal of Behavioral Development, 15,* 527–553.

Raine, A., & Mednick, S. A. (1989). Biosocial longitudinal research in antisocial behavior. *Revue of Epidemiology, 37,* 515–524.

Robins, L. N. (1966). *Deviant children grown up: A sociological and psychiatric study of sociopathic personality.* Baltimore, MD: Williams & Wilkins.

Satterfield, J. H. (1978). The hyperactive child syndrome: A precursor to adult psychopathy? In R. D. Hare & D. Schalling (Eds.), *Psychopathic Behavior: Approaches to research* (pp. 329–346). New York: Wiley.

Satterfield, J. H. (1987). Childhood diagnostic and neuro-physiological predictors of teenage arrest rates: An 8-years prospective study. In S. A. Mednick, T. E. Moffit, & S. A. Stack (Eds.), *The causes of crime: New biological approaches* (pp. 147–167). Cambridge, England: Cambridge University Press.

Satterfield, J. H., Hoppe, C. M., & Schell, A. M. (1982). A prospective study of delinquency in 110 adolescent boys with attention deficit disorder and 88 normal adolescent boys. *American Journal of Psychiatry, 139,* 795–798.

Schuckit, M. A., Petrich, J., & Chiles, J. (1978). Hyperactivity: Diagnostic confusion. *Journal of Nervous and Mental Disease, 166,* 79–87.

Stattin, H., & Magnusson, D. (1991). Stability and change in criminal behaviour up to age 30. *The British Journal of Criminology, 31,* 327–346.

Stattin, H., Magnusson, D., & Reichel, H. (1989). Criminal activity at different ages. A study based on a Swedish longitudinal research population. *The British Journal of Criminology, 29,* 368–385.

Susman, L. (1989). Biology–behavior interactions in behavioral development. *ISSBD Newsletter, 15,* 1–3.

von Eye, A. (1990). *Introduction to configural frequency analysis: The search for types and antitypes in cross-classifications.* New York: Cambridge University Press.

Weiner, H. (1989).The dynamics of the organism: Implications of recent biological thought for psychosomatic theory and research. *Psychosomatic Medicine, 51,* 608–635.

Weiss, G. (1983). Long-term outcome: Findings, concepts and practical implications. In M. Rutter (Ed.), *Developmental neuropsychiatry.* New York: Guilford.

Weiss, G., Hechtman, L., Perlman, T., Hopkins, J., & Wenar, A. (1979). Hyperactives as young adults: A controlled, prospective ten year follow-up of 75 children. *Archives of General Psychiatry, 6,* 675–681.

Weiss, G., Hinde, K., Werry, J., Douglas, V., & Nemeth, E. (1971). Studies on the hyperactive child. VIII: Five year follow-up. *Archives of General Psychiatry, 24,* 409–414.

Weiss, G., & Trockenberg Hechtman, L. T. (1986). *Hyperactive children grown up. Empirical findings and theoretical considerations.* New York: Guilford.

Woodman, D., Hinton, J., & O'Neill, M. (1977). Relationship between violence and catecholamines. *Perceptual and Motor Skills, 45,* 702.

15

Intractable Tangles of Sex and Gender in Women's Aggressive Development: An Optimistic View

Kathryn E. Hood

Pennsylvania State University

When we connect gender and sex, are we comparing something social with something natural, or are we comparing something social with something which is also social (in this case, the way a given society represents "biology" to itself)?

—Delphy (1993)

Biological sex often serves as an explanatory concept for sex-typed behaviors, and this is especially true of aggressive behavior. Since the influential reviews of Maccoby and Jacklin (1974, 1980), many developmental psychologists have held the view that sex-related differences in aggressive behavior are biologically caused to a significant extent. The counterposed view (for example, Tieger, 1980) challenges the strong hypothesis of biological causation by citing inconsistencies in the experimental animal work and counterexamples from other cultures, to demonstrate that factors such as social contingencies of reward or punishment, methods of child rearing, and cultural beliefs and practices can vary in ways that accentuate or eliminate sex differences in aggressive behavior.

Given the array of mixed findings in the literature on biology and aggressive behavior (Archer, 1991; Hyde, 1986), this difference of interpretation may not be resolved by the continued accumulation of evidence. The arguments on each side seem to proceed by a different logic. For some, the perceived ubiquity of gender differences is sufficient to support or prove biological causation. For example, Gove (1985) notes that gender differences seem to be stable across time and place so that "their ubiquitous nature would suggest a ubiquitous base" (p. 139) of biological sex differences. He then proposes that women's low rate of aggressive behavior is due largely to "their affiliative nature, their physique, and to their lack of assertiveness, all of which have a biological base" (p. 138). Here the seeming shift to (biological) certainty is a subtle closing move of induction. By the logic of induction, this conclusion requires that the contingent (social) conditions influencing aggressive behavior will never change.

For others addressing the same issue, the logic proceeds differently: If the hypothesis is about essence—"all crows are black"—then one white crow is sufficient to disconfirm. From this deductive view, failures to confirm stand out in a literature of disparate findings and counterinstances, sufficient to forestall any weighty conclusion. For example, Macaulay (1985) remarks on her 1977 review with Frodi and Thome: "There were far too many studies with no gender differences to support any theory that strong biological factors, deeply ingrained personality traits, or well-learned gender roles make even a majority of women reliably or consistently very much less aggressive than men" (Macaulay, 1985, p. 192). Jeanne Block (1983) asserts that until the "spiraling, reciprocating, bidirectional effects . . . of differential socialization are specifically evaluated by cultural, subcultural, or individual family changes, the role of biological and bidirectional factors cannot be assessed." From this logical perspective, the argument from contingency to essence (or necessity) is not valid.

The intricacies of this impasse reflect the challenges to science posed by the complexity of human development. In humans, sex as a biological factor is completely intertwined with gender, a social-psychological factor. The resulting tangles of biological and cultural factors are intractable to analysis. In particular, causal analysis is limited in this case (Rutter, 1988). As Tieger (1980) notes, the relationship between sex and gender is "a dialectical one insofar as biological attributes and cultural concepts could not become analytically disentangled in a simple cause-effect relationship." (For a dialectical conception of development, see Eccles, 1987; Hood, 1995.) Gender as a social-psychological construct operates to organize expectations about an individual's abilities, appropriate behavior, academic and employment potential, family and social roles, and self-concepts. Because of the complexity of these social factors, and the complexity of their interrelationships across families and cultures and historical periods, the concept of gender entails the strong possibility of individual plasticity and social change.

To join in this debate, the present discussion offers a brief review of studies in women's aggressive development, which serves as a prelude to considering genes, hormones, puberty, menstrual cycle effects, and socialization. The focus is on studies using direct behavior observation. Questions about sex and biological causation are put into comparative perspective because nonhuman animals presumably are not influenced by social-psychological factors related to gender roles, and because animals can be used in powerful experimental designs. Applying the same or similar questions and methods of study to different species can provide a test of the generality of findings, and a source of new hypotheses. Ultimately, girls' development is the focus: What happens to girls' aggressive behavior during the course of maturation and anticipatory socialization for adult roles? The concluding section assesses the significance of these findings for supporting aggressive or assertive behavior as a component of girls' and women's healthy development. Gender-specific developmental pathways leading to problematic outcomes such as violence or depression are considered with a view to clinical interventions that might prevent or ameliorate problems in development.

The perspective is an optimistic one because it is set in the present era of social transformation, as women by their own efforts are entering public positions of authority. Women scientists and practitioners can disclose, define, and interpret for themselves the dialectic of sex and gender, and the actual or potential significance of women's aggressive behavior.

SEX AND GENDER DIFFERENCES IN AGGRESSIVE BEHAVIOR

A pervasive assumption in the study of aggressive behavior has been that males have an appetite for aggressive encounters with same-sex conspecifics, whereas females fight only to protect offspring (Moyer, 1976). Moreover, the apparent prevalence of sex differences implies that the sources are fixed biological factors, according to Maccoby and Jacklin (1974, 1980). Even in experimental social psychology (Frodi, Macaulay, & Thome, 1977), biological factors are invoked to "lay the groundwork for an understanding of the phenotypic expression of whatever genetic differences may exist." However, higher levels of male aggressiveness are not found in 44 of the 72 studies reviewed in that work (Frodi et al., 1977). The findings indicate that women are equally likely as men to report feelings of aggressiveness or hostility (also see Werner & Smith, 1992). These feelings are manifested as aggressive behavior only when the situation is seen as justifying an aggressive response. If subjects are provoked or angered, or if subjects are assured anonymity, then women are equally as aggressive as men (Frodi et al., 1977). Otherwise, self-reported anxiety and guilt stops women from acting on their angry feelings.

Fear of retaliation also stops women's aggression. From a meta-analysis of 81 findings from 63 studies, Eagly and Steffen (1986) conclude that gender differences in aggressive behavior arise from women's and girls' expectation of punishment for aggressive acts. In these meta-analyses and in the meta-analyses of 143 studies using nonclinical samples by Hyde (1984, 1986), gender accounts for about 5% of the variance in aggressive behavior, with average male values one third to one half of a standard deviation higher than female values.

Are these gender differences the result of "whatever genetic differences may exist" between females and males? A direct test of genetic effects has been carried out with an animal model.

GENES: X'S, Y'S, AND OTHERWISE

Sex differences in morphology, hormones, and behavior may follow from the developmental expression of sex differences in genes. In mammals, a female develops unless a Y chromosome is present, in which case testosterone is produced by the gonads during prenatal and perinatal development, organizing the genitalia and some specific brain areas as male. At puberty, increased levels of gonadal hormones activate the process of sexual differentiation into adult forms. These sex-differential processes suggest the possibility that sex-related differences in aggressive behavior are linked to the Y chromosome. Without a Y chromosome, and without high levels of testosterone, the argument follows, nonmaternal females are not stimulated to fight.

Selective breeding studies have been informative on this point. One coordinated series of studies (Cairns, Gariépy, & Hood, 1990; Hood, 1988, 1992b; Hood & Cairns, 1988, 1989) has presented genetic, hormonal, developmental, neurochemical, and social-contextual analyses of the development of aggressive behavior. (For a discussion, see Gariépy, Lewis, and Cairns, chap. 3, this volume.) Selective breeding for high or for low levels of aggressive behavior in male mice produced durable changes in a few generations in the aggressive behavior of males, compared to control line males bred without selection for aggressive behavior.

Initial studies of female aggression supported the then-prevalent view that females never fight. Young females tested at day 46 (postpubertal) in the standard dyadic test for aggressiveness did not attack (Cairns, MacCombie, & Hood, 1983; also see Lagerspetz & Lagerspetz, 1975; van Oortmerssen & Bakker, 1981). In the fifth generation of selective breeding, older females reared in isolation showed no attacks in the standard dyadic test at late maturity, age 200 days (Hood & Cairns, 1988).

That finding, however, was limited to the dyadic test setting. When female mice were housed in groups and tested at maturity in the home cage with same-age, same-sex intruders, female aggressive behavior was robust and identical in form to male aggressive behavior, with attacks, wrestling, and biting. Moreover, females from the line of high-aggressive males were more likely to attack than females from the line of low-aggressive males. Most pronounced line differences were found in studies of postpartum aggression, with maternal females showing *higher* levels of attacks than males (Table 15.1; Hood & Cairns, 1988; also see Lagerspetz & Lagerspetz, 1975; Sandnabba, 1992).

Sex Effects Depend on Age

Female aggressive development follows a different pattern than males: Females are more likely to fight later in life. To define that pattern, a life-span longitudinal study was implemented using testing procedures appropriate for females: group rearing and 10-minute home cage intruder tests with same-sex intruders. Selective breeding effects in males first appeared when male aggressiveness increased

TABLE 15.1
Attacks by Females (Postpartum) and Males (Dyadic Test)
in the Eighth Generation of Selective Breeding
for Differential Male Aggressiveness in Mice

	Selective Breeding		
Measure	High Aggressive	Control	Low Aggressive
Attack Frequency			
Female			
Mean	15.40[a]	3.93	.20
SE	2.13	1.04	.14
Male			
Mean	7.61	1.35	.00
SE	1.43	.75	.00
Attack Latency (seconds)			
Female			
Mean	15.33[a]	82.00	170.67
SE	4.15	17.41	7.67
Male			
Mean	81.09	155.88	180.00
SE	13.53	11.53	44.96

Note. [a]This cell is different from all others, for both sex and line comparisons.
n = 15 to 23 per group. The first 5 minutes of behavior tests are compared. From Hood and Cairns (1988).

early in life, after puberty, at age 46 days. Selective breeding effects in females first appeared when female aggressiveness increased later in the lifespan, at early maturity, age 90 days, and increased over maturity. Females in the high-aggressive line showed more attacks (but not decreased latency) at late maturity, age 270 days, compared to high-line females at early maturity, age 90 days (Hood, 1988, 1992b; Hood & Cairns, 1988; Table 15.2).

The most recent life-span research confirms the earlier findings. To clarify the relationship between maturation and the experience of repeated testing, two independent sets of animals were reared in small groups and tested in five intruder trials, which were given at 1-week intervals. One set of animals was tested early in life, beginning just after weaning at age 23 days and continuing through puberty to young adulthood. The other set was tested at late maturity, beginning at age 200 days. The results confirm the life-span longitudinal findings. In older mature females, aggressive behavior increased over trials until female attack frequency was equal to male frequency in the fifth trial (Fig. 15.1). Analyses of variance showed a significant interaction: Sex differences depend on age, but age by itself is not a significant factor (Hood, in preparation a; Hood, 1992b).

We can conclude that ability and willingness to fight does not require a Y chromosome. These results suggest a reinterpretation of sex-related factors in

TABLE 15.2
Attack Frequency in Selectively Bred Mice Over the Life Span:
Repeated Intruder Trials* ($\bar{x}$)

Line	Age (days)					
	30	46	90	210	270	500
High aggressive						
Females	3.33	2.44	4.56	4.56	9.44	6.14
Males	6.66	10.78	10.22	9.89	9.00	—
Low aggressive						
Females	0	0	1.22	0	.66	0
Males	4.88	5.44	1.33	1.11	.33	—

Note. *In a mixed-model ANOVA, the effect of line is significant ($p < .001$). The sex-by-age interaction shows a trend ($p < .10$). Analyses at each age show a significant effect of sex at day 46 only ($p < .05$). From Hood and Cairns (1988).

aggressive behavior, conceived not as differences in quantity of a unitary trait of aggressiveness, or in quality of aggressiveness, but rather as differences in the ecological contexts and developmental stages that support aggressive expression for each sex. Two conditions of testing, group rearing with intruder trials and maternal aggression tests, may be laboratory analogues to natural settings for female aggressiveness in wild mice. In these settings, forms of female aggression are identical to male aggression. These developmental-genetic analyses have revealed both sex-similarities—mature high-aggressive line females are behaviorally more similar to their brothers than they are to females from the other lines—and sex-differences in contexts that support aggressive behavior.

HORMONES, PUBERTY, AND FEMALE SOCIALIZATION

Sex-related developmental changes in aggressive behavior over the life span can be used as a basis for assessing hormonal effects on behavior. In animal models, sex differences in aggressive behavior do not appear until puberty, when male aggressiveness increases (Hood & Cairns, 1988). This pattern depends on testosterone in pubertal males, and also depends on genetic background, social context, previous social experience, individual responsiveness to hormones, and bidirectional effects of behavior on hormones. Social interactions such as winning or losing a conflict are sufficient to increase or decrease circulating levels of testosterone. Representative experimental studies and reviews are convergent on these points (Archer, 1991, Beeman, 1947; Brooks-Gunn, Graber, & Paikoff, 1994; Huntingford & Turner, 1987; Johnson & Whalen, 1988; Leshner, 1983; Sapolsky, 1987; Sherwin, 1988; for girls in particular, see Udry, 1988).

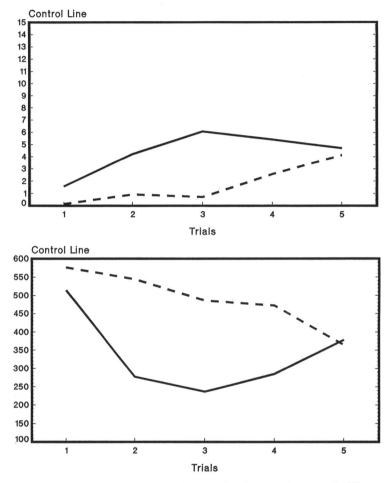

FIG. 15.1. Aggressive behavior by female and male mice at late maturity. Mice
are from the control line, the line not selectively bred for aggressive behavior.
(Parallel effects are evident in the selected lines, as presented in Hood, 1992b.)
For attack frequency (top figure) and attack latency in seconds (bottom
figure), sex differences diminish over five weekly 10-minute trials. Females =
dashed lines. Males = continuous lines.

It is important to note that in humans, the pubertal patterns are opposite to
those found in some animal studies; aggressive behavior decreases as boys
mature, and hormone–behavior relationships at puberty are not straightforward
(Buchanan, Eccles, & Becker, 1992; Inoff-Germain et al., 1988; Nottelmann et al.,
1987). In one investigation, boys who were more aggressive had low gonadal
hormones, reflecting their earlier stage of pubertal maturation compared to
other boys. Their aggressive behavior was related to anxiety, not anger, and to

higher levels of stress-related adrenal hormones (Susman, Inoff-Germain, Nottel-mann, Cutler, & Chrousos, 1987).

What happens to girls' aggressiveness at puberty? Social development is transformed when girls start to date. They leave their small groups of close girlfriends and thus may learn from older peers about smoking, drinking, having sex, or skipping school. However, direct effects of female pubertal–hormonal development on aggressive behavior are less well understood. Furthermore, little is known about maternal aggression in humans (but see the following discussion of depression). Evidence on life-span changes in hormones and aggressiveness is sparse, especially from the longitudinal designs that would be most informative. (One early study used a projective method to address women's aggressiveness in later maturity; see Neugarten & Gutmann, 1964).

Female Aggressiveness At Puberty

Female behavior at puberty has been recently investigated in nonhuman animals (Hood, in preparation b), as well as in humans. A series of experiments using young females from a line of mice bred for high-aggressiveness (discussed earlier) showed no pubertal change in attack frequency or latency. From post-weaning age until postpuberty, females had seven longitudinal intruder trials with same-age females, and were examined daily to determine first ovulation (by changes in vaginal cells). No pubertal changes were found in attack frequency (4.88 in prepubertal trials; 5.82 in postpubertal trials); latency scores showed a trend to faster attacks postpubertally. Neither accentuation nor suppression of female aggressiveness at the onset of puberty was evident in these comparative studies.

More direct effects were found in humans in an observational study of peripubertal girls, ages 9 to 14, in a series of interactions with their parents. Girls with high aggressiveness also showed high estrogen in blood samples drawn 1 or 2 days after the behavior observation (Inoff-Germain et al., 1988). In that investigation, girls were equally aggressive as boys, and their aggressive behavior was not related to age or to visible stage of pubertal development (by Tanner rating; most were not menstruating). Girls with low aggressiveness ("shows no signs of anger when aggressed against") were low in testosterone. Hormonal relationships were sparse for boys in this study.

A different set of relationships resulted from the use of self-report measures of adjustment and mothers' ratings of children's behaviors at ages 9 to 14, in an investigation by the same research team (Nottelmann et al., 1987). Girls who were rated by their mothers as aggressive or cruel were in earlier stages of pubertal development, without regard to age. Girls in earlier stages of puberty with problems in family relationships and coping had high levels of circulating andros-tenedione (a stress-related androgen of adrenal or ovarian origin). Among older girls, those in earlier stages of puberty who had problems in social relationships with peers had high levels of luteinizing hormone (of pituitary origin). Independent of age or pubertal status, girls (but not boys) with acting out or depression problems showed low levels of the stress-related adrenal hormone DHEAS.

The interpretation of these relationships is furthered by the evidence from another set of studies. Nonlinear relationships of estrogen and aggressive affect were suggested by findings of Brooks-Gunn and Warren (1989). For girls age 10 to 14, each tested one time, those with higher levels of self-reported aggressive affect showed lower levels of estrogen, independent of visible pubertal stage (by Tanner rating; most were not menstruating), and affect increased with estrogen before leveling off and declining. Girls with high aggressive affect had low DHEAS: In particular, low DHEAS girls with high aggressiveness reported negative life events related to peers. Followed up a year later, those girls were no longer reporting high aggressive affect; stressful events did not persist. However, a parallel nonlinear relationship between the first year's estrogen level and aggressive affect in the second year did persist, with increasing aggressive affect associated with low and/or rising levels of estrogen (Paikoff, Brooks-Gunn, & Warren, 1991). In the second year, physical maturation partially mediated the estrogen-aggressive affect relationship, as girls' bodies manifested the developmental changes wrought by puberty during the year.

These results are interpreted by Paikoff et al. as reflecting the perturbation of girls' psychological equilibrium by rising titres of estrogen at early puberty, with later adjustment by girls to adult patterns of hormonal ebb and flow. Similarly, in the work by Inoff-Germain et al. (1988), girls in early stages of pubertal maturation might have been activated by first exposures to rising estrogen, and then adapting after some months of exposure. The two findings of low DHEAS and high aggressiveness recall Magnusson's (1988) finding of low adrenaline in stimulus-seeking high aggressive boys, and Udry's (1988) findings with low-DHEA girls. Interestingly, in a cross-sectional design (Udry and Talbert, 1988), both girls and boys showed an *extraversion* personality factor related to high testosterone during puberty, and girls in particular showed a relationship between follicular progesterone and self-reported aggression, independent of age or pubertal stage.

However, just as in studies of hormone–behavior relationships in males, these findings are subject to uncertainty about the direction of effects: Are events or changing life situations causing hormonal–behavioral responses? The animal literature supports this interpretation: for example, females may delay puberty in response to stressful social conditions (Bronson, 1985). The conclusion reached by Buchanan et al. (1992) in their careful review applies: "Are adolescents the victims of raging hormones?" It is "still an open question" (p. 98). Those authors call for longitudinal research to address the issues of social or biological priority in relation to behavioral change. Whether most longitudinal designs are sufficiently discriminating to characterize the nexus of event-related hormonal changes at puberty remains to be seen.

Social Transformation of Girls' Aggressive Behavior

What happens in the lives of children and adults to produce and maintain the reliable (if modest) gender difference in aggressive expression? To consistently shape this most energetic and effective form of social interaction, the engendering process must be both pervasive and powerful. The physiological transformation of girls into women is accompanied by explicit and implicit programs of socialization from peers, teachers, parents, and media. The values transmitted in middle-class Euro-American gender socialization are designed to transform rambunctious girls into sedate young ladies who are nice, caring of others, and cooperative. This socialization process is a potential source of behavior change in adolescence. In addition, as the child grows tall and begins to resemble a woman, the instantaneous responses of social partners are altered, to produce another likely source of change in girls' behavior. These social factors can be considered in tandem with the increase of sex hormones and the onset of menstrual cycles as possible causes of behavior change in adolescent girls.

Developmental analyses contrasting children and college students show an age-related decline. Overt aggressive behavior is more likely in children than in college students, and gender differences are larger in children (studies of older adults are scarce). These developmental changes are interpreted as the result of sanctions against overt aggression in adolescence and adulthood (Hyde, 1984, 1986; Maccoby & Jacklin, 1974). If the age-related decline in aggressive behavior results from social sanctions, might children's gendered patterns also result from social sanctions? Evidence to support that possibility (Perry, Perry, & Weiss, 1989) shows that girls expect more parental disapproval for aggression than boys.

Comprehensive longitudinal designs are required to fully address these issues. Findings from one major investigation, the Carolina Longitudinal Study, are presented to illustrate the unique contributions of that design (Cairns & Cairns, 1994). One method employed in that study is to pursue the obvious, to chart the phenomenon of interest over development by directly observing overt manifestations of aggressive behavior in social interactions. Another method is to ask people whether and why they act aggressively. The tantalizing outcome is that with the same subjects, the two methods produce incompatible results. For another example, a common and puzzling discrepancy is the finding that teachers and other observers rate boys as more aggressive than they rate girls, while girls and boys rate themselves as equally aggressive (for another recent example, see Pulkkinen & Pitkanen, 1993). Why is there disagreement on such a salient feature of social life?

The use of multiple methods in the Carolina Longitudinal Study gives some purchase on the question. An unexpected bonus of the extensive contextual analysis developed in this work is that the combination of methods—direct observation of behavior, self-ratings, teacher ratings, and peer nominations—reveals a developmental process particular to girls, a subtle segue that explains the puzzling discrepancy, and more.

Silence and Social Sabotage Among Girls

An obvious pattern of gender differences in aggressive behavior emerges from direct behavior observations of early adolescent girls. In one set of school-based observations, subjects were the center of focal observations for 30 to 60 minutes daily on four consecutive days (Cairns, Perrin, & Cairns, 1985). Girls showed very high rates of positive interactions among their friends (Table 15.3) However, negative interactions by girls were relatively rare. Most notably, girls almost never retaliated overtly against other girls when provoked, but they were quite likely to retaliate against boys (Table 15.4; Cairns, Perrin, & Cairns, unpublished manuscript).

What was not obvious was revealed, by contrast, spontaneously in conversations. Retaliation against girls did occur, and powerfully, in a qualitatively different form than retaliation against boys. The girls reported in interviews that when a girl made them angry, they would not retaliate directly (as shown in girls' low rates of retaliation in Table 15.4). However, when asked, "What do you do when a girl makes you angry?", girls spontaneously described a different tactic of retaliation—by social sabotage. "I call her names—not to her face, but behind her back." "I just don't talk to her, and I tell my friends not to talk to her." "Most of us get along, and if we don't get along with that person, we just don't talk to 'em" (Cairns, Perrin, & Cairns, unpublished manuscript). What girls do to girls is to use social sabotage, ostracism, and in-group shunning, forms of behavior that are invisible to an outside observer, but readily apparent to the target of aggression. Against the background of very high rates of friendly interaction among girlfriends (Table 15.3), omissions of friendly behavior and acts of deliberate social exclusion would be obvious to those embedded in the social network. The data show that girls are capable of overt fighting: They

TABLE 15.3
Positive and Negative Interactions With
In-group and Out-group Peers: Rate Per Hour

| | Positive (Compliment, help, play, etc.) | | Negative (Hit, insult, argue, etc.) | |
	In-group	Out-group	In-group	Out-group
Girls	5.16	1.18	0.29	0.19
Boys	2.68	0.59	0.57	0.27

Note. Junior high students observed in an academic classroom and a physical education classroom (n = 5 girls and 5 boys as focal subjects) for 3.7 hours each, on average. In-group = cluster of friends. Out-group = other peers. Adapted from Cairns, Perrin, and Cairns (1985). Reprinted with permission.

TABLE 15.4
Behavioral Observation of Negative Acts Against Same-Sex
or Opposite-Sex Peer Aggressors: Conditional Probability
of Behavioral Response After Provocation

	Behavioral Response	
Subjects	Retaliate	Ignore
	Same-Sex Aggressor	
Girls	.03	.97
Boys	.18	.79
	Opposite-Sex Aggressor	
Girls	.28	.68
Boys	.30	.78

Note. Junior high students observed in an academic classroom and a physical education classroom ($n = 10$ girls and 10 boys as focal subjects) for about 4 hours each, on four consecutive days. Adapted from Cairns, Perrin, and Cairns (unpublished manuscript). Reprinted with permission.

retaliate with direct aggression against offending boys. However, what they do to offending girls is a form of covert aggression, a socially sophisticated form of social sabotage that also is intended to harm.

Girls' Aggression Goes Underground

The developmental progression of this pattern of social sabotage is clear in the longitudinal assessments of 220 children from age 10 (Grade 4) to age 13 (Grade 7; Cairns, Cairns, Neckerman, Ferguson, & Gariépy, 1989). In behavior observations, girls were equal in overt aggression to boys in fourth grade, and girls were equal to boys in being nominated as aggressive by teachers and by peers. In interviews, 33% of girls reported fighting with boys, compared to 45% of boys who fought with boys. By the seventh grade, girls were less overtly aggressive than boys and less likely to be nominated by teachers as aggressive (Cairns & Cairns, 1986). In interviews, girls reported less physical aggression (24%), while boys did not change. However, by the seventh grade, these same girls had developed a new form of aggressive behavior. In fourth grade, 10% of girls reported that they used ostracism, social exclusion, or character defamation to express conflict. In the same girls 3 years later, about 50% reported using these tactics, a significant developmental increase. Girls are the primary targets of this new form: 46% of girls reported ostracizing other girls, and 23% of girls reported ostracizing boys. Boys reported this method of aggression significantly less often: 18% reported ostracism against other boys and 9% reported ostracism against girls (Cairns & Cairns, unpublished manuscript).

Factor analyses of aggression measures show that a distinctive *social aggression* (ostracism) factor emerges for seventh-grade but not fourth-grade girls, and not for boys at any age. The developmental emergence of social sabotage marks a developmental shift in girls' expression of aggression. "Social manipulation and ostracism—as involved in alienation, rumors, and social rejection—emerges as a major property of aggressive behavior in early adolescence, especially for girls. . . . Rather than report everyday offenses of peers to adults as they did in childhood, adolescent girls report to each other" (Cairns et al., 1989, p. 328).

This developmental transformation of the expression of aggression in girls is key to resolving the puzzling disparity of self-reports and others' reports of children's aggressiveness. Here, teacher ratings and peer nominations show gender differences while self-ratings do not. Lower ratings by teachers and peers are correlated with lower levels of observed aggressive acts for girls ($.69 < r < .94$), while self-ratings are not. Girls rate themselves as significantly more aggressive than teachers rate them. Boys do not. These patterns make sense once it is known that girls' aggression has gone underground, invisible to nonintimate peers, and to adult authorities. For teachers, an expected social greeting that does not occur is not a classroom management problem. Even to the target, the source of the social sabotage may not be known. "And what is hidden to the victim may also be hidden to the researcher" (Cairns et al., 1989, p. 329; also see Loeber & Schmaling, 1985). However, girls know what they do to hurt others, with full intent, and they report themselves accordingly as equal in aggressiveness to anyone.

The reality of these "hidden" effects is demonstrated in studies showing peak levels of social sabotage in 11-year-old girls (Björkqvist, Lagerspetz, & Kaukianen, 1992; Lagerspetz & Björkqvist, 1994; Lagerspetz, Björkqvist, & Peltonen, 1988; Paul & Baenninger, 1991). For example, among girls in 7th to 11th grades, "feeling left out of a group" was by far the most frequently reported of a variety of stressful circumstances. Over 70% of girls reported this as a negative circumstance in their life. Such negative circumstances were found to predict depressed moods months later, especially for seventh grade girls (Siegel & Brown, 1988). Other longitudinal studies provide additional support. In the multiethnic sample of Werner and Smith (1992), adolescent girls, but not boys, reported stressful conflicts with peers (Table 27). In the prospective study by Gjerde, Block, and Block (1988), a subset of depressed girls described themselves as highly aggressive, but without any overt expressions of aggressiveness (also see Block, Gjerde, & Block, 1991).

In the qualitative research of Brown and Gilligan (1992), the voices of the girls experiencing this "relational treachery" are revealed: "So she has this group of all the people that she thinks are pretty and nice and very smart, and she takes them into her group and teaches them not to like certain people, and then she uses other people to get information out of some people . . . she's just mean . . ." (p. 101). Asked how she would deal with a disagreement with a friend, one girl said, "I don't know, by doing probably what you wanted to do in a way that would be discreet enough so that you wouldn't like—so that you wouldn't . . . I don't know, make it too obvious." She said she prefers "a pleasant fight, you know, where you kind of ignore the person or just try to step back" (Brown & Gilligan, 1992, p. 205).

Strong corroboration of these findings was presented by Crick and Grotpeter (1995), in their valuable descriptive study of children's "relational aggression" or social sabotage. Girls in grades 3 to 6 who practice relational aggression report more depression and less acceptance by peers. Those girls are likely to be classified as controversial, that is, strongly liked by some peers and strongly disliked by others. Based on this finding, Crick and Grotpeter raise concern about serious maladjustment for girls, but not boys, who practice relational aggression. They also offer an alternative interpretation: Relationally aggressive girls are invested with "social authority" in their peer group to determine who joins and who leaves.

Because of the co-occurrence of factors in their naturalistic setting, Crick and Grotpeter (1995) used covariance analysis to statistically remove the effects of overt aggressive behavior. With overt aggression effects controlled for statistically, the additional factors that characterize relational aggression might be revealed. By this method, overt (boys') aggression is characterized by *higher* levels of social adjustment (footnote 2, p. 716) while relational (girls') aggression is characterized by *lower* levels of social adjustment. However, statistically removing the effects of gender and gender norms is not simple because many more boys than girls (in the sample) practice overt aggression and many more girls than boys practice relational aggression. The portion of these sex differences in aggression-adjustment relationships that is due to more general gender-related differences in adjustment, and the portion that is due to qualities specific to relational or overt aggression is not clear. Perhaps spirited girls who violate gender norms early in life by using overt aggression are disliked by some peers. Those girls might later learn to substitute relational aggression to achieve their ends. The issue of individual continuity—whether young girls high in overt aggression later are high in relational aggression—remains to be considered.

Developmental Sequelae of Social Sabotage by Girls: Increased Depression?

The increase of depression in girls and women in adolescence and early adulthood is well documented (Petersen et al., 1993; Moffitt, 1993). Twice as many females as males become depressed after age 13 and stay depressed through midlife, for reasons that are not clear (Nolen-Hoeksema, Girgus, & Seligman, 1991; Petersen, Sariagni, & Kennedy, 1991). Longitudinal prospective analyses show that for girls, but not boys, it was the more intelligent children, and those with close long-term friendships who at age 14 lost poise, felt inadequate, and at age 18 became depressed (Gjerde & Block, 1991; also see Siegel & Brown, 1988). Though not viewed by observers as aggressive, depressed girls in that study rated themselves as highly aggressive. Evidence for denial of anger and masked depression was found through nonlinear relationships. These patterns may follow from the oversocialization of girls (Block, 1983), constraints on agency, and the redirection of anger inward to produce passivity, dependence, and low self-esteem (Allgood-Merton, Lewinsohn, & Hops, 1990; Gjerde & Block, 1991; Leadbeater, Blatt, & Quinlan, 1995; Levit, 1991; Nolen-Hoeksema, 1994; Zahn-Waxler, Cole, & Barrett, 1991).

In a subsequent report, Gjerde (1995) found that depression at age 23 is predictable from girls' passive and intropunitive personality at age 7, and from boys' active and aggressive personality at age 7. Predictors for womens' depression are few and are less coherent over time than are predictors for mens' depression. Gjerde proposed that there are different gender pathways to depression. As girls enter puberty the newly imposed and more extensive constraints of adult gender roles most powerfully affect the empathic, intelligent girls; these girls, at ages 18 and 23, show higher levels of depression. Gjerde further noted that maladjustment may consist of either overaggressiveness or underaggressiveness, with a balanced expressive style most beneficial for both girls and boys.

Social relationships with boys and with adults also become more complex. Sexual harassment at school and elsewhere increases at adolescence, and continues through adulthood. An outstanding majority, 80%, of adolescent girls report having experienced sexual harassment (Cutler & Nolen-Hoeksema, 1991). Girls report feeling afraid and less confident, and less likely to speak in class as a consequence; they are likely to alter their activities at school to avoid male harassers (*Hostile Hallways*, 1993). These gendered patterns may also contribute to the coincident increase in depression in girls at that age. Ironically, Gilligan (1991) discloses that it is adult women whose socialization silenced girls in the all-female environment of one girls' school. These dynamics are best understood in the larger context of the social environment of both women and girls. (For a cultural and literary analysis of traditional suppression of girls by women, see Walker, 1992.) Why do girls practice social sabotage? The answer may relate to gendered patterns of sexual debasement in the tangle of attitudes about sex and gender that presently constitute sex-role socialization.

Social sabotage continues in gendered patterns in adulthood. In a study of harassment in the workplace, Björkqvist, Osterman, and Lagerspetz (1994) found that women and men are equally aggressive, but women are more likely to use "social manipulation" and men are more likely to use "rational-appearing" aggression (interrupting others, directly criticizing others). Their scale of "social manipulation" includes omission of acts as well as commission of acts: backbiting, spreading of false rumors, insinuations without direct accusation, not being spoken to, and "do-not-speak-to-me" behavior. This finding suggests that girls' aggression goes underground and stays underground through adulthood, even in professional settings.

MENSTRUAL–BEHAVIORAL CHANGE
AND BELIEFS ABOUT PMS

Female aggressiveness in adulthood has been investigated rarely, and more often in the context of pathology than normative development. One reason may be the assumption that menstrual-related hormonal factors influence women's aggressive behavior. However, tracking natural variations in hormones during the ovulatory cycle and assessing the extent of corresponding behavior changes is a reasonable strategy for studying biological factors in aggressiveness.

Menstrual Cycles and Observed Behavior Change

During the ovulatory cycle in females, the sex hormones estradiol and progesterone, show large and predictable changes. Behavior observations of female rats show increased attacks on other females when subjects are in the postovulatory phase of low progesterone (Hood, 1984). Because this phase of the estrus cycle corresponds to the premenstrual phase of the menstrual cycle, the finding seems to parallel the stereotype of premenstrual syndrome (PMS) which includes, among other changes, a hypothesized increase in irritability and aggressiveness during the days before menstruation. By current stereotypes, and by some clinical reports, this syndrome afflicts most women. However, many studies of nonclinical samples find that when women are not aware of the purpose of the study, their daily self-reports of mood do not show PMS. Most recently, studies with hormonal assessments and self-reports include Laessle, Tuschi, Schweiger, and Pirke (1990) and Gallant, Popiel, Hoffman, Chakraborty, and Hamilton (1992). (See also Abplanalp, Donnelly, & Rose, 1979; Golub & Harrington, 1981; Koeske, 1983; Lahmeyer, Miller, & DeLeon-Jones, 1982; Mansfield, Hood, & Henderson, 1989; McFarlane, Martin, & Williams, 1988; Rossi & Rossi, 1977; Sanders, Warner, Backstrom, & Bancroft, 1983; Wilcoxon, Schrader, & Sherif, 1976; Woods, Dery, & Most, 1982; see Parlee, 1982, for a review.)

   To extend the study of menstrual cycle effects to direct observations of social behavior, rather than self-reports, a prospective longitudinal observational study of 30 female college students was implemented (see Hood, 1992a, for a brief report). Four videotaped weekly meetings were designed to present two different social contexts, one of unstructured social interaction, and one structured to provoke social conflict during a challenging discussion. In addition, daily self-reports of mood were collected. Subjects were naive about the purpose of the experiment.

   Were women more aggressive or assertive during the premenstrual phase? Occasions on which women stated their own opinions during the challenging discussions were coded. By this measure, women's assertiveness, or efficacy (Table 15.5) does not change during the menstrual cycle. Menstrual cycle changes in behavior do occur, but not in patterns that support the stereotype of PMS.

TABLE 15.5
Contextual Determinants of Menstrual Cycle
Effects in Observations of Social Interactions

	Outcome by Context	
Observed Behaviors	Unstructured Situation	Structured Discussion
Efficacy	—	no change
Assertive style	menstrual phase < midcycle	no change
Responsive style	no change	no change
Nonverbal-social	no change	no change
Nonverbal-activity	no change	premenstrual > midcycle

Note. Midcycle = Days 8–14 (follicular phase) plus Days 15–21 (luteal phase).
Unstructured situation: 5 minutes of social interaction with no task orientation.
Structured discussion: 5 minutes of discussion of an assigned moral or social problem of significant complexity. Topics were chosen based on individual subjects' self-reported opinions so that each subject disagreed with the two other group members during the coded discussion.

Context-dependent changes are found during the menstrual phase, the period of menstrual flow. The frequency of assertive-style social participation (coded if the subject asked a question, answered a question, or told a story) is lower during the menstrual phase but only during the unstructured interactions. In the context of structured discussions, assertive-social participation does not show menstrual phase effects. Responsive style participation (the subject answered a question, or agreed with someone) and nonverbal behaviors expressing social interest do not change by phase or by context. However, nonverbal activity scores (arm, leg, and foot movement) are elevated during the structured discussions, with significantly higher activity in the premenstrual phase than in the follicular phase.

At the end of the study period, subjects were asked to describe their changes during their most recent menstrual cycle, using a standard instrument. Retrospective self-reports of "feeling aggressive" during the weeks around menses showed a PMS-like pattern, with significantly higher levels in the premenstrual week. However, in daily self-reports collected over 30 days, no corresponding effect is found in the same subjects' reports of "feeling aggressive" for those same days, and no corresponding behavior change is noted in the weekly observations of social interactions.

In this study, the only one (to our knowledge) using direct observations of social behaviors, women who believe they are more aggressive during the premenstrual phase do not show behaviors corresponding to their beliefs about PMS. Women's beliefs about their own biology (perhaps based on comparative studies with animal models) do not reflect their own behavior, by this finding. In addition, women's daily self-reports of mood do not reflect increased aggressiveness in the premenstrual phase of the cycle. In this situation, subjects' beliefs about the effects of PMS seem to influence their retrospective accounts more substantially than do their actual experiences during their menstrual cycle. (For an impressive demonstration of PMS belief effects on self-report, see Ruble, 1977; see also Bains & Slade, 1988. Alternatively, real behaviors may be attributed to physiology. Zoccolillo [1993] reported that girls with conduct disorder are prone to somatization, with "unexplained somatic complaints.")

The social consequences of popular beliefs about biology and behavior may obscure the analysis of bidirectional effects, and even prevent scientific detection or correction of popular misconceptions. For example, beliefs about women's impairment due to PMS might obstruct women's access to high-status positions, and thereby deny women the psychological and physiological benefits that accrue from high-status positions (Rodin & Ickovics, 1990). If that were the case, then those beliefs about biological causation would become self-fulfilling entirely through social processes.

FEMALE BIOLOGY AND AGGRESSION IN CONTEXT

Biological sex is a concrete category that is used every day to organize social life. Individuals can identify their own correct sex category—female or male—with exceptionally high reliability. The relative lack of intermediate sex categories (but see Unger, 1993) lends credibility to the presupposition that sex-typed behaviors are exclusive, nonoverlapping sets. In fact, the opposite is more accurate. The distribution of even the most extreme sex-typed behaviors, such as aggressive behavior, are 95% overlapping, with large sex differences only at the extremes. The apparent confusion of biological and behavioral categories is further perpetuated by the use of clinical and criminal populations to characterize normal developmental patterns.

Criminal and Clinical Outcomes
and Developmental Interventions

In both criminal violations and clinical diagnoses, the gendered pattern is clear: Women are 2 to 9 times less likely than men to become violent offenders or antisocial personalities, and 2 times more likely to have depressive or affective disorders (Eaton et al., 1989; Gove, 1985; Regier et al., 1988; Robins, 1986). For example, in a longitudinal British sample, 18% of males and 2.5% of females had been arrested by age 25, and self-reports of violent acts were 4.5 times more frequent in males than females (Rutter & Giller, 1983). Arrests for criminal violence reflect these gendered patterns. Manslaughter arrests are 90% male, and assault arrests are 86% male. The most prevalent female crimes are nonviolent ones: larceny (32% female) and fraud (43% female; Maguire, Pastore, & Flanagan, 1993). Female crimes of property have increased in recent years, but not violent crimes (Gove, 1985). The evidence for biological causation of female crime is inconclusive (Widom & Ames, 1988).

Nevertheless, women can and occasionally do murder and maim. The developmental consequences of serious aggression by girls are equally dire as they are for boys (Cairns et al., 1989; Tremblay, 1991; Robins, 1986; Zoccolillo, 1993). For example, aggressive girls may as adults apply strong punishment to their children, perpetuating the cycle (Huesmann, Eron, Lefkowitz, & Walder, 1984). Girls with behavior problems are less likely than boys to have access to therapy (Offord, Boyle, & Racine, 1991). Choosing the most helpful intervention strategies for aggressive or depressed women and girls depends on understanding the development of the problem, imagining other possible pathways in development, and how to bring those about.

The prospective longitudinal study by Werner and Smith (1992) provides a rich, comprehensive account of gendered developmental pathways. In frequent assessments from age 1 year to age 31 years, girls and boys show quite distinct and different ensembles of protective factors and risk factors for criminal outcomes and poor adaptation. For 31-year-old women, protective factors reflect an easy and sociable temperament at age 1 year and adolescent girls' strong sense of self: high self-esteem and a strong sense of efficacy. Risk factors derive from conflict among peers and family during adolescence, especially for delinquent girls (see Werner & Smith, 1992, Table 13, p. 226 and Table 20, p. 232). For the subgroup of high-risk girls, social support, especially by teen peers, functions as a protective factor (see Werner & Smith, 1992, and Fig. A4, p. 245 and Table 28, p. 241).

It might be assumed that for girls at risk from poverty or family discord, compliance to external authority would provide a path to safety. Surprisingly, for high-risk girls (but not boys), an important protective factor is having a strong internal locus of control. Rather than supporting delinquent behaviors, such an inner focus acts to preserve healthy goals of girls in high-risk or low-opportunity situations until those goals can be implemented, often later in life when women are in their late 20s.

Although delinquent girls at age 18 report feelings of anger equal to boys, and equal proportions of girls and boys commit violent crimes, more of the girls had recovered by age 31, suggesting greater resilience by women in early adulthood. For at-risk girls in the sample, the most resilient are significantly *more* assertive and independent than other girls in that cohort. (By contrast, resilient boys are more nurturant than other boys.) It seems that by transcending the limits of sex roles, resilient youths were enabled to assemble support from a wider range of abilities (Werner & Smith, 1992).

The present discussion, based on studies of normative patterns, may usefully inform the process of intervention. The interpretation proposed is that girls' healthy aggression and confidence is socially suppressed at puberty or before. Subverted, it goes underground, with subsequent depression and vicious social sabotage (Cairns et al., 1989; Gjerde, 1995; Gjerde & Block, 1991). Social exclusion and acts of social sabotage produce pervasive effects distributed widely, and cannot be countered effectively. They derive from hurtful intentions to damage the target psychologically and socially in that most important social setting of adolescence, the peer group. For girls in early adolescence, a time of heightened self-consciousness, vulnerability to sexual abuse, and vulnerability to depression, social sabotage may produce pain more intense than a bust in the chops. As Cairns et al. (1989) noted, this new tactic of social sabotage may account for emergence in early adolescence of trust and loyalty as central components of friendship.

If girls abjure physical attack, these other formidable powers are available to them in the reckoning of social accounts. However, the indirect quality of the attack by sabotage may prolong anger in girls compared to boys (Lagerspetz, Björkqvist, & Peltonen, 1988), undermine self-efficacy (Campbell, Muncer, & Coyle, 1992), and prevent conflict resolution. The depression that may result in victims and in perpetrators is rarely recognized, even by those closest to youngsters: For example, Paikoff et al. (1991) found no correlation between mothers' and daughters' reports of girls' depression. In the work by Gjerde, Block, and Block (1988), depressed girls were rated as highly aggressive by their own report, but not by others. The loss of liveliness in a dull, unresponsive, uncommunicative adolescent may be overlooked by teachers and parents.

How can one prevail with an intangible foe? Can anger provide its own cure? By clinical accounts, some kinds of anger can cure. But, it is not the humiliated fury of the suppressed or inferior-status person that will release such a gnarly knot, it is the expression of "righteous indignation" by a person with self-worth, supported by significant others, with reasonable expectation of success (Lewis, 1986). The therapeutic context can provide a haven for the expression of righteous indignation, perhaps thereby preventing the explosions of humiliated fury that characterize violent and assaultive behavior (Franks, 1979). For example, in the current research literature on self-concept, highest attainment of mental health is found in girls and women who describe themselves as androgynous, with features of both female and male stereotyped traits (Bem, 1985) as in the assertive resilient girls in Werner and Smith (1992). Accordingly, the course of therapy might turn from accepting the limits of the feminine sex role stereotype to supporting an unconstrained exploration of women's individual interests and abilities (Eccles, 1987). Rather than dosing clients with Valium or Prozac, progressive therapists might employ assertiveness training and peer-based consciousness-raising for promoting mental health. The transition from childhood to adolescence may be an especially crucial developmental moment for preserving girls' agency through intervention, education, and social support.

The pervasive and unconscious quality of gender stereotypes often obscures their influence in clinical practice (see Kaplan, 1992, and following discussions: Fodor, 1993; Mirkin, 1994; Pugliesi, 1992. Also see the journal *Women and Therapy*, volumes 5 and 9). A continuous and exacting scrutiny of gender stereotypes offers the possibility of reexamining their basis and correcting their harmful effects.

Healthy Forms of Women's Aggressive and Assertive Behavior

Assertive behavior, which consists of socially appropriate forms of aggressive behavior, is an important asset in competitive social situations. This is evident in advertisements seeking to employ "aggressive sales managers" and "aggressive self-starters." In educational settings, also, assertiveness is an asset. In a longitudinal study of 173 girls from age 8 to age 26 (Pulkinnen & Pitkanen, 1993), those judged by peers and teachers to be high in aggressiveness at age 8 were more likely to continue in higher education than girls in the midaggressive group. This surprising finding was explicated by contrasting physically aggressive girls, who were likely to quit school after the ninth grade (and then to become involved in criminal activities), and verbally and facially aggressive girls, who were more likely to go on to university-level studies. Boys did not show meaningful differences on this dimension. The result is interpreted as indicating that verbal and facial aggression may be an indicator in girls of a "strong temperament which is needed for academic achievements." (See also Purifoy & Koopmans, 1980; Werner & Smith, 1992, p. 56, for examples of resilient assertive girls; by contrast, for examples of depressed girls who are impaired in schoolwork and peer relationships see Nolen-Hoeksema & Girgus, 1994.)

Self-defense is a form of healthy aggressive behavior. Presently in the United States, acts of sexual violence against women are more likely to be committed by familiar than unfamiliar mates (Maguire, Pastore, & Flanagan, 1993, Table 3.27, p. 267). Comparative studies show that appropriate defensive aggression is abundantly available to females: Maternal aggression by females is fast and furious, and aggression against strange female intruders is formidable (Hood, 1992b). In humans, Pulkkinnen (1987) has shown that defensive aggression is associated with good adjustment in girls, whereas offensive aggression is associated with poor adjustment. An instance of healthy resistance by girls, from Orenstein's (1994) vivid documentary, employed social sabotage: ". . . he made an obscene comment to one of the girls in the class. All of the girls immediately bonded together and stopped speaking to him, even though he subsequently apologized . . . (because) 'He always apologizes, but then he does it again. We don't have to take that any more.' " Increased societal support for women and children to appropriately defend themselves may increase assertive, constructive responses to threat, and reduce the prevalence of desperate violent reactions.

Cross-cultural comparisons offer some insights into the range of possible social arrangements. In contemporary populations in the United States, gender differences in aggressive behavior, depression, influenceability, dominance, and leadership styles are less pronounced in African-American than Euro-American populations. Some studies show more androgynous mixtures of personality traits, with high levels of agentic and instrumental abilities in African-American women compared to White women. Black women are more likely than White women to endorse nonsubordinate roles for women, with higher goals for employment and education, more expectancies for success, and less conflict about combining work and family roles. (The valuable review by Lips, 1993, provides documentation for these outcomes; but see the debate in Tieger, 1980, and Maccoby & Jacklin, 1980.) The contemporaneous reality of more gender-egalitarian groups underscores the possibility of attaining gender equity for all groups. Contextual analysis and diversity-focused research aimed at understanding the sources of variability among groups can reveal the processes that maintain gender differences, and those that support gender–role transcendence.

A more complete account of the social conditions that constrain appropriate assertive expression for women, and the conditions that support it, will expand the present understanding of possible and optimal futures. This expanded vision is the context in which global conceptions of biological gender differences can be evaluated. Placing women at the center of the analysis, rather than in the margins as a special case, puts into perspective the potential contribution of free expression to women's healthy development.

ACKNOWLEDGMENTS

Grateful acknowledgments are due to Bonnie Barber, Bob Cairns, Lisa Crockett, Marcy Lansman, Susan McHale, Peter Molenaar, Anne Petersen, and Jacki Weinstock for their support of the research reported here and their help in the preparation of this chapter.

REFERENCES

Abplanalp, J. M., Donnelly, A. F., & Rose, R. M. (1979). Psychoendocrinology of the menstrual cycle. I. Enjoyment of daily activities and moods. *Psychosomatic Medicine, 41*, 587–604.

Allgood-Merton, B., Lewinsohn, P. M., & Hops, H. (1990). Sex differences and adolescent depression. *Journal of Abnormal Psychology, 99*, 55–63.

Archer, J. (1991). The influence of testosterone on human aggression. *British Journal of Psychology, 82*, 1–28.

Bains, G. K., & Slade, P. (1988). Attribution patterns, moods, and the menstrual cycle. *Psychosomatic Medicine, 50*, 469–476.

Beeman, E. A. (1947). The effect of male hormone on aggressive behavior in mice. *Physiological Zoology, 20*, 313–405.

Bem, S. (1985). Androgyny and gender schema theory: A conceptual and empirical integration. In T. B. Sonderegger (Ed.), *Nebraska Symposium on motivation: Vol. 32. Psychology and gender* (pp. 179–226). Lincoln: University of Nebraska Press.

Björkqvist, K., Lagerspetz, K. M. J., & Kaukianen, A. (1992). Do girls manipulate and boys fight? Developmental trends in regard to direct and indirect aggression. *Aggressive Behavior, 18*, 117–127.

Björkqvist, K., Osterman, K., & Lagerspetz, K. M. J. (1994). Sex differences in covert aggression among adults. *Aggressive Behavior, 20*, 27–33.

Block, J. H. (1983). Differential premises arising from differential socialization of the sexes: Some conjectures. *Child Development, 54,* 1335–1354.

Block, J. H., Gjerde, P. F., & Block, J. H. (1991). Personality antecedents of depressive tendencies in 18-year-olds: A prospective study. *Journal of Personality and Social Psychology, 60,* 726–738.

Bronson, F. H. (1985). Mammalian reproduction: An ecological perspective. *Biology of Reproduction, 32,* 1–26.

Brooks-Gunn, J., Graber, J. A., & Paikoff, R. L. (1994). Studying links between hormones and negative affect: Models and measures. *Journal of Research on Adolescence, 4,* 469–486.

Brooks-Gunn, J., & Warren, M. P. (1989). Biological and social contributions to negative affect in young adolescent girls. *Child Development, 60,* 40–55.

Brown, L. M., & Gilligan, C. (1992). *Meeting at the crossroads: Womens' psychology and girls' development.* Cambridge, MA: Harvard University Press.

Buchanan, C. M., Eccles, J. S., & Becker, J. B. (1992). Are adolescents the victims of raging hormones: Evidence for activational effects of hormones on moods and behavior at adolescence. *Psychological Bulletin, 111,* 62–107.

Cairns, R. B., & Cairns, B. D. (unpublished manuscript). Aggressive behavior, social structure, and social cognition: Gender similarities and differences in highly aggressive elementary school children. University of North Carolina, Chapel Hill.

Cairns, R. B., & Cairns, B. D. (1986). The developmental-interactional view of social behavior: Four issues of adolescent aggression. In D. Olweus, J. Block, & M. Radke-Yarrow (Eds.), *Development of antisocial and prosocial behavior* (pp. 315–342). New York: Academic Press.

Cairns, R. B., & Cairns, B. D. (1994). *Lifelines and risks: Pathways of youth in our time.* Cambridge, England: Cambridge University Press.

Cairns, R. B., Cairns, B. D., Neckerman, H. J., Ferguson, L. L., & Gariépy, J.-L. (1989). Growth and aggression: I. Childhood to early adolescence. *Developmental Psychology, 25,* 320–330.

Cairns, R. B., Gariépy, J.-L., & Hood, K. E. (1990). Development, microevolution, and social behavior. *Psychological Review, 97,* 49–65.

Cairns, R. B., MacCombie, D. J., & Hood, K. E. (1983). A developmental-genetic analysis of aggressive behavior in mice: I. Behavioral outcomes. *Journal of Comparative Psychology, 97,* 69–89.

Cairns, R. B., Perrin, J. E., & Cairns, B. D. (unpublished manuscript). Social cognition and social behavior in adolescence: Aggressive patterns. University of North Carolina, Chapel Hill.

Cairns, R. B., Perrin, J. E., & Cairns, B. D. (1985). Social structure and social cognition in early adolescence: Affiliative patterns. *Journal of Early Adolescence, 5,* 339–355.

Campbell, A., Muncer, S., & Coyle, E. (1992). Social representation of aggression as an explanation of gender differences: A preliminary study. *Aggressive Behavior, 18,* 95–108.

Crick, N. K., & Grotpeter, J. K. (1995). Relational aggression, gender, and social-psychological adjustment. *Child Development, 66,* 710–722.

Cutler, S. E., & Nolen-Hoeksema, S. (1991). Accounting for sex differences in depression through female victimization: Childhood sexual abuse. *Sex Roles, 24,* 425–438.

Delphy, C. (1993). Rethinking sex and gender. *Women's Studies International Forum, 10,* 1–9.

Eagly, A. H., & Steffen, B. J. (1986). Gender and aggressive behavior: A meta-analytic review of the social psychological literature. *Psychological Bulletin, 100,* 309–330.

Eaton, W. W., Kramer, M., Anthony, J. C., Dryman, A., Shapiro, S., & Locke, B. Z. (1989). The incidence of specific DIS/DSM–III mental disorders: Data from the NIMH Epidemiologic Catchment Area Program. *Acta Psychiatrica Scandinavican, 79,* 163–178.

Eccles, J. S. (1987). Adolescence: Gateway to gender-role transcendence. In D. B. Carter (Ed.), *Current conceptions of sex roles and sex typing: Theory and research* (pp. 225–241). New York: Praeger.

Foder, I. G. (1993). A feminist framework for integrative psychotherapy. In G. Strickler & J. R. Gold (Eds.), *Comprehensive handbook of psychotherapy integration* (pp. 217–235). New York: Plenum.

Franks, V. (1979). Gender and psychotherapy. In E. S. Gomberg & V. Franks (Eds.), *Gender and disordered behavior: Sex differences in psychopathology* (pp. 453–485). New York: Brunner/Mazel.

Frodi, A., Macaulay, J., & Thome, P. R. (1977). Are women always less aggressive than men? A review of the experimental literature. *Psychological Bulletin, 84*, 634–660.

Gallant, S. J., Popiel, D. A., Hoffman, D. M., Chakraborty, P. K., & Hamilton, J. A. (1992). Using daily ratings to confirm premenstrual syndrome/late luteal phase dysphoric disorder. Part 1. Effects of demand characteristics and expectations. *Psychosomatic Medicine, 54*, 149–166.

Gilligan, C. (1991). Women's psychological development: Implications for psychotherapy. *Women and Therapy, 11*, 5–31.

Gjerde, P. F. (1995). Alternative pathways to chronic depressive symptoms in young adults: Gender differences in developmental trajectories. *Child Development, 66*, 1277–1300.

Gjerde, P. F., & Block, J. (1991). Preadolescent antecedents of depressive symptomatology at age 18: A prospective study. *Journal of Youth and Adolescence, 20*, 217–232.

Gjerde, P. F., Block, J., & Block, J. H. (1988). Depressive symptoms and personality during late adolescence: Gender differences in the externalization–internalization of symptom expression. *Journal of Abnormal Psychology, 97*, 475–486.

Golub, S., & Harrington, D. M. (1981). Premenstrual and menstrual mood changes in adolescent women. *Journal of Personality and Social Psychology, 41*, 961–965.

Gove, W. R. (1985). The effect of age and gender on deviant behavior: A biopsychosocial perspective. In A. Rossi (Ed.), *Gender and the life course* (pp. 115–144). New York: Aldine.

Hood, K. E. (1984). Aggression among female rats during the estrus cycle. In K. J. Flannelly, R. J. Blanchard, & D. C. Blanchard (Eds.), *Biological perspectives on aggression*. New York: Alan R. Liss.

Hood, K. E. (1988). Female aggression in [albino ICR] mice: Development, social experience, and the effects of selective breeding (*Mus musculus*). *International Journal of Comparative Psychology, 2*, 27–41.

Hood, K. E. (1992a). Contextual determinants of menstrual cycle effects in observations of social interactions. In A. J. Dan & L. L. Lewis (Eds.), *Menstrual health in women's lives* (pp. 83–97). Chicago: University of Illinois Press.

Hood, K. E. (1992b). Female aggression in mice: Developmental, genetic, and contextual factors. In K. Björkqvist & P. Niemelä (Eds.), *Of mice and women: Aspects of female aggression* (pp. 395–402). Orlando, FL: Academic Press.

Hood, K. E. (in preparation a). Life-span aggressive behavior in mice: Sex and selective breeding effects.

Hood, K. E. (in preparation b). Female aggressive behavior over the life span: Pubertal and mid-life changes.

Hood, K. E. (1995). Dialectical and dynamical systems of approach and withdrawal: Is fighting a fractal form? In K. Hood, G. Greenberg, & E. Tobach (Eds.), *Behavioral development: Concepts of approach-withdrawal and integrative levels. The T. C. Schneirla Conference Series, Vol. 5.* New York: Garland.

Hood, K. E., & Cairns, R. B. (1988). A developmental-genetic analysis of aggressive behavior in mice: II. Cross-sex inheritance. *Behavior Genetics, 18*, 605–619.

Hood, K. E., & Cairns, R. B. (1989). A developmental-genetic analysis of aggressive behavior in mice: IV. Genotype-environment interaction. *Aggressive Behavior, 15*, 361–380.

Hostile hallways: The AAUW survey on sexual harassment in America's schools. (1993). P.O. Box 251, Annapolis Junction.

Huesmann, L. R., Eron, L. D., Lefkowitz, M. M., & Walder, L. O. (1984). Stability of aggression over time and generations. *Developmental Psychology, 20*, 1120–1134.

Huntingford, F. A., & Turner, A. K. (1987) *Animal conflict.* New York: Chapman & Hall.

Hyde, J. S. (1984). How large are gender differences in aggression? A developmental meta-analysis. *Developmental Psychology, 20*, 722–736.

Hyde, J. S. (1986). Gender differences in aggression. In J. S. Hyde & M. C. Linn (Eds.), *The psychology of gender: Advances through meta-analysis* (pp. 47–65). Baltimore, MD: Johns Hopkins Press.

Inoff-Germain, G. E., Arnold, G. S., Nottelmann, E. D., Susman, E. J., Cutler, G. B., Jr., & Chrousos, G. P. (1988). Relations between hormone levels and observational measures of aggressive behavior of young adolescents in family interactions. *Developmental Psychology, 24*, 129–139.

Johnson, F., & Whalen, R. E. (1988). Testicular hormones reduce individual differences in the aggressive behavior of male mice: A theory of hormone action. *Neuroscience and Biobehavioral Reviews, 12*, 93–99.

Kaplan, M. (1992). A woman's view of DSM–III. *American Psychologist, 38*, 786–803.

Koeske, R. H. (1983). Lifting the curse of menstruation: Toward a feminist perspective on the menstrual cycle. In S. Golub (Ed.), *Lifting the curse of menstruation* (pp. 1–16). New York: Haworth.

Laessle, R. G., Tuschl, R. J., Schweiger, U., & Pirke, K. M. (1990). Mood changes and physical complaints during the normal menstrual cycle in healthy young women. *Psychoneuroendocrinology, 15*, 131–138.

Lagerspetz, K. M. J., & Björkqvist, K. (1994). Indirect aggression in boys and girls. In L. R. Huesman (Ed.), *Aggressive behavior: Current perspectives* (pp. 131–150). New York: Plenum.

Lagerspetz, K. M. J., Björkqvist, K., & Peltonen, T. (1988). Is indirect aggression typical of females? Gender differences in aggressiveness in 11- to 12-year-old children. *Aggressive Behavior, 14*, 403–414.

Lagerspetz, K. M. J., & Lagerspetz, K. Y. H. (1975). The expression of the genes of aggressiveness in mice: The effects of androgen on aggression and sexual behavior in females. *Aggressive Behavior, 1*, 291–296.

Lahmeyer, H. W., Miller, M., & DeLeon-Jones, F. (1982). Anxiety and mood fluctuation during the normal menstrual cycle. *Psychosomatic Medicine, 44*, 183–194.

Leadbeater, B. J., Blatt, S. J., & Quinlan, D. M. (1995). Gender-linked vulnerabilities to depressive symptoms, stress, and problem behaviors in adolescents. *Journal of Research on Adolescence, 5*, 1–29.

Leshner, A. I. (1983). The hormonal responses to competition and their behavioral significance. In B. Svare (Ed.), *Hormones and aggressive behavior* (pp. 393–400). New York: Plenum.

Levit, D. B. (1991). Gender differences in ego defenses in adolescence: Sex roles as one way to understand the differences. *Journal of Personality and Social Psychology, 61*, 992–999.

Lewis, H. (1986). The role of shame in depression. In M. Rutter, C. E. Izard, & P. B. Read, (Eds.), *Depression in young people: Developmental and clinical perspectives* (pp. 325–339). New York: Guilford.

Lips, H. (1993). *Sex and gender* (2nd ed.). Mountain View, CA: Mayfield.

Loeber, R., & Schmaling, K. B. (1985). Empirical evidence for overt and covert patterns of antisocial conduct problems: A meta-analysis. *Journal of Abnormal Child Psychology, 13*, 337–352.

Macaulay, J. (1985). Adding gender to aggression research: Incremental or revolutionary change? In V. E. O'Leary, R. K. Unger, & B. S. Wallston (Eds.), *Women, gender, and social psychology* (pp. 191–224). Hillsdale, NJ: Lawrence Erlbaum Associates.

Maccoby, E. E., & Jacklin, C. N. (1974). *The psychology of sex differences.* Stanford, CA: Stanford University Press.

Maccoby, E. E., & Jacklin, C. N. (1980). Sex differences in aggression: A rejoinder and reprise. *Child Development, 51*, 964–980.

Magnusson, D. (1988). *Individual development from an interactional perspective: A longitudinal study.* Hillsdale, NJ: Lawrence Erlbaum Associates.

Maguire, K., Pastore, A. L., & Flanagan, T. J. (1993). *Sourcebook of criminal justice statistics—1992.* Washington, DC: U.S. Government Printing Office.

Mansfield, P. K., Hood, K. E., & Henderson, J. (1989). Women and their husbands: Mood and arousal fluctuations across the menstrual cycle and days of the week. *Psychosomatic Medicine, 51*, 66–80.

McFarlane, J., Martin, C. L., & Williams, T. M. (1988). Mood fluctuations: Women versus men and menstrual versus other cycles. *Psychological Women Quarterly, 12*, 201–223.

Mirkin, M. P. (Ed.). (1994). *Women in context: Toward a feminist reconstruction of psychotherapy.* New York: Guilford.

Moffitt, T. E. (1993). Adolescence—limited and life-course persistent antisocial behavior: A developmental taxonomy. *Psychological Review, 100,* 674–701.

Moyer, K. E. (1976). *The psychobiology of aggression.* New York: Harper & Row.

Neugarten, B., & Gutmann, D. (1964). Age–sex roles and personality in middle age: A thematic apperception study. In B. L. Neugarten (Ed.), *Personality in middle and late life: Empirical studies* (pp. 44–89). New York: Atherton.

Nolen-Hoeksema, S. (1994). An interactive model for the emergence of gender differences in depression in adolescence. *Journal of Research on Adolescence, 4,* 519–534.

Nolen-Hoeksema, S., & Girgus, J. S. (1994). The emergence of gender differences in depression during adolescence. *Psychological Bulletin, 115,* 424–443.

Nolen-Hoeksema, S., Girgus, J. S., & Seligman, M. E. P. (1991). Sex differences in depression and explanatory style in children. *Journal of Youth and Adolescence, 20,* 233–245.

Nottelmann, E. D., Susman, E. J., Inoff-Germain, G. E., Cutler, G. B., Jr., Loriaux, D. L., & Chrousos, G. P. (1987). Developmental processes in early adolescence: Relationships between adolescent adjustment and chronologic age, pubertal stage, and puberty-related serum hormone levels. *The Journal of Pediatrics, 110,* 473–480.

Offord, D. R., Boyle, M. C., & Racine, Y. A. (1991). The epidemiology of antisocial behavior in childhood and adolescence. In D. J. Pepler & K. H. Rubin (Eds.), *The development and treatment of childhood aggression* (pp. 31–54). Hillsdale, NJ: Lawrence Erlbaum Associates.

Orenstein, P. (1994). *SchoolGirls: Young women, self-esteem, and the confidence gap.* New York: Doubleday.

Paikoff, R. L., Brooks-Gunn, J., & Warren, M. P. (1991). Effects of girls' hormonal status on depressive and aggressive symptoms over the course of one year. *Journal of Youth and Adolescence, 20,* 191–215.

Parlee, M. B. (1982). The psychology of the menstrual cycle: Biological and psychological perspectives. In R. C. Freeman (Ed.), *Behavior and the menstrual cycle* (pp. 77–99). New York: Dekker.

Paul, L., & Baenninger, M. (1991). Aggression by women: Mores, myths and methods. In R. Baenninger (Ed.), *Targets of violence and aggression* (pp. 401–441). New York: North-Holland.

Perry, D. G., Perry, L. C., & Weiss, R. J. (1989). Sex differences in the consequences that children anticipate for aggression. *Developmental Psychology, 25,* 312–319.

Petersen, A. C., Compas, B. E., Brooks-Gunn, J., Stemmler, M., Ey, S., & Grant, K. E. (1993). Depression in adolescence. *American Psychologist, 48,* 155–168.

Petersen, A. C., Sarigiani, P., & Kennedy, R. E. (1991). Adolescent depression: Why more girls? *Journal of Youth and Adolescence, 20,* 247–271.

Pugliesi, K. (1992). Women and mental health: Two traditions of feminist research. *Women and Health, 19,* 43–68.

Pulkkinen, L. (1987). Offensive and defensive aggression in humans: A longitudinal perspective. *Aggressive Behavior, 13,* 197–212.

Pulkkinen, L., & Pitkanen, T. (1993). Continuities in aggressive behavior from childhood to adulthood. *Aggressive Behavior, 19,* 249–263.

Purifoy, F. E., & Koopmans, L. H. (1980). Androstenedione, T and free T concentrations in women of various occupations. *Social Biology, 26,* 179–188.

Regier, D. A., Boyd, J. H., Burke, J. D., Rae, D. S., Myers, J. K., Kramer, M., Robins, L. N., George, L. K., Karno, M., & Locke, B. Z. (1988). One-month prevalence of mental disorders in the United States. *Archives of General Psychiatry, 45,* 977–987.

Robins, L. N. (1986). The consequences of conduct disorder in girls. In D. Olweus, J. Block, & M. Radke-Yarrow (Eds.), *Development of antisocial and prosocial behavior* (pp. 385–409). New York: Academic Press.

Rodin, J., & Ickovics, J. R. (1990). Women's health: Review and research agenda as we approach the 21st century. *American Psychologist, 45,* 1018–1034.

Rossi, A. S., & Rossi, P. E. (1977). Body time and social time: Mood patterns by menstrual cycle phase and day of week. *Social Science Research, 6*, 273–308.

Ruble, D. N. (1977). Premenstrual symptoms: A reinterpretation. *Science, 197,* 291–292.

Rutter, M. (1988). Longitudinal data in the study of causal processes: Some uses and some pitfalls. In M. Rutter (Ed.), *Studies of psychosocial risk: The power of longitudinal data* (pp. 1–28). New York: Cambridge University Press.

Rutter, M., & Giller, H. (1983). *Juvenile delinquency: Trends and perspectives.* New York: Penguin.

Sanders, D., Warner, P., Backstrom, T., & Bancroft, J. (1983). Mood, sexuality, hormones, and the menstrual cycle: I. Changes in mood and physical state: Description of subjects and method. *Psychosomatic Medicine, 45,* 487–581.

Sandnabba, N. K. (1992). Aggressive behavior in female mice as a correlated character in selection for aggressiveness in male mice. In K. Björkqvist & P. Niemela (Eds.), *Of mice and women: Aspects of female aggression* (pp. 367–379). New York: Academic Press.

Sapolsky, R. M. (1987). Stress, social status, and reproductive physiology in free-living baboons. In D. Crews (Ed.), *Psychobiology of reproductive behavior* (pp. 291–322). Englewood Cliffs, NJ: Prentice-Hall.

Sherwin, B. B. (1988). A comparative analysis of the role of androgen in human male and female sexual behavior: Behavioral specificity, critical thresholds, and sensitivity. *Psychobiology, 16,* 416–425.

Siegel, J. M., & Brown, J. D. (1988). A prospective study of stressful circumstances, illness symptoms, and depressed mood among adolescents. *Developmental Psychology, 24,* 715–721.

Susman, E. J., Inoff-Germain, G. E., Nottelmann, E. D., Cutler, G. B., Jr., & Chrousos, G. P. (1987). Hormones, emotional dispositions, and aggressive attributes in young adolescents. *Child Development, 58,* 1114–1134.

Tieger, T. (1980). On biological basis of sex differences in aggression. *Child Development, 51,* 943–963.

Tremblay, R. E. (1991). Aggression, prosocial behavior, and gender: Three magic words, but no magic wand. In D. J. Pepler & K. H. Rubin (Eds.), *The development and treatment of childhood aggression* (pp. 71–78). Hillsdale, NJ: Lawrence Erlbaum Associates.

Udry, J. R. (1988). Biological predispositions and social control in adolescent sexual behavior. *American Sociological Review, 53,* 709–722.

Udry, J. R., & Talbert, L. M. (1988). Sex hormone effects on personality at puberty. *Journal of Personality and Social Psychology, 54,* 291–295.

Unger, R. H. (1993). Alternative conceptions of sex (and sex differences). In M. Haug, R. E. Whalen, C. Aron, & K. Olsen (Eds.), *The development of sex differences and similarities in behavior* (pp. 457–476). Boston: Kluwer.

van Oortmerssen, G. A., & Bakker, C. M. (1981). Artificial selection for short and long attack latencies in wild *Mus musculus domesticius. Behavior Genetics, 11,* 115–126.

Walker, A. (1992). *Possessing the secret of joy.* New York: Harcourt Brace Jovanovich.

Werner, E. E., & Smith, R. S. (1992). *Overcoming the odds: High risk children from birth to adulthood.* Ithaca, NY: Cornell University Press.

Widom, C. S., & Ames, A. (1988). Biology and female crime. In T. E. Moffitt and S. A. Mednick (Eds.), *Biological contributions to crime causation* (pp. 308–331). Boston: Martinus Nijhoff.

Wilcoxon, L. A., Schrader, S. L., & Sherif, C. W. (1976). Daily self-reports on activities, life events, moods, and somatic changes during the menstrual cycle. *Psychosomatic Medicine, 38,* 399–417.

Woods, N. F., Dery, E. K., & Most, A. (1982). Stressful life events and perimenstrual symptoms. *Journal of Human Stress, 8,* 23–31.

Zahn-Waxler, C., Cole, P. M., & Barrett, K. C. (1991). Guilt and empathy: Sex differences and implications for the development of depression. In J. Garber & K. A. Dodge (Eds.), *The development of emotion regulation and dysregulation* (pp. 243–272). Cambridge: Cambridge University Press.

Zoccolillo, M. (1993). Gender and the development of conduct disorder. *Development and Psychopathology, 5,* 65–78.

CONCLUSION: A SYNTHESIS OF STUDIES ON THE BIOLOGY OF AGGRESSION AND VIOLENCE

Robert B. Cairns
University of North Carolina

David M. Stoff
National Institute of Mental Health

Over the past 2 decades, remarkable progress has been achieved in research on the biological influences that underlie the dynamics of aggressive behavior. These advances have been generated by recent technological developments in the neurosciences and molecular genetics as well as by innovative longitudinal and experimental analysis of aggressive interchanges. The upshot is that progress can be claimed in virtually every domain of genetic, neurobiological, and biosocial investigation.

Any brief summary of the contents of this volume runs the risk of distorting the subtlety and power of the analyses found in the separate chapters. Yet the total findings should be viewed in context in order to take stock of the present and to establish priorities for the future. Toward this end, we first comment on the application of a biopsychosocial framework to aggression and violence that was proposed over 2 decades ago by investigators working in diverse domains of medicine, behavioral biology, medical genetics, and evolutionary and developmental psychology (e.g., Borgaonkar & Shah, 1974; Cairns, 1972, 1979; Engel, 1977; Scott, 1977).

An Integrative Approach

Within the traditions of the biological sciences, aggression has been classically viewed as an inevitable consequence of evolutionary, genetic, or physiological forces. Hence the focus of early biological research on aggression was concerned with evolutionary, genetic, neurobiology, endocrine, or morphological processes, most often with these levels of analysis considered singly. At the same time, the social sciences provided quite a different perspective. Within the behavioral sciences, human aggression has been commonly viewed as a pathological outcome of early experiences or a product of social learning processes gone awry. Hence individual psychological, familial, or societal processes were implicated and viewed as the primary causative agents. The result was that the concepts and findings on aggression that emerged from these two domains of science appeared to come from different worlds.

Modern biobehavioral science has demanded a more integrative account of behavioral processes, including aggression and violence. The task is to understand how configurations are formed across genetic–neurobiological–behavioral–social pathways. A biobehavioral science recognizes that behaviors are simultaneously determined by processes within the individual, in the social ecology, and in interactions between the two. A focus on either social or biological factors can yield only part of the story of aggressive and violent behaviors; integrative investigations are essential to complete the picture.

A central feature of the contemporary perspective is that aggressive and violent behaviors represent the melding of biological and environmental sources of influence. Biological and social factors typically collaborate rather than compete in the establishment and regulation of aggressive patterns. Accordingly, the prediction of aggressive behavior requires precise information on how social contexts and social actions influence biological states, and how biological states affect behavior. As circumstances and social relationships change over time and space, the actions and internal states of individuals become aligned with contemporary contexts.

In brief, the modern biobehavioral perspective holds that:

• Genetic, neurobiological, experiential, and cultural influences on behavior are fused at each developmental stage. Biological influences are not pasted onto otherwise intact structures.

• Behavioral organization and experiences contribute directly to the development, instigation, and organization of biological processes and vice versa. Behavioral–biological relations do not occur on a one-way street.

• Influences on aggressive behavior may be observed at multiple levels in the biobehavioral system. Because single aspects of genes, neurobiology, and context do not develop and function in isolation, they should not be divorced from the whole in analysis. One corollary of this propostiion is that investigations of the biological biases of aggressive behavior should include, but not be limited to, the brain sciences.

Taken in overview, these propositions help bring together the accounts of aggression and violence in this volume that have quite different starting points—from molecular genetics and neurohormones to development and microevolution.

TAKING STOCK

Aggressive behavior has been viewed here as a key feature of biological adaptation. Although there is general agreement among investigators on the significance of biological contributions, the specific hypotheses that have been offered in this volume cannot be reduced to a single model. Moreover, the hypotheses are not necessarily mutually exclusive. As Convit and his colleagues (chap. 9, this volume) observe, "the separate contributions [to violence research] from biological and environment as well as their resulting interactions make this a very complex issue . . . To compound these problems investigators from these different disciplines frequently do not read each others work, and consequently the amount of cross-fertilization has been, until quite recently, somewhat limited" (pp. 169–170). We agree, and that is one of the reasons for this volume. Although it would be premature at this juncture to attempt to organize the models proposed into a single framework, the primary ideas, as well as the differences and similarities among them, can be outlined in an overview of hypotheses and findings.

Alleles, Serotonin, and Impulsive Aggression

Neurogenetic investigations have been recently propelled by significant advances in the techniques of molecular genetic analysis. In his chapter describing the pursuit for genetic alleles contributing to aggressive behavior, Goldman provided a succinct account of the procedures now available and a summary of the early research returns. With the development of automated sequencing methods and rapid procedures for scanning for genetic variants, the direct scanning of candidate genes has now become a practical and productive enterprise. If employed in conjunction with other methodologies, which have different advantages and limitations, the procedures can provide convergent evidence with respect to the neurogenesis of aggressive behavior. In discussing how discrete genetic loci may be linked to disturbed behavioral phenomena, Goldman cites recent findings of population associations between specific genetic loci, cerebral spinal fluid (CSF) 5-HIAA concentrations, and suicidal behavior. A population association between a DNA marker of the TPH gene to CSF 5-HIAA concentration was recently reported by Nielson et al. (1994). The association was discovered in a population of alcoholic Finnish prisoners who, by the nature of their crimes, were deemed impulsive.

There are also some qualifications that complicate the search for connections between genetic loci, neurotransmitter activity, aggressiveness, and impulsiveness. For example, consider the intriguing discovery from Brunner, Nelen, Breakefield, Ropers, and Van Oost (1993) that males from a Dutch family suffering from borderline mental retardation, inability to control their impulses, and aggressive behaviors exhibit a mutation within the structural gene for monoamine oxidase A (MAO-A; which normally degrades serotonin). This particular mutation causing an MAOA deficiency would appear to be associated with a flooding of transmitters in the brain, including serotonin. If the transmitters were to accumulate abnormally in the brain, then those responses that are normally inhibited would be in high gear all of the time. One outcome may be heightened aggression and reduced CSF 5-HIAA concentrations (i.e., decreased brain serotonin turnover), as noted in the foregoing studies. However, studies are needed to determine the various neurochemical alterations induced by selective MAOA deficiency and to ascertain whether there is an increase or decrease in brain serotonin turnover. Moreover, even if the suspected mutation found in this Dutch family should be found in other families, its expression might well be modified by social, economic, and cultural factors.

Evidence consistent with the serotonin–impulsivity–suicide–aggression proposal was first reported by Asberg and colleagues in Sweden (e.g., Asberg, Schalling, Traskman-Bendz, & Wagner, 1987; Asberg, Traskman, & Thoren, 1976). In addition, a strong inverse correlation between CSF 5-HIAA and a history of aggressive behavior was found in young male recruits for the U.S. Navy (Brown et. al., 1982; Brown, Goodwin, Ballenger, Goyer, & Major, 1979). Similar findings have been reported for Finnish impulsive violent offenders (Linnoila et al., 1983). This set of studies was summarized by Virkkunen and Linnoila (chap. 5, this volume) in the following statement: "A low concentration of cerebrospinal fluid (CSF) 5-hydroxy-indoleacetic acid (5-HIAA) has been associated with an increased risk of suicide attempts, unprovoked interpersonal violence and early onset alcoholism in men" (p. 87).

However, as Soubrie (1986) indicated, neurotransmitters are themselves interrelated in origin and function, rendering it unlikely that specific behavioral actions will be supported by a single neurotransmitter. To be sure, a single neurotransmitter does not act in isolation. In this regard, Virkkunen and Linnoila proposed that deficient serotonin turnover leads to disturbances in the regulation of glucose metabolism and diurnal activity cycles. In a fresh comprehensive study, Finnish male subjects were classified into three groups of alcoholic offenders (impulsive, nonimpulsive, and antisocial personality disorder) and one normal male control group. The study found that the mean CSF 5-HIAA concentration of impulsive, alcoholic offenders was lower than that of nonimpulsive, alcoholic offenders. This outcome replicates the basic serotonin–impulsive–alcoholic phenomenon cited earlier. In addition, healthy, nonimpulsive, nonalcoholic volunteers apparently had mean CSF 5-HIAA concentrations between those of the impulsive and nonimpulsive alcoholics. Why was no difference obtained between the normal controls and the high-impulsive or low-impulsive groups? The latter finding invites speculations about the range and role of variations in serotonergic concentrations and impulsivity in a normal population.

Among the different groups of offenders, measures of glucose metabolism yielded outcomes that were not consistently linked to CSF 5-HIAA concentration. This outcome apparently was inconsistent with expectations. As Virkkunen and

Linnoila indicate, the obtained difference on mean blood glucose nadir between impulsive, alcoholic offenders and healthy volunteers might be secondary to alcoholic dependence. Moreover, no differences were obtained between the four groups in other measures of glucose metabolism, contrary to what had been expected. In brief, the findings of this carefully constructed comparison among groups provided only modest support for the hypothesized role of glucose metabolism in the serotonin–impulsivity–aggression proposal. The reasons for the discrepancy clearly require further research on glucose metabolism in highly aggressive subjects.

Extending the serotonin–impulsivity–suicide–aggression proposal, Coccaro and Kavoussi (chap. 4, this volume) took advantage of the neuroendocrine challenge strategy to support the reduced brain serotonin hypothesis in personality disordered patients with impulsive–aggressive and suicidal behavior. They noted that if serotonin serves to inhibit impulsive–aggressive behavior, there may be other central neurotransmitters that serve to excite impulsivity and aggression. In a review of biochemical, brain receptor, platelet receptor, and neuropsychopharmacologic challenge studies, they concluded that "the behavioral constructs of 'irritability' and 'assaultiveness' appear to be critical to the relationship between 5-HT and impulsive aggressive behavior." They also observe that the evidence on the excitatory role of other neurotransmitter systems—including dopamine, norepinephrine, and opiates—is more limited. Yet the experimental findings from nonhuman animal studies is provocative with respect dopamine and GABA, and the whole story remains to be adequately told (see Barros and Miczek, chap. 12, this volume).

In reviewing studies of the functional status of brain serotonergic systems in children and adolescents with aggressive behavior, Stoff and Vitiello (chap. 6, this volume) stated that "the relatively few studies of central 5-HT indices in child and youth aggression [only four; two by the same research group] do not reveal the consistent pattern of reduced 5-HT function that has been found in numerous reports of adult aggression" (for references see chapters by Coccaro & Kavoussi, and Virkkunen & Linnoila, this volume). There was a hint of a relation between lower CSF 5-HIAA levels and aggression of youth with disruptive behavior disorders, but these data must be replicated under more controlled conditions by other investigators. These authors also noted that the relatively few peripheral 5-HT studies in aggressive children and youth do not reveal consistent 5-HT abnormalities in blood elements, as might be predicted from the adult studies. However, peripheral 5-HT indices are limited by the unacceptably low correlations with central 5-HT indices. Stoff and Vitiello (chap. 6, this volume) also discussed methodologic reasons that complicate conducting central 5-HT studies of aggression in children and youth (e.g., difficulty in repetitive measurement, age or developmental changes, influence of ongoing social context). Their chapter concluded with a review of the relatively scarce literature for the use of serotonergic agents in the treatment of childhood and adolescent aggression and suggested prospects for new 5-HT drug development, based on results of specific disturbances in 5-HT physiology.

Alcohol and Aggression

As Barros and Miczek observed, "ethanol clearly stands out as the drug most frequently associated with violent and aggressive behavior in humans" (p. 237). It shows up in higher mortality risks in suicide, homicide, motor vehicle accidents, and domestic violence. These epidemiological data are correlational, however, and the causative mechanisms are poorly elucidated. Moreover, there are large environmental, cultural, gender, and individual difference effects, including the phenomenon that many persons show less aggressive behavior after drinking.

Animal models have enabled more precise analyses of relationships between ethanol, neurotransmitter activity and aggression. Such animal studies are especially useful because of the relative infrequency and periodic nature of aggressive acts in humans. Moreover, from a neuropharmacological point of view, animal studies permit the direct manipulation of brain serotonin concentrations as well as pre- and postsynaptic receptor activation and blockade. Although the nonhuman research has clearly implicated the role of serotonergic mechanisms in aggressive behaviors of animals, the story is not a simple one because the effects are sometimes in the opposite direction to the expectation, and more than one pathway seems to be involved (see Barros and Miczek, this volume). In this regard it was noted that ethanol stimulates the activity of serotonin releasing neurons. The paradox is that ethanol *stimulates* serotonin release and *enhances* (rather than diminishes) aggressive behavior in many individuals.

In the line of research described by Barros and Miczek, an attempt was made to disaggregate samples of CFW mice into subgroups which showed alcohol-heightened aggression (20%–30% of the mice), alcohol-suppressed aggression (15%–20%), and nonreliable effects of aggression (the remaining 50% + of the mice). Only when this split is made is it possible to identify the experimental effects of low-moderate doses of alcohol in CFW mice. Although the low-dose effects seem robust and replicable, the classification procedures themselves are determined by the animals' prior aggressive response to alcohol. Obviously the evidence would be more compelling if the classification were independent of the response.

In this regard, three matters seem to demand high priority in further research. First, there is a compelling need to clarify, using procedures that extend beyond alcohol-aggressive assessments, which individuals are likely to respond to low doses of alcohol with heightened aggression. Second, the precise neurochemical changes that are produced by alcohol need to be elucidated. Third, systematic, multiple-level analyses are required. There is now broad agreement that the one gene–one neurotransmitter–one behavior formula is too simple (Goyer & Semple, this volume). As Barros and Miczek remarked:

> Nowadays it is recognized that more than one neurotransmitter system participates in the expression of a designated behavior [and] that different neurotransmitters, neuromodulators or hormones contribute to the fine control of one neurotransmitter actions. Further exploration of multiple systems interactions in the expression of ethanol-heightened aggression will be easier from now, due to the development of diverse laboratory and clinical in vivo methods able to detect minute changes of several neurotransmitters and their metabolites at the same time. (p. 254)

Fronto-Temporal Abnormalities, Brain Imaging, and Violence

Advances in brain-imaging techniques have greatly enhanced our ability to plot the structural and functional properties of the central nervous system. As Raine and Buchsbaum (see chap. 10) indicate, these procedures offer "the potential for a revolution in our understanding of the neurophysiological and neuroanatomical underpinnings of crime and violence" (p. 195). But much remains to be done before the revolution can occur. To date, only a handful of studies have been conducted with specific reference to violence and antisocial behaviors. However limited, the work completed to date has yielded intriguing albeit preliminary findings.

In a PET analysis of brain functioning, Raine et al. (1994) compared 22 murderers with individually matched controls. Their findings indicate a selective reduction in prefrontal glucose metabolism in the murderers. This outcome is consistent with neuropsychological studies that have implicated frontal cortex damage in nonmurderous though highly aggressive and violent youth. However, as Raine and Buchsbaum observed, the evidence is hardly conclusive, and "such dysfunction may be best viewed as a predisposition to violence rather than prefrontal dysfunction, in and of itself, causing violence . . . requiring other environmental, psychological, and social factors to enhance or diminish this biological predisposition." In addition, there is only a modest relationship between imaging measures of brain function and brain structure. Assessments of both structure and function can be productively combined in future brain-imaging work.

Although the literature is still sparse, Goyer and Semple report PET findings that support an inverse relationship between aggressive–impulsive behavior and regional cerebral metabolic rate of glucose in the frontal lobe. On the basis of their own results and related investigations, Goyer and Semple suggest that the orbital frontal, upper prefrontal, and left insular temporal-parietal regions may be involved in the regulation of aggressive behavior. They view these results as consistent with the serotonin–impulsivity–aggression proposal, yet they also indicate that the other transmitters are likely to be involved. These authors also reported that a small group of patients with borderline personality disorder were characterized by a unique combined pattern of decreased glucose metabolic rate in the B plane frontal lobes and increased glucose metabolic rate in the D plane frontal lobes. Similar studies are being extended to combat veterans with posttraumatic stress disorder. It has not yet been determined whether patients with aggressive–impulsive difficulty demonstrate a correlation of regional brain function with pharmacological treatment response.

Following Luria (1966), the anterior frontal lobes are proposed to be responsible for executive functions in virtually every complex behavioral activity, and frontal lobe damage should be associated with deficits in judgment, insight, abstraction, reasoning, and planning. Convit and his colleagues present information on the specific hypothesis that frontotemporal abnormality is related to violent behavior. As these authors observed, there is now a substantial clinical literature to suggest linkage between frontotemporal lobe regions, impulsivity, and, possibly, a common central serotonin mechanism. But there are also multiple pathways of influence, and the relations among systems transcends focus on a single locus of dysfunction. One task for future research is to clarify the network of causal relationships for humans. Toward this end, multilevel longitudinal studies of the biology and behavior can be productively combined, in conjunction with parallel experimental analyses of nonhumans.

Autonomic Responsivity

About a century ago, William James (1890) set the stage for modern day psychophysiology when he raised questions about the relation between physiological events and molar psychological or behavioral processes such as emotion. The psychophysiological approach capitalizes on links between the behavioral and physiological domains in an attempt to develop integrated theoretical perspectives on behavioral–physiological relationships by employing physiological measures to illuminate behavioral states and processes. Over the last several decades technological advances in bioelectronics, imaging methods, and laboratory computing have made it possible to record signals from the brain and peripheral physiological systems with greater sensitivity and fidelity than ever before. It has become clear that psychological variables can significantly impact on physiological function and that physiological processes are important determinants of behavior. Much of this work has been complicated by the assumption of psychophysiological isomorphism when, in fact many physiological responses are multiply determined. Despite this stumbling block and other limitations for inferring psychological significance from physiological signals (Cacioppo & Tassinary, 1990), an extensive body of research on psychophysiological measures (principally electrodermal, cardiovascular, event related potentials, EEG) has emerged in relationship to aggressive, violent behavior. Although much progress has been made, it is fair to say that a better understanding of the many-to-one mappings between the psychological and physiological realms is essential for psychophysiology to realize its full potential as an interface science bridging the clinical, cognitive, and neuroscience domains.

Raine's chapter 8 is an updated review of all studies measuring skin conductance and heart rate activity in aggressive, violent, populations. He noted that in these populations skin conductance was characterized by reduced arousal, poorer classical conditioning, and long half-recovery times and resting heart rate was consistently lower. It was hypothesized that heart rate may predispose to the development of fearlessness, which in turn predisposes to aggressive, violent behavior. This fearlessness may in turn underlie the skin conductance arousal and conditioning deficits found in antisocial populations. It was also argued that low resting heart rate in noninstitutionalized offenders is a highly replicated finding that may be relatively specific to violent offending and may interact in important ways with social variables in the prediction of violence. An alternative interpretation is that delinquent, antisocial males are not easily frightened, and this shows up in both their heart rates and their behaviors.

In exploring the utility of heart rate and heart rate variability as a methodological tool, Mezzacappa, Kindlon, and Earls (chap. 7, this volume) related heart rate regulatory patterns to disruptive, aggressive, antisocial behaviors as well as to the cognitive and motivational domains. These authors discussed the utility of spectral analysis techniques for the construction of models of individual difference in the relationship of autonomic nervous system activity to behavior. They noted that the major problem in interpreting heart rate–behavior relationships was a general absence of a developmental perspective and not in conceptual models of behavior nor of autonomic regulatory function. The developmental theme, admirably expressed by Mezzacappa et al., recurs throughout this volume.

Quantitative Genetics and the Epidemiology of Aggression

Researchers investigate possible genetic components of aggression and violence by studying populations and families as well as genetic, biochemical, and neurobehavioral markers and characteristics. A central idea behind these studies is to separate genetic and environmental components of variance. Comparisons of the similarities of familial, twin, and adopted children have been traditionally concerned with estimating the magnitude of genetic contributions to behavior rather than identifying the mechanisms by which the similarities are produced. Insofar as traditional personality tests are concerned, the results of aggressive measures are unambiguous. Across studies, similarities between MZ twins are consistently higher than among DZ twins on personality measures of aggression. As Carey (chap. 1, this volume) concluded, "there is an important genetic influence on personality scales that measure aggression and sociopathy in adults. The results for children are more variable and suggest that common environment may play a more important role than it does for adults" (p. 7).

There remain some puzzles in this picture, however. For example, research on criminal arrests in adults suggest only modest genetic similarities, if the behavioral outcome is limited to violence. Between-MZ similarities on violence are less than, say, between-MZ similarities on property crimes. As Carey indicates, various factors potentially contribute to the lower levels of genetic relationship for violence (e.g., reliance on official records, low baserate of violent behavior). In any case, it seems important to identify why the apparent discrepancy is observed.

In the long run, behavioral–genetic investigations may be as useful in pointing to research on environmental effects as in pointing to studies of biological influence. For example, the MZ–DZ findings suggest that much is still to be learned about the extent and continuance of direct interactions among identical twins, and the outcomes of such interactions on their shared behaviors, attitudes, and beliefs. Although these effects may be most pervasive for commonplace behaviors, truly violent acts may require another form of analysis. When the phenotype is restricted to violent offenses, several qualifications must be made in the interpretation of a possible role for genetics. As Carey concluded, "genetically informative designs using multivariate techniques will become increasingly important for understanding the complicated pathways for human aggression" (p. 16).

Development and Aggression

Developmental studies of aggressive behavior begin with the assumption that social actions are multidetermined and dynamic over time. Social interactions, including aggressive behaviors, occur at the interface between organismic and environmental sources of influence (Gariépy, Lewis, and Cairns, chap. 3, this volume). The developmental perspective promotes a focus on the plasticity of the biology of the organism and its environment. The impressive stability of aggressive behavior across time and generation is a product of correlated biological and environmental constraints.

This perspective has implications for the proposals summarized before, including the developmental-genetics of aggression. According to Gariépy et al., direct experimental manipulations across ontogeny show that the effects of genetic background on aggressive behavior can be modified, neutralized, or reversed by experiences. Interactions between environments and genetic background are the rule, not the exception. A high priority for future research should be to track these correlated changes in neurobiology and behavior.

One of the findings reported in Gariépy et al. provides a clue on how it is possible for genetic, rearing, and pharmacological contributions to have similar neurobiological and behavioral effects on aggression, albeit through different pathways. In this regard, the selective breeding studies of the NC lines of aggressive mice point to a correlated and possibly contributing role of heightened dopaminergic activity in specific areas of the brain, including the nucleus acccumbens. These effects were produced by genetic manipulation. Moreover, a seemingly parallel effect (i.e., heightened dopamine activity in the nucleus accumbens) can also be produced by the intake of alcohol (Yoshimoto, McBride, Lumeng, & Li, 1992). Further, Gariépy and his colleagues reported that heightened dopamine activity and heightened aggression can also be produced by environmental manipulations of rearing and attack.

At a more speculative level, these findings on "phenotypic equifinality" are consistent with Fuller's (1967) proposal that the aspects of behavior most modifiable by variation in experience may also be particularly sensitive to genetic variation. The same adaptations in aggressive behavior can be reached by different avenues. This proposal has considerable merit when one considers that very rapid behavioral changes may be required for survival in ontogeny and evolution.

Another robust phenomena that has been explored from a developmental perspective is the close relationship between the developmental onset of steroid hormones in adolescent males and the onset of aggressive and violent behavior. Susman and her colleagues (chap. 13, this volume) provide a careful analysis of how experience and neuroendocrine factors collaborate in the development of aggressive behaviors in males and females. Addressing the notion of reciprocal influences of hormones and behavior, this research group questions the conventional idea that biology is a determinant of behavior by presenting data that it works in the other direction as well, that is, behavioral experiences and contexts lead to neuroendocrine changes that, in turn, lead to increases or decreases in aggressive behavior. Susman concluded that "Theories are needed to integrate antecedents and consequences of aggressive and antisocial behavior and neurobiological processes at all stages of the life span. Specifically, environmental factors, known to affect neuroendocrine development in subhuman species, should be included in the development of theories and hypotheses of aggressive behavior in humans" (p. 285). It is also noted that better neuroendocrine–behavior links need to be established to generalize what we know from laboratory studies to aggression in naturalistic settings.

Kathryn Hood (chap. 15) observed that there has been a curious and pervasive gender bias in research on aggression. Violence, aggression, and antisocial behavior have been investigated primarily in males. This gender preference seems to hold regardless of samples investigated (mice or men), domains explored (genes, neurohormones, hormones), or theoretical issues tackled (nature or nurture). Hood argues that this bias has needlessly handicapped our understanding of biobehavioral processes in general and our understanding of gender and aggression in particular.

Hood's own research on the behavioral biology of aggression in mice and rats nicely illustrates the point. She shows that fluctuations in hormonal states have a large effect upon variations in attacks among nonhuman females. Accordingly, Hood finds (a) there are significant changes in the likelihood of attacks as a function of stage of parturition (i.e., prepartum, postpartum, and nonpregnancy), (b) there are increased attacks after estrous cessation among older females, and (c) differences in the probability of attacks by females are associated with their stage of the estrous cycle. Ironically—given the gender bias in prior research—the evidence on the relations between attacks and hormonal states indicates that the phenomena is probably more robust in females than in males. Moreover, Hood concluded that "the willingness to attack does not require a Y chromosome" (chap. 15, this volume). This conclusion is consistent with Lagerspetz and Lagerspetz's (1975) proposal that autosomal genetic mechanisms are involved in the heritability of attacks and violence in these selectively bred lines.

But it is hazardous to leap from mice to men, or women. Extending her research to humans, Hood finds little support for a direct translation of the cyclic hormone-behavior findings. Specifically, systematic studies yield scant support for the stereotypic premenstrual syndrome (PMS), no matter how it is measured. There are, however, different aggressive strategies that girls and boys tend to employ: Direct physical confrontation is more likely to occur in male-male conflicts, and indirect social aggression is likely in female-female conflicts. These gender differences, while robust, are not invariant with respect to context, ethnic background, or measurement strategy. In the light of the social-contextual relativity of gender aggressive strategies in human beings, Hood argues that there is only modest utility in continuing to refer to global conceptions of innate or biological gender differences. She concludes: "Placing women at the center of the analysis, rather than in the margins as a special case, will clarify the potential value of free expression for women's healthy development" (chap. 15, p. 330).

Beyond the finding of reasonable stability and predictability over time, the broader point in Magnusson's chapter 14 (this volume) is that it is folly to divorce the study of aggressive behaviors from other characteristics of the individual. Magnusson (1988) and his colleagues find that it is a configuration of aggression, restlessness, and autonomic reactivity that provides the strongest predictions of subsequent antisocial behavior. Single variables, including assessments of aggression, are misleading because they provide only part of the effective configuration. This finding and the insight it supports is consistent with the proposition that both behavior and biology represent the operation of dynamic systems over time. These systems are poorly represented by focus on separate variables. In describing the role of low autonomic reactivity in the development of antisocial behavior, Magnusson proposed an interactional model of individual functioning. He remarks: "The model indicates a multideter-mined stochastic process in which biological factors are involved in a constant, reciprocal interaction with other factors in the individual and the environment" (p. 301).

Magnusson and his colleagues have taken the lead in formulating an integrative model of aggressive behavior development (see Magnusson, 1988, 1995). The Stockholm group has pioneered the development of methods of person analysis, which permits researchers to move beyond the variable-oriented approach in order to identify configurations of biological-contextual characteristics that operate over time (e.g., Bergman & Magnusson, 1991). This research illustrates how measurement strategies and analytic techniques can be consonant with a holistic interdisciplinary approach.

LOOKING AHEAD

Because each chapter in this book concludes with a section on "Future Research Prospects," the reader is referred to the respective chapters for a recommended research agenda. Here, we highlight some important principles that could be followed in future biological studies of aggression and violence. These principles are common to the various research strategies discussed in this book.

Aggression and violence are essentially social acts; hence, their analysis cannot be reduced solely to biological events. Nonetheless, biological influences do contribute some variance to their occurrence. Because of their heterogeneity and complexity, aggression and violence do not lend themselves readily to reductionistic thinking, as experiential and sociocultural forces exert a major influence upon this phenomenon. It is highly unlikely that the problem of aggression and violence can be reduced to a single gene or dysfunction in a single enzyme, receptor, or molecular component of a nerve cell. More than likely, multiple biological systems are involved and these systems act in concert with the more molar social realm. It is necessary to go beyond the conventional notion that biological variables not only influence behavior and environment to the more modern notion that behavioral and environmental variables also impact on biology. Maturation and developmental processes may provide the common ground for understanding the processes of biological–social integration. On the one hand, it is virtually impossible to conceptualize developmental changes without recognition of the inevitable internal modifications that occur within the organism over time. On the other hand, it is misleading to focus on the individual's biology in the absence of detailed information about the interactional and social circumstances in which the behavior occurs.

It would be fruitful to evaluate biological influences in an ongoing pattern of aggressive violent behavior. This is a challenging task because of the often episodic occurrence of such behavior and the problem in assessing biological variables during its actual occurrence. It is, however, important to approximate the naturalistic situation as best as possible. Unfortunately, almost all studies of biological variables have attempted to correlate these variables with past behavioral events despite the strong possibility that biological factors may influence the risk for aggression and violence at the moment of the behavior or, far earlier, during infant development. More prospective studies are in order to assess whether or not biological factors directly cause aggression and violence. A related point is that it would be useful to characterize biological variables as patterns of development over time rather than the typical method of measuring them as single values at a given time point. Innovative research designs will incorporate biological variables in longitudinal studies of aggression and violence. Recurrent biological testing will require more rigorous psychometric evaluation and employment of relatively noninvasive methods.

Biological studies of prosocial behavior may shed more light on the mechanisms responsible for aggression and violence and on its intervention. To date, biological studies have emphasized negative outcomes. However, contemporary prevention research relies heavily on enhancing protective factors to promote positive social development and reduce risk. It is therefore important to determine whether biological variables are associated with prosocial behavior and development. Biological factors may underlie social and familial processes as well as the more conventionally studied negative risk variables of antisocial behavior and other correlated risks, such as alcohol abuse.

Behavioral and biological measures should be simultaneously collected in aggressive and violent subjects and members of their families. Patterns of inheritance need to be traced across generations, particularly in view of strong evidence for the intergenerational transmission of aggression. Unfortunately, this has previously been done on few, if any, occasions. It becomes necessary to go beyond the two-group (experimental vs. control), single biological measure design to determine linkages between behavioral and biological variables over time.

In conclusion, we reiterate our belief that the scientific advances in genetics and neurobiology will not be realized unless they are incorporated with development, context, and sociocultural events that play a powerful role in aggression and violence. Such a multilevel integrative approach is essential to incorporate neurobiological advances with findings from longitudinal and experimental analysis of aggression. To the extent that it enhances understanding, consolidates information, and smooths the transition to the next generation of integrative studies on biology, behavior, and development, this volume will have achieved its goal. As such, this volume is a progress report, not a final statement.

REFERENCES

Asberg, M., Schalling, D., Traskman-Bendz, L., & Wagner, A. (1987). Psychobiology of suicide, impulsivity and related phenomena. In H. Y. Meltzer (Ed.), *Psychopharmacology: Third generation of progress* (pp. 655–658). New York: Raven.

Asberg, M., Traskman, L., & Thoren, P. (1976). 5-HIAA in the cerebrospinal fluid: A biochemical suicide predictor? *Archives of General Psychiatry, 33*, 1193–1197.

Bergman, L. R., & Magnusson, D. (1991). Stability and change in patterns of extrinsic adjustment problems. In D. Magnusson, L. R. Bergman, G. Rudinger, & B. Törestad (Eds.), *Problems and methods in longitudinal research: Stability and change* (pp. 323–346). Cambridge, MA: Cambridge University Press.

Borgaonkar, D., & Shah, S. (1974). The XYY chromosome male—or syndrome? *Progress in Medical Genetics, 10,* 135–222.

Brown, G. L., Ebert, M. H., Goyer, P. F., Jimerson, D. C., Klein, W. J., Bunney, W. E., & Goodwin, F. K. (1982). Aggression, suicide, and serotonin: Relationships to CSF amine metabolites. *American Journal of Psychiatry, 139,* 741–746.

Brown, G. L., Goodwin, F. K., Ballenger, J. C., Goyer, P. F., & Major, L. F. (1979). Aggression in humans correlates with cerebrospinal fluid amine metabolites. *Psychiatry Research, 1,* 131–139.

Brunner, H. G., Nelen, M., Breakefield, X. O., Ropers, H. H., & Van Oost, B. A. (1993). Abnormal behavior associated with a point mutation in the structural gene for monoamine oxidase A. *Science, 262,* 578–580.

Cacioppo, J. T., & Tassinary, L. (1990). Inferring psychological significance from physiological signals. *American Psychologist, 45,* 16–28.

Cairns, R. B. (1972). Fighting and punishment from a developmental perspective. In J. K. Coles & D. D. Jensen (Eds.), *Nebraska Symposium on Motivation, Vol. 20* (pp. 59–124). Lincoln: University of Nebraska Press.

Cairns, R. B. (1979). *Social development: The origins and plasticity of interchanges.* San Francisco, CA: Freeman.

Engel, G. L. (1977). The need for a new medical model: A challenge for biomedicine. *Science, 196,* 129–136.

Fuller, J. L. (1967). Experiential deprivation and later behavior. *Science, 158,* 1645–1652.

James, W. (1890). *Principles of psychology* (Vol. 2). New York: Holt.

Lagerspetz, K. M. J., & Lagerspetz, K. Y. H. (1975). The expression of the genes of aggressiveness in mice: The effects of androgen on aggression and sexual behavior in females. *Aggressive Behavior, 1,* 291–296.

Linnoila, M., Virkkunen, M., Scheinin, M., Nuutila, A., Rimon, R., & Goodwin, F. K. (1983). Low cerebrospinalfluid 5-hydroxyindoleacetic acid concentration differentiates impulsive from nonimpulsive violent behavior. *Life Sciences, 33,* 2609–2614.

Luria, A. R. (1966). *Higher cortical functions in man.* New York: Basic Books.

Magnusson, D. (1988). *Individual development from an interactional perspective.* Hillsdale, NJ: Lawrence Erlbaum Associates.

Magnusson, D. (1995). Individual development: A holistic, integrated model. In P. Moen, G. H. Elder, Jr., & K. Lüscher (Eds.), *Examining lives in context: Perspectives on the ecology of human development* (pp. 19–60). Washington, DC: American Psychological Association.

Nielsen, D. A., Goldman, D., Virkkunen, M., Tokola, R., Rawlings, R., & Linnoila, M. (1994). Suicidality and 5-hydroxyindolacetic acid concentration associated with a tryptophan hydroxylase polymorphism. *Archives of General Psychiatry, 51,* 34–38.

Raine, A., Buchsbaum, M. S., Stanley, J., Lottenberg, S., Abel, L., & Stoddard, J. (1994). Selective reductions in prefrontal glucose metabolism in murderers. *Biological Psychiatry, 35,* 365–373.

Scott, J. P. (1977). Social genetics. *Behavior Genetics, 7,* 327–346.

Soubrie, P. (1986). Reconciling the role of central serotonin neurons in human and animal behavior. *Behavior and Brain Sciences, 9,* 319–364.

Yoshimoto, K., McBride, W. J., Lumeng, L., & Li, T.-K. (1992). Alcohol stimulates the release of dopamine and serotonin in the nucleus accumbens. *Alcohol, 9,* 17–22.

Author Index

A

Aaronson, R., 177, *191*
Aasman, J., 129, *141*
Abbott, D. H., 244, *263*
Abel, L., 89, 90, 98, 150, 161, *167*, 204, 206, 209, 210, *216*, 232, 234, 235, 343, *351*
Abeling, N. G. G. M., 5, *17*, 31, 32, 34, 36
Aberg-Wistedt, A., 108, *123*
Abplanalp, J. M., 324, *330*
Abrams, N., 300, *307*
Achenbach, T. M., 110, *118*, 283, 286
Achte, K. A., 25, *39*
Ackenheil, M., 30, 31, *39*
Adam, D., 126, 127, *142*
Adams, J. J., 176, *188*
Adams, P. B., 105, 115, *118*
Adamson, D., 35
Adesso, V. J., 238, *258*
Adinoff, B., 69, 79, 83, 84
Adler, G. K., 281, *287*
Aghajanian, G. K., 28, 35
Agmo, A., 249, *260*
Ahn, H., 183, *190*
Ait Amara, D., 4, *19*, 245, *257*, *261*
Akhtar, L., 30, 31, *37*, 246, *257*
Akiskal, S. H., 109, *121*
Akselrod, S., 126, 127, *140*
Alarcon, R. D., 114, *118*

Albaugh, B., 30, 31, *37*, 246, *257*
Albrecht, P., 126, 127, 128, 129, *143*
Alessi, N. E., 105, 114, *119*, *123*, 197, *214*
Alexander, M., 173, *188*
Alicandri, C., 127, *141*
Allan, A. M., 250, *254*
Allen, N., 300, *307*
Allen, T., 89, 97
Allgood-Merton, B., 322, 323, *330*
Allikmets, L. H., 249, *254*
Allolio, B., 79, 83
Alpert, N. M., 90, 98
Altemus, M., 230, 231, 233
Altman, H., 175, *189*
Amara, D. A., 33, 39
American Psychiatric Association, 92, 96, 237, *254*
Amery, B., 113, *118*
Ames, A., 326, *335*
Amsel, R., 294, *306*
Anderson, G. M., 108, 112, 114, *118*, 120, *121*
Anderson, L., 105, 115, *118*
Andersson, T., 294, 302, 303, *306*
Andreason, P. J., 89, 90, 97, 150, 163, *165*, 206, *215*, 221, 222, 223, 225, 226, 227, 230, 231, 233, *234*
Andres, A. H., 112, *118*
Andrews, H., 175, *191*
Andrews, M. J., 244, *260*

353

Subject Index

A

Q

QNS, *see* Quantified Neurological Scale
Quantified Neurological Scale (QNS), brain
    dysfunction and violence in psychiat-
    ric populations, 178, 181–182, 184

R

Rank, testosterone levels and experiential influ-
    ences, 273
Raphe neurons, firing rate and ethanol, 245,
    see also Ethanol intoxication
RCBF, *see* Regional cerebral blood flow
rCMRG, *see* Regional cerebral metabolic rate
    of glucose
Reactivity, mice selectively bred for aggression,
    43, 46
Rearing conditions
    aggressive behavior in mice selectively bred
        for aggression, 42, 45–46
    early and aggressive behavior, 27–28
Receptors, brain and serotonin activity associ-
    ated with aggression, 71
Recidivism, violent offenders, 162, *see also*
    Violent offenders
Reciprocal influences, hormone–behavior in-
    teractions, 270
Regional cerebral blood flow (rCBF)
    homicidal aggression, 232
    measurement in personality disorders and
        other nonpsychotic patients,
        226–228, 230
    serotonin activity measurement, 220
    violence studies, 204–208
Regional cerebral metabolic rate of glucose
    (rCMRG), *see also* Glucose meta-
    bolism
    homicidal aggression, 232
    measurement in personality disorders in
        other nonpsychotic patients,
        226–228, 230
    serotonin activity measurement, 220
Regional energy usage, aggression link, 220
Regions of interest (ROI), positron emission
    tomography, 222, 223, 226–228
Relational aggression, females, 321–322
Remoxipride, dopamine antagonist and reac-
    tivity to social stimuli in mice,
    55–56

Reproduction, stress system and behavior,
    280–282
Resident-intruder paradigm, rodents and alco-
    hol-heightened/suppressed aggres-
    sion, 241–242, *see also* Intruder
    studies
Respiration, heart rate variability, 129–132
Respiratory sinus arrhythmia (RSA), influ-
    ences affecting and heart rate vari-
    ability, 127, 139, *see also* Heart
    rate
Resting heart rate, violent vs. nonviolent of-
    fenders, 159, *see also* Heart rate
Retaliation, fears and female aggression, 311,
    319
Revised Behavior Problem Checklist, heart
    rate-disruptive behavior relationship
    in children, 137, *see also* Child Be-
    havior Checklist
Rhesus monkeys, 5-hydroxyindoleacetic acid
    levels, 70, 244, *see also* Nonhuman
    primates
Righteous indignation, expression and female
    aggression, 328
Risk factors
    criminal behavior by females, 327
    violence
        identifying in society, 185
        lack of descriptive and correlation hy-
            potheses, 170
        psychophysiological, 162
Rival aggression, laboratory animals and etha-
    nol, 239
RO-15-4513, ethanol and aggression, 252,
    see also Ethanol intoxication
Rodents, *see also* Mice
    amphetamine and dopamine relation to ag-
        gression, 246
    behavioral biology of aggression, 347–348
    dominance and territorial aggression and
        ethanol, 241
    dopamine correlation with aggression,
        78–79
    genetic factors and aggression, 3–4
    5-hydroxyindoleacetic acid
        ethanol intoxication related to aggres-
            sion, 244
        impulsive-aggressive behavior, 28–29
    norepinephrine correlation with aggres-
        sion, 78